GREYSON DAUGHTREY

Director, Health, Physical Education and Safety,
Norfolk Public Schools, Norfolk, Virginia;
Formerly, Visiting Professor of Physical Education,
University of South Dakota

Second Edition

1973

W. B. SAUNDERS COMPANY · PHILADELPHIA · LONDON · TORONTO

EFFECTIVE TEACHING IN PHYSICAL EDUCATION

FOR SECONDARY SCHOOLS

W. B. Saunders Company: West Washington Square
Philadelphia, PA 19105

12 Dyott Street
London, WC1A 1DB

833 Oxford Street
Toronto 18, Ontario

All photographs which do not have a credit line are from the Norfolk City Schools.

Original cover artwork by Kay White Baker, Supervisor, Department of Art Education, Norfolk Public Schools, Norfolk, Virginia.

Effective Teaching in Physical Education   ISBN 0-7216-2881-8
for Secondary Schools

Print No: 9   8   7   6   5   4   3   2   1

To My Wife

ANNE SCOTT DAUGHTREY

PREFACE

The second edition of this text has been completely revised. In this edition, emphasis has been placed on physical education rather than on combining physical education with health education, as in the first edition. Health education is an important part of the school curriculum, and in many places it is taught in conjunction with physical education. However, the recent increased emphasis in health education has generated such a vast amount of material that it is not feasible to cover both areas adequately in one book. Moreover, physical education is today involved with such innovative concepts as modular scheduling, team teaching, movement education, and elective programs; and additional space is needed to treat these trends.

As physical education approaches the twenty-first century, many problems remain unsolved. Just as education in general faces austere budgets and public scrutiny, so must physical education justify its inclusion in the educational program. In the first edition of the text, the need for effective instruction was stressed. The second edition reiterates this stand and throughout the text emphasis is placed on methods through which quality teaching may be attained. Through quality instruction, physical education will achieve a position of strength in the curriculum and support from the community.

The experience of the author covers almost half a century of teaching in both secondary and college levels, and in directing the physical education program in a large city. These years of observation have clearly revealed the need for greater emphasis on teacher preparation. Many teachers entering the teaching profession are devoid of purpose and lack the ability to select and execute the appropriate techniques for effective teaching. This situation discloses the need for a text which will provide the teacher with the necessary background to perform satisfactorily in the teaching assignment. Such a background is provided in this text.

This book, although primarily a methods text, is something more. During the professional years, courses in curriculum, measurement, methods, principles and kinesiology are offered in preparation for teaching. Basic concepts from these courses need to be consolidated and taught concurrently with methods if teaching is to be effective.

Part One, *Why* Teach Physical Education?, is designed to show the need for physical education in a technological society. The areas of concern that have plagued education for many years are discussed. The importance of community-school relations and the role of the teacher are included in the section.

Part Two, *What* to Teach in Physical Education, takes the student from the formation of a philosophy through the scientific development of a curriculum to his role in the overall school organization. An overview of the importance of motivation and theories of learning from the traditional to a modern concept of how children learn are presented. This section also includes a discussion of the innovative programs and organizational patterns mentioned earlier.

Part Three, *How* to Teach Physical Education, begins with the first day the teacher meets the class and shows how the class may be organized effectively. Many aids to assist the teacher with the numerous problems which occur are discussed and 75 daily lesson plans for 15 individual and team activities are developed. It is here that behavioral objectives in the psychomotor, cognitive and affective domains are presented.

Part Three also includes methods of planning and organizing the intramural laboratory; the evaluation of the program, the teacher, and the student; a brief overview of the teacher's role in planning facilities; methods of teaching the exceptional child; and techniques for requisitioning equipment and supplies.

The materials and points of view described throughout the text are based on research and actual laboratory experimentation; they are, therefore, practical as well as scientific.

Finally, teachers and administrators searching for guidance in implementing an effective physical education program need to be familiar with procedures that have been tried and proved successful. This text provides such assistance by describing many successful innovations and programs which have been developed throughout the country.

GREYSON DAUGHTREY

ACKNOWLEDGMENTS

The writer is indebted to many people for the initial inspiration in writing this text. However, the dedicated teachers the author has been privileged to supervise and work with provided the necessary motivation for the second edition of the text.

The influence of the great leaders in physical education on the writer resulted in much of the philosophy contained in the book. The author frankly admits that without the professional guidance and assistance of the late Tucker Jones, former chairman of the Department of Physical Education at The College of William and Mary, there would have been no professional background for teaching or writing. The philosophy of Jesse Feiring Williams has so affected the thinking of the author that threads of his teachings are interwoven throughout the text. Other leaders such as Clark Hetherington and Jay B. Nash, whose leadership in physical education is recorded in history, influenced some of the trends discussed in various sections of the text.

Grateful acknowledgment is given to the many teachers and administrators who contributed photographs and diagrams to illustrate particular points of emphasis.

The author is indebted to Anne Orrell for typing the manuscript and to Pauline Wiley for editing it. The printing firms of Oliver and Smith and Pentecost, Wade, and McLellan provided valuable assistance in technical matters. Teagle and Little, Printers, kindly assisted with photographic details.

CONTENTS

PART ONE

WHY TEACH PHYSICAL EDUCATION?

Chapter 1

THE NEED FOR PHYSICAL EDUCATION

---

*Lack of activity destroys the good
condition of every human being,
while movement and methodical physical
exercise save it and preserve it.*

Plato

Courtesy Cedar Rapids Community School District

HISTORICAL SIGNIFICANCE

History records many instances of nations that started from crude civilizations and progressed step by step to cultures of wealth and ease. At the pinnacle of ease and prosperity, those great civilizations perished, not from conquest or other external influences but because of deterioration from within.

Modern American society has in 300 years reached a plateau of prosperity that took thousands of years for other civilizations to attain. Because of today's highly industrialized way of life, the physical labors of individual men that brought this country to the high peak of plenty we now enjoy have been forgotten. Our masses no longer have to use their muscles to provide a livelihood. Moreover, 80 percent of our population is concentrated around the industrial life of our great cities. Many other people have become victims of the atomic age, with its emphasis on speed of travel, the convenience of home and office appliances, television, and other facets of sedentary living that involve little muscular activity. It is amazing to find how much of our daily routine requires little or no physical activity.

Hours are spent eating, viewing television, working at a desk, and riding buses or automobiles rather than walking, running, or performing physical labor in which muscles are used in the many ways necessary for normal healthy living.

VICTIMS OF SCIENTIFIC INGENUITY

This nation and its people have achieved greater scientific advances and a higher standard of living than any other nation on earth. Nowhere else are average people able to afford such luxuries as automobiles, radios, television, and telephones. A comparison of the number of people using these commodities in 25 nations is shown in Table 1–1.

While other nations have failed to develop or have been restricted in their development by inadequate education, political strife, war, and disease, this country under a democratic system of free enterprise has channeled scientific and technological advances toward more ease and higher living standards in a peaceful society. Surely these accomplishments are desirable. How, then, are we becoming victims of our scientific ingenuity? It is indeed a paradox that as scientific advances bring increasing ease, comfort, and pleasure to our lives, the greater are the deteriorating influences such as delinquency and crime, crises in public education, lack of physical activity and high incidence of drug usage and venereal disease among young people, all

3

TABLE 1–1. COMPARATIVE NUMBERS OF PEOPLE POSSESSING AUTOMOBILES, TELEPHONES, AND TELEVISION SETS IN 25 NATIONS*

25 Largest Nations	Population	People per		
		Automobile	*Telephone*	*Television*
CHINA	780,000,000	20,803	3,196	7,800
INDIA	523,893,000	1,150	527	74,842
SOVIET UNION	237,914,000	216	26	12
UNITED STATES	203,000,000	2.5	2	2.4
PAKISTAN	130,000,000	981	799	3,250
INDONESIA	113,650,000	614	672	1,578
JAPAN	101,090,000	26	6	5
BRAZIL	88,209,000	58	60	15
NIGERIA	62,300,000	853	837	1,175
GERMANY (WEST)	59,949,000	6	6	3
GREAT BRITAIN	55,283,000	5	5	4
ITALY	53,748,000	7	8	6
FRANCE	50,320,000	5	7	6
MEXICO	47,267,000	53	45	21
PHILIPPINES	35,993,000	180	173	103
THAILAND	33,693,000	302	342	153
TURKEY	33,100,000	271	77	3,310
SPAIN	32,411,000	24	10	10
POLAND	32,207,000	103	21	10
EGYPT	31,300,000	288	93	63
SOUTH KOREA	30,470,000	1,870	103	305
IRAN	27,900,000	171	127	108
BURMA	27,000,000	915	1,299	0
ETHIOPIA	24,400,000	837	754	4,067
ARGENTINA	23,617,000	20	15	9

*From *World of Facts:* "How 134 Nations Around the Globe Compare in Geography, Industry, Government and Living Conditions." Washington, D.C., Civic Education Service, 1969.

of which affect the health and physical fitness of the nation.

Our achievements have not gone unnoticed by others. This nation's actions and attitudes affect and are affected by other societies in the world about us. Although the impact has perhaps not reached home as it should, we are generally aware that America is today fighting for survival politically and economically in a world seeking self-expression and individual betterment. In this battle for survival, there are two immediate forces that threaten our people: aggression from without and deterioration from within. Perhaps no other institution can offer a greater deterrent to these threatening forces than education.

THE ROLE OF EDUCATION IN THE WORLD CRISIS

Education in the United States has a twofold responsibility in educating students for able citizenship. Students must be prepared to meet the threat of aggression—which will always be with us—and at the same time be able to concentrate on skills necessary to life in a peaceful world and the demands of a highly competitive society.

It is important that the urgency of the world crisis not be minimized. However, it must be realized that the efforts of this country center around living in a culture designed for peace. Whether living at peace or preparing for conflict, the nation must be physically, emotionally and mentally fit.

Educators need to be concerned with upgrading all phases of the educational curriculum. To place major emphasis on mental growth and development without recognizing the fact that boys and girls need guidance in their physical development is a serious mistake. It is disturbing to note that while educational administrators have for years been planning and improving the curriculum in academic education they have left physical growth to chance. A recent report shows that approximately 60 percent of the nation's school children do not participate in a daily program of vigorous activity.[1] To substantiate the charge that physical education is treated in a lackadaisical manner, a very simple survey may be used. Answers to the following questions help to reveal the status of physical education in the schools of America:

1. Does the program have the same daily requirement as the academic curriculum?
2. Is the teaching load comparable to that in other areas of the curriculum?
3. Does the program have a separate budget divorced from athletics?
4. Does the program have teaching stations comparable in number to those allotted to other subjects?

5. Are teachers chosen for teaching ability or are they selected for coaching performance?
6. Are adequate supplies and equipment available?
7. Are physical education teachers supervised?
8. Are both inside and outside facilities adequate?
9. Are physical education teachers evaluated on quality instruction rather than on coaching success?
10. Is the girls' program given the same attention as the boys'?

If the questions listed above can be answered affirmatively, then the program should be adequate. However, very few schools in the country can boast of programs that meet these criteria. How, then, can boys and girls attain and maintain the strength, skill, and endurance so necessary for normal growth and development if they do not have the opportunity to participate in a well-planned program of physical education? How will they be able to meet the challenge of the twenty-first century without the health and fitness needed for survival?

This imbalance in the guidance of the mental and physical growth of boys and girls has created many serious problems that are contributing to the disintegration of the health and fitness of our youth.

History reveals that political leaders have been concerned with the disintegrating influences that have destroyed civilizations. In an address to news executives from 13 midwestern states in Kansas City, Missouri, July 6, 1971, President Richard M. Nixon stated that the United States is approaching the decadence that destroyed history's great civilizations. He pointed out that great civilizations of the past, as they have become wealthy, as they have lost their will to live, to improve, have become subject to the decadence that eventually destroys the civilization. The United States is now reaching that period.[2]

In addition to these problems, failure to understand the growth, development and needs of young people in the planning of curriculum content has placed education in a position of actually contributing to the revolt of youth rather than assisting to stabilize learning and develop acceptable social behavior. Educators must accept the challenge that confronts them and make the necessary curriculum adjustments to assist our youth not only mentally but also physically and emotionally in their preparation for a changing world. Some of the more serious areas of concern that exist in the American culture are discussed in this chapter.

AREAS OF CONCERN IN THE AMERICAN CULTURE

All societies are beset by problems. In advanced countries many of the areas of concern are materialistic outgrowths of invention and progress. Other problems, the disintegrating by-products of a progressive and permissive culture, are related to the mental, physical and emotional factors involved in the growth and development of children. Some of these areas of concern that are apparent in the United States are educational problems, emotional instability, physical inactivity and delinquency.

There are others, but those mentioned above may be identified in large part as the outgrowths of inadequate physical activity, a situation which may be alleviated through wide participation in a well-organized physical education program. The seriousness of these problems, which pose a tremendous challenge to American education, and their relationship to physical education will be discussed on the following pages.

EDUCATIONAL PROBLEMS

School Dropouts

Educators are deeply concerned with the apparent lack of desire for scholastic achievement on the part of many pupils in school today. The appalling number of dropouts, particularly in the secondary schools, has reached a stage so critical that efforts are being made both locally and nationally to do something to correct the situation. One source shows that approximately one-fourth of the students who enter the ninth grade do not graduate.[3] Efforts have been made to ascertain the causes of dropping out. A majority of the studies show that lack of interest is the major reason that pupils are quitting school.

Lack of Interest. When students lose interest in school, the curriculum should be examined and evaluated. The traditional curriculum, which does not provide opportunity for the development of individual potentialities, discourages students and causes them to leave school. The curriculum must be interesting, flexible, and realistic if the needs of today's youth are to be met. Many leaders in education, sociology, and psychology are strongly urging changes in curriculum content. During the 1950's, Bossing, a renowned educator, realized the need for curriculum changes. He stated that "when the unreal verbal emphasis so common today is rejected and attention is focused upon the vital problems of life in the contemporary world, the curriculum will become more challenging to youth."[4]

Students today, because of television and other media of communication outside the school, are more knowledgeable and sophisticated than students of the past. Experiences within the school must relate to and offer solutions for the many problems and needs confronting them. If the school cannot provide this assistance, youth will seek help elsewhere. Attention in recent years has been focused on disadvantaged children, culturally deprived children and physically, mentally and emotionally handicapped pupils. Schools have always been faced with the special problems of such children. Now, with the many federal programs designed for innovative curriculum procedures, concentrated efforts to improve the education of these pupils are being undertaken. The traditional curriculum is clearly not designed to meet the needs of disadvantaged or handicapped children. Recent opinion substantiates this premise as shown by Torrence and Strom:

It is obvious that actual curriculum change has not kept pace with educational objectives. . . . In some cases educators have shown a remarkable ability to resist new knowledge and research findings. This has been especially true in the area of individual differences, where resistance to innovations of proven value would seem to indicate a belief that it might be easier for youngsters to modify their minds than for the school to change its requirements.[5]

Skinner, an outstanding behavioral psychologist, feels that education is failing because of what he calls aversive control. In the following observation he discusses how teachers fail:

The teacher does not teach; he simply holds the student responsible for learning. The student must read books, study texts, perform experiments, and attend lectures, and he is responsible for doing so in the sense that, if he does not correctly report what he has seen, heard, or read, he will suffer aversive consequences. Questions and answers are so staple a feature of education that their connection with teaching almost never occasions surprise, yet as a demand for a response which will meet certain specifications, a question is almost always slightly aversive. An examination, as a collection of questions, characteristically generates the anxiety and panic appropriate to avoidance and escape. Reading a student's paper is still likely to be called correcting it. Examinations are designed to show principally what the student does not know.[6]

For many years the traditional academic curriculum has been geared to the I.Q.

Until recently many educators believed that there was a correlation between a low intelligence quotient and dropping out of school. Current studies show that this is not true.[7] Moreover, it is known today that the I.Q. is not the only measure of ability. What about creativity? An emerging concept is that the typical I.Q. test does not measure creative giftedness except perhaps indirectly in some areas of cognition and memory.[8] All children, and the disadvantaged in particular, may find a new world of joy and happiness when allowed to develop their creative potential. Creativity may be identified and can be taught. Do present teaching methods and procedures lend themselves to cultivating creativity? Frost and Rowland express their opinions regarding the need for a re-evaluation of the school environment if the needs of the creative child are to be met:

> Often the creative, like others who deviate from expectations of the educational system, are stifled, restless and disappointed with the school environment . . . the thwarted creative mind may well find its gratification in destructive behavior.[8]

> There is only one subject matter for education, and that is Life in all its manifestations. Instead of this single unity, we offer children—Algebra, from which nothing follows; Geometry, from which nothing follows; Science, from which nothing follows; History, from which nothing follows; a couple of Languages, never mastered; and lastly, most dreary of all, Literature, represented by plays of Shakespeare, with philological notes and short analyses of plot and character to be in substance committed to memory. Can such a list be said to represent Life as it is known in the midst of the living of it? The best that can be said of it is, that it is a rapid table of contents which a Deity might run over in his mind while he was thinking of creating a world, and had not yet determined how to put it together. . . .
>
> Alfred N. Whitehead

A review of curriculum offerings and teaching methods based on the individual needs of children may lead to programs of teaching that should stimulate interest and motivate children to learn those essentials so necessary for living in today's complex social structure. Lack of interest can be alleviated to a measurable degree through an effective program in physical education. The relationship of physical education to the dropout problem is pointed out in a statement by Conant:

> If I had to choose one department in high school that can do most to reduce dropouts and to hold the youngster emotionally to the institution, it would be physical education.[9]

Physical education can do this because it is natural for growing children to be active; there will inevitably be tremendous pupil interest in a program that is properly designed to meet their needs. The holding power of physical education is shown in the popularity of and the massive participation in intramural sports which are an extension of physical education instruction. In addition to participating in organized intramural activities, secondary school pupils are self-motivated. To substantiate this, one has only to watch the thousands of skill-thirsty pupils on the playgrounds after school, practicing, on their own, the fundamentals of basketball. The physical education class in the school is the only place in which the masses of students may receive competent instruction for satisfactorily participating in these after-school programs.

At this point, the interschool athletic program as it relates to the school dropout needs to be discussed. Competitive athletic contests provide dramatic appeal to the rugged, daring and masculine nature of many students. If outlets for these aggressive drives cannot be found, students will leave school to find satisfaction in other activities outside the school. It was shown earlier that the traditional philosophy of the curriculum which permeates the high schools of America forces many students out of school. Faris clarifies this situation in the following statement:

> In almost all of a modern educational system there is little visible substantive connection between studying to be something and actually being that thing. There is formal connection, both direct and indirect, but the tasks of study and preparation bear little resemblance to concrete tasks in any particular occupation. Consequently, though adults expect youth to aspire, the very meaning of aspiration, and thus its impact, is obscure to youth. An important function of

athletics is to make real the conception of aspiration. . . . The substance of athletics contains within itself — in its rules, procedures, training and sentiments — a paradigm of adult expectations regarding youth.[10]

Although relatively few students are able to participate in interschool athletics, the same principles may be applied more extensively to the instructional and intramural phases of physical education programs. This is true since interschool athletics are designed for gifted individuals, and physical education, when planned properly, meets the needs of all students. Table 1–2 illustrates this premise.

Leaders in educational thought have for many years realized the need for making the school a natural environment for pleasant experiences. Early in this century, Dewey pointed the way for retaining students in school. He stated that experience has shown that when children have a chance to participate in physical activities which bring their natural impulses into

play, going to school is a joy; management is less of a burden; and learning is easier.[11]

Academic Achievement

Even if the dropout problem could be solved overnight, educators would still be faced with the problems posed by the great variance in the learning rates of those who remain in school. Reading deficiency, failure to retain acquired knowledge, and lack of creative effort are some areas that teachers and administrators are studying. Many innovations, such as programmed teaching, machine teaching, and team teaching, are being used in an effort to upgrade the teaching process and develop the student's academic achievement potential. Administrators and teachers should become thoroughly acquainted with accepted theories about the learning process and they should review the many studies

TABLE 1–2. COMPARISON OF OBJECTIVES OF INTRAMURAL SPORTS WITH THOSE OF INTERSCHOOL ATHLETICS

Objectives	Interschool Athletics	Intramural Sports
Develop and maintain maximum physical efficiency.	Rates high during the competitive years, for the gifted few. However, team sports activity usually ends when school years are over.	Rates high throughout life, since program is designed for the masses and level of physical efficiency is geared to individual needs.
Develop useful skills.	Rates high for the particular sport. Rates low if there is not a varied participation.	Rates high, since a varied program is always available.
Conduct himself in socially acceptable ways.	Could rate high or low. Pressure on winning sometimes brings about antisocial behavior.	Rates high, since winning is not so important.
Enjoy wholesome recreation.	Too often athletes have limited experience in a variety of activities. Team sports participants usually have little experience in individual sports.	Rates high, since intramurals are geared to recreation and lifetime sports.
Other Objectives		
Physical Fitness	Rates high.	Rates high.
Sportsmanship	Rates high and low.	Rates high.
Health and Fitness	Rates high for a few.	Rates high.
Spectator Appeal	Rates high. Necessary for financial survival.	Rates low. Not necessary.

showing the relationship between academic achievement and physical growth and development. A brief analysis of the relationship may help to clarify this point of view.

Lack of Physical Education Impedes Mental Development. The tendency to place emphasis on the development of the mind without attention to physical growth and development is one of the major reasons so many pupils are inattentive in class, make poor grades, and lose interest in school. Moreover, lack of muscular coordination hinders mental development. Nason, in a survey of 237 gifted children, showed that failure to develop good muscular coordination puts a very definite ceiling on genius.[12]

To further substantiate the concept of the unity of mind and body, Jacobson reports that in every case when a subject thought about movement, slight contractions occurred in the muscles that would have been involved in the activity about which the subject was thinking.[13]

The Mind Develops as the Body Develops. Much has been written about the development of the mind as the basic objective of education. If this premise is accepted, there should be some clarification as to the manner in which the brain cells are involved in the process. In studying the structure of the mind and the body and the relationship between them, one learns that all knowledge is acquired through the physical senses. For example, we acquire mathematical and scientific concepts through our ears, our eyes, and our kinesthetic sense. Therefore, every effort should be made to learn more about maintaining the health and efficiency of our avenues of learning. This premise is substantiated by Chaney and Kephart in their observation that:

Both embryologically and psychologically the motor system is there first. It represents the initial system in the developmental hierarchy. As with all other developments in nature more advanced systems do not begin from scratch but represent expansions and elaborations of existing systems. In the human organism, the system which because of its prior development must be used as the basis for such expansion and elaboration is the motor system. It is logical, therefore, to expect that the earliest generalizations with which we must be concerned in child training are motor generalizations.[14]

There can be no doubt of the importance of the kinesthetic sense in mental develop-

ment. Steinhaus, throughout his years of research, continually points out that much knowledge of the world comes to us through our muscle sense, and that our very life depends on it. He elaborates on this thesis by pointing out that one can live without eyes or ears, but one cannot breathe, talk or acquire skill without muscle sense.[15] Experimentation with mentally retarded children indicates the correlation between physical education and intellectual development. Studies of these handicapped children have produced considerable evidence that well-planned programs in physical education

Figure 1–1. Research has shown that, other things being equal, activities which involve use of arms and legs in a coordinated effort are an important prerequisite for good scholastic achievement. (Courtesy Richmond Senior High School, Richmond, Indiana.)

improve learning capacity. A research program undertaken in 1965 in Nashville, Tennessee, revealed that a systematic physical education program of 20 days' duration enhanced the intellectual development of educable mentally retarded boys.[16] Similar results were reported in experiments in England in which the I.Q.'s of institutionalized mentally retarded boys increased as a result of the program.[16]

The Mental Expresses Itself Through the Physical. The development of the mind can be studied in another way. After accumulating knowledge about science, mathematics, or other fields, the individual next expresses or makes use of this knowledge. Further, as the relationship of mind and body is studied, it is found that all thoughts and mental impulses must be manifested through the body. All knowledge, all flashes of genius, and in fact, all communication have to be expressed vocally, by writing, or

by some physical behavior. This fact necessitates efforts to develop the body's ability to express the mental manifestations of the glorious heritage of civilization. The Greeks and Romans, thousands of years ago, knew the answer: a sound mind in a sound body.

The Mind and Body Are Inseparable. Many great thinkers have pointed out the importance of physical education and its relationship to mental development. Many years ago Lumley stated: "Play develops, in an all-round fashion, that part of man which is his distinctive glory, the nervous system and the brain."[17]

Studies have been made showing the correlation between normal physical development and mental acceleration. Mitchell and Mason have pointed this out:

Educators have made a study of the relationship between mental and physical growth and have found that on the whole, children retarded in their physical development are backward mentally, or vice versa, that well-developed and healthy children are apt to be precocious in their school work.[18]

Latarjet in the early 1930's experimented with scholastically retarded children to determine the effects of exercise on intellectual progress. He chose the most retarded and placed them in a special class which the children named "the health class." The classes usually consisted of six hours of intellectual work. During the experiment two of the six hours were devoted to physical education, leaving four hours for intellectual work. In less than three months, improvements occurred not only in the children's physical condition but also in their intellectual progress, memory and attention, writing and drawing, and, to the astonishment of teachers and parents, in their character as well. Latarjet concluded that the experiment suffices to show the positive effects of exercise on intellectual progress for the retarded. He also pointed out that comparable results could be observed with normal children.[19]

Recent research has shown the high correlation between the gifted mind and a healthy body. Gallagher states:

A large body of research collected in different places and at different times suggests that gifted children are equal to, or slightly better than, their average-ability classmates on such physical characteristics as height, weight, strength of grip and resistance to physical illness.[20]

Arthur H. Steinhaus

Although internationally known as a physiologist, Dr. Steinhaus will be remembered for his contributions to both physiology and health. His research over the years provided groundwork for developing physical education programs on a scientific basis.

Buhler and Guirl make this observation:

The more able student is characterized by his early physical development. He has a tendency to be taller, heavier and has fewer physical defects. Not only does he enjoy outdoor games preferred by average children, but tends to excel in these games. He usually enjoys superior health and, as a result, has fewer absences from school due to illness. He also possesses especially good eye-hand coordination.[21]

Further evidence of the close relationship between the mental and physical development of the body is discussed by Hebb:

It is obvious that the growth of the mind and its later stability depend upon conditions which make for physical health, just as they depend upon the genetic development with which the organism begins its career, but it is now clear that mental function also depends essentially on sensory stimulation, upon the experience of the organism by way of smelling, hearing, feeling, tasting and seeing.[22]

Williams records several studies which show the relationship between the child's physical development and his mental condition. In each of these studies the intellectually superior child was heavier and taller.[23]

There is documented evidence showing the importance of organized physical education in mental development. Joseph Gruber, in an address to the American Association for the Advancement of Science, stated that youngsters who exercise and are fit do better in academic achievement.

His research shows that exercises that involve coordinated movements of the arms and legs are the key to promoting academic achievement. The report shows that those coordinated movements that require a child to think through the performance patterns before execution are the types of activities that tap the same learning mechanisms that are utilized when learning to read and write. Coordinated movements, requiring reflective thinking, exercise the mind, and thus open up wider avenues for mental development. All school children should receive daily instruction in appropriate physical activities carefully selected to increase their physical fitness; to deny such a program to all people may have the effect of placing a ceiling on their future potential.

Gruber, in his summary, pointed out that the results of the study have far-reaching implications for physical education teachers, as shown in the following statements:

1. Motor aptitude test items correlate positively and significantly with intellectual performance.

2. Items measuring coordination of the arms and legs contribute more to the mind-body relationship than do items measuring growth, strength, speed and power.

3. It is possible to predict a child's level of academic achievement from a motor aptitude test battery utilizing multiple regression techniques.

4. Several experimental programs have demonstrated a significant improvement in the academic performance of children exposed to a physical education program.

5. Items measuring certain aspects of motor performance, intellectual achievement and certain personality components appear to be interrelated.

6. There appears to be a significant positive relationship between physical fitness and grade point average.

7. There is a significant positive relationship between mental and motor performance in the mentally retarded.[24]

In view of the overwhelming evidence pointing to the improvement of intellectual achievement through increased physical fitness, Gruber states that:

Since the theory of integrated development has validity it is recommended that all school children receive daily physical education designed to stimulate those mechanisms that are accounting for increased academic productivity.[24]

Gruber concludes that a large number of studies clearly show that recess periods are not only undesirable but inexcusable as substitutes for physical education. He feels that administrators, principals, and parents should be aware that recess periods do not provide the optimal stimuli needed to further academic achievement.[24]

A study by Hopwood and Van Iden should be reported here. They used 134 boys with 10 or more years of continuing attendance to show the relationship between academic performance and growth. The study was made in the Shaker Heights, Ohio, school district, grades 3 through 12. The school is recognized as having ideal teaching conditions and has a reputation for high scholarship, excellent facilities and a fine curriculum.

The Wetzel Grid (see Appendix) was used in evaluating physical growth. Standards for body size, physique, direction and speed development based on 50 plotted points for each boy were determined. In documenting academic performance three approaches were used: 60 teachers' marks for each boy summarized three intra-semester reports; 50 periodic I.Q. test scores and profile ratings; and 240 achievement test results.

Several findings of this study are:

1. Scholastic achievement, as measured by teachers' marks in required courses, is directly associated with how successfully a pupil main-

tains acceptable growth performance over a 10-year, grade 3 to 12 career.

2. Unacceptable forms of growth were characteristically accompanied by academic under-achievement which grew worse as the years of poor growth continued to accumulate.[25]

The authors claim that the results of the study leave no room for an alternative view. They are firm in their opinion that: "Other things being equal, physical fitness appears to be an important prerequisite for good scholastic achievement."[25]

Figure 1–2. Daily instruction in planned physical education is essential for increased academic productivity. (Courtesy Richmond Senior High School, Richmond, Indiana.)

As a result of the study the authors recommend greater cooperation among academic, guidance and physical education departments. They feel that the ground-work for preventing scholastic under-achievement which is associated with sub-par physical growth may be developed through this cooperation.

A final statement made by the authors further emphasizes the importance of physical fitness in academic performance:

The academic aftermath of unsatisfactory physical growth was, very plainly, sub-par scholastic achievement, apparently for the quite plausible reason that a child too tired or weak to grow properly can hardly be expected to possess either the will or the strength to develop his physique or to improve his mind.[25]

Bucher outlines a sequence of studies dating back to the turn of the century that reveals a close affinity between physical education and academic achievement. He reviews research by Lewis Terman, H. H. Clark, Boyd Jarman, David Brace, F. R. Rogers, Clayton Shay, Marcia Hart, G. L. Rarick, Robert McKee, A. H. Ismail, C. C. Cowell, Arnold Gesell, Arthur T. Jersild, Jean Piaget, D. H. Radler, and Newell Kephart. In all instances these studies confirm the direct relationship between physical education and academic achievement.[26]

A more recent report by Clark, consisting of 33 studies, showed the relationship between physical fitness and learning potential. The report included research projects taken from educational, psychological and medical journals. The conclusion drawn from an analysis of these studies maintains that:

As a consequence of the evidence presented ... it may be contended that a person's general learning potential for a given level of intelligence is increased or decreased in accordance with his degree of physical fitness.[27]

The report produces evidence which relates the individual's general learning potential to fitness and shows the need for maintaining physical fitness as an objective of physical education.

As a summary to the relationship of physical education to the development of the intellect, the eminent physiologist Steinhaus makes the following observations:

1. The neocortex contains nerve centers that make possible seeing, hearing, and localization of touch, speaking, and delicate movements of face, hands and other body parts, memory, reasoning, and awareness of self. Here are stored memories of the past, here are learned rules and skills of sports that cause one person to differ from another, here are correlated the sensory experiences that acquaint us with objects and events in the world around us, thus giving meaning to concepts and ideas. *Here is located the least understood yet most important of our senses; namely, the muscle sense.*

2. More important to life than vision and hearing, this propioception, kinesthesia, or muscle sense, provides the mind with its understanding of stretch, tension, movement, and the third dimension.

3. Without the sensations that arise from activity in muscles and joints, our inner world of concepts would be flat and completely unreal. Herein lies the most important contribution of physical activity to the mind of man. Every movement, every body position, every tension in muscle and joint structure contributes to the formation of concepts or ideas that form the building stones with which we construct our thought life.[15]

The physical education program in our schools is the only medium for providing adequate physical activity for the nation's children, since the majority of children are required to attend schools and physical education in some form is found in most schools. Through a sequential program in physical education, proper instruction designed to meet the needs of children may be initiated.

EMOTIONAL INSTABILITY

Fifty percent of all hospital beds in this country are occupied by emotionally disturbed people. Authorities state that one person in every 10 (a total of 20,000,000 in the United States) has some form of mental or emotional illness that needs psychiatric treatment. Many of the causes of this problem are known. The results of two World Wars, the economic and social reversals of the Depression of the 1930's, the American involvement in the Asian and Viet Nam conflicts, and the tension created by the continuing cold war have contributed to the unrest. Looming above all these is the terrific strain created by the nuclear

CONSERVATIVE ESTIMATE OF INCIDENCE (in millions)	ABNORMAL BEHAVIOR
300,000	TRANSIENT DISORDERS (civilian, each year)
10,000,000	PSYCHONEUROSES
20,000,000	PSYCHOPHYSIOLOGIC DISORDERS
700,000	PSYCHOTIC DISORDERS (functional)
300,000	CHARACTER DISORDERS (psychopathic, criminal)
5,000,000	PROBLEM DRINKING
1,000,000	CHRONIC ALCOHOLISM
60,000	DRUG ADDICTION
100,000	ACUTE BRAIN DISORDERS
1,000,000	CHRONIC BRAIN DISORDERS
5,500,000	MENTAL RETARDATION (mental deficiency)

(Scale: 20, 15, 10, 5, 0)

Figure 1-3. Incidence of abnormal behavior in the United States. (From Coleman, James: *Abnormal Psychology and Modern Life.* Chicago: Scott, Foresman and Company, 1964.)

age in which we live; we simply have not had time to develop our emotional stamina sufficiently to bear up under the strain of the uncertainty we have created. The fast pace at which Americans live, the emphasis on individual effort, the lack of proper recreation and exercise, and the improper use of leisure time are deteriorating influences that take their toll from the emotional well-being of the American people.

An intensive research project conducted at the University of Illinois reports the anatomical, physiological and psychological changes induced by exercise programs. The findings indicate that:

Persistent physical training negates some of the poorly rated parasympathetic nervous tendencies and if not carried too far into over-training, develops positive dynamic qualities of psychological value.[28]

After considerable research Bortz found that through exercise the body is more able to withstand tension. He states:

It would appear that exercise strengthens the adaptive mechanisms of the body. In a physically fit person, there appears to be a better adrenal reserve with an increased amount of steroids available to counter prolonged tension.[29]

A more extensive discussion of emotional health and the importance of physical education in developing emotional stability will be found in Chapter 4.

NEED FOR PHYSICAL ACTIVITY

Exercise and Growth Patterns

Recent studies in physiology and medicine reveal that sequentially planned programs in physical education influence growth patterns in children[30] and contribute to the physiological health of adults.[28] These studies emphasize not only the importance of vigorous exercise programs but also the need for teaching the skills of those activities which can be used beyond school years and throughout life.

The development of neuromuscular skill, improvement of muscular movement and increased working capacity of the body are the results of systematic programs of exercise.[30] Exercise is also necessary for the normal growth and maintenance of the protoplasmic integrity of the tissues, the decline of fatty tissue and the normal growth of the bones.[30]

Exercise and Heart Disease

Although many factors are involved in degenerative circulatory diseases, recent research indicates the value of regular exercise in the prevention of such disorders. It is generally recognized that poor diet, heredity, lack of rest, smoking, stress and obesity are linked to circulatory disorders. Lack of exercise also seems to be a very important factor. Authoritative study and opinion support the premise that regular physical activity may prevent and postpone cardiovascular degenerative changes.[31] Authoritative studies have also documented the positive effects of exercise on circulation; on the tone of the diaphragm, which in turn improves heart function; on the capacity of the small blood vessels; on digestion and elimination; and on the nervous system.[32]

Figure 1–4.   Heredity aside, the only way to develop a strong nervous system is through vigorous exercise during the formative years.

Figure 1–5.   Evidence shows that the American youth requires instruction in more activities designed to meet the needs of all students and not the gifted few alone.

Surgeon General Urges More Exercise

The Surgeon General of the United States, Dr. Jessie L. Steinfeld, is one of the nation's leaders in physical fitness. He feels that prevention should receive more attention. He states many of our health problems stem from the fact that Americans are not as health conscious as they should be. We must provide them with more accurate information about health care and health maintenance. One way to do this is by pointing out that regular exercise is a form of health insurance, or preventive medicine.

Newsletter, President's Council on
Physical Fitness and Sports, March 1971

Further evidence showing the beneficial results of exercise on the heart and blood vessels is supplied by Klump. He reports that coronary disease is not a problem in those sections of the world where physical activity is necessary throughout life, and that the hearts of active individuals have a greater network of arteries than those of sedentary individuals. The more active individual stands a better chance of escaping a heart attack.[33] What we usually call a heart attack is not an organic heart condition but is the result of a blockage of the coronary artery caused by arteriosclerosis. Proper diet and physical activity seem to lower the incidence of arteriosclerosis.

The eminent cardiologist, Paul Dudley White, has this to say about the need for vigorous exercise in the prevention of arteriosclerosis:

We do not have all the information we need about preventive measures, but we are quite sure that we do have some clues. One of these is the maintenance of physical fitness, including the avoidance of obesity and the establishment of regular habits of vigorous exercise . . . In order to establish good habits which

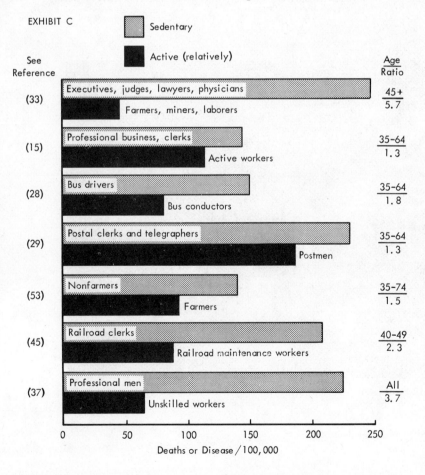

Figure 1-6. Coronary heart disease and CHD deaths related to sedentary versus active occupation: summary of studies. "Age" refers to the age range of subjects; "ratio" is the ratio of sedentary to active. Data are from references cited on the ordinate. (From Johnson, Perry, Updike, Wynn F., Stolberg, Donald C., and Schaeffer, Maryellen: *Physical Education: A Problem-Solving Approach to Health and Fitness.* Copyright © 1966 by Holt, Rinehart and Winston, Inc. Reprinted by permission of Holt, Rinehart and Winston, Inc.)

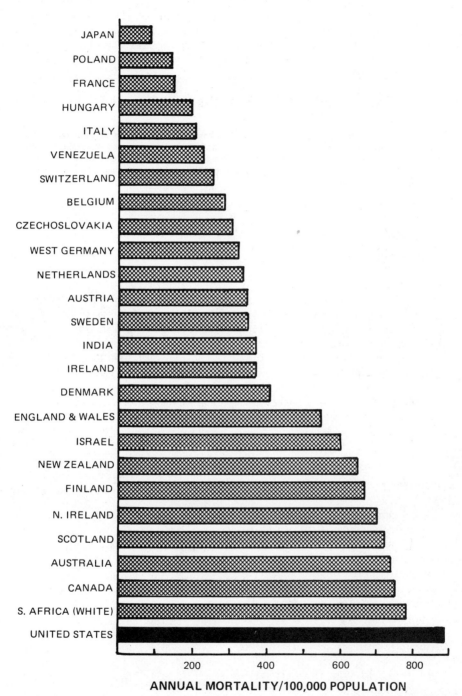

Figure 1-7. Average annual mortality due to arteriosclerotic heart disease in men aged 55–64. Figures represent either 1956–1958 or 1957–1959. Adapted from Yudkin. (From James, Thomas N., and Keyes, John W. (Eds.): The Etiology of Myocardial Infarction. Boston: Little, Brown and Company, 1963.)

are protective throughout life, we must . . . train the young, no older than their teens and also vigorously through their twenties.[34]

Recent research substantiates the opinion of Paul Dudley White. Dr. Alfredo Lopez, physician-researcher for the Department of

Medicine at the State University of Medicine in New Orleans, feels that exercise is more important than diet in preventing heart attacks. Dr. Lopez states that "in comparative studies, physical activity seems to negate the vascular impairment associated with dietary habits.[35]

Tendency Toward Heart Disease Begins Early

The tendency toward heart disease and arteriosclerosis begins early in life. This was revealed by post mortem studies among United States casualties in Viet Nam. The studies show that the incidence of hardening of the arteries is higher in the eighteen–twenty-five age bracket in the Viet Nam war than in Korea. Kenneth H. Cooper who made the study attributes this condition to <u>lack of exercise,</u> high-fat diets and cigarette smoking.

Physical Education Newsletter
October 1, 1969

Exercise and Tension

Ninety-one percent of the respondents to a survey of the opinions of 54 psychiatrists showed that they believed moderate exercise would assist in relieving tension. The activities to which the respondents gave the highest priorities were walking, swimming, bowling, golf, tennis, square dancing, social dancing, folk dancing, creative dancing, calisthenics, bag punching, basketball, fishing, boating, gardening, and relaxing exercises.[36]

Physical Fitness

Efforts have been made to compare the fitness of American youth with those of other nations. These studies show that our children may not be as fit as they should be. Tests by Kraus and Hirschland reveal that approximately 60 percent of the 4000 American boys and girls tested failed simple tests of minimum strength as contrasted with failure in only eight percent of the 2000 European youth that were tested (Fig. 1–8).[37]

The draft in World War II rejected 40 percent of all inductees for reasons of physical and mental health.[23] Larson reported that the physical condition of inductees into the Army Air Force was such that 90 percent needed special training to meet minimum standards. He found that 40 to 50 percent did not possess sufficient

skill to stimulate interest in any sport to the extent of participation. Only three to five percent had varsity experience, and from 30 to 40 percent were unable to swim. These surveys also indicated that sports such as golf, tennis, bowling, and handball were not taught in most schools.[38]

The Equitable Life Assurance Society reports that each year more entering college freshmen fail to meet minimum physical achievement tests.[39] In 1958–59 the American Association for Health, Physical Education and Recreation tests were administered to 10,000 British and American children. The results showed that the British children were superior to American boys and girls in all events except the softball throw.[40]

Although there is disagreement among physical education leaders concerning the validity of the Kraus-Hirschland tests (see Figure 1–8), these did serve as a catalyst to arouse the nation to the need for more physical activity. Alarmed by the findings of those tests, President Eisenhower created the President's Council on Youth Fitness. The initial conference, which was held at Annapolis, made recommendations that:

1. The President of the United States create a top-level committee of Federal departments having programs and activities relating to the fitness of youth.

2. A Citizens Advisory Committee be appointed by the President of the United States to advise the President and the American people of the fitness of American youth.

3. The adoption of recommendations one

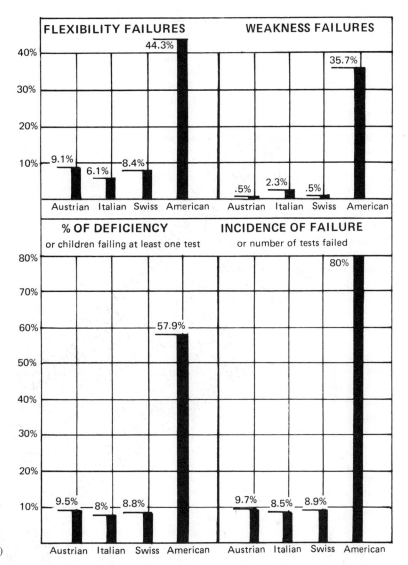

Figure 1–8. Comparison of test failures in different countries. (From Hans Kraus and Ruth Hirschland: Minimum Muscular Fitness Tests in School Children, *Research Quarterly*, May, 1954, p. 184.)

and two supra, or the activation of any other group, must never cloud the fact that the prime and continuing responsibility for fitness of youth is in the home and local community.

4. All organizations, public or private, education or recreation, in their own particular areas of application and working cooperatively with one another, interpret in various ways the need for and the value of physical fitness. They must avoid a narrow definition of fitness yet take into account the value of simple approaches to this complex problem—building toward complete understanding and support.

5. Coordinated reasearch be conducted to ascertain the dimensions and complications of the fitness of our American youth.

6. Television, radio, and other media of communications be used to tell the story of youth fitness to the people—including our young people.

7. Federal, state and local governments sponsor and conduct demonstration projects to dramatize the practicality of steps to aid the fitness of youth.

8. Sufficient funds be provided by public and private sources to initiate and promote the plans, programs, and activities essential for attainment of fitness of American youth.[41]

In his message to the conference, President Eisenhower stated:

That national policies will be no more than words if our people are not healthy of body, as well as of mind, putting dynamism and leadership into carrying out major decisions. Our young people must be physically as well as mentally and spiritually prepared for American citizenship.[41]

The Council has continued its function in the administrations of Presidents Kennedy, Johnson and Nixon. President Kennedy made the following statement in support of the Council:

It is of great importance, then, that we take immediate steps to ensure that every American child be given the opportunity to make himself physically fit—fit to learn, fit to understand, to grow in grace and stature, to fully live.[42]

The Council received its greatest support under the administration of President Kennedy. Through his efforts the Council initiated recommendations for a basic school program which have had a tremendous effect on physical education throughout the country. The recommendations are for health appraisals, identification of physically-underdeveloped pupils through screening tests, re-emphasis on physical development through developmental exercises and finally, tests for evaluating physical development.[42]

In 1961 the Council, in its bulletin *Youth Physical Fitness*, recommended guidelines for an effective physical fitness program:

1. Programs to improve physical fitness must provide vigorous activities that will develop the physique, increase the efficiency of the cardiovascular system, and contribute to the development of physical skills.
2. Progressive resistive exercises involving increased work loads for longer periods are essential to increase the level of fitness.
3. Endurance develops in proportion to the total work done over a period of time.
4. Strength is increased through activities requiring more than 50 per cent of the total strength capacity.
5. Organic efficiency is improved where rhythmical muscular activity is continued over long, unbroken periods.
6. Physical fitness is directly proportional to the levels of strength, power and endurance achieved.
7. The school physical education program should include a core of developmental and conditioning activities, appropriate to each grade level. These activities should be carefully identified and stressed in progressive order.
8. The school health education program provides knowledge and understanding based on scientific facts and principles in order to develop desirable health attitudes and behavior for promotion of physical fitness.[42]

The Council has provided the impetus necessary for focusing attention on the need for fitness. It recognizes the existence of many excellent programs in the country and has assisted those communities where programs are inadequate. Probably the most important contribution the Council has made is in alerting the nation to the need for sound physical education programs in the schools.

In May, 1971, operating under the new name of President's Council on Physical Fitness and Sports, with C. Carson Conrad as executive director and astronaut James A. Lovell as chairman, the Council adopted a statement of basic beliefs. The first of these statements was devoted to school programs for grades kindergarten through 12. It is reproduced here in its entirety:

All school children in grades K–12 should be required to participate in daily programs of physical education emphasizing the development of physical fitness and sports skills.

1. Medical authorities recommend unequivocally regular vigorous exercise during school years, as such is essential to healthy development of individuals.
2. In order to enjoy a sport, master the necessary skills and participate safely, a person must be physically fit. The popular slogan, *Get Fit by Playing*, should be: *Get Fit to Play Safely.*
3. Within the educational context of physical education programs, students should develop knowledge of the effects of activities for conditioning as well as the relation of activities to various aspects of health throughout life. Students need to understand the basic elements of physiology of exercise and the value of participating in regular vigorous activities. The need to continue activities in adulthood should be stressed at an early age and throughout the school physical education experience. Knowledge, understanding and participation should result in the development of desirable attitudes concerning the values of participation in regular vigorous physical activity.
4. Special programs of physical education should be provided those pupils with orthopedic problems, obesity, perceptual motor problems, and other health-related problems. Such students must first be identified, along with those who may suffer from physical underdevelopment, malnutrition or inadequate coordination.
5. Physical education programs should be

planned to include physiological fitness goals along with other educational aims needed to meet the developmental needs of children; thus, activities must be adapted to individual needs and capacities and be vigorous enough to increase energy utilization and heart rate significantly.

6. The school physical education program should include a core of developmental and conditioning activities appropriate for each grade level. Activities should be identified and stressed in progressive order. Demonstration standards for survival activities, particularly including swimming, should be established and competence maintained by periodic testing and training.

7. Every pupil should have continuing supervision by his family physician and dentist, including periodic examinations and correction of remediable defects.

Through these resources, supplemented wherever necessary and feasible by school and community services, the health appraisal procedures should include:

1. Identification of pupils with correctable orthopedic defects and other health problems and subsequent referral to medical authorities.

2. A posture check, including foot examination; pupils with acute problems should be referred to medical authorities.

3. Height and weight measurements, interpreted in terms of individual needs; pupils who are obviously obese, underweight or malnourished should be identified and referred to medical authorities.[43]

The Lifetime Sports Foundation. The Lifetime Sports Foundation was organized in 1965 with the purpose of emphasizing fitness through sports that last a lifetime. It is intended to assist educational and recreational organizations and other agencies in improving their programs. Working through administrators and supervisors, the Foundation assists with in-service programs to improve instruction in teaching lifetime sports. Through the Foundation, valuable information is distributed to school personnel to impress them with the importance of teaching sports skills.

The Foundation was created by two large industries, American Machine and Foundry Corporation and the Brunswick Corporation. These industries for many years have been interested in the health and fitness of the nation. Through their efforts they hope to improve the fitness of the American people through increased interest and participation in lifetime sports.

Exercise and Older People

Too often, physical education leaders devise programs for elementary and secondary school pupils without taking into consideration the need for exercise in later years. The life span of people in this country is increasing each year. In the past 69 years the life expectancy of a newborn infant has increased from 47.3 to 70.5 years.

Objectives of the Lifetime Sports Foundation from the Foundation's Charter

1. To encourage participation and competition in sports activities which maintain fitness and develop habits of exercise which provide the physical health, vitality, and emotional outlets which are necessary and basic to mental well-being and intellectual vigor.

2. To provide opportunities for youth to develop sports skills in games which can be played and enjoyed throughout life.

3. To encourage appropriate research into the physical benefits of sports activities to conclusively prove the value of exercise to health and mental well-being.

4. To establish instructional opportunities to qualify men and women to teach effectively those sports and games which lack adequate numbers of competent coaches.

5. To work with and assist the athletic organizations of schools and colleges to enlarge their competitive programs to include more games and activities to increase the number of participants.

6. To promote international understanding through the establishment of competition between citizens' teams in as many sports as possible.

7. To encourage the Pan American and Olympic Games Committees (and other like organizations) to enlarge their competitive programs to include all sports played world-wide.

8. To promote and improve recreational and sports participation opportunities for American citizens.[44]

The importance of exercise from birth to old age is unquestioned. Paul Dudley White reemphasizes the reasons for exercise in later years:

1. It maintains muscle tone throughout the body, including the heart itself.
2. It provides relaxation by relieving nervous tension and strains, anxiety, and mental concentration.
3. It aids digestion by reducing nervous tension and has a favorable effect on bowel function.
4. It helps to control obesity, especially where a few grams of fat are in the wrong places, such as the walls of the coronary and other important arteries.
5. Deepening of the respiration improves the function of the lungs.[45]

The physiological and psychological effects of exercise listed above are necessary for all age groups. Since the skills learned during adolescence are those usually practiced in later life, it becomes necessary to plan instruction in those activities that may be used in maturity. It is rare that new skills are learned efficiently after age 60.

Health and fitness for older adults is becoming a problem, and more than ever before we are confronted with the challenge of providing recreational programs for these people. A basic part of the answer to this challenge is to provide secondary pupils with instruction in those leisure-time activities that will be enjoyed by them in later life.

DELINQUENCY AND CRIME

Whether there actually is a higher incidence of delinquency and crime today or whether we merely have better statistics is beside the point. The fact remains that there is too much delinquency. In 1971 the incidence of juvenile crime was alarming. The following facts pertaining to juvenile crime were revealed by the Federal Bureau of Investigation in the publication, *Crime in the United States, 1972:*

1. The national crime rate, or the risk of being a victim of crime, has increased 74 percent since 1960. Murder increased 76 percent since 1966.
2. Ten percent of all persons arrested for murder were under 18 years of age in 1971.
3. Forcible rape committed by persons under 18 years of age increased 42 percent since 1966.
4. In 1971, 32 percent of the persons arrested for robbery were under 18 years of age.
5. Fifty percent of the arrests in 1971 for larceny were under 18 years of age.
6. In 1971, 53 percent of arrests made for auto theft were 18 years of age or under.
7. A brief summary shows that, in 1971, 26

Figure 1–9. Instruction in activities which provide for participation in later life should be a part of the physical education curriculum. (Courtesy Richmond Senior High School, Richmond, Indiana.)

Figure 1–10. Proper guidance in socially accepted activities plays an important role in combating delinquency. (Courtesy Washington High School, Germantown, Wisconsin.)

percent of all crimes which were solved involved persons under 18 years of age.[46]

Many years ago Hetherington stated, "Play gone wrong is the source of most of the bad habits known to children and youth."[47] Children are pressured toward activity by innate drives. They will engage in some form of activity whether we want them to or not. Their play life may be clean, socially acceptable and healthful, or it may be activity outside acceptable social standards. It is the responsibility of adults to provide opportunity for and to guide children into the kind of play and activity that is socially acceptable. Proper guidance in activities through a well-planned physical education program plays an important role in combating delinquency.

It is logical to assume that if the social structure of the country, through the media of clubs, schools, recreational centers, the home and other community organizations, should plan purposeful activity for youth, many delinquent acts would be curtailed. The schools are in a better position than any other medium to render preventive programs. Williams says that "If the school population of this generation of Americans could become addicted to wholesome play and recreation, many of our present social ills relating to work would disappear."[23] Irrespective of such opinions as those expressed in the Task Force Report,[48] which claims that the schools play an unimportant role in deterring delinquency, there are several reasons to support the premise that the school is effective in this area and that physical education has a leading role:

1. A school exists in every community.
2. The school works with children from all backgrounds.
3. The school receives children at an early age and has daily contact with them for 10 or 12 years.
4. Teachers are trained to work with children.
5. The school has a more natural rela-

tionship with parents than the police.

6. The school is in a position to detect children's emotional problems early enough to prevent such problems from leading to delinquency.

Physical education provides the greatest socializing medium in the school. The various games, sports, dances, and activities that constitute the curriculum are areas in which boys and girls can find natural outlets for tension, suppressed desires and aggressive urges. Through wise counsel and direction the teacher may direct these urges into socially acceptable channels.

The Educational Policies Commission in its landmark report entitled Education for All-American Youth strongly emphasizes the importance of physical education in American schools. The Commission proclaims that physical education is an indispensable part of the health program but it also has other purposes. Physical education serves as the medium for developing a variety of recreational skills, provides socializing experiences and builds desirable attitudes of teamwork, sportsmanship and respect for other people.

Medical opinion supports the importance of the role of physical education in guiding and assisting adolescents in their social adjustments. Shaffer, an eminent physician, has this to say about the need for physical activity:

The need for activity is present from earliest infancy but it is heightened in adolescence, I believe, because muscular activity, creative or aggressive, is a mechanism for relief from the stresses and anxieties which occur at this time.[49]

Several experiments have been made to determine the effects of recreational programs on delinquent behavior. One made in Anaheim, California, in 1924, revealed that when playgrounds opened in this city, juvenile delinquency decreased 70 percent during the first six months.[18] Educators since the turn of the century have expressed strong convictions concerning the importance of the play life of children. Dewey explained the need for activity:

If education does not afford opportunity for wholesome recreation and train capacity for seeking and finding it, the suppressed instincts find all sorts of illicit outlets, sometimes overt, sometimes confined to the indulgence of the imagination.[50]

Mental hygiene reports show the need for physical education as an important part of the educational curriculum, for the development of a wholesome personality. Burnham states that:

Thus physical education is the oldest, the simplest, the wholesomest, of all kinds of formal training. Its results are recorded not in ranks and parchments but in muscle, sinew, red blood, in neurones, behavior patterns, interest, attitudes, and ideals, artistic and personal.[51]

The assertion that physical education involves the teaching of skills which in turn are expressed in the intramural and recreational programs should be properly interpreted. Merely to teach skills and organize games and contests is not a guarantee of preventing delinquency. Solving the problem is not this simple. However, the guidance of individuals through their play life, emphasizing the values of fair play, the need for fitness and the personal satisfaction in physical performance may very well serve as a substitute for antisocial behavior. This premise is expressed by Layman, who states:

It may be said that participation in athletics and physical education activities appears to have potentialities for encouraging the development of favorable personality and character traits but probably will be effective only if the programs involved are based on social values and a recognition of individual differences.[52]

Considerable support is given to physical education as a deterrent to delinquency and school dropouts by Paul Briggs, Superintendent of Schools, Cleveland, Ohio. He makes the following comments:

1. The last place to cut a budget is in the areas of health, physical education, recreation and athletics.

2. We have to be active in physical education, health, recreation and athletics.

3. We have to use our programs to break the isolation of the ghetto.

4. We have to use our programs to keep children in school, to teach them discipline, and how to live with each other.

5. We have to use the wholesomeness of the athletic field and the athletic plant to do these things.

6. We are putting our money where our mouth is in this respect because we believe in health, physical education and recreation.[53]

A Superintendent Speaks

Paul Briggs, Superintendent of Schools, Cleveland, Ohio, finds that physical education and athletics do things for pupils that cannot be equaled elsewhere in school. He says:

I have seen young men headed for trouble, academic trouble, personal trouble, legal trouble, until they had a real experience in physical education or athletics, and suddenly begin to find themselves.

He refers to a survey of five high schools in Cleveland which shows how participation in sports keeps youngsters in school.[53]

The American Medical Association has emphasized the need for physical education. In June, 1969, The House of Delegates of the Association passed a resolution outlining its stand. The resolution states:

WHEREAS, The medical profession has helped to pioneer physical education in our schools and colleges and thereafter has encouraged and supported sound programs in this field;

WHEREAS, There is increasing evidence that proper exercise is a significant factor in the maintenance of health and the prevention of degenerative disease; and

WHEREAS, Advancing automation has reduced the amount of physical activity in daily living, although the need for exercise to foster proper development of our young people remains constant, and

WHEREAS, There is a growing need for the development of physical skills that can be applied throughout life in the constructive and wholesome use of leisure time; and

WHEREAS, In an age of mounting tensions, enjoyable physical activity can be helpful in the relief of stress and strain, and consequently in preserving mental health; therefore be it

RESOLVED, That the American Medical Association through its various divisions and departments and its constituent and component medical societies do everything feasible to encourage effective instruction in physical education for all students in our schools and colleges.[54]

Civilized man works hard to achieve ease and comfort in later life. The tragedy is that when he reaches this goal, he often becomes mentally and physically inactive, a state not conducive to longevity. The problem for adults is: What kind of exercise? Many individuals would play golf and tennis, bowl and swim if they had learned the rudiments of such sports during their school years. Unless infectious disease is a factor, health and fitness result when an effort to exercise regularly is sustained throughout life. However, in a modern society it is harder to maintain health than in less civilized cultures. Attitudes toward habits of exercise, as well as other good health practices must be formed early in life. Later chapters will show how these attitudes and practices can be achieved through physical education.

Other evidence that we are victims of our own ingenuity is the sedentary life into which the products of our technology have forced us. The American people are sitting themselves into a state of inertia, weakness, and poor health. The advent of television and the emphasis on spectator entertainment have greatly contributed to this unwholesome situation. The lack of exercise is evident everywhere. Physicians prescribe exercise; "health studios" and reducing salons have become a million dollar industry because of the lack of simple exercise in our daily lives.

There is a need in our culture for greater *participation.* We are rapidly becoming a nation of spectators. One hundred thousand spectators will watch one football game with only 22 players participating. The great emphasis placed on interscholastic and intercollegiate participation is acceptable only if equal emphasis is also placed on activity for the masses. Dr. Edwin Burdell, president of Cooper College, in a speech at the National Council of Higher Education in Chicago in 1957, stated that "spectatorship is perhaps the most deadening influence in our society."

WHAT MUST BE DONE?

Administrators must establish and maintain in the curriculum an equal balance between mental education and physical education. Educators, authors, and other leaders advocate the development of the whole child mentally, physically, and emotionally. Yet in such vital matters as curriculum, monetary expenditures, and provision for facilities and staff, the greatest emphasis is too often placed on the offerings that are intended to train only the mind. Health and fitness may be developed only by systematic use of the muscles of the body and by continual instruction in good health habits and practices. Unless the program of physical education is given a proper place in the curriculum, our boys and girls will continue to be physically and emotionally unfit.

Physical development and mental growth are simultaneously occurring natural functions. We do not leave mental growth to chance, and we cannot afford to leave physical growth and development to chance. Guidance in physical development through required physical education classes scheduled during the school day is as necessary as guidance in mental development through such scheduled courses as English, science, or mathematics.

The program in physical education cannot be restricted to interscholastic athletics, which involves only a few gifted pupils. Neither should it be left to outside agencies, such as Boys' clubs, Y.M. or Y.W.C.A.'s and recreation groups. This approach to fitness places the program on a permissive basis, leaving teaching and participation to chance.

The Need for Physical Education

The imperative need for physical education in the school curriculum is scientifically advanced by Williams, Brownell and Vernier:

1. Aside from the influence of heredity and nutritive conditions, physical education is the sole source for the development of vitality. Organic power is dependent in large part upon the activities of youth, and neglect of physical education in childhood produces abnormal adult types.

2. Physical education is the sole organized means for the development of neuromuscular skills so essential for the proper functioning of the individual as a moving, motor mechanism. There are, also, vast contributions from these skills to the complete orientation of the individual as a thinking, feeling, and acting organism.

3. Physical education is indispensable as the most important agency to develop attitudes toward play and to combat the sedentary life and its associated evils. No subject in schools and no agency outside the schools is so well prepared to promote the idea that play is a part of the good life. There is no need to argue the necessity for such teaching. Society gives numerous signs that play and recreation are essential. To keep alive the play motive requires education of people in skills and attitudes that provide satisfactions in the activities of recreation.

4. Physical education is indispensable for setting standards of sportsmanship. Games offer the laboratory where vital attitudes are formed and the teaching of these, so essential for sport, is equally demanded in all walks of life.[55]

This chapter has pointed out several trends and influences that must be counteracted if we are to offset the internal deteriorating forces that threaten us. The remaining chapters in this book will show how a quality physical education program, regularly scheduled every day in every grade, can go a long way toward alleviating the ills of man and society that have been discussed here.

QUESTIONS FOR DISCUSSION

1. Explain the paradox that we are victims of our scientific ingenuity.
2. Discuss some of the educational challenges in the present world crisis.
3. What is meant by a deteriorating trend and how does it affect the American culture?

4. Why is physical education a deterrent to school dropouts?

5. What is the chief cause of school dropouts? Why?

6. What is meant by mind-body unity?

7. Discuss emotional stability.

8. Discuss the role of physical education in developing emotional stability.

9. What is the stand taken by the American Medical Association on physical education?

10. What is the relationship of physical education to diseases of later life?

11. What is meant by the statement, "Play gone wrong may produce delinquency"?

SUGGESTED ACTIVITIES

1. Chart a comparison of trends in American culture with those in ancient Greece.

2. Study the dropout problem in the local high school.

3. Visit several doctors and report on their opinions of the importance of physical education.

4. Construct a graph or chart showing the incidence of crime in the various age groups in your locality.

REFERENCES

1. Charles Bucher, *Foundations of Physical Education*, 5th ed., p. 493 (St. Louis: The C. V. Mosby Company, 1968).

2. Address by Richard M. Nixon, Kansas City, Missouri, July 6, 1971.

3. Glen F. Ovard, *Administration of the Changing Secondary School*, p. 289 (New York: The Macmillan Company, 1966).

4. Nelson L. Bossing, *Principles of Secondary School Education*, p. 293 (Englewood Cliffs, New Jersey: Prentice-Hall, Inc. 1955).

5. E. Paul Torrence and Robert D. Strom (eds.) *Mental Health and Achievement*, p. 29 (New York: John Wiley and Sons, 1965).

6. B. F. Skinner, *The Technology of Teaching*, pp. 99–100 (New York: Appleton-Century-Crofts, 1968).

7. Chris DeYoung and Richard Wynn, *American Education*, p. 480 (6th ed.; New York: McGraw-Hill Book Company, 1968).

8. Joel L. Frost and G. Thomas Rowland, *Curricula for the Seventies*, pp. 181; 187 (Boston: Houghton Mifflin Company, 1969).

9. James B. Conant, *JOHPER*, p. 41 (March, 1963).

10. Robert Faris, *Handbook of Modern Sociology*, p. 206 (Chicago: Rand McNally and Company, 1966).

11. John Dewey, *Democracy in Education, An Introduction to the Philosophy of Education*, p. 194 (New York: The Macmillan Company, 1916).

12. Leslie Nason, *Physical Education Newsletter*, p. 1 (Croft Educational Services, Inc., September 27, 1958).

13. E. Jacobson, "Electrophysiology of Mental Activities," *American Journal of Psychology*, pp. 693–694 (Vol. XLIV, No. 44, 1932).

14. Clara M. Chaney and Newell C. Kephart, *Motoric Aids to Perceptual Training*, p. 4 (Columbus: Charles E. Merrill Publishing Company, 1968).

15. Arthur H. Steinhaus, *Toward an Understanding of Health and Physical Education*, pp. 32–33; 10 (Dubuque, Iowa: William C. Brown Company, 1963).

16. Julian Stein, "The Potential of Physical Activity for the Mentally Retarded Child," *JOHPER*, p. 26 (April, 1966).

17. Frederick Lumley, *Principles of Sociology*, p. 375 (New York: McGraw-Hill Book Company, 1928).

18. Elmer Mitchell and Bernard Mason, *Theory of Play*, pp. 251; 205 (New York: A. S. Barnes and Company, 1948).

19. A. Latarjet, "Physical Education, Athletics and Mental Hygiene," (Washington, D.C.: *Journal of the American Association of Health, Physical Education, Recreation*, p. 28, November, 1932).

20. James Gallagher, "What Are Gifted Children Like?" *In* Lester D. Crow and Alice Crow (eds.), *Educating the Academically Able*, p. 41 (New York: David McKay Company, 1963).

21. Ernest O. Buhler and Eugene N. Guirl, "The More Able Student, Described and

Rated," *In* Lester D. Crow and Alice Crow (eds.), *Educating the Academically Able*, p. 49 (New York: David McKay Company, 1963).

22. Donald O. Hebb, "Role of Experience," *Control of the Mind, Man and Civilization*, p. 42. Seymour M. Forbes (ed.) (New York: McGraw-Hill Book Company, 1961).

23. Jesse, F. Williams, *Principles of Physical Education*, pp. 149; 85; 115 (8th ed.; Philadelphia: W. B. Saunders Company, 1964).

24. Joseph J. Gruber, "Exercise and Mental Achievement," (From an address before the American Association for the Advancement of Science, Dallas, December, 1968).

25. Howard H. Hopwood and Starr S. Van Iden, "Scholastic Underachievement as Related to Sub-par Physical Growth," *The Journal of School Health*, pp. 337–348 (October, 1965).

26. Charles Bucher, "Health, Physical Education and Academic Achievement," *Journal of the National Education Association*, pp. 38–40 (May, 1965).

27. H. Harrison Clark (ed.), *Physical Fitness Research Digest*, President's Council on Physical Fitness and Sports (October, 1971).

28. Thomas E. Cureton, "Anatomical, Physiological and Psychological Changes Induced by Exercise Programs (exercises, sports, games) in Adults," p. 152. *Exercise and Fitness*, Chairman Seward C. Staley (Chicago: The University of Illinois and the Athletic Institute, 1960).

29. Edward L. Bortz, "Exercise, Fitness and Aging," p. 8. *Exercise and Fitness*, Seward C. Staley, Chairman (Chicago: The University of Illinois and the Athletic Institute, 1960).

30. G. Lawrence Rarick, "Exercise and Growth," pp. 441; 460 *Science and Medicine of Exercise and Sports*, Warren G. Johnson (ed.) (New York: Harper and Brothers, 1960).

31. Perry Johnson *et al.*, *Physical Education—A Problem Solving Approach to Health and Fitness*, p. 109 (New York: Holt, Rinehart and Winston, 1966).

32. Paul Dudley White, "RX for Health: Exercise," *In* Perry Johnson *et al.*, *Physical Education—A Problem Solving Approach to Health and Fitness*, pp. 394–397 (New York: Holt, Rinehart and Winston, 1966).

33. Theodore Klump, "Heart Attacks and High Blood Pressure," *Think*, p. 5 (International Business Machines Company, March, 1958).

34. Paul Dudley White, "Health and Sickness in Middle Age," *JOHPER*, p. 22 (October, 1960).

35. *Today's Health*, p. 7 (Chicago: American Medical Association, July, 1971).

36. Oliver Byrd, "A Survey of Beliefs and Practices of Psychiatrists on the Relief of Tension by Moderate Exercises," *Journal of School Health*, p. 426 (November, 1963).

37. Hans Kraus and Ruth P. Hirschland, "Minimum Muscular Fitness Tests in School Children," *Research Quarterly*, pp. 178–187 (May, 1934).

38. Leonard Larson, "Some Findings Resulting from the Army Air Force Physical Training Program," *Research Quarterly*, p. 144 (October, 1946).

39. "Fitness Facts," *Equitable Life Assurance Society of the United States*, p. 1 (New York, n.d.).

40. Richard H. Pohndorf, "Physical Fitness of British and United States Children," pp. 8–16 *The Athletic Institute*, 1961.

41. *Fitness of American Youth*, A Report to the President of the United States, President's Council on Youth Fitness, pp. 7–8; 13 (June, 1956).

42. *Youth Physical Fitness: Suggested Elements of a School-Centered Program*, pp. 6–7; 4–5 President's Council on Youth Fitness, 1961.

43. President's Council on Physical Fitness and Sports, *Newsletter*, pp. 14–16 (June, 1971).

44. Bud Wilkinson, "The Lifetime Sports Foundation," *JOHPER*, p. 66 (April, 1965).

45. Paul Dudley White, "The Role of Exercise in the Aging," *Journal of the American Medical Association* (September 7, 1957).

46. *Crime in the United States 1971* (Washington, D.C.: Federal Bureau of Investigation, 1972).

47. Clark Hetherington, *A School Program in Physical Education*, p. 87 (New York: World Book Company, 1922).

48. The President's Commission on Law Enforcement and Administration of Justice, *Task Force Report: Juvenile Delinquency and Youth Crime* (Washington: U.S. Government Printing Office, 1967).

49. Thomas E. Shaffer, "The Adolescent's Health and Activity Needs," *Background Readings in Physical Education*, p. 367. Ann Paterson and Edmond C. Hallberg (eds.) (New York: Holt, Rinehart and Winston, 1966).

50. John Dewey, *Democracy in Education*, p. 241 (New York: The Macmillan Company, 1921).

51. W. H. Burnham, "The Development of the Wholesome Personality," Mental Hygiene Bulletin, September 1930, from John Eisele Davis and William Rush Dunton, *Recreational Therapy*, p. 40 (New York: A. S. Barnes and Company, 1936).

52. Emma M. Layman, "Contributions of Exercise and Sports to Mental Health and Social Development," *Science and Medicine of Exercise and Sports*, p. 576. Warren R. Johnson (ed.) (New York: Harper and Brothers, 1960).

53. "An Inner City Superintendent Supports Physical Education," *Physical Education Newsletter* (Croft Educational Services, Inc., June 1, 1971).

54. *Report*, American Medical Association House of Delegates (Miami, 1969).

55. Jesse F. Williams *et al.*, *Administration of Health Education and Physical Education*, 6th ed., p. 10 (Philadelphia: W. B. Saunders Company, 1964).

SELECTED READINGS

Bookwalter, Karl W. and Harold J. Vanderzwaag. *Foundations and Principles of Physical Education*. Philadelphia: W. B. Saunders Company, 1969.

Carroll, Herbert. *Mental Health: The Dynamics of Adjustment*. Englewood Cliffs, New Jersey: Prentice-Hall, Inc., 1951.

Caswell, Hollis. *The American High School: Its Responsibilities and Opportunity*. New York: Harper and Brothers, 1946.

Paterson, Ann, and Edmond C. Hallberg. *Background Readings for Physical Education*. New York: Holt, Rinehart and Winston, 1966.

Steinhaus, Arthur H. *Toward an Understanding of Health and Physical Education*. Dubuque, Iowa: William C. Brown Company, 1963.

Thayer, V. T. *The Role of the School in American Society*. New York: Dodd Mead and Company, 1961.

Toynbee, Arnold T. *A Study of History*. New York: Oxford University Press, 1957.

Van Dale, Deobold, Elmer Mitchell, and Bruce Bennett. *A World History of Physical Education*. Englewood Cliffs, New Jersey: Prentice-Hall, Inc., 1953.

Williams, Jesse F. *The Principles of Physical Education*, 8th ed. Philadelphia: W. B. Saunders Company, 1964.

Woodring, Paul, and John Scanlon (eds.). *American Education Today*. New York: McGraw-Hill Book Company, 1964.

Chapter 2

AREAS OF CONCERN IN PHYSICAL EDUCATION

*Life is not to live
but to be well.*
Martial

For years the curriculum in physical education has been subjected to various pressures and misunderstandings that have had adverse effects on the program. Because of these pressures, many programs have become weak, unscientific, and lacking in direction.

The author, while teaching graduate students in physical education at the University of South Dakota, conducted in the classes an extensive survey on the crucial issues in physical education. Out of the research accomplished in the classes grew recommendations for positive procedures that may be initiated to improve the overall situation. The findings and recommendations are discussed in the following paragraphs.

KEEP THE SCHOOL CURRICULUM IN BALANCE

Periodically, attention is focused on educational curriculum changes and revisions in order to meet new academic objectives. The need for more time for various academic subjects or the addition of new programs sometimes results in the relegation of physical education to a place of insecurity or obscurity.

In many locations, teaching stations assigned to physical education have been reassigned to other disciplines to expand academic programs. Physical education classes have been uprooted from their stations and assigned to study halls or other inadequate locations.

It is not sound educational procedure to expand the instructional offering in one essential subject at the expense of crippling or curtailing another essential area of instruction. It is the duty of administrators to provide enough time, space and teachers to upgrade *all* areas of instruction. Teachers may assist in upgrading physical education instruction by developing a program of public relations to inform the administrators and the community of their activities and of the importance of these activities for the students. Chapter 3 elaborates on the importance of public relations.

ESTABLISH REQUIREMENTS IN PHYSICAL EDUCATION

If any subject is to maintain a permanent place in the curriculum, it must be ranked as a required subject. Since health is a basic objective of education and necessary for preparing boys and girls for effective living, physical education should be required.

Figure 2-1. Daily physical education is necessary both for health and as insurance for the future.

The United States Office of Education showed that in 1943 and 1944 only 50 per-cent of all the boys in the 11th and 12th grades were provided with organized physi-cal education programs.[1] The situation has not improved since then. In 1958, the year Sputnik was launched, emphasis on science stimulated many administrators to down-grade the requirement in physical educa-tion. In 1960 Bookwalter showed that 50 percent of the boys and girls in high school were receiving no program of physical education at all.[2] Because of the emphasis on physical fitness by the President's Coun-cil on Physical Fitness and Sports, many parochial and private schools have in-creased their physical education offerings. The public school requirement has, how-ever, remained about the same.

SECURE CREDIT

Offering credit for physical education gives added meaning to the program. Very few systems grant credit for physical educa-tion comparable to that given for academic subjects. This attitude places the program in a bad light and causes pupils to lose respect for it.

If physical education is to assume the importance it rightly deserves, credit com-parable to that accorded to other subjects in the curriculum must be granted. This will come about only when teachers place

sufficient emphasis on teaching and when the program of teaching is of a caliber de-manding recognition.

IMPROVE TEACHER PREPARATION

Teachers who are adequately prepared for teaching in their chosen fields have little difficulty in doing an effective job. How-ever, teachers too frequently enter the pro-fession inadequately prepared to teach effectively. Not only do they lack knowledge of many activities, they also are not pre-pared to teach skills to large groups. This is particularly true in teaching the skills of individual sports, such as golf, tennis, tumbling, swimming, and wrestling. Teachers are usually able to teach the skills of an activity to a small group of five or six pupils. Problems arise when the teacher meets a class of 50 and is expected to teach the same skill to this large group. He in-variably attempts to teach only a few pupils while a large group remains idle. This procedure, if allowed to continue in-definitely, creates disciplinary problems and leads to ineffective instruction. The way to correct this and other similar de-ficiencies in the teacher is through a pro-gram of professional preparation. Colleges and universities which prepare teachers are attempting to improve their programs; their efforts should be intensified.

IMPROVE FACILITIES

Although adequate facilities are necessary for effective instruction in physical education, there are few places in America where teaching facilities are comparable to those of the academic program. The science department in a high school having 1200 pupils probably has a classroom and a teacher for every 150 pupils (eight teachers). A school of this size should have at least six stations and six teachers for physical education, based on 40 pupils per teacher, five periods per day, with one free period (see Chapter 15). Very few schools have such an arrangement.

However, teachers should not use inadequate facilities as an excuse to resort to poor teaching; instead they should learn to improvise and use the existing facilities as effectively as possible. It is only by using inadequate facilities to their best advantage that the teacher will be able to justify the need for better facilities.

ESTABLISH OBJECTIVES

Teachers need to have clearly established objectives if effective teaching is to be achieved. They often launch or are launched into a program without established goals; too often, also, the program follows tradition rather than serving current needs. The teacher who selects activities for children that are outdated and that may be injurious to health does so through poor planning of objectives. If instruction in leisure-time activities is to be a basic objective, teachers must teach skills in those activities that the student will engage in long after his school career has ended.

IMPROVE INSTRUCTION

Good instruction is important in all subjects and it is more than ever before necessary for the survival of physical education as a profession. The quality of instruction in many places is so poor and the program has deteriorated to such an extent that administrators and the public will no longer support it. Many years ago LaPorte made the observation, "In many instances a physical education class consists merely of a period of supervised play with no thought of instruction."[3] This situation still exists, and physical education as a profession has suffered because of either poor instruction or no instruction at all.

Poor teaching shows up more readily in a physical education class than in other areas of instruction. The informal, free-play, loosely organized class is not only nonproductive in attaining excellence in skill performance but it is also fraught with situations adversely affecting the health and safety of pupils. A well-planned, smoothly organized, well-taught program in physical education is something beautiful to see; a poorly taught program, on the other hand, is sadly lacking in its contributions to education.

ESTABLISH NORMAL TEACHING LOADS

If teachers of physical education are expected to do a satisfactory job, they must have a teaching load comparable to teachers of other subjects in the curriculum. Although teachers of academic subjects have reasonable teaching loads, physical education teachers are frequently given 50, 70, and sometimes 100 pupils per period to teach. Not only is it impractical to teach a group as large as this effectively but the problem of safety also exists in such large classes. The safety of pupils should always be of prime concern to a teacher, and it is a serious mistake to expect a teacher to be responsible for teaching unreasonably large classes. But, as in the case of inadequate facilities, teachers should not become apathetic in situations that are deplorable. They should continually strive to correct the situation; until the conditions are alleviated, the teachers should do their best by using newer methods of organizing in order to meet the challenge of large classes. One of the purposes of this book is to show how this can be done.

EMPHASIZE SCIENTIFIC PROGRAMS

Physical education activities have a pronounced effect on the health of boys and girls, and teachers should strive to include only those activities in the curriculum that are best suited to the growth needs of pupils.

Programs of the past were often mass exercises in which the teacher performed all the planning and direction, giving pupils little opportunity either to express themselves or to develop their innate potentialities. The emphasis was on developing muscle; little if any thought was given to the close relationship of the physical with the mental and emotional. Those programs became unpopular because students were continually asking: Muscles for what? Why lift weights, tumble, or chin the bar? Why perform for many hours the various exercises included in the calisthenic program? Developing muscle with strength as the basis was the end objective rather than the means through which to achieve a goal. Many teachers today still feel that developing muscle is the sole objective of the physical education program.

The present trend toward the formal, unnatural program just noted, which is evident in many places, may very well place physical education in the same uncertain position it was in 50 years ago. This trend cannot be criticized too strongly. Many individuals and groups, aided by manufacturers of various contrivances for use in physical education classrooms, are not only causing irreparable damage to the physical education program, but are also preventing boys and girls from receiving the type of instruction they should have. Physical education leaders must take a stand and voice their opinions regarding this trend, which is unscientific, unrealistic, and contrary to research findings.

It is difficult to understand why supposedly trained teachers will impose on boys and girls unnatural calisthenics and other uninteresting movements that are as antiquated as the model-T Ford. It could perhaps be understood if nothing else were available, but excellent programs based on the needs and interests of the pupils are easily initiated. This point of view is developed more fully in Chapter 6.

One of the most difficult problems in physical education is the use of the empirical approach to content selection. Individual opinions without scientific background have had an adverse effect on the curriculum content. An illustration of this is the teacher who, during high school and college, was an outstanding basketball player. He accepts a position teaching physical education and coaching basketball. In his opinion basketball should occupy a dominant position in the program because he likes it. This point of view could be the factor that would cause the teacher to exclude from the curriculum such carry-over activities as tennis, bowling, golf, and swimming.

The author has seen entire programs consisting of a single activity, such as weight lifting, football, or various gymnastics and calisthenics. Another example of such a program was published showing an entire program of physical education that consisted of 45 minutes of calisthenics and a shower.[4] These programs, based entirely on the individual whims or opinions of an administrator, coach, or physical education teacher, are completely without scientific foundation.

KEEP THE INTERSCHOLASTIC PROGRAM IN PROPER PERSPECTIVE

Interscholastic athletics are an important part of the school program, and teachers should be encouraged to make every effort to develop the best programs possible. It is unfortunate, however, when the interscholastic program dominates the physical education curriculum. Too often pressure is placed on coaches to win contests. If the coaches teach physical education, they may concentrate on their coaching assignments and neglect the instructional program. They frequently are more interested in their teams than in instruction and use class time for varsity practice or use pupils in various classes for developing players for the varsity program. Teachers who coach also frequently use teaching time to plan schedules, view films of games and plan plays and strategies for future games, thus leaving classes to their own devices, and resorting to the "throwing-out-the-ball" type of program. Many programs in physical education throughout the country have suffered because of these practices.

The antagonism that exists between the physical education teacher and the coach may hurt the instruction program in physical education. Thomas Hamilton, Executive Director of Athletic Associations of Western

Universities, makes the following observation: "We, the physical educators and coaches, spend most of our time selling ourselves or bickering between ourselves."[5]

Physical education should not be confused with the interscholastic program. Athletics are for the gifted few; physical education is designed for everyone. Physical Education is an instructional program; interscholastic athletics are extracurricular activities. There is a place and a need for both programs in the schools; with thoughtful administration and supervision, the two programs can assist each other tremendously.

MOTIVATE THE PLAY URGE

The play urge, which is one of the basic drives of boys and girls, should be motivated by the physical education program.

Some people are of the opinion that the play urge, the urge for physical activity, is diminishing; and when one observes the ways many teenagers spend their time today, one must agree. Juniors and seniors in the large high schools enjoy entertainment involving sitting, riding, and viewing more than activities requiring a great deal of movement. At some point in their lives the urge for play and physical activity has been discouraged and inhibited either because of poor, artificial programs based on unnatural activities or because of the lack of any program at all. Teachers must initiate sound programs of physical education based on the needs and interests of pupils from the first grade through high school. The play urge is instinctive, but it must be continually motivated during the school years if pupils are to remain physically active throughout life.

COUNTERACT THE PLAY CONNOTATION

Many people associate the word "play" with activity that lacks purpose and educational benefits. The play concept has hurt the program in physical education. Vestiges of old religious beliefs which frowned on play still prevail in some places and influence those who are responsible for administering educational funds. Some are unwilling to support a program that is basically a play program.

Teachers, in attempting to provide actual play for all pupils in their classes, are prone to neglect one important objective of physical education—the teaching of skills. The play program that dominates many classes in physical education usually results in a situation in which a group of pupils is given a ball. Then, after spending valuable time choosing sides, the pupils attempt to play a game with the teacher either officiating or standing on the sidelines observing. This procedure has a deleterious effect on the entire physical education program. Teachers are not needed to watch a group of pupils play a game; they are needed to teach.

IMPROVE PUBLIC RELATIONS AND INTERPRETATION

A well-planned public relations program is a sure way of bringing the purposes of the instructional program in physical education before the public.

The athletic program is self-perpetuating, but the instructional program in physical education rarely is interpreted to the public. A well-planned, dynamic public relations program is imperative if the program is to survive. The public, administrators, teachers, and pupils should be shown why physical education is essential to a well-developed educational program and basic to personal fitness and health. These objectives should be discussed, and the manner in which the program attempts to reach these objectives should be explained.

When teachers are able to show evidence that the quality of students' lives after school and after graduation has been improved through physical education programs taken in school, then and then only will the programs assume the desired level of recognition and authority in the school and the community.

MOTIVATE PUBLIC INTEREST

A well-informed and interested public is desirable if schools are to provide adequate instruction in physical education. The public has never been overly concerned with the school physical education program. Indeed, there is evidence all around us indicating that the public is not particularly concerned with health in general. A case in point is the recent information concerning cigarette smoking and health. Despite the overwhelming evidence pointing to the high correlation between excessive smoking and lung cancer, smoking increased during the year the study was released.

Although adults are sometimes negligent in their own health habits, they are usually concerned with the health of their children. Physical Education teachers need to interpret the program sufficiently in order to acquaint parents with the importance of physical education and its relation to their children's normal growth and development. Teachers should have a strong background in the advances in health practices that will enable them to assist pupils in the acquisition of proper health knowledge and the formation of correct health habits. The results of these procedures will eventually reach the home and help to direct public opinion toward greater interest in health and fitness and support for physical education programs.

INFORM COMMUNITY PRESSURE GROUPS

Community groups play a powerful role in assisting the public schools with their many problems, and these groups should be informed of the content of the physical education program. Sometimes local groups become enthusiastic about some selected activities and pressure school authorities to include these activities in the program. Teachers and administrators should be aware of this trend and attempt to show the group how certain activities are beneficial whereas others may be injurious to the health and fitness of children.

An illustration of this type of pressure was recently experienced by the author. Several parent groups became emotionally concerned about the safety of young girls and women because of several assault incidents. They initiated a campaign to teach the deadly art of karate to young girls through the instructional physical education classes. If these groups had not been shown the objectives of physical education,

the criteria for selecting activities scientifically, and the dangers of this sport, karate would have been placed in the curriculum.

Physical education programs are concerned primarily with the health and fitness of individual boys and girls. These programs may affect the health of young people as seriously as the regimen prescribed by a member of the medical profession. The wrong prescription of exercise or activity may have an adverse effect on the health of boys and girls equal to that which the wrong prescription or diagnosis in medicine may have. Activities included in the program of physical education will affect the health of boys and girls either adversely or favorably. Community groups who seek to amend the curriculum should therefore be shown why some activities are included and others excluded.

If physical education is to maintain its proper place in the school curriculum, it must make a consistently positive contribution to students' health. This premise should continually be brought to the attention of the community in order that the program be interpreted properly.

EDUCATE THE MANUFACTURERS

Members of the profession should continuously include the equipment manufacturers in their public relations programs in order to acquaint them with the objectives of physical education and to encourage them to design and market equipment that will help to carry out these objectives.

Through the years, many manufacturers have cooperated with teachers in a joint effort to improve equipment and make it more functional. However, some manufacturers through extensive advertising have flooded the market with equipment and gadgets that have no value in teaching physical education. Buyers frequently purchase this equipment without considering its usefulness to the activity involved, to see whether it contributes to recognized objectives. An illustration of this point is the extensive use of swings on playgrounds. Swinging offers very little exercise and can be extremely dangerous. The amount of time and money spent on swings could be more wisely invested, for example, in climbing apparatus, which is less dangerous and provides opportunity for a much greater amount of activity. Teachers should be extremely careful before including activities and equipment that do not meet the basic objectives in physical education. Many items of equipment now used in the program are of little real value, as the teacher in the average community will readily see if he makes a survey of his program and his community. Only through careful study by the teacher of the needs of pupils and discussion of these needs with the manufacturers may equipment be constructed that continues to serve the purposes of the program.

MAINTAIN PRESTIGE

The status that a program enjoys in the school curriculum contributes tremendously to the effectiveness of teaching.

Physical education has not occupied the level of prestige enjoyed by academic subjects since the days of the ancient Grecian civilization. This is partially because of the nature of the subject itself and the types of programs that have dominated teaching for many years. In those places where physical education is properly organized and effectively taught, and where the content is in keeping with recognized objectives, the program is appreciated and occupies a respected place in the curriculum.

It is the teacher's job to develop the climate of teaching in such a way that the program will gain prestige. The teacher's grooming, his speech, his personality, and his effectiveness in teaching and in interpreting his program will influence the level of respect that physical education achieves in his community.

Physical education teachers should employ the rich background of their field in their associations with their colleagues. When a group of science teachers meet during the day for lunch or an assigned period, they discuss the technicalities involved in nuclear energy and other phases of the science curriculum. Physical education teachers usually discuss why Joe Jones did not make the extra point after the touchdown or why they lost five dollars on Saturday's game. Teachers of academic subjects are not favorably impressed by such trivia. These teachers of physical education might

discuss such items as why the law of reciprocal innervation is violated in an isometric movement or why the principle of opposition is not followed in fencing. Discussing such topics may help the teachers understand their own field better; moreover, it will help to correct the fallacy that there is no depth of content in physical education. The program of physical education has important implications which permeate other phases of education, but teachers too often fail to include these implications in their "shop talk" with their colleagues from other disciplines.

Another point in developing prestige is the professional terminology. Sometimes teachers and administrators refer to the physical education program as "gym" or "fizz-ed." These terms are not at all descriptive or complimentary. Teachers should continually try to remedy this unfortunate choice of terms by using the proper terminology themselves. To bring the program out of the dressing-room connotation to the main floor of acceptance, it should be called by its proper title—physical education.

ESTABLISH COLLEGE ENTRANCE REQUIREMENTS

The entrance requirements established by the colleges and universities insure a permanent place for academic subjects in the high school curriculum. If a certain number of credits in physical education were required for college entrance, the program would immediately assume prestige and improvement in quality would follow. Although teachers are not in a position to influence this situation directly, they should use their local and national associations to assist with the problem.

WORK TOWARD UNANIMITY OF PHILOSOPHY

College leaders play an important role in determining the philosophy of physical education; however, a few institutions of higher education share a common philosophy in preparing students for teaching. Some teacher-preparation programs are dominated by athletic activities; some emphasize recreation; others stress gymnastics with emphasis on calisthenics and apparatus. More colleges should offer intensive instruction in how to teach effectively the important carry-over sports, such as tennis, golf, wrestling, bowling, and swimming, which are basic to current objectives in physical education.

In some teacher-training programs, the approach for many years has been to present two points of view and to allow pupils to make their own decisions on what is right or wrong. In preparing teachers for the challenge of the future, teacher-training institutions should prepare students to decide which point of view is right. Successful teaching cannot exist on indecision. If there is one phase of the educational curriculum in which unanimity of purpose is needed, it is in the field of physical education. Teachers must know what is currently accepted as the correct method of teaching a skill. It is possible that research may, at a later date, improve on this procedure; but until this is done, there is only one correct method at a given moment.

As an illustration, let us examine the procedure for teaching the front somersault in tumbling. It is generally accepted that a performer must tuck neatly at just the right moment, and also at just the right moment come out of the tuck, landing in the upright position. For a teacher to fail to teach the somersault the right way might very well result in tragedy. If the teacher fails to emphasize the urgency of tucking properly, the performer may land on his neck and a serious injury or death may be the result. Accident statistics point out the many tragedies resulting from improper teaching procedures.

The tumbling illustration may be applicable in establishing a basic philosophy in physical education. If research and logic show that natural activities involving the fundamental movements of man are essential for normal growth and development, then all teachers should emphasize such activities. If certain calisthenic and gymnastic movements are unsafe and do not contribute to normal physiologic growth and development, then all teachers must know why, and must establish criteria for selecting the right activities.

Boxing offers an illustration of this point of view. For many years boxing was one of the top priority activities, which was not only taught in the classroom but was also an important intercollegiate and interscholastic sport. Today, because of safety factors, boxing is no longer found in the curriculum. Physical educators agree that the sport is counter to current philosophy in physical education. This kind of general agreement should be encouraged for all aspects of the physical education curriculum.

Teachers, if they are to be successful, must know the proper way to teach skills. They must also have a sound basic philosophy regarding the overall program if their efforts are to bring about the desired results. Preparation for teaching should include a study of the latest findings in physical education research in order to approach the desired objectives in teaching. Teachers must realize that they are dealing with the health and fitness of children and this fact demands a rather high degree of consistency in the philosophy under which they work toward their objectives.

The purpose of Chapters 1 and 2 has been to point out the need for physical education in the 20th century and to show why programs of physical education in many cases are not fulfilling their mission. It is interesting to note that several of the crucial issues presented in Chapter 2 are issues of public relations. The next chapter will show how an effective public relations program for physical education can be initiated and maintained.

QUESTIONS FOR DISCUSSION

1. Why is good health a major objective of education?
2. What groups have listed good health as a major objective?
3. What is the chief cause of the decline in fitness of the American youth?
4. What has been the influence of the manufacturers on the health of the American youth?
5. How does personal opinion affect the curriculum adversely?

6. What effect does the interscholastic program have on physical education?

7. How are community groups able to affect the program?

8. What is meant by the scientific program? The natural program?

9. How does the philosophy of the college affect the program in the secondary school?

10. Discuss several ways of improving the prestige of the physical education program.

SUGGESTED ACTIVITIES

1. Visit a local business and search for examples of automation. Show how the workers are affected.

2. Make a survey of schools that have reassigned physical education teaching stations to other departments. List the conditions that have led to the change.

3. Compile a list of manufacturers' items that affect the physical education program adversely.

4. Study the facilities in a high school in the community. If you feel that they are inadequate, show what improvements should be made.

REFERENCES

1. United States Office of Education, *Education for Victory*, III Bulletin No. 1 (Washington, D.C.: Government Printing Office, July 3, 1944).

2. Karl Bookwalter, *Basic Activities for Secondary Physical Education* (Unpublished paper, Indiana University, 1960).

3. W. Ralph LaPorte, *The Physical Education Curriculum* p. 58 (Los Angeles: The University of Southern California Press, 1940).

4. Editorial, *Physical Education Newsletter* (December, 1964).

5. Thomas J. Hamilton, "An Athletic Director Looks at Fitness," *JOHPER*, p. 14 (September, 1957).

SELECTED READINGS

Brunner, Burton C. "How Will Today's Physical Education Classes be Remembered in 1989?" *JOHPER,* February, 1969, p. 42.

"Current Administrative Problems." *National Association of Secondary School Principals.* Washington, D.C.: AAHPER, 1960.

Francis, Robert J. "1956 Study of Basic Issues Facing the Profession." *JOHPER*, December, 1960.

Griffith, Daniel E. "The Ten Most Significant Educational Research Findings in the Past Ten Years." *Executive Action Newsletter,* Croft Educational Services, Inc., May, 1967.

Larson, Leonard A., *et al. Problems in Health, Physical Education, and Recreation.* Englewood Cliffs, New Jersey: Prentice-Hall, Inc., 1953.

Paterson, Ann, and Edmond C. Hallberg. *Background Readings for Physical Education.* New York: Holt, Rinehart and Winston, 1966.

Sanborn, Marian A., and Betty G. Hartman. *Issues in Physical Education.* Philadelphia: Lea and Febiger, 1964.

Steinhaus, Arthur H. *Toward an Understanding of Health and Physical Education.* Dubuque, Iowa: William C. Brown Company, 1963.

Chapter 3

SCHOOL-COMMUNITY RELATIONS

It is appalling that the story of education is being told so poorly, when it is told at all.

C. K. Hodenfield

Courtesy Richmond Senior High School, Richmond, Indiana

Education in America's public schools has weathered many social and economic storms. The depression of the 1930's, World Wars I and II, and the Korean and Viet Nam conflicts have all left their marks on education. Every upheaval in the social structure in the past 50 years has been reflected in the schools, often resulting in lowered teacher morale, inadequate facilities, sub-standard instruction and in some instances the closing of schools.

The front pages of the nation's newspapers carry headlines that reveal the crucial status of public education:

"Quick Bus Ruling Predicted"
"100 U.S. Teachers Drop Under for Jobs, Australia Needs Them"
"Teacher Job Report Ordered"
"Teachers to Press for Raises"
"School Aid Policy Vote Set Today"

Education in America is big business. Projected enrollments by 1977 are expected to reach 63 million students from kindergarten through college. A staggering 41 percent of local taxes is used for schools.[1]

Onrushing events focus the attention of teachers and administrators on the need for and importance of public support for education. The problem is greater today because of the many sensitive issues, such as busing, integration, riots, drugs and other social turbulences, all of which involve the public schools. In addition to these problems, teachers and administrators face public and student opinion concerning the curriculum itself. Grave concern is voiced with regard to equal educational opportunity for minority groups, special education for the handicapped, and the teaching of controversial subjects, such as sex education.

Never in the history of American education have the schools and the community needed each other as much as they do now. The schools must rely on the taxpayer for support of education, and the taxpayer needs the expertise of educators to assist with the education of his children in a turbulent society. Cutlip and Center give three reasons for strengthening the schools in order to enlist the support of the community:

1. In the battle for freedom and peace, United States citizens face problems of unequaled perplexity and difficulty. The need for educated, informed citizens capable of charting a safe course for the nation was never greater. One of the prime functions of education is to develop informed citizens equal to their responsibilities. Schools should offer every child an education up to his capacity.

2. Because our system is grounded in free education, schools represent the first point of

Figure 3–1. Education is big business in the United States. The magnitude of education in this country is revealed in the headlines of the nation's newspapers.

attack. Vigilance and common sense are required to safeguard against subversion and against injury from well-intentioned but ignorant zealots.

3. The educational system, from kindergarten to university, is confronted with a lack of adequate facilities and qualified teachers. The accelerated birth rate since World War II has swamped present facilities and staffs. There are more young people, more of them going to school and more going longer. In 1967, there were nearly 44 million pupils in public schools. In 1977, there will be 48 million children enrolled. For a typical city of 100,000, this means one new school building every few years. For example, in Huntsville, Alabama, school enrollment increased rapidly enough to require one additional teacher and one additional classroom a week for five years out of ten. Urban mobility also complicates the building problems for school boards.[1]

The California Report on School-Community Relations

A recent report compiled by the California Bureau of Health Education, Physical Education, Athletics and Recreation showed that visits to more than 500 high schools in the past six years revealed that those which had outstanding programs had also developed excellent community support.

Interpreting educational purposes to the community is vital; to ignore it could very well lead to the demise of education. Studies show why this opportunity for two-way communication is necessary. Carter compiled interviews with community leaders in 82 school districts and interviews with sample voters in four cities. The following results reflect the opinions of taxpayers regarding education:

The voter thinks schools are good in general, but he criticizes them in particular areas: frills, too much play, curriculum and discipline.

The voter thinks the most important tasks of schools are to teach the fundamentals—reading, writing, spelling, arithmetic, and speaking—and to instill loyalty to the United States. He also thinks that these are the jobs done best.

The voter thinks the least important tasks of the schools are to teach about the local region, to afford enjoyment of cultural activities—art and music—and to provide industrial arts education.

The voter's evaluation of the local schools, his evaluation of school costs, and his pride in the schools are most closely associated with likelihood of voting and of voting favorably.

About half the voters show no evidence of any participation in school affairs and no interest in such participation. About a third of the voters participate actively. The more the voter participates, the more knowledge he has of school performance.[2]

The issues involved in the program of physical education discussed in Chapter 2 demonstrate both the need for a stronger professional relationship between the

---

Physical Education During the Sixties

Richard H. Pohndorf, a leader in physical education who is concerned with the status of physical education, feels there has been a national decline in physical fitness. The many reports on both the national and international level have given the public cause for concern. He feels the condition exists because of the following conditions:

1. Two percent of the high school population has physical education five times per week.

2. Less than 50 percent of the 12 million boys and girls in 30,000 high schools have physical education two or three times a week.

3. Fifty percent of the high school population has no physical education in the curriculum.

4. More than 80 percent of all skills necessary for sports participation, which an individual develops during his lifetime, are acquired between the ages of seven to 17. These "ten" skill and fitness years are highly important and currently being neglected by school authorities.

Richard H. Pohndorf, "The Erosion of Physical Education," Physical Education Newsletter (June 12, 1961).

Will the Program Improve in the Seventies?

teacher, the administrators, and the colleges and the need for interpreting the program to the community. Moreover, implicit in the recommendations for meeting the issues is the fact that the survival of physical education may very well depend upon how well teachers and leaders in the field are able to arouse people and acquaint them with the importance to our youth of an effective program of physical education in the schools. This chapter is devoted to showing how the program may be interpreted through the various public relations media.

PLURAL PUBLICS

The school public relations program should be carefully planned to reach certain groups who have influence over the administration of the school. Too often "the public" is referred to as one large, all-inclusive body. However, there is no one public. There is, instead, an infinite number of publics; and just as there are many publics, there are also many opinions. Opinions also vary *within* a given public or group. Public relations is a way of influencing public opinion. If the public relations program effectively reaches each of the publics, many of the problems confronting the profession will cease to exist. Two-way communication should be established between the schools and the following groups which comprise most of the plural publics.

Community

Every community is composed of organizations concerned with the operation of the schools within the community. Some of these groups are the civic clubs, parent-teacher organizations, youth groups, church-affiliated groups, chambers of commerce, manufacturers, medical associations, public health organizations, patriotic agencies, business and industry, fraternal groups, and various health, cultural and governmental agencies.

Administrators

This group of people consists of the principals, directors of instruction, coor-

dinators, supervisors, assistant superintendents, and superintendents. Many administrators are academically oriented and perhaps unaware of the importance of physical education. They are usually specialists in a particular subject who have been selected from the classroom. It is important that they understand the need for a well-planned program of physical education and the importance of this program in relation to the growth and development of children. The media used to reach this group may be entirely different from the media used to reach the general public.

Faculty

The faculty in a particular school, although not directly responsible for the program, may influence the success of the program by their attitude toward physical education and toward the physical education teacher. A well-organized program in which the physical education teacher is constantly striving to improve will go a long way toward favorably impressing other teachers, who in turn will support the program. In addition, a quality program should include announcements, bulletins and other materials, which should be disseminated among the school faculty.

Students

Students comprise the single most important public. They must understand the program and the need for it. When each activity is explained to them, they will cooperate more willingly and benefit more directly from the instruction. Too often teachers impose activities on a class without explanation; and the students, not realizing the importance of the activity, are uncooperative and perhaps rebel.

The Physical Education Teacher

The school-community relations program can be no better than the teacher. An enthusiastic, knowledgeable teacher can exude so much enthusiasm that the importance of the program will be understood by his students, who in turn carry the program home to their parents. This interpretation of the program through pupils is a most effective public relations tool. The teacher must continually strive to make his class meaningful to the pupils. How interesting and effective the program is to pupils may be determined by asking questions such as the following:

1. Do my pupils seem happy with the program?
2. Is my teaching enthusiastic?
3. Do I arrange for individualized instruction?
4. Do I explain the purpose and value of each activity taught?
5. Do I vary the program content?
6. Do I provide ways for each child to experience success?
7. Do I group pupils by ability?
8. Do I set an example in morals, character and fitness that students and others admire?
9. Do I practice what I preach regarding sportsmanship?
10. Do I actually teach rather than "throw out the ball"?
11. Do I utilize available time for instruction?

If you, as a teacher, can answer these questions affirmatively, then you may be assured that you have the admiration of your pupils. If you teach 200 students per day, you will then have 200 public relations agents interpreting the program in favorable terms to their parents and others.

Figure 3–2. Every student is a school-community relations agent. (Courtesy Richmond Senior High School, Richmond, Indiana.)

School-Community Relations, Teacher Challenge

Tom York, sports director of WBRC-TV, Birmingham, Alabama, and a long time advocate of health and fitness, describes his philosophy in informing the public about physical education:

You can't sell the program by telling them that they will develop terminal diseases and die if they don't participate. A few may buy it but not many.

I'm convinced that you sell it the same way you sell soap, cereal, automobiles, and clothes. You sell the sizzle instead of the steak; you sell the aroma instead of the coffee; you sell the bouquet instead of the wine.

York, a member of the original PEPI Committee (Physical Education Public Information Project), challenges the teacher to sell the program. He says:

And finally—let's face it. The whole physical education program, and the professionals in it, have long been considered a back-of-the-bus proposition by the rest of the academic community.

I submit that if you are to become a meaningful force in the physical development of future generations, this image must necessarily be upgraded—and you have within yourself the ability, the tools, and the potential for forging this concept of the "New Physical Education."

Tom York, "Who Buys Physical Education?"

Figure 3–3. The teacher is the driving force behind the school-community relations program.

THE POWER STRUCTURE IN THE COMMUNITY

Research has shown that communities and cities usually have a few individuals who constitute the power structure. In the past it was thought that the general public had the power, but recent studies show this to be untrue. A relatively few individuals frequently constitute the "hidden" power and wield final authority over public affairs. When planning the public relations program, teachers should understand the power structure and try to reach those few individuals who constitute the "hidden" authority over public functions.

DEFINITION OF SCHOOL-COMMUNITY RELATIONS

Kindred defines school public relations as a process of communication between the school and the community. He says:

School public relations is a process of communication between the school and community for the purpose of increasing citizen understanding of educational needs and practices and encouraging intelligent citizen interest and cooperation in the work of improving the school.[3]

The goal, of course, is to improve education and through it to improve society. Such a goal provides a foundation for school-community cooperation. The public relations program is a two-way communications system through which these two segments of society acquaint each other with their needs. Because society moves slowly, even in its own interests, educators need to have an organized public relations program through which it can influence public opinion to support quality education.

When working with the various publics, school leaders should be aware that each one is opinionated and sensitive. This is not a derogatory accusation, but the statement of a simple truth of human nature. Indeed, who among us does not have some bias? It is obvious that people who work with the community and try to influence public opinion can accomplish their purpose much more easily if they begin with a recognition of this fact. It is considered a good public relations approach to begin where the public is and lead it to the desired goal. Such an approach necessitates the establishment of objectives to assist the teacher in planning a school-community relations program.

The School-Community Relations Creed

In the long run, schools secure the best kind of public relations by maintaining the highest professional standards, by dealing honestly, tactfully, fairly, sympathetically and courageously with all. In all contacts with the press and the public, educators stand to lose nothing and to gain everything by being thoroughly frank and forthright, and by doing everything possible to demonstrate that the schools' paramount concern is the growth and welfare of the pupils and the community.[4]

THE OBJECTIVES OF SCHOOL-COMMUNITY RELATIONS

The teacher, before initiating a program in school-community relations, should establish definite objectives. These objectives may be used to evaluate the program and assist in determining the progress made in reaching desired goals. The following guidelines should be helpful to the teacher in acquainting the public with the needs and importance of physical education:

1. People should know the purposes of physical education in a democratic culture. These purposes should be interpreted with emphasis on the importance of physical education in the survival of our country. Representatives from the various organizations within the community should be involved in developing the curriculum. During this developmental process they become acquainted with the aims and objectives of physical education.

2. The school-community relations program should develop within the community a deeper insight and understanding of the physical education curriculum. This may be accomplished by actual presentation of effective teaching methods showing the influence of the instruction on the growth and development of pupils. This may be done through practical use of the media outlined in this chapter.

3. Parents should be periodically apprised of the status and performance of their children. They want to know the accomplishments of their children, the progress they have made, how these achievements compare with those of other children and other systems, and the results of today as compared with performance in the past. An illustration of reporting physical education to parents is shown in Chapter 14.

4. The school-community relations program should acquaint the many publics of the problems facing physical education. All should know about crowded classes, inadequate facilities, poor equipment and ineffective instruction.

5. The program in school-community relations should inform the people of the results attained in the existing teaching setting. Through the use of appropriate media parents should know just how much is being accomplished in spite of handicaps and obstacles.

6. The value of physical education in our country should be re-emphasized. The publics should be made to realize that the most powerful nation on earth reached this status through the constructive efforts of millions of people who received their education in the nation's schools. The role of physical education in developing health and fitness as aspects of this country's greatness should be shown.

7. The citizens should understand the responsibilities of teachers of physical education. This is more important today than in the past both because of the great demands made on teachers in a changing society and because of the increased cost of education.

8. The school-community relations program should involve citizens in assuming a greater responsibility for quality instruction. This can be done by showing citizens that the solution to many problems in our society depends on public support of education, which in turn attempts to provide quality instruction in an effort to alleviate these problems. Enlisting groups to sponsor various activities (Figure 3–10) is an illustration of one way to implement this objective.

9. School-community relationships

should develop a two-way system of communications between the school and the community. This may be accomplished by initiating a partnership between parents and teachers, promoting cooperative efforts of the schools and the publics and providing joint committees for parents and teachers to work together in planning programs.

UNDERLYING PRINCIPLES OF SCHOOL-COMMUNITY RELATIONS

There are many approaches to school-community relations. The program of physical education has several facets, each of which may be of tremendous interest to the public if presented properly. The very magnitude of the program necessitates the formulation of basic principles to guide the teacher who is attempting to interpret the program.

School-community relations cannot be left to chance. Interpreting the program to the plural publics is too important to the survival of physical education to be allowed to operate in an erratic or haphazard manner. Every contact that teachers have with the pupils, parents, and the community develops an attitude, positive or negative, toward the teacher, the physical education program and the school. The American Association of School Administrators has compiled a list of basic principles for public relations, which should be helpful to the teacher in determining the character of the school-community relations program:

1. School public relations must be honest in intent and execution.
2. School public relations must be intrinsic.
3. School public relations must be continuous.
4. School public relations must be positive in approach.
5. School public relations should be comprehensive.
6. School public relations should be sensitive to its public.
7. The ideas communicated must be simple.[4]

SPECIFIC GUIDELINES IN REACHING THE PUBLICS

The general principles listed above establish a foundation for a sound school-community relations program. However, in addition to these principles, the teacher should have some simple but specific guidelines to assist him in interpreting the program. Because of the uniqueness of the program and its important relationship with community health, these guidelines should be understood by the teacher before initiating any plan of educating the public. In other words, the teacher must first educate himself about every facet of his program before he attempts to intepret it to others. The following guidelines are suggested.

The Teacher Must Realize His Responsibility for School-Community Relations. The key to successful school-community relations is the teacher. He is in a strategic position for initiating a sound program of instruction which challenges the pupil, appeals to parents and satisfies the taxpayer. It is the teacher who in the final analysis must answer to the parent, the administrator and the public regarding the need and the importance of the program. The teacher in his everyday contacts with parents and lay people will impress them either positively or negatively depending on his ability to win friends and interest them in his profession. The teacher may use the following practices in developing lines of communication between the school and the community. He should:

1. Belong to community groups, become interested in the various committees of the organization and assist them in their efforts. These groups will eventually become his most valuable allies.
2. Enlist the support of various groups and individuals in the program by inviting them to speak to classes, participate in school programs and assist in planning the program.
3. Be available to make talks before the various clubs on such topics as physical fitness, exercise and health, and the importance of learning leisure time skills. He should develop some of the material discussed in Chapter 1 and present it to clubs and other organizations.
4. Become acquainted with the criticisms aimed at physical education and counter those criticisms with scientific information which shows the need for the program.
5. Be able to justify some of the demands made by physical education leaders

such as requirements, credit, and adequate money for facilities, equipment and supplies.

6. Study the various media of public relations discussed in this chapter and develop them in interpreting the program.

The Teacher Should Know the Relationship of Physical Education to Health. We have already emphasized the need for a revitalization of programs in physical education instruction. The facts are available from various sources, such as popular news media, regarding malnutrition, the need for more exercise, and the urgency of educating the masses in wiser use of their leisure time. Although advances in medical science have practically eliminated many diseases and have increased our life span, the ever-increasing incidence of heart disease, emotional instability, and diseases of the aged caused by lack of exercise paint an alarming picture. The truth of these general health conditions must be realized and carried to the home and to the leaders in every community. Moreover, these leaders must be shown the important contribution school physical education programs make in combating these conditions.

The Teacher Should Use His Knowledge to Establish Quality Instruction. There are too many poorly planned and meaningless programs throughout the country today. It is difficult to justify the expenditure of tax money for the employment of a highly trained college graduate to "throw out a ball" and then stand around watching a group of pupils play a game. The program of physical education can survive only when it is based on instruction in the skills of those activities and areas that have meaning and value to the pupil, the administrators, and the public.

In September, 1970, an article appeared in Family Health which carried the following heading:

Physical Education
ARE OUR CHILDREN BEING CHEATED?

They certainly are. Some gym classes aren't very physical or educational, even for the few youngsters who can make the school team.

The heading alone is enough to show how badly people are misinformed about physical education. It refers to "gym classes" which is a distasteful term used for physical education. It is terminology such as this that lessens the respectability of the profession.

In the article serious charges are leveled at physical education. The author, Jackson Pollack, states that the program instead of planning to build health and fitness for all children concentrates on the athletically elite few. He claims that millions of taxpayers' dollars are wasted on these programs and that the average child who needs a good physical education is neglected to such an extent that his future health may be impaired.

The author cites the results of studies by experts throughout the country which disclose the reasons physical education in so many places has deteriorated. Because of these conditions many students dislike the program, find excuses for avoiding it and if they are not excused waste precious time loafing and clowning. The reasons referred to are:

1. Most school "gym" programs are geared to benefit 10 percent of the children who need it least—the hotshot athletes who hog the gyms, playing fields, and coaches' time.

2. The other more than 41 million children—including the underweight, overweight, shy, scrawny, awkward, handicapped, poorly coordinated, and just plain normal—get short shrift from most of their "gym" teachers.

3. Instructors are mainly concerned with developing athletes because this adds to their own stature and because they are incapable of teaching the ordinary child. Some of them can hardly be described as teachers. Former athletes themselves, they are actually trainers and coaches.

The article indicts teachers, administrators and colleges. Although a national poll by the National Education Association of 1.5 million public school teachers disclosed that a majority of them felt that pupils need more exercise, 70 percent were not willing to devote school time to alleviate the situation. Administrators appoint unqualified instructors to teach physical education and allow coaches to overemphasize competitive sports rather than devote time to physical education. Finally, the colleges need to improve the caliber of instruction in the preparation of teachers.[5]

What Students Think About Physical Education

Many teachers enter the profession and for years meet their classes without knowing just what their students think of them or their program. Pollack revealed in his article, "Are Our Children Being Cheated?" how students feel about them and their program.

A Junior High School girl:
"We have two 45 minute periods per week. We spend 25 minutes getting dressed and undressed, and taking a shower. The rest of the time, we 75 girls mostly stand in line for roll call and inspection. Gym is a silly bore. All we do is march around like they do in the Army."[5]

There are many situations similar to the one shown above which reveal the opinions held by pupils regarding the physical education program. Years of inferior programs have produced the unfavorable status which physical education presently occupies in some sections of the country.

The Teacher Must Educate the Plural Publics. Too often excessive time is spent trying to educate and interpret the program to one's own group. Although it is important to interpret the program continually to one's colleagues, it is even more important to reach the general educators, the parents, and the community, for they are the groups who in the final analysis control the progress of the educational curriculum.

Admiral Thomas J. Hamilton, executive director of the Athletic Associations of Western Universities, made the following observation:

I have observed that, most of the time, physical educators busy themselves with selling other physical educators on the virtues of their programs. Coaches sell other coaches; directors sell other directors. But how much time and opportunity is grasped to sell the education leaders who make the final decisions? Not enough.

Physical Education Newsletter,
August 15, 1970.

The Teacher Must Understand the Importance of Human Relations. Teachers should be aware of the need for continually practicing good human relations. They must be unselfish, cooperative, understanding and able to work with the citizenry. Sometimes teachers allow their prejudices and jealousies to seep into their professional efforts and sway them into decisions and actions that place their public relations program in jeopardy.

The Teacher Must Understand the Need for Planning. Planning is the requisite for a successful school-community relations program. Teachers need to establish goals, evaluate the existing program in physical education, determine the media to be used, select the activities which reflect the needs for physical education and inventory existing efforts in interpreting physical education before initiating programs in school-community relations.

Various studies disclose the need for planning school-community relations programs. Education is the only big enterprise that does not approach public relations in a scientific, aggressive manner. A 1967 survey of 43 states was made to determine the status of school-community relations on the state level. The survey revealed the following inadequacies in interpreting education at the top level:

1. Most state school chiefs emphasized publicity and media relations in their concept of public relations. Few of them embraced the mature concept of public relations. Few had provisions for feedback from the public.

2. These state school heads, when asked to indicate the immediacy of their public information needs, placed an effective external communications program first, an internal communications program second.

3. Ten state departments of education said they could not provide public relations assistance to local districts, despite the growing demand for such counsel.

4. In 17 states, the superintendent said the public relations officer was included in the administrative council of the department; in 15 states he was not.

5. Of the 33 information officers covered in the survey, only two had over 10 years' experience in their present jobs. The median level of experience was less than one year.[1]

On the local level the picture is just as bad. An example of the lack of effective planning in school-community relations is disclosed in a study made of 395 school districts in Wisconsin in 1963. Questionnaires sent to both elementary and secondary schools noted that:

1. Few Wisconsin public school districts follow a predetermined information policy. Concern for such a policy may be increasing; but, as yet, most school districts handle communications problems as they arise.
2. Most school districts have some method of allocating informational duties, but in many cases communicating is considered as just another duty to be performed.
3. The attitudes of school district administrators are not always on the side of the people's right to know.

4. The most frequently used channel of communication of the school districts is written press releases, whether or not an information specialist is employed.
5. Only three school districts in Wisconsin employed full-time practitioners. Many schools use teachers on a part-time basis to handle publicity. Most specialists replying in the study said that they needed more time to do their public relations tasks, particularly for external communications.[1]

The Teacher Should Be Acquainted with the Power Structure. As explained earlier, there are usually a few individuals who exercise considerable control over community affairs. Although it may be difficult, teachers, in addition to reaching the many publics, should know the people who comprise the power structure and apprise them of the objectives and purposes of physical education before initiating a program in school-community relations.

Physical Education Public Information Project
(PEPI)

In an effort to interpret and enlighten the public regarding the need for physical education, the American Association for Health, Physical Education, and Recreation has established a public relations program. This effort, known as the Physical Education Public Information Project, was formed to reach the many publics, including students, administrators and supervisors, boards of education, teachers and professors, parent-teacher associations, civic organizations, industrial organizations and health foundations. The main thrust of the Project will be made through the radio and television media, particularly on the national networks. Material available to teachers, directors and administrators has been developed to assist them in sponsoring local programs.

PEPI developed the following concepts which may serve as guidelines for developing school-community relations programs:

1. A physically educated person is one who has knowledge and skill concerning his body and how it works.
2. Physical education is health insurance.
3. Physical education can contribute to academic achievement.
4. A sound physical education program contributes to development of a positive self-concept.
5. A sound physical education program helps an individual attain social skills.[6]

MEDIA FOR REACHING THE PLURAL PUBLICS

The teacher who understands the program and has planned and organized his work carefully is ready to interpret the

program to one or all of his publics. The problem confronting him is determining how the many publics can be reached. A public relations program in physical education must utilize a medium that will effectively portray the philosophy and objectives of the program and the contributions it makes. The media must be types that will convey the message in such a manner that the various publics will understand and support the efforts of teachers and administrators.

Lines of communication must be established between the school and the publics. This, of course, requires educational leadership. The publics seek leadership; therefore, when leadership is available, lines of communication may be fairly easily established. Some media are better suited for one group than for others. The following criteria should be helpful in selecting the proper medium for the particular public:

1. FACILITY OF PREPARATION. The medium selected should be one which can be planned and developed with the minimum amount of time and with few materials. The time element is all-important in writing most news stories, as well as in preparing other materials.

2. IMMEDIACY OF PREPARATION. In planning the release schedule, time should be allowed for printing or other finishing operations. Production time should be brief.

3. DISSEMINATION TO CHANNELS. It is advisable to use materials which can be routed immediately after their completion to the agencies which distribute them: press, radio, homeroom teachers, or post office.

4. DISTRIBUTION. The medium selected should reach the maximum number of people in the shortest time and in the most effective manner.

5. COST. All materials must be developed at the lowest possible cost. Experience and care in planning will make this possible.

6. UNDERSTANDABILITY. The message should be intelligible to every person in the community.

7. POPULAR INTEREST AND APPEAL. The message which is pertinent, meaningful, and personalized will gain ready and instant support.

8. ADAPTABILITY. Wherever possible, the materials used for one medium should be adaptable to others. Efficient planning will make good materials available for many purposes.

9. COMPREHENSIVENESS. The medium used should be one with which it is possible to cover the subject thoroughly.

10. EFFECTIVENESS. Favorable response is the primary concern of public relations. The degree to which the medium achieves this objective is the measure of its success.[4]

JOHN B. VAN WHY

John Van Why was a dedicated leader in physical education. His imprint on students and physical education in the midwest will be visible for years. Although known as a "students'" professor, his contributions in public relations were recognized throughout the country.

Television and Radio

Television programs have a powerful effect on the viewing audience. Well-planned programs may be of tremendous value in presenting the purposes and objectives of physical education. There are some people who rarely read newspapers, relying solely on other media for their information. This group of people may be easily informed by television programs that are carefully planned and presented in an interesting manner. For example, programs involving pupils participating in the activities from a particular program in physical education might create considerable interest. This medium is one of the best for educating large masses of people within the community.

The radio is still an effective medium of communication with the various publics. Although not so popular as it was before the advent of television, it is unequalled for the presentation of continuous programs and spot announcements.

Newspapers

Just as television and radio are designed to reach large numbers of people, so is the newspaper a medium for communicating with the many publics. It is an excellent public relations medium not only for those individuals who view television but also for those people who do not rely on television for their information. Newspapers may be used for reporting results of various aspects of the program, such as the results of a demonstration, the winners of an intramural meet or of a specific activity involving more than one school, through a special news story or feature article. Since news articles reach many of the publics, the value of this medium should never be minimized. It provides a written record of physical education events and has special appeal for both pupils and parents, who enjoy seeing their names in print (Fig. 3–4).

Although parents are interested in reading about the various aspects of good instruction, too often adequate space is not provided in the news items. Ovard pointed this out in a survey of 13 topics of school news. He ranked them according to expressed interests by parents and compared this rating to the space allotted to them in the leading newspapers.[7] The results are shown above:

Pupil progress and achievement ranked first in parental interest but ranked fourth in space devoted to it. Extracurricular activities ranked 13th in parental interest but were first in allotted space. Teachers of physical education should learn the procedures of reporting that will be of sufficient appeal to receive adequate space in the news.

Topics of School News	Rank According to Patron's Interest	Space in News
Pupil progress and achievement	1	4
Method of instruction	2	10
Curriculum	3	6
Health of pupils	4	9
Value of education	5	12
Discipline and behavior of pupils	6	11
Teachers and school officials	7	2
Attendance	8	13
Building and building program	9	8
Business management, finance	10	7
Board of education and adm.	11	5
P.T.A.	12	3
Extracurricular activities	13	1

Speakers

Teachers of physical education may appear before civic clubs and parent teacher groups and explain the purpose of physical education. They may use visual aids or pupils to assist in getting the message across. Speeches by physical education teachers or directors are usually most effective when made before small groups.

Teachers may enlist the assistance of outstanding speakers in the city, acquaint them with the purpose and objectives of physical education, and plan appearances for them before the various organizations within the city.

School Papers

School newspapers are in the same category with public newspapers, except that they reach smaller, more select groups. Informative school papers are important for reaching teachers, parents, and pupils.

Assembly Programs

Assembly programs are an excellent medium for educating pupils and teachers. A tumbling demonstration or a simple play illustrating how physical education instruction is conducted can play a vital role in public relations.

Figure 3–4. Local newspapers are valuable media for interpreting the program to the public.

An interesting illustration of public relations through the medium of the assembly program was tried in the Norfolk Public Schools, Norfolk, Virginia. The program which follows was designed by teachers and planned to interpret physical education to all the teachers in the high schools of the city.

THE PROGRAM
CREATIVITY AND FITNESS THROUGH RHYTHMICS

This program is an outgrowth of the physical education intramural program. Its theme is "Creativity and Fitness Through Rhythmics." Rhythmics are combinations of natural movements put in rhythmic patterns which allow for creativeness and contribute to physical fitness.

The numbers of this program are forms of creative rhythmics. These students will use movements to interpret and express a variety of ideas, feelings, and moods. You will see different types of movements ranging from the religious to the syncopated.

Most movements use music as an impetus and as accompaniment. Now you will see a religious interpretation of a poem using spoken words instead of music. These words will serve as both content and accompaniment. A group of Washington High School students will interpret the poem "The Creation" by James Weldon Johnson. You are familiar with this poem. It is in your Literature Book.

Ole Man River

Folk movements are noted chiefly for their recreational values. This type of movement originated with the common people of a country or sections of a country. They depict some of the traditional beliefs, legends, and customs of peoples. The Mississippi River is the Ole Man River of our country. Folk movements found their way into the songs and stories of the pioneering people along the Mississippi.

Let's watch the students of Madison Junior High School interpret some of the customs of the people along the Mississippi to the folk tune of "Ole Man River."

Delicado

Latin American movement is shown in this presentation. Latin America is the part of the American continent south of the United States. Every country has an abundance of customs and lore. These movements have a Spanish flavor, because the Latins are descendants of Spain. The Latins move for pleasure and enjoyment of keeping up with a beautiful rhythmic beat. Ruffner Junior High School will interpret some Latin American movements to the tune of "Delicado."

Quiet Village

Movement has filled a fundamental need in man since the beginning of civilization. Some of the movements of primitive man seem to be a magical ceremony. They are done close to the ground with a typical crouched position that seems to establish a relationship between man and earth. Washington High School will perform some semi-primitive movements to the tune of "Quiet Village."

Precision Plus

These are skilled movements performed to syncopated rhythm. These are locomotive movements that are lusty and vigorous. These movements call for coordination of arms, legs, and body.

Rosement Junior High School will perform some skilled syncopated movements which we have named "Precision Plus."

Bashin'

More syncopated movements are presented here. These are popular movements put together just for fun. They are an outgrowth of exploration, experimentation, and manipulation of popular movements.

Madison Junior High School will perform some syncopated movements to the tune of "Bashin'."

Exodus

Some movements do not follow any special idea. They are done to music for rhythm's sake only. Washington High School has used ballet-type movements and fitted them to music. These are semi-ballet movements done to the tune of "Exodus."

Scarf Dance

Aesthetic movements are movements that are presented for appreciation. They are classic in nature and because of their serenity, they appeal to the beautiful in us. These movements are enhanced by the use of scarves and falling snow. Jacox Junior High School will perform some aesthetic movements to the tune of "Let It Snow."

These rhythmic movements were developed in the individual schools mentioned in the program. A schedule was made and the groups from all schools were presented during the planned auditorium period at each school. Not only was the physical education program interpreted effectively, but the entire presentation gave the hundreds of academic teachers a chance to witness a demonstration that was elegant, aesthetic, and far removed from the locker-room connotation.

Demonstrations

Demonstrations involving many pupils may be of tremendous help in interpreting physical education. Not only will these presentations provide a culmination of the physical education offering, they will give parents and other groups a realistic, first-hand insight into the purpose, objectives, and content of the physical education curriculum (see Chapter 13).

Raymond Welsh, director of Physical Education at East Orange (New Jersey) High School, reports on a "Red and Blue Night" for freshman, sophomore, junior, and senior boys. The boys are divided into two teams, red and blue. The teams compete on a point basis. The program for the demonstration incorporates a variety of activities and is described below:

EAST ORANGE HIGH SCHOOL
BOYS' PHYSICAL EDUCATION
DEPARTMENT

presents

RED AND BLUE NIGHT

featuring

FRESHMAN, SOPHOMORE, JUNIOR,
AND SENIOR BOYS
(all volunteers)

PHYSICAL EDUCATION STAFF
Ray Welsh   Red Team
Thomas Nolen   Blue Team
Elliott Edelstein Blue Team

Robert B. Redman Memorial Gym: 7:45 P.M.

1. Freshman Physical Fitness Exercises
   Reds: Welsh   Blues: Edelstein
2. Upperclass Physical Fitness Exercises
   Reds: Welsh   Blues: Nolen
3. Mass Games — Reds vs. Blues
   Jump the Shot (freshmen)
   Crab Ball (sophomores and freshmen)
   Number Ball (junior and seniors)
4. Team Games — Reds vs. Blues
   Volleyball (two games — all classes)
   Floor Hockey (juniors and seniors)
   Basketball (juniors and seniors)
     Warriors (Reds) — Taylor Culver vs.
     Panthers (Blues) — Melvin Sanders
   Basketball (freshmen — small boys)
5. Relays — Reds vs. Blues
   Jack Rabbit (freshmen and sophomores)
   Wheelbarrow (freshmen and
     sophomores)
   E. O. Scooters (freshmen)
6. Sweet Georgia Brown — Dribbling Contest —
   Reds vs. Blues

INTERMISSION
10 minutes

7. Rope Climbing — Reds vs. Blues
8. Apparatus — Reds vs. Blues
   Parallel bars, horse, buck
9. Apparatus — Reds vs. Blues
   Long horse and springboard

(Please remain seated until all students leave the gymnasium.)

Figure 3–5. Demonstrations provide parents with an opportunity to understand the purposes of the health and physical education program.

Figure 3–6. City-wide tournaments are used effectively in interpreting the intramural program.

City-wide Intramurals

This phase of the intramural program brings together pupils from the various schools and provides a medium allowing the more gifted pupils to participate. City-wide intramurals as public relations media are similar to demonstrations but differ in that they involve a more specialized and somewhat smaller group. They are important for reaching a smaller group of parents. Examples of city-wide programs are described in Chapter 13.

Parent-Pupil Programs

Some teachers have been successful in developing programs in which parents and their children meet in the school for playdays, awards, banquets and similar occasions. The program is planned to allow parents and their children to participate together. Such a program exists at Northeast High School in Lincoln, Nebraska. Under the direction of Mrs. Vietta Short, a Girls' Athletic Association Mother-Daughter Playday is held each October. Mothers are invited to be teammates with their daughters in tennis, relays, softball, archery, volleyball, shuffleboard and other activities. In addition, a father-daughter awards banquet is held each year involving about 100 fathers and daughters.[8]

Handbooks

The handbook is a relatively new medium of public relations. It is inexpensive and extremely effective if distributed to parents. At the beginning of each term teachers may send this handbook home by the pupils and ask parents to send their comments back to the teachers. The handbook provided by the Norfolk City Schools is an example of an effective use of this medium. It has proved to be an invaluable aid in interpreting the program to parents. Thirty thousand copies of these handbooks are sent home to parents each year. The brochure outlines the entire school program from the elementary through the high school and includes a section on intramurals. It also includes the various physical education requirements pertaining to uniforms, lockers, excuses, towel fees, and other items of importance (Fig. 3–7).

The Indiana State Board of Health publishes a brochure for parents entitled *Physical Education: An Interpretation for Parents.* This handbook includes the following topics:

What is Physical Education?
Why Physical Education?
  1. Physical Growth and Development
  2. Social-Psychological Benefits
  3. Recreational Skills for Leisure Living
  4. Safety and Survival Skills
  5. Citizenship and Character Education
  6. The Push-Button Age
What Should Parents Expect:
  1. From the School
  2. From the Community
Characteristics of an Educated Person

Clifford Barnes, director of Physical Education in South Bend, Indiana, Community School Corporation, also uses a handbook to describe his program. The cover and contents of this handbook are also shown in Chapter 9.

Special Publications

Certain publications are aimed at a particular audience and are presented in a more sophisticated manner than is usually the case in other media. Such a publication is shown in Figure 3–8. The brochure is available on request. This medium

PHYSICAL EDUCATION REQUIREMENTS

Health and Physical Education is required of all students in grades seven through twelve. One credit each year is given towards graduation in grades eight through ten. Pupils in grade seven in the Junior High Schools must have satisfactorily completed this course in the seventh before entering the eighth grade program.

Health and Physical Education is elective, with credit, in the eleventh and twelfth grades. These credits may be used for graduation credit.

EXCUSES

Pupils may be excused from the activity program by a note from physician. They will attend the health classes and make up the work missed in the activity program through activity knowledge tests devised by the teacher. Full credit will be granted in these cases.

PHYSICAL EDUCATION UNIFORMS

A standardized uniform has been adopted for all high schools in the city. Each pupil is required to have a complete physical education uniform prior to participation in class activities. These uniforms may be purchased from any store which carries this equipment.

Boys	Girls
White Shirt and Blue Trunks	One-Piece Blue Uniform
Shoes	Shoes
Socks	Socks
Combination Locks	Combination Locks
(Buy through school)	(Buy through school)

TOWEL FEES

The fee for laundering and use of towels is $1.00 per semester. Pupils are required to take showers, but may be excused by a note from the parent. However, the towel fee must be paid since a towel is necessary for various reasons. Pupils sometimes get dirty when playing outside, they perspire and whether they shower or not, they need a towel.

PARENTS PLEASE TEAR, SIGN AND RETURN

Dear Teacher:

I have read the Handbook, am familiar with the contents and should like to make the following comments:

_____
_____
_____
_____
_____

Signature   Telephone   Date

Printed by TEAGLE & LITTLE, Norfolk, Va.

**HEALTH - SAFETY
AND
PHYSICAL EDUCATION**

HANDBOOK
for
PUPILS and PARENTS

NORFOLK PUBLIC SCHOOLS
Norfolk, Virginia

Figure 3–7. The handbook, designed for parents as well as pupils, is also an excellent means of providing better understanding of physical education programs.

Building Healthier Youth

Department of
Health Education — Physical Education — Safety Education
NORFOLK CITY SCHOOLS
Norfolk, Virginia

Health Education and Physical Education

RESOLVED, *That the American Medical Association reaffirm its longstanding and fundamental belief that HEALTH EDUCATION should be an integral and basic part of school and college curriculums and that state and local medical societies be encouraged to work with the appropriate health and education officials and agencies in their communities to achieve this end.*

RESOLVED, *That the American Medical Association through its various divisions and departments and its constituent and component medical societies do everything feasible to encourage effective instruction in PHYSICAL EDUCATION for all students in our schools and colleges.*

Passed by House of Delegates of the American Medical Association, Miami Beach, June 1960

Figure 3–8.

should be used for members of the power structure and other key individuals in the community.

Homework in Physical Education

It has been noted that the time allotted for instruction in physical education is inadequate to provide for normal child growth and development. The time necessary to realize the benefits of exercise must be found outside the school day. This technique has been applied to academic subjects for many years; we recognize it as "homework." Only recently has the need for additional time away from school been recognized as necessary by the physical education profession.

A plan that has proved to be of immense value in motivating pupils to practice after school is the assignment of homework in physical education. Pupils are given various proficiency tests in the instructional classes and are encouraged to practice at home those skills that need to be improved. The plan has proved to be an outstanding public relations medium, since the pupils carry the program and purposes into the home. An illustration of homework assignments in physical education is shown in Chapter 10.

Pupils

Pupils are the best single medium for interpreting the program. They constitute at the same time a public and a medium for public relations. When the physical education class is well-organized and taught effectively, and when the pupils enjoy it, the report they carry home has tremendous value. The teacher who teaches 200 pupils daily has 200 public relations agents who may either raise or lower the prestige of the program, depending upon the quality of instruction.

The lesson must always be meaningful to the pupils. Objectives should be explained and the purposes of each phase of the program clarified in order that pupils assist in the realization of the objectives. The importance of the lesson should be brought out in terms of pupil needs — what it does to and for them. It is only through this approach that the majority of pupils will understand why physical education is important. It is necessary that pupils realize how the instruction in the skills of the various activities helps them become better adjusted to the rigors of life in the 20th century. When pupils see physical education in this light, the information carried home enlists the support of their parents.

Figure 3–9.   An exhibit of projects constructed in the classes is an effective means of interpreting the program.

Projects and Exhibits

Dedicated teachers usually inspire pupils to produce work that is worthy of special attention. Certain areas, particularly in safety instruction, as related to physical education, are particularly adaptable to the project approach in teaching. Teachers may have safety booklet contests and exhibits within the classes. These projects may be displayed and invitations sent to the administrators, parents, and other teachers on the school faculty.

In addition, exhibits may be set up in local civic buildings, the town library, store windows, and the like. This is a popular public relations medium for special observances, such as Education Week.

Tours

A particular week during the year may be set aside for inviting various groups to see what is being accomplished by the offering in physical education. The week may be labeled "Health and Fitness Week." Tours may be arranged to carry groups to the various schools where they can actually see the program in action. An entire civic club could visit the schools; the school bus or a chartered bus could transport the members. A sponsor might be procured to defray the cost of transportation.

Sponsors

Bringing the community into the program is a powerful public relations program in itself. Not only does this approach allow a particular group to feel it has a part in the program, but its material assistance with the operation of the program is invaluable.

As explained earlier, the teacher is the spark plug in developing the various media which are available for interpreting the program. Enlisting the support of community groups to sponsor various programs has been described. In addition to this, individuals in the community sometimes are able to provide tremendous assistance for an otherwise unheard-of program. A layman in Paterson, New Jersey, developed a public relations program so

Figure 3–10. Sponsors may not only contribute excellent teaching materials, but they also lend their support to the program.

unique that it should be mentioned here. Don Nizza, owner of a personnel agency in Ridgewood, New Jersey, set a goal of improving the physical education program in the area. He sent 380 questionnaires to physical education teachers, administrators, school board members, and sports writers asking for their opinions on specific questions relating to the public schools in New Jersey. He received 101 answers which served as a basis for articles in the local newspaper. The questions and findings follow:

1. Does the average layman understand the objectives of good physical education?

Responses:	92.0%	No
	3.0%	Probably not
	2.5%	Yes
	2.5%	Don't know

Some general comments from the respondents:

"I believe that the average layman thinks of physical education as a recreation period where the students play games."

"Average laymen consider athletics as the Physical Education program. To them the objective of Physical Education is win, win, win or replace the coach."

"We have no one to blame but ourselves. We as physical education teachers take too much for granted and will not try to educate the community on what it really means to operate a sound physical education program."

"I believe the professionals do not sell their discipline in physical education to the public by action and practice!"

"No, even the average professional teacher does not understand good physical education."

Other respondents noted that administrators tend to minimize physical education, that some teachers tend to throw out the ball, and that many feel physical education is a play period rather than a phase of education designed to help students.

2. What do you feel are the objectives of good physical education?
Results: Objectives most repeated:
a. Physical fitness (sound body) — over 60%
b. Knowledge of game skills and sports — about 45%
c. Knowledge of leisure time carryover sports — about 40%
d. Attitudes, cooperation, leadership — about 25%
e. Individual responsibility, respect for authority, moral views, and so on — about 25%
f. Mental alertness — about 20%
g. Confidence, achievement, pride — about 15%

3. Are all schools meeting these objectives?

Results:	81.75%	No
	3.75%	Very Few (some)
	5.0%	Yes (most are)
	9.5%	Don't Know

Some general comments:

"I would think most fail badly."

"Physical education always has been a second-class citizen in the curricula."

"Absolutely not! Very few are able with the facilities and equipment available. Many schools are staffed with 'throw out the ball and bat' types of teacher."

"Despite excellent facilities and equipment in our school, we still play touch football all fall, softball all spring."

"Apparently not . . . otherwise the public would view physical education in a better light."

"Parents do not support or see the necessity of good physical education."

"Yes, I am certain."

Other respondents noted that the school board and administration tended to downgrade physical education and inhibit the quality of programs.

4. If not, what steps can be taken now and in the future to achieve these objectives?

General comments most repeated in one form or another:

"Improve community relations, meetings, demonstrations, information."

"Develop a progressive program of studies for total development of a youngster."

"Most physical education personnel do not learn their gymnastics in a gym or their wrestling on a mat . . . most learn out of books."

"Fewer physical education people in coaching. They have little time for meetings, curriculum development, program evaluation."

"Better preparation at the college level. 'Knowing how' has been minimized."

"Reduce class sizes . . . schedule physical education first!"

"Permit those expert in the area a greater role in decision making."

"Boards of education must review and evaluate frequently in order to have an ongoing progressive program."

"More stringent course for teachers."

"Let the grade for physical education be included in determining the honor roll."

"The insistence of a well-rounded program by the state, instead of just so many minutes."

"Be cognizant of new research and methods."

"Review courses for teachers every five years."

"Professional preparation of teachers dedicated to physical education rather than coaching."

"The sincerity of the individuals involved important. Can you teach the old dogs new tricks? Do they just claim professionalism?"

"Every school system should have a physical education coordinator who is divorced from all coaching or other forms of athletics. He should have the power to hire and fire."

As shown by the questions and replies, Mr. Nizza was able to discuss many facets and shortcomings of the program in his articles in the newspaper. He enlightened the publics on such phases of the program as fitness, professional standards, analysis

of the curriculum and the difference between physical education and athletics. Mr.
Nizza has this to say about the questionnaires:

**Generally, the physical educators who answered
my questionnaire were frank . . . They told me things
they wouldn't have told other educators because they
knew that I was a layman and not involved in professional controversies. In addition to answering my questions, many of the physical education teachers and
administrators took the time to write me long letters
analyzing the state of physical education in their
respective schools and districts.[9]**

Information such as that gathered from
the survey discussed above paves the way
for similar procedures in other sections of
the country. The specific items listed in the
study should help teachers to improve their
immediate programs and to plan programs
for the future.

Bulletin Boards

Bulletin boards are an excellent medium
for interpreting the program to pupils,
teachers, and parents. The bulletin board
may be planned by a group of pupils working with the teacher; items of interest should
be artistically displayed. The bulletin board
may be used to portray various aspects of
the program, such as announcements of
activities, results of contests, and pictures
of pupils in action. Many phases of the program are adaptable to such visual presentation.

Visitations

A most effective medium for reaching
parents is the scheduling of time for parents
to visit the school and see students in classes
actually learning the skills and movements
necessary for attaining the objectives of
health and physical education.

Pupils in each class are asked to carry
notices home to parents inviting them to
visit the school during the period in which
the pupil is scheduled for physical education. This plan allows the parent to see his
child perform without taking too much of
the parent's time. Since only a small group
visits any period, seating arrangements are
usually easily arranged. Other media are
incorporated in the visitation technique;
bulletin boards should be decorated, notices
and exhibits placed at strategic spots, and
educational material given to the parents
to take home.

An example of an effective visitation program is the one developed by Joel T. San-
toro, co-chairman of the Physical Education
Department at the Isaac E. Young Junior
High School, New Rochelle, New York. He
invites the principal, parent-teacher groups,
teachers and civic leaders to visit the school
and observe specific lessons. Speaking of the
benefits of public relations, he says:

**When the time comes for the department to request
a larger annual budget or the community is voting on a
referendum to enlarge physical education facilities,
it is often too late to tell all aspects of the physical
education story. However, if the physical education
staff has conducted a continuous and organized public
relations effort over the years, the chance of winning
public approval for a proposed project is excellent.[10]**

SUMMARY

The public relations concepts presented
in this chapter constitute a major portion
of the *Why* of physical education. When
one understands the need for an effective
school physical education program (Chapter 1) and the difficulties involved in achieving such a program (Chapter 2), he appreciates the importance of good public
relations. Even so, he must first know *what*
constitutes a good physical education curriculum. Part II will discuss the *what* phase.

QUESTIONS FOR DISCUSSION

1. What is the relationship of interpretation to public relations?
2. What is meant by "plural publics"?
3. What are the most important groups to be reached in a public relations
program?
4. In your opinion, which is the most important medium of public relations? Elaborate.

5. Why are principles necessary in establishing a public relations program?

6. Discuss the guidelines that the teacher might use in initiating a public relations program.

7. Why are sponsors important?

8. Do you know of a school that has a good public relations program? What media are used?

9. What is meant by the power structure of a community? How does it affect school public relations?

SUGGESTED ACTIVITIES

1. Plan an assembly program interpreting physical education.

2. Develop a public relations idea for one of the media discussed.

3. Visit a local school and study its public relations program. Report the findings to the class.

4. Visit a newspaper and study its operation. List the departments through which a school public relations program could be channeled.

5. Study a physical education class and list the phases that could be used for a television program.

6. Plan a physical education exhibit.

7. Talk with several local organizations and list those that are willing to sponsor various phases of the program in your community.

REFERENCES

1. Scott M. Cutlip and Allen H. Center, *Effective Public Relations,* 4th ed., pp. 563; 567; 568 (Englewood Cliffs, New Jersey: Prentice-Hall, Inc., 1971).

2. Richard Carter, "Voters and Their Schools," *Stanford University Institute of Communication Research*, pp. 4–16 (Stanford, California, 1960). From Scott M. Cutlip and Allen H. Center, *Effective Public Relations,* 4th ed. (Englewood Cliffs, New Jersey: Prentice-Hall, Inc., 1971).

3. Leslie W. Kindred, *School Public Relations,* pp. 16–17 (Englewood Cliffs, New Jersey: Prentice-Hall, Inc., 1955).

4. American Association of School Administrators, *Public Relations for America's Schools* pp. 171; 16–30; 280 (28th Yearbook; Washington, D.C., 1950).

5. Jack Pollack, "Are Our Children Being Cheated?" *Family Health*, p. 15 (September, 1970).

6. Physical Education Public Information Project, *JOHPER*, p. 54 (September, 1971).

7. Glen Ovard, *Administration of the Changing Secondary School,* p. 453 (New York: The Macmillan Company, 1966).

8. "Public Relations—The Key to Parental Support," *Physical Education Newsletter* (Croft Educational Services, Inc., November 1, 1966).

9. "The Public's Finding Out What PE's All About," *Physical Education Newsletter* (Croft Educational Services, Inc., May 1, 1970).

10. "Tips on Winning Recognition for Your Program," *Physical Education Newsletter* (Croft Educational Services, Inc., January 1, 1968).

SELECTED READINGS

American Association of School Administrators. *Public Relations for America's Schools.* Twenty-eighth Yearbook. Washington, D.C., 1950.

Baley, James. "Public Relations." *JOHPER* (November, 1961), p. 27.

Bendiner, Robert. *The Politics of Schools: A Crisis in Self-Government.* New York: Harper and Row, 1970.

Bennett, Bruce, "Tell It To Mom and Dad." *JOHPER*, p. 31. (March, 1962).

Cutlip, Scott M., and Allen H. Center. *Effective Public Relations,* 4th ed. Englewood Cliffs, New Jersey: Prentice-Hall, Inc., 1971.

Dubin, Robert. *Human Relations in Administration.* Englewood Cliffs, New Jersey: Prentice-Hall, Inc., 1961.

Fine, Benjamin. *Educational Publicity.* New York: Harper and Brothers, 1943.

Graham, Grace. *The Public School in the American Community.* New York: Harper and Row, 1963.

Grinnell, J. E. and R. J. Young. *School and the Community.* New York: The Ronald Press, 1955.

Harlow, Rex and Marvin Black. *Practical Public Relations.* New York: Harper and Brothers, 1947.

Jennings, Kent M. "Parental Grievances and School Politics." *Public Opinion Quarterly,* Vol. 32, Fall, 1968.

Jones, James. *School Public Relations.* New York: Center for Applied Research in Education, Inc., 1966.

Kerth, Dorothy. "A Symposium on Interpreting Programs to Educators, Parents, and Students." *JOHPER*, pp. 34–35. (November, 1958).

Kimbrough, Ralph. *Political Power and Educational Decision Making.* Chicago: Rand McNally and Company, 1964.

Kindred, Leslie W. *School Public Relations.* Englewood Cliffs: Prentice-Hall, Inc., 1955.

Luffman, Helen. "Use the Experts." *JOHPER*, p. 29. (November, 1961).

McClosky, Gordon. *Education and Public Understanding*, 2nd ed. New York: Harper and Row, 1967.

Miller, Ben. "Public Relations." *JOHPER*, p. 22. (January, 1961).

Stearns, Harry L. *Community Relations and the Public Schools.* Englewood Cliffs, New Jersey: Prentice-Hall, Inc., 1955.

Sumption, Merle R., and Yvonne Engstrom. *School-Community Relations: A New Approach.* New York: McGraw-Hill Book Company, 1966.

Thompson, William. "Pass the Word." *JOHPER*, p. 32. (February, 1961).

Chapter 4

THE TEACHER OF PHYSICAL EDUCATION

A Teacher affects Eternity; he can never tell where his influence stops.

Henry Brooks Adams

Courtesy Richmond Senior High School, Richmond, Indiana

The teacher of physical education probably assumes more responsibility than teachers of other subjects. Not only is he required to know the content of his field, but he must also be aware of other aspects of teaching that are peculiar to physical education. For example, the element of danger is always present in most physical education activities, and teachers must be familiar with the correct teaching procedures that may prevent accidents and injury. In addition to the danger involved in the activities taught, the environment of the physical education class, unlike that of other subjects, is such that serious accidents may occur if the teacher does not develop preventive measures for safety.

The physical education teacher before beginning instruction must be familiar with the many details involved in organizing his class, such as supervision of the locker room and dressing procedures. He must be able to demonstrate the skills and techniques of the many activities that constitute the physical education curriculum. These demonstrations must be correct and also in keeping with findings of kinesiology and

the latest research in safety education. Finally, physical education is the only movement program in the curriculum. Since movement is involved, the teacher of physical education must be prepared for the many special problems that will arise.

The purpose of this chapter is to discuss the qualities that characterize good teachers and suggest guide lines that will assist them in their efforts to develop quality instruction in a changing society.

CHARACTERISTICS OF GOOD TEACHERS

The faculty of any secondary school today is composed of all kinds of teachers. Some are there because they are dedicated and have a genuine interest in working with young people. On the other hand, many are teaching who place physical education in a secondary role, who are unqualified and who are using their position as an interim job before assuming other responsibilities. Regardless of why they are there, however, the importance of quality

67

instruction is so great that emphasis must be placed upon improving the program.

The survival of physical education in the American culture depends largely on quality programs in the schools throughout the nation. Quality programs will exist only where good teachers are continually doing a commendable job. The urgent need for physical education teachers to meet the challenge of quality instruction is obvious. Throughout America, particularly in large cities, the public is refusing to support education. Budgets are being cut, and in some instances entire school systems are closing because of insufficient funds to support the educational effort and to pay teachers' salaries. A recent survey of the plight of education is shown in Figure 4–1, which shows the effect of discontinuing the tax on real estate as a means of supporting education.

Unfortunately, when budgets are cut, physical education is often the first to get the axe. Among the reasons for this action is the poor quality of instruction practiced in some physical education classes. The teacher who uses the physical education class for extra practice for the varsity, who resorts to the play program instead of teaching and who leaves the class to function without him is the teacher who is contributing to the demise of physical education.

Fortunately, there are teachers who believe in the importance of quality instruction and who continually attempt to improve their status as a teacher. These teachers have many characteristics in common, which will be discussed in this chapter.

Emotional Stability

One of the most important attributes of a good teacher is a stable personality. A nervous, irritable teacher will create disciplinary problems and compound the seriousness of an otherwise trivial incident that might occur in the class. The fact that many teachers who are presently teaching should not be in the classroom is revealed in a study published in *Today's Health*. The study reveals that nine percent of today's teachers are maladjusted, create serious problems

in their classes and should be removed.[1] Teachers who are well-adjusted, happy, enthusiastic and understanding usually develop the buoyant and relaxed atmosphere which is essential for effective teaching.

Pleasing Personality

In addition to being emotionally stable, successful teachers are friendly and extroverted and relate to their pupils. The days are past when teachers who are embittered and unfriendly with pupils can produce the types of programs necessary for quality education.

Knowledgeable

Teachers of physical education must be familiar with all skills and techniques that are necessary for satisfactory instruction in physical education. Students enrolled in physical education are hungry for knowledge of correct techniques in skill performance and have little respect for teachers who cannot provide this knowledge. It is possible for teachers to teach an activity without actually demonstrating it, but the ability to show students the correct form is a sure way of gaining the admiration and respect of students.

Dedication

Unless teachers are dedicated, it is difficult for them to maintain the enthusiasm and aggressiveness necessary for teaching. Students do not respond to the teacher who lacks interest in attending to the many little details involved in class management and teaching. A poorly managed class that offers inadequate instruction prompts students to turn their interests in directions unrelated to instruction. Not only do classes conducted by unenthusiastic teachers provide little instructional value for the students, they create a climate that is conducive to anti-social behavior and disciplinary problems.

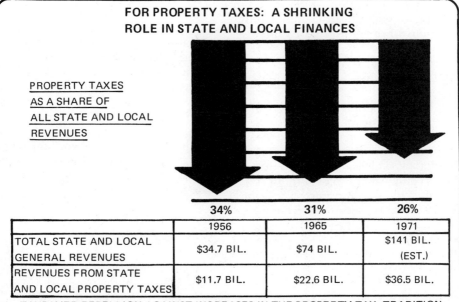

FOR PROPERTY TAXES: A SHRINKING ROLE IN STATE AND LOCAL FINANCES

PROPERTY TAXES
AS A SHARE OF
ALL STATE AND LOCAL
REVENUES

34% 31% 26%

	1956	1965	1971
TOTAL STATE AND LOCAL GENERAL REVENUES	$34.7 BIL.	$74 BIL.	$141 BIL. (EST.)
REVENUES FROM STATE AND LOCAL PROPERTY TAXES	$11.7 BIL.	$22.6 BIL.	$36.5 BIL.

TAXPAYER REBELLION AGAINST INCREASES IN THE PROPERTY TAX--TRADITION-
ALLY THE MAJOR SOURCE OF FUNDS FOR SCHOOLS -- HAS FORCED STATES AND
LOCALITIES TO TURN, INSTEAD, TO OTHER SOURCES OF REVENUES: SALES AND
INCOME TAXES AND HELP FROM THE FEDERAL GOVERNMENT.   RESULT: LESS
AND LESS RELIANCE ON THE PROPERTY TAX, NOW THE TARGET OF NATIONWIDE
LEGAL ATTACKS.
BASIC DATA: U.S. DEPT. OF COMMERCE; 1971 ESTIMATE BY USN&WR ECONOMIC UNIT

Figure 4–1. Effects of discontinuing property taxes on financing education. (Courtesy *U.S. News and World Report*, November 8, 1971, p. 48.)

Gregarious

Successful teachers are usually fond of children and other people and enjoy associating with them. If teachers dislike children and the people with whom they work, it is extremely difficult for them to develop the rapport necessary for teaching. Day-by-day problems that occur in teaching become unbearable if teachers cannot relate to their students. Although knowledge of skills is extremely important, teachers must be able to break through the barriers that may exist between them and their students. This is best accomplished by the teacher's friendly and gregarious attitude toward the students.

Individual Differences

Although it is generally understood that students who comprise a physical education class vary physically, mentally, and emotionally, teachers rarely consider this fact in planning their daily teaching procedures. Effective teaching cannot exist without considering individual differences in the process. Students progress at different rates in the acquisition of skills, and procedures must be developed that provide opportunity for each student to proceed at his own rate.

Professional Interest

Teachers who constantly seek to improve their status through research, study and participation in professional efforts are usually superior teachers. By keeping abreast of the latest findings in research on learning theories and the best methods in teaching skills, the teacher is better equipped to achieve the level of performance expected of a superior teacher. The superior teacher is also one who is active in national teaching associations (Figs. 4–2 and 4–3).

Professional Dignity

The degree of respectability that physical education enjoys in a given school is determined by the teacher. Successful teachers of physical education are articulate, have a command of the English language and leave a good impression with their fellow teachers. The teacher who calls the program "fizz-ed" or "gym," refers to teaching wrestling as "rassling" or who "throwed" the ball should not be surprised when he finds that in the eyes of his colleagues the program has very little prestige.

Goals and Objectives

A successful teacher knows where he is going. He plans his work and is aware of each step that takes the performance of his class a little closer to his goal. Without specific objectives, instruction is erratic and meaningless.

Teachers Must Become Personally Involved

Physical education teachers in Denver, Colorado, feel that teachers must be more concerned with what they teach children through physical education than how they teach activities. They suggest that each teacher must ask himself the following questions:

1. How do I develop an atmosphere of learning which is encouraging and supportive?
2. What activity sequence is most effective in helping the child develop a positive self-image?
3. What are the best methods for helping each child to make his contribution to the group?
4. How can I gradually help to develop a feeling of confidence in those children who tend to be timid and reluctant to participate?
5. What do I really stand for—demonstrated by the example I set by my own behavior and the kinds of organizational procedures and teaching methods I use to give every child a "fair shake?"

Physical Education Newsletter (October 1, 1966).

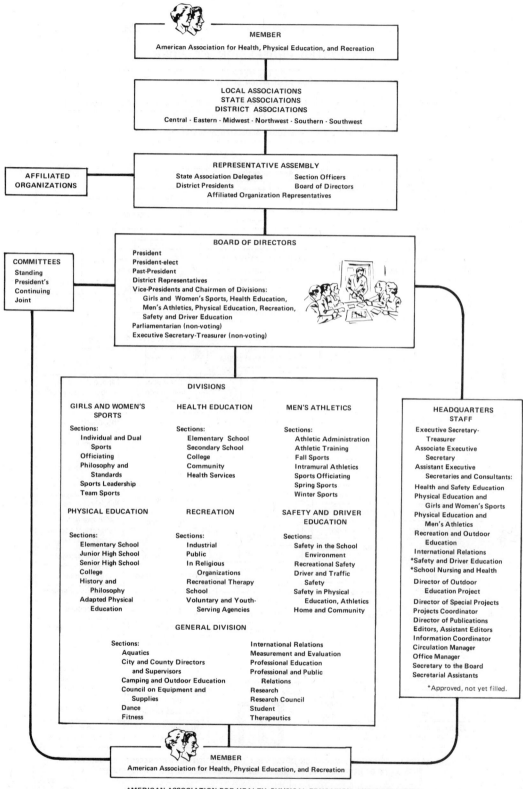

Figure 4–2. Organization chart of the American Association for Health, Physical Education, and Recreation.

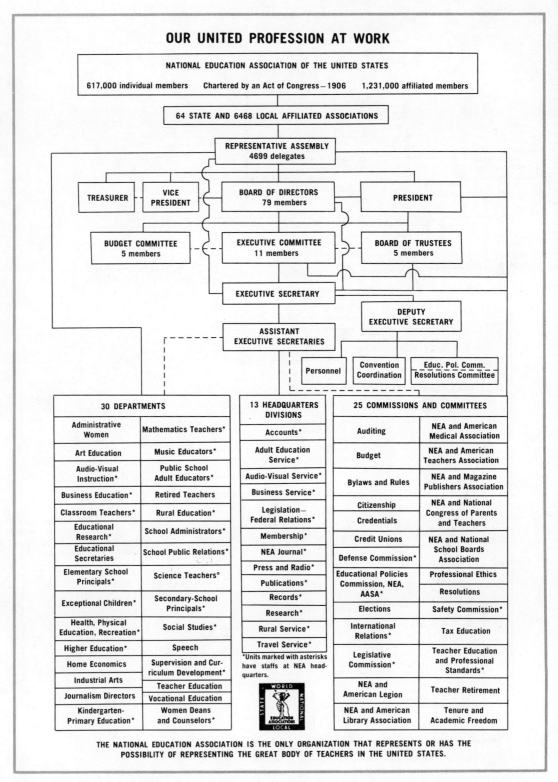

Figure 4–3. The National Education Association is the only organization that can represent the great body of teachers in the United States.

Code of Ethics of the Education Profession

Preamble

The educator believes in the worth and dignity of man. He recognizes the supreme importance of the pursuit of truth, devotion to excellence, and the nurture of democratic citizenship. He regards as essential to these goals the protection of freedom to learn and to teach and the guarantee of equal educational opportunity for all. The educator accepts his responsibility to practice his profession according to the highest ethical standards.

The educator recognizes the magnitude of the responsibility he has accepted in choosing a career in education, and engages himself, individually and collectively with other educators, to judge his colleagues, and to be judged by them, in accordance with the provisions of this code.[2]

Selection of Activities

The teacher who thinks in terms of quality instruction and successful teaching selects activities scientifically, using recommended criteria to assist in their selection. In many teaching situations the individual teacher is responsible for developing the curriculum, although too often he is not qualified for such work. The inclusion of unscientific activities in the program may not only be harmful educationally but may also result in serious health and safety problems. (See Chapter 6 for an extensive discussion of this topic.)

Creativity

Successful teachers are creative. They may not be satisfied with the traditional approach in teaching and may feel that there is a better way than that described in the text or guidebook. In such a situation they will experiment, groping for a superior method of motivating students to learn, and at the same time experience a greater thrill in the process.

Character

Successful teachers in physical education set examples in how to live the good life. Teachers who are involved with dissipation, who openly drink, and who smoke in the presence of their students find it difficult to enlist respect and admiration from their students. Physical education is the one area in the curriculum which should personify those character traits and the moral fiber that are essential for health, fitness, and happiness. The teacher must set the example in this way of life.

Related to this characteristic is the element of fair play and honesty in all teacher-pupil relationships. In making awards, giving marks for the report card, and rendering decisions in play and discipline, fairness and firmness should prevail.

Health

The teacher of physical education must be healthy, not only because he must set an example, but also because the nature of his work demands excellent health at all times. Physical education is the most physically and emotionally demanding subject in the curriculum. Teachers who do not establish standards of healthful living cannot meet the challenge of teaching physical education for long.

General Appearance

Sometimes physical education teachers in their efforts to relate to their students disregard good taste in their dress and mannerisms. This is bad, since teachers are not students. Their job is to set examples, not to try to gain popularity with their students by adopting every whim and fad that the students may subscribe to. A student, for example, may wear a certain type of clothing that to his peers is acceptable, but should the teacher adopt it also, he would place himself in an untenable position, having by the move lost both dignity and respect.

Voice

The tone in which the teacher addresses his students is of extreme importance. A successful teacher is able to talk to a large class in a normal, well-modulated tone. A teacher should not attempt to talk over the noise of a class. He should establish the type of rapport with students in which students remain quiet and attentive while he is talking to them. Nothing irritates students more than a screaming teacher who attempts to reach students by pitching his voice higher and higher as the noise of the class increases.

Commitments

All teachers have certain commitments which are basic to success. These commitments involve their relations with students, with the public, and in the profession, as well as their obligations to professional and employment practices. These commitments, set forth by the National Education Association, are reproduced here:

PRINCIPLE I — Commitment to the Student

The educator measures his success by the progress of each student toward realization of his potential as a worthy and effective citizen. The educator therefore works to stimulate the spirit of inquiry, the acquisition of knowledge and understanding, and the thoughtful formulation of worthy goals.

In fulfilling his obligation to the student, the educator:

1. Shall not without just cause restrain the student from independent action in his pursuit of learning, and shall not without just cause deny the student access to varying points of view.
2. Shall not deliberately suppress or distort subject matter for which he bears responsibility.
3. Shall make reasonable effort to protect the student from conditions harmful to learning or to health and safety.
4. Shall conduct professional business in such a way that he does not expose the student to unnecessary embarrassment or disparagement.
5. Shall not on the ground of race, color, creed, or national origin exclude any student from participation in or deny him benefits under any program, nor grant any discriminatory consideration or advantage.

6. Shall not use professional relationships with students for private advantage.
7. Shall keep in confidence information that has been obtained in the course of professional service, unless disclosure serves professional purposes or is required by law.
8. Shall not tutor for remuneration students assigned to his classes, unless no other qualified teacher is reasonably available.

PRINCIPLE II — Commitment to the Public

The educator believes that patriotism in its highest form requires dedication to the principles of our democratic heritage. He shares with all other citizens the responsibility for the development of sound public policy and assumes full political and citizenship responsibilities. The educator bears particular responsibility for the development of policy relating to the extension of educational opportunities for all and for interpreting educational programs and policies to the public.

In fulfilling his obligation to the public, the educator:

1. Shall not misrepresent an institution or organization with which he is affiliated, and shall take adequate precautions to distinguish between his personal and institutional or organizational views.
2. Shall not knowingly distort or misrepresent the facts concerning educational matters in direct and indirect public expressions.
3. Shall not interfere with a colleague's exercise of political and citizenship rights and responsibilities.
4. Shall not use institutional privileges for private gain or to promote political candidates or partisan political activities.
5. Shall accept no gratuities, gifts, or favors that might impair or appear to impair professional judgment, nor offer any favor, service, or thing of value to obtain special advantage.

PRINCIPLE III — Commitment to the Profession

The educator believes that the quality of the services of the education profession directly influences the nation and its citizens. He therefore exerts every effort to raise professional standards, to improve his service, to promote a climate in which the exercise of professional judgment is encouraged, and to achieve conditions which attract persons worthy of the trust to careers in education. Aware of the value of united effort, he contributes actively to the support, planning, and programs of professional organizations.

In fulfilling his obligation to the profession, the educator:

1. Shall not discriminate on the ground of race, color, creed, or national origin for membership in professional organizations,

nor interfere with the free participation of colleagues in the affairs of their association.

2. Shall accord just and equitable treatment to all members of the profession in the exercise of their professional rights and responsibilities.

3. Shall not use coercive means or promise special treatment in order to influence professional decisions of colleagues.

4. Shall withhold and safeguard information acquired about colleagues in the course of employment, unless disclosure serves professional purposes.

5. Shall not refuse to participate in a professional inquiry when requested by an appropriate professional association.

6. Shall provide upon the request of the aggrieved party a written statement of specific reason for recommendations that lead to the denial of increments, significant changes in the employment, or termination of employment.

7. Shall not misrepresent his professional qualifications.

8. Shall not knowingly distort evaluations of colleagues.

PRINCIPLE IV — Commitment to Professional Employment Practices

The educator regards the employment agreement as a pledge to be executed both in spirit and in fact in a manner consistent with the highest ideals of professional service. He believes that sound professional personnel relationships with governing boards are built upon personal integrity, dignity, and mutual respect. The educator discourages the practice of his profession by unqualified persons.

In fulfilling his obligation to professional employment practices, the educator:

1. Shall apply for, accept, offer, or assign a position of responsibility on the basis of professional preparation and legal qualifications.

2. Shall apply for a specific position only when it is known to be vacant, and shall refrain from underbidding or commenting adversely about other candidates.

3. Shall not knowingly withhold information regarding a position from an applicant or misrepresent an assignment or conditions of employment.

4. Shall give prompt notice to the employing agency of any change in availability of service, and the employing agent shall give prompt notice of change in availability or nature of a position.

5. Shall not accept a position when so requested by the appropriate professional organization.

6. Shall adhere to the terms of a contract or appointment, unless these terms have been legally terminated, falsely represented, or substantially altered by unilateral action of the employing agency.

7. Shall conduct professional business through channels, when available, that have been jointly approved by the professional organization and the employing agency.

8. Shall not delegate assigned tasks to unqualified personnel.

9. Shall permit no commercial exploitation of his professional position.

10. Shall use time granted for the purpose for which it is intended.[2]

A superintendent once listed what he expected of a teacher. Although these observations were made 35 years ago, they are as important now as they were then. He felt that a successful physical educator should:

Know the world in which he and the school in which he may work are to serve. He should know how to proceed in giving aid and encouragement to those influences that are for the good of men, and at the same time receive aid in the promotion of the work that he is doing in the school world.

Not turn out to be one of those narrow-groove workers in the organization. This second quality which I would look for in the physical education candidate I call, for lack of a better term, *breadth* — a breadth of vision that sees within one's task many roads leading out to many places.

Become a teacher in the physical education department who can and will participate in the interests common to the members of the whole teaching staff. I am convinced that this quality is necessary before real, genuine cooperation can be secured from those other teachers. When you find a school that has such cooperation, you will have a master teacher of physical education, one who not only teaches children successfully, but who has imbued his fellow teachers with all the wonderful possibilities of a complete physical education program.[3]

SEEKING A POSITION

Applying for a Position

It is advisable for the college student to write a letter early in his senior year to the superintendent of the district in which he wishes to teach. Sometimes students are prone to postpone applying for a position and as a result will find the best jobs already taken. Upon receipt of the letter, the school administration will send an application blank to the student.

The application should be carefully filled in with special attention to spelling and neatness. An application carelessly worded and hastily filled in may have an adverse effect on the candidate's chance of securing a position. If possible, it would be advantageous for the student to type the requested information.

Interviewing

After graduation, the interview is the most important step in the prospective teacher's career. The manner in which he approaches the superintendent, principal, or supervisor is extremely important. He may be a dedicated person, highly endowed with the capabilities of a superior teacher, yet he may not be offered a position because of the impression he makes on the individual who is interviewing him. The following suggestions should be of value for the teacher when interviewed by the principal or supervisor. The applicant should:

Be Familiar with the Philosophy of the System. Before he reports for the interview, the applicant should, if at all possible, learn something about the philosophy of the program. Is emphasis placed on instruction? Does the administration believe in quality education? Does the school program include or sponsor innovative plans such as flexible scheduling, educational television, and team teaching? If these plans exist, are they successful? Gaining knowledge about questions such as these will be of invaluable aid to the prospective teacher.

Be Able to Answer Questions About Physical Education. The applicant should be able to answer in a straightforward manner questions about physical education. He should have established a philosophy of his own and be able to discuss it. He should be able to demonstrate how to teach certain

activities if asked to do so. The interview gives the applicant a chance to impress the interviewer with his capabilities as a teacher. Some questions that may be asked are:

1. Why did you decide to teach physical education?
2. What activities are you best able to teach?
3. What is your feeling about teaching as opposed to play?
4. Do you intend to make the teaching of physical education your life's work?
5. Are you married? Does your wife work?
6. What is the status of your health?
7. What is your experience in physical education?
8. Why did you seek employment in this area rather than in some other place?
9. Briefly what is your philosophy of physical education?

Be Personable. The prospective teacher can make a good impression on the interviewer by exhibiting good taste in his dress and in the manner in which he responds to the queries of the principal, supervisor, or superintendent. The candidate should realize that the interviewer is observing and appraising him as an addition to the teaching staff in a particular school. In view of this, the prospective teacher should be careful in answering questions; he should be alert, poised and relaxed. He must assure the employer that he possesses the confidence, ability and professional background to perform a satisfactory job if given a contract.

Become Familiar with the School System. The interview is a two-way procedure. Although the basic purpose of the interview is to provide the administrator with knowledge of the applicant, it should also provide the prospective teacher with the advantages and disadvantages of the particular position. The applicant has the right to know what the system has to offer as an inducement for him to accept a position. In a diplomatic way the candidate should find answers to the following questions:

1. Is the physical education program required? If so, what is the requirement?
2. Do the students receive credit for graduation? If so, how much credit?

3. Does the department have a supervisor?
4. Is there a Guidebook available?
5. Does physical education have its own budget, or does it depend on gate receipts for survival?
6. What is the status of the girls' program?
7. What are the facilities for physical education? Does each teacher have a teaching station?
8. Is there sufficient equipment available for conducting a quality program?
9. What are the retirement, insurance, sick leave, and personal leave plans?
10. Does the system provide an intramural program? If so, who is in charge?
11. Are teachers evaluated?

THE TEACHER AND THE COMMUNITY

Although a large portion of time is spent in the school where the teacher is employed, the community plays an important role in the teacher's life. One of the biggest problems both single and married teachers have in a new community is the development of an interesting social life. It is sometimes difficult for strangers in a city to meet people and make new friends. This can be a real problem, as shown by instances in which teachers have resigned and left their jobs because of the lack of friends and a normal social life.

Teachers who are accepting positions in the large cities should be familiar with the community. They will need assistance in finding living accommodations, the church of their choice, shopping areas, amusement centers, and other facets of the community. Some systems provide this information during orientation programs which are held prior to the opening of schools.

Immediately upon arrival, teachers should find out from the department head, another teacher, or the Chamber of Commerce, the location of churches and the various clubs in the city. Some of the most lasting friendships are made in the church and in the civic and service clubs. By attending these organizations, teachers should be able to develop friendships and enroll in committee work which will provide a medium for social involvement.

Involvement of new teachers in the community not only facilitates the teachers' own adjustments, but it also brings the physical education program and the community together for a more effective relationship. Successful teachers accept this challenge. Because they are an integral part of community life, they learn about the needs of students and the attitudes of parents toward education in general and physical education in particular. The inquisitive teacher learns about the environment in which students live and uses this information to provide a more effective teaching program. He uses the community as a laboratory and a resource for enriching instruction with those essentials that provide for quality education.

In Chapter 3 it was pointed out that the teacher is the key to interpreting the program to the many publics. He is the source that provides the parents with information depicting the needs and purposes of physical education. He accomplishes this by providing students with a quality program of instruction, they in turn acquainting parents with the purposeful program that exists in the class. In addition to effective instruction, the teacher through his community contacts and associations is able to develop a positive attitude toward physical education. His personality, the spirit in which he relates to his community associates, the speeches he makes, his willingness to work in community organizations and his leadership in community affairs go a long way toward creating a positive image of physical education and providing a more effective instructional program.

THE TEACHER IN THE SCHOOL

General Duties

In addition to his teaching assignments, the teacher is usually expected to assist with other responsibilities in school life. He may be asked to sponsor some student activity, hold a homeroom, or coach a team. His cooperation in these assignments not only

Figure 4–4. The teacher is the key to developing a sound school-community relations program.

provides opportunities for learning about students in a different perspective, but gives the teacher a broader insight into the administration of the school. A large number of administrators are selected from physical education, and all assignments which provide organizational and administrative experiences enhance the teacher's chances of becoming an administrator. It was shown earlier in the chapter that one of the outstanding qualities of a successful teacher is the willingness to assist in the total operation of the school.

It is interesting to note the changes that have been made in the teacher's contractual responsibilities over the years. Many of the duties that were required in the 1930's are unheard of today. For example, a contract issued in 1931 showed the following responsibilities:

A salary of $65 a month for a school year of nine months.

Teach pre-primary through the eighth grade in all subject areas (reading, penmanship, arithmetic, hygiene, agriculture, grammar, spelling).

Teach the evils of smoking and alcohol.

Ring the school bell once at eight o'clock and twice at eight-thirty (the bell was in a tower and was pulled by a rope).

Teach from eight-thirty in the morning until four o'clock in the afternoon with a half-hour for lunch at noon.

Chop wood for the potbellied stove that stood in the back of the schoolhouse, light the fire whenever heat was needed.

Daily clean and scrub the sitting boards of the two outhouses.

Sweep the floor daily and wash the floor each Friday before leaving the schoolhouse.

Wash the windows (there were twelve) at least once a month.

Have fresh drinking water in the two buckets (pump was in the school yard).

Keep a pot of stew going on the stove (lunch for the poor children in the school district).

Mow the grass around the school as need arose.

Attend church each Sunday and teach a Sunday school class.

Be sure that each eighth grader passed the county examinations (your next year's contract depended on this).[4]

Administrators such as principals and supervisors who work with and evaluate teachers are aware of the qualities that teachers must possess if they are to be successful. A questionnaire prepared by John Barringer, Director of Physical Education, Tucson, Arizona, was sent to seventy-six city and county directors asking them to indicate what they expected of a new teacher. The results revealed that they expected a new teacher should:

1. Have a strong personality that reflects integrity, character, and emotional stability.
2. Be professionally prepared to teach physical education.
3. Have a broad cultural background.
4. Understand and appreciate the environment in which he expects to teach.
5. Be more concerned with teaching children than with teaching subject matter.
6. Have a knowledge of child growth and development as a foundation upon which to plan learning experiences.
7. Possess the ability to establish effective professional relationships with students, colleagues, and parents.
8. Understand the place and function of physical education in the total curriculum and display an active interest in the whole school program.
9. Take an active interest in his own professional growth and strive continuously to improve professionally.
10. Understand the *why* of physical education and be able to interpret it to others.
11. Demonstrate a desire to work with all students, not just with talented athletes.
12. Have the ability to demonstrate basic skills and movements in a wide variety of physical education activities.
13. Be free of prejudice and show respect for all, especially disadvantaged students and those with below average ability.[5]

Specific Duties

In addition to meeting the general expectations mentioned above, teachers are expected to assume certain specific responsibilities. These responsibilities are related to the day-by-day instruction and may be used as an integral part of teacher evaluation. Irrespective of how they are used, effective instruction cannot exist without them. Various schools develop different specific responsibilities, depending on the philosophy of the school and the department. One guidebook expects teachers to comply with the following:

1. Attend faculty and departmental meetings.
2. Be responsible for all supplies for classes.
3. Check to see that each pupil has a proper uniform.
4. Evaluate pupils with the plan outlined.
5. Enter grade and intramural records on permanent record cards.
6. Have pupils carefully fill out individual record cards.
7. See that leaders in each class are appointed or elected and have meetings with them at designated times.
8. Cooperate to the fullest extent with other teachers in the department.
9. Supervise dressing room while being used by class.
10. Be responsible for safety of pupils and proper facilities.
11. Acquaint pupils with their responsibilities.
12. Stay with their classes at all times.
13. Cooperate with department head in his efforts to improve instruction.[6]

THE TEACHER IN CHANGING TIMES

The Changing Curriculum

Just as teachers of academic areas adapt their curricula to fit the times, so must physical education teachers be responsive to changing concepts and procedures. A leading educator has stated that:

> The art of teaching is in about the same state as was the art of war in the 15th century when the Roman legion had been supplemented by the English long bow, cross bow, and gunpowder. Educationally we now have other instruments—equivalent to the tank and the airplane—which we try out now and then. But we put out trust in the old weapons and an occasional cavalry charge.[7]

Chapter 7 explains the need for curriculum change if education assumes the responsibility of educating *all* children. Some of the changes would involve more elective programs and fewer required subjects. The schools of tomorrow will place more emphasis on performance objectives, greater use of technology and audiovisual aids, greater specialization in teaching, more attention given to individualized instruction, development of ungraded schools and classes, lengthening of the school day, and adoption of the 12-months school. These are just a few of the changes that are beginning to creep into our present educational system, and will be the nucleus of education in the 21st century.

All educational change will be reflected in the physical education program. As a matter of fact, some of these changes have existed in physical education for years. Although probably not aware of it, physical education teachers have long been conducting programs involving behavioral objectives. Physical education is basically centered around the psychomotor domain, and students have been evaluated on their performance in the skills which constitute the program.

The physical education teacher in changing times must have a flexible attitude toward teaching and must be able to hold his own in the curriculum battle which is sure to develop in the not too distant future.

The Changing Student

Rapidly changing social conditions and influences in the past few years have completely changed the climate of education in the nation's schools. Teachers can no longer rely on traditional methods and approaches for teaching *all* students. For 50 years, teaching was more or less concerned with perpetuating the same curriculum content presented in the same traditional way. Although textbooks discussed individual differences, practice reveals very little application of this important facet of teaching. The major portion of the curriculum is still designed for students who are contemplating college. Little attention is given to students who are more concerned about developing skills to make a living now rather than about attending college.

Recent emphasis on the importance of developing programs that will provide for equal opportunity in education has revealed glaring inequities in the present system. Antiquated content and procedures must give way to innovations and approaches that will provide education with a new look which will eventually change the entire complexion of the present educational scheme. High on the list of teaching priorities is the development of methods and procedures for teaching the disadvantaged student. Although there are other students in the changing student body who should receive special attention, the need for curriculum change to meet the needs of the disadvantaged student is of utmost importance.

Teaching the Disadvantaged. Attention was drawn to the special problems involved in teaching the disadvantaged by experiments in the early 1960's which revealed that the disadvantaged child is preconditioned to failure because of his background. He is exposed neither to the rich, varied environment nor to the parental encouragement that enhance the success of the middle-class child. When placed in the predominantly middle-class public school, the chances of the slum child to progress and learn successfully were then extremely remote.[8]

Through the efforts of Project Head Start, attempts were made to offset the disadvantages which plagued the ghetto child. One of these efforts was the summer enrichment program for preschool children. The program showed promise, and studies of those children who participated revealed improvement. However, unless carried on through the traditional school curriculum, the program could probably do more harm than good. This is true since the gains made in the summer program tend to fade unless the regular school program in the primary grades is excellent and is adjusted to meet the needs of the disadvantaged.

However, from all of the studies and experiments, a new image of the disadvantaged child as well as more suitable teaching methods have emerged. According to Biehler, the disadvantaged child psychologically suffers from:

1. *Poor Motivation.* The ghetto child does not have the same desire to learn and become educated as does the middle-class child. He learns to hate school and to compensate by resorting to anti-social behavior.
2. *Lower Expectations on Part of Teachers.* Teachers are prone to expect less of the ghetto child, and the treatment which follows this expectation causes the child to develop a negative attitude toward learning.

3. *Poor Self-Perception on Part of Pupils.* Children from the ghetto, because of the affluence portrayed on television which is in sharp contrast with the environment in which they live, develop a poor self concept. They must be provided with the opportunity to live in more acceptable situations and have a chance to develop their innate potentialities. Some of the most outstanding accomplishments in sports have been made by school children from the ghetto when given the opportunity.

4. *Antagonism Toward School and Teachers.* Disadvantaged children develop a negative attitude toward school and antagonism toward their teachers. This is easily understood when individual study reveals that their parents were dropouts and cared little for school and education. In addition, the middle-class child by the time he enters junior high school is already thinking about college. This is not true of the ghetto child. He does not have parents who are prodding him to further his education; nor are the members of his peer group college-bound.[8]

If the present trend in our public schools continues, then all teachers must learn how to teach and work with disadvantaged children. Physical education teachers have a tremendous opportunity to assist in the education of the disadvantaged child. The self-image of the ghetto child in sports is superb. There are few high school, college and professional teams in the country that do not have among their members many players from the ghetto. Physical performance is an area in which these children can excel and develop a positive self-concept. The physical education programs throughout the country have done a tremendous job in providing opportunity for the disadvantaged child to develop his potential. However, these programs are not developed to the level they should reach. Chapters 6 and 7 describe some of the needs of physical education if it is to meet the challenge.

Implications for Teaching the Disadvantaged. In view of the foregoing discussion, there are certain implications for teaching disadvantaged children. Biehler lists them:

1. Help disadvantaged pupils feel secure in the classroom, experience success, and gain confidence.
2. Keep expectations high. Be alert to the influence of stereotypes and preconceptions.
3. Help the disadvantaged child develop a positive image and satisfy his need for esteem.
4. Keep in mind that many disadvantaged pupils are predisposed to be hostile toward teachers and school.
5. Take into account the lack of roots and the likelihood of discontinued education when dealing with disadvantaged children.
6. Keep in mind the poor physical health and conditions of many disadvantaged children.
7. Don't assume that the disadvantaged child has been exposed to what is so often wrongly taken for granted.
8. Help the disadvantaged child get into the habit of studying.
9. Encourage parents to take an interest in what their children are learning.
10. Be aware of the limited readiness of the disadvantaged child.
11. In giving and interpreting tests of all kinds, keep in mind the handicaps under which the disadvantaged labor in test situations.
12. Keep in mind the verbal deficit of the disadvantaged.
13. Be conscious of the physical, practical orientation of the disadvantaged.
14. Don't forget the slower learning pace typical of the disadvantaged.
15. Keep parents informed of what is going on in school in an effort to arouse interest in the day-to-day aspects of schooling.[8]

Theory and Practice

The gap that exists for new teachers between theory and practice is sometimes insurmountable. Teachers, as the day approaches for their first teaching assignment, need practical answers to the many problems that confront them. A background in theory is desirable, but success in teaching is measured by sound practical methods and procedures. The teacher facing his class for the first time needs to have a basic knowledge of kinesiology, philosophy, history of physical education and other subjects, but without an equal knowledge of effective procedures of organizations and methods of teaching, the results will be unsatisfactory. It was mentioned earlier that physical education is a movement program; and when a class of 40 to 50 students begin to move into the techniques of skill acquisition, common sense and practical experience are essential for success.

The need for students to acquire practical knowledge in how to teach is so great that the importance of the student teaching program in college cannot be overemphasized. Teachers should take advantage of every opportunity in their student teaching to learn about the day-to-day problems that occur and to devise ways to alleviate them. In those situations where the teacher is closely supervised, he may receive valuable assistance. If he is doing his student teaching in a school where he is given considerable freedom with little supervision, he may profit by experimentation. Irrespective of the manner in which the student teaching program is handled, the student will find that the experience may prove invaluable when he begins his teaching career.

Accountability

A trend that teachers must face when they begin their teaching assignment is accountability to the public for the effectiveness of their instruction. Parents have been concerned with the quality of instruction for many years, but the pressure for measuring the actual results of teaching is intense. The taxpayers are insisting on knowing how much education can be acquired for their investment.

As teachers enter the profession they become aware of the trend and should be apprised of the kinds of accountability that presently exist. Boutwell discusses four types:

1. *National Assessment of Educational Progress.* National Assessment is an organization that assists school boards and educators with the problems of accountability by measuring what students do and can do with what they learn. It attempts to show what children carry away from the classroom.
2. *The Voucher System.* The Voucher System provides assistance to parents who believe private schools offer a better education than the public schools. The parent is provided a voucher which is equal to the cost of educating a child in the public school and permitted to use it in a private school.
3. *Performance Contracting.* The late 1960's saw the beginning of performance contracting in which areas of instruction such as reading were placed in the hands of private, commercial firms to teach. Education received a jolt which history may reveal as the greatest catalyst to improved instruction in 50 years. It grew out of the failure of many disadvantaged children to read and learn arithmetic and the failure of education to make changes to meet the needs of *all* children. Probably the most noticeable result in performance contracting is that it is producing educational reform.
4. *PPBS.* This venture into accountability is a type of systems planning that was introduced into General Motors and the Pentagon. The initials stand for Program Planning Budgeting System. The system is applied to school operations tied to specific goals.[9]

The movement to provide the taxpayer with evidence to justify the expenditure of money for education has initiated the development of performance objectives in many places throughout the country. Performance or behavioral objectives are discussed in Chapter 5 and are written for the lesson plans shown in Chapter 12.

In the past, physical education has held back and waited to follow academic trends in education which means that it is late in showing the results of educational change. However, in the use of performance objectives, it should not wait for academic areas to experiment before taking action. Physical education operates in the psychomotor domain and has been relying on performance measuring for many years. Teachers should use this medium of measuring motor performance in their teaching and also in their school-community relations programs. Parents can understand results that are available in the performance testing and by relating these results to the need for physical education, teachers can

Figure 4-5. Quality instruction in physical education is essential for accountability.

easily justify the expenditure of money for the physical education program.

THE TEACHER AND THE SUPERVISOR

Dedicated teachers are quite frank both in stating that they need help and in stating the type of help and guidance they want from their supervisors. *Physical Education Newsletter* has compiled some of the areas in which teachers feel that supervisors can help them. Beginning teachers should expect this assistance and should not hesitate to make their wants known:

1. Teachers want more contact with their supervisors.
2. Teachers want their supervisors to help them become better teachers by supplying the leadership and inspiration.
3. Teachers want their supervisors to help them learn the proper lines of authority and supervision.
4. Teachers want their supervisors to help them find the compromise point between the ideal and the practical.

5. Teachers want their supervisors to keep them informed about new equipment, instructional materials, trends, and techniques.
6. Teachers want their supervisors to provide and coordinate the K–12 program.
7. Teachers want their supervisors to have the courage to lead, to make decisions, to try new ideas.
8. Teachers want their supervisors to give them some responsibility for developing the core program of activities based on a sequential progression.
9. Teachers want their supervisors to make better use of individual teachers' talents and specialties.
10. Teachers want their supervisors to give expert advice and guidance and to make constant, forceful (but not authoritarian) efforts to improve the teaching situation.
11. Teachers want their supervisors to provide more opportunity for physical education teachers to share ideas and teaching techniques with each other.
12. Teachers want their supervisors to keep the lines of communication between them and the staff open and functioning smoothly at all times.
13. Teachers want their teaching performance evaluated by a specialist in physical education.[10]

QUESTIONS FOR DISCUSSION

1. Why does the physical education teacher have more responsibility than other teachers?
2. What are some of the characteristics of a successful teacher?
3. What are the major commitments of a teacher?
4. Why should physical education teachers become involved in community projects and organizations?
5. What is meant by accountability? Why should physical education teachers be concerned with performance contracting?

SUGGESTED ACTIVITIES

1. Develop a chart listing the responsibilities of a physical education teacher as compared with those of academic teachers.
2. Visit a school and after observing several teachers, list those attributes that seem to be producing quality instruction.
3. Write several school systems and request application blanks. Study these blanks and make a chart listing questions which appear on each.

REFERENCES

1. Myron Brenton, "Troubled Teachers Whose Behavior Disturbs Our Kids," *Today's Health*, p. 17 (November, 1971).
2. "Code of Ethics of the Education Profession," *National Education Association* (Adopted by the Representative Assembly, July, 1968).

3. R. W. Bardwell, "What I Expect of a Teacher of Physical Education," *JOHPER*, p. 16 (September, 1935).

4. Jessie B. Dypka, "Who Taught in a One Room School in the Depression," *Innovator* (The University of Michigan School of Education, October 14, 1971).

5. Elmore Vernier, "Better Teacher Preparation Means Better Teaching in Physical Education," *Physical Education Newsletter* (Croft Educational Services, Inc., February, 1969).

6. "Building Healthier Youth," *Norfolk Public Schools*, p. 5 (1971).

7. William Clark Trowe, "New Educational Arsenal," *Innovator* (The University of Michigan School of Education, October 14, 1971).

8. Robert F. Biehler, *Psychology Applied to Teaching*, pp. 350; 352; 353–361 (Boston: Houghton Mifflin Company, 1971).

9. William Boutwell, "Happenings in Education," *The PTA Magazine*, pp. 13–14. National Congress of Parents and Teachers (November, 1971).

10. "What Physical Education Teachers Want From Their Supervisors," *Physical Education Newsletter* (Croft Educational Services, Inc., September 15, 1964).

SELECTED READINGS

Bucher, Charles A. *Foundations of Physical Education*, 5th ed. St. Louis: The C. V. Mosby Company, 1968.

McClosky, Mildred G. (Ed.). *Teaching Strategies and Classroom Realties.* Englewood Cliffs, New Jersey: Prentice-Hall, Inc., 1971.

Phi Delta Kappan (March, 1971).

"Preparing Teachers for a Changing Society" (From the proceedings of the Seventh National Conference of City and County Directors, AAHPER, 1970).

PART TWO

WHAT TO TEACH IN PHYSICAL EDUCATION

Chapter 5

PHILOSOPHY OF PHYSICAL EDUCATION

Thy purpose firm is equal to the deed.
Edward Young

Courtesy of Norfolk City Schools.

UNANIMITY OF PURPOSE

The author for a number of years has interviewed, taught, and supervised hundreds of teachers and college students who have majored in the field of physical education. Prospective teachers and those already teaching were asked to state briefly, in writing, their philosophy of physical education. They were asked what they would attempt to do or what they were trying to accomplish.

It is revealing, in studying the comments of those students and teachers, to find such a wide variance of philosophy and such an appalling lack of unanimity of purpose. Although some responses were good, the comments ranged from those reflecting no purpose at all to the most fantastic concepts having no scientific basis whatsoever.

The following excerpts from the responses of these students and teachers illustrate the thinking of many teachers and students today and point to a great need for assisting teachers in formulating basic concepts in physical education.

STUDENT AND TEACHER PHILOSOPHIES

I believe that physical education, if properly taught and supervised, can do more for an individual than any other activity offered by the school.

My philosophy of physical education is that the physical education program should provide for all students a means of having fun and developing appreciation of athletic and recreational activities.

I believe physical education is the necessary weld to make the education of the individual a more complete process.

I believe that a sound physical education program can teach a youngster, through the physical, and do as much for him as any other course in school.

To instill into the individual a basic liking for some activities so that he will have some carry-over value to make him better adjusted to society and take care of his leisure time wisely.

I believe that we need physical education in the school system more than ever. With the way our society tends to pamper its young—

89

with their lack of "chores" to do—we are fast becoming an unhealthy nation.

I believe that physical education "well taught" can contribute more to the educational program than any other subject.

These are only a few of the responses, of course, but they are representative. If all the varying concepts and philosophies were listed, many pages would be necessary. A study of these conflicting points of view clearly indicates the need for teachers to formulate a basic purpose or philosophy. Some of the more pertinent questions all prospective teachers should ask themselves are:

1. Do I know where I am headed? What is my aim?
2. Can I scientifically justify the activities I wish to teach?
3. Am I willing to abandon the teaching of certain activities if they are shown to be educationally unsound?
4. Is my program self-centered or pupil-centered?
5. Are the activities safe?
6. Is my program a play program or is it a teaching program?

Teachers must have a basic philosophy to achieve the goal of effective teaching. Programs based on uncertainty, unrealistic objectives, or no objectives at all will not meet the needs of the pupils. Moreover, teachers, directors, and principals are frequently asked by superintendents and school boards to justify various programs and to show why vast amounts of money must be spent on certain activities. It is imperative that administrators and teachers have a sound, practical basic philosophy through which to justify their programs when these questions are raised. This premise is emphasized by the Educational Policies Commission in the following statement:

Educational purposes, then, are a form of social policy, a program of social action based on some accepted scale of values. . . . Only the broadest lines of policy can have more than temporary and local application, but these controlling principles are of prepotent importance. Everything, in fact, depends upon them.[1]

Since the purpose of this chapter is to assist teachers in their efforts to develop a practical philosophy of physical education, it is logical to assume that an overview of the aims, definitions and objectives of education and physical education should be first in order. The remainder of this chapter will be devoted to this premise.

GENERAL OBJECTIVES OF EDUCATION

Individuals and groups from time to time have endeavored to formulate the general purposes of education. One of the most outstanding definitions was offered in 1918, when the Cardinal Principles of Secondary Education were designed to serve as a guide at a time when education was undergoing a transition from the more formal curriculum to one designed to meet the needs of a changing society.[2] These cardinal principles are:

Health
Command of the Fundamental Processes
Worthy Home Membership
Vocation
Citizenship
Worthy Use of Leisure
Ethical Character

Just prior to and during World War II, the need for another look at the purposes of education became evident. In 1938, the Educational Policies Commission of the National Education Association condensed the purposes of education into four broad areas. These four purposes are still widely accepted objectives of education:

1. The objectives of self-realization.
2. The objectives of human relations.
3. The objectives of economic efficiency.
4. The objectives of civic responsibility.[1]

Physical education, like all other disciplines, plays an important role in the attainment of all four of these broad divisions; however, the first, the objective of self-realization, is the one to which physical education makes its greatest contribution.

The Objectives of Self-Realization

The Inquiring Mind. The educated person has an appetite for learning.

Speech. The educated person can speak the mother tongue clearly.

Reading. The educated person reads the mother tongue efficiently.

Writing. The educated person writes the mother tongue effectively.

Numbers. The educated person can solve problems of counting and calculating.

Sight and Hearing. The educated person is skilled in listening and observing.

Health Knowledge. The educated person understands the basic facts concerning health and disease.

Health Habits. The educated person protects his own health and that of his dependents.

Public Health. The educated person works to improve the health of the community.

Recreation. The educated person is participant and spectator in many sports and other pastimes.

Intellectual Interests. The educated person has mental resources for his leisure time.

Esthetic Interests. The educated person appreciates beauty.

Character. The educated person gives responsible direction to his own life.

Another group of objectives was developed by the Educational Policies Commission and published in 1944. These 10 objectives were entitled "Imperative Educational Needs of Youth," and have had a tremendous influence on the organization of the secondary curriculum. Of the 10 needs, numbers two and eight have a direct bearing on the physical education program. These imperative needs are reproduced in their entirety:

1. All youth need to develop salable skills and those understandings and attitudes that make the worker an intelligent and productive participant in economic life. To this end, most youth need supervised work experience as well as education in the skills and knowledge of their occupations.

2. All youth need to develop and maintain good health and physical fitness.

3. All youth need to understand the rights and duties of the citizen of a democratic society, and to be diligent and competent in the performance of their obligations as members of the community and citizens of the state and nation.

4. All youth need to understand the significance of the family for the individual and society and the conditions conducive to successful family life.

5. All youth need to know how to purchase and use goods and services intelligently, understanding both the values received by the consumer and the economic consequences of their acts.

6. All youth need to understand the methods of science, the influence of science on human life, and the main scientific facts concerning the nature of the world and of man.

7. All youth need opportunities to develop their capacities to appreciate beauty in literature, art, music and nature.

8. All youth need to be able to use their leisure time well and to budget it wisely, balancing activities that yield satisfactions to the individual with those that are socially useful.

9. All youth need to develop respect for other persons, to grow in their insight into ethical values and principles, and to be able to live and work cooperatively with others.

10. All youth need to grow in their ability to think rationally, to express their thoughts clearly, and to read and listen with understanding.[3]

The purpose of listing these general objectives, which have influenced the secondary curriculum, is to show that good health is a constant goal of education. Although the program in physical education makes contributions to all the objectives of education, its unique contribution is made to the health objective.

GENERAL THEME THROUGH THE YEARS

The health of boys and girls is always given high priority by every group that has studied the needs of pupils in relation to their educational development. It is a general theme brought out in all the statements of aims of education. Health is basic to all living. In every walk of life, no matter what the profession or avocation may be, health is basic to success and happiness.

In terms of total health, three components must be considered. These components are mental health, physical health, and emotional health; they should always be included in planning a curriculum in physical education.

Total health cannot be the aim of physical education if by health we mean physical vigor only. The desirable outcomes of vigorous exercise may make a contribution to health, but not enough to make health a basic aim. If, on the other hand, we consider health as an integration of the mental, physical, and emotional processes and then consider how physical education contributes to the total health of the individual, we must place health as a major goal of physical education.

PHYSICAL EDUCATION DEFINED

Physical education teachers should be familiar with the nature of physical education, how it relates to and how it differs from other areas in the school curriculum, what contributions it makes to the development and growth of children, and to what extent it should be recognized in the educational scheme. Briefly, physical education needs to be defined. A definition that is acceptable and which is appropriate for this chapter is proposed by Nixon and Jewett:

Physical Education should be defined as that phase of the total process of education which is concerned with the development and utilization of the individual's movement potential and related responses, and with the modifications or stable behavior changes in the individual which result from these responses.[4]

OVERVIEW OF THE BASIC AIM OF PHYSICAL EDUCATION

Before attempting to initiate any program of physical education, a basic aim or purpose has to be determined. The basic aim of any subject is the result of years of thought, the application of principles, and the final analysis obtained through the practical application of all known phenomena around which the existing programs revolve. The basic aim is the rudder of the ship of theories that continually sails the sea of education. It is the basic aim that really sets the direction for what is to be accomplished and helps to determine whether the effort is approaching the desired goal.

In a democracy, in which health and fitness are part of the culture, each individual should have the opportunity of manifesting and developing his potential. Attention is centered on the individual in an effort to educate him for his immediate and future years of life in a democratic society. This principle calls for a broader, richer curriculum content based on the needs of the individual. In physical education, especially, a broad perspective is needed, viewing the pupil as an individual who also has to har-monize with the group. With this overview, we see the individual in his home, in school, and in all community activities. The curriculum should be constructed from this broad perspective, with the health needs of the individual serving as the nucleus of the program.

A look at some of the aims of physical education proposed by leaders within the past 50 years should be helpful for teachers in developing a philosophy of physical education:

WILLIAM RALPH LAPORTE:
The ultimate aim of physical education may well be to so develop and educate the individual through the medium of wholesome and interesting physical activities that he will realize his maximum capacities, both physically and mentally, and will learn to use his powers intelligently and cooperatively as a good citizen even under violent emotional stress.[5]

JESSE FEIRING WILLIAMS:
Physical education should aim to provide skilled leadership and adequate facilities which will afford an opportunity for the individual or group to act in situations which are physically wholesome, mentally stimulating and satisfying, and socially sound.[6]

LESLIE IRWIN:
The general function of physical education in the public schools is to assist in providing a medium for normal growth and natural development of each pupil.[7]

KARL W. BOOKWALTER:
The aim of physical education is the optimum development of the physically, mentally and socially integrated and adjusted individual through guided instruction and participation in total-body activities selected according to social and hygienic standards.[8]

AAHPER
The American Association for Health, Physical Education and Recreation lists five major purposes of physical education which clearly show the transformation of the profession from the old program of *physical training* to a comprehensive and modern program of *physical education:*

1. *To help* children learn to move skillfully and effectively not only in exercises, games, sports, and dances but also in all active life situations.
2. *To develop* understandings of voluntary movement and the ways in which individuals may organize their own movements to accomplish the significant purposes of their lives.
3. *To enrich* understanding of space,

time, mass-energy relationships, and related concepts.

4. *To extend* understanding of socially approved patterns of personal behavior, with particular reference to the interpersonal interactions of games and sports.

5. *To condition* the heart, lungs, muscles, and other organic systems to respond to increased demands by imposing progressively greater demands upon them.[9]

A condensation of the aims listed above might result in one general aim that would link physical education more closely to the total health and well-being of the individual:

Physical education in a democratic culture should place before all pupils those phases of activity, guidance and instruction which allow for manifestation and development of inherent potentialities, contributing to the total health and well-being of the individual and allowing him to become adjusted to immediate and long-term problems of living — physically, mentally, emotionally, and socially.

The statement of an aim is the statement of an ideal goal, the complete attainment of which would bring about the perfect realization. This state of perfection will never be attained. However, it is necessary to set the goal of any effort far enough out of reach so that it serves as a challenge. The performance in a program in which participants strive for an unattainable goal will be far better than it would be if the goal were too easily reached. For example, it is generally assumed that the "Western Roll" is the best type of high jump to teach when elements of safety as well as performance are considered. An experienced coach, having had training in kinesiology, will have a mental picture of the perfect form in the "Western Roll," which would involve per-

fect timing, perfect approach, perfect landing, perfect opposition of arms and legs, and so on. In reality there is no such thing as perfection. However, the coach who is never satisfied with the immediate performance and who is constantly seeking improvements will produce better results than one who is satisfied with mediocre attainment and a goal easily reached.

The same principle applies to the program in physical education. If the individual is continually striving for a better, a more ideal program, the result will be better than if he were satisfied with low standards.

While teachers should always have an ideal aim, they must deal practically with stark reality. Scheduled to attend their classes are all kinds of pupils — short, slender, fat, strong, weak — and teachers have to provide a program to suit all of them. In order to do this, the teachers must have guidelines to help them utilize to the best advantage the time allotted for instruction. These guidelines or steps leading toward the ultimate aim are the objectives of the program. These objectives should always be brought to the attention of teachers, administrators, and the public when programs in physical education are planned and executed.

OBJECTIVES OF PHYSICAL EDUCATION — HISTORICAL DEVELOPMENT

1920–1930

Hetherington, one of the early pioneers in the modern program of physical education, classifies all objectives in five major groupings:

The Common Objective

As objectives in physical education are developed, consideration should be given to the fact that the objectives of physical education are to a degree the same as those of education. There is only one basic problem in civilization — the human problem. The aim of everything should be to develop better humans. The first objective would then be to make the world a better place for these humans to live in.

Although physical education and education have similar objectives, physical education occupies a unique place in education and, therefore, is more specific in its objectives.

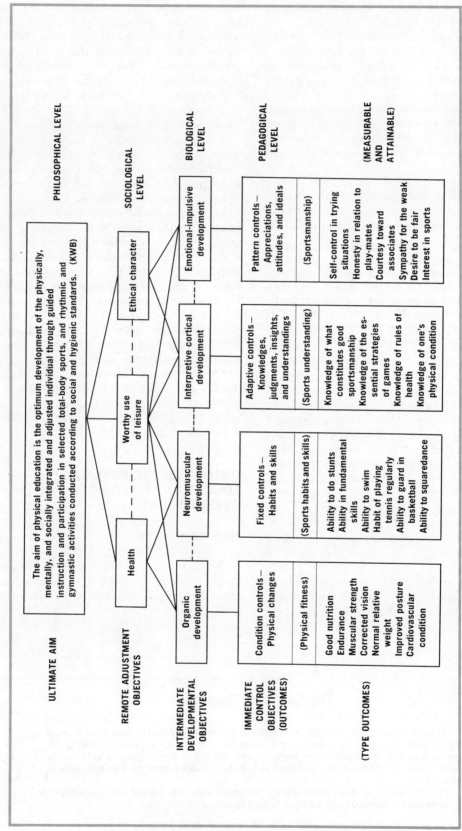

Figure 5-1. The purposes of physical education. From Bookwalter, K. W.: Physical Education in the Secondary Schools. © 1964 by The Center for Applied Research in Education, Inc.

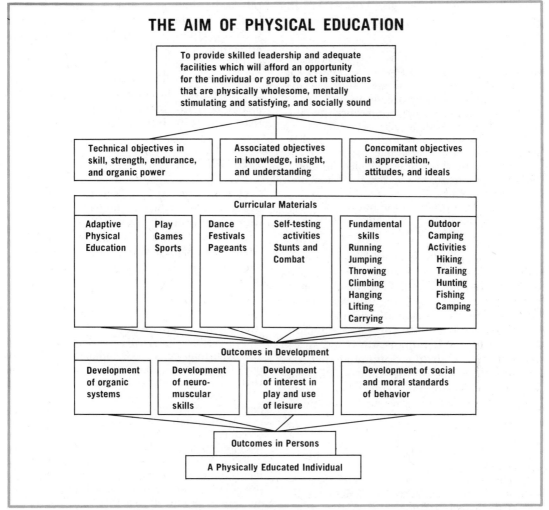

THE AIM OF PHYSICAL EDUCATION

To provide skilled leadership and adequate facilities which will afford an opportunity for the individual or group to act in situations that are physically wholesome, mentally stimulating and satisfying, and socially sound

Technical objectives in skill, strength, endurance, and organic power	Associated objectives in knowledge, insight, and understanding	Concomitant objectives in appreciation, attitudes, and ideals

Curricular Materials

Adaptive Physical Education	Play Games Sports	Dance Festivals Pageants	Self-testing activities Stunts and Combat	Fundamental skills Running Jumping Throwing Climbing Hanging Lifting Carrying	Outdoor Camping Activities Hiking Trailing Hunting Fishing Camping

Outcomes in Development

Development of organic systems	Development of neuro-muscular skills	Development of interest in play and use of leisure	Development of social and moral standards of behavior

Outcomes in Persons

A Physically Educated Individual

Figure 5–2. The aim of physical education. (From Williams, Jesse F.: *Principles of Physical Education.* Philadelphia: W. B. Saunders Company, 1971, p. 331.)

1. The immediate objectives in the organization and leadership of child life as expressed in big muscle activities.

2. The remote objectives in adult social adjustment and efficiency.

3. The objectives in development.

4. The objectives in social standards as applied to the activities, the development and the adjustment.

5. The objectives in the control of health conditions.[10]

1930–1940

Sharman outlined three general objectives of physical education:

1. To provide opportunities for controlled participation in physical activities that will result in educative experiences.

2. To develop the organic systems of the body, to the end that each individual may live at the highest possible level.

3. To develop skills in activities and favorable attitudes toward play that will carry over and function during leisure time.[11]

1940–1950

Williams proposed four standards for assessing or judging the physical education program that revealed the thinking during the war years. These standards are as effective for judging outcomes today as they were many years ago. As set forth in these four statements, physical education should:

1. Provide physiological results, scientifically determined, indicative of wholesome, functional activity of organic systems, and sufficient for the needs of the growing organism.
2. Have meaning and significance for the individual and provide a carry-over interest.
3. Provide opportunity for the individual to satisfy those socially desirable urges and impulses of nature through engagement in motor activities appropriate to age, sex, condition, and stage of development.
4. Offer opportunity to the individual under wise leadership to meet educative situations as one of a social group.[6]

No list of objectives would be complete without the efforts of committee or group study and deliberation. One of the most outstanding projects ever undertaken in curriculum design was made during World War II and reported in the *Physical Education Curriculum.* This report was based on 14 years of research by the Committee on Curriculum Research of the College Physical Education Association. The Committee proposed the following wartime objectives:

1. The development of fundamental skills in aquatic, gymnastic, rhythmic, and athletic activities for immediate educational purposes — physical, mental, and social.
2. The development of useful and desirable skills in activities suitable as vocational interests for use during leisure time.
3. The development of essential safety skills and the ability to handle the body skillfully in a variety of situations for the protection of self and of others.
4. The development of a comprehensive knowledge of rules, techniques and strategies in the above activities suitably adapted to various age levels.
5. The development of acceptable social standards, appreciations and attitudes as the result of intensive participation in these activities in a good environment and under capable and inspired leadership.
6. The development of powers of observation, analysis, judgment, and decision through the medium of complex physical situations.[5]

World War II created an increased emphasis on health and fitness. Stimulated by the high proportion of rejections from military service because of physical deficiencies, many educators lent their support to the physical education effort. After the war, leaders in the profession came forward with objectives that influenced the physical education program. Bucher reflected the thinking of those years in his list of four objectives: (1) the physical development objective; (2) the motor development objective; (3) the mental development objective; and (4) the human relations objective.[12]

1950–1960

During the 1950's, several leaders in physical education made contributions to the philosophical approach to physical education. Cowell advocated a balanced curriculum and grouped both general and specific objectives in the following categories:

1. Organic power or the ability to maintain adaptive effort — in which one attempts to strengthen muscles, develop resistance to fatigue, and increase cardiovascular efficiency.
2. Neuromuscular development — in which one attempts to develop skills, grace, a sense of rhythm, and an improved reaction time.
3. Personal-social emotional attitudes and adjustment — in which one attempts to place pupils in situations that encourage self-confidence, sociability, initiative and self-direction, and a feeling of belonging.
4. Interpretative and intellectual development — in which pupils are encouraged to approach whatever they do with active imagination and some originality, so that they contribute something that is their own.
5. Emotional responsiveness — in which pupils express joy and "fun" in games and sports, get a thrill out of cooperative success or team work, and develop an increased appreciation of aesthetic experiences in the dance, game or water ballet.[13]

Nash, one of the foremost leaders in physical education for many years, provided direction in the 1950's with the following classification of objectives:

1. Immediate objectives
2. Intermediate objectives
   a. Organic development
   b. Neuromuscular development
   c. Interpretive development
   d. Emotional development
3. Remote objectives
   a. Health
   b. Recreation
   c. Citizenship.[14]

1960–1970

The 1960's saw a revival in objectives that not only affected the thinking of physical education leaders for that era but also influenced planning for the 1970's. Among those writers was Willgoose, who maintained that physical education is the development of (1) physical fitness and motor skills; (2) social efficiency; (3) culture; (4) recreational competency; and (5) intellectual competency.[15] Nixon and Jewett proposed five broad, general objectives which were designed for use in the creation of immediate or specific objectives. These objectives were designed to serve as forerunners in the design of performance objectives and are duplicated below:

1. *To develop a basic understanding and appreciation of human movement.* This broad objective involves (a) the development of understanding and appreciation of the deeper, more significant human meanings and values acquired through idea-directed movement experience; (b) an appreciation of human movement as an essential non-verbal mode of human expression; (c) the development of a positive self-concept and body image through appropriate movement experience; and (d) the development of key concepts through volitional movements and closely related non-verbal learning activities.

2. *To develop and maintain optimal individual muscular strength, muscular endurance and cardiovascular endurance.* It is customary to refer to this purpose as the "physical fitness" objective. Many authors expand it to include such factors as flexibility, balance, agility, power, and speed. It is essential to develop not only skills but also knowledge and understanding relevant to physical fitness.

3. *To develop individual movement potentialities to the optimal level for each individual.* Physical education instruction concentrates on the development of selected neuromuscular skills, and on the refinement of fundamental movement patterns basic to specific skills.

4. *To develop skills, knowledge, and attitudes essential to satisfying, enjoyable physical recreation experiences engaged in voluntarily throughout one's lifetime.* Normal mental and emotional health are enhanced by participation in voluntary physical recreation.

5. *To develop socially acceptable and personally rewarding behavior through participation in movement activities.* Physical education instruction seeks to develop desirable social habits, attitudes, and personal characteristics essential to citizens in a free, democratic society.[4]

Irwin describes four objectives which state the philosophy of physical education in a simple manner. He feels that the objectives of physical education should be closely associated with those of education. His objectives are outlined as follows:

1. The physical objective
   a. The health of youth
   b. The development of skill
   c. Physical growth and development
2. The social objective
3. The emotional objective
4. The recreational objective
   a. Recreational activities in the school program
   b. Development of habits of participation in recreational activities
5. The intellectual objective
   a. Knowledge of fundamentals, rules and strategy of sports
   b. Providing a medium for the most efficient and effective intellectual development
6. Citizenship through physical education.[7]

The author has intentionally presented a large number of objectives designed by past and present leaders. Physical education had its greatest growth during the years discussed in the preceding paragraphs. The contributions made by the authors cited above and by others, including Wood, Oberteuffer, Cassidy, Abernathy, Hughes and French, cannot be discarded or forgotten. Indeed, the "new physical education" is not new at all but has its roots in the philosophy of the 1920's and 30's. Many of the ideas and programs advanced today are merely restatements in newer terms of earlier theories. An example of this is the "isometrics" system that is advocated presently. It is a restatement of one application of the overload principle that was advanced 75 years ago. Perceptual-motor learning, which is receiving considerable attention, was discussed in early texts on kinesiology and the physiology of exercise.

It is with the foregoing overview of the aims and objectives of education in general and physical education in particular that the author has developed four modern objectives of physical education. These objectives are realistic and should therefore be helpful in planning programs not only for the 1970's but also for the oncoming 21st century.

A Matter of Survival

Our nation stands at the crossroads of whether we survive or follow the paths of those civilizations that perished because of internal disintegration. Survival to a large degree depends on the health and fitness of its citizenry. The stamina, strength, endurance and motor development so necessary for health and fitness are developed during the formative years. This development can take place only in a quality physical education program that is required daily of all pupils from the first grade through graduation.

OBJECTIVES FOR A MODERN PROGRAM IN PHYSICAL EDUCATION

There is a great need for research in the scientific determination and development of objectives in physical education. Present methods include studying the physiological and psychological needs of children as shown by authorities in the field, observing boys and girls in their work and play, selecting objectives from those listed by leaders in physical education, and developing objectives that parallel social needs with emphasis on recreation. In addition to the foregoing methods, which are typically used in developing objectives, *teachers should determine to just what extent the program contributes to the survival of our country.*

Teachers need assistance in developing guidelines and in establishing a philosophy of physical education. Without direction the program is unrewarding, permissive, and lacking in the necessary content so important for the growth needs of children. Somewhere close to the actual teaching situation teachers must have directional guides in the form of objectives or goals to give meaning to the instruction. If they begin teaching without direction they become easy prey for unqualified individuals who may impose on them scientifically unsound activities, programs and equipment.

In the development of objectives teachers may become disheartened because of the many types involved. Literature reveals objectives designed for administrators, teachers, pupils, lesson plans, activities and so on. For clarification and practicality, the present discussion treats two classes, which should be sufficient for teachers to use at this stage of development. These classes consist of general objectives, which establish goals for the total program in physical education, and specific objectives, which serve as guides and provide direction for the instructional class. These two groups are interrelated and dependent on each other.

In an attempt to summarize the many objectives that are scientifically sound and educationally acceptable, the two groups, (1) General Objectives and (2) Performance Objectives, are discussed.

GENERAL OBJECTIVES

Objective One: The Program Should Provide Opportunity for the Desirable Manifestation of the Play Urge

Play is synonymous with movement and is one of the four basic urges or drives of man. Play, exercise, activity, or movement— the name does not matter—is basic to all life. Whereas basic drives have been broken down into rather extensive categories by some psychologists, they can generally be grouped into four basic urges: sex, ego, gregariousness, and play. The play urge is the first to manifest itself. A newborn baby takes its first and most important fitness test when it utters its first cry at birth. This manifestation of life is a muscular demonstration and initiates the child's career in fitness for survival. In quick order, this muscular movement is followed by rolling, sitting, crawling, pulling up, walking with support, standing alone and walking alone. The development in these movements is orderly and 95 percent of all individuals pass through these stages in 14 months.[16] As children grow, fundamental movements such as walking, running, hanging, carrying, jumping, leaping, climbing, and other movements, which are the natural inherited movements of all human beings, are developed. It is through such movements that organic vigor is developed.

These desires for activity are self-motivated. The dynamic urge for activity is a natural biological impulse of all normal healthy individuals and is manifested by outward responses in play activities. Play activities provide a means of normal self-expression for the natural biological drives so dominant in children.

Providing opportunity includes the provision of well-qualified teachers who are versed in physiology, anatomy, and kinesiology and who understand the needs and interests of children. It includes provision of the best equipment and facilities available. Adequate opportunity above all calls for a diversified program of activities suitable for both the immediate and remote needs of the pupil. As Moehlman states, "Education within a democratic culture must provide for equality of individual opportunity in accord with inborn capacity."[17]

Desirable manifestation of the play urge includes participation in all activities that have meaning and are socially acceptable. It takes into consideration those activities that are suitable for the individual anatomically, physiologically, and emotionally and that contribute to his total well-being. It excludes those activities that are detrimental to health, or that are unsafe, or antisocial in nature. *Desirable manifestation* includes those activities that are educationally sound and excludes those that are not acceptable educationally. For example, boxing could not be considered because any sport having as its objective the damage of the human brain is not educationally sound. The term *desirable* should limit the definition of play to distinguish it from a program in which time would be wasted because of inadequate organization and poor instruction.

The fundamental movements of man which are part of man's inheritance and which have been basic in our culture for thousands of years include activities that are interesting because they are natural activities which provide the movements necessary for normal growth and develop-

CLARK W. HETHERINGTON

Clark Hetherington was a leader in developing the primary aims of physical education through the organization of big muscle activities. He was a pioneer in the natural program of physical education as opposed to the unnatural systematized programs which dominated the curriculum early in this century. History will reveal Hetherington to be one of the outstanding philosophers of the century. His greatest contribution was the construction of a physical education curriculum.

ment. Williams points out the importance of these natural activities:

. . . the fact that man presents in the racial patterns of his nervous system certain underlying predispositions to function in well-defined motor activities characterized in type and quality by his motor experiences over thousands of years, that he is urged on by his very nature to exploit these established organizations, and that, under proper guidance, such expressions may be made to serve high causes and noble ends is of outstanding import.[6]

The program of physical education for

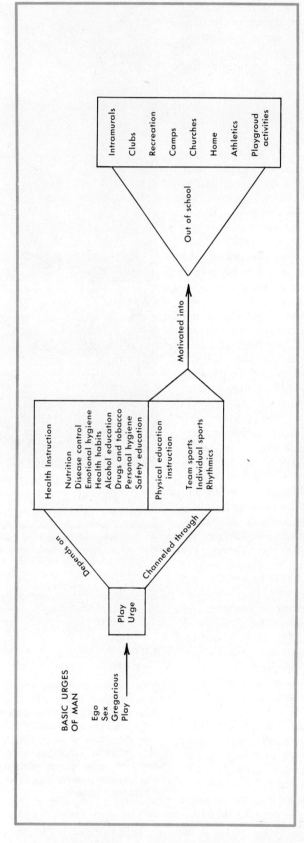

Figure 5-3. Development of the play urge.

children should consist of those big-muscle activities found in games, sports, and rhythms that incorporate these fundamental movements of man. These movements are outlined by Sapora and Mitchell:

Locomotion	Handling Objects
Creeping	Throwing
Walking	Catching
Running	Striking
Dancing	Swinging
Jumping	Pushing
Climbing	Pulling
Swimming	Lifting
Diving	Carrying[18]

Latchaw and Egstrom suggest a more comprehensive outline of the fundamental movements. They speak of gross movement skills and classify these into three groups: (1) basic movements; (2) skills of locomotion; and (3) skills for overcoming inertia of external objects. The classifications and movements involved are shown below:

Basic Movements	Skills of Locomotion	Skills of Overcoming Inertia
Bending	Walking	Pushing
Stretching	Running	Pulling
Twisting	Leaping	Throwing
	Jumping	Kicking
	Hopping	Striking
	Skipping	Batting
	Sliding	Catching
	Galloping	Blocking[19]

The classification of fundamental movements developed by Godfrey and Kephart deserves inclusion in this section. Although similar to the other groups, these authors use a different terminology for the general headings and include several sub-headings. Their classification outline follows:

A. *Body Handling Patterns*
 1. Locomotor Movements
  a. Crawling
  b. Walking
  c. Running
  d. Climbing
  e. Jumping
  f. Rolling
  g. Hopping
  h. Skipping
 2. Balance Patterns
  a. Standing
  b. Sitting
  c. Twisting
  d. Bending
  e. Stretching
  f. Swinging
  g. Rotating

B. *Object Handling Patterns*
 1. Propulsion Patterns
  a. Throwing
  b. Hitting
  c. Kicking
  d. Pushing
  e. Lifting
 2. Absorption Patterns
  a. Catching
  b. Carrying[20]

This concept of play shows that children do not need external, artificial programs imposed upon them by parents, teachers, or others. What they need is guidance. Opportunity has to be provided for pupils to participate in activities that allow for desirable manifestation of their natural play urge. These activities need to be scientifically selected in order that children have opportunity for the fullest mental, physical, emotional and social growth. Chapter 6 shows how the selection of activities can be made.

Although play is one of the basic urges of life, literature does not offer sufficient explanation as to why humans play. Since manifestation of the play urge is a basic objective of physical education, teachers should have knowledge and understanding of the existing theories of why children play.

A recent survey showed 15 theories purporting to explain why children play.[21] These theories were classified into groups and evaluated. A description of each theory is made in Figures 5–4, 5–5, and 5–6. An examination of these theories may be of assistance to teachers in relating play to the physical education program.

Objective Two: The Program Should Contribute to Physical Fitness

Physical fitness is a phase of total fitness and an integral part of the physical education program. The problem confronting many teachers and administrators is interpretation. Many individuals have their own definitions of physical fitness and the activities that should be used to achieve it. Those interpretations in many instances are without scientific foundation and represent an empirical approach in teaching.

Fitness for What? Recent emphasis on physical fitness at both local and national levels has had such far-reaching implica-

(Text continued on page 106.)

CLASSICAL THEORIES OF PLAY

Name	Play is caused:	This explanation assumes:	It can be criticized because:	Verdict
Surplus Energy I	by the existence of energy surplus to the needs of survival	1. energy is stored 2. storage is limited 3. excess energy must be expended 4. expenditure is made on play, by definition.	1. children play when fatigued or to the point of fatigue so a surplus is not necessary for play 2. the process of evolution should have tailored the energy available to the energy required.	Inadequate
Surplus Energy II	by increased tendency to respond after a period of response deprivation.	1. response systems of the body all have a tendency to respond 2. response threshold is lowered by a period of leisure.	after periods of disuse, eventually all available responses should reach a low enough threshold to be discharged. Some responses available to the person are never used.	Inadequate as written but has been incorporated in learning theory.
Instinct	by the inheritance of unlearned capacities to emit playful acts.	1. the determinants of our behavior are inherited in the same way that we inherit the genetic code that determines our structure 2. that some of those determinants cause play.	1. it ignores the obvious capacity of the person to learn new responses that we classify as play 2. the facile naming of an instinct for each class of observed behavior is to do no more than to say "Because there is play, there must be a cause which we will call an Instinct."	Inadequate

Preparation	by the efforts of the player to prepare for later life.	1. play is emitted only by persons preparing for new ways of responding, and in general is the preserve of the young 2. the player can predict what kinds of responses will be critical later 3. instincts governing this are inherited imperfectly and are practiced during youth.	1. it requires that the player inherit the capacity to predict which responses will be critical. This requires the inheritance of information about the future. 2. play occurs most frequently in animals that live in rapidly changing circumstances. 3. when acceptably prepared the person should stop playing.	Inadequate. However play may have by-products that are advantageous later.
Recapitulation	by the player recapitulating the history of the development of the species during its development.	1. critical behaviors occurring during evolution of man are encoded for inheritance. 2. person emits some approximation to all these behaviors during his development. 3. since they are currently irrelevant they are play. 4. the stages in our evolution will be followed in the individual's development.	1. no linear progression in our play development that seems to mirror the development of a species. At one point, late boyhood and adolescence, there may be similarity between sports and games and the components of hunting, chasing, fighting, etc., but before and after there seems little relation. 2. does not explain play activities dependent on our advanced technology.	Inadequate
Relaxation	the need for an individual to emit responses other than those used in work to allow recuperation.	1. players work 2. play involves the emission of responses different to those of work.	1. it does not explain the play of children—unless they are clearly working some part of their day. 2. does not explain the use in play of activities also used in work.	Inadequate

Figure 5–4. Classical Theories of Play. (From Ellis, M. J.: "Play and its theories re-examined." *Parks and Recreation*, National Recreation and Parks Association, August, 1971.)

RECENT THEORIES OF PLAY

Name	Play is caused:	This explanation assumes:	It can be criticized because:	Verdict
Generalization	by the players using in their play, experiences that have been rewarding at work.	1. that there are at least two separable categories of behavior. 2. that the players transfer to play or leisure, behaviors that are rewarded in another setting. 3. that to be useful we understand what rewards an individual at work.	1. it seems to exclude play of preschool children. 2. it assumes that at least some aspects of work are rewarding.	1. Data tend to support this as a view of leisure behavior preferences in adults, providing a chronic or long-term view of their behavior is taken. 2. We must wait for more data.
Compensation	by players using their play to satisfy psychic needs not satisfied in or generated by the working behaviors.	1. that there are at least two separable categories of behavior. 2. the player avoids in play or leisure behaviors that are unsatisfying in the work setting. 3. the player selects leisure experiences that meet his psychic needs. 4. that to be useful we understand the mismatch of needs and satisfactions in the work setting (or vice versa).	1. it seems to exclude the play of preschool children. 2. it assumes that work is damaging, does not satisfy some needs.	1. Such data as exists gives support to the idea in the long term. 2. We must wait for data.
Catharsis	in part by the need to express disorganizing emotions in a harmless way by transferring them to socially sanctioned activity. This concept has almost entirely been limited to questions of aggression, and will be so here.	1. frustration of an intention engenders hostility towards the frustrator. 2. this hostility must be expressed to reduce psychic and physiological stress. 3. this frustration or hostility can be redirected to another activity.	1. it is a partial explanation for only the compensatory behavior engendered by hostility. 2. the data show conclusively that sanctioning aggression increases it. 3. the planning of activities to provide outlets for aggression constitutes its sanctioning.	As an explanation for some aspects of play and leisure pursuits (usually vigorous games), it has no support in the aggression literature.

Psycho-analytic I	in part by the players repeating in a playful form strongly unpleasant experiences, thereby reducing their seriousness and allowing their assimilation.	1. simulating unpleasant experiences in another setting reduces the unpleasantness of their residual effects.	Both ignore play that is not presumed to be motivated by the need to eliminate the products of strongly unpleasant experiences.	There are few data, or conceptual analyses of these tenets. The work is strongly clinical and concerned with individuals. We need clear formulations of what the psycho-analytic view of play is, so that it may be tested.
Psycho-analytic II	in part by the player during play reversing his role as the passive recipient of strongly unpleasant experience, and actively mastering another recipient in a similar way, thus purging the unpleasant effects.	1. achieving mastery, even in a simulated experience, allows the elimination of the products of an unpleasant experience by passing similar experiences on to other beings or objects.		
Developmentalism	the way in which a child's mind develops. Thus play is caused by the growth of the child's intellect and is conditioned by it. That play occurs when the child can impose on reality his own conceptions and constraints.	1. that play involves the intellect. 2. that as a result of play, the intellect increases in complexity. 3. that this process in the human can be separated into stages. 4. that children pass through these stages in order.	1. it doesn't account for play when and if the intellect ceases to develop.	The best known thinker in this school is Paiget who is concerned with the cause of play, but more importantly with its content. This concept must be integrated with a more precise theory of motivation and learning.
Learning	the normal processes that produce learning.	1. the child acts to increase the probability of pleasant events. 2. the child acts to decrease the probability of unpleasant events. 3. the environment is a complex of pleasant and unpleasant effects. 4. the environment selects and energizes the play behaviors of its tenants.	1. it doesn't account for behavior in situations where there are no apparent consequences. (However this theory would maintain that there are no such settings.) 2. it doesn't account for the original contributions to behaviors made by an individual's genetic inheritance.	Cultural, sub-cultural and familial differences support the view that quantity and content of play behavior is learned. The theory can account for the content of an individual's play if not his inherited tendencies to play.

Figure 5–5. Recent theories of play. (From Ellis, M. J.: "Play and its theories re-examined." *Parks and Recreation,* National Recreation and Parks Association, August, 1971.)

tions for teachers, administrators, and lay people that sound professional scrutiny of the subject is in order.

The physical education program in the schools of America has woven a tortuous path toward the establishment of a basic scientific philosophy and a sound approach to content. The time has come for physical education leaders to assert their professional leadership by stating clearly and loudly the proper interpretation of physical fitness and the importance of protecting the gains that have been made in formulating a scientific foundation for physical education in this country.

As the educational pendulum swings from one extreme to another, the physical education program is in danger of losing ground if the term *physical fitness* is not interpreted clearly and scientifically. In the past few years many contraindicated activities have been included in the curriculum that are supposed to contribute to physical fitness. Some manufacturers through high-pressure advertising have introduced numerous fads and artificial contrivances and have capitalized on the present emphasis on fitness. These ideas have infiltrated the curriculum to such an alarming extent that physical education in some cases has been placed in an awkward position in order to defend them.

First, it should be clearly borne in mind that physical fitness is only one basic objective of physical education. It should also be understood that physical fitness is a *relative* state and varies from individual to individual and from program to program. There are varying degrees of fitness, from the least fit to the most fit, depending on the type of fitness the individual is seeking. In discussing the problem of fitness, one must ask, "Fitness for what?" Is the program planned in terms of fitness for war? If so, this means that individuals must be educated to kill and to keep from being killed. Or is the program designed for living in a peaceful society? The objectives of educating for war are entirely different from those designed for living in peace. Is the program of fitness planned for interscholastic athletics? If so, what phase of athletics? The training for a golf program is entirely different from the training necessary for a wrestling program. The level of fitness for the interscholastic program is neither neces-sary nor desirable for the great mass of pupils involved in the physical education program.

Many programs advocated at present are based on the findings of certain "fitness tests," many of which are scientifically unsound and which may place physical education in the same uncertain status it had many years ago. As an outgrowth of these tests, groups and individuals are advocating programs in calisthenics and gymnastics used in Europe during the latter part of the 19th century when the major objective was preparation for war. These programs were transplanted to this country and for many years dominated our physical education efforts.

These programs were unpopular and unsatisfactory in the old countries, and they were no more popular in America. They are undemocratic, dictatorial, militaristic, and contrary to the natural movements of man and the fundamental concepts of the democratic way of life.

Early in the 20th century, through the efforts of Clark Hetherington, Jesse Feiring Williams, Jay B. Nash, and Thomas Wood, the scientific approach to physical education began to gain recognition and programs of physical education based on the fundamental movements of man replaced the artificial, unnatural, arm-swinging era. Calisthenics, unnatural gymnastics, and various systems were replaced by sports and games involving the fundamental movements. These natural movements will always prevail over the unnatural programs in the play life of children. The sports program that includes these movements is the natural, scientific approach to physical fitness. Many leaders subscribe to this philosophy. Williams summarizes scientific thought on present programs:

> This does not mean that sound programs should be replaced by stupid calisthenics, most of which are not vigorous at all; they may appear to be effective only because they require the individual to move in unnatural ways.[6]

At a conference on youth and fitness, a prepared statement pointed out that:

> It is not possible to design a single set of standards of fitness for all age groups and persons with diversified tasks. . . . For each individual at each developmental stage, there is a desirable level of total fitness to be sought according to the person's role in life.[22]

MODERN THEORIES

Name	Play is caused:	This explanation assumes:	It can be criticized because:	Verdict
Play as Arousal-Seeking	by the need to generate interactions with the environment or self that elevates arousal (level of interest or stimulation) towards the optimal for the individual.	1. stimuli vary in their capacity to arouse 2. there is a need for optimal arousal. 3. change in arousal towards optimal is pleasant 4. the organism learns the behaviors that result in that feeling and vice versa.	1. it is very general and handles equally well questions of work and play. In fact it questions the validity of separating work from play.	Together with learning, and developmentalism as a package is a very powerful theoretical base for our professional operations.
Competence/Effectance	by a need to produce effects in the environment. Such effects demonstrate competence and result in feelings of effectance.	1. demonstration of competence leads to feelings of effectance. 2. effectance is pleasant. 3. effectance increases the probability of tests of competence.	1. for the organism to constantly test whether it can still competently produce an effect seems to require uncertainty as to the outcome. Uncertainty or information seem to be the very attributes of stimuli that are arousing. 2. thus it can be argued that competence/effectance behavior is a kind of arousal-seeking.	Is best subsumed as an explanation that developed as theorists moved towards the arousal seeking model.

Figure 5–6. Modern theories of play. (From Ellis, M. J.: "Play and its theories re-examined." *Parks and Recreation,* National Recreation and Parks Association, August, 1971.)

It is the opinion of the author that the so-called "fitness tests" have nothing to do with total fitness and should be called, therefore, physical proficiency tests.

Obvious flaws in physical fitness tests, formal activities such as calisthenics, certain types of gymnastics, and other unnatural activities are the overemphasis on strength, which is only *one* factor in the development of physiological fitness, and the lack of a scientific approach to the various other components of fitness. There are three components of fitness—anatomical, psychological, and physiological (Fig. 5–7). All three of these components are vitally important in the approach to physical fitness.

Anatomical Component. The anatomical component has to do with the individual's heredity. Certain anatomical structures may handicap an individual in the performance of a given "fitness test." Individuals with long arms are usually unable to do as many pull-ups as those with short arms. For the long-armed individual, the pull-up would not be a fair test. Exceptions such as this occur throughout the "fitness test" procedure. Individuals with handicaps, such as loss of an arm or leg or varying degrees of deformities, do not perform as well in certain "fitness tests," yet they may be as fit physiologically as an Olympic athlete.

Psychological Component. This component relates to the emotional factors involved in fitness performances. Competition may so affect an individual that his emotions may hinder his performance. It would not be scientifically sound to say that one who fails to start quickly, because of some emotional deviation, and who thereby gives a poor performance in the 50-yard dash is not physically fit.

Physiological Component. The physiological component involves four factors: strength, skill, speed, and endurance. This component is the one which physical education teachers and lay people seem to understand and to which they give the most recognition. It must be emphasized at all times that physiological fitness is relative; it varies between extremes from the least fit to the most fit according to the activity involved. The fitness needed for a steel worker is entirely different from that needed for a salesman. The question should always be asked, *Fitness for what?* Who can

say that a basketball player is more fit than a wrestler or vice versa? Which is the more fit, the elephant, which travels four or five miles per hour and is capable of phenomenal strength, or the cheetah, which cruises at 75 miles per hour and has little strength?

Physiological performance involving feats of strength, speed, skill, and endurance, whether singly or in combination, is limited by various anatomical and psychological components. The anatomy of the individual always limits the degree of performance, and emotional factors as well have a direct bearing on performance.

In order to develop physiological fitness, a large variety of activities must be included in the program. Physiologically, anatomically, and psychologically, there is no "best" activity for development and neither is there any single activity that is suitable for every individual. Boys and girls, after having participated in many different types of activities, form likes and dislikes for certain activities. This is natural if only for anatomical reasons. Success in performance motivates interest, and anatomical structure plays an important role in successful performance.

This principle necessitates the careful classification of all pupils in order to assure proper participation in the activities necessary for physiological development. Teachers must continually remember that no two pupils are alike in interest, ability, structure, or temperament. Each class will have average, gifted, handicapped, skillful, highly combative, unskilled, tall, slender, fat, and nervous students, with varying degrees of ability. An effective program should be designed to meet the needs of all types and should allow for the manifestation of their innate abilities.

Four factors of physiological fitness will be considered separately in the following paragraphs. The curriculum should include activities that involve all of these factors, for all of them are important in the quest for physiological fitness. Although other factors such as power, agility, and flexibility have been mentioned, the four described below may be considered as basic to all physical education programs.

SKILL. The attainment of skill in various activities may be called the epitome of physical fitness. A varied curriculum of skills if taught properly will develop strength,

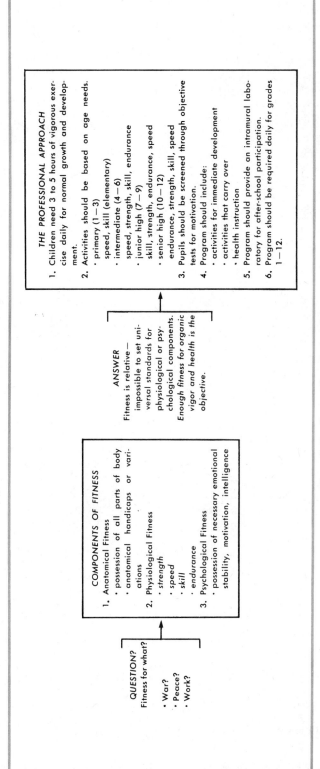

Figure 5-7. Pattern for physical fitness.

L. TUCKER JONES

Tucker Jones was both a philosopher and a teacher of physical education, who believed that learning skills was the most important objective of physical education. He felt that "high level performance lends an appreciation of all skills; it means keener judgment."

speed, and endurance. Not only does the practice of skill activities develop other factors of fitness, but such activities also are interesting to the participant.

The importance of skill education has been pointed out in the professional literature for many years. At the turn of the century, leading physiologists were emphasizing the value of teaching skills. Schmidt discusses this early thinking during the era of formal gymnastic training. He states: "Exercises of skill, however, have as their principal aim the improvement of coordination between the brain and nerves so as to control the body through will power."[23]

Morehouse and Miller summarize recent thinking on the importance of teaching skills:

The development of motor skills of various types, one of the major objectives of physical education, consists primarily of improvement in the speed and

accuracy with which the nervous system coordinates activity.[24]

The teaching of skills is not easy; it requires careful planning and continuous effort by the teacher. Some of the criticism of our field has stemmed from the fact that some teachers have ignored the teaching-of-skills approach in favor of activities less demanding of the teacher's time and energy.

Many activities, such as marching, certain types of calisthenics, strength tests, and other tests of a formal nature, should be carefully evaluated before they are included in the program. The development of skill is the essence of physical education and the backbone of the program. Without the skill approach, there would be no need for physical education teachers. A college graduate is not needed to check the number of times a group of pupils chin the bar or perform the standing broad jump, or to time pupils in "circuit training." However, a well-trained teacher is needed to teach the intricate movements of basketball, tennis, swimming, wrestling, and rhythms. If physical education is to serve the pupils, if the program is to maintain a position of prestige in the school, if, indeed, the program is to survive, physical educators must strive for a *teaching* program that emphasizes the teaching of skills.

Teaching skills to assist pupils in after-school participation is extremely important. Pupils who learn skills are motivated to practice them out of school, since the skills offer a challenge and may provide an opportunity for a person to compete with others and with himself. The skills which allow the pupils to practice at or near the home in preparation for participating with other persons at a later time are the most desirable. Williams points to the need for after-school participation by stating:

Provision for physical exercise of school children is not enough. These children must learn skills and acquire interests in physical activities which they will be disposed to continue after school days are over.[6]

Brownell and Hagman further substantiate this premise:

The basic element in physical education emphasizes skill. Skill is fundamental to all other attributes. . . . Skill in a broad range of motor activities presents the best single index of an enduring interest in physical education that leads on to wider participation in wholesome recreation.[25]

In addition to the need for skills instruction in physiological development, the importance of skills to intellectual achievement is well documented. The teaching of skills involves perceptual motor movements which are vitally important in learning to read and write. For a discussion of the relationship of physical education to academic performance, see Chapter 1, p. 8.

SPEED.   In most life situations, muscular speed is necessary in varying degrees. For growing boys and girls, to be able to run fast, to throw fast, and to combine speed with strength, skill and endurance are basic for normal growth and development.

Speed is based on quick muscular reaction. Practicing speed activities improves coordination and reaction time. Through participation in activities combining endurance and strength, the organs of the body are developed during the formative years, enabling individuals to perform the tasks of later life. In many instances, speed combined with skill may offset a lack of strength. This is one way individual differences are provided for in physical education; the compensating factor motivates greater interest in participation.

Speed, according to Mitchell, has always been an important factor in man's survival. He says: "Speed is just as essential in the industrial and social life of today. In the play of children it is most often speed that brings success and the same is true in athletic competition."[26]

ENDURANCE.   To be able to compete, to participate, to prolong certain efforts with a minimum of fatigue is important in the development of physical fitness. There are two kinds of endurance: muscular endurance and circulatory-respiratory endurance. The former is the ability of the muscles to perform work, as in pull-ups; and the latter is the ability of muscle groups to contract for long periods of time, as in distance running. Exercises of endurance, therefore, are essential. They develop the heart, promote metabolism, and provide an overall physiological development that is not attained through exercises of skill, speed, or strength. Schmidt shows that a man may have acquired through training an athletic,

muscular development of great strength, but little endurance. He states:

> Since it is the purpose of physical education to increase the metabolism of the body, to stimulate the activities of the organs and especially to train the circulatory and respiratory organs, exercises of speed and endurance are the most effective. They cannot be replaced by exercises of strength and skill, because these serve a different purpose and must be evaluated in a different way.[23]

STRENGTH.   Strength is basic to performance and is essential in the development of muscular efficiency. The ability to lift, to carry, to hold, to squeeze, and to push are important factors in the development of strength.

It must be constantly borne in mind that strength should be developed concurrently with speed, skill and endurance. Overemphasizing strength while neglecting the other components produces undesirable results. The type of strength illustrated by bulging muscles is no longer considered as an example of good development. The strength developed through vigorous participation in sports and games is much closer to the physiological ideal. Williams says:

> What, then, is to be said of the efforts of certain persons to develop large and bulging muscles or to pursue certain odd skills that have no useful function in life? The satisfactions derived from such exercises serve only whimsical values such as exhibitionism. At times they are outlets for maladjusted personalities.[6]

As far back as the early 1930's, when strength activities and strong men with bulging muscles were the fashion, outstanding physiologists were concerned with the overemphasis on strength. Schmidt shows that:

> It is, however, a grave error to confuse this development of the musculature, in its various groups, with the development of the body as a whole, including the important vital organs and their function. Such mistakes prevail today in many gymnastic systems.[23]

Strength alone is not an indication of fitness. Fitness involves the development of all the factors that contribute to fitness of which strength is only one. Karpovich and Sinning have this to say: "Strength tests do not permit us to draw satisfactory conclusions regarding the efficiency of the entire body."[27]

At this point it would be well to discuss

an aspect of training that is confusing to many teachers and students. Recently, various terms such as "isometrics," "isotonic training," and "weight training" and the various procedures involved in these systems have received considerable attention.

There is nothing new in these programs. During the early years of this century, Swoboda employed the same principle and called the system "conscious evolution." A little later Charles Atlas called it "dynamic tension." The physiological principle involved in all these systems of developing strength is the *principle of overload*. Advocates of muscle-building have taken the long established principle of overload and have manufactured new titles for it in an effort to promote their programs and to sell mechanical equipment, and contrivances.

The principle of overload is simple. All individuals have definite patterns of physical activity. They walk so much, climb so many stairs, run a certain amount, dance so much, sit a certain portion of the time and participate in other routines, which comprise the usual schedule of work or play. When this program is increased, employing more work and more muscle effort, the increment of activity is known as overload. Overload may be described as any type of exercise program that is an increase over the previous or usual pattern of activity. There are many ways of overloading a muscle in order to develop strength. Some of these methods are acceptable as sound physical education procedures and some are of questionable value. In order to discriminate between them, the teacher should be familiar with the three types of overload:

1. *Natural Overload.* Any time that a muscle is required to perform or contract with greater effort than before, the overload principle is used. A person who has been walking a mile daily will be overloading various muscle groups if he runs the mile instead of walking. Sprinters practice overloading more than distance runners. The natural method of overload involves movement and is physiologically sound. The natural sports instruction program that constitutes the bulk of the physical education curriculum provides sufficient overload for normal growth and development.

2. *Special Overload for Sports Training.* For developing the strength of a specific group of muscles to improve performance in a skill, certain types of overload methods have been found to be of great help and are acceptable. An illustration of this method is the training of basketball players. Medicine balls should be used for developing the shoulder and arm muscles, a heavy basketball for strengthening the fingers and then the standard ball for practicing the skills. This procedure may be applied to other sports skills, such as swinging a heavy bat for developing hitting strength in baseball, jumping with weights on the shoulder for developing jumping. The point to remember here is to apply the overload to the muscles involved rather than resort to weight lifting with the assumption that lifting weights will

JESSE FEIRING WILLIAMS

Jesse Feiring Williams, an outstanding leader in physical education, emphasized the importance of educating the whole person through physical education, rather than concentrating solely on the physical.

assist in developing better performance in all sports. Weight lifting is a good overload activity for training in lifting weights.

3. *Nonfunctional Overload.* This type of overload includes many "systems," which have been practiced under various names but which still involve the physiological principle of overload. *Isometric training* includes all methods in which a muscle is stimulated but either is not allowed to contract or is contracted a little and then held. Isometric training does not allow or develop flexibility; it excludes natural movements and is physiologically unsound as a physical education activity. Even as a training program for sports, it is of questionable value.

Steinhaus refers to this:

As training aid for various sports activities, isometric exercises are rarely superior to other more functional ways of overloading. This is due to the fact that the development of strength is very particulate, i.e., confined to the actual muscle group that is overloaded. Consequently, throwing a medicine ball to develop arm and shoulder muscles used in basketball is much more likely to develop a "basketball musculature" than would any form of isometrics or weight lifting. In fact the latter are likely to develop muscles of the kind and strength that may even be a handicap to the nth degree basketballer. Judged in this way, isometrics are functional in a very limited way and weight lifting is truly functional only for weight lifting.[28]

Another form of overload known as *isotonic training* is the method that overloads the muscle but allows complete contraction. Isotonic contraction is more functional but is of questionable value as a physical education activity. Clark and Clark state that neither isometric nor isotonic exercise improves circulatory endurance; this is a deficiency of both types of exercise in the development of physical fitness.[28]

Each of the two types will improve muscular strength. Many studies have been made to show the superiority of one type over the other. These studies reveal that one group is about as effective as the other in developing strength. Clark and Clark state, "However, the evidence shows little if any difference in the effectiveness of the two forms in achieving strength increase."[29]

Physical Education and Overload

Physical education teachers are faced with the problem of whether to include the overload program of isometrics involving weights and mechanical equipment in the program. Considerable evidence shows the inadvisability of incorporating these activities in the physical education curriculum. For training athletes, there may be a need for some type of overload, such as the special overload. However, there is a difference between the level of strength needed for normal growth and development and that needed for training athletes. Physical education is concerned with the responsibility of developing strength on the level necessary for normal growth and development and not the level for competitive athletics.

Years ago Schmidt showed that extreme exercises of strength are questionable:

For organs which are located in the chest cavity, i.e., the lungs and heart, the practice of extreme strength exercises is much more serious. . . . In educational gymnastics of youth the pursuit of strenuous exercise is inadvisable, as an athletic development of individual muscle groups is unnecessary and even undesirable.[23]

More recently, Clark and Clark have pointed out that "based upon present knowledge, it might be well to go slow in advocating isometric exercise."[28] Williams scientifically explains how the entire group of activities violates the law of reciprocal innervation:

Now the use of exercises at times is made to violate this very clear fact. So-called "resistive exercises" are advocated in certain systems and in so-called "educational exercises" the individual is asked to hold the active and antagonistic muscle groups in a state of contraction. Thus, these movements are stiff, rigid and hence unphysiological.[6]

Law of Reciprocal Innervation. The law of reciprocal innervation has been defined by Sherrington and has served as a guideline in teaching for many years.[30] It is involved in all movements. When an impulse is sent from the brain to a muscle to contract, a corresponding impulse is sent to the antagonistic muscle to relax. In the flexion of the arm, for example, the stimulus sent to the biceps has a corresponding impulse sent to the triceps to relax. This physiological phenomenon is the natural way for producing smooth coordination and is basic for attaining excellence in all skills and movements. There are many resistance movements, labeled as isometric and isotonic exercises, that violate this principle; nevertheless, they are included in some physical education programs. Because they violate established principles of movement, they should be excluded from the curriculum of physical education.

As a part of the physical education program, isometric exercises are inadvisable, since they impede the normal range of joint movements and do not incorporate the natural body movements necessary for normal growth and development. Overload may be involved in all physical education activities without excluding the natural movements, which have been described. Wrestling, as an illustration, not only provides a more acceptable overload for developing strength but also includes the speed, skill, and endurance factors. Different types of running provide overload and develop physiological endurance, which is not found in isometric exercises.

Wilbur shows that games are better than formal gymnastics in building strength in the arms and shoulder girdle, in establishing body coordinations, agility and control, and in reaching a high degree of physical fitness.[31] It is the purpose of physical education to seek those activities that develop the body as a whole and not isolated areas of the body.

Weiss shows why sports are essential to the fitness effort. He explains that "We need to revise our strategy. We do not seem to be succeeding very well in making our youth take their fitness medicine. We should turn more and more to sports—through intramurals, playdays, and community recreation programs."[32]

Bender, Kaplan and Johnson in a recent article point out that isometric programs should be evaluated very carefully. They state, "An isometric conditioning program using gross exercises is often more detrimental than beneficial."[33]

Recent medical opinion places isometrics in an unfavorable light, particularly for those with circulatory problems. Schultz states that:

Isometrics, for example, are now considered inadvisable; such exercises tend to raise both blood pressure and pulse rate to an unsafe degree. Most authorities feel that rhythmical exercise is best.[34]

This observation is substantiated by Clark. He reports the results of studies made of isometric and isotonic exercises on the circulatory system. The studies reveal that isometric exercises are more likely than isotonic exercises to produce irregular heart beats, premature ventricular contractions, abnormally fast heart beat in heart disease patients, and rise in blood pressure. He also concluded that:

In overall assessment of the relative merits of isometric and isotonic conditioning of muscle groups, the isotonic form has a definite advantage. This form of exercise is superior for the improvement of muscular strength and muscular endurance in those phases of the physical fitness program. The extravagant claims of physical fitness benefits from isometric exercise as commonly practiced are far from justified.[35]

Definition of Physical Fitness

In summarizing the foregoing considerations of physical fitness, it may be stated that *physical fitness is a relative condition, which varies from individual to individual and which depends on the ability of the individual to adjust to the tasks demanded of him with as little effort as possible and without undue fatigue.*

In striving for physiological fitness, physical education teachers must continually search for the scientific approach in the selection of activities that make the greatest contribution to strength, speed, skill, and endurance. They must also constantly seek to determine which of these four factors plays the greatest role in each individual's fitness needs.

In light of these considerations, teachers should adjust the content of the curriculum to meet the individual's capacity as based on his individual health needs.

The Health Objective

The student of physical education may be at a loss as to what his role is regarding physical fitness in its relation to physical education. He may ask, "How much fitness is necessary?" To what extent should he pursue the various testing programs? What should be his objectives relative to fitness?

Teachers and administrators should always be concerned with the health needs of individual boys and girls and they should guide their programs toward the health objectives of physical education.

Professional leaders should be concerned with the positive health objective of fitness. If they are not, the program does not contribute to the health of boys and girls. In that case, how can they justify the expenditures of money for playgrounds, gymnasia, and teachers and the demands for time in the crowded school curriculum? In other words, if the program of physical education does not contribute to good health, it is difficult to justify its inclusion in the curriculum since health is a basic objective of education.

With the health objective as a goal, physical fitness may be viewed more clearly and scientifically. A recent committee of the American Medical Association and the American Association for Health, Physical Education and Recreation stated: "Along with exercise, adequate nutrition, sufficient rest and relaxation, suitable work, the use of medical and dental services and the avoidance of excesses are all important in maintaining fitness."[36] This clearly shows that the exercise approach to fitness is not enough. Supporting services and instruction are also important. To initiate a vigorous exercise program without sound medical examination and health instruction in some instances may do more harm than good. Karpovich and Sinning make the following observation:

. . . **Beyond a certain indispensable minimum of physical fitness, an additional improvement in physical fitness has no effect upon health, no matter how one defines the word. Excessive physical activities, on the other hand, may be definitely detrimental to persons with some diseases.**[27]

Teachers should seek the level of physical fitness needed for each pupil and provide the opportunity for sufficient exercise to meet the health needs of every individual.

Objective Three: The Program Should Provide Instruction in Leisure Time Skills

Highly competitive team sports, such as basketball, football, and hockey, although vitally important during the formative years, have critical limitations for partici-

pation in later years. On the other hand, activities such as swimming, bowling, golf, tennis, table tennis, and dancing offer life-long opportunity for participation. However, it is important that the skills involved in these activities be learned during school years.

Immediate Carry-Over

When considering the value of leisure and carry-over activities, teachers should always remember that leisure-time participation means today, tomorrow, next year, and many years from now. Activities should be taught that will allow pupil participation in the immediate future in order that they can derive the greatest amount of physiological development. Carry-over value is frequently thought of in terms of what the individual may do many years from now; at the same time, teachers should not lose sight of the need for participation in the present and immediate future. Many team activities are essential for physiological development and should be considered for immediate carry-over. Proper instruction in these activities should be provided in the curriculum.

The program should also include activities that can be practiced at home and near the home. The health and fitness of American youth will be more nearly achieved through instruction in such activities, since the home and its environs are where pupils spend most of their leisure time. Individual activities, such as chinning, broad and high jump, dashes, individual basketball shooting and dribbling, stroking the tennis ball against a wall, and practicing the golf swing in the garage or on the lawn, are examples of the activities that can be practiced at home after instruction has been given during the physical education period.

Carry-Over Beyond School Years

Activities that set the pattern for exercise many years after the students leave school should also be taken into consideration when planning the curriculum. Team sports may be essential for immediate carry-over, but for use beyond school years they are valueless. Individual sports, such as golf,

Figure 5–8. Golf is one of the best carry-over sports and can be a life-long activity. (Courtesy Los Angeles City Schools.)

tennis, bowling, swimming, dancing, and table tennis rate high in adult participation and should be included in the program. Moreover, these activities also make a great contribution during the formative years.

Norfolk City Survey. The physical education department of the Norfolk City Public Schools surveyed the opinions of 16,000 parents to determine which activities they would like to have been taught when they were in school. The findings were overwhelmingly in favor of instruction in individual activities, such as golf, tennis, bowling, swimming, dancing, and table tennis. Team sports were scored very low[37] (see Figures 5–9, 5–10, 5–11, and 5–12).

Opinions of Outstanding Leaders. Through the years a great number of leaders and groups have emphasized the importance of teaching the skills of individual sports that will carry over into later life.

Nixon and Jewett explain the need for teaching skills of individual sports in the high school:

There is greater emphasis on the so-called carry-over activities, such as swimming, bowling, tennis, golf, archery, badminton and others. . . . these carry-over activities are introduced at earlier grade levels, such as in beginning junior high school years.[4]

Other leaders in health and physical education have corroborated this opinion. Karl and Carolyn Bookwalter show the need for instruction in individual sports and why such sports are not necessarily less developmental than the more rugged team sports.[38]

Nash shows how, historically, no great civilization has ever developed leisure and survived. According to Nash:

The increase in leisure and the decline of civilization have synchronized so many times in history that the outlook so far as America is concerned is none too bright. . . . given leisure man will go to sleep; that is, he will let down, get soft, become an onlooker, cease to be vigorous and then lose initiative.[39]

Brownell and Hagman point to physical education as a teaching program in which children learn skills for carry-over beyond school years.[25]

Mitchell and Mason describe how the football or basketball athlete in college may be inadequately equipped for participation after college because he had not learned to play tennis or to swim.[26] Oberteuffer and

(Text continued on page 121.)

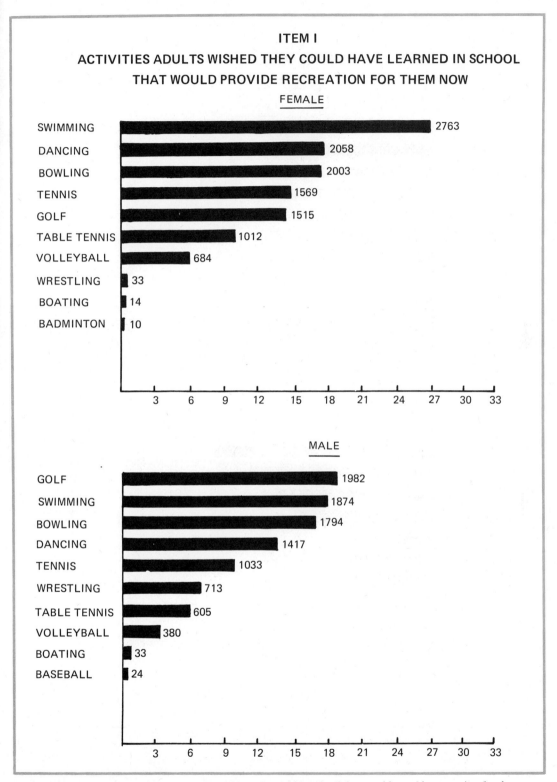

Figure 5–9. Activities adults wished they could have learned in school that would provide recreation for them now.

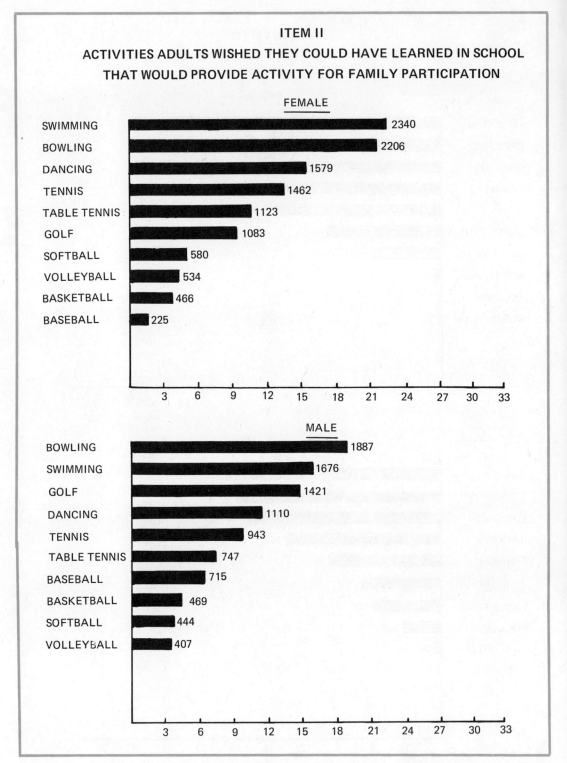

Figure 5–10. Activities adults wished they could have learned in school that would provide activity for family participation.

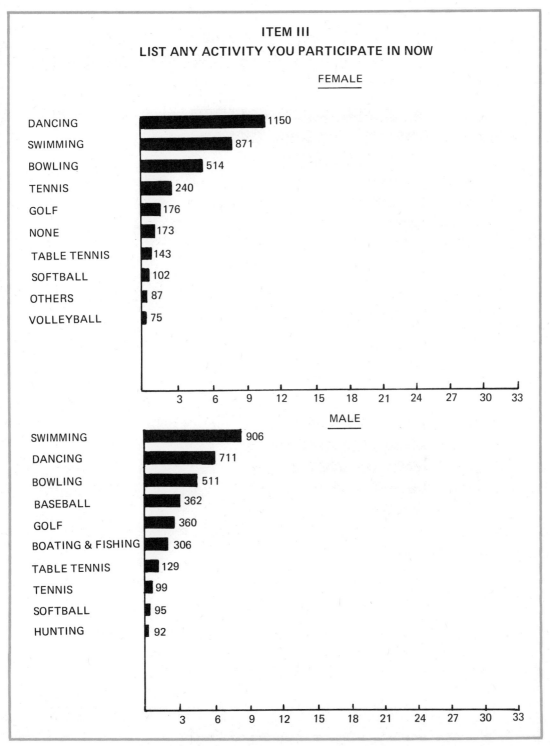

Figure 5–11. List any activity you participate in now.

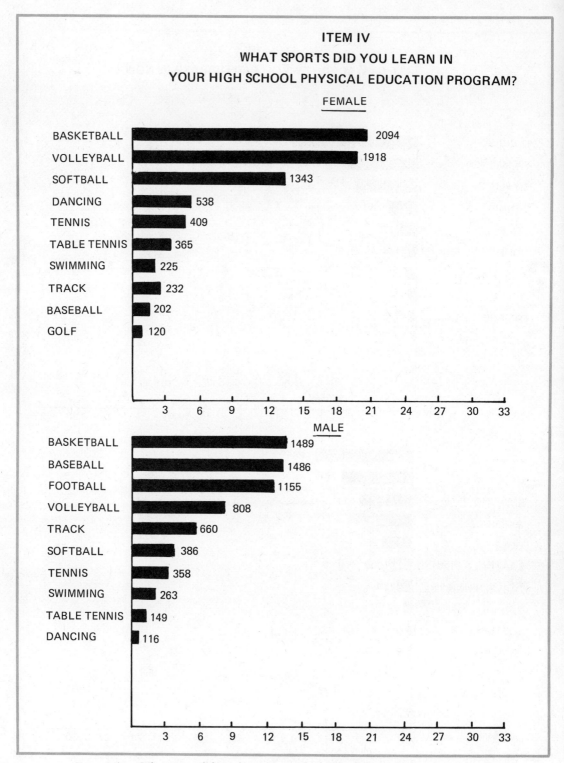

Figure 5–12.   What sports did you learn in your high school physical education program?

Ulrich show why the carry-over activities are far superior to "blind alley" activities, which lead nowhere after the class period is over.[40]

Finally, Williams summarizes by stating that:

No child can be considered educated unless he has acquired in childhood and youth familiarity and skill in a large number of games and sports which give satisfaction and lead to their pursuit in recreational ways out of school.[6]

One of the criticisms of physical education today is that it fails to teach the skills of individual sports that have great carry-over value. Devising procedures for including individual sports in the curriculum and teaching the skills needed in them should be of prime concern to teachers of physical education.

Objective Four: The Program Should Contribute to Emotional Stability

Through guidance in the situations arising from participation in play, pupils learn to adjust to situations and to each other. In no other phase of school life is the opportunity so great for emotional guidance as in the day-by-day experiences which arise in the physical education program.

Hetherington states, "The degree of the development of nervous functional power in any individual is determined, within the limits of heredity, by the variety, amount and intensity of activities during the years of growth."[10] Not only do certain activities develop nerve strength, but through them the qualified and interested teacher may be able to provide an environment and instruction which will contribute to emotional stability.

It is extremely important that the program contain a great variety of vigorous activities and that all children be afforded the opportunity of learning the skills involved in these activities. Heredity aside, there is no way to develop a strong, stable nervous system other than through vigorous exercise during the formative years. It seems logical, therefore, that participation in those activities which arouse the deeper emotions, tempered by the inhibitory ele-

JAY B. NASH

Jay Nash was one of the great leaders in physical education who believed that the program should assist the individual in developing play skills for leisure-time activity. It was pointed out in his writings that no nation could survive without purposeful leisure-time participation.

ments of rules, penalties and restrictions, and guided by the teacher would furnish a fertile environment for developing emotional stability.

Hetherington shows the importance of continuous activity in the development of the nervous system:

Nervous development must be gained through continuous activity during the whole period of childhood and youth. It cannot be gained after maturity, and it cannot be gained in any one year or group of years in either childhood or youth.[10]

Sociologists, physicians, psychologists, and psychiatrists say that a well-planned program in physical education is the best medium of alleviating emotional disturbances. Their findings are expressed in the statement of Layman:

Any type of activity which can provide a wholesome outlet for the fundamental physiological drives and satisfaction of the psychological needs is a valuable

Figure 5–13. Vigorous activity contributes to emotional stability.

tool to the mental hygienist. Of all subjects in the educational curriculum, physical education is the one which can best accomplish this function and it is not dependent on adult motivation.[41]

Morehouse and Miller, in describing the importance of exercise to emotional health, state:

If exercise is pleasant in itself, as in games, part of the benefit derives from the relief of tensions and the monotony of daily activity.[24]

Voltmer and Esslinger state:

Emotional stability is only achieved through practice in controlling and modifying the feelings released. Physical education makes a substantial contribution to education in providing a laboratory setting in which emotional control is practiced.

In view of this fact, the curriculum of physical education should include those activities which are particularly valuable in arousing and offering an outlet for emotional expression. Body-contact activities, such as football, basketball, soccer, and wrestling, are very effective in this respect because they exercise deeper, more powerful emotions than many of the non-contact activities.[42]

Observations and studies at the Menninger Clinic prompted W. C. Menninger to make the following statements regarding

the value of play in the prevention of emotional illness:

Recreation has not only played an important part in the treatment program of many mental illnesses but it has been a considerable factor in enabling former patients to remain well. Therefore, psychiatrists believe that recreative activity can also be a valuable preventive of mental and emotional ill health.

Good mental health is directly related to the capacity and willingness of an individual to play. Regardless of his objections, resistances, or past practices, any individual will make a wise investment for himself if he does plan time for his play and take it seriously.

Competitive games provide an unusually satisfactory social outlet for the instinctive aggressive drive. Psychiatrists postulate the existence in the personality of an aggressive instinct which constantly seeks expression. Where its direct expression is denied, symptoms may develop. There are perhaps specific values in varying degrees and types of competitive activity.

In this troubled world today, so filled with unhappiness, distress, anxiety and restlessness, to whom can one look for help? It is my firm conviction that if we could encourage and teach and guide more people to more effective recreative activity, we could and would make a major contribution to our national and international peace of mind. That, it seems to me, is the big challenge to recreation workers today.[43]

Johnson and Hutton gave personality tests to a group of college wrestlers. The study showed that before wrestling, the functional intelligence of the group dropped from a mean average of 110 to a low of 92; there were increased neurotic tendencies and aggressive feelings, which were inhibited. After wrestling, the functional intelligence returned to normal, the neurotic feelings disappeared, and aggressive tendencies were reduced. This study further substantiates the effectiveness of physical education activity in re-shaping human behavior along socially accepted channels.[44]

Ninety-one percent of the respondents to a survey of the opinions of 54 psychiatrists showed that they believed that moderate exercise would assist in relieving tension. The activities to which the respondents gave the highest priorities were walking, swimming, bowling, golf, tennis, square dancing, social dancing, folk dancing, creative dancing, calisthenics, bag punching, basketball, fishing, boating, gardening, and relaxing exercises.[45]

Outstanding educators are deeply concerned with the development of emotional stability. Kilpatrick summarizes this concern. He states: "No aim for education is more vital or essential than the proper care of the emotions, the building of properly adjusted personalities."[46] He feels that all human beings have personal wants and inner urges and that to satisfy them results in a happy and useful life while to deny them reasonable expression leads to maladjustment. Kilpatrick describes these wants as follows:

1. The craving for interesting and even exciting activity.
2. The demand for security against anxieties and fears.
3. The desire for response (the most social of these urges).
4. The desire for recognition.[46]

Kilpatrick stresses the importance of using the first as a tool to achieve the others. He explains in this way:

That the healthy child craves activity of a kind interesting to him has been known from the beginning of time, but only in recent years has this craving been recognized as itself a necessary and therefore a proper and healthy manifestation of life. In our social heritage, compulsory restraint of children was until recently the common procedure.[46]

He shows how modern educators use the craving for activity as a primary basis for teaching and says that in steering the child, consideration of the child's interests and desire for activity should be the starting point.[46]

The power of the intellect over bodily functions is vitally important in modern civilization. The intellect should always control the emotions; intellectual decision is constructive decision whereas emotional decision in many instances is destructive decision. Activities in the curriculum that do not allow for successful performances will foster frustration, which in turn will affect the intellect to the extent that emotional decision will dominate intellectual decision. This being true, it is important that the activities that are included in the curriculum be those that contribute to the manifestation of the individual's innate potentialities and allow him some measure of accomplishment.

Teachers should have a working knowledge of emotional health and emotional disorders. Familiarity with the various emotional disturbances found in all strata of our society may enable the teachers of physical education to make greater contributions to the health and fitness of their students.

As teachers study the emotional problems in the classroom, they will find that pupils are integral parts of the environment. The ways in which pupils adjust to their environment determines, to a great extent, their emotional development.

PERFORMANCE OBJECTIVES

Having established an overview of the philosophy of physical education through general aims and objectives, the teacher is ready to focus his attention on devising performance objectives for the instructional program. These objectives are not only necessary for providing direction and meaning for each class period, but they are desirable for evaluating pupil performance and teacher efficiency. The terms "performance" and "behavioral" will be used interchangeably to discuss objectives.

Behavioral Domains

Evaluation is the motive behind the recent emphasis on improving the quality of instruction. Evaluation can be approached successfully through behavioral or performance objectives. Behavioral objectives have been classified into three large groups or domains: cognitive, affective and psychomotor. In the mid-1950's a committee of college and university leaders published the *Taxonomy of Educational Objectives* which developed the cognitive domain.[47] During the early 1960's objectives in the affective domain were published,[48] but very little material has been published in the psychomotor domain. The three domains are briefly discussed below. Students who wish to explore these areas further may refer to the references at the end of the chapter.

The Cognitive Domain. The cognitive domain consists of behavior involving the intellectual process of the learner symbolized by knowledge, comprehension, application, analysis, synthesis and evaluation.

In physical education the cognitive domain includes learning and solving problems related to objectives, materials, methods, procedures, rules, guidelines, and other related areas which involve students of physical education. Evaluation in these areas should be made in behavioral terms.

The Affective Domain. The affective domain consists of behavior involving the attitudes, emotions and values of the learner and is reflected in the learner's interests, appreciations, and adjustments. It is symbolized by response, organization and characterization.

In physical education the affective domain refers to attitudes which may be expressed in interests, appreciations and values that may be developed toward physical education. In evaluation behavioral objectives should be written measuring such areas as leadership, self-discipline, responsibility, sportsmanship, self-concept and respect for rules of the game.

The Psychomotor Domain. The psychomotor domain places emphasis on neuromuscular skills and is symbolized by frequency, energy and duration. Physical education is built around the development of neuromuscular skills and has always been evaluated by performance in these skills. Although instructional objectives in the psychomotor domain include some cognitive and affective elements, the performance in motor skills is the basic outcome of the learner's response.

In writing performance objectives in the psychomotor domain such fundamental movements as those shown on page 101 of this chapter should be included. The individual and group activities which constitute the bulk of physical education incorporate these fundamental movements. To a large extent the popularity of a sport is determined by the number of fundamental movements included in the activity. Sports such as football, basketball, and track enjoy universal popularity because they involve many of the fundamental movements discussed earlier in the chapter. Compare the popularity of these sports with fencing, which involves no fundamental movements. Swimming, which does not involve the fundamental movements but is extremely popular, is one exception to this general rule. This is probably due to the fact that swimming is a survival activity and has become a necessity for reasons of safety. However, it is much more difficult to learn how to swim than it is to become proficient in those activities involving the fundamental movements such as running, throwing, catching, dodging, etc.

Behavioral Categories

Many books and articles have been written describing the domains and the categories which may be included in writing behavioral objectives. Teachers and students may find it difficult to formulate a working procedure to assist them in writing these objectives. The objectives should be written and graded from the most simple to the most complex. Gronlund has devised a format which arranges the categories for classification in this way. Figure 5–14 illustrates how this is done. For example, the cognitive domain starts with the knowledge category and proceeds through the increasingly more complex categories—comprehension, application, analysis, synthesis and evaluation.

Teachers need a guide to assist them in writing behavioral objectives. As they write objectives vital questions are raised. Are the objectives desirable for the particular unit? Is the list adequate? Are the objectives clearly worded? Criteria are necessary to assist teachers in answering these questions. A practical approach in determining the value of the final list of objectives is the use of a check list, such as the one shown in Figure 5–15.

The writing of behavioral objectives for the physical education program may have some advantages, particularly in the psychomotor domain. On the other hand, considerable opinion as to the disadvantages of using behavioral objectives should be weighed carefully before definite decisions are made as to the advisability of developing such objectives. Eisner discusses the disadvantages of curriculum construction and teaching based on behavioral objectives. He argues that the theory has four limitations:

1. The dynamic and complex process of instruction yields outcomes far too numerous to be specified in behavioral and content terms in advance.

2. A limitation of theory concerning educational objectives is its failure to recognize the constraints various subject matters place upon objectives. In some subject areas, such as mathematics, languages, and the sciences, it is possible to specify with great precision the particular operation or behavior the student is to perform after instruction. In other subject areas, especially the arts, such specification is frequently not possible and when possible may not be desirable.

3. The assumption that objectives can be used as standards by which to measure achievement fails, I think, to distinguish adequately between the application of a standard and the making of a judgment. Not all—perhaps not even most—outcomes of curriculum and instruction are amenable to measurement. . . . The judgment by which a critic determines the value of a poem, novel or play is not achieved merely by applying standards already known to the particular product being judged; it requires that the critic or teacher view the product with respect to the unique properties it displays and then, in relation to his experience and sensibilities, judge its value in terms which are incapable of being reduced to quantity or rule.

4. Educational objectives need not precede the selection and organization of content. The means through which imaginative curriculums can be built is as open-ended as the means through which scientific and artistic inventions occur. Curriculum theory needs to allow for a variety of processes to be employed in the construction of curriculums.[49]

The task of writing behavioral objectives could become unsurmountable if the objectives had to be stated in specific detail. If each area of instruction were to be developed around all of the possible outcomes, too much time would be spent in writing them. There are many people who feel that a few general objectives satisfactorily serve the cause of education and that minute objectives are not necessary. Ebel feels that "there is no skeleton key that gives easy access to all storehouses of knowledge."[50] He feels that to state objectives to evaluate a student's knowledge is commendable. However, he claims that:

There are others who conceive behavioral objectives as definitions of the ultimate purposes of education, which is to change the pupil's behavior in the direction of certain specified patterns of desirable behavior. It is this conception that we would challenge, for it raises some disturbing questions.[50]

Ebel raises the question of the right of imperfect individuals to attempt to implant in other individuals the responses they would make in later life. He follows this line of reasoning by referring to a totalitarian society in which the edicts of the ruler impose patterns of behavior on individual members of the society. His concept of education is to help students determine their own behavior rather than merely to mold their behavior to suit the purposes of the group.[50]

DESIRABLE OUTCOMES OF THE PROGRAM

As the program begins to function, certain outcomes should be observed. These outcomes may also be classified as evaluative criteria. At this point, the reader might review the basic aim of physical education discussed on page 93. Note the important role these desirable outcomes play in the philosophy of physical education. Although there are many desirable outcomes of health and physical education, the more outstanding ones, discussed briefly in the following paragraphs, are good health and character, sportsmanship and socialization.

Good Health

Good health is one of the aims of education and is the basic aim of physical educa-

(Text continued on page 132.)

MAJOR CATEGORIES IN THE COGNITIVE DOMAIN OF THE TAXONOMY OF EDUCATIONAL OBJECTIVES (BLOOM, 1956)

DESCRIPTIONS OF THE MAJOR CATEGORIES IN THE COGNITIVE DOMAIN

1. **Knowledge.** Knowledge is defined as the remembering of previously learned material. This may involve the recall of a wide range of material, from specific facts to complete theories, but all that is required is the bringing to mind of the appropriate information. Knowledge represents the lowest level of learning outcomes in the cognitive domain.

2. **Comprehension.** Comprehension is defined as the ability to grasp the meaning of material. This may be shown by translating material from one form to another (words to numbers), by interpreting material (explaining or summarizing), and by estimating future trends (predicting consequences or effects). These learning outcomes go one step beyond the simple remembering of material, and represent the lowest level of understanding.

3. **Application.** Application refers to the ability to use learned material in new and concrete situations. This may include the application of such things as rules, methods, concepts, principles, laws, and theories. Learning outcomes in this area require a higher level of understanding than those under comprehension.

4. **Analysis.** Analysis refers to the ability to break down material into its component parts so that its organizational structure may be understood. This may include the identification of the parts, analysis of the relationships between parts, and recognition of the organizational principles involved. Learning outcomes here represent a higher intellectual level than comprehension and application because they require an understanding of both the content and the structural form of the material.

5. **Synthesis.** Synthesis refers to the ability to put parts together to form a new whole. This may involve the production of a unique communication (theme or speech), a plan of operations (research proposal), or a set of abstract relations (scheme for classifying information). Learning outcomes in this area stress creative behaviors, with major emphasis on the formulation of new patterns or structures.

6. **Evaluation.** Evaluation is concerned with the ability to judge the value of material (statement, novel, poem, research report) for a given purpose. The judgments are to be based on definite criteria. These may be internal criteria (organization) or external criteria (relevance to the purpose) and the student may determine the criteria or be given them. Learning outcomes in this area are highest in the cognitive hierarchy because they contain elements of all of the other categories, plus conscious value judgments based on clearly defined criteria.

Figure 5–14. Tables for evaluating behavioral (performance) objectives. (From Gronlund, Norman E.: *Stating Behavioral Objectives for Classroom Instruction.* Toronto: Collier-Macmillan, Ltd., 1970.)

Figure 5–14 continued on opposite page.

EXAMPLES OF GENERAL INSTRUCTIONAL OBJECTIVES AND BEHAVIORAL TERMS FOR THE COGNITIVE DOMAIN OF THE TAXONOMY

Illustrative General Instructional Objectives	Illustrative Behavioral Terms for Stating Specific Learning Outcomes
Knows common terms Knows specific facts Knows methods and procedures Knows basic concepts Knows principles	Defines, describes, identifies, labels, lists, matches, names, outlines, reproduces, selects, states
Understands facts and principles Interprets verbal material Interprets charts and graphs Translates verbal material to mathematical formulas Estimates future consequences implied in data Justifies methods and procedures	Converts, defends, distinguishes, estimates, explains, extends, generalizes, gives examples, infers, paraphrases, predicts, rewrites, summarizes
Applies concepts and principles to new situations Applies laws and theories to practical situations Solves mathematical problems Constructs charts and graphs Demonstrates correct usage of a method or procedure	Changes, computes, demonstrates, discovers, manipulates, modifies, operates, predicts, prepares, produces, relates, shows, solves, uses
Recognizes unstated assumptions Recognizes logical fallacies in reasoning Distinguishes between facts and inferences Evaluates the relevancy of data Analyzes the organizational structure of a work (art, music, writing)	Breaks down, diagrams, differentiates, discriminates, distinguishes, identifies, illustrates, infers, outlines, points out, relates, selects, separates, subdivides.
Writes a well organized theme Gives a well organized speech Writes a creative short story (or poem, or music) Proposes a plan for an experiment Integrates learning from different areas into a plan for solving a problem Formulates a new scheme for classifying objects (or events, or ideas)	Categorizes, combines, compiles, composes, creates, devises, designs, explains, generates, modifies, organizes, plans, rearranges, reconstructs, relates, reorganizes, revises, rewrites, summarizes, tells, writes
Judges the logical consistency of written material Judges the adequacy with which conclusions are supported by data Judges the value of a work (art, music, writing) by use of internal criteria Judges the value of a work (art, music, writing) by use of external standards of excellence	Appraises, compares, concludes, contrasts, criticizes, describes, discriminates, explains, justifies, interprets, relates, summarizes, supports

Figure 5–14. *Continued.*

Figure 5–14 continued on following page.

MAJOR CATEGORIES IN THE AFFECTIVE DOMAIN OF THE TAXONOMY OF EDUCATIONAL OBJECTIVES (KRATHWOHL, 1964)

DESCRIPTIONS OF THE MAJOR CATEGORIES IN THE AFFECTIVE DOMAIN

1. Receiving. Receiving refers to the student's willingness to attend to particular phenomena or stimuli (classroom activities, textbook, music, etc.). From a teaching standpoint, it is concerned with getting, holding, and directing the student's attention. Learning outcomes in this area range from the simple awareness that a thing exists to selective attention on the part of the learner. Receiving represents the lowest level of learning outcomes in the affective domain.

2. Responding. Responding refers to active participation on the part of the student. At this level he not only attends to a particular phenomenon but also reacts to it in some way. Learning outcomes in this area may emphasize acquiescence in responding (reads assigned material), willingness to respond (voluntarily reads beyond assignment), or satisfaction in responding (reads for pleasure or enjoyment). The higher levels of this category include those instructional objectives that are commonly classified under "interests"; that is, those that stress the seeking out and enjoyment of particular activities.

3. Valuing. Valuing is concerned with the worth or value a student attaches to a particular object, phenomenon, or behavior. This ranges in degree from the more simple acceptance of a value (desires to improve group skills) to the more complex level of commitment (assumes responsibility for the effective functioning of the group). Valuing is based on the internalization of a set of specified values, but clues to these values are expressed in the student's overt behavior. Learning outcomes in this area are concerned with behavior that is consistent and stable enough to make the value clearly identifiable. Instructional objectives that are commonly classified under "attitudes" and "appreciation" would fall into this category.

4. Organization. Organization is concerned with bringing together different values, resolving conflicts between them, and beginning the building of an internally consistent value system. Thus the emphasis is on comparing, relating, and synthesizing values. Learning outcomes may be concerned with the conceptualization of a value (recognizes the responsibility of each individual for improving human relations) or with the organization of a value system (develops a vocational plan that satisfies his need for both economic security and social service). Instructional objectives relating to the development of a philosophy of life would fall into this category.

5. Characterization by a Value or Value Complex. At this level of the affective domain, the individual has a value system that has controlled his behavior for a sufficiently long time for him to have developed a characteristic "life style." Thus the behavior is pervasive, consistent, and predictable. Learning outcomes at this level cover a broad range of activities, but the major emphasis is on the fact that the behavior is typical or characteristic of the student. Instructional objectives that are concerned with the student's general patterns of adjustment (personal, social, emotional) would be appropriate here.

Figure 5–14. *Continued.*

Figure 5–14 continued on opposite page.

EXAMPLES OF GENERAL INSTRUCTIONAL OBJECTIVES AND BEHAVIORAL TERMS FOR THE AFFECTIVE DOMAIN OF THE TAXONOMY

Illustrative General Instructional Objectives	Illustrative Behavioral Terms for Stating Specific Learning Outcomes
Listens attentively Shows awareness of the importance of learning Shows sensitivity to human needs and social problems Accepts differences of race and culture Attends closely to the classroom activities	Asks, chooses, describes, follows, gives, holds, identifies, locates, names, points to, selects, sits erect, replies, uses
Completes assigned homework Obeys school rules Participates in class discussion Completes laboratory work Volunteers for special tasks Shows interest in subject Enjoys helping others	Answers, assists, complies, conforms, discusses, greets, helps, labels, performs, practices, presents, reads, recites, reports, selects, tells, writes
Demonstrates belief in the democratic process Appreciates good literature (art or music) Appreciates the role of science (or other subjects) in everyday life Shows concern for the welfare of others Demonstrates problem-solving attitude Demonstrates commitment to social improvement	Completes, describes, differentiates, explains, follows, forms, initiates, invites, joins, justifies, proposes, reads, reports, selects, shares, studies, works
Recognizes the need for balance between freedom and responsibility in a democracy Recognizes the role of systematic planning in solving problems Accepts responsibility for his own behavior Understands and accepts his own strengths and limitations Formulates a life plan in harmony with his abilities, interests, and beliefs	Adheres, alters, arranges, combines, compares, completes, defends, explains, generalizes, identifies, integrates, modifies, orders, organizes, prepares, relates, synthesizes
Displays safety consciousness Demonstrates self-reliance in working independently Practices cooperation in group activities Uses objective approach in problem solving Demonstrates industry, punctuality and self-discipline Maintains good health habits	Acts, discriminates, displays, influences, listens, modifies, performs, practices, proposes, qualifies, questions, revises, serves, solves, uses, verifies

Figure 5–14. *Continued.*

Figure 5–14 continued on following page.

EXAMPLES OF GENERAL INSTRUCTIONAL OBJECTIVES AND BEHAVIORAL TERMS FOR THE PSYCHOMOTOR DOMAIN OF THE TAXONOMY

Taxonomy Categories	Illustrative General Instructional Objectives	Illustrative Behavioral Terms for Stating Specific Learning Outcomes
(Development of categories in this domain is still underway)	Writes smoothly and legibly Draws accurate reproduction of a picture (or map, biology specimen, etc.) Sets up laboratory equipment quickly and correctly Types with speed and accuracy Operates a sewing machine skillfully Operates a power saw safely and skillfully Performs skillfully on the violin Performs a dance step correctly Demonstrates correct form in swimming Demonstrates skill in driving an automobile Repairs an electric motor quickly and effectively Creates new ways of performing (creative dance, etc.)	Assembles, builds, calibrates, changes, cleans, composes, connects, constructs, corrects, creates, designs, dismantles, drills, fastens, fixes, follows, grinds, grips, hammers, heats, hooks, identifies, locates, makes, manipulates, mends, mixes, nails, paints, sands, saws, sharpens, sets, sews, sketches, starts, stirs, uses, weighs, wraps

Figure 5–14. *Continued.*

CHECK LIST

	Yes	No

Adequacy of the List of General Objectives

1. Does each general instructional objective indicate an appropriate outcome for the instructional unit? (See recommendations of curriculum and subject experts.)
2. Does the list of general instructional objectives include all logical outcomes of the unit (knowledge, understanding, skills, attitudes, etc.)?
3. Are the general instructional objectives attainable (do they take into account the ability of the students, facilities, time available, etc.)?
4. Are the general instructional objectives in harmony with the philosophy of the school?
5. Are the general instructional objectives in harmony with sound principles of learning (e.g., are the outcomes those that are most permanent and transferrable)?

Statement of General Objectives

6. Does each general instructional objective begin with a verb (e.g., knows, understands, appreciates, etc.)?
7. Is each general instructional objective stated in terms of student performance (rather than teacher performance)?
8. Is each general instructional objective stated as a learning product (rather than in terms of the learning process)?
9. Is each general instructional objective stated in terms of the students' terminal behavior rather than the subject matter to be covered?
10. Does each general instructional objective include only one general learning outcome?
11. Is each general instructional objective stated at the proper level of generality (i.e., is it clear, concise, and readily definable)?
12. Is each general instructional objective stated so that it is relatively independent (i.e., free from overlap with other objectives)?

Behavioral Definition of General Objectives

13. Is each general instructional objective defined by a list of specific learning outcomes that describes the terminal behavior students are expected to demonstrate?
14. Does each specific learning outcome begin with a verb that specifies definite, observable behavior (e.g., identifies, describes, lists, etc.)?
15. Is the behavior in each specific learning outcome relevant to the general instructional objective it describes?
16. Is there a sufficient number of specific learning outcomes to adequately describe the behavior of students who have achieved each of the general instructional objectives?

Figure 5–15.   Check list for evaluating behavioral objectives. (From Gronlund, Norman E.: *Stating Behavioral Objectives for Classroom Instruction.* Toronto: Collier-Macmillan, Ltd., 1970.)

tion. It is largely because of physical education's tremendous contribution to health that physical education leaders continue to demand time in the curriculum. Improvement in health habits and attitudes, therefore, should be an outcome of a well-planned scientific program of physical education.

Positive Character Traits

A well-planned, carefully organized program of physical education will incorporate qualities that will assist the pupil in developing a well-integrated personality, which is a major factor in his total health. It may very well be that positive character traits will be an outgrowth of such a program. Hetherington expressed the value of physical education in developing character when he said, "The values of physical education in character training bulk large, because natural big-muscle activities are the outcroppings of the most fundamental instincts and emotions in human nature."[10]

However, the mere participation in physical education activities does not insure positive character traits. The exact opposite may take place. The very nature of partici-

pation and competition may develop negative character manifestations. It is at this point that guidance by the teacher is necessary if positive character traits are to be developed. Participants must be guided and educated along channels of socially acceptable behavior.

Sportsmanship

The practice of good sportsmanship has been an aspect of physical education for many years and the teacher should use proper methods of guidance to assist pupils in developing good sportsmanship.

Socialization

Participation in physical education activities provides one of the truly natural media for social adjustment and behavior. Through the ages, man, being a gregarious animal, has used sports, dancing, and other play activities as outlets for his social drives. The physical education program, when organized carefully and taught properly, can make an outstanding contribution to the socialization process in the school curriculum.

QUESTIONS FOR DISCUSSION

1. What is meant by unanimity of purpose?
2. Why is a basic philosophy necessary?
3. What is the difference between aim and objectives?
4. What is your aim or purpose in physical education?
5. What is meant by the health objective?
6. Discuss the fundamental movements of man.
7. What is the relationship of physical education to juvenile delinquency?
8. What is physical fitness?
9. What are the components of physical fitness?
10. What are the factors in physiological fitness?
11. What are the types of overload? Explain each.
12. Why are carry-over activities important?
13. How does physical education contribute to emotional stability?
14. Distinguish between objectives and desirable outcomes.
15. What are performance objectives?
16. What is meant by behavioral domains?
17. Which domain is more closely related to physical education? Why?
18. What are the advantages of performance objectives? Disadvantages?

SUGGESTED ACTIVITIES

1. Write your philosophy of physical education.
2. Prepare a list of activities showing how each contributes to the factors in physiological fitness.

3. Give each member of the class a simple fitness test composed of the dash, sit-up, and standing broad jump. Divide the class into two groups: Those who are "fit" and those who are "unfit." Analyze and point out the shortcomings of such a program.

4. List examples of the application of reciprocal innervation.

5. Write to the Juvenile Court in several cities and ask them to show the effects of a good physical education program on juvenile delinquency.

6. Use yourself in an experiment. Perform some type of isometric exercise for one week; then participate in a natural activity, such as swimming, tennis, or golf. Decide which gives the greater satisfaction.

7. Write performance objectives in the three domains for the skills of one team and one individual sport.

8. Use the objectives listed above to evaluate a secondary school class.

REFERENCES

1. Educational Policies Commission, *The Purposes of Education in American Democracy*, pp. 2; 50–108 (Washington, D.C.: National Education Association, 1938).
2. Commission on the Reorganization of Secondary Education, *Cardinal Principles of Secondary Education*, Bulletin No. 35, p. 9 (Washington, D.C.: Bureau of Education, Government Printing Office, 1918).
3. Educational Policies Commission, *Education for All American Youth*, pp. 225–226 (Washington, D.C.: National Education Association, 1944).
4. John E. Nixon and Anne E. Jewett, *An Introduction to Physical Education*, 7th ed. pp. 56; 90; 173 (Philadelphia: W. B. Saunders Company, 1969).
5. William Ralph LaPorte, *The Physical Education Curriculum*, 3d ed., p. 37 (Los Angeles: The University of California Press, 1942).
6. Jesse Feiring Williams, *Principles of Physical Education*, 8th ed., pp. 325; 476–481; 185; 225; 108; 186; 219; 354 (Philadelphia: W. B. Saunders Company, 1964).
7. Leslie Irwin, *The Curriculum in Health and Physical Education*, pp. 42–53 (Dubuque, Iowa: William C. Brown Company, 1969).
8. Karl W. Bookwalter, *Physical Education in Secondary Schools*, p. 3 (New York: The Center for Applied Research in Education, Inc., 1964).
9. American Association for Health, Physical Education and Recreation, *This Is Physical Education* (Washington, D.C., 1965).
10. Clark W. Hetherington, *School Program in Physical Education*, pp. 20; 27; 34 (New York: World Book Company, 1922).
11. Jackson Sharman, *Introduction to Physical Education*, pp. 66–68 (New York: A. S. Barnes & Co., 1934).
12. Charles A. Bucher, *Foundations of Physical Education*, pp. 144–150 (St. Louis: C. V. Mosby Company, 1952).
13. Charles C. Cowell, *Scientific Foundations of Physical Education*, p. 173 (New York: Harper and Brothers, 1953).
14. Jay B. Nash *et al.*, *Physical Education: Organization and Administration*, pp. 60–64 (New York: A. S. Barnes & Co., 1951).
15. Carl E. Willgoose, *The Curriculum in Physical Education*, p. 27 (Englewood Cliffs, New Jersey: Prentice-Hall, Inc., 1969).
16. Ernest Hilgard, *Introduction to Psychology*. 3d ed., p. 71 (New York: Harcourt, Brace and World, 1962).
17. Arthur B. Moehlman, *School Administration*, p. 127 (New York: Houghton Mifflin Company, 1940).
18. Allen V. Sapora and Elmer D. Mitchell, *The Theory of Play and Recreation*, 3d ed., pp. 131–140 (New York: The Ronald Press Company, 1961).
19. Marjorie Latchaw and Glen Egstrom, *Human Movement*, pp. 29–39 (Englewood Cliffs, New Jersey: Prentice-Hall, Inc., 1969).
20. Barbara B. Godfrey and Newell C. Kephart, *Movement Patterns and Motor Education*, p. 40 (New York: Appleton-Century-Crofts, 1969).
21. M. J. Ellis, "Play and Its Theories Re-examined," *Parks and Recreation*, p. 51 (National Recreation and Park Association, August, 1971).
22. American Association for Health, Physical Education and Recreation, *Youth and Fitness*, Report of the National Conference on Fitness for Secondary School Youth, p. 73 (Washington, D.C., 1958).
23. Ferdinand A. Schmidt and Carl B. Sputh, *Physiology of Exercise*, pp. 176; 174; 71; 102 (Philadelphia: F. A. Davis Company, 1931).
24. Laurence E. Morehouse and Augustus T. Miller, *Physiology of Exercise*, 6th ed., p. 21; 300 (St. Louis: C. V. Mosby Company, 1971).
25. Clifford L. Brownell and E. Patricia Hagman, *Physical Education*, pp. 210; 52 (New York: McGraw-Hill Book Company, 1951).

26. Elmer,D. Mitchell and Bernard S. Mason, *The Theory of Play*, pp. 236; 210 (New York: A. S. Barnes & Co., 1948).

27. Peter V. Karpovich and Wayne E. Sinning, *Physiology of Muscular Activity*, 7th ed., pp. 282; 270 (Philadelphia, W. B. Saunders Company, 1971).

28. American Association for Health, Physical Education and Recreation, *Operation Fitness U. S. A.—Isometric and Isotonic Exercises*, pp. 4; 3 (Washington, D.C., 1963).

29. Harrison H. Clark and David H. Clark, *Developmental and Adapted Physical Education*, p. 165 (Englewood Cliffs, New Jersey: Prentice-Hall, Inc., 1963).

30. Charles Sherrington, *The Integrative Action of the Nervous System*, p. 88 (New Haven: Yale University Press, 1961).

31. E. A. Wilbur, "A Comparative Study of Physical Fitness Indices as Measured by Two Programs of Physical Education: The Sports Method and the Apparatus Method," *Research Quarterly* (October, 1943).

32. Raymond A. Weiss, "Do Sports Produce Fitness?" p. 20, *JOHPER* (March, 1961).

33. Jay A. Bender, Harold M. Kaplan and Alex J. Johnson, "Isometrics," p. 21, *JOHPER* (May, 1963).

34. Dodi Schulz, "Family Doctors Health Guide," *Ladies' Home Journal*, p. 38 (August, 1971).

35. Harrison Clark, "Basic Understandings of Physical Stress," *Physical Fitness Research Digest* (Washington, D.C.: President's Council on Physical Fitness and Sports, July, 1971).

36. American Medical Association and American Association of Health, Physical Education and Recreation, *Exercise and Fitness*, *JOHPER*, pp. 40–41 (April, 1958).

37. Greyson Daughtrey, *Preferences of 16,000 Parents* (Norfolk, Virginia: Norfolk City Schools, 1959).

38. Karl Bookwalter and Carolyn Bookwalter, *Fitness for Secondary School Youth*, p. 52 (Washington, D.C.: American Association for Health, Physical Education and Recreation, 1956).

39. Jay B. Nash, "Leisure for What?," *JOHPER*, p. 11 (May, 1935).

40. Delbert Oberteuffer and Celeste Ulrich, *Physical Education*, 3rd ed., p. 298 (New York: Harper and Bros., 1962).

41. Emma M. Layman, *Mental Health*, p. 191 (Minneapolis: Burgess Publishing Company, 1955).

42. Edward F. Voltmer and Arthur A. Esslinger, *The Organization and Administration of Physical Education*, 4th ed., p. 105 (New York: Appleton-Century-Crofts, 1967).

43. W. D. Menninger, M. D., "Recreation and Mental Health," *Recreation*, pp. 340; 345, National Recreation Association, Inc. (November, 1948).

44. Warren Johnson and Daniel Hutton, "Effects of Wrestling Upon Personality." In Oliver Byrd, Ed., *Health Yearbook*, p. 49 (Stanford: Stanford University Press, 1955).

45. Oliver Byrd, "A Survey of Beliefs and Practices of Psychiatrists on the Relief of Tension by Moderate Exercises," *Journal of School Health*, p. 427 (November, 1963).

46. William H. Kilpatrick, *Philosophy of Education*, p. 371; 380; 381 (New York: The Macmillan Company, 1963).

47. Benjamin Bloom (ed.), *Taxonomy of Educational Objectives, Handbook 1, Cognitive Domain* (New York: David McKay Co., Inc., 1956).

48. David R. Kralhwohl (ed.), *Taxonomy of Educational Objectives, Handbook 2, Affective Domain* (New York: David McKay Co., Inc., 1964).

49. Elliot W. Eisner, "Educational Objectives Help or Hindrance?," *The School Review*, Vol. 75, No. 3, pp. 254–259 (Autumn, 1967).

50. Robert Ebel, "Comments," *The School Review*, Vol. 75, No. 3, pp. 262; 263 (Autumn, 1967).

SELECTED READINGS

Bloom, Benjamin S., et al. *Handbook on Formative and Summative Evaluation of Student Learning*. New York: McGraw-Hill Book Company, Inc., 1971.

Bookwalter, Karl W., and Harold J. Vanderzwaag. *Foundations and Principles of Physical Education*. Philadelphia: W. B. Saunders Company, 1969.

Cratty, Bryant J. *Movement Behavior and Motor Learning*, 2d ed. Philadelphia: Lea and Febiger, 1967.

Coleman, James C. *Abnormal Psychology and Modern Life*. Chicago: Scott, Foresman and Company, 1964.

Felshin, Janet. *Perspectives and Principles for Physical Education*. New York: John Wiley and Sons, 1967.

Gerhard, Muriel. *Effective Teaching Strategies with the Behavioral Outcomes Approach*. West Nyack, New York: Parker Publishing Company, Inc., 1971.

Godfrey, Barbara B., and Newell C. Kephart. *Movement Patterns and Motor Education.* New York: Appleton-Century-Crofts, 1969.

Gorlow, Leon, and Walter Katkovsky (eds.). *Readings in the Psychology of Adjustment.* New York: McGraw-Hill Book Company, Inc., 1959.

Gronlund, Norman E. *Stating Behavioral Objectives for Classroom Instruction.* Toronto: The Macmillan Company, 1970.

Lansley, Keith L., and Maxwell Howell. "Play Classification and Physical Education. *JOHPER,* September, 1970.

Layman, Emma M. *Mental Health Through Physical Education and Recreation.* Minneapolis: Burgess Publishing Company, 1955.

MacKenzie, Marlin M. *Toward a New Curriculum in Physical Education.* New York: McGraw-Hill Book Company, Inc., 1969.

Oberteuffer, Delbert, and Celeste Ulrich. *Physical Education.* New York: Harper and Brothers, 1962.

Plowman, Paul D. *Behavioral Objectives.* Chicago: Science Research Associates, 1971.

Popham, W. James. *Systematic Instruction.* Englewood Cliffs, New Jersey: Prentice-Hall Inc., 1970.

Popham, W. James. "Objectives '72," *Phi Delta Kappan,* March, 1972, p. 432.

Singer, Robert N. *The Psychomotor Domain, Movement Behavior.* Philadelphia: Lea and Febiger, 1972.

Thayer, V. T. *The Role of the School in American Society.* New York: Dodd, Mead and Company, 1961, Chaps. 5, 6, and 7.

Willgoose, Carl E. *The Curriculum in Physical Education.* Englewood Cliffs, New Jersey: Prentice-Hall, Inc., 1969.

Chapter 6

DEVELOPMENT OF CURRICULUM CONTENT

The value of bodily health and vigor no modern-minded person can deny.
William Kilpatrick

Courtesy Richmond Senior High School, Richmond, Indiana.

Developing the curriculum in physical education is a very tedious and challenging task. Social pressures, lack of facilities, overcrowded curriculums, and austere budgets are a few of the pressures that affect curriculum content. Other factors such as local philosophy pertaining to the subjects that should be included in the total curriculum, purposes of physical education, public opinion regarding physical education, divisions of the physical education program, and time allotment are factors that influence curriculum construction.

In designing the curriculum in physical education questions are raised relative to procedures involved, who should be responsible for the construction, and who should provide the leadership. These questions and others show the necessity for careful planning in developing the curriculum. Although many colleges and universities offer courses in curriculum, it is extremely difficult to separate methods from curriculum. This necessitates the inclusion in this text of the rudiments of curriculum construction.

PRINCIPLES IN CURRICULUM CONSTRUCTION

Oberteuffer and Ulrich feel "that the end of education is the improvement of society as a whole and the effective development of the individual as he seeks to enrich that society." Using this, then, as a base, they suggest nine principles of curriculum construction:

1. The curriculum should be planned to allow for progression in learning, with a minimum of repetition of activities.
2. The curriculum should be arranged so that students have consecutive time to learn.
3. There should be cooperative planning in conceiving and executing the curriculum.
4. The curriculum should consist of activities in which values are inherent, which are intrinsically interesting and with which the student can develop a compatibility.
5. The curriculum should be constructed in relation to community needs and facilities and with some consideration given to the interests which may be engendered by national backgrounds or ethnic characteristics.
6. The curriculum should provide activities which are susceptible to informal rather than formal teaching methods.
7. Curriculum materials should be selected in relation to age, sex, and physical condition of students.
8. The curriculum should make ample provision for those learnings associated with motor activity.
9. Integration as an educational process and concept has a bearing on physical education, and its premise should be examined.[1]

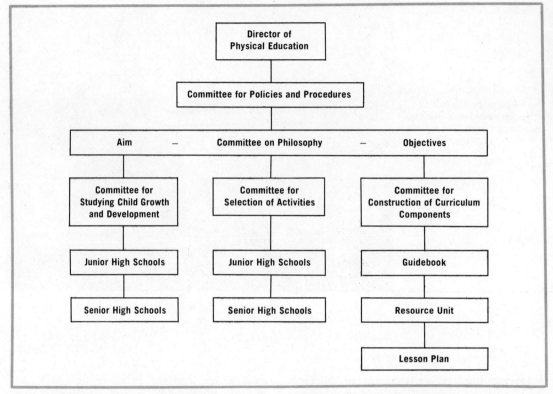

Figure 6–1. An arrangement of committees for designing a curriculum in physical education.

COMMITTEES IN CURRICULUM PLANNING

In the past experts were usually given the responsibility for curriculum construction. However, this proved unsatisfactory and in recent years, instead of one person being assigned to write the curriculum, many persons are given this responsibility. Administrators, physical education teachers and other interested persons are assigned to various committees. These committees have specific responsibilities for study of the various components in curriculum construction. Figure 6–1 suggests an arrangement of committees for designing a curriculum in physical education, a plan that will be used throughout this chapter.

POLICIES AND PROCEDURES

The committee is responsible for the overall planning of the curriculum in physical education. It studies the needs of the community, evaluates the existing program and determines present weaknesses. Other responsibilities of the committee include arranging schedules, coordinating the efforts of the other committees, procuring materials for committee work and editing the final materials compiled by other committees.

PHILOSOPHY

The importance of determining the basic philosophy of the physical education program was discussed in Chapter 5, which should be reviewed at this time.

CHILD GROWTH AND DEVELOPMENT

Effective teaching has its roots in the growth and development of children. The very foundation of education is the attempt to assist children in their mental, physical, and emotional development as they grow from early childhood to adulthood. Therefore, teacher-preparation programs should include a thorough background in child growth and development.

Teachers of physical education have a serious responsibility for guiding pupils through these years of growth; in order that the program influence children properly, the content must be geared to their growth needs. You are probably aware of programs in which adult-type activities are imposed upon young children—you may even have had a personal experience with such a program. If you have read the previous chapters in this book, you are aware by now that such practices violate all medical research and common sense and may adversely affect the health of children.

Most teacher-preparation programs include several hours in such courses as child growth and development, child and adolescent psychology, and the like. These courses provide knowledge of the growth needs of the age group appropriate to the prospective teacher's career goals. A general overview of the growth and needs of children should be carefully studied before curriculum construction begins. References at the end of this chapter will provide sources for such a review. A comprehensive list of concepts of child growth, completed by a curriculum workshop, is shown below:

1. There are ideas, feelings, and ways of acting through which all children go at certain stages of their growth, but no two children are alike in the way in which they pass through these stages.
2. Children do not grow evenly in all aspects of their development.
3. Differences in mentality, personality, and temperament are greater than physical differences.
4. Children's psychological needs are as important as their physical needs.
5. A child reacts as a total being.
6. Early training greatly influences basic behavior patterns and personality traits.
7. Children will grow no matter what care is provided for them, but they will grow best if they are loved and made to feel needed.
8. A child reflects his family life. Family life and culture can vary in different areas so that what is accepted by one may be rejected by the other.
9. If a child's growth seems to differ greatly from that of most children of his age, he should be given special consideration: if he has a high level of general maturity, leadership qualities, a wide range of creative skills and special interests, and achievement beyond grade placement, he may be classified as mentally gifted; if he is unable to profit from classroom instruction because of limited mentality, he may be classified as retarded.[2]

During the growth period there are developmental tasks that are necessary if boys and girls are to experience achievement. Havighurst lists eight developmental tasks encompassing the age span from the junior high school through the senior high school. They are as follows:

1. Achieving new and more mature relations with age-mates of both sexes
2. Achieving a masculine or feminine social role
3. Accepting one's physique and using the body effectively
4. Achieving emotional independence of parents and other adults
5. Preparing for marriage and family life
6. Preparing for an economic career
7. Acquiring a set of values and an ethical system as a guide to behavior—developing an ideology
8. Desiring and achieving socially responsible behavior[3]

Task number three has challenging implications for physical education. Many problems in behavior and achievement may be alleviated if students are shown that, although their particular developmental patterns may differ from those of the average person, they are still normal. Physical education has a responsibility to help students develop their self-image. Havighurst suggests the following guidelines:

1. Use criteria of skill and physical development in grouping students for physical education.
2. Teach about the physical changes of adolescence, stressing the normality of variability.
3. Apply criteria of physical development in grouping students at the junior high school level.
4. Use dancing to build up appreciation of the beauty of the human body.
5. Make it easy for a student to ask for information and assurance with respect to his own physical development.[3]

These concepts and developmental tasks present a capsule review of the broad field of child growth and development throughout the school years. They also emphasize the range of problems a teacher may face in guiding students assigned to him for instruction during these years. Our major concern then is with the growth and development needs in the junior and senior high school years.

As a background for developing the curriculum, a study of child growth and development is necessary. Since physical education is concerned with the health and fitness of children, learning about their mental, physical, social and emotional characteristics facilitates the task of developing relevant and effective curriculum content. Teachers should use the information presented on the following pages to assist them in the construction of the curriculum guide.

The Junior High School Pupil

The junior high school pupil has certain characteristics that affect the procedures used in teaching. An understanding of these characteristics is necessary in the construction of the curriculum. Boys and girls as they approach adolescence undergo anatomical and physiological changes that have a definite bearing on their psychological attitudes toward school and society in general. The characteristics of the junior high school pupil which are discussed in the following paragraphs illustrate the importance of understanding the growth and development of children of this age before constructing the content for the guide.

Physical Characteristics
1. Most girls complete their growth spurt at the beginning of this period. The boys' growth spurt, however, usually is not completed before the eighth or ninth grade, and it may be precipitous. Some boys add as much as six inches and 25 pounds in a single year.
2. Puberty is reached by practically all girls and by many boys so that secondary sex characteristics become increasingly apparent. These include the development of breasts and hips in girls and the deepening of voice and development of shoulders in boys. Concern about the physical and psychological changes associated with puberty is almost universal.
3. There is likely to be a certain amount of adolescent awkwardness—probably due as much to self-consciousness as to sudden growth—and a great deal of concern about appearance. Both boys and girls take pains with their grooming, and what they may lack in finesse,

they more than make up for in imagination and verve.
4. Although this age period is marked by relatively good health, the diet and sleeping habits of many junior high students are poor. In a television interview one dietitian estimated that only 10 percent of all pupils at this age have an adequate diet.
5. Physical and mental endurance is limited at this time, probably as a result of several factors: the diet and sleeping habits just mentioned; the draining of energy by the process of growth; and the disproportionately small size of the heart. Although there is no clear-cut agreement on this last point, many authorities stress that the heart does not spurt in its development as the rest of the body does.

Social Characteristics
1. The peer group becomes the source of general rules of behavior. There is frequently a conflict between the peer code and the adult code, owing partly to the drastic cultural changes which have taken place within the last 20 years.
2. Junior high school students feel a need to conform because they want to be part of the crowd; cliques are common.
3. Students are greatly concerned about what others think of them. Therefore, both friendships and quarrels become more intense, and best friends may replace parents as confidants.
4. Girls are more advanced socially than boys of the same age and therefore tend to date older boys who are at about the same point of maturation. In reaction to this, many younger boys may try to cover up their immaturity and lack of confidence by teasing and being obstreperously critical of girls.

Emotional Characteristics
1. At this age a student is likely to be moody and unpredictable—partly as a result of biological changes associated with sexual maturation and partly because of his own confusion about whether he is a child or an adult.
2. Students may behave boisterously to conceal their lack of self-confidence.
3. Anger outbursts may be common. These often result from a combination of psychological tension, bio-

logical imbalance, fatigue caused by over-exertion, lack of proper diet, and/or insufficient sleep.

4. Adolescents tend to be intolerant and opinionated, probably because of lack of self-confidence. It is reassuring for them to think that there are absolute answers—and that they know them.

5. In junior high school, students begin to look at parents and teachers more objectively and may be angry that they have been deluded into attributing omniscience to mere mortals.

Mental Characteristics

1. Students at this age can comprehend abstract concepts to an increasing degree and therefore are better able to understand moral and ethical principles.

2. Although the attention span of junior high students can be quite lengthy, there may be a tendency to daydream. Such detours into fantasy and "dreams of glory" probably take place because the students lack the real thing and also because their opportunities for excursions into fantasy are limited.[4]

AGNES WAYMAN

Agnes Wayman, one of the outstanding leaders in physical education, was a philosopher and will be remembered for her vision and tireless efforts to give physical education status in education. Her contributions in curriculum construction have greatly influenced the thinking of physical education leaders over the years.

The Senior High School Pupil

Senior high school pupils have to be considered differently from those in junior high school. Their needs are different, and problems that were of a minor nature in junior high school may be of major concern in the senior high school years. Conversely, problems that perplexed the junior high school pupil diminish or disappear as the pupil matures into senior high school age.

Physical Characteristics

1. Most students reach physical maturity, and virtually all attain puberty. While almost all girls reach their ultimate height, some boys may continue to grow even after graduation. Tremendous variation exists in height and weight and in rate of maturation.

2. The physical changes associated with puberty cause the older adolescent to have the appearance of an adult. His realization that there will be no further physical changes due to growth may add to an already extreme self-consciousness.

3. Sexual maturity is linked to glandular

changes and imbalance. According to Kinsey (1948), the male sex drive is at a peak between 16 and 17.

4. General health is quite good—again, in spite of the eating and sleeping habits of most adolescents.

Social Characteristics

1. The peer group dominates the lives of students, and the conflict between the peer and adult codes increases. Pressures to conform are extreme, the most obvious sign of this being fads in dress.

2. The most pervasive preoccupation for many students is the opposite sex. Dating, going steady, and marriage dominate their thoughts and conversation during this period.

3. Girls are still more mature socially than boys of the same age and continue to date older boys. Girls tend to have a small number of close girl friends, and boys usually have a wider circle of male friends on a more casual basis. But because of the competitive

nature of both dating and school-work, neither boys nor girls may feel that they can completely trust these friends.

Emotional Characteristics

1. The adolescent revolt is an expression of the universal changeover from childhood to adulthood. In our society we do not have any clearly prescribed forms of behavior for making this difficult change. As a result, the adolescent must take matters into his own hands.
2. Because of their increasing independence, many adolescents are in frequent conflict with their parents. They may turn to the teacher for sympathy and advice.
3. Students at this age are given to daydreaming, especially about their future. Many tend to over-estimate their abilities and their chance of entering the professions or of holding other status jobs.

Mental Characteristics

1. At this age young people have close to maximum intellectual efficiency, but lack of experience limits both their knowledge and their ability to use what they know.
2. Students' realization that they need to develop their own "philosophies of life" in regard to ethical, political, and religious matters may be threatening to them, but it offers an excellent opportunity for guided discussion.[4]

Although the preceding characteristics may provide a general overview of typical characteristics of junior and senior high school pupils, there is need for a source of more specific guides to enable teachers to relate these characteristics to the actual program in physical education. The guidebook for physical education devised by the Boys' Department of the New York City Public School System provides such a source. This outline incorporates the characteristics of pupils, their needs and the meaning for physical education.

CHARACTERISTICS OF THE EARLY ADOLESCENT
(Ages 12–14 – Grades 7–8–9)

1. *Characteristics:* Rapid, uneven growth
   Needs: Knowledge of physical changes taking place

Understanding that the changes are normal
Avoidance of extreme fatigue
Meaning for Physical Education:
Regular daily period of physical education
Explanation of growth processes and their effect upon the individual

2. *Characteristics:* Increase in heart size
   Needs: Avoidance of undue fatigue
   Understanding of physiological changes
   Physical activity to give tone to heart muscle
   Adequate rest and sleep
   Meaning for Physical Education:
   Frequent health examination
   Develop ability to pace himself in competitive sports and games
   Extended running, jumping, and developmental exercises

3. *Characteristics:* Awkwardness, lack of balance, poor coordination
   Needs: Understanding of changes
   Practice in skills leading to better coordination
   Meaning for Physical Education:
   Daily practice of skills
   Exercises and activities such as gymnastics, tumbling, dancing

4. *Characteristics:* Less energy, tires easily, unable to sustain strenuous activity
   Needs: Balance of work and rest
   Graded activity gradually pushed to capacity
   Understanding of the body processes causing fatigue
   Meaning for Physical Education:
   Balanced program of activity
   Graded and progressive activity
   Gradation in skill development and achievement

5. *Characteristics:* Restless, moody, displays apparent laziness, overcritical of adults, changeable, uncooperative, rebellious, aggressive
   Needs: Warm affection and understanding by adults
   Sense of humor
   Sympathetic understanding
   Security and understanding at home
   Meaning for Physical Education:
   Give assurance, encouragement, and praise for accomplishment and effort
   Opportunity to reach achievable goals in the program

6. *Characteristics:* Desire to excel in physical skills and athletics
   Needs: To learn how to play games well

Experience success

Develop some special game and sports skill

Meaning for Physical Education:

Provide a wide variety of games, sports, skills

Sufficient practice time for improved skill performance

Opportunity to utilize skills in the "laboratory" aspect of the program

7. *Characteristics:* Desire to try many new experiences, excitement, and adventure

Needs: Opportunities for independent thought and action

Opportunity to belong to a group

Opportunity to participate in organized play as a member of the group

Opportunity for competition

Meaning for Physical Education:

Introduce new gymnastics, stunts, games

Provide broad intramural program

Wide variety of activities with opportunity to experience some success

Motivation for skills and team play

8. *Characteristics:* Developing interest in girls

Sexual tensions increase

Needs: Sustained physical activity

Opportunity to participate in coeducational activity

Meaning for Physical Education:

Offer a variety of coeducational activities, such as bowling, tennis, volleyball, dancing

9. *Characteristics:* Changes in appetite and habits of nutrition

Needs: An understanding of reasons for physiological changes

Meaning for Physical Education:

Incidental teaching of nutrition

Development and motivation of sound practices in nutrition for improved skill performance

10. *Characteristics:* Enjoys practice for improvement

Needs: Opportunities provided for sustained skill practice

Meaning for Physical Education:

Opportunities for squad practice, lead-up games and drills, review of skills in game situations

11. *Characteristics:* Hero worship prevalent

Desire for group status is strong

Needs: Utilization of athletic heroes and identification with athletic stars

Meaning for Physical Education:

Motivating device for improved skill performance

Provision for group status as member of a team

Recognize skill improvement

Acceptance dependent upon skill development and ability

12. *Characteristics:* Permanent friendships begin to develop

Needs: Identification as member of a peer group because of common interests

Meaning for Physical Education:

Provision for organization of the class by squads and teams with recognition for successful team effort

Opportunity to play in organized games and tournaments

CHARACTERISTICS OF THE LATER ADOLESCENT
(Ages 15–18 — Grades 10–11–12)

1. *Characteristics:* Rapid weight gain

Bone growth almost complete

Needs: Knowledge of changes taking place in the body

More adult activity

Meaning for Physical Education:

Regular daily period of physical education

Explanation of growth processes and their effects on the individual

Expanded opportunities for self-direction and selection of activities

2. *Characteristics:* Increase in strength

Improved motor coordination

Desire to develop strong bodies

Needs: Development of more advanced skills

Greater emphasis upon body building activity

More sustained activity

Meaning for Physical Education:

Greater stress on conditioning and fitness activities

More advanced skills with finer coordinations taught

More contact sports offered

3. *Characteristics:* Tendency towards less fatigue

Needs: Adequate program of sleep and rest

Meaning for Physical Education:

Provision for a balanced program of activity and rest

4. *Characteristics:* Desire to make a good appearance

High interest in physical attractiveness

Needs: Feelings of social status and competence

Meaning for Physical Education:
Greater stress on developing healthy bodies
Incidental teaching in good grooming
Stress poise and graceful movement

5. *Characteristics:* Desire to accept more adult responsibility

Needs: Greater independence of thought and action

Meaning for Physical Education:
Provide greater opportunity for student leadership and for playing the game as a culmination of learning experiences

6. *Characteristics:* Interest in coeducational activities
Development of adult sex characteristics

Needs: Develop skills in social coeducational activities such as bowling, dancing
To join others in the group in co-recreational activities

Meaning for Physical Education:
Expand and provide opportunities for corecreational program

7. *Characteristics:* Strong identification with admired adult

Needs: To join adults in their activities and act like adults

Meaning for Physical Education:
Teach carry-over leisure sports, such as tennis, golf, bowling

8. *Characteristics:* Desire for excitement and adventure

Needs: Opportunity for competitive activity
Opportunity to try activities involving skill and daring

Meaning for Physical Education:
Provide a wide variety of competitive activities
Emphasize gymnastics, tumbling, wrestling

9. *Characteristics:* Greatly influenced by group opinion

Needs: To gain status as part of the group

Meaning for Physical Education:
Provide status developing activities
Full development of skill and athletic ability
Testing program to determine skill development status [5]

SELECTION OF ACTIVITIES

If there is one phase of teaching physical education that stands out as the most important and to which the least attention is given, it is the selection of activities for the program. Program after program throughout the country consists of activities that can be shown to have no place in the curriculum when analyzed scientifically.

Activities that are not suited for the growth and development patterns of boys and girls, those that are unsafe, and all those that do not meet the objectives of physical education should be excluded from the curriculum. Activities are frequently included in the program simply because a teacher or coach likes them. Allowing the teacher freedom of choice in the selection of activities can be a serious mistake. Often the individual is not qualified to make a choice; and when the choice is made, it is based on the empirical approach and not on scientific analysis.

Several methods have been used to determine content for the physical education curriculum. Some of these methods have influenced the curriculum, while others have had relatively little effect. Probably the most commonly used methods are (1) the survey of participants method, (2) the committee construction method, and (3) the arbitrary selection by teachers. These methods will be discussed in the following paragraphs.

Survey of Participants

Surveys reflecting the opinions of participants are of great value in curriculum construction because the participants are the ones for whom the programs are designed. They know which activities best suit their own abilities and interests.

The Norfolk City Survey. In the spring of 1958, the Department of Health and Physical Education of the Norfolk Public Schools made a survey of 16,000 parents to find just what, in their opinion, were desirable activities for the high school program. The results of the survey showed that although many parents had participated in team sports in school, they wished that they had received instruction in individual sports that they could presently enjoy. The individual sports they selected were golf, swimming, bowling, tennis, and dancing (see Chapter 5).

The significance of this survey is strengthened by the following factors:

1. A very large sample of parents was involved.
2. The opinions came from thousands of people who were able to make comparisons between what they had in high school and what they wished they had been taught.
3. The opinions were not made by teachers who, because they like an activity and participate in it, might want to superimpose it on their pupils.
4. The city in which the survey was taken is classified as largely transient because of the many military installations; the respondents, therefore, reflect to a great degree a national opinion.[6]

The College Survey. Fox showed the preferences of college graduates for various activities after graduation. Questionnaires were sent to graduates of 18 colleges, who were asked several questions pertaining to the activities in which they were participating, the recreational facilities available, the activities in which they did not participate, and finally, the activities in which they wished they could have had instruction. The following activities were listed as the ones they wished they could have learned in college: swimming, golf, tennis, bowling, and social dancing. This study also is important because it again shows the preferences of participants rather than those of teachers.[7]

The Recreation Survey. Sharman reports a study of leisure-time activities of 5000 people made by the National Recreation Association. The study showed that there is a great difference between the activities in which people *actually* participate and those in which they *really* want to engage. The activities in which people participated, in order of frequency, were: listening to radio, reading magazines and newspapers, attending movies, visiting and entertaining, reading fiction, auto-riding for pleasure, reading nonfiction, writing letters, swimming, and conversation. The 10 activities in which they desired to engage were, in order of frequency: swimming, tennis, boating, auto-riding, caring for flower garden, playing golf, camping, playing a musical instrument, attending a theatre, and listening to the radio. It is interesting that the desire for participation in carry-over physical education activities was high.[8]

University of South Dakota Survey. Dr. John Van Why, formerly Chairman of the Health and Physical Education Department of the University of South Dakota, made a study of physical education students at the university to determine what factors are conducive to voluntary participation in active play. A report of the study states that the data seem to justify the following conclusions:

1. The most popular physical education activities in order of popularity are golf, softball, swimming, and tennis.
2. One of the chief reasons that individuals do not participate in play activities after leaving school is *lack of skill*.
3. Most of the individuals who still participate on a voluntary basis in golf, softball, swimming, and tennis possess average or above-average ability in these activities. (Hence, it appears that skill is conducive to voluntary play.)
4. There is more interest in individual physical education activities, such as golf, swimming, tennis, and bowling, than in group activities, such as softball, basketball, and volleyball.
5. The type of physical education programs in high school and college is a determining factor in voluntary participation in later life. This is especially true with references to individual activities.
6. The data show that many individuals would have chosen to participate in activities having a high degree of carry-over value, such as golf and bowling, but they had no opportunity to do so.
7. There is a relationship between those individuals who participated in the intramural athletic program and those who participated on a voluntary basis after leaving school. (This would appear to give added importance to intramural athletic programs.)
8. The reasons for voluntary participation in sports after the student leaves school were listed (in order of importance) as follows: the fun and enjoyment, the socialization, the desire for competition, and the physical benefits derived.[9]

Committee Construction Method

From time to time, groups of individuals acting as a committee have attempted to select activities for physical education. These efforts have had very little constructive effect on the program, perhaps because of a failure to use the scientific approach, which would rule out personal likes and dislikes in the selection of content.

The LaPorte Study. Probably the most extensive attempt to select activities in physical education was made by a committee chaired by William Ralph LaPorte. The committee, composed of many outstanding leaders in physical education, took nine years to complete its work. The study was a tremendous effort on the part of these leaders to formulate a program in physical education.[10]

Although the resulting report was a step forward in curriculum construction, recent evidence shows the desirability of eliminating several activities included in the report. For instance, the report recommended boxing. By all current criteria, boxing should be excluded from the physical education program because its ultimate objective is to score a knockout. The knockout is caused by a concussion of the brain, which permanently damages brain tissue. Any activity that has as its aim the damage of the human brain is educationally unsound and should be excluded. Activities which involve hanging by the arms are not suitable for most girls as they approach puberty. This is true because of the weakness of the arms and the large amount of weight around the center of gravity. These contraindicated activities include movements on the parallel bars, long horse, flying rings, horizontal ladder and weight lifting.[11]

When activities are selected scientifically, the personal likes and dislikes of individuals are minimized. Because the health of boys and girls is at stake in deciding those activities to be included in the curriculum, the most scrupulous care in selection is essential.

Arbitrary Selection by Teachers

Usually the activities which constitute the curriculum in physical education are determined by the individual teacher. Observation of programs throughout the country reveals that balanced programs are rare. When the individual teacher selects the activities for instruction, the resulting program usually consists of activities which he likes and which he feels sufficiently knowledgeable to teach. Situations such as this are to be condemned since the health and fitness of boys and girls should be the determining factors in curriculum construction rather than the personal likes and dislikes of teachers. Voltmer and Esslinger substantiate this opinion:

The physical educator usually builds his own program. The activities that he teaches will depend upon his training and philosophy. Whether the program is good or bad, it is usually accepted. School administrators are usually alert to deficiencies in other aspects of the curriculum but have a lack of critical judgment in regard to physical education, which has led to the acceptance of very inadequate service programs. This opportunity for physical educators to construct their own programs has often been exploited. If it is desired to build up the varsity athletic teams, the entire program may be shaped toward this end with no consideration for educational outcomes. This has been a common practice.[12]

The need for a program consisting of a variety of activities is extremely important. The needs and interests of children should be considered when designing curriculum content. Children vary anatomically, psychologically and physiologically and no one activity is best for all pupils.

A committee of the American Medical Association strongly supports a varied program of activities in the physical education program. It offers the following recommendations:

1. A varied physical education program is the key to encouraging lifelong interest in vigorous activities.

2. Adequate programs of physical education are based on the variety of interests, activity needs, abilities, levels of coordination, speed, physical size, and strength of boys and girls.

3. The development of emotional maturity can be aided by comprehensive physical education programs. Sports activities can help fill a child's apparent need for adventure, train him to meet and accept challenge, provide a basis for comparison with his peers, teach him to accept limitations, and increase his self-esteem.

4. Intramural programs, a logical competitive extension of physical education classes, provide continuing satisfying activity and usually lead to increased skill and fitness.[13]

The Scientific Approach in Selecting Activities

Although contributions made by some committees are limited, surveys are helpful in the selection of activities for the curriculum content. However, the chief fault of the survey method is that in the past the surveys were made up of the opinions of individuals other than the participants. The Norfolk, College, and South Dakota surveys are significant because the investigators went directly to the participants. College professors, teachers, and supervisors should initiate more of these participant-oriented surveys in order to improve the content in physical education.

It is the purpose of this chapter to show how activities *may be selected scientifically. It should not be construed that the plan shown is the only way to select activities. Nevertheless, the information should help the teacher realize the importance of the scientific approach in the selection of activities and emphasize his need to be able to justify everything included in the curriculum.*

Criteria Through the Years. In the selection of activities it is important that definite criteria be selected and used to evaluate each activity considered for inclusion in the curriculum. These criteria, to be fundamentally sound, must be based on the educational needs of boys and girls.

Criteria are different from objectives. Objectives are the *guides* that assist in the step-by-step approach to the ultimate goal. Criteria are the *standards* used to select the material that is needed in carrying out the objectives.

1930–1940. An early group of criteria was devised in 1934 by the American Physical Education Association which provided the standards for selecting activities for the curriculum during the 1930's. The importance of these criteria was enhanced because they were compiled by a committee rather than by an individual. The criteria are as follows:

1. Select activities of a wide variety that are interesting.
2. Select only those not likely to cause physical or social injury.
3. Select big muscle activities which pupils will be apt to use in later life.
4. Select those activities that have interest in them, elements that make them educationally valuable.
5. Select activities which stimulate the vital organs.
6. Select activities that can be used in an extensive intramural program including such minor activities as dancing, sports clubs, and hiking.[14]

1940–1950. In the early 1940's the results of one of the greatest efforts to select activities for the physical education curriculum were published. A committee consisting of national leaders working for nine years evaluated 20 activities and ranked them according to an evaluation made by outstanding experts throughout the country. The following criteria were used in the study and served as the bases for making evaluations of the activities by showing:

1. The contribution to the *physical* and *organic* growth and development of the child and the improvement of body function and body stability.
2. The contribution to the *social traits* and qualities that go to make up the good citizen and the development of sound moral ideals through intensive participation under proper leadership.
3. The contribution to the *psychological* development of the child including satisfaction resulting from stimulating experiences both physically and socially.
4. The contribution to the development of *safety skills* that increase the individual's capacity for protection in emergencies, both in handling himself and in assisting others.
5. The contribution to the development of *recreational skills* that have a distinct function as hobbies for leisure-time hours, both during school years and afterwards.[10]

1950–1960. Other authors have selected criteria for the evaluation and selection of activities. Brownell and Hagman used 11 criteria based on the thinking of leaders during the 1950's:

1. Does the activity contribute directly to the achievement of program objectives?
2. Does the activity have greater relative value than any other possible choice?
3. Does the activity have meaning for the current social life of the learner?
4. Does the activity have carry-over value for the out-of-school and adult life of the learner?
5. Is the activity of interest to the learner?
6. Is the activity within the range of ability of the learner?
7. Does the activity grow out of previous experience and will it lead to further developmental experiences?
8. Has the activity been adequately presented in a previous grade or within a previous experience of the learner?
9. Can the activity be learned better through an available non-school agency?
10. Does the activity contribute to a correla-

tive function with other experiences in the curriculum?

11. Is the activity reasonably safe or does it lend itself to reasonable safety precautions?[15]

Hughes and French list four criteria, which they use to evaluate a number of activities, and suggest which could be used. Their criteria are (1) physical and organic, (2) social and moral, (3) psychological, and (4) safety.[16]

Cowell and Hazelton outline eight criteria with several subheadings. Evaluation for each element is made by checking one of three columns headed "A great deal," "Somewhat," and "Only slightly." These criteria are shown in Figure 6–2.

1960–1970. During the 1960's, leaders began to develop criteria that would reflect the times and serve as indicators for the '70's. Bookwalter and Vanderswaag proposed 11 criteria that provide teachers and others who are designing curriculums a comprehensive set of principles for selecting curriculum content. These criteria are reproduced in their entirety:

Validity. The activities selected must contribute to one or more of the objectives of physical education.

Totality. The total of the activities selected for each sex and any grade level must have the potential for making an optimum contribution to all valid objectives for each sex and for that grade level.

Relativity. Activities must be selected according to their relative contribution to the totality of the purposes for physical education and for the needs of the learner.

Acceptability. Activities must be meaningful and purposeful to the learner and thus acceptable to him even if they are not of greatest interest.

Continuity. Activities must lead on to continued use of more of the same and to related activities.

Desirability. Activities must be of interest to the child. Contribution to other desires enhances potential or latent interest.

Utility. Activities must have carry-over value today and in the future, out of school, and in after-school years.

Capacity. Activities must be within the ability of the learner according to his age, sex, and physical capacity.

Intensity. Activities should be treated sufficiently intensively to assure that the learner acquires the proper degree (beginning, intermediate, or advanced) of competence set for the grade or course level.

Social Adaptability. Activities must offer leadership-followership opportunities in a social situation such as will promote social adaptability in life activities.

Feasibility. Activities must be feasible in a particular school in terms of time allotment, facilities, teacher competence, and geographical or community differences.[17]

Jesse Feiring Williams, for many years an outstanding leader in physical education, proposed several criteria which not only affected the selection of content for the 1960's but served as standards for earlier years. They are (1) relative worth, (2) interest, (3) functional utility, (4) maturity, (5) experience, (6) safety, and (7) achievement.[11]

1970–1980. The criteria shown above were devised by leaders in physical education. It seems appropriate to reflect the opinion of leaders in general education in the activities that should be included in the physical education curriculum. The following criteria, formulated by Frost and Rowland, were developed to serve as standards for selecting content in the seventies:

1. Provision must be made for individual differences in physical ability.

2. Care must be taken to ensure the safety of partially disabled children and of smaller children playing with larger ones.

3. Provision for gradual progressions must be made.

4. Natural play activities must supplement more structured activities.

5. The program should provide experiences in planning one's own activities.

6. Activities should have some relation to the child's out-of-school life, providing bases for his continued activity after he has left school.

7. The program should provide for great variety in the use of the different muscle groups.

8. Separation of the sexes for certain activities should become desirable in the upper elementary grades.[18]

Criteria for the Future. The criteria listed on the preceding pages reflect the thinking of physical education leaders over the past 50 years. The purpose of preparing such a large list is twofold: (1) to show the importance of criteria in the selection of activities, and (2) to assist in the development of a group of criteria that will stand the test of the future. This double purpose is accomplished by using the criteria that are most prevalent through the years. By this procedure, the following criteria have

	A great deal	Somewhat	Only slightly
1. Does the activity have a direct relationship to the overall objectives of the school?			
a. The development of physical health			
b. The inculcation of social attitudes (courtesy, etc.)			
c. The development of social sensitivity (respect for humanity, social justice, devotion to democracy)			
d. The development of better personal-social adjustment (friendships, acceptance, status)			
e. The development of effective methods of thinking			
f. The cultivation of work habits and study skills			
g. The acquisition of important information			
h. The acquisition of a wide range of significant interests			
i. The development of an increased appreciation of music, art, literature, and other aesthetic experiences			
2. Does the activity satisfy the immediate interests of pupils?			
3. Does the activity capitalize on previously acquired knowledge, skill, and interests of pupils, and simplify and promote learning in further learning situations?			
4. Does the activity abound in possibilities for concomitant learnings?			
a. Ideals			
b. Attitudes			
c. Tastes			
d. Appreciations			
5. Does the activity provide for the variations which exist among human beings?			
a. Age			
b. Sex			
c. Skill			
6. Does the activity satisfy the various important needs of youth? what opportunity does the activity offer for:			
a. Recognition, approval, appreciation, status			
b. New experience, excitement, adventure			
c. Affection, being wanted, a sense of belonging			
d. Power, a sense of achievement, mastery, accomplishment			
e. A sense of protection and security, a release from anxiety and tension			
7. Does the activity have "carryover" value? Do children tend to engage in the activity in their "out-of-school" hours?			
8. Does the activity make unreasonable administrative demands in terms of:			
a. Space			
b. Equipment			
c. Time allotment			
d. Leadership			

Figure 6–2. Tentative form for evaluating curriculum experiences in physical education. (From Cowell, Charles C., and Hazelton, Helen W.: *Curriculum Designs in Physical Education.* Englewood Cliffs, New Jersey: Prentice-Hall, Inc., 1955, p. 83.)

been selected as a guide in the selection of activities for programs of the future.

MAJOR CRITERIA. Several criteria are so important that they may be classified as major criteria. These should be given more weight than others in selecting activities, those that do not measure up being excluded from the curriculum. These major criteria are:

1. Does the activity meet the basic objectives? No activity should be included in the curriculum if it does not contribute to the attainment of the basic objectives and purposes of physical education. (See Chapter 4 for basic objectives.)

2. Is the activity reasonably safe? Another area that should receive major consideration is safety. It is the responsibility of the teacher to assure parents and children that the environment for the physical education program is safe and that activities that have been found to be dangerous have been ex-

cluded. Teachers are responsible by law for the safety of their pupils and may be liable if negligence can be shown in the conduct of the program. Many accidents that occur in the physical education class could have been prevented if the proper safety precautions had been taken.

Teachers should seriously consider their legal responsibilities for the safety and welfare of their pupils. A further discussion of teacher negligence will be found in Chapter 10.

3. Are the activities teachable? An inventory of the various movements of which the human body is capable would show thousands of possibilities. Natural play activities alone involve hundreds of kinds of movements. When all the movements using machines, gadgets, and "frill" activities are added, the selection of activities becomes increasingly complicated. *Teachers should be exceedingly careful in*

Figure 6–3. It is the teacher's responsibility to supervise activities and to use correct teaching procedures. (Courtesy Los Angeles City Schools.)

promoting activities that may be included in the curriculum. Activities that do not involve instruction should be carefully scrutinized before being used. Not only is this important because of the growth and development needs of children, but for teacher security as well. Calisthenics is an example. A school might employ two teachers to teach the skills of wrestling and basketball to groups of 50 pupils each, but the teachers might instead use their time to emphasize calisthenics. Now, any average person (a *teacher* is not needed) with the use of a public address system could give commands for calisthenics to the entire student body at one time for one period as effectively as he could do so to a class of 50 for five periods daily. This procedure would release five periods that had been devoted to physical education to other subjects and alleviate a crowded school day. In addition, the calisthenics could be done without employing a professional teacher, or at most only one. There is evidence to show that calisthenics-dominated programs are not uncommon.[19]

This criticism applies to many activities such as the type of circuit training in which a pupil runs a distance, chins the bar, climbs a piece of apparatus, and jumps a ditch. A professional teacher is not needed for activities of this nature. Nor do the so-called "fitness tests" require a qualified teacher. This is proved by the fact that in many programs the tests are given by students. Very little instruction is involved in the standing broad jump and the pull-up, which are usually included in these tests.

Many activities, such as hiking and camping, have doubtful value in the teaching program. Physical education programs throughout the country have suffered because teachers have attempted to include new fads without subjecting the activities to scientific criteria.

LOCAL CRITERIA. After having been subjected to the *major* criteria, each activity must be evaluated by *local* criteria. Many activities may be considered acceptable until they are evaluated by local criteria, which may necessitate excluding some from the program.

1. *Is the activity too expensive?* The cost of any activity must, of course, be considered. If several activities measure up to all criteria but one is less costly, then this should be the grounds for selecting it in preference to the others. Lack of facilities may be the determining local factor for including or excluding an activity. An illustration is the teaching of swimming. Swimming meets all criteria, but in some localities it might have to be eliminated because of the cost or the lack of the proper facilities.

2. *Is the activity generally interesting?* Other things being equal, the interest of pupils should be considered. However, interest fluctuates with age and experience. Proper instruction can also change interest. An activity that is not accepted today may be interesting next week, depending on how well it has been presented and what degree of success pupils have had in it.

Pupil interest is important for motivation in physical education. Thousands of dollars are spent annually on equipment and items that are uninteresting to pupils and therefore are not used. Recently, a recess recreational program was observed. On the playground were six items of traditional equipment: swings, jungle gym, slide, ladder, merry-go-round, and chinning bar. The cost of the equipment was about $2000. Not one pupil was using the apparatus. The entire group was participating in a kickball game involving the fundamental movements— running, throwing, kicking, and catching. If instruction is provided, pupils will invariably resort to activities involving the greatest number of natural movements when they are left alone.

Teachers too often impose on pupils what they think the pupils should have. The teachers themselves do not participate in these activities, yet they expect the pupils to do so. Physical education must be interesting to pupils or the exercise program ends with the immediate class period.

3. *Does the community accept the activity?* The schools belong to the people. An activity may be safe and meet all basic objectives, but still not be acceptable

to the community. An illustration is dancing. Various dance forms conform to all objectives; yet in an intensely religious community dancing may not be acceptable. There are other activities, which the community will accept, that make the same contribution. These acceptable activities should be included in the program and an effort made to educate the community to accept dancing at a later time.

4. *Is the activity too time-consuming?* There are many activities which would meet all the criteria, but because of large classes are too time-consuming. An illustration is the apparatus program that is included in some schools. The parallel bars, for instance, are seldom purchased in multiple sets; a school would be fortunate to have one set. It would take an instructor many weeks, therefore, to teach the skills involved on the parallel bars to a class of 40 to 50 pupils. In order for the program to be effective, all pupils should reach some degree of proficiency on the bars. This would involve a tremendous amount of time, making the value of this activity doubtful. On the other hand, the same large group could be taught the skills of wrestling much more quickly and effectively, with far less expenditure of money and with greater realization of basic objectives.

Criterion of Relative Value. Sometimes two or three activities meet all the established criteria. However, because the time element allows the inclusion of only one, a decision must be made as to which has the greatest relative value. An illustration would be touch football, speedball, and soccer. All three of these activities meet the accepted criteria. However, touch football might be selected since it is an American activity or since it would be more acceptable in a given locality; it also provides greater motivation for after-school participation because of the national interest developed through television.

Procedures for Selecting Activities for the Program

Several steps should be followed in the selection of activities for the curriculum, not only to achieve a more scientific ap-

proach to the formation of curriculum content but also to initiate a more cooperative effort by teachers in planning and teaching after the activities have been selected.

Formation of a Committee. A committee should consist of teachers of physical education and administrators who have vision and are sincere, dedicated, unselfish, unbiased, and experienced. The committee should be assigned to perform the following steps:

1. *List activities for study.* Each member should list the activities he feels should be studied, from which the curriculum content would be selected.
2. *Eliminate certain activities.* All activities that are extremely hazardous should be ruled out immediately.
3. *Formulate criteria.* Evaluative criteria should be set up to measure each activity.
4. *Assign weight values.* The committee should assign to each criterion a weight value in points. It is obvious that certain criteria should have greater weight than others.
5. *Evaluate activities by major criteria.* The activities that have not been eliminated because of the safety factor should be evaluated by the major criteria that have been selected (page 153). Forms should be made up, listing the criteria and activities to be evaluated.
6. *Arrange activity by rank.* From the total points given activities by the various members of the committee, the activities should be arranged by rank. These activities may be recommended for use anywhere.
7. *Evaluate activities by local criteria.* Each member of the committee, or each teacher in the system, or teachers in other systems may subject the group of activities to local criteria for the selection of activities for the individual school or schools.
8. *Evaluate activities by relative value.* Several activities may meet all criteria, but not all can be included. The activities should be subjected to the criterion of relative value and a decision made as to the one to be retained.

A Suggested Curriculum. While teaching in the graduate school of South Dakota University, the author experimented in scientific curriculum construction by having classes of graduate students spend several weeks exploring this approach, using a plan similar to the one just outlined. The results of the study are shown in Figure 6–4 and are further explained below.

1. **List activities to be studied.** Each member of the class submitted a group of activities he wished to study and evaluate. In many instances, these activities constituted the curriculum used in the school where the student taught. The activities were tennis, swimming, basketball, volleyball, touch football, rhythmics, golf, tumbling, table tennis, bowling, calisthenics, wrestling, fitness tests, skiing, boxing, trampoline, riflery, rope walking, softball, horseshoes, soccer, hockey, badminton, archery, weight lifting, apparatus, body mechanics, hiking, camping, judo, dashes, hurdles, distance run, weights (track), jumps, and handball.

2. **Eliminate certain activities.** For various reasons, which are shown below, a number of activities were eliminated immediately:

    a. *Unsafe activities.* Several studies show that certain activities are extremely dangerous and may adversely affect the health and fitness of boys and girls. This ruled out boxing, judo, trampoline, and certain types of gymnastics and apparatus, as well as various activities not suitable for girls.

    b. *Non-physical education activities.* Some activities, such as camping, hiking, and skiing, were not considered to be physical education teaching activities and were dropped at the beginning. The premise established in class was that *teaching* should be the basis of all physical education and that non-teachable activities should not be included in the curriculum.

    c. *Conditioning exercises.* The class agreed that conditioning exercises should be a part of each lesson in physical education for the purposes of "warming-up" for greater efforts later. This group of movements should be studied scientific-

ally, and the class voted to consider them separately. (Some leaders feel that many so-called conditioning movements in this group should be excluded. These exercises will be further discussed later in this chapter.)

    d. *Remaining activities.* The following activities, remaining after all that had originally been submitted were subjected to evaluation in Step 2, were used for evaluation:

Tennis	Swimming
Bowling	Golf
Badminton	Handball
Basketball	Touch football
Rhythmics	Volleyball
Softball	Body Mechanics
Table tennis	Distance Runs
Wrestling	Tumbling
Horseshoes	Jumps
Dashes	Archery
Soccer	Fitness tests
Hockey	Apparatus (limited)
Hurdles	Weights (track)

3. **Develop weight for major and local activities.** It is essential that weight be established for major and local criteria.

    a. *Major criteria.* The major criteria for this study were divided into two sections: *objectives* and *safety*. Safety was thought to be important enough to be used as a major criterion, even though it was used at the beginning of the project to exclude all extremely dangerous activities.

Objectives (See Chapter 5)	Weight in Point Range
a. Desirable outlet for the play urge	1–75
b. Leisure-time development	1–75
c. Development of emotional stability	1–75
d. Development of physical fitness	75–total
(1) Skill	1–30
(2) Endurance	1–20
(3) Strength	1–15
(4) Speed	1–10
Safety	1–100

    b. *Local criteria.* The activities that may qualify under the major criteria form a group of activities that could be used in most situations.

Totals	Time consuming	Community acceptance	Cost Expensive / Inexpensive	Interest Low / High	Local Criteria	Safety	Speed 1-10	Strength 1-15	Endurance 1-20	Physical fitness Skill 1-30	Development of emotional stability	Leisure time development	Desirable outlet for the play urge	Major Criteria — To what degree does the activity contribute to:
(1-30)	1-30	1-30		1-30		1-100		1-75			1-75	1-75	1-75	Weight Value
3423						955	79	71	135	165	600	698	720	Tennis
3302						920	77	60	120	250	545	680	650	Badminton
3286						928	44	80	93	203	510	778	650	Bowling
3265						860	82	68	160	250	701	479	665	Basketball
3252						780	64	77	191	208	592	685	655	Swimming
3239						870	39	69	102	276	600	663	620	Golf
3234						885	81	78	195	245	633	490	627	Handball
3146						630	94	100	150	242	670	560	700	Touch Football
3122						920	42	59	114	164	555	610	658	Volleyball
3067						810	62	56	110	204	555	620	650	Softball
3052						920	39	96	94	175	520	500	708	Rhythmics
2925						935	19	44	44	288	520	645	430	Horseshoes
2881						627	80	97	135	266	645	330	701	Soccer
2870						961	40	31	54	198	463	663	460	Table Tennis
2867						800	78	138	177	244	620	130	680	Wrestling
2702						885	99	98	124	96	505	285	610	Dashes
2697						680	71	93	170	206	578	276	623	Hockey
2625						795	99	96	138	192	480	165	660	Hurdles
2472						946	19	41	90	140	338	375	523	Body Mechanics
2467						840	69	107	170	101	465	115	600	Distance Run
2440						595	48	98	114	255	515	225	590	Tumbling
2421						840	67	96	88	200	395	125	610	Jumps
2335						775	22	58	52	239	379	620	190	Archery
2283						880	66	92	121	116	225	138	645	Fitness Tests
2228						820	46	115	100	174	395	110	468	Weights (Track)
2204						665	43	113	142	229	415	96	501	Apparatus

Figure 6–4. Selection of activities for the secondary school.

How to Evaluate

1. **Major Criteria.** If the activity contributes little to each objective, give it a low score. If it makes a great contribution, give a high score.
2. **Local Criteria**
   Interest. If interest is low, give a low score; if high, give a high score.
   Cost. If the activity is expensive, give a low score; if inexpensive, score high.
   Community Acceptance. If activity is accepted, score high; if not, score low.
   Time Consumption. If activity consumes too much time, score low; if not, score high.
3. Please score by using your best scientific knowledge and not by personal likes and dislikes.
4. Each teacher will score both girls' and boys' activities.

Description of the Criteria

1. **Desirable Outlet for the Play Urge.** The activity should include one or more of the natural fundamental movements of man, such as running, jumping, throwing, dodging, climbing, and hanging.
2. **Leisure Time Development.** The activity should have great carry-over value so that exercise does not stop when the pupil finishes school
3. **Development of Emotional Stability.** The activity should be such that the pupil is able to achieve success and have the feeling of accomplishment. If the pupil is frustrated in his efforts, he may become emotionally upset and hence unstable.

154

However, local conditions would affect the inclusion of some in the curriculum. This would necessitate the establishment of other criteria used to select from the activities a group that could be used locally. The local criteria with their weight values are:

Interest	1–30
Cost	1–30
Community Acceptance	1–30
Time Consumption	1–30

4. **Evaluate by Major Criteria.** The activities remaining from the first screening were evaluated by the major criteria (Fig. 6–4). They were then ranked in decreasing order with the activity having the highest score at the top as shown below. *The author wishes to emphasize that the activities selected comprise a suggested curriculum. The intent of the author is to motivate teachers and administrators to experiment with designing curriculum content scientifically.*

1. Tennis (boys and girls)
2. Badminton (boys and girls)
3. Bowling (boys and girls)
4. Basketball (boys and girls)
5. Swimming (boys and girls)
6. Golf (boys and girls)
7. Handball (boys and girls)
8. Touch football (boys only)
9. Volleyball (boys and girls)
10. Softball (boys and girls)
11. Rhythmics (boys and girls)
12. Horseshoes (boys and girls)
13. Soccer (boys only)
14. Table tennis (boys and girls)
15. Wrestling (boys only)
16. Dashes (boys and girls)
17. Hockey (boys and girls)
18. Hurdles (boys only)
19. Body mechanics (boys and girls)
20. Distance runs (boys only)
21. Tumbling (boys only)
22. Jumps (boys only)
23. Archery (boys and girls)
24. Fitness tests (boys and girls)
25. Weights (track) (boys only)
26. Apparatus (limited) (boys only)

5. **Evaluate by Local Criteria.** Each student, using the local criteria established in class, selected a group of activities that could be used in his own teaching situation. The students submitted a ranked list of activities (note that of three selections shown no two had the same activity listed first):

Student One

Dashes	Bowling	Golf
Softball	Swimming	Basketball
Soccer	Badminton	Volleyball
Tumbling	Archery	Tennis
Touch Football	Wrestling	

Student Two

Touch Football	Basketball	Dashes
Softball	Volleyball	Table Tennis
Wrestling	Soccer	Hockey
Tumbling	Bowling	Badminton
Body Mechanics	Archery	Swimming
Golf	Rhythmics	Tennis
Apparatus	Handball	Horseshoes

Student Three

Tennis	Swimming	Basketball
Handball	Track	Badminton
Volleyball	Wrestling	Rhythmics
Touch Football	Bowling	Softball
Tumbling	Golf	Soccer
Table Tennis	Hockey	Body Mechanics
Archery	Horseshoes	Apparatus

6. **Evaluate by Relative Value.** The teachers decided that they might find it necessary to further refine their selection, subjecting the activities to the criterion of relative value as described on page 152. This would be done when they returned to their teaching positions.

Students in the Methods Class at Lynchburg College, Lynchburg, Virginia, scientifically selected a group of activities for the physical education curriculum. This approach illustrates the thinking and planning that should be involved in devising a curriculum in physical education. Briefly, the procedures in the process were as follows:

1. The students, after considerable study, selected six criteria which would be used in evaluating physical education activities.
2. Importance was evaluated and a percentage assignment made as to opportunity for the development of the criteria. This was done as follows:

Safety	29%
Basic Skills	21%
Physical Fitness	18%
Total Involvement	15%
Social Interaction	9%
Leisure Time Skill Development	8%

3. Each student in the class gave a rank

order to particular activities within the framework on a 1–5 low-high ranking.

4. The activities were ranked by total scores and the top 12 are shown below. The actual rank of each activity and the totals are shown in Tables 6–1 and 6–2.

Jr. High School Girls
Basketball
Tennis
Soccer
Bowling
Volleyball
Modern Dance
Square Dance
Folk Dance
Tap Dance
Softball
LaCrosse
Paddle Tennis

Jr. High School Boys
Track
Basketball
Tennis
Volleyball
Folk Dance
Square Dance
Flag Football
Running
Jogging
Soccer
Modern Dance
Badminton

Sr. High School Girls
Tennis
Basketball
Folk Dance
Square Dance
Modern Dance
Soccer
Floor Exercise
Volleyball
Swimming
Softball
Badminton
Tap Dance

Sr. High School Boys
Basketball
Speedball
Soccer
Volleyball
Flag Football
Softball
Calisthenics
Square Dance
Running
Modern Dance
Wrestling
Badminton
Jogging

Further information relative to procedures involved in this study may be obtained by writing to Mrs. Jacqueline W. Asbury, Lynchburg College, Lynchburg, Virginia.

In addition to the suggested procedures discussed above, the following paragraphs offer other assistance in selecting activities

TABLE 6–1. SCIENTIFIC SELECTION OF A CURRICULUM IN PHYSICAL EDUCATION *(Girls)**

Activity	Safety 1–5 29%		Basic Skills 1–5 21%		Physical Fitness 1–5 18%		Total Involvement 1–5 15%		Social Interaction 1–5 9%		Leisure Time Skills Development 1–5 8%		Total
Senior High Girls													
Tennis	4.3	124.7	3.7	77.7	3.8	68.4	4.3	64.5	3.1	27.9	3.5	28.0	391.2
Basketball	3.2	92.8	4.0	84.0	4.3	77.4	3.9	58.5	4.6	41.4	4.2	33.6	387.7
Folk Dance	4.6	133.4	3.2	67.2	2.8	50.4	3.1	46.5	4.3	38.7	4.3	34.4	370.6
Square Dance	4.6	133.4	3.1	65.1	2.5	45.0	3.4	51.0	4.3	38.7	4.3	34.4	367.6
Modern Dance	4.6	133.4	3.2	67.2	2.6	46.8	3.4	51.0	3.8	34.2	4.3	34.4	367.0
Soccer	3.1	89.9	4.0	84.0	4.7	84.6	3.9	58.5	3.6	32.4	1.8	14.4	363.8
Floor Exercise	4.1	118.9	4.6	96.6	3.5	63.0	3.1	46.5	2.3	20.7	1.8	14.4	360.1
Volleyball	4.6	133.4	3.8	79.8	2.7	48.6	3.7	55.5	3.3	29.7	1.4	11.2	358.2
Swimming	3.4	98.6	3.2	67.2	3.1	55.8	4.2	63.0	4.7	42.3	3.7	29.6	356.5
Softball	3.6	104.4	3.8	79.8	3.8	68.4	3.6	54.0	2.9	26.1	2.6	20.8	353.5
Badminton	4.3	124.7	3.6	75.6	2.8	50.4	2.7	40.5	2.9	26.1	3.9	31.2	348.5
Tap Dance	4.6	133.4	3.0	63.0	2.7	48.6	2.9	43.5	2.7	24.3	4.3	34.4	347.2
Junior High Girls													
Basketball	4.4	127.6	4.1	86.1	4.0	72.0	3.9	58.5	3.7	33.3	2.3	18.4	395.9
Tennis	4.9	142.1	3.7	77.7	2.9	52.2	3.5	52.5	3.7	33.3	3.5	28.0	385.8
Soccer	3.4	98.6	3.9	81.9	4.4	79.2	4.6	69.0	4.2	37.8	1.4	11.2	377.7
Bowling	4.9	142.1	2.8	58.8	2.5	45.0	3.7	55.5	3.9	35.1	4.7	37.6	374.1
Volleyball	4.9	142.1	2.6	54.6	2.9	52.2	3.9	58.5	3.8	34.2	3.2	25.6	367.2
Modern Dance	5.0	145.0	2.7	56.7	2.1	37.8	3.3	49.5	3.6	32.4	4.9	39.2	360.6
Square Dance	5.0	145.0	2.7	56.7	2.1	37.8	3.2	48.0	3.5	31.5	4.7	37.6	356.6
Folk Dance	5.0	145.0	2.7	56.7	2.1	37.8	3.2	48.0	3.5	31.5	4.6	36.8	355.8
Tap Dance	5.0	145.0	2.8	58.8	2.5	45.0	3.2	48.0	3.5	31.5	3.1	24.8	353.1
Softball	4.1	118.9	3.0	63.0	2.2	39.6	3.4	51.0	3.8	34.2	3.2	25.6	332.3
Lacrosse	1.8	52.2	4.3	90.3	4.7	84.6	3.6	54.0	2.6	23.4	2.2	17.6	322.1
Paddle Tennis	4.9	142.1	2.6	54.6	2.3	41.4	2.0	30.0	1.9	17.1	2.8	22.4	307.6

*Courtesy of Mrs. Jacqueline W. Asbury, Lynchburg College, Lynchburg, Virginia.

TABLE 6–2. SCIENTIFIC SELECTION OF A CURRICULUM IN PHYSICAL EDUCATION *(Boys)**

Activity	Safety 1–5 29%		Basic Skills 1–5 21%		Physical Fitness 1–5 18%		Total Involvement 1–5 15%		Social Interaction 1–5 9%		Leisure Time Skills Development 1–5 8%		Total
Senior High Boys													
Basketball	3.5	101.5	4.3	90.3	4.5	81.0	4.0	60.0	4.0	36.0	4.1	32.8	401.6
Speedball	3.9	113.1	3.7	77.7	4.0	72.0	3.8	57.0	3.6	32.4	2.1	16.8	369.0
Soccer	2.9	84.1	4.2	88.2	4.1	73.8	4.0	60.0	3.9	35.1	2.8	22.4	363.6
Volleyball	4.0	116.0	3.4	71.4	3.0	54.0	3.9	58.5	3.7	33.3	3.6	28.8	362.0
Flag Football	3.0	87.0	4.0	84.0	3.7	66.6	4.0	60.0	3.9	35.1	2.7	21.6	354.3
Softball	3.5	101.5	3.9	81.9	3.0	54.0	3.4	51.0	3.6	32.4	3.8	30.4	351.2
Calisthenics	4.2	121.8	2.3	48.3	4.1	73.8	3.8	57.0	2.2	19.8	2.8	22.4	343.1
Square Dance	4.5	130.5	2.6	54.6	2.0	36.0	3.9	58.5	3.9	35.1	3.0	24.0	338.7
Running	4.2	121.8	1.9	39.9	4.2	75.6	3.9	58.5	1.7	15.3	3.4	27.2	338.3
Modern Dance	4.5	130.5	2.7	56.7	2.8	50.4	3.3	49.5	3.3	29.7	2.6	20.8	337.6
Wrestling	2.7	78.3	4.2	88.2	4.5	81.0	3.1	46.5	2.4	21.6	2.0	16.0	331.6
Badminton	4.2	121.8	3.1	65.1	2.8	50.4	3.0	45.0	2.5	22.5	3.3	26.4	331.2
Jogging	4.3	124.7	1.6	33.6	4.0	72.0	3.6	54.0	1.5	13.5	3.4	27.2	325.0
Junior High Boys													
Track	4.6	133.4	4.7	98.7	4.1	73.8	4.0	60.0	2.8	25.2	3.0	24.0	415.1
Basketball	3.0	87.0	5.0	105.0	4.8	86.4	3.8	57.0	4.3	38.7	4.2	33.6	407.7
Tennis	5.0	145.0	4.2	88.2	3.4	61.2	3.0	45.0	2.8	25.2	5.0	40.0	404.6
Volleyball	4.9	142.1	3.2	67.2	2.4	43.2	4.8	72.0	4.9	44.1	4.3	34.4	403.0
Folk Dance	5.0	145.0	2.3	48.3	2.7	48.6	4.7	70.5	4.5	40.5	4.9	39.2	392.1
Square Dance	5.0	145.0	2.3	48.3	3.1	55.8	4.0	60.0	5.0	45.0	4.7	37.6	391.7
Flag Football	3.1	89.9	4.6	96.6	4.0	72.0	4.4	66.0	4.2	37.8	3.5	28.0	390.3
Running	4.7	136.3	3.3	69.3	4.9	88.2	2.4	36.0	2.1	18.9	4.7	37.6	386.3
Jogging	4.9	142.1	2.0	42.0	5.0	90.0	3.7	55.5	2.1	18.9	4.7	37.6	386.1
Soccer	3.2	92.8	4.1	86.1	4.7	84.6	4.3	64.5	3.3	29.7	2.9	23.2	380.9
Modern Dance	5.0	145.0	2.3	48.3	3.0	54.0	4.0	60.0	4.1	36.9	4.1	32.8	377.0
Badminton	4.9	142.1	3.5	73.5	3.0	54.0	3.0	45.0	3.0	27.0	4.1	32.8	374.4

*Courtesy of Mrs. Jacqueline W. Asbury, Lynchburg College, Lynchburg, Virginia.

for instruction. These guidelines, involving extremely sensitive and important aspects of the physical education curriculum, should be carefully studied. The areas of concern are activities for girls, gymnastics and contraindicated activities.

Activities for Girls. The program for girls beyond the 6th grade should be different from the boys' program. Although the emotional and physiological characteristics of girls play an important role in the difference, the chief concern is anatomical.

On approaching puberty, girls begin to differ anatomically from boys to a marked degree. The structure of the pelvis and the large amount of weight around the hips handicap girls in their efforts to run; they no longer run as easily and successfully as boys do. The tilt of the pelvis limits the forward motion in running. This does not mean that girls should not run, but it does mean they should not run the way that boys do. They should participate in running activities suited for girls. Activities such as tennis incorporate the appropriate type of running suitable for girls; the dash and hurdles do not.

As they approach puberty, girls also find it more difficult to perform those activities involving hanging by the arms. This is because of the weakness of the arms and the amount of weight around the center of gravity. Many of the movements involved in the traditional apparatus program, therefore, are unsuited for junior and senior high school girls. Williams gives medical opinion about these activities:

Many of the activities on the parallel bars, long horse, flying rings, traveling rings and horizontal ladder, that girls can do equally as well as boys before puberty, become wholly undesirable for them afterward.[11]

He goes on to show that girls and women should:

... not be asked to engage in weight lifting, to perform muscular feats on the apparatus. ... The strength developed in modern dance is not only more suitable for girls and women than the strength acquired for stunts on heavy apparatus, but also it will arrive sooner and stay longer. The strength developed in swimming, hockey, skating and tennis is not only far preferable in type for girls than the strength acquired in weight-lifting but also more efficient and enduring.[11]

A recent issue of the *Physical Education Newsletter* contained a statement from the American Medical Association concerning activities for girls, summarized as follows:

The day has long since passed when it was permissible to make girls' physical education a carbon copy of what is offered to boys. Girls need a program that is geared to their particular physiological and emotional structure and that will stimulate a desire to participate.[21]

ETHEL PERRIN

Ethel Perrin for over 75 years was a leader in physical education. Although trained in formal gymnastics, she became an ardent supporter of the natural program designed to meet the needs of a democratic culture. Through her friendship with young people and her powerful influence during the early years she helped to pave the way for a dynamic program in physical education as we know it today.

Gymnastics. To clearly understand the nature of conditioning exercises (calisthenics), which are commonly used in the United States, teachers should study the origin of these exercises. These movements are part of a general gymnastics program; gymnastics constitutes one phase of the total physical education offering.

Gymnastics, as practiced in the United States, has its origin in European culture. Generally there are four large divisions of gymnastics: *calisthenics, apparatus, tumbling,* and *marching.* Gymnastic movements had as their primary aim preparation for military service. There were many systems of gymnastics, but four of them seem to have survived and have influenced the physical education program in this country. These systems are the German, Swedish, Danish, and Expressive. Sharman outlines three of them.[8]

GERMAN
  a. Marching and similar work
  b. Free standing exercises, with or without use of hand apparatus
  c. Apparatus work (comprising suspension and arm support exercises; balance and suppleness tests; jumping, vaulting and tumbling)
  d. Class running and running games such as relay, obstacle races and hand tag

SWEDISH
The Day's Order
1. Preparatory
    a. order movements
    b. leg movements
    c. arch flexions
    d. heave movements
    e. balance movements
2. Body of lesson
    a. back exercises
    b. abdominal exercises
    c. lateral trunk movements
    d. the climax: running, jumping, and games
3. Quieting
    a. slow leg movements
    b. breathing exercises

DANISH
  a. Class arrangement
  b. Exercises for legs
  c. Exercises for arms
  d. Exercises for neck
  e. Lateral exercises
  f. Abdominal exercises

g. Dorsal exercises

h. Marching and running

i. Vaulting and agility exercises

EXPRESSIVE GYMNASTICS

Expressive gymnastics are a variation of the German system and are more modern than the original version. Williams, Dambach, and Schwendener outline the Expressive system:

1. Relaxation exercises consisting of drooping and low swinging movements to correct tenseness.

2. Contraction exercises. These aim to teach the natural contractions, to strengthen various joints and ligaments. They involve a fixation of certain joints, and allow the greatest possible energy to flow into the arms and legs. They usually have a central origin.

3. Progressive exercises. These fluctuate between relaxation and contraction, and incorporate a feeling of unity, elasticity and harmony.

4. Dancing movements, that coordinate the whole musculature by swinging, leaping or running exercises.[22]

Leaders of these systems brought them to this country during the latter part of the 19th century, and for many years such programs dominated physical education in the United States.

Although these systems served a purpose, they could not satisfy the needs of a culture based on democratic principles. At the end of World War I, physical education pioneers such as Clark Hetherington, Jesse Feiring Williams, and Jay B. Nash began to eliminate the formal pattern of gymnastics. They and others introduced the natural program of physical education based on the fundamental movements, using sports, games, dancing, and swimming as the media for expression.

Calisthenics survived this transformation and Williams explains why:

... school people set up a number of conditions that reflected the ideas they had concerning the function of education. In effect, the schoolmen proposed that any physical training that was to be taken into the school must require very little time, must be inexpensive and not demand specially trained teachers, must conduct its activities in the classroom (activity carried on outside the school building could not be educative), and must not require apparatus.

Unfortunately, the experts in physical training of the time came forward and said in effect: We have just what you want. We propose systematic exercises that can be taught by the regular teacher in the classroom. No apparatus will be required, and the expense is very moderate. These exercises will correct the schoolroom stoop, provide relief for the mind, and bring health and vigor to the body. The antiseptic request of the schoolmen was accorded a sterilized program, vestiges of which remain today as "10 minutes a day of calisthenics."

Now, this in brief, represents the beginning of physical education in the schools of the United States. No study was made of the kind of activities boys and girls need for developmental purposes, nor of the usages to which physical activities may be put in the setting up and acquirement of standards of conduct. The schoolroom stoop and physical weakness loomed large as the problems. A ready cure was proposed for a very complex disturbance with the usual unsatisfactory results when unscientific methods are proposed.

This type of physical training (for it was nothing more than a training procedure) never caught the imagination of boys and girls. They were asked to go through an innumerable number of stupid posturings when their whole being was calling for a kind of activity based in the neuron connections already set up and organized in their nervous systems. Consequently, from time to time, youth took into its own hands the business of physical education. In colleges and high schools, teams were organized for the playing of games, meets were held with other teams, and soon the institutions represented found themselves involved in disputes, financial arrangements, and real embarrassments. Not yet appreciating the place of physical education in the education of young people, schoolmen set up faculty advisers, or managers, to control an activity with which they had little sympathy and no understanding.[11]

Conditioning exercises when related to teaching a sport are important for warm-up values and should be given a place in the curriculum. But they do not produce fitness, and the individuals who subscribe to this philosophy need to study what constitutes fitness.

Irwin has similar views in evaluating calisthenics. He states:

Marching, calisthenics and apparatus work are usually known as formal activities. Experience with these activities in regular physical education classes in the public schools of America shows that they are inferior to the free, rugged sports activities in accomplishing the objectives of physical education in a democracy.[23]

Hetherington also emphasizes the need for natural movements:

The natural physical-training activities arise out of

children's play tendencies. They are satisfying because they meet growth needs. These needs are not met by any other kind of activity. The natural activities are an essential part of the child life. On the other hand, gymnastic drills or calisthenic movements are pure adult inventions. They are artificial or invented movements derived from the army idea of "training" and were incorporated into the school program in Germany and Sweden when formal discipline was in vogue.[24]

Cowell has this to say about the matter:

When we gave up "physical training" and formal gymnastics for physical education and a richer program of natural activities, we did it in order to bring education into greater harmony with biological laws and therefore to better meet the basic personality needs of children and youth.[25]

Hetherington states that "children do not rush together spontaneously at recess or after school hours and start a gymnastic drill."[24] Children must be motivated to extend the instructional program beyond the school day if they are to meet the hourly activity requirement of normal growth and development. This motivation will be achieved by teaching pupils to better perform those natural play movements they would undertake anyway.

Recently, leaders have studied the problem and many criticisms are leveled at the artificial programs existing today. Flint discusses the problem of promoting various systems of calisthenics:

. . . most exercise series are planned to accomplish certain purposes. In some cases, however, the type of movements involved often make it impossible to meet these objectives. Too often different muscles from those intended will execute the action, or the principles or mechanics will work in direct opposition to that predicted and the results will consequently be unsatisfactory.[26]

These opinions show rather conclusively that many of the unnatural calisthenic movements are in the physical education curriculum for no scientific reason. Instead, they have been handed down from year to year and teachers have accepted them without question. Although some of the movements have been derived from experiments that have been used for corrective purposes, they are not desirable for the majority of students.

Natural movements are prescribed by nature and are beneficial for normal growth and development. However, various unnatural calisthenics may cause serious damage to the alignment of the body if used improperly. Many teachers do not know which muscles are actually used in calisthenic exercises, and so more harm than good is frequently the result (Fig. 6–6).

Figure 6–5.   Activities involving natural movements are safe, meet the objectives of physical education, and are interesting to pupils.

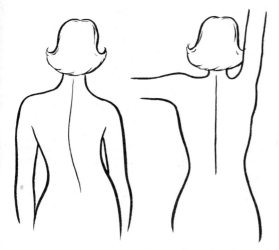

Figure 6-6. The lateral curvature shown is a form of spinal curvature known as scoliosis. The curve is convex to the left, and the exercise shown in the picture with the left arm extended sideward and right arm extended upward will tend to straighten the spine. However, if a teacher uses certain artificial exercises with emphasis on extending the right arm to the side, the condition may be exaggerated. (Adapted from Bowen, Wilbur P.: *Applied Anatomy and Kinesiology,* 7th ed. Revised by Henry A. Stone. Philadelphia: Lea and Febiger, 1955, p. 345.)

Exercises for warming-up purposes should incorporate as nearly as possible the actual movement that will be involved in the major activity that follows. For example, a batter swings one or two bats before batting; a pitcher warms up by pitching with moderate speed.

Finally, Flint summarizes in a brief statement a sensible point of view relative to calisthenics:

To exercise just for the sake of exercising, however, can be a poor and sometimes dangerous practice unless the exercises have been carefully selected for each individual need and unless their execution is supervised with a trained and critical eye.[26]

Contraindicated Exercises. Many traditional exercises used universally by teachers and coaches have been examined recently and have been found to be undesirable for use in the physical education program. Not only do they not do what they are supposed to do, but they may seriously injure the individual. Some exercises falling in this category are the deep knee bend, leg lift, sit-up, toe touching, dips (unless correctly executed), and back arch.

Lowman has shown why such movements as the duck waddle, Russian bounce, and full squats, which involve the deep knee bend, put undue strain on the knee joints:

. . . it is still a common practice to use such exercises as "deep knee bends" or full squats—duck waddle or Russian bounce—without regard to body weight, faulty leg or foot alignment, when it should be obvious to anyone who has had any physics that the "stress on a joint is specifically related to the degree of angulation or rotation in that joint in certain positions and likewise the angle of the application of the force." If, for example, a fat boy aged 12 to 15 with relaxed arches and moderate knock knees does a deep knee bend, he will make undue stress on the knee ligaments, as well as pressure on the synovial linings. He will in all probability toe out somewhat; so, in consequence, he will increase tension on the upper tibial growth plate, as well as applying a terrific breaking stress on his midtarsal area, further flattening the long arch. This will lower both front and back abutments and necessitate a further adaptive shortening of his calf muscles as well as the anterior tibials.[27]

The Committee on Medical Aspects of Sports of the American Medical Association points out the danger of the deep knee bend and the duck waddle:

Both exercises have a potential for serious injury to the internal and supporting structures of the knee joint, one of the most vulnerable parts of the athlete's body.[27a]

Flint explains why the leg lift is questionable, since it is not an abdominal exercise:

Since a large number of individuals have some degree of lordosis in which there is a shortening of the hip flexors, a tightening of the erector spinae in the lumbar region, and a lengthening of the abdominals, this exercise only tends to aggravate an existing condition and may perpetuate skeletal faults.[26]

Lowman also shows the questionable value of the leg lift:

Supine lying—leg raising done with the mistaken idea that it develops the abdominal muscles—may if there is any degree of lordosis, increase the lordosis with the exercise.[27]

Nelson discusses the inadvisability of using the leg lift:

Since sway back and lower back strain are mentioned as dangers, it should also be pointed out that straight leg raises contribute to these conditions and should not be used as abdominal exercises.[28]

The sit-up as a physical education activity is discussed by Flint:

The additional strength which the hip flexors gain in performing this exercise will only tend to accentuate a postural condition of lordosis.[26]

Flint also explains why the toe-touching exercise is contraindicated:

Of all the exercises performed, the one which is most commonly used, accomplishes the least toward body development and maintenance, and causes the most damage to all involved joints is the forward bending of the trunk with forceful bouncing movements in attempting to touch the hands to the toes. This is not an abdominal exercise, as is often claimed, because the movement is accomplished by gravity, momentum, and eccentric contraction of the back extensors.

The position forces the knees into hyperextension and the anterior portions of the lumbar vertebrae are subjected to tremendous amounts of pressure, a factor believed by many to have either a direct or an indirect effect on low-back complaints. A certain amount of lengthening of the back and hip extensors may result by modifying this exercise so that the trunk is flexed forward with controlled movements from the long sitting position. However, this does little to qualify it as an abdominal strengthening exercise.[26]

The dips or push-ups are questionable unless performed correctly. These movements are discussed by Lowman:

. . . unless most cautiously done and carefully supervised, push-ups will cause the trunk to sag and a lordotic curve increase, as well as over-stretching the abdominals. Purportedly, this exercise is supposed to strengthen the shoulder girdle. Because about 75 percent of all students have varying degrees of round shoulders their rhomboids and lower trapezii will be stretched and their opponents, the pectorals and serrati, will be adaptively shortened, as well as the anterior shoulder joint ligaments. When the major need is to strengthen all antigravity muscles because of the general malposture, this exercise will only make these anterior muscles more shortened, which is contraindicated.[27]

Flint shows the serious consequences that may result from including the back arch in the program:

The purpose of exercises such as prone lying with trunk extension (the swan exercise), prone lying with leg extension, and backward circling of the trunk is to increase flexibility of the trunk and to strengthen the posterior thoracic and hip muscles. These and all exercises which force the back into hyperextension should be eliminated from an exercise program for the general population. For the large number of individuals who have varying degrees of sway back with weakened abdominals, movements which hyperextend the back will only exaggerate the condition and at the same time place unnecessary strain on the overused lumbar joints. The low back extensors are shortened, the tilting of the pelvis forward is increased, and the lumbar vertebrae are pulled forward. The anterior longitudinal ligament of the vertebrae is also put on a stretch. If subjected to repeated periods of stretching, it will become permanently lengthened, consequently weakening the joint structures. Only if a functional flattened lumbar curve exists can the "back bend" exercise be used advantageously.[26]

A recent development has been the formation of a committee by the American Association of Health, Physical Education and Recreation to study the entire field of contraindicated activities. This committee should make a tremendous contribution to the scientific selection of activities for the physical education program.

After several years of indecision and planning, the committee adopted the title: *The Committee to Evaluate Practices and Concepts in Health Education, Physical Education and Recreation.*

The Committee developed plans for surveying and evaluating questionable practices in physical education. As reported in the January, 1971, issue of the *Journal*, the Committee is in the process of initiating evaluations of some commonly criticized practices such as the deep knee bend, isometric exercises and 15 minutes of daily exercises for physical fitness benefits.

An evaluation of procedures and practices form has been developed and may be procured from the Association. The form is shown in Figure 6–7.

DEVELOPING CURRICULUM COMPONENTS

As discussed earlier in this chapter, the responsibility for developing the curriculum in physical education is usually vested in the school administration. In the past, the actual construction was done by administrators. However, recent trends give the teacher a more vital role in assisting with the development of the curriculum. In many schools the physical education teacher is given the entire responsibility for the program. Whether the teacher is partially or fully responsible for this planning, he should be familiar with the procedures for the construction of (1) the curriculum guide, (2) the resource unit, and (3) the daily lesson plan.

This chapter presents a brief outline to assist the teacher. There is considerable additional material available on the various aspects of planning and selected references are provided at the end of the chapter for students who wish to read more about curriculum development.

The Curriculum Guide

Chapter 1 outlined the many problems and areas of concern that may be involved in the physical education curriculum and Chapter 4 developed a working philosophy. The first part of this chapter shows *one way* in which activities may be scientifically selected for the program. The next logical step is to place the content sequentially in a guide so that teachers can use it effectively.

Each system or school should have a guidebook outlining the areas that are to be taught in the physical education program. The guidebook should be written by teachers and administrators who have a background in physical education and should cover those areas recommended by various national education organizations, successful school systems, and current authors; in addition, it must be designed to meet local needs. The procedures and methods for studying these areas should be determined by the committees constructing the guidebook.

The construction of a physical education guide serves many purposes. The end result not only provides a necessary guide for instruction, but it also gives teachers valuable experience in the democratic processes involved in educational procedures. The research and interaction involved develops leadership on the part of individual teachers, increases their in-depth knowledge and assures better usage of the document since many people participated in its construction.

Definition. The curriculum guide may be defined as a written outline of the essential content to be covered in a specific discipline, or of a course within that discipline; the guide serves as an aid to instruction. The guide usually contains units of instruction relating to a central theme. For example, a guide in physical education would contain such units as Bowling, Golf, Tennis, Wrestling, Modern Dance, and Basketball. As an aid to teaching, it may also contain suggestions for methods of presentation, pupil activities, supplementary resources, and the like.

Although some authors differentiate between such terms as curriculum guide, teacher's guide, guidebook, or the term "course of study," all serve essentially the same function described in our definition. Most common today are the terms curriculum guide and guidebook; these will be used interchangeably in this text.

Characteristics of the Curriculum Guide. The curriculum guide should reflect the local emphasis on teaching procedure. If the school system emphasizes the subject matter approach, this approach will dominate the development of the guidebook. On the other hand, if the experience curriculum is dominant, the guidebook will reflect the more informal experience approach. Irrespective of the type of curriculum, a number of elements are common to effective guidebooks, including the following:

1. A definition of curriculum
2. A statement of the philosophy of physical education, including aims and objectives
3. Selection of areas of instruction
4. Scope, sequence, and time allotment
5. Organization of program content
6. Suggested teaching procedures
7. Reference materials
8. Evaluation procedures
9. Anticipation of future needs

A definition of the physical education curriculum is essential and should be the first step in curriculum construction. The definition should be consistent with the overall policy of the school, and efforts should be made to relate the physical education curriculum to the general school program.

Chapter 5 discussed the importance of developing a philosophy in physical education. The aims of physical education and the procedures necessary for achieving these aims should be incorporated in the philosophy. Without a basic philosophy the curriculum would be without direction and valuable time would be wasted on needless effort.

The selection of areas of instruction is the nucleus of the curriculum. Later in the chapter the importance of determining which activities should be included and which should be excluded will be pointed out.

After curriculum content has been de-

QUESTIONNAIRE

1. Identify and briefly describe the concept or practice (use additional paper if necessary).

2. Cite an actual example of this concept or practice if possible.

3. Where is the concept or practice most prevalent?

_____ ELEMENTARY SCHOOLS   _____ SECONDARY SCHOOLS   _____ COLLEGES/UNIVERSITIES

_____ YOUTH AGENCIES   _____ NEWS MEDIA   _____ COMMERCIAL ESTABLISHMENTS

OTHER _____

4. Is there a specific target group involved?

_____ MALE   _____ FEMALE   _____ AGE GROUP _____

_____ SOCIOECONOMIC GROUP _____

Figure 6–7.   *See opposite page for legend.*

Figure 6–7 continued on opposite page.

termined, the orderly arrangement of the activities is in order. The traditional philosophies of (1) simple to complex, (2) chronological order, and (3) placement of activities based on the internal sequential plan are the usual criteria for arrangement of content. These three criteria together with developmental needs of children should determine the orderly arrangement of activities.

The organization of activities involves an overlapping of numbers three and four. Materials must be adapted to the curriculum structure of the school. The various types of curriculum such as the broad fields, or core, must be taken into consideration as the curriculum develops. A study should be made concerning the extent to which the unit plan is used. There are other problems involved in the organization of activities and these should be studied carefully so that the curriculum provides solutions to the problems, rather than merely stating them.

Teaching procedures related to the objectives of the curriculum content should be

5. Is there a particular geographical location?   _____ YES   _____ NO

If yes, section of the country: _____

_____ URBAN ONLY   _____ RURAL ONLY   _____ SUBURBAN ONLY

6. To the best of your knowledge, what is the original source of the concept or practice?

_____ EXPERT'S OPINION (name): _____

_____ RESEARCH ARTICLE(S) author(s): _____

_____ FOLKLORE (source, if known): _____

_____ UNKNOWN

7. What is the potential of the concept or practice?

FOR HARM:

FOR GOOD:

8. What is the extent of the practice?

_____ WIDESPREAD   _____ FAIRLY COMMON   _____ ISOLATED

SIGNATURE   DATE

TITLE

ADDRESS

Representing the following group (if applicable):

Figure 6–7. *Continued.* Questionnaire for procuring information regarding questionable practices and concepts in physical education. (*JOHPER*, January, 1971, p. 28.)

discussed. Suggestions may be made concerning these procedures, but teachers should feel free to approach teaching situations individually as they see fit.

No guide is complete without a list of useful references, including texts, periodicals and sources of visual aid materials.

Evaluation of pupil progress is essential in all physical education programs. The policies and procedures of evaluating the program and of grading pupils should be studied carefully. A valid plan for marking pupils in physical education and determin-

ing whether they pass or fail is a rare thing. Marking pupils fairly is one of the most perplexing problems facing physical educators today.

It is generally agreed that no curriculum guide is complete. Education itself is a dynamic function, and physical education is continually changing its emphasis and direction. Curriculum planners should anticipate changes in the future and make recommendations that will be easily adaptable to these changes.

The Curriculum Guide Committee. Curriculum specialists today generally agree that the development of the guidebook should be the cooperative effort of specialists and teachers. Not only does the participation of teachers promote *esprit de corps* but it also provides valuable in-service training. The committee technique, therefore, is widely used in the construction of curriculum guides.

The selection of the committee is very important in the construction of the guidebook. It is obviously more expedient to select teachers who are interested in the project. The more effective teachers with good professional backgrounds in physical education usually make valuable contributions. This suggests, of course, a continuing supervisory function to stimulate all the teachers to be both interested in and qualified for curriculum committee service. Nevertheless, for both expediency and effectiveness of the final product, the committee members selected should be both willing and able to do the job. Arbitrary

selection before studying the background of the members frequently creates problems and delays production of an effective guidebook.

Although the general development of the guidebook should be undertaken by a large group, it is advisable to delegate the actual writing to a small group or perhaps to one member who is qualified to perform this function. This will provide for better continuity and for consistency of style and level of content.

The general committee is divided into subcommittees that study the various areas of instruction to be included in the curriculum guide. A uniform pattern of reporting is agreed upon in the general committee. Results reported by subcommittees go to an editing committee that prepare the final product for printing.

Many systems and schools that have prepared guidebooks for physical education instruction, although their committees are organized in various ways, have the same

Arkansas State Department[29]

SECTION I—EVALUATIVE CRITERIA FOR PHYSICAL EDUCATION

Part I. Organization
    Background Information
    Recommended Standards and Procedures
    Evaluative Criteria
    Evaluations

Part II. Nature of Offerings
    Background Information
    Evaluative Criteria
    Evaluations

Part III. Physical Facilities
    Background Information
    Evaluative Criteria
    Evaluations

Part IV. Direction of Learning
    Instructional Staff
      Background Information
      Evaluative Criteria
      Evaluations
    Instructional Activities
      Evaluative Criteria
      Evaluations
    Instructional Materials and Equipment
      Evaluative Criteria
      Evaluations
    Methods of Evaluation
      Evaluative Criteria
      Evaluations

SECTION II—THE PHYSICAL EDUCATION CURRICULUM

Types of Activities and Time Allotments
Suggested Yearly Program by Grades
Suggested Plan for Class Period
Modified Program

SECTION III—PHYSICAL EDUCATION ACTIVITIES

Part I. Team Sports
Part II. Individual or Dual Activities
Part III. Dance
Part IV. Gymnastics and Tumbling
Part V. Developmental Activities
Part VI. Outdoor Education
Part VII. Extra-Class Activities

Seattle Public Schools[30]

1. Purposes, Administration and Organization
   Philosophy
   Aims and Objectives
   Administration of the Program
     State Law
     Seattle School District Policies
     In-District Relationships
     In-School Relationships
   Organization of the Physical Education Program
     General Organization
     Class Organization

2. Special Situations and Hints
   Skill Practice in Large Classes
   Activities for Large Classes
   Discipline Hints
   Bulletin Boards
   Growth and Development in Early Adolescence
   Gifted Students
   Students of Low Skill
   Coeducational Activities

3. Team Sports
   Soccer
   Speedball
   Speed-a-way
   Volleyball
   Basketball
   Softball
   Floor Hockey
   Games of Low Organization

4. Individual and Dual Sports
   Track and Field
   Badminton
   Tennis
   Table Tennis
   Shuffleboard

5. Gymnastics, Tumbling, Rope Climbing
   Objectives
   Suggested Skill and Knowledge Sequence
   Safety Procedures
   Class Organization
   Side Horse Vaulting
   Parallel Bars
   Balance Beam
   Uneven Parallel Bars
   Free Exercise
   Tumbling
   Rope Climbing

6. Rhythms
   Dance
     Modern and Social Dance
     Round Dances and Mixers, Folk Dances
     Tap Dancing
     Other Rhythmic Activities

7. Body Mechanics, Movement Exploration,
   Weight Training, Circuit Training
   Body Mechanics
   Movement Exploration
   Weight Training
   Circuit Training

8. The Intramural Program
   Schedule
   Grouping
   Leadership
   Equipment
   Safety
   Activities
   Awards
   Points
   Optional Awards Points
   Tournaments

New York City[5]

INTRODUCTION

ORGANIZATION OF THE PROGRAM

TEAM SPORTS
  Basketball
  Baseball and Softball
  Soccer
  Football
  Volleyball
  Track and Field

CONDITIONING AND PHYSICAL FITNESS

GYMNASTICS AND TUMBLING

INDIVIDUAL AND DUAL SPORTS
  Tennis
  Golf
  Bowling
  Handball

Other Individual and Dual Sports
  Fencing
  Badminton
  Deck and Ring Tennis
  Paddle Tennis
  Shuffleboard
  Table Tennis
  Tetherball

DANCE AND RHYTHMICS
  Social Dance
  Folk Dancing
  American Country Dances

GAMES

Jacksonville, Florida[31]

PART I. ORGANIZATION AND ADMINISTRATION
    Objectives
    Characteristics and Implications
    Organization Plan
    Accreditation Standards
    Safety Responsibilities of Instructor
    Sources of Money for Purchasing
        Equipment and Supplies
    Care of Equipment and Supplies
    Information Card
    Policies and Procedures
    County Policies
    Grading System
    Rainy Day Program
    Adaptive Program

PART II. INSTRUCTIONAL UNITS
    Self-Testing Activities
        Physical Fitness Test
        Body Mechanics
        Weight Training
        Wrestling
        Track and Field
        Gymnastics, Stunts, and Tumbling
    Team Sports
        Basketball
        Boundball
        Gator Ball
        Speedball
        Soccer
        Softball
        One Pitch Softball
        Touch Football
        Volleyball

    Recreational Activities
        Archery
        Badminton
        Bowling
        Cork Ball
        Deck Tennis
        Golf
        Handball
        Horseshoes
        Paddle Tennis
        Shuffleboard
        Table Tennis
        Tennis
    Rhythms
    Aquatics
    Outing Activities
        Camping and Casting

PART III. SUGGESTED PROGRAMS
    Junior High Boys
    Senior High Boys
    Junior High Girls
    Senior High Girls

PART IV. EVALUATION OF PROGRAM
    Construction of Examinations
    An Evaluation in Physical Education

PART V. RESOURCES AND BIBLIOGRAPHY
    AAHPER Resources
    Other Resources
    Bibliography

---

general pattern for appointing the committees and for studying the various areas to be included in the guidebook. It should be helpful for teachers to study guides from other cities as they proceed with their planning. On the preceding pages are four outlines of guides from areas that have outstanding programs. One state outline and three city programs are shown.

The curriculum guide should be developed along lines that will help teachers to improve instruction and to provide more meaningful instruction for the pupil. It should be regularly evaluated to determine whether it is serving its purposes. Several criteria may be used to evaluate the guide. The following criteria reflect current thinking in developing the guide:

The guide should be

1. Constructed by committees composed of teachers and administrators with a background in physical education.
2. Broad in scope, containing the necessary resource units that will be helpful to all teachers.
3. A reservoir of suggestions, references, teaching aids, and physical education problems that teachers may refer to when the need arises.
4. So constructed that sequential treatment of content will be provided.
5. Flexible, allowing for teacher creativity, yet maintaining unanimity of purpose throughout.

The curriculum guide, in which content is broken down into various topics, provides the framework within which the teacher presents the units of instruction.

Unit Teaching

The unit approach to physical education instruction is practical, functional, and motivating. Teachers of physical education should therefore become skilled in construction of resource units. The many advantages of unit teaching are well documented in educational literature; therefore, we will not repeat them here.

Unit teaching, when planned properly, provides a thorough sequential approach to instruction. Pupils no longer are subjected to the hit-or-miss, unrelated method of participating in physical education. The unit method takes into account their different interests and abilities and motivates them to learn. Teachers enjoy their work more because they are better able to stimulate the interest and enthusiasm of the pupils; in addition, both they and the pupils are able to see progress more readily.

Selecting the Material. The philosophy of the school, purposes of the course, and available resources influence the selection of the central problems around which the resource units are to be developed. The needs of pupils should always be foremost in the planning.

Physical education is so close to everyday living and so vital for health and happiness that material for developing a unit is always available. The resourceful teacher need not look far to tap the vast reservoir of materials. A few of them are:

TEXTBOOKS. Current textbooks from reputable publishers serve as authoritative sources for facts and information. There are many excellent health education texts that may be used to aid the teacher in construction of the unit.

NEEDS OF PUPILS. Many of the physical education needs of pupils are obvious. Pupils who are physically weak, poorly coordinated, and emotionally unstable are noticed by the observant teacher. The needs of such pupils should guide the teacher in the selection of instructional units.

COURSES OF STUDY. Teachers may secure curriculum guides from other sections of the country to assist in the development of local resource units. Many guides are composed of resource units that can be adapted to the local teaching situation.

COMMUNITY. The community is a rich source of materials for developing resource units. Many community groups such as the local health organization, sports club, medical association, and department of public health are most cooperative in supplying materials and data.

RECORDS. Many schools keep records of students' progress through the years. Medical records, guidance studies, and other demographic data provide a fertile reservoir of materials for the guidebook.

Divisions of the Unit. There is no single outline that is best for developing all resource units. The number and titles of sections vary with different authors. One leader in education suggests the following divisions for the content of the unit: Title, Introduction, Basic Problems, Objectives, Content and Methods of Implementation, Evaluation, and Bibliography.[32]

The guidebook of the New York City Public Schools uses the following organizational pattern for its units of instruction. Units for two areas are outlined below:

BOYS	GIRLS
Basketball	*Modern Dance*
Introduction	History and development
Objectives	Place in the program
Approach and motivation	Organization of the unit
Charts of scope and sequence	Objectives
Instructional materials	Approach and motivation
Class organization and management	Instructional materials
General teaching suggestions	Class organization
Safety precautions	Teaching suggestions
Grade 7: skill analysis, teaching cues, applications	Safety precautions
Grade 9: skill analysis, teaching cues, applications	Charts of scope and sequence
Grade 10: skill analysis, teaching cues, applications	Analysis, teaching cues, and applications
Grade 12: skill analysis, teaching cues, applications	Evaluation
Evaluation	Bibliography and references[33]
Bibliography and references[5]	

Many authors in the physical education field have outlined divisions of content for the education resource unit. An example is the outline suggested by Nixon and Jewett as shown below:

1. Educational Philosophy
2. Needs of Individuals or Groups
   Physiological
   Psychological
   Social
3. Considerations in the Selection of Learning Experiences
   The level of fundamental skill performance by pupils
   The physical condition of the participants
   The size and maturity of the individuals with whom the program deals
   The general interest each pupil has in physical education
   Sex must be considered
   The relative emphasis to be given to each of the general objectives at each grade level
   The teacher load
   Available instructional areas
   Available equipment
   The time allotment
   Geographical and climatic conditions
4. Scope
5. Sequence and organization
6. Evaluation.[34]

Guidelines for Developing the Unit. Several elements are common to all good resource units. These provide a means for establishing guidelines that will assist the teacher in developing a unit to serve local purposes. Some of the important points to consider in the planning of the unit are:

1. Needs of pupils should always be the basic consideration. They should be encouraged to participate in developing the unit.
2. Desirable outcomes and objectives should be established; all materials and activities should contribute to the realization of these goals.
3. Content should be current, factual, and appropriate.
4. Content should include a wide variety of materials, activities, and resources that will meet individual needs, interests, and abilities.
5. Material should be extensive and detailed enough to provide for ease in using the unit.

Unit in Volleyball

I. **Objectives**
   1. To learn teamwork
   2. To develop the basic skills of volleyball
   3. To teach an intensive type of game
   4. To develop carry-over desire
   5. To learn the physiological values of volleyball
   6. To learn the rules of volleyball
   7. To learn the history of volleyball

II. **Basic Skills**
   1. Passing
   2. Serving
   3. Set-up
   4. Spike
   5. Blocking
   6. Net recovery

III. **Equipment Needed**
   1. Nets
   2. Outside area
   3. Inside area
   4. Balls
   5. Blackboard
   6. Charts
   7. Lime for marking areas
   8. Pump
   9. Score sheets

Unit continued on opposite page.

IV. Values
   1. Provides emotional release
   2. Provides an excellent recreational game
      for immediate carry-over
   3. Develops postural muscles
   4. Develops skill
   5. Develops speed
   6. Develops endurance
   7. Develops teamwork

V. Teaching Procedures
   Orientation
   1. Acquaint class with the history and importance of the game.
   2. Explain why skills should be learned before activity is played.
   3. Use visual aids and have pupils read about volleyball.
   4. Allow pupils to participate in game briefly to show the need for skills.
   5. Emphasize pupil-teacher discussion.
   Demonstration
   1. The skill should be carefully and correctly
      demonstrated by the teacher or pupils.
   2. The skills should then be analyzed and discussed.
   3. The teacher decides whether to use the whole or part method.
   Organization for Instruction
      There are many formations which may be used in organizing for teaching. Some of the
      well known ones are shown in Chapter 12.
   Inventory
   1. Each pupil should be allowed to try the skill.
   2. Pupils should try the skills in groups to avoid
      wasting of time and prevent standing around.
   3. Teacher should walk around the groups and evaluate.
   Ability Grouping
   1. Pupils (after the inventory) should be grouped
         into as many sections based on ability as space,
         facilities, and safety permit.
   2. Pupils practice the skill and advance from the less proficient to the most proficient or
         from one component of an activity to another more advanced component, as in a tumbling
         sequence.
   3. Pupils who perform skills well may assist others or serve as checkers in dangerous activi-
         ties such as tumbling.
   Skills Laboratory
   1. Skills taught in the instructional phase should be placed in a competitive situation.
   2. Activity should reach its peak intensity in this phase.
   3. Relay races and mass participation should constitute this phase.

VI. Evaluation
   1. Knowledge tests on all skills
   2. Objective tests on all skills
   3. Evaluation of attitudes and behavior

VII. References
   Fait, Hollis F., et al.: A Manual of Physical Education Activities, 3d ed. Philadelphia: W. B.
      Saunders Company, 1967.
   Seaton, Don Cash, et al.: Physical Education Handbook, 4th ed. Englewood Cliffs, New Jersey:
      Prentice-Hall, Inc., 1965.
   Slaymaker, Thomas, and Virginia H. Brown: Power Volleyball. Philadelphia: W. B. Saunders
      Company, 1970.
   Stanley, D. K., and I. W. Waglow: Physical Education Activities Handbook. Boston: Allyn and
      Bacon, Inc., 1966.
   Visual Aids
   1. Film strips on volleyball. Athletic Institute, 209 South State Street, Chicago, Illinois
   2. Play Volleyball. Association Films, 347 Madison Avenue, New York.
   3. Volleyball for Boys. Coronet Instructional Films, Palmolive Building, Chicago, Illinois
   4. Volleyball Guide for Girls. American Association for Health, Physical Education and Recrea-
      tion, Washington, D.C., 1963–1965.

6. Content should motivate the pupils to carry their interests and efforts in the topic beyond the class period.

7. Evaluation should include a variety of techniques involving the pupils, the teacher, and the parents. Emphasis should be on pupil growth in health awareness and health habits.

STEPS IN DEVELOPING THE UNIT. Although the elements described above provide an overview of what should be contained in the unit, assistance is needed with procedures involved in designing the unit. The following steps are suggested:

1. Diagnosing needs
2. Formulating specific objectives
3. Selecting content:
   Topics
   Basic ideas
   Specific content
4. Organizing content
5 & 6. Selecting and organizing learning experiences:
   Introduction, opener, orientation development
   Analysis, study application, generalization
   Summary, culmination
   Rhythm of learning activities
7. Evaluating
8. Checking for balance and sequence.[35]

A Physical Education Unit.   It is extremely important for teachers to develop resource units in physical education. A universal lack of unit planning in physical education is probably one of the reasons that the program has never been accorded the level of prestige it deserves. The resources unit on pages 170–171 is presented to serve as a guide in developing other physical education units.

After the guidebook and the units it is composed of are completed, the next consideration is the planning necessary for the day-to-day instruction.

The Daily Lesson Plan

The unit is a collection of materials, activities, and resources and covers a block of time within the school term. Obviously it must be broken down into smaller sections for daily presentation. The true test of effective teaching is the manner in which the teacher introduces the body of knowledge from the unit into the daily class routine. The value and importance of daily planning, therefore, cannot be overestimated.

Definition.   The daily lesson plan is the teacher's day-to-day guide to effective teaching. The plan should be concise and should be developed to utilize every moment of class time. Nothing is more conducive to poor instruction than the teacher who faces the class without specific preparation. Pupils can readily tell when a teacher is floundering, wasting time, or waiting for the bell to announce the end of the period. No doubt every reader has experienced this at some time in his school career. It is better that the teacher reach the end of the period with considerable information uncovered than to finish his lesson halfway through the period and then assign aimless work to await the end of the period. Both of these situations, however, can be avoided with proper planning.

Evaluation of the Lesson Plan.   Evaluation is a part of all phases of teaching; the lesson plan is no exception. The teacher should have some standards by which to measure its effectiveness. The following criteria may be used to evaluate daily lesson plans.

THE LESSON PLAN MUST HAVE MEANING FOR THE LEARNER.   The teacher should construct the plan on the basis of the pupil's needs, interests, and abilities. Chapter 11 emphasizes the importance of multisensory appeals in making the lesson more meaningful to the learner. This means that pupil participation should be stimulated by the presentation of the material.

THE PLAN SHOULD BE BRIEF.   The teacher already has the guidebook, which serves as a reservoir of material, and the teaching unit, which specifies the material to be learned. The daily lesson plan should be taken from the unit and should be a simple guide for the day's lesson.

THE LESSON PLAN MUST BE INTERESTING. The plan should be organized in such a manner that all of the appropriate tools of learning can be brought into the presentation. The type of plan that provides for the teacher to lecture the entire period will fail because it does not utilize the methods necessary for effective teaching. Modern teaching principles point out that interest is generated more readily when the learner actively participates in the learning process.

THE PLAN MUST STIMULATE EXTRA-CLASS ACTIVITY. Motivation is the key to all learning. The lesson should be so planned that pupils will desire to continue learning beyond the class period.

THE PLAN SHOULD BE COMPLETE. Although brief, the lesson plan should be complete and should include all the essentials. Included in the plan should be the title of the lesson, objectives, equipment and supplies needed, values of the activity, time allowed for each phase, homework and evaluation.

Refer to Chapter 12 for a more compre-hensive discussion of the procedures for developing a daily lesson plan.

The Professional Challenge

The author wishes to emphasize that the method of selecting activities shown in this chapter is only a beginning in this most important phase of teaching. The scientific selection of cur-riculum content in physical education is an intricate procedure and requires consider-able research. Teachers should accept the challenge and carefully devise other methods of curriculum construction with emphasis on the scientific approach.

QUESTIONS FOR DISCUSSION

1. Why should activities in the physical education program be selected scientifically?
2. Do surveys of participants indicate the types of activities that should be included in the curriculum?
3. What are criteria?
4. Distinguish between criteria and objectives.
5. What are some major criteria for selecting activities?
6. Why are local criteria important?
7. Discuss safety in relation to physical education activities.
8. Discuss the selection of activities for girls.
9. What is the purpose of calisthenics?
10. What is meant by contraindicated activities? Discuss.
11. Why should the teacher be involved in the construction of the guidebook?
12. What are the characteristics of a good curriculum guide? Outline a sample guide.
13. Discuss the criteria for evaluating a curriculum guide.
14. What is meant by unit teaching?
15. What are the divisions of the resource unit?
16. Why is the daily lesson plan important?

SUGGESTED ACTIVITIES

1. Make a survey of a school to find out how its physical education activities were selected.
2. Construct a chart using accepted criteria and list the activities that are usually included in the curriculum. Evaluate them and arrange the remaining activities by rank.
3. List activities that are not suitable for girls. Show why.
4. Make a survey of a program in physical education and point out the contraindicated activities that are used.
5. Develop a unit in physical education.
6. Develop a daily lesson plan for physical education.

REFERENCES

1. Delbert Oberteuffer and Celeste Ulrich, *Physical Education*, 3rd ed., pp. 289–302 (New York: Harper and Row, 1962).
2. *Curriculum Construction* (Norfolk Public Schools, 1957).

3. Robert J. Havighurst, *Developmental Tasks and Education,* 3rd ed., pp. 45–75 (New York: David McKay Company, 1972).

4. Robert Biehler, *Psychology Applied to Teaching,* pp. 128–140 (Boston: Houghton Mifflin Company, 1971).

5. "Physical Education for Boys, Grades 7–12," pp. 5–7 (Board of Education of the City of New York, 1964).

6. Greyson Daughtrey, "Preferences of 16,000 Parents" (Survey, Norfolk Public Schools, 1959).

7. Margaret G. Fox, "Activities They Wish They'd Had in College," *Journal of the American Association of Health, Physical Education and Recreation,* p. 14 (January, 1957).

8. Jackson Sharman, *The Teaching of Physical Education,* pp. 170; 209 (New York: A. S. Barnes & Company, 1939).

9. John Van Why, "A Study to Determine Factors Conducive to Voluntary Participation in Active Play" (University of South Dakota, 1953).

10. William R. LaPorte, *The Physical Education Curriculum,* p. 8 (Los Angeles: The University of Southern California Press, 1942).

11. Jesse F. Williams, *Principles of Physical Education,* 8th ed., pp. 119; 351; 205; 306 (Philadelphia: W. B. Saunders Company, 1964).

12. Edward E. Voltmer and Arthur A. Esslinger, *The Organization and Administration of Physical Education,* 4th ed., p. 97 (New York: Appleton-Century-Crofts, 1967).

13. "Need for Varied Activities in Physical Education Programs, A Committee Report," *JOHPER,* p. 6 (Washington, D.C.: American Association of Health, Physical Education and Recreation, June, 1965).

14. Mabel Lee, *The Conduct of Physical Education,* p. 100 (New York: A. S. Barnes and Company, 1937). From *Research Quarterly* of the American Physical Education Association, "Objectives and Policies, A Committee Report" (December, 1934).

15. Clifford L. Brownell and E. Patricia Hagman, *Physical Education,* p. 193 (New York: McGraw-Hill Book Company, 1951).

16. William L. Hughes and Esther French, *The Administration of Physical Education,* p. 69 (New York: A. S. Barnes and Company, 1954).

17. Karl W. Bookwalter and Harold J. Vanderzwaag, *Foundations and Principles of Physical Education,* p. 217 (Philadelphia: W. B. Saunders Company, 1969).

18. Joe E. Frost and G. Thomas Rowland, *Curriculum for the Seventies,* p. 416 (Boston: Houghton Mifflin Company, 1969).

19. *Editorial (Physical Education Newsletter,* December 15, 1964).

20. Paul Vogel, "Battle Creek Physical Education Curriculum Project," *JOPHER,* Vol. 40, No. 7 (September, 1969).

21. "Suitable Physical Activity for Girls and Women" (*Physical Education Newsletter,* November, 1964).

22. Jesse F. Williams, John Dambach, and Norma Schwendener, *Methods in Physical Education,* p. 172 (Philadelphia: W. B. Saunders Company, 1932).

23. Leslie Irwin, *The Curriculum in Health and Physical Education,* p. 132 (St. Louis: C.V. Mosby Company, 1960).

24. Clark Hetherington, *School Program in Physical Education,* pp. 54; 57 (New York: World Book Company, 1922).

25. Charles C. Cowell, *Scientific Foundations of Physical Education,* p. 44 (New York: Harper and Brothers, 1953).

26. M. Marilyn Flint, "Selecting Exercises," *Journal of the American Association of Health, Physical Education and Recreation,* pp. 19; 20; 21 (February, 1964).

27. Charles L. Lowman, "A Message to School Health Services," *Journal of School Health,* pp. 17; 18 (January, 1962).

27a. Health Education Service. American Medical Association, September, 1961, p. 26.

28. Dale O. Nelson, "Focus on Two Fitness Exercises," *Journal of the American Association of Health, Physical Education and Recreation,* pp. 20; 23 (May, 1964).

29. *Physical Education, A Guidebook for Secondary Schools* (Arkansas State Department of Education. Little Rock, Arkansas, 1968).

30. *Physical Education Guide, Junior High School Girls* (Seattle Public Schools, Seattle, Washington, 1968).

31. *Physical Education Curriculum Guide, Grades 7–12* (Duval Board of Education, Jacksonville, Florida, 1968).

32. Stephen Romine, *Building the High School Curriculum,* p. 300 (New York: The Ronald Press Company, 1954).

33. *Physical Education for Girls, Grades 7–12* (Board of Education of the City of New York, New York, New York, 1964).

34. John E. Nixon and Anne E. Jewett, *An Introduction to Physical Education,* 7th ed., pp. 163–169 (Philadelphia: W. B. Saunders Company, 1969).

35. Hilda Taba, *Curriculum Development,* pp. 347–349 (New York: Harcourt, Brace & World, Inc., 1962).

SELECTED READINGS

Cowell, Charles. *Scientific Foundations of Physical Education.* New York: Harper and Brothers, 1953.

Doll, Ronald C. *Curriculum Improvement: Decision Making and Process.* Boston: Allyn and Bacon, Inc., 1964.

Inlow, Gail M. *The Emergent Curriculum.* New York: John Wiley and Sons, Inc., 1966.

Irwin, Leslie W. *The Curriculum in Physical Education.* Dubuque, Iowa: Wm. C. Brown Company Publishers, 1969.

Nixon, John E., and Ann E. Jewett. *Introduction to Physical Education,* 7th ed. Philadelphia: W. B. Saunders Company, 1969.

Oberteuffer, Delbert, and Celeste Ulrich. *Physical Education.* New York: Harper and Brothers, 1964.

Willgoose, Carl E. *The Curriculum in Physical Education.* Englewood Cliffs, New Jersey: Prentice-Hall, Inc., 1969.

Chapter 7

THE TEACHER'S ROLE IN ORGANIZATION AND ADMINISTRATION

Living is learning and growing is learning. The human individual learns his way through life.

Robert Havighurst

Courtesy Richmond Senior High School, Richmond, Indiana

The subject of curriculum content development was initiated in Chapter 6. The many problems involved in the selection of activities were discussed, with emphasis placed on the need for using recognized criteria to make the selection. *The importance of carefully selecting materials for the physical education curriculum cannot be overemphasized.*

The teacher is now in the position of implementing the content which has been selected. However, before any type of instruction can be used, the internal organization of the school must be studied and discussed with the administrative head of the school. Although the responsibility for organizing subject content in the school rests with the principal, the teacher plays a vital role in initiating any constructive change that may be necessary. The teacher can do his best work when he has an overview of the mechanics underlying the total school organization and the way in which physical education relates to it. This chapter will discuss some of the more pertinent organizational problems which face teachers as they begin their teaching career.

GUIDELINES FOR THE OVERALL PROGRAM

Several aspects of the total physical education program must be determined and approved by the administrative head of the school or school system. Such overall factors will largely determine whether or not the program will be effective and conducive to good teaching. Many programs have failed because the proper administrative framework has never been fully established. *Teachers have a responsibility to assist administrators with the formulation of policies that will provide a strong foundation for the program.* They should have access to authoritative opinion on the various factors necessary for the development of such a program. These factors are discussed on the following pages.

Requirement

The first policy to be considered is the status of physical education in the school program. Chapter 2 listed this as one of the crucial issues in physical education and emphasized the need for requiring physical education daily in all grades from one through twelve. *Establishing the requirement, therefore, is the first and most important step in planning and organizing a program.*

Educational leaders and groups constantly stress the importance of required physical education. Conant says that "I am convinced that ideally a period of physical education should be required for all pupils in grades one through twelve every day...."[1]

Emphasizing the need for continuing the instruction beyond the elementary years, the National Conference for the Mobilization of Health Education, Physical Education and Recreation recommended that "a daily program of directed physical education should be provided for all high school pupils."[2]

In 1958, the National Conference on Fitness of Secondary School Youth also underlined the need for a secondary school requirement. The Conference made the following recommendation:

It is recommended that a minimum time allotment of one period per day from grades seven through twelve be devoted to the areas of health and safety education and physical education.[3]

The President's Council on Youth Fitness as a guideline recommended for grades 7 through 12 one standard class period per day, five days per week.[4]

A National Medical jury of the President's Council in 1964 unanimously recommended daily physical education in grades K–12. In 1972 the Council reorganized, and, operating under the new name of President's Council on Physical Fitness and Sports, reaffirmed the previous stand on requirements.[5]

Lloyd Michael, speaking to the Seventh National Conference on Physicians and Schools said that "in the junior and senior high school, it is proposed that there should be a daily program of directed physical education for all pupils."[6]

Gruber, in a paper prepared for presentation before the American Association for the Advancement of Science held in Dallas, Texas, December 1968, refers to a large number of studies that show a "significant improvement in the academic performance of children exposed to a physical education program."[7] He refers to documented evidence which indicates that the mind and body are related and that a daily program of physical education is essential for academic achievement. The author shows that if children are not provided with such a program the result may be a retardation of future potential. Gruber concludes that:

Coordinated movements requiring reflective thinking are potential carriers of mind, and as such open up wider avenues for mental development ... (hence) all school children should receive daily instruction in appropriate physical activity carefully selected to increase their physical fitness.[7]

These recommendations strengthen the position of the teachers in proposing a requirement for physical education to their administrators. The teachers must continually strive for adequate requirements.

Through effective interpretation and presentation of the logical reasons for requirements based on health needs, administrators may be convinced of the importance of placing the physical education program on a required basis in all grades. The case is strong, and it is not difficult to convince administrators and boards of education of the need for requiring the program when the facts are effectively presented.

The author feels that a requirement in physical education in all grades from kindergarten through grade 12 is not an end in itself. Physical education should not stop at the end of the twelfth grade, but should continue throughout life. It is misleading to say that physical education should begin or end at any specific time. Exercise in varying degrees begins with birth and ends only at death. It is the responsibility of physical educators to guide children through an effective program during the school years and thus motivate them to continue their physical education throughout life.

Credit

An essential corollary to the requirement is the awarding of credit for physical education (see Chapter 2). If physical education is ever to attain the status it should have in education, it must carry the same credit as any other subject in the curriculum. Teachers and physical education leaders have for too long been apathetic about the matter of credit for physical education and must therefore assume a large share of the blame for the status of the program in this respect. Even at the risk of being repetitious, it must be emphasized again that the strongest source of improvement lies within the profession itself: the program must be interpreted and the objectives explained in a continuing effort to convince the administrators that, in education, the physical is as important as the mental. Credit for physical education must therefore equal that given for academic subjects.

Class Size

Another important policy to be established for the overall organization is the matter of class size. Although the ideal class size for any subject has not yet been determined, optimal limitations for effective classroom instruction have been empirically established. These limitations apply to physical education as well as to the so-called academic subjects. In some respects, class size for physical education is even more crucial than for other subjects. Teachers of physical education are concerned not only with excellence of instruction but also with the safety of each boy and girl in the class. Large numbers of pupils cannot be taught effectively. Moreover, there is a high correlation between large classes and accidents.

The optimal class size for physical education is between 30 and 40 pupils per teacher.

Scheduling

Pupils should be scheduled by grades in order that the proper sequence of teaching be maintained; that is, each class should be composed of students from only one grade level. Effective teaching demands sequential treatment of content. Although there may be some topical overlap, repetition will be avoided through the spiral of learning, an educational principle long accepted as fundamental to good teaching (Figure 7–1). Each succeeding grade should require a little more content, a different approach, and higher goals.

Teaching Stations — Teachers Needed

Proper organization for teaching dictates the need for a particular place for each teacher and his class. This is called a teaching station. Teachers should work with administrators to secure an adequate number of teaching stations for the program. Just as other subjects have stations or classrooms, so must physical education. Here is a simple formula for providing adequate teaching stations: For every 240 pupils (six periods daily, 40 pupils per period), one station and one teacher are needed. A school with 1200 to 1400 pupils would, therefore, have six teachers (for the average school) — three men and three women — and six stations. Without a teacher-station plan for teaching, teachers cannot do an effective job; administrators must be kept aware of this.

A more accurate plan is shown in the following formula:

$$\frac{\text{Number of students assigned to physical education}}{\text{Class load}} \times \frac{\text{Number of periods class meets weekly}}{\text{Total number of class periods in school week}} = \frac{\text{Number of stations needed}}{}$$

In a junior high school with 1200 pupils enrolled in physical education, a class size of forty pupils per teacher and a six-bell day, the number of stations would be calculated as follows:

$$\frac{1200}{40} \times \frac{5}{30} = \frac{6000}{1200} \text{ or five stations needed}$$

Teaching stations need not be elaborate. A careful survey of a building often discloses many areas that can be used as teaching stations. If necessary, basement space, hallways, a locker room, a gymnasium fitted with a dividing door, or other spaces may be converted into teaching stations. Improvisation is often necessary until adequate facilities can be provided, but care should be taken not to allow the improvisations to become accepted as permanent facilities. The problem of teaching stations will be discussed at length in Chapter 15 under facilities. Figures 7–2, 7–3 and 7–4 show how folding partitions may be used for making less expensive teaching stations.

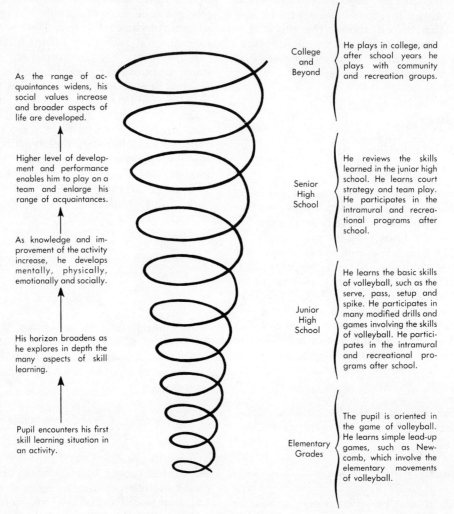

As the range of acquaintances widens, his social values increase and broader aspects of life are developed.

Higher level of development and performance enables him to play on a team and enlarge his range of acquaintances.

As knowledge and improvement of the activity increase, he develops mentally, physically, emotionally and socially.

His horizon broadens as he explores in depth the many aspects of skill learning.

Pupil encounters his first skill learning situation in an activity.

College and Beyond

He plays in college, and after school years he plays with community and recreation groups.

Senior High School

He reviews the skills learned in the junior high school. He learns court strategy and team play. He participates in the intramural and recreational programs after school.

Junior High School

He learns the basic skills of volleyball, such as the serve, pass, setup and spike. He participates in many modified drills and games involving the skills of volleyball. He participates in the intramural and recreational programs after school.

Elementary Grades

The pupil is oriented in the game of volleyball. He learns simple lead-up games, such as Newcomb, which involve the elementary movements of volleyball.

Figure 7-1. The spiral of learning, when applied to teaching skills, begins with a simple movement and proceeds to the complex game situation. Throughout the learning process a continuous thread of multipatterned fabric is noticed. This thread denotes the spiral-of-learning concept. (Adapted from Daughtrey, Anne S.: *Methods of Basic Business and Economic Education.* Cincinnati: Southwestern Publishing Co., 1965, p. 151.)

Figure 7–2.   A pupil-choice program involving team teaching that uses four choices, four stations, and four teachers. The group in the foreground chose basketball instruction; the second group chose volleyball (nets put in place after developmental exercises); the third group chose tumbling; and the group in the auxiliary gymnasium, seen through the door of the equipment room, elected to receive wrestling instruction.

Figure 7–3.   Team-teaching and elective programs in a three-station situation.

Guidelines for Secondary School Physical Education

A position paper published in 1970 by the American Association of Health, Physical Education and Recreation provides a rationale for developing sound programs in physical education. The stands taken on scheduling, time allotment and class size are included in the following recommendations.

Scheduling, time allotment, and class size have a direct bearing on the health, safety, and extent of participation by students, on the type of activities that can be offered, and on the student outcomes which can be expected.

A daily instructional period of directed physical education should be provided for all secondary school students equivalent in length to that found in the regular school pattern.

Schools organized on other than the traditional schedule should provide physical education experiences for each pupil comparable in time to that allocated to other major courses.

The instructional program should be scheduled to allow for maximum participation and adequate time for each pupil to have an opportunity to gain the satisfaction that comes from achievement.

All students should be enrolled in physical education classes. Time should be scheduled in the physical education program for pupils handicapped by functional or structural disorders and those who find it difficult to adjust to the regular program.

Assignment to physical education classes should take into consideration sex, skill, maturation, grade level, and health status.

The pupil/teacher ratio should be the same for physical education classes as for other subject areas with variations possible depending upon the activity.

There should be no substitute for the instructional program.

The teacher's schedule should allow time for preparation.

Figure 7–4. Team teaching in a two-station situation.

Placement of Content

There are three current plans for including activities in the curriculum: *cycle plan, grade placement,* and *seasonal placement.*

The Cycle Plan. In the cycle plan the program is arranged to offer certain activities in yearly cycles. For example, in a school requiring physical education in grades 7 through 12, swimming may be offered during the 7th, 9th, and 11th grades; bowling may be taught in the 8th, 10th and 12th grades (Fig. 7–5).

The major criticism of this plan is the large interval of time which exists between cycles. To teach an activity and then wait a semester or even a year before it is offered again is not a sound instructional procedure.

Grade Placement. In this plan, activities are assigned to specific grades. However, systems that use this plan usually resort to repetition in several grades by breaking certain activities into elementary and advanced fundamentals.

Placement of activities according to grade is often unsatisfactory to students, since they may not continue to participate in a sport that they like once they have completed the grade for it. This situation can be avoided by using the seasonal placement of content.

Seasonal Placement. This plan calls for introduction of the same activities each year on a seasonal schedule. Although the activities are the same each year, the approach, lead-up, and other instructional techniques vary from grade to grade. Content is sequentially developed. Pupils are guided toward improvement each time the activity is offered; progressively higher goals would therefore minimize repetition. (See the Spiral of Learning, Fig. 7–1.)

For instance, assume that basketball is a basic activity. The curriculum content in an 8th grade class might consist of foul shots, various shots from the floor, dribbling, basic passes, and so forth. If, after taking an inventory of performance in the class, it is found that dribbling was adequately covered in a previous grade, it should not be necessary to continue dribbling instruction except for an occasional review. Briefly, in the seasonal approach the activity remains the same each year, but the method of instruction and the skills content develop progressively upward.

The seasonal plan is the most practical

SEQUENCE	1ST SEMESTER	2ND SEMESTER
7	Conditioning Exercises Touch Football Hockey Soccer Swimming Basketball Volleyball	Conditioning Exercises Tennis Rhythms Fitness Tests Badminton Golf Horseshoes Handball

8	Conditioning Exercises
	Bowling
	Table Tennis
	Tumbling
	Archery
	Apparatus
	Wrestling
		Softball
		Fitness Tests
		Body Mechanics
		Track
		    Dashes
		    Hurdles
		    Distance Running
		    Jumps
		    Weights

9	Conditioning Exercises Touch Football Hockey Soccer Swimming Basketball Volleyball	Conditioning Exercises Tennis Rhythms Fitness Tests Badminton Golf Horseshoes Handball

10	Conditioning Exercises
	Bowling
	Table Tennis
	Tumbling
	Archery
	Apparatus
	Wrestling
		Softball
		Fitness Tests
		Body Mechanics
		Track
		    Dashes
		    Hurdles
		    Distance Running
		    Jumps
		    Weights

11	Conditioning Exercises Touch Football Hockey Soccer Swimming Basketball Volleyball	Conditioning Exercises Tennis Rhythms Fitness Tests Badminton Golf Horseshoes Handball

12	Conditioning Exercises
	Bowling
	Table Tennis
	Tumbling
	Archery
	Apparatus
	Wrestling
		Softball
		Fitness Tests
		Body Mechanics
		Track
		    Dashes
		    Hurdles
		    Distance Running
		    Jumps
		    Weights

Figure 7–5. A scope and sequence arrangement of physical education activities using the cycle plan for placement.

Figure 7–6. The seasonal approach not only provides motivation but also allows adequate time for learning intricate skills.

and the most satisfactory for the following reasons:

1. The fact that many schools do not have more than one or two grades of physical education rules out the use of the grade placement plan in various activities.
2. Some activities are popular at certain times every year. To progressively teach skills of the activity at these times would greatly stimulate the interest and participation in the activities as an after-school effort.
3. A great deal of time is needed for teaching the skills of sports and for learning them properly. If they are taught progressively each year, the results will be more satisfying.

Yearly Calendar

For an effective balance of the various activities included in the curriculum, each activity or group of activities should receive an allotted amount of time. Some activities require considerably more time for instruction than others. Local and national emphasis on certain activities can affect the amount of time necessary for adequate instruction. Activities that receive great national attention, such as football and basketball, may not require as much instructional time as a leisure-time activity that has received little attention.

If teachers are to teach effectively, they should develop yearly calendars that include the sequential placement of content and time allotment for each activity or group of activities. Without such a calendar no orderly arrangement of material or equal-time emphasis of activities is possible. Effective teaching depends on this arrangement. To show how activities may be incorporated into a yearly calendar, several examples of how emphasis differs from one activity to another are shown on the following pages.

An example of the way in which a small city plans its yearly calendar is shown in the program of the Cedar Rapids (Iowa) Community School District. The program offers the following yearly curriculum, which includes the time allotted to each activity for boys and girls.[9] (See calendars on pages 186 and 187.)

The New York City Public School System has developed a comprehensive calendar of activities. Because of the magnitude of the task involved, this calendar was designed for two types of programs: one for schools with adequate facilities and one for schools whose facilities are limited.[10] (See pages 188–190.)

(Text continued on page 191.)

BOYS

GRADE 10

First Semester

BOY X	Weeks	BOY Y	Weeks
Orientation	1	Orientation	1
Swimming	18	Physical fitness	2
	19	Touch football	6
		Speedball	3
		Volleyball	5
		Rhythms	2
			19

Second Semester

	Weeks		Weeks
Orientation	1	Orientation	1
Physical fitness	2	Swimming	18
Basketball	6		19
Tumbling, apparatus	4		
Track and Field	3		
Softball	3		
	19		

GRADE 11

First Semester	Weeks	Second Semester	Weeks
Orientation	1	Orientation	1
Physical fitness	2	Basketball	5
Touch football	4	Tumbling and apparatus	5
Speedball	2	Track and field	4
Volleyball	2	Softball	2
Wrestling	4	Physical fitness and	2
First aid (Red Cross)	4	evaluation	
	19		19

GRADE 12

First Semester

	Weeks		Weeks
Orientation	1	Orientation	1
Physical fitness	2	Wrestling	6
Touch football	5	Volleyball	4
Tennis	3	Electives in minor ·	
Badminton, table tennis		games and recreation	6
and recreational games	5	Physical fitness and	
Tumbling and apparatus	3	Evaluation	2
	19		19

(See legend on opposite page.)

GIRLS

GRADE 10

First Semester

GIRL X	Weeks	GIRL Y	Weeks
Orientation	1	Orientation	1
Swimming	18	Physical fitness	2
	19	Speedball	5
		Volleyball	6
		Rhythms	5
			19

Second Semester

	Weeks		Weeks
Orientation	1	Orientation	1
Physical fitness	2	Swimming	18
Volleyball	5		19
Basketball	5		
Recreational games	4		
Tennis	2		
	19		

GRADE 11

First Semester	Weeks	Second Semester	Weeks
Orientation	1	Orientation	1
Physical fitness	2	Basketball	4
Soccer	4	Table Tennis and	
Field hockey	4	Recreational Games	3
Volleyball	4	Softball	3
Tumbling and trampoline	4	Tennis	2
	19	Physical Fitness and	
		Evaluation	2
		First Aid (Red Cross)	4
			19

GRADE 12

First Semester	Weeks	Second Semester	Weeks
Orientation	1	Orientation	1
Physical fitness	2	Basketball	5
Field hockey	6	Badminton, deck	
Volleyball	5	tennis, etc.	5
Modern dance	5	Archery	3
	19	Tennis	3
		Physical fitness	
		and evaluation	2
			19

Yearly calendar for a small city. (Courtesy Cedar Rapids (Iowa) Community School District.)

SEASONAL PROGRAM—Grades 7, 8, 9*
For Junior High Schools with outdoor facilities

GRADE 7—No. Periods	GRADE 8—No. Periods	GRADE 9—No. Periods
FALL SEMESTER		
OUTDOOR SEASON (September, October, November)		
Organization and Orientation—10 Conditioning—15 Tennis—15 Touch Football—15	Organization and Orientation—15 Soccer—30	Organization and Orientation—15 Football—5 Conditioning and Fitness Testing—15
INDOOR SEASON (December, January)		
Conditioning and Fitness Testing—10 Basketball—15	Gymnastics—30 Volleyball—15	Gymnastics—15 Volleyball—15 Dance, Social—15
SPRING SEMESTER		
INDOOR SEASON (February, March)		
Organization and Orientation—5 Gymnastics—30 Folk and Square Dance—15	Volleyball—5 Conditioning and Fitness Testing—15	Conditioning and Fitness Testing—15 Bowling—15
OUTDOOR SEASON (April, May, June)		
Conditioning and Fitness Testing—15 Other Individual Sports—15 Softball—15 Track and Field—15	Softball—15 Track and Field—15 Golf—15 Handball—15	Basketball—30 Softball—15 Track and Field—15

*From Physical Education for Boys, Grades 7–12. By permission of the Board of Education of the City of New York.

SEASONAL PROGRAM: Grades 10, 11, 12*
For Senior High Schools with outdoor facilities

GRADE 10 — No. Periods	GRADE 11 — No. Periods	GRADE 12 — No. Periods
FALL SEMESTER		
OUTDOOR SEASON (September, October, November)		
Organization and Orientation — 10	Organization and Orientation — 10	Organization and Orientation — 10
Conditioning and Fitness Activities — 5	Soccer — 15	Conditioning and Fitness Activities — 5
Soccer — 15	Football — 30	Volleyball — 15
Football — 15		Soccer — 15
INDOOR SEASON (December, January)		
Conditioning and Fitness Testing — 10	Conditioning and Fitness Testing — 15	Conditioning and Fitness Testing — 10
Dance — 15	Volleyball — 15	Basketball — 30
Volleyball — 15		
SPRING SEMESTER		
INDOOR SEASON (February, March)		
Organization and Orientation — 5	Organization and Orientation — 5	Organization and Orientation — 5
Gymnastics — 15	Gymnastics — 30	Gymnastics — 15
Basketball — 15		Dance — 15
OUTDOOR SEASON (April, May, June)		
Basketball — 15	Softball — 30	Track and Field — 30
Softball — 15	Bowling — 15	Golf — 15
Track and Field — 15	Other Individual and Dual Activities — 15	Tennis — 15
Handball — 15		

*From Physical Education for Boys, Grades 7–12. By permission of the Board of Education of the City of New York.

SEASONAL PROGRAM: Grades 7, 8, 9*
For Junior High Schools
with limited or no outdoor facilities

GRADE 7 — No. Periods	GRADE 8 — No. Periods	GRADE 9 — No. Periods
FALL SEMESTER		
Organization and Orientation — 10 Conditioning and Fitness Testing — 15 Football — 15 Gymnastics — 30 Dance — 15	Organization and Orientation — 10 Gymnastics — 15 Soccer — 30 Volleyball — 30	Organization and Orientation — 10 Conditioning and Fitness Testing — 15 Football (Touch) — 15 Gymnastics — 15 Dance — 15
SPRING SEMESTER		
Organization and Orientation — 5 Basketball — 15 Conditioning and Fitness Testing — 15 Track and Field — 15 Softball — 15 Other Individual and Dual Sports — 15 Tennis — 15	Organization and Orientation — 5 Conditioning and Fitness Testing — 15 Gymnastics — 15 Track and Field — 15 Softball — 15 Handball — 15 Golf — 15	Organization and Orientation — 5 Conditioning and Fitness Testing — 15 Basketball — 30 Track and Field — 15 Bowling — 15 Softball — 15

*From Physical Education for Boys, Grades 7–12. By permission of the Board of Education of the City of New York.

SEASONAL PROGRAM: Grades 10, 11, 12*
For Senior High Schools
with limited or no outdoor facilities

GRADE 10 — No. Periods	GRADE 11 — No. Periods	GRADE 12 — No. Periods
FALL SEMESTER		
Organization and Orientation — 10 Conditioning and Fitness Testing — 15 Soccer — 15 Football — 15 Volleyball — 15 Gymnastics — 15	Organization and Orientation — 10 Conditioning and Fitness Testing — 15 Soccer — 15 Football — 15 Volleyball — 15	Organization and Orientation — 10 Conditioning and Fitness Testing — 15 Soccer — 15 Basketball — 30 Dance — 15
SPRING SEMESTER		
Organization and Orientation — 5 Basketball — 30 Dance — 15 Track and Field — 15 Softball — 15 Handball — 15	Organization and Orientation — 5 Gymnastics — 30 Softball — 30 Bowling — 15 Other Individual and Dual Sports — 15	Organization and Orientation — 5 Gymnastics — 15 Volleyball — 15 Track and Field — 30 Golf — 15 Tennis — 15

*From Physical Education for Boys, Grades 7–12. By permission of the Board of Education of the City of New York.

An illustration of how one state classifies and allots time to the various groups is shown in the guide developed by the Arkansas State Department of Education. The guide includes six classification groups in grades 7 through 12 and time allotments for both boys and girls.[11] See Figure 7–7.

It should be interesting for teachers to use the criteria in Chapter 6 to evaluate the activities included in the yearly calendars outlined above. Also the teacher may wish to study the calendars and determine which of the three or which combination of the three plans should be used.

Now that teachers are familiar with the yearly calendar and time allotment of activities, they should have an overview of the various patterns for including these activities in the school program. The following section of the chapter provides this overview.

Scope and Sequence

A successful curriculum depends largely on the scope and sequence of the instructional content. *Scope* means the materials, areas and body of knowledge that will be included in the total curriculum (see Chapter 6). *Sequence* refers to the way in which the body of knowledge is placed in the various grades. Using the activities selected in Chapter 6, p. 154 (scope), Figure 7–5 shows how these may be arranged (sequence) in a school with physical education required in grades 7 through 12.

One scope and sequence arrangement of a year's program for the junior and senior high school including the time allotment is shown in Figures 7–8 and 7–9. Another arrangement is shown in Figure 7–10, which was taken from the Guidebook of the Grace M. Davis High School, Modesto, California.

In addition to arranging curriculum content as shown in Figures 7–8, 7–9, and 7–10, scope and sequence can be further developed to include the skills of the various activities as they appear in the various grade levels. This phase of curriculum construction, as described in a section from the guidebook used by the New York City Public Schools, is shown in Figure 7–11.

ORGANIZATIONAL PATTERNS

An arrangement commonly known as the 6-3-3 plan is prevalent throughout the country. The 6-3-3 plan places the first six grades in the elementary school, grades 7 through 9 in the junior high school and 10 through 12 in the senior high school.

Junior High School—Orientation of Activities

The purpose of physical education in junior high school is to orient the pupil in a wide variety of activities with emphasis on the teaching of skills. The actual participation in the activity should take place during the intramural, recreational, or other programs outside the class, since there is sufficient time for such activities only in after-school hours. The class instruction should be thorough in the teaching of skills and planned so as to motivate the pupil to practice after school what he learned in the instruction class. Nash, Moench, and Sauborn define junior high school instruction in this way: "The junior high school period is best adapted to the learning of a large number of fundamental skills. . . . Generalization rather than specialization is advised . . ."[12]

Bossing and Cramer describe how orientation and exploratory courses may provide new learning experiences, stimulating personal interest in the junior high school. They emphasize this point of view in discussing the purpose of the junior high school:

It is increasingly evident that the personal interest program is being assigned an integral role in the junior high school curriculum and is required to be as broad as is feasible for effective accommodation of the needs of all students . . . and it should be the concern not only of special teachers but of all school staff members, particularly those participating in block-time or core programs.[13]

In the late 1940's the Norfolk City Public Schools developed a program of orientation and student choice (electives) that has proved successful, having operated continuously in fifteen junior and senior high schools despite austere budgets and rapidly changing times. Since the Norfolk system is organized around the 6-3-3 concept and the physical education program

(Text continued on page 197.)

TYPE OF ACTIVITY	SEVENTH GRADE		EIGHTH GRADE		NINTH GRADE		TENTH GRADE		ELEVENTH GRADE		TWELFTH GRADE		SAMPLE ACTIVITIES
	Boys	Girls	Boys	Girls	Boys	Girls	Boys	Girls	Boys	Girls	Boys	Girls	
Rhythmic Activities	15%	30%	15%	30%	15%	30%	10%	30%	10%	30%	10%	30%	Fundamentals of rhythms, folk games, mixers, square dancing, modern dance, singing games.
Team Activities (Highly organized team sports)	30	25	30	25	30	30	35	30	35	30	35	30	Basketball, baseball, touch football, volleyball, soccer, speedball, field hockey, field ball, speed-a-way.
Individual activities (Individual sports and recreational activities)	20	20	20	20	20	20	30	30	30	30	30	30	Tennis, golf, badminton, bowling, archery, table tennis, handball, shuffle board, track and field, horseshoes, deck tennis, aerial darts, paddle tennis, fly and bait casting, swimming, skating, quiet games, camping, canoeing and boating.
Self Testing Activities	15	10	15	10	15	10	20	5	20	5	20	5	Tumbling, pyramid building, apparatus activities, wrestling, individual and dual stunts, rope climbing, rope jumping, and trampoline activities.
Games and Relays	15	10	15	10	15	5							Wheelbarrow relay, two-legged relay, crab walk race, obstacle race, leap frog relay, overhead relay goalthrowing relay, dodge ball, keep-away.
Body Mechanics and Conditioning Activities	5	5	5	5	5	5	5	5	5	5	5	5	Fundamentals and practice of walking, running, sitting, lifting, pushing, carrying, standing. Exercises for strength and endurance. Example: push-ups, sit-ups, chinning.

Figure 7-7. Time allotments for activities for boys and girls according to grade. (Courtesy of State Department of Education – A Guide for Secondary Schools in Arkansas. Little Rock, Arkansas.)

CHART I: NORMAL PROGRAM

Time Allotment for Activities Based on 5 periods per week; every semester.

This chart offers suggested time allotment for the entire course of study. Adjustment may be made in accordance with local facilities, equipment, and personnel. On a basis of 180 periods per year, 15 have been allotted for organization and orientation, 10 periods in the Fall and 5 in the Spring.

ACTIVITY	Jr. H.S. (Per. per year)			Sr. H.S. (Per. per year)		
	7th	8th	9th	10th	11th	12th
CONDITIONING AND PHYSICAL FITNESS TEST	30	15	30	15	15	15
DANCE Folk and Square	15			15		
Social			15			15
GYMNASTICS Apparatus, Tumbling, Ropes, Rebound Tumbling	30	30	15	30	30*	15
INDIVIDUAL AND DUAL SPORTS Bowling			15		15	
Handball		15		15		
Golf		15				15
Tennis	15					15
Others: (Ping-Pong, Badminton, Paddle Tennis, Tetherball, etc.)					15*	
TEAM SPORTS Basketball	15		30	30		30
Soccer		30		15	15*	15
Softball (Baseball)	15	15	15	15	30*	
Touch Football	15		15	15	30*	
Volleyball		15	15	15	15*	15
TRACK AND FIELD	15	15	15	15		30
AQUATICS	(If facilities are available)					
GAMES Low Organization, Contests,	(If time permits)			(If time permits)		
Relays, Self-Testing,						
Mass Games						
TOTALS	165	165	165	165	165	165

*Schools offering Hygiene (Health Teaching) in the 11th Year should omit these 15-period units and give 30-period units for only 15 periods.

Figure 7–8. *Physical Education for Boys, Grades 7–12.* Board of Education of the City of New York, 1964.

MODIFYING THE NORMAL PROGRAM (CHART I)

Schools offering Physical Education five times per week in alternate semesters will multiply the suggested time allotment in Chart I by 0.5. Schools which offer four periods per week every semester will multiply the time allotment by 0.8. Schools with three periods per week will multiply by 0.6. A short program based on the needs of some junior-high schools is shown below.

CHART II. SHORT PROGRAM

Time Allotment for Activities based on 2 periods per week, every semester. Nine periods have been allotted for organization and orientation of the class.

ACTIVITY	Jr. H.S. (Per. per year)			Sr. H.S. (Per. per year)		
	7th	8th	9th	10th	11th	12th
CONDITIONING AND PHYSICAL FITNESS TESTING	12	6	12	6	6	6
DANCE Folk and Square	6		6	6		6
Social						
GYMNASTICS Apparatus, Tumbling, Ropes, Rebound Tumbling, Pyramids, Stunts	12	12	6	6	12	6
INDIVIDUAL AND DUAL SPORTS Bowling			6		6	
Golf		6				6
Handball		6		6		
Tennis	6				6	
Others: (Ping-Pong, Badminton, Paddle Tennis, Tetherball, etc.)	6				6	
TEAM SPORTS Basketball	6		12	12		12
Soccer		12		6	6	6
Softball (Baseball)	6	6	6	6	12	
Touch Football	6		6	6	12	
Volleyball		12	6	6	6	6
TRACK AND FIELD	6	6	6	6		12
AQUATICS	(If facilities are available)					
GAMES Low Organization, Relays, Mass Games, Self-Testing	(If the time permits)					
TOTALS	66	66	66	66	72	60

Figure 7–9. *Physical Education for Boys, Grades 7–12.* Board of Education of the City of New York, 1964.

BOYS' PHYSICAL EDUCATION BLOCKS

Vacation	Block	Dates	Days	Freshmen	Sophomore	Juniors	Seniors
		Sept. 10 to Sept. 15	4	ORIENTATION			
	1	Sept. 16 to Oct. 10	19	Gymnastics	Basketball	Speedball	Volleyball
	2	Oct. 13 to Oct. 31	15	Basketball	Gymnastics	Volleyball	Kanaki
Nov. 11 — — — Nov. 27–28	3	Nov. 3 to Nov. 28	17	Track	Speedball	Gymnastics	Basketball
	4	Dec. 1 to Dec. 19	15	Volleyball	Kanaki	Wrestling	Golf
		Dec. 22 to Jan. 2		CHRISTMAS VACATION			
	5	Jan. 5 to Jan. 26	16	Football	Volleyball	Coed. Dance – Basketball	Speedball
		Jan. 27 to Jan. 30	4				
Feb. 12 — — — Feb. 23	6	Feb. 2 to Feb. 27	18	Swimming	Wrestling	Badminton	Softball
	7	March 2 to March 20	15	Wrestling	Swimming	Golf	Co-ed. Badminton
		March 23–27		EASTER VACATION			
	8	March 30 to April 17	15	Speedball	Softball	Swimming	Weight Training
	9	April 20 to May 8	15	Softball	Track	Kanaki	Swimming
May 29	10	May 11 to June 8	21	Optional	Optional	Optional	Optional
		June 9 to June 12	4	FINALS			

Note: 1. Mass Exercises—1st 10 min. of each period.
2. Rainy Day Schedule—Boys in Gym area.
3. Physical Fitness Days—Fresh.-Soph., Mon. & Wed.
   Juniors-Seniors, Tues. & Thurs.

Figure 7–10. Scope and sequence arrangement of activities. (Courtesy Grace M. Davis High School, Modesto, California.)

SCOPE AND SEQUENCE:
(Grade Placement of Skills in Bowling)

	JUNIOR HIGH SCHOOL			SENIOR HIGH SCHOOL		
GRADE:	7	8	9	10	11	12
KNOWLEDGE						
History of the game			B		R	
Scoring Techniques			B		R	
Basic rules of the game			B		R	
Equipment and care of equipment						
Selection of a ball			B		R	
Selection of shoes			B		R	
Glossary of terms used			B		B	
Safety precautions			B		B	
Etiquette of the game			B		B	
SKILLS						
Position for delivery			B		R	
Straight ball			B		R	
Hook ball					ADV.	
Four step delivery			B		R	
Three and five step deliveries					O	
Release of the ball						
Straight ball			B		R	
Hook ball					ADV.	
Curve ball					ADV.	
Follow through			B		R	
Pin bowling			B		R	
Spot bowling					B	
Pin falls						
Left side spares			O		B	
Right side spares			O		B	
Converting the splits			O		ADV.	
KNOWLEDGE AND SKILL TESTS			B		B	
LEADUP GAMES AND DRILLS			B		B	
CULMINATING ACTIVITY (Visit to local alley; Intramural Tournament)			B		B	

Figure 7–11.   Scope and Sequence of skills of an individual activity. (From *Physical Education for Boys, Grades 7–12.* Board of Education of the City of New York, 1964.)

operates within that structure, a discussion of the program seems appropriate. The two phases, junior high school and senior high school, will be discussed separately.

In Norfolk, physical education and health are required daily subjects with full academic credit (one credit per year) from grades 7 through 10, which become elective in grades 11 and 12. Pupils may earn as many credits in physical education as they do in English or other academic subjects.

The following yearly calendar shows how the orientation plan works in the Norfolk program. The seasonal organizational calendar incorporates the time allotment and placement of activities. Note that some of the academic instruction in skills, such as presentation of rules of the game, are offered in the health classes.

Overview of the Program. The orientation procedure, which is used in the junior high school, is described as follows:

1. All junior high schools in Norfolk have six teaching stations (three gymnasia, three health rooms) and six teachers (three men and three women). The activity alternates weekly with health instruction.
2. In the activity program, each of the three teachers and his class rotate around each activity, spending the allotted time as shown below.
3. In the third cycle, because of the time element, all three teachers teach tumbling or body mechanics at the same time for two weeks.[14]

Weeks	Boys	Girls
ONE WEEK:	ORGANIZATION	ORGANIZATION
Each teacher spends one week organizing classes and planning for the semester's work.	1. Fill out individual cards. 2. Send handbooks home—parents sign and return. 3. Collect money for towels. 4. Set deadline for suits (one week). 5. Explain the program (use handbook). 6. Fill out permanent cards (new pupils). 7. Explain and promote intramurals. 8. Explain alternate use of facilities with health instruction.	1. Fill out individual cards. 2. Send handbooks home—parents sign and return. 3. Collect money for towels. 4. Set deadline for suits (one week). 5. Explain the program (use handbook). 6. Fill out permanent cards (new pupils). 7. Explain and promote intramurals. 8. Explain alternate use of facilities with health instruction.
ONE WEEK:	PROFICIENCY TESTS	PROFICIENCY TESTS
These tests may be given at another time if desired.	1. Pull-ups 2. Dash (50 yd.) 3. Sit-ups (per min.) 4. Standing broad jump 5. Agility run (40 yd.)	1. Wall push (30 sec.) 2. Sit-ups (30 sec.) 3. Dash (40 yd.) 4. Agility run (30 yd.) 5. Pull-up (modified)
FIRST CYCLE (THREE WEEKS): Each teacher spends one week on each activity.	Touch football skills—one week Rules—Friday during health class 1. Stance 2. Blocking formations 3. Passing formations 4. Receiving passes formation 5. Carrying ball 6. The touch 7. Punting	Hockey skills—one week Rules—Friday during health class 1. Grip 2. Dribble 3. Passing 4. Dodging 5. Tackle 6. Goal shooting 7. Relays employing skills
Remember: teaching the skills is the chief aim.	Bowling skills—one week Rules—Friday during health class	Bowling skills—one week Rules—Friday during health class

(Program continued on following page.)

Weeks	Boys	Girls
Teachers will arrange skills by days as they wish. It is imperative that all skills be taught in the time allowed. Encourage pupils to enter the intramural program.	1. Grip 2. Stance 3. Approach 4. Delivery 5. Follow through 6. Aiming Table tennis skills—one week Rules—Friday during health class 1. Grip 2. Serve 3. Footwork 4. Return 5. Spins	1. Grip 2. Stance 3. Approach 4. Delivery 5. Follow through 6. Aiming Table tennis skills—one week Rules—Friday during health class 1. Grip 2. Serve 3. Footwork 4. Return 5. Spins

SECOND CYCLE (SIX WEEKS):
 	
Each teacher spends two weeks on each activity.
 	
Remember: Teaching the skills is the chief aim.
 	
Teachers will arrange skills by days as they wish. It is imperative that all skills be taught in the time allowed.
 	
Encourage pupils to enter the intramural program.
 	
Teacher and class rotate to new activity every two weeks.
	Basketball skills—two weeks
	Rules—Friday during health class
	
	1. Foul shots
	2. Shooting
	3. Dribbling
	4. Basic passes
	5. Pivot
	6. Guarding
	   (man to man)
	
	Wrestling skills—two weeks
	
	Scoring—Friday during health class
	
	1. Referee position
	2. Break downs
	3. Reverses and escapes
	4. Pins
	5. Counters
	6. Scoring
	
	Volleyball skills—two weeks
	
	Rules—Friday during health class
	
	1. Underhand serve
	2. Passing
	3. Set-ups
	4. Recover from net
	5. Rotation
		Basketball skills—two weeks
		Rules—Friday during health class
		
		1. Passes
		2. Foul shots
		3. Dribbling
		4. Pivot
		5. Set shot
		6. Lay-up
		7. Guarding
		
		Rhythmic skills—two weeks
		
		1. Warm-up exercises and techniques of rotation, stretching, and flexion
		2. Forms of locomotion: skip, hop, slide, gallop, walk, run, leap, and jump
		3. Traditional steps:
		   two-step, waltz, mazurka, polka, and schottische
		4. Interpretive movements
		
		Volleyball skills—two weeks
		
		Rules—Friday during health class
		
		1. Underhand serve
		2. Passing
		3. Set-ups
		4. Recover from net
		5. Volleying
		6. Rotation

(Program continued on opposite page.)

Senior High School—Election of Activities

The purpose of the senior high school program is to allow pupils to follow their interests in particular activities and to assist them in attaining a high degree of performance in those activities in which they wish to excel.

Pupils reaching the senior high school should have had an extensive orientation in a great number of skills during their elementary and junior high school years.

Weeks	Boys	Girls
THIRD CYCLE (TWO WEEKS):	Tumbling skills—two weeks	Body mechanic skills—two weeks
Each teacher spends two weeks on tumbling. Remember: teaching the skills is the chief aim. Encourage pupils to enter the intramural program	1. Forward roll 2. Shoulder roll 3. Back roll 4. Squat balance 5. Hand stand 6. Head stand	1. Conditioning exercises 2. Balances; jump and turn, Chinese get-up, knee dip, cartwheel, hand stand, and head stand 3. Rolls: human roll, forward roll, backward roll, combination, Eskimo roll, and forward roll through arch 4. Walks: seal crawl, duck walk, wheel barrow, and crab walk 5. Simple stunts: flying angel, back to back and over, scooter, and back bend
FOURTH CYCLE (SIX WEEKS):	Tennis skills—two weeks Rules—Friday during health class	Tennis skills—two weeks Rules—Friday during health class
Each teacher spends two weeks on each activity Remember: teaching the skills is the chief aim.	1. Grip 2. Forehand 3. Backhand 4. Serve 5. Volley 6. Lob	1. Grip 2. Forehand 3. Backhand 4. Serve 5. Volley 6. Lob
Teachers will arrange skills by days as they wish. It is imperative that all skills be taught in the time allowed.	Track skills—two weeks Rules—Friday during health class 1. Starts 2. Dash 3. Low hurdles 4. Running broad jump 5. Relay	Archery skills—two weeks Rules—Friday during health class 1. String 2. Stance 3. Nock 4. Draw 5. Anchoring 6. Aim
Encourage pupils to enter the intramural program. Teacher and class rotate every two weeks.	Golf skills—two weeks Rules—Friday during health class 1. Grip 2. Stance 3. Swing 4. Follow through 5. Putting 6. Drive 7. Scoring	Golf skills—two weeks Rules—Friday during health class 1. Grip 2. Stance 3. Swing 4. Follow through 5. Putting 6. Drive 7. Scoring

Preferences change with age. As the years pass by, the pupils form likes and dislikes for various activities based on their individual anatomical structures, physiological limitations, and psychological attitudes.

Thus, it is good educational procedure to periodically allow pupils in high school to make a *choice of activities within the requirement and from a scientifically selected list of activities which constitute the curriculum.* Teachers should make every effort to assist pupils in improving their skill performance and in motivating them to participate in the intramural program. Nash, Moench, and

Sauborn point to the importance of the elective program:

It is predicted that the high school of tomorrow will provide each student with an area of free choice of physical education activities, beyond the conditioning program, based on student's health and physical fitness. Students will be allowed to follow their own interests and teachers will give attention to instructing students in activities of their own choice. The aim — everyone able to do well whatever he chooses to do.[12]

A recent study of physical education curricula by Hermann and Osness showed the advantages of the elective program over the traditional curriculum. They state that:

There is considerable doubt that traditional programs of physical education are equipped by design or intent to serve the needs of children and youth today. The programs are almost exclusively activity oriented with little or no attention given to developing concepts about physical activity itself or an understanding of the mechanics of movement.[15]

They continue with their analysis of content arrangement and elaborate fully on the laboratory approach by suggesting the need for blocks of activities with emphasis on the acquisition of skills:

The student would be able to choose any two of these blocks during the two semesters. Complete

FALL AND WINTER

Weeks	Boys	Girls
ONE WEEK: Each teacher spends one week organizing classes and planning for the semester's work.	ORGANIZATION 1. Fill out individual cards. 2. Send handbooks home — parents sign and return. 3. Collect money for towels. 4. Set deadline for suits (one week). 5. Explain the program (use handbooks). 6. Fill out permanent cards. 7. Explain and promote intramurals. 8. Explain alternate use of facilities with health instruction.	ORGANIZATION 1. Fill out individual cards. 2. Send handbooks home — parents sign and return. 3. Collect money for towels. 4. Set deadline for suits (one week). 5. Explain the program (use handbooks). 6. Fill out permanent cards. 7. Explain and promote intramurals. 8. Explain alternate use of facilities with health instruction.
ONE WEEK:	PROFICIENCY TESTS 1. Chin 2. Dash (50 yd.) 3. Sit-ups (min.) 4. Standing broad jump 5. Agility run (40 yd.)	PROFICIENCY TESTS 1. Wall push (30 sec.) 2. Sit-ups (30 sec.) 3. Dash (40 yd.) 4. Agility run (30 sec.) 5. Pull-up (modified)
FIRST CHOICE PERIOD (THREE WEEKS): Pupils choose which of three activities they wish to participate in for two weeks. Teachers decide which activity they will teach. The teacher with the most experience in an activity teaches that activity.	Bowling — inside 1. Review junior high skills 2. Advanced skills: deliveries, aim, spare bowling Volleyball — outside 1. Review junior high skills 2. Advanced skills: overhand serve, spiking, attack, defense, handling Touch football — outside 1. Review junior high skills 2. Advanced skills	Bowling — inside 1. Review junior high skills 2. Advanced skills: deliveries, aim, spare bowling Volleyball — outside 1. Review junior high skills 2. Advanced skills: overhand serve, spiking, attack, defense, handling Hockey — outside 1. Review junior high skills 2. Advanced skills

(Program continued on opposite page.)

coverage of a few activities would be achieved rather than skimming a large number, some of which may not be suited to the individual.[15]

However, it is imperative that pupils learn how to select activities wisely. All choices should be preceded by a period of orientation, preferably in the junior high school. If this is not possible, each free-choice period in the senior high school should be preceded by an appropriate orientation period during the first year of the high school program.

The elective plan has been used in all of the senior high schools in Norfolk, Virginia, for 22 years and operates in conjunction with the junior high school orientation program. The program is described on the following pages.

Overview of the Program. The senior high school physical education program allows pupils a choice of activities from the approved curriculum and assists the pupil in attaining a higher degree of performance than that developed in the junior high school. After the pupils make their choices of the activities available in the seasonal category, the teachers are assigned to the activity for which they are best qualified. Pupils are allowed to make three choices each semester.[14]

Weeks	Boys	Girls
SECOND CHOICE PERIOD (THREE WEEKS): Pupils choose which of three activities they wish to participate in for three weeks. Teachers teach activity they are best qualified to teach.	Wrestling—inside 1. Review junior high skills 2. Advanced skills: basic position, methods of going behind, take-downs	Body mechanics—inside 1. Review junior high skills 2. Advanced skills: exercises, stunts, roll progression, dive progression, inverted balances, balances, combat stunts, stunts for groups, figures
	Volleyball—outside 1. Review junior high skills 2. Advanced skills: overhand serve, spiking, attack, defense, handling	Volleyball—outside 1. Review junior high skills 2. Advanced skills: overhand serve, spiking, attack, defense, handling
	Touch football—outside 1. Review junior high skills 2. Advanced skills	Hockey—outside 1. Review junior high skills 2. Advanced skills
THIRD CHOICE PERIOD (TWO WEEKS): Pupils choose which of three activities they wish to participate in for two weeks. Teachers teach activity they are best qualified to teach.	Wrestling—inside 1. Review junior high skills 2. Advanced skills: basic positions, methods of going behind, take downs	Body mechanics—inside 1. Review junior high skills 2. Advanced skills: exercises, stunts, roll progression, dive progression, inverted balances, balances, combat stunts, stunts for groups, figures
	Tumbling—inside 1. Review junior high skills 2. Advanced skills: dive and rolls, kip or snap-up, hand spring (back and front), front flip, back flip, round off, combinations	Basketball—inside 1. Review junior high skills 2. Advanced skills: zone defense, man-to-man defense, offensive strategy, team plays, formations, relays
	Basketball—inside 1. Review junior high skills 2. Advanced skills: zone defense, man-to-man defense, team plays, formations, offensive strategy, relays	

SPRING

Weeks	Boys	Girls
ONE WEEK:	ORGANIZATION	ORGANIZATION
Each teacher spends each week organizing classes and planning for the semester's work. Teachers teach activities they are best qualified to teach.	1. Fill out individual cards. 2. Send handbooks home—parents sign and return. 3. Collect money for towels. 4. Set deadline for suits (one week). 5. Explain the program (use handbook). 6. Fill out permanent cards (new pupils). 7. Explain and promote intramurals. 8. Explain alternate use of facilities with health instructions.	1. Fill out individual cards. 2. Send handbooks home—parents sign and return. 3. Collect money for towels. 4. Set deadline for suits (one week). 5. Explain the program (use handbook). 6. Fill out permanent cards (new pupils). 7. Explain and promote intramurals. 8. Explain alternate use of facilities with health instructions.
FIRST CHOICE PERIOD (TWO WEEKS): Pupils choose which of three activities they wish to participate in for two weeks. Teachers teach activity they are best qualified to teach.	Wrestling—inside 1. Review junior high skills 2. Advanced skills: basic positions, methods of going behind, take downs Tumbling—inside 1. Review junior high skills 2. Advanced skills: dive and roll, kip or snap-up, hand spring Basketball—inside 1. Review junior high skills 2. Advanced skills: zone defense, man-to-man defense, offensive strategy, team plays, formations, relays	Body mechanics—inside 1. Review junior high skills 2. Advanced skills: exercises, stunts, roll progression, dive progression, inverted balances, balances, combat stunts, stunts for groups, figures Basketball—inside 1. Review junior high skills 2. Advanced skills: zone defense, man-to-man defense, offensive strategy, team plays, formations, relays Rhythmics—inside 1. Review junior high skills 2. Advanced skills: use elementary skills and create movements, sports skills to music and athletic rhythms
SECOND CHOICE PERIOD (THREE WEEKS): Pupils choose which of three activities they wish to participate in for three weeks.	Track—inside, outside 1. Review junior high skills 2. Advanced skills: high hurdles, high jump (Western roll), shot put, pole vault, 220 dash, 440 dash	Track, relays, dashes—inside, outside 1. Review junior high skills 2. Advanced skills: relays, dashes, starts

(Program continued on opposite page.)

Weeks	Boys	Girls
Teachers teach activity they are best qualified to teach	Tennis—inside, outside 1. Review junior high skills 2. Advanced skills: court positions (singles and doubles), smashing, half volley, stop volley, baseline play Table tennis—inside 1. Review junior high skills 2. Advanced skills: strokes, half volley, forehand spin, backhand drive, forehand chop, backhand chop, drop shot, smash shot, doubles, strategy	Tennis—inside, outside 1. Review junior high skills 2. Advanced skills: court positions (singles and doubles), net play (singles and doubles), smashing, half volley, stop volley, baseline play Table tennis—inside 1. Review junior high skills 2. Advanced skills: strokes, half volley, forehand spin, backhand drop, forehand chop, backhand chop, drop shot, smash shot, doubles, strategy
THIRD CHOICE PERIOD (THREE WEEKS): Pupils choose which of three activities they wish to participate in for three weeks. Teacher teach activities they are best qualified to teach.	Track—outside 1. Review junior high skills 2. Advanced skills: high hurdles, high jump (Western roll only), shot put, pole vault, 220 dash, 440 dash Tennis—outside 1. Review junior high skills 2. Advanced skills: net play (singles and doubles), smashing, half volley, stop volley, baseline play Golf—outside 1. Review junior high skills 2. Advanced skills: clubs and distances, approaches, individual and groups, etiquette, play	Archery—outside 1. Review junior high skills 2. Advanced skills Tennis—outside 1. Review junior high skills 2. Advanced skills: court positions (singles and doubles), net play (singles and doubles), smashing, half volley, stop volley, baseline play Golf—outside 1. Review junior high skills 2. Advanced skills: clubs and distances, approaches, individual and groups, play, etiquette
ONE WEEK:	PROFICIENCY TESTS 1. Chin 2. Dash (50 yd.) 3. Sit-ups (min.) 4. Standing broad jump 5. Agility run (40 yd.)	PROFICIENCY TESTS 1. Wall push (30 sec.) 2. Sit-ups (30 sec.) 3. Dash (40 yd.) 4. Agility run (30 yd.) 5. Pull-up (modified)

Advantages of the Elective Program.
Pupil selection of activities has many advantages on the senior high school level. Experience in the Norfolk program reveals these advantages:

1. It allows the pupils to specialize.
2. It provides for individual differences.
3. It provides better staff utilization through team teaching and allows the teachers to teach those activities that they are best qualified to teach.
4. It eliminates most discipline problems because pupils participate in the activity of their choice.
5. It minimizes organizational difficulties.

ALLOWS PUPILS TO SPECIALIZE. Pupils are able to spend more time on the activity they enjoy and for which they are best suited. This free-choice participation encourages them to become proficient in an activity they can carry over into later life.

PROVIDES FOR INDIVIDUAL DIFFERENCES. It has been shown that boys and girls are by nature more successful in some activities than in others. When pupils select activities, they select those activities which experience has shown them they excel in because of anatomical, physiological, and psychological factors.

PROVIDES FOR BETTER STAFF UTILIZATION THROUGH TEAM TEACHING. If the purpose of the senior high school is to assist pupils in attaining superior performance in those activities in which they are predisposed to excel, then the teacher who is best qualified to teach the activity should be assigned to it. Team teaching allows for a reassignment of the teacher's time, placing the best qualified teacher in the proper activity. Although teachers are expected to teach many activities, they are rarely expert in all. However, each teacher is usually expert in one or two activities, and through the team teaching procedure his special talents may be used to assist groups in attaining a higher degree of performance.

Team teaching and pupil choice go hand in hand, and the combination of these two procedures will improve the quality of instruction. Twenty-two years of experimentation with the team teaching-pupil choice plan in the Norfolk Public Schools corroborates this premise. In the plan, the teachers not only teach the activity for which they are best qualified, but they also work cooperatively in planning the mechanics of organization, teaching procedures, assisting pupils in the selection of activities and in attending to other details that are involved in the teaching of physical education.

MINIMIZES DISCIPLINARY PROBLEMS. Since they are participating in the activities of their choice, pupils are more inclined to report to class promptly, dress properly, refrain from bringing notes to be excused, enter into the learning situation with more interest, and cooperate with the teacher. Many time-consuming chores—checking tardy pupils, questioning pupils as to why they are not dressed properly—will tend to disappear when pupils are allowed to participate in activities of their choice.

MINIMIZES ORGANIZATIONAL DIFFICULTIES. When pupils select activities they like, teachers do not have to spend precious time checking tardy pupils, inquiring about dress, and becoming involved in many of the organizational difficulties that stem from student lack of interest in the teacher-imposed activity.

Other Elective Programs. The following paragraphs are examples of four elective programs in the following cities: Livonia, Michigan; Racine, Wisconsin; Modesto, California; and Tucson, Arizona.

LIVONIA, MICHIGAN. Believing that students should be allowed choice in the selection of activities, the girls' department of physical education at Stevenson High School, Livonia, Michigan, developed a curriculum based on electives. The program grew out of dissatisfaction with the traditional approach in which a teacher had dominated the instruction with the result that he had to continually explain the necessity for each phase of instruction.[16]

After one week of introductory units, the format consists of day-by-day choices by each student for participating in the areas of interest. Three different activities are covered during each of three six-weeks marking periods. The school year is divided into two semesters as shown:

FIRST SEMESTER

1st six weeks
Tennis
Field Hockey
Self Testing #1

2nd six weeks
Basketball ⎫ Elective for Intermediate-
Folk and Square Dance ⎭   Advanced Ability Group
Swimming   Beginner-Intermediate
   Ability Group

3rd six weeks
Basketball ⎫ Elective for Beginner-
Folk and Square Dance ⎭   Intermediate Ability Group
Swimming   Intermediate-Advanced
   Ability Group

SECOND SEMESTER

1st six weeks
Health ⎫ Elective for Beginner-
Modern Dance ⎭   Intermediate Ability Group
Gymnastics   Intermediate-Advanced
   Ability Group

2nd six weeks
Health ⎫ Elective for Intermediate-
Modern Dance ⎭   Advanced Ability Group
Gymnastics   Beginner-Intermediate
   Ability Group

3rd six weeks
Softball
Track and Field
Self Testing #2

Pupils are allowed to earn credits for marking purposes through performance and participation. These credits are awarded as follows:

2 standard performances = $1/4$ credit
3 quality performances = $1/2$ credit
4 standard performances = $1/2$ credit
5 standard performances = $3/4$ credit
5 quality performances = 1 credit
Officiating = $1/4$ credit
Standard Participation = $1/4$ credit
Quality Participation = $1/2$ credit

Marks are based on the following plan:

A = $1\frac{1}{2}$ credits
B = $1\frac{1}{4}$ credits
C = 1 credit
D = $1/2$ credit

The girls are shown how credits may be earned by studying sheets which are developed for this purpose. Sample sheets are shown for one team sport and one individual sport.

BASKETBALL ELECTIVE

	Standard Performance	*Quality Performance*
AREA 1 Rules Test	Pass with 70%	Pass with 80%
AREA 2 Participation	7 days practice, 1 of which is full court	11 days practice, 1 of which is full court
AREA 3 Shooting		
1. Short shots, any technique	6 baskets in 30 seconds	10 baskets in 30 seconds
2. Free throws, any technique	1 out of 4	2 out of 4

BASKETBALL ELECTIVE (*Continued*)

AREA 4 Passing

1. Chest pass to target (1 block in wall, chest high), 10' from wall	5 accurate passes in 10 seconds	8 accurate passes in 10 seconds
2. Two-hand overhead throw to wall and catch from 5' restraining line (no batting)	8 passes in 10 seconds	12 passes in 10 seconds

AREA 5 Dribbling

Dribble alternately around 4 markers placed 8' apart and start to first marker is 5' start to fourth marker is 45'	14.0 seconds	12.1 seconds

AREA 6 Playing ability   Instructor rated

AREA 7 Officiating
1. Pass rules test with 90%
2. Officiate tests
3. Officiate 4 days, 1 of which is an official game
4. Instructor's recommendation

REQUIRED SWIMMING
BEGINNER AND INTERMEDIATE

	Standard Performance	Quality Performance
AREA 1 Front crawl Coordinated stroke Rhythmic breathing on alternate sides for at least 2 lengths	4 lengths	10 lengths
AREA 2 Crawl *or* Elementary back stroke	4 lengths 4 lengths	10 lengths 10 lengths
AREA 3 Breaststroke	4 lengths	10 lengths
AREA 4 Sidestroke *or* Overarm sidestroke Half the distance swum on each side	4 lengths 4 lengths	10 lengths 10 lengths
AREA 5 Distance Any coordinated stroke or combination of strokes swum without stopping at ends for rest	¼ mile (18 lengths)	½ mile (36 lengths)
AREA 6 Supplementary strokes Butterfly Inverted breaststroke Double trudgeon Single trudgeon Trudgeon crawl	2 lengths 2 lengths 4 lengths 4 lengths 4 lengths	5 lengths 5 lengths 10 lengths 10 lengths 10 lengths
AREA 7 Special credit Basic dive Pass 4 written tests (short ones)	¼ credit for each of these	

RACINE, WISCONSIN. An example of how high school students may profit by allowing them choice in selecting activities is well illustrated by the program at J. L. Case High School, Racine, Wisconsin.

Although the program is required for three years (grades 10 through 12), activities may be selected *within* the program. All activities are grouped into five categories: team sports, conditioning exercises, swimming, gymnastics, lifetime sports and coeducational activities. Each student must choose nine activities each year with a stipulated number from each category.

The program at Case High School is unique. All students are required to have a 55 minute program daily. Each teaching unit runs from three to five weeks, and choices are made at the end of each unit.

Varied facilities exist at the school, including a field house, an auxiliary gymnasium, an Olympic-size swimming pool, and outdoor fields and courts. The staff consists of six women teachers, seven men, one full-time and one half-time aide.

The following curriculum, which is used at Case High School, shows the required and elected activities:[17]

GIRLS' PROGRAM

Grade Ten

Team Sports — Girls are required to take field hockey and one of the following: volleyball, basketball, softball, or speedball.

Conditioning — Girls must take two of the following activities: individual study, body mechanics, track and field.

Dance — Girls must participate in either modern dance or folk dance.

Swimming — Girls must participate in a nonswimmer, beginner, intermediate, or advanced swimming unit.

Gymnastics — Beginning tumbling is required.

Lifetime Sports — Girls must take part in one of the following: badminton, tennis, or archery.

Coeducation — Dancing is required.

Fitness — Girls must participate in a two-week fitness unit, which includes time for fitness testing.

Grade Eleven

Team Sports — Girls are required to take two of the following: field hockey, volleyball, basketball, softball, and speedball.

Conditioning — Girls must elect one of the following: individual study, body mechanics, track and field, or speedball.

Dance — Girls must take either modern dance, folk dance, or tap dance.

Swimming — Girls must take one of the following swimming courses: nonswimmer, beginner, intermediate, advanced, lifesaving, swimming and fitness, or synchronized swimming.

Gymnastics — During the junior or senior year, girls must take one of the following: intermediate tumbling, advanced tumbling, or apparatus work.

Lifetime Sports — Girls must participate in two of the following: badminton, tennis, archery, golf, and fencing.

Coeducation — Girls are required to take one of the following coeducation courses: dance, swimming, volleyball, or recreational games.

Fitness — Girls must participate in a two-week fitness unit, which includes time for fitness testing.

Grade Twelve

Team Sports — Girls must participate in one team sport. The same sports are offered as for 11th grade girls with the addition of advanced courses in volleyball and basketball.

Conditioning — Girls must select one of the conditioning activities from the same list of four choices offered to 11th graders.

Dance — Girls may elect to take modern dance, folk dance, or tap dance. A dance activity is not required in the senior year.

Swimming — Girls may elect one swimming course from the same list offered to 11th graders. Swimming is not required in the senior year for girls who can pass the swimming test. Girls who can't pass the test are required to take beginning swimming.

Gymnastics — See the 11th grade requirements.

GIRLS' PROGRAM (*Continued*)

Lifetime Sports — Girls are required to participate in three of the following lifetime sports: badminton, tennis, (I or II), archery, golf, fencing, ice skating, or bowling.

Coeducation — Girls must select one coeducational activity from the same list offered to 11th graders.

Fitness — Girls must participate in a one-week fitness unit.

BOYS' PROGRAM

Grade Ten

Team Sports — Boys must select three of the following: football, soccer, speedball, volleyball, basketball, and softball.

Conditioning — Boys are required to participate in two of the following: cross-country, wrestling, weight lifting, independent study, and track and field.

Swimming — Boys must take either beginning or intermediate swimming.

Gymnastics — Beginning tumbling is required.

Lifetime Sports — Boys must take one of the following: archery, tennis, or badminton.

Coeducation — Dance is required.

Fitness — Boys must participate in a two-week fitness unit, which includes time for fitness testing.

Grade Eleven

Team Sports — Boys must participate in two of the following: football, speedball, soccer, volleyball, basketball, and softball. Advanced units are offered in volleyball and basketball.

Conditioning — Boys must select two activities from the same list offered in grade 10.

Swimming — Boys must participate in one of the following swimming units: beginning, advanced, diving, or lifesaving.

Gymnastics — During the junior or senior year, boys must participate in one of the following gymnastics units: beginning tumbling, advanced tumbling, apparatus work, or combatives.

Lifetime Sports — Boys are required to take part in two of the following lifetime sports: tennis, badminton, bowling, archery, golf, and paddle ball.

Coeducation — Boys must select one of the following four coeducational activities: dance, swimming, volleyball, or recreational games.

Fitness — Boys must participate in a two-week fitness unit, which includes time for fitness testing.

Grade Twelve

Team Sports — Boys are required to select one of the following team sports: football, speedball, volleyball, basketball, or softball. Advanced units are offered in volleyball, basketball, and softball.

Conditioning — Boys must participate in one of the five conditioning activities offered in grades ten and eleven.

Swimming — Boys may elect to participate in swimming and may choose from the following courses: beginning, advanced, diving, lifesaving, or water polo. Swimming is not required in grade twelve unless a boy fails in swimming test, in which case he is required to take beginning swimming.

Gymnastics — See 11th grade requirements.

Lifetime Sports — Students are required to select three of the following courses: tennis (beginning or advanced), badminton, paddle ball, handball, bowling, golf, and "gunology" (bascially gun safety with some shooting practice).

Coeducation — Boys are required to participate in one of four coeducational activities listed under 11th grade offerings.

Fitness — Boys are required to take part in a one-week unit.

MODESTO, CALIFORNIA. Students at the Grace M. Davis High School in Modesto, California, are allowed to elect their activities in physical education. They are given two choices both in the regular program and in the athletic program. Figures 7–12, 7–13, 7–14 and 7–15 provide practical examples of how the elective program operates. The schedule for both boys and girls is shown in Figure 7–16.[18]

TUCSON, ARIZONA. The girls enrolled in physical education at Catalina and Rincon High Schools in Tucson, Arizona, participate in activities based on their individual needs and interests. They elect at least one activity from each of the three categories: individual sports, team sports, and rhythmics and fitness. Notice, for example, in Figure 7–17 how one girl chose modern dance, gymnastics, and softball for her junior year.

The program is built around the following administrative procedures:

1. All students are assigned to a Physical Education period. The number of students assigned per period is determined by the physical facilities and the activities elected.

2. One instructor is assigned as period coordinator and she is responsible for making teaching assignments to other staff members under the guidance of the department heads. The period coordinator is the teacher of record for students assigned to her particular period.

3. The staff schedule is set up to make the best possible use of staff talent for teaching particular activities during each period.

4. Each student is assigned to a particular class within her physical education period on the basis of her interest, ability, or need. The interest is indicated by the student's Interest Inventory form. Ability is determined by skill tests and teacher evaluation. The need is reflected by posture pictures, health screening, fitness tests, and self-evaluation. Students who have particular physical limitations participate in Physical Education activities modified to fit their specific problem.

5. Girls generally are assigned to a specific activity for six weeks, although some units last for nine or even 12 weeks.[19]

A permanent record card is kept on each girl which records (1) activities the girl has taken, (2) the student's skill level, (3) the grade received, (4) physical fitness scores, and (5) skill test marks. The reader may refer to Chapter 9, p. 282 for the permanent record card which is used in the program.

Orientation and Electives in Other Patterns

The Traditional High School. Many schools are organized on the 8–4 plan; others operate on a 6–6 or 7–5 plan. In these systems, which do not have the separate junior and senior organization, a variation must be made in the orientation-elective plan that has been recommended. One way in which the program may be organized to include orientation and electives is to use the first year of the high school program for orientation. Pupils should rotate periodically in a planned curriculum during this year and then be allowed to make a choice in the remaining year or years.

Schools Requiring Only One Year of Physical Education. In schools having only one year of required physical education, it is extremely difficult to provide a sound orientation and elective program.

However, if the teacher responsible for the program has access to the elementary school, he may initiate an orientation program in the last year of elementary school. Access is usually not difficult to obtain, but the teacher wishing to initiate a program with the elementary school providing the orientation phase should follow protocol. After he plans his program, which should be clear, thorough, and substantiated by authoritative references, he should next present the idea to his principal. The director, or superintendent, should then be contacted by the principal, the teacher or both. With approval at this level, the teacher is then ready to approach the elementary school principal and teacher. The teachers involved should then meet to work out details of implementing the program.

If the system has a director or supervisor, the orientation program can be initiated from the top. Nevertheless, all administrators and teachers involved should understand the proposed plan so that it can be incorporated into the program enthusiastically and effectively.

Although the orientation program in the elementary school may be somewhat more limited than one in a higher school, there

(Text continued on page 216.)

GRACE M. DAVIS HIGH SCHOOL
MODESTA, CALIFORNIA
ELECTED ACTIVITIES

BOYS' PHYSICAL EDUCATION Class	9	10	11	12	ESTIMATED Fall Students	ESTIMATED 1971 Classes	EXPLANATION	ACTUAL Fall Students	ACTUAL 1970 Classes
Boys' Physical Education 1	322				322	6		230	7
Boys' Physical Education 3								224	5
Boys' Physical Education 5								227	5
Boys' Physical Education 7								180	5
Gymnastics		5	14	7	26	1		31	1
Freshman Football								57	2
Sophomore Football		73			73			50	2
Varsity Football		1	34	23	58	*		53	3
Cross Country		10	9	8	27			36	1
General Physical Education (7th period)		5	7	30	42	2		151	3
Wrestling		12	7	5	24				

(Program continued on opposite page.)

Activity				Adjusted Total		Notes
Freshman Basketball						
Sophomore Basketball	8		8		*	
Varsity Basketball	9	7	16		6	
Team Sports	104	85	72	261		
Individual Sports	30	39	17	86	2	
Co-ed Physical Education	2	12	20	34	1	26 / 1
Life Saving (Co-ed)	13	13	31	57	2	Combined with girls for 2 classes
Modern Dance						1-Boys } (Both Co-ed) 1-Girls }
Tumbling (Trampoline)	5	6	10	21	½	(Pertains to Life Saving only)
Weight Training	33	52	46	131	4	
Co-ed Swimming (Diving)	18	14	14	46	1	
Gymnastics (Wrestling)	3	2	7	12	½	
Modified Physical Education	4	6	4	18	1	15 / 1
Basic Skills					1	
Totals	326	326	309	**Adjusted Total** 1262	28	Includes Coaching Assignment 36

	301 → 1280

*Does not include Coaching Assignment

Includes Coaching Assignment

Figure 7–12. How students elect activities. (Courtesy Grace M. Davis High School, Modesto, California.)

GIRLS' PHYSICAL EDUCATION BALLOT   Year in School
_____

Spring Semester, 1971

Name_____, _____, _____
                    Last   First   Initial
          (Please Print)

ALL STUDENTS: CIRCLE first choice; UNDERLINE second choice.

CO-ED PROGRAM	GIRLS' PROGRAM (girls only)
1) Dance (square, folk, social) — Badminton	1) Body Mechanics
2) Tumbling — Trampoline	2) Team Sports (basketball, softball)
3) Individual Sports (badminton, archery, table tennis, golf)	3) Gymnastics
4) Track	4) Basic Skills
5) Beginning Swimming	5) Modified PE
6) Advanced Swimming	
7) Life Saving	
8) Synchronized Swimming	
9) Modern Dance (2)	
10) Modern Dance (4)	
11) Modern Dance (6)	

- -

Please check the following questions if they apply to you. This is information to be used by the Girls'
Physical Education Department only and does not affect the choices made above.)

_____ I am interested in working in the Physical Education Office as an office girl.

_____ I am interested in assisting a teacher as a teacher assistant in (_____).
                                                                    name the activity

_____ I am interested in a career in teaching physical education, or recreation, or health.

Figure 7–13.   Girls' Physical Education Ballot. (Courtesy Grace M. Davis High School, Modesto, California.)

BOYS' PHYSICAL EDUCATION BALLOT

Spring Semester, 1972

Name_____, _____, _____
                              Last   First   Middle
                    (Please Print — no nicknames)

ALL students complete this section.	Boys who wish to participate in a Spring

ALL students complete this section.
Circle first choice.
Underline second choice.

Boys who wish to participate in a Spring sport, please circle the sport in which you wish to participate. YOU MUST COMPLETE THE LEFT HAND SIDE OF THIS FORM EVEN IF YOU ARE GOING OUT FOR A SPORT.

Regular Program — Coed Classes

1. Dance — Badminton (Square-Folk-Social)
2. Tumbling — Trampoline
3. Individual Sports (Badminton, Archery, Ping Pong, Golf)
4. Track
5. Beginning Swimming
6. Life Saving
7. Advanced Swimming
8. Synchronized Swimming
9. Modern Dance

Athletic Program

1. Varsity Baseball
2. Sophomore Baseball
3. Freshman Baseball
4. Track
5. Swimming
6. Golf
7. Tennis
8. Gymnastics

Regular Program — Boys' Classes Only

1. Wrestling — Recreational Games
2. Weight Training
3. Team Sports — Softball, Kanaki, Football, Basketball, Volleyball, Speedball
4. Gymnastics
5. Body Mechanics
6. Modified Physical Education

For Coach's Use Only

The above circled Spring sport is:

_____Approved

_____Unapproved

_____
            (Signature of Coach)

Figure 7–14. Boys' Physical Education Ballot. (Courtesy Grace M. Davis High School, Modesto, California.)

Year in School
Next Year
(Fall, 1971)

_____

BOYS' PHYSICAL EDUCATION BALLOT

Fall Semester, 1971

Name_____, _____, _____
             Last   First   Middle
        (Please Print)

REGULAR PROGRAM	ATHLETIC PROGRAM
ALL STUDENTS COMPLETE THIS SECTION.	Boys who wish to participate in a fall sport please circle the sport in which you wish to participate. YOU MUST COMPLETE THE LEFT HAND SIDE OF THIS FORM EVEN IF YOU ARE GOING OUT FOR A SPORT.

ALL STUDENTS COMPLETE THIS SECTION.

Circle first choice.

Underline second choice.

All students must make two selections.

1. Team Sports (Basketball, Speedball, Football, Volleyball, Kanaki, Softball)
2. Individual Sports (Golf, Badminton, Archery, Track)
3. Co-ed PE
4. Life Saving (Co-ed)
5. Modern Dance (Co-ed)
6. Tumbling — Trampoline
7. Weight Training
8. Swimming and Diving
9. Gymnastics — Wrestling
10. Modified Physical Education

Boys who wish to participate in a fall sport please circle the sport in which you wish to participate. YOU MUST COMPLETE THE LEFT HAND SIDE OF THIS FORM EVEN IF YOU ARE GOING OUT FOR A SPORT.

1. Varsity Football
2. Sophomore Football
3. Cross Country
4. Varsity Basketball
5. Sophomore Basketball
6. Wrestling
7. Gymnastics

_____

For Coach's Use Only — The above circled fall sport is

_____Approved

_____Unapproved

_____
(Signature of Coach)

Figure 7–15.   Boys' Physical Education Ballot. (Courtesy Grace M. Davis High School, Modesto, California.)

GRACE M. DAVIS HIGH SCHOOL
FALL SCHEDULE—1971
CO-ED PHYSICAL EDUCATION

BOYS

Name	1	2	3	4	5	6	7
Laun	Co-ed Physical Education	Team Sports	Weight Training	Modified Physical Education	Lunch	Preparation	Sophomore Football
Crum	Individual Sports (Boys)	Weight Training	Swimming Diving (Co-ed)	Lunch Preparation	Physical Education 1	Physical Education 1	Freshman Football
Erler	Gymnastics Team	Health Science	Health Science	Gymnastics Wrestling Trampoline	Lunch	Basic Skills (Boys)	Varsity Football
Gonsalves	Physical Education 1	Physical Education 1	Team Sports	Weight Training	Lunch	Preparation	Varsity Football
Parrill	Math	Individual Sports (Girls)	Physical Education 1	Team Sports	Lunch	Preparation	General Physical Education
Torre	Weight Training	Driver Education	Driver Education	Preparation	Lunch	Individual Sports (Boys)	Varsity Football
Windemuth	Team Sports			Physical Education 1	Team Sports	Team Sports	General Physical Education

GIRLS

	1	2	3	4	5	6	7
Johnson	Co-ed Physical Education		Basic Skills	Body Mechanics	Body Mechanics		Body Mechanics
Azevedo	Tumbling	Physical Education 1	Physical Education 1	Tumbling	Individual Sports (Girls)		
Finley	Physical Education 1	Physical Education 1	Team Sports			Team Sports	Physical Education 1
Hodge		Body Mechanics	Gymnastics	Modified Physical Education	Gymnastics	Gymnastics	
Gregory		Gymnastics		Physical Education 1	Tumbling	Physical Education 1	Gymnastics
Bloom	Modern Dance 1	Modern Dance 1	Modern Dance 3			Modern Dance 3	Modern Dance 5
Nugent	Swimming Diving (Co-ed)				Life Saving (Co-ed)	Live Saving (Co-ed)	

Figure 7–16. Physical Education Schedule. (Courtesy Grace M. Davis High School, Modesto, California.)

CATALINA HIGH SCHOOL
INTEREST INVENTORY

NAME *Mary Smith*
GRADE *Junior*
PERIOD *2*
DATE *September, 1966*

NUMBER 1, 2, 3 IN ORDER OF PREFERENCE IN EACH CATEGORY. CIRCLE YOUR
FIRST CHOICE OF ALL ACTIVITIES. PUT ANY ADDITIONAL COMMENTS UNDER
BOTTOM "COMMENTS".

INDIVIDUAL SPORTS	RHYTHMICS AND FITNESS	TEAM SPORTS
____ ARCHERY	*1* (MODERN DANCE)	____ BASKETBALL
____ BADMINTON	*2* ROUND, FOLK AND	____ FIELD HOCKEY
3 CAMPING	SQUARE DANCE	*1* SOFTBALL
____ GOLF	*3* CONDITIONING	*3* SPEED-A-WAY
1 GYMNASTICS		*2* VOLLEYBALL
____ REC. SPORTS		
____ SWIMMING		
____ TENNIS		
2 TRACK AND FIELD		

HEALTH STATUS

WILL YOUR PHYSICAL EDUCATION ACTIVITY BE LIMITED IN ANY WAY? *No*
EXPLAIN: _____
COMMENTS: _____
ARE YOU INTERESTED IN PREPARING FOR ANY OF THE ADVANCED OR SPECIAL
CLASSES? *Yes* ____ IN WHAT? *Advanced Basketball*

SPECIAL CLASSES IN PHYSICAL EDUCATION
ADVANCED TENNIS
ADVANCED DANCE
ADVANCED GYMNASTICS
ADVANCED SPORTS
PEP LEADERSHIP

Figure 7–17. Pupil Interest Inventory Form. (Courtesy Catalina High School, Tucson, Arizona.)

are many devices and procedures that can be used to acquaint the students with a variety of activities. For example, pupils may be shown films of various sports, and a short introductory program may be developed in order to determine where their interests lie.

Trends Affecting Physical Education

New patterns of organizing physical education programs have become widespread in many sections of the country. All of them have been tried in the field of general education, and some of them seem to offer a welcome change in the traditional curriculum. These patterns may affect an entire system or merely a single school. Irrespective of how they are used or to what extent they are applied, they should have passed the experimental stage before being applied to physical education. Sometimes physical educators, in their efforts to improve their programs, are likely to subscribe to many experiments made by general educators.

Although physical education has some common aims with general education, it is a different discipline. Physical education is basically a *movement* program. As such, it is planned differently, organized differently and makes unique contributions to the education of children.

New procedures in organizing programs in physical education should be based on scientific guidelines or practices which have proved to be successful. Some of the more promising procedures are discussed in the following pages of this chapter.

Educational Television. Probably no educational medium offers greater promise for the presentation of material than television, which provides almost unlimited opportunities for studying new material that would otherwise be unavailable. In the area of physical education so many experiments and discoveries are projected through television that an alert teacher has only to familiarize himself with program schedules to bring these findings to the class.

Closed circuit television in many places has already been included in the overall curriculum planning. Although experimentation is still going on, some form of educational television seems to be here to stay. Many people feel that closed circuit television, when used properly, is an outstanding tool for assisting the teacher in bringing the best procedures and materials to the classroom.

There is no doubt that as a medium of instruction, educational television has many advantages. In those areas of the curriculum in which teachers are scarce, television may provide instruction for many pupils who otherwise would not have it. Scanlon reports that through the "Continental Classroom" at least 35,000 high school teachers watched programs that were designed to upgrade the teaching of physics, chemistry, and mathematics.[20]

Television has been used in many cities to provide excellent programs in art, music, sciences, and foreign languages that heretofore were impossible because of the lack of qualified teachers.

A major advantage of educational television as a medium of instruction is the ease with which it brings to the classroom educational experiences that traditional teaching could never provide. Many supplementary teaching aids — museum items, governmental documents, actual experiments, industrial research, photographs, international broadcasts, public health programs and hundreds of special programs and projects that were unavailable because of expense and space — are now within reach of the classroom.

Admittedly, educational television has several disadvantages. DeYoung and Wynn advance the following criticisms:

First, many teachers fear that TV may eventually reduce the number of teaching positions or convert teachers into glorified monitors, and are therefore skeptical of it. Second, the alleged advantages of educational television have been grossly exaggerated. The Ford Foundation, which has subsidized educational television with heretofore unknown generosity, was unequivocally convinced of its advantages almost as soon as the demonstrations began.[21]

Many people feel that the programs have failed to measure up to the claims advanced by proponents of this medium. Alberty and Alberty support this view in the following statements:

1. The claims that educational television provides more effective instruction are based on questionable procedures, which fail to take into account such intangibles as attitudes, ideals and values that are important in the education of children.
2. Televised lectures by "master teachers" to large groups of students are but a modification of the time-honored "lecture-method" which has been largely repudiated in the secondary school.[22]

DeYoung and Wynn report that several school systems that experimented with educational television have eliminated it from their budgets. New Jersey was one of the first to drop it because it failed to meet the claims advocated by its proponents. The District of Columbia after several years of enthusiastic experimentation dropped it completely because of its inadequacy as a tool of instruction.[21]

Probably one of the basic reasons why educational television fails is its inability to hold the attention of the pupils. Pupils look upon television as a medium of entertainment. After the first few lectures in the classroom, television loses its entertainment appeal. In order to offset this criticism, teachers attempt to make the programs more entertaining. This procedure not only places them in direct competition with commercial entertainment but also weakens the educational objectives.

Trowe presents several disadvantages of educational television:

1. It is a viewing and listening device only.
2. Pupils may daydream or sleep.
3. It provides for no pupil participation.
4. Notes may be scanty since the pupil must watch the picture.
5. The instructor proceeds at his rate of speed with no possibility of adapting instruction to the individual.[23]

Although educational television has been used rather extensively in teaching academic subjects, it is rarely used in teaching physical education. The advantages and disadvantages of educational television described for use in teaching academic subjects may also be applied to teaching physical education.

In addition to giving consideration to the pros and cons of teaching academic subjects by educational television, attention should be focused on the difficulty of teaching physical education by educational television. Physical education is basically a movement program as contrasted to the non-movement aspect of academic subjects. The procedures used in teaching physical education are different from those used in academic subjects. Methods and procedures used for teaching academic subjects are usually planned around the cognitive domain, whereas those applied to physical education are in the psychomotor domain. One exception to this is the health-knowledge aspect of teaching physical education.

A study to determine how extensively educational television programs for physical education were utilized throughout the United States revealed that television programs for physical education were utilized more often in the elementary than in the secondary grades. The report, which showed the results of questionnaires from 42 directors, revealed that 15 of the directors reported that television was utilized, while 27 stated that television was not utilized.[24] The failure to utilize television in physical education is another illustration of the difficulty arising when methods designed for teaching academic subjects are used in teaching physical education.

The teacher of physical education should study the issue carefully and be familiar with the advantages and disadvantages before launching into an educational television approach to teaching. Probably the most sensible view is offered by DeYoung and Wynn, who suggest: "A willingness to experiment further, an objective open-mindedness, and a patient delay in judgment until more experience is gained would seem to be in order."[21]

Programmed Learning. Programmed teaching takes the learner on a step-by-step venture into the acquisition of knowledge. In a controlled environment he proceeds from one step to another, giving responses that indicate that he knows what the information is. The teacher observes the step-by-step learning process, and when incorrect answers are given, the teacher is aware of it and makes changes in the controlled environment.

Proponents of programmed instruction feel that they have the answer to effective teaching. Klaw notes several arguments for programmed teaching:

1. Pupils will learn in about half the time.
2. Programmed instruction will have a sharp impact on the way textbooks are written.
3. Programmed instruction may be used to enlarge curriculum content in a school. Children may begin to study languages in the elementary school.
4. Programmed study allows students to proceed at their own speed. This enables teachers to group by ability. Small schools may adapt their curriculum to individual needs and abilities.
5. Programmed study not only allows bright students to proceed faster but may assist the slow learner even more.
6. Teaching machines and programmed study may help to reduce dropouts and contribute to the goal of educating all children to the limit of their capabilities.[25]

Gardner believes in the use of teaching machines if they are used wisely. However, he feels that the title is misleading and that they should be called "self-teaching devices." He says:

The best self-teaching devices and programs have proved remarkably effective, and students seem to enjoy working with them . . . the self-teaching device can individualize instruction in ways that are not now possible.[26]

Educational technology is developing so rapidly that programmed teaching has already passed from the machine stage to the programming of textbooks into another educational breakthrough that may completely revolutionize education. The use of computerized electronic teaching devices is the latest development. Gerald Grant reports that the educational technology market has already reached the 500 million dollar a year mark with a potential of five to 15 billion dollars within a decade.[27]

Those who advocate the computerized classroom claim that it will provide for individual instruction and eliminate the shortcomings of the teaching machine. Some of the advances in computerized instruction have been listed by Grant:

1. Systems Development Corporation has brought out a computer program that will "counsel" a student by predicting his grade average from past performance and matching these against his choices of school programs.

2. Reading and mathematics will be taught by computers . . . to youngsters in the first three grades at the Brentwood Elementary School in Palo Alto, California.

3. Oakley Elementary School in a Pittsburgh suburb will soon convert to a computerized base for nearly half of its instructional load. Development of both these programs, using primarily Westinghouse and IBM equipment, was financed by the U.S. Office of Education.

4. O.E.A. recently provided funds to the Chicago Welfare Department to buy talking typewriters that have proved particularly effective in teaching deprived children and adult illiterates to read and write.

5. Because up to 500,000 pages of printed material can be stored on a small videotape, many libraries are converting to computerized "information retrieval systems."

6. At the Mohansic Elementary School in Westchester County, N.Y., and in seven junior high schools in Philadelphia this fall students will be taking computer-aided courses in mathematics, science, and economics.[27]

According to Grant, indications are that companies are writing program proposals for some local school officials with many equipment sales also. Unless it is stopped, this trend may have serious effects on education in the nation's schools.[27]

Physical education teachers must proceed with caution in subscribing to any suggested program of teaching that carries with it implications of profiteering and programming that are not in the best interests of children.

There is some feeling among educators that unless limitations are placed on the use of programmed instruction and teaching machines, education may suffer. They feel that commercial interests and educational foundations are gaining control over instruction through the mass production of films, teaching machines, and videotapes. DeYoung and Wynn discuss this point of view in the following criticisms of teaching machines:

1. Pressure for the right answers may snuff out the revolt of skepticism that has so often led to new discovery.

2. They permit no fanciful excursions into unprogrammable speculation or discovery prompted by a student's fleeting glance and caught by an alert teacher.

3. They discover no new knowledge and have no power of discrimination.

4. Television, massed film systems and teaching machines threaten the local school system's control over what should be taught.

5. James Finn, Chairman of the Department of Audio-Visual Education at Southern California, raises the horrifying possibility of total educational automation on a national basis. By combining mass instruction technology, i.e., teaching machines, it would be possible, says Finn, to eliminate not only the teacher but the entire school system.[21]

Very little research has been done to show the extent to which programmed instruction has been used in teaching motor skills. The available research showing the effectiveness of programmed instruction has been done in cognitive learning. Physical educators interested in innovative procedures in teaching skills should know what has been done in programmed instruction. Locke analyzed seven studies which described the programmed approach in teaching sports skills. He showed that, in general, programming may be as effective for some purposes as traditional methods.[28]

One particular aspect of this study should be noted. According to the report, instructors in some of the studies merely observed the experiments and did not take an active part in the instruction. The report stated that if the experiments had been used as a supplement to the regular instruction, just as audiovisual aids are, with the teacher assuming the role as the leader in teaching, the results might have been better. However, the fact that teachers were passive and thus added nothing to the instruction reinforces the arguments against programmed instruction listed in this chapter.

Programmed instruction is another effort

to free students from the traditional sameness of the classroom and provide more individualized effort allowing students to proceed at their own pace. At its best this type of instruction can be effective only as a supplementary device.

Team Teaching.   In those schools where more than one teacher is employed for the program, team teaching may be used to teach groups more effectively. Team teaching brings together two or more teachers who cooperatively plan and devise better ways of teaching groups of pupils. When planning for individual sports instruction, for example, one teacher might teach a small group in golf while another teacher or teachers could teach volleyball or basketball skills.

Team teaching has been tried successfully in some places. One of these is the girls' department at Sehome High School in Bellingham, Washington. The department consists of two women. Available facilities are one half of the gymnasium large enough for three volleyball courts and a small area with one court. Two classes of approximately 35 pupils each are scheduled together. The 70 students are grouped by ability into eight squads and assigned to the four courts. For four days (Monday through Thursday) the squads rotate around the four stations, with all pupils reporting to the large gymnasium on Friday for tournaments.

Individualized instruction is provided in the small gymnasium by one of the two teachers. The unit consists of three weeks' instruction in volleyball skills, with tests given at the end of the unit.

The teachers, Karel Thompson and Lora Lindgren, because of the successful team approach in volleyball, have expanded the program team-teaching concept to include track and gymnastics. A further expansion of the team teaching approach included men in the planning, thus providing better staff utilization.

Miss Thompson lists the following advantages of the team-teaching concept:

1. Each teacher has the time to do extensive research and develop units in her area of specialty.
2. Students receive far more individual help. This is particularly true in the volleyball unit, and Miss Thompson has found that skill development has increased substantially.

3. Individual instruction, geared to the level of each homogeneous group, makes it possible for each group to advance as rapidly as possible.
4. Homogeneous grouping for team games, such as volleyball, prevents one highly skilled individual from dominating play.

Miss Thompson continues:

Perhaps the main disadvantage of our volleyball unit is the structured one day in five of concentrated skill development. The slow learner often needs four days to practice and master a new skill, but the top squads are often ready for new techniques and skills before their turn in the small gym rolls around again. We recognized this as we moved along in our team teaching efforts and adjusted so that the instructor in the main gym would introduce new challenges to keep the top students interested.[29]

The Evergreen Park Community High School, Evergreen, Illinois, uses the team teaching approach in teaching physical education. The school schedule consists of seven 56-minute periods each day. The physical education schedule is arranged as follows:

Period 1	Freshmen
Period 2	Sophomores
Period 3	Planning Period
Period 4	Lunch
Period 5	Seniors
Period 6	Juniors
Period 7	Conference

Freshmen, sophomores and juniors have three periods of physical education each week and two periods of health; senior students have five periods of physical education weekly.

The schedule allows the four teachers to teach each class. This arrangement provides time for conferences and planning and a better arrangement for supervision. The supervision plan looks like this at the beginning of the period:

1. One teacher supervises the dressing room.
2. One teacher stays in the health room.
3. One teacher is stationed in the gym for taking the roll.
4. One teacher remains in the office to be available for problems that may arise.

Within each class small groups and large groups are arranged which provides for more individualized instruction for those pupils who need it. Figures 7–18 and 7–19 show the schedules which are used at Evergreen.[30]

GRADE 10 – DECEMBER 3-7 – PERIOD 2

GROUP	MONDAY	TUESDAY	WEDNESDAY	THURSDAY	FRIDAY
"A" Weight Classification 0–110 lbs.	HEALTH LECTURE (Auditorium) Instructor IV	Health (Classroom) Inst. IV	Basketball Round Robin Tournament (Station A) Inst. II Student Leaders	Basketball Round Robin Tournament (Station A) Inst. II Student Leaders	Basketball Round Robin Tournament (Station A) Inst. II Student Leaders
"B" Weight Classification 111–125 lbs.		Wrestling Round Robin Tournament (Balcony) Inst. I Student Leaders	Health (Classroom) Inst. IV ·	Wrestling Round Robin Tournament (Balcony) Inst. I Student Leaders	Wrestling Round Robin Tournament (Balcony) Inst. I Student Leaders
"C" Weight Classification 126–150 lbs.		Weight Training Isometrics (Station B) Inst. III Student Leaders	Weight Training Isometrics (Station B) Inst. III Student Leaders	Health (Classroom) Inst. IV	Weight Training Isometrics (Station B) Inst. III Student Leaders
"D" Weight Classification 151-over lbs.		Basketball Round Robin Tournament (Station A) Inst. II Student Leaders	Wrestling Round Robin Tournament (Balcony) Inst. I Student Leaders	Weight Training Isometrics (Station B) Inst. III Student Leaders	Health (Classroom) Inst. IV

Indoor Team Teaching Assignments and Programs at Evergreen Park Community High School

Figure 7–18. Courtesy Evergreen Park Community High School, Evergreen, Illinois.

ADVANTAGES OF TEAM TEACHING. Many teachers and educational leaders in physical education strongly endorse the advantages that accrue from team teaching. Trump and Baynham, using the results of studies in team teaching made in several schools, endorse this procedure. They summarize the results of their findings in two statements:

1. Team teaching provides the setting in which individual teachers can best use and further develop their individual talents.
2. Students can benefit from the best that teachers have to offer.[31]

Experiments in team teaching by the National Association of Secondary School Principals revealed the following advantages:

1. Teachers learned the strengths and weaknesses of traditional teaching procedures.

2. Talented teachers were utilized to a better advantage.
3. Teachers were under pressure to do a better job.
4. There was greater communication among classes.
5. Students enjoyed the plan.[32]

Arguments for team teaching based on research are advanced by Meyer. According to him:

1. Team teaching has a tremendous potential as the vehicle essential for transformation of interdisciplinary teaching from the state of theory to one of fact.
2. The major thrust of teaming for instruction of youth is to improve the quality of instruction and individualize it; to extend specialized teaching competencies of staff; and to provide a more flexible basis or organization in terms of student, staff, time and curriculum.[33]

DISADVANTAGES OF TEAM TEACHING. Leaders in education do not agree on the

GRADE 11—MAY 27-31—PERIOD 6

GROUP	MONDAY	TUESDAY	WEDNESDAY	THURSDAY	FRIDAY
"A" Weight Classification 0-125 lbs.		First Aid (Classroom) Inst. III	Softball (Athletic Field) Inst. V Student Leaders	Track & Field: Shot Put Discus (Track Areas) Inst. I Student Leaders	Track & Field: Broad Jump High Jump (Track Areas) Inst. II Student Leaders
"B" Weight Classification 126-145 lbs.	FIRST AID LECTURE (Auditorium) Instructor............III	Track & Field: Broad Jump High Jump (Track Areas) Inst. II Student Leaders	First Aid (Classroom) Inst. III	Softball (Athletic Field) Inst. V	Track & Field: Shot Put Discus (Track Areas) Inst. I Student Leaders
"C" Weight Classification 146-165 lbs.		Track & Field: Shot Put Discus (Track Areas) Inst. I Student Leaders	Track & Field: Broad Jump High Jump (Track Areas) Inst. II Student Leaders	First Aid (Classroom) Inst. III	Softball (Athletic Fields) Inst. V Student Leaders
"D" Weight Classification 166-over lbs.		Softball (Athletic Fields) Inst. V Student Leaders	Track & Field: Shot Put Discus (Track Areas) Inst. I Student Leaders	Track & Field: Broad Jump High Jump (Track Areas) Inst. II Student Leaders	First Aid (Classroom) Inst. III

Outdoor Team Teaching Assignments and Programs at Evergreen Park Community High School

Figure 7-19. Courtesy Evergreen Park Community High School, Evergreen, Illinois.

effectiveness of team teaching. In opposition to the advantages shown in the paragraphs above, Vars points out several disadvantages:

1. Those who expect team teaching to give the teacher more time for planning and for counseling with students are doomed to disappointment.
2. The many complicated administrative decisions that are delegated to the team are tremendously time consuming.
3. Even large group instruction, which is supposed to give teachers some released time, may fail to deliver. Teachers who are not directly responsible for the lesson must be present anyway, or involved in the planning, in order to insure articulation of lessons that precede or follow.
4. It is also difficult to see how small groups could carry out their own plans and still keep their schedules close enough together to profit from large group instruction.[34]

Saylor and Alexander report other shortcomings of team teaching:

1. Teachers may overemphasize the mastering of content and neglect other major objectives of the school.
2. Teachers may not have close relationships with pupils so that the social, emotional and character development of the child may be neglected.
3. The hierarchal organization may result in discontent and loss of morale among teachers.
4. Team teaching may result in rigidity and inflexibility with pupils shunted around in a highly mechanistic manner.
5. Schools may use the plan to increase pupil-teacher ratio, reducing the opportunities for individual instruction.[35]

Teachers themselves have expressed opposition to team teaching. Some of these objections of teachers who have had experience with team teaching are listed by Douglass:

1. In many schools, the large groups are not sectioned by ability and the instruction is directed to the students of average or superior ability.
2. Professional teachers have not been given a reduced class load, nor have they been paid higher salaries.
3. The small-group instruction is ineffective, because there are not enough teachers and assistants to work at it.
4. The large-group instruction casts the student in a passive role; he is occupied mostly with taking lecture notes.
5. Provisions are not made for individual differences, especially for low-ability students.
6. Large-group instruction is inappropriate for such courses as basic English and mathematics, where teachers need to know and to work closely with individual students.
7. Costly space for large-group instruction has been designed so that it is difficult to use for other purposes.[36]

Modular Scheduling. Probably the most popular innovation in education today is modular or flexible scheduling. This plan was developed to assist administrators and teachers in their efforts to provide more flexibility in the daily schedule and to give teachers more time for individual instruction. This plan eliminates the traditional allocation of one daily period, usually 50 or 60 minutes, to each subject. It substitutes for this daily period a number of modules which do not have to be allocated each day. Some subjects will be given more modules than others, depending on the needs of the subject. These modules usually consist of 20 minutes; but they may vary, depending on local needs.

In developing modular scheduling, three phases of learning are usually involved. They are (1) large group instruction, (2) small group instruction, and (3) independent study.

LARGE GROUP INSTRUCTION. Large group instruction involves instruction to large groups of pupils ranging from 75 to 300. The instruction, provided by a team of teachers, is given once or twice each week. Various teaching media are used, including films, filmstrips, overhead projectors and the like. The pupils are not given the opportunity to ask questions, but are required to take notes and study the materials provided by the team.

SMALL GROUP INSTRUCTION. This phase of instruction organizes the pupils in small groups with from five to 20 pupils in each group. The teacher actually teaches, answers questions, develops discussions, and evaluates both pupil progress and the instruction itself. These groups usually meet two or three times per week.

INDEPENDENT STUDY. This is the third phase of the modular plan, in which the pupil is unscheduled and is allowed to pursue his own interests. He may do research, visit the laboratory, study independently or work with another pupil. In the case of physical education, he would report to the gymnasium, playground, or pool.

Physical educators should ask several questions relative to flexible scheduling. Who determines the number of modules allocated to each subject? How many modules will physical education be allowed? Will successful programs have to lose their hard-earned gains for some experiment that has not, as yet, proved to be successful? These questions and others should be resolved if physical education is to maintain its respectability in the curriculum.

Examples of Modular Scheduling. Some examples of modular scheduling are shown on the following pages. Students and teachers should study the plans and evaluate them, remembering that change is not always progress.

GERMANTOWN, WISCONSIN. Washington High School, located in Germantown, Wisconsin, adopted the modular scheduling plan in 1968. The plan includes the three phases of modular scheduling: large group instruction (Fig. 7–20), small group instruction (Fig. 7–21), and independent study (Fig. 7–22).

The purpose of adopting the modular scheduling plan was to achieve the following objectives:

1. To provide for students' greater opportunity for individualized instruction.
2. To foster more student responsibility.
3. To allow opportunity for student self-discipline.
4. To allow opportunity for student self-direction.

Figure 7–20.   Large group instruction at Washington High School, Germantown, Wisconsin.

Instead of a traditional five-day schedule with seven periods in a day, the system operates within a six-day cycle with each day consisting of twenty-one 20-minute modules. Each of the six days is given a letter "A" through "F" to complete the six-day cycle. For example, beginning with the first of the week, Monday is "A"; Tuesday is "B," Wednesday, "C" day; Thursday, "D" day; Friday, "E" day; and the following Monday would be "F" day; Tuesday, "A" day, and so on.

The students are required to attend physical education four days for three modules out of the six-day cycle. Three classes involve instruction, while the fourth is a laboratory class. The type of instruction that is presented within a laboratory situation depends on the type of unit, length of unit, number of students and number of skills to be learned.

Twelve laboratories exist within the six-day cycle. Students are scheduled into these laboratories at the beginning of the school year. The laboratories are combinations, freshman-sophomore and junior-senior.

Figure 7–21.   Small group instruction at Washington High School, Germantown, Wisconsin.

Figure 7-22. Independent study at Washington High School, Germantown, Wisconsin.

All teachers are required to teach within each laboratory. The laboratories provide for a smaller teacher-student ratio, more individualized instruction, and better personal contact with students. The program at Washington High School operates on a master schedule which is shown in Figure 7-23.[37]

MINNEAPOLIS, MINNESOTA. The modular scheduling program for the girls' physical education department at Regina High School in Minneapolis, Minnesota has an innovated scheduling plan which should be discussed. Because of modular scheduling, the girls are able to receive instruction in leisure-time activities that would be impossible in the traditional schedule. They have developed a modular schedule of electives, six of which are off-campus courses that utilize community recreation centers.

The program began in 1968, when the curriculum was expanded to include off-campus activities such as horseback riding, golf, bowling, skiing, and swimming. Students use a check sheet (see below) for their course selections. The starred courses are off-campus courses which are offered to sophomores, juniors, and seniors. The other courses are offered to sophomores only. The form consists of four sections, the student selecting sections in order of preference. Within each section she chooses one course for each quarter (Fig. 7-24).

A master physical education schedule is used which includes the number of modules, time allowed each module, and the daily assignment of physical education. A copy of the schedule is reproduced in Figure 7-25.

A Critical Look at Modular Scheduling. Modular scheduling has been in existence long enough to make possible some hard, practical observations concerning its relative value. Students like modular scheduling, and for bright students it offers positive advantages. However, there appears to be no significant difference in mean achievement scores between students in flexible modular schools and those in traditional schools.[38]

It seems that the independent phase of modular scheduling has been abused, since it does not offer promise for certain students. When allowed free time, these students invariably choose activities of either a social or an antisocial nature. For them, independent study is not synonymous with individualization of instruction.[38]

The need for serious consideration of a realistic plan to provide for those students whose needs are not met by modular scheduling is obvious. Such a plan is described by Thomson as the client-centered plan.[38] In the client-centered school, a diagnostic center is available to determine interests, skills, attitudes, needs and other pertinent data concerning students. Using the information gathered from the center, student types are deter-

GERMANTOWN HIGH SCHOOL
PHYSICAL EDUCATION SCHEDULE
1971–72

MOD	TIME	A	B	C	D	E	F
1	7:50						
2	8:10	11	12	11	12	11	12
3	8:30	Sec 1	Sec 1	Sec 1	Sec 1	Sec 1	Sec 1
4	8:50						
5	9:10		11–12				
6	9:30		LAB				
7	9:50	9–10	11–12		9–10		
8	10:10	LAB	LAB		LAB		
9	10:30	9–10	9–10	9–10	9–10	9–10	9–10
10	10:50	SPECIAL					→
11	11:10						
12	11:30						
13	11:50	9–10	11–12	9–10	11–12	9–10	11–12
14	12:10	LAB	LAB	LAB	LAB	LAB	LAB
15	12:30	9	9	9	9	9	9
16	12:50	Sec 1	Sec 2	Sec 1	Sec 2	Sec 1	Sec 2
17	1:10						
18	1:30	10	10	10	10	10	10
19	1:50	Sec 1	Sec 2	Sec 1	Sec 2	Sec 1	Sec 2
20	2:10						

Figure 7–23. Master schedule for the physical education program at Washington High School, Germantown, Wisconsin.

COURSE SELECTIONS

(931)

	1	2	3	4
	**Swimming_____	Volleyball_____	Gymnastics_____	Archery_____
Choice no.	1 Recreational Games_____	2 **Bowling_____	3 Basketball_____	4 **Golf_____
	1 Tennis_____			

(932)

	1	2	3	4
	**Swimming_____	**Bowling_____	Fun, Fitness, Tumbling_____	**Golf_____
Choice no.	1 Tennis_____	2 Archery_____	3 Skiing_____	4 Track and Field_____
	1 Trampoline_____			
	1 Balance Beam_____			

(933)

	1	2	3	4
	Volleyball-Basketball_____	Archery_____	Modern Dance or Roller Skating_____	Softball_____
Choice no.	1 **Horseback Riding_____	2 **Bowling_____	3 Gymnastics_____	4 Tennis_____

(934)

	1	2	3	4
	**Swimming_____	Gymnastics_____	Archery_____	Tennis_____
Choice no.	1 Campcraft and Recreation_____	2 **Bowling_____	3 **Skiing_____	4 Softball_____
	1 Modern Dance_____			

Figure 7–24. Course selections at Regina High School, Minneapolis, Minnesota.

REGINA HIGH SCHOOL
1970–71 BASIC SCHEDULE

Mod	Time	A	B	C	D	E
1	8:20	homeroom	homeroom	homeroom	homeroom	homeroom
2	8:40		925/06 Phys. Ed. I	925/02 Phys. Ed. I	925/06 Phys. Ed. I	925/02 Phys. Ed. I
3	9:00		925/06 Phys. Ed. I	925/02 Phys. Ed. I	925/06 Phys. Ed. I	925/02 Phys. Ed. I
4	9:20	resource center	925/06 Phys. Ed. I	925/02 Phys. Ed. I	925/06 Phys. Ed. I	925/02 Phys. Ed. I
5	9:40	resource center				
6	10:00	resource center	925/03 Phys. Ed. I	925/04 Phys. Ed. I	925/04 Phys. Ed. I	925/03 Phys. Ed. I
7	10:20	resource center	925/03 Phys. Ed. I	925/04 Phys. Ed. I	925/04 Phys. Ed. I	925/03 Phys. Ed. I
8	10:40	resource center	925/03 Phys. Ed. I	925/04 Phys. Ed. I	925/04 Phys. Ed. I	925/03 Phys. Ed. I
9	11:00	925/07 Phys. Ed. I	resource center		resource center	resource center
10	11:20	925/07 Phys. Ed. I	resource center		resource center	resource center
11	11:40	925/07 Phys. Ed. I	resource center	925/07 Phys. Ed. I	resource center	resource center
12	12:00			925/07 Phys. Ed. I	resource center	
13	12:20			925/07 Phys. Ed. I	resource center	
14	12:40	Health			hall duty	
15	1:00	Health			hall duty	
16	1:20	932 Phys. Ed. II	933/01 Phys. Ed. II	931/01 Phys. Ed. II		934 Phys. Ed. II
17	1:40	932 Phys. Ed. II	933/01 Phys. Ed. II	931/01 Phys. Ed. II		934 Phys. Ed. II
18	2:00	932 Phys. Ed. II	933/01 Phys. Ed. II	931/01 Phys. Ed. II		934 Phys. Ed. II
19	2:20	932 Phys. Ed. II	933/01 Phys. Ed. II	931/01 Phys. Ed. II		

Figure 7–25.　Basic schedule in physical education at Regina High School, Minneapolis, Minnesota.

Figure 7–26. Horseback riding is an example of off-campus activity which is possible because of flexible scheduling. (Courtesy Regina High School, Minneapolis, Minnesota.)

mined. Instructional modes are developed from these typologies to provide a degree of individualization. The instructional system operating in the client-centered school is shown in Figure 7–27.

The instructional mode is essential to the success of the client-centered school. The effectiveness of the mode depends on its adaptability to the success of the individual student. The modes must provide for bright and dull students, attitudes, values, psychological patterns and life styles. An instructional mode is shown in Figure 7–28.

Although no research is available to point the way for solutions to the inadequacies of modular scheduling, Thomson feels that:

What does appear to be true from the present vantage point, however, is that unscheduled time and independent study at present do not benefit a significant number of students. Alternative arrangements must be found. The search will continue for new ap-

proaches. The client-centered school seems to be a promising direction to pursue.[38]

An important two year study commissioned by the California Bureau of Health Education, Physical Education, Athletics and Recreation revealed the advantages of daily scheduling over modular scheduling in physical education. The study involved 2400 students in 12 high schools of which six were on modular scheduling and six on daily scheduling.

H. Harrison Clark, the chairman of the project, stated that "the results . . . supported the value of the daily physical education requirement."[39]

The director of the project, Stan LeProtti, made the following analysis of the study:

. . . the advantage alluded to by exponents of flexible scheduling . . . is not attainable under the conditions which presently exist. Students do not respond ac-

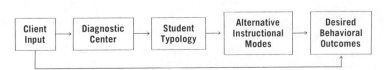

Figure 7–27. The instructional system operating in the client-centered school. (Courtesy of Scott Thomson, *Phi Delta Kappan*, April, 1971, p. 484.)

PROFILE OF AN INSTRUCTIONAL MODE

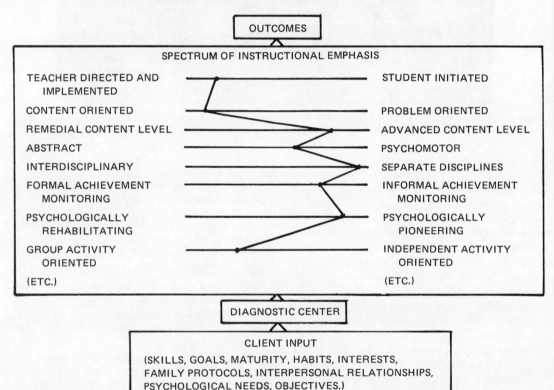

Figure 7–28.   Profile of an instructional mode. (Courtesy of Scott Thomson, *Phi Delta Kappan*, April, 1971, p. 484.)

cording to theory; staff does not function effectively to the extent claimed; and existing facilities do not accommodate the scheduling practice.

In those flexible schedules which provide elongated time periods, i.e., 90 or 120 minutes for physical education on an irregular basis, the process of program administration and instruction is simply slowed down. That is, students take longer to dress, teachers take longer to take the roll, and students spend more time standing or sitting during the instructional phase of the program.[39]

The major problem in modular scheduling revealed by the committee was the use of unscheduled time. A large number of students, instead of reporting for independent study, resource centers and conferences, were found visiting friends, sitting around, and actually leaving the campuses.

The unscheduled time also contributed to increased locker room theft which necessitated the need for more supervision of parking lots, hallways, dining areas and other places where students meet. The report showed that in one school teachers were scheduled for 36 modules of instruction and 43 modules of general supervision per week. Situations such as this are not only expensive but are a gross misuse of professional time that should be used for instruction.

Gard, in a timely analysis of flexible scheduling, discusses the problems that arise when administrators attempt to handle all the variables which are involved in daily scheduling. He shows that only through the use of a computer-produced schedule can a flexible scheduling plan become a reality. Although there are advantages to such a system, Gard points out the problems of additional time, space and personnel which involve huge outlays of money.

In addition to the areas and personnel involved in the scheduled subjects, space and personnel are needed for *unscheduled* time. Whether the students are in large groups, small groups or independent study, the ratio of students to seats does not change and the need for additional personnel to supervise these groups is evident.

Gard also discusses the human element in flexible scheduling. In the flexible scheduling plan there is the opportunity for planning for team teaching, supervising independent work and meeting with small groups. Working with these groups may

demand 25 to 40 percent more teacher time. However, this problem may be offset by the use of aids and the result may be a greater service for a lower cost than the traditional schedule.

However, Gard also points to the 40 percent of unassigned time in which students are released from supervision. This phase of flexible scheduling too often results in vandalism, off-campus problems, petty theft, loitering on the premises of homeowners and businesses, and absenteeism. In addition to the problems mentioned, the incidence of smoking of cigarettes and marijuana is greater.

For those schools that are determined to initiate a flexible scheduling approach, Gard feels that the following arrangements should be made:

1. Planning of the "master schedule" should be truly adequate to minimize the number of impossible student schedules.
2. Students should not be scheduled for larger loads than the school can support.
3. Faculty members should expect to work harder and to put in longer hours with students.
4. Administrators, board members, students, and community should recognize the price of reduced control—in absenteeism, failure, and even possible violence to person and property. (The community must be prepared for the cost and unpopularity of firm grounds-control measures should this eventually prove necessary.)
5. Ample space should be available for study and research—adequate even for the necessary inefficiency of voluntary usage—and to accommodate the one in four who probably will need full-time supervision.
6. Faculty support measures (aides, supervisors, materials, services) should be adequate to leave teachers free to teach and to plan.[40]

Modular scheduling thus has been successful in some schools and failed dismally in others. The major concern of physical education in considering this plan is the status given to physical education. As was pointed out earlier in the chapter, it is generally recognized that approximately 60 minutes of physical education is necessary every day. Many school systems have achieved this goal. Will modular scheduling affect this daily allotment of time? Authorities in medicine and leaders in education and physical education emphasize the need for physical education every day, as daily exercise is important for the normal growth and development of children. If modular scheduling interferes with fulfilling this requirement, then teachers should urge that the administration provide sufficient modules to allow physical education the minimum recommended time each day.

Movement Education

Since the mid-1950's some leaders in physical education have given impetus to movement exploration and education. Although not a phase of physical education, it has been an underlying concept and the new emphasis is definitely a trend which affects the curriculum in physical education.

Physical education is basically movement. Vigorous movement is the characteristic that distinguishes physical education from other areas in the school curriculum. Although movement exploration has always been synonymous with physical education, many leaders feel that performance in sports skills, rhythms, and other activities is not the ultimate goal if the individual is to become physically educated.

The supporters of movement education advocate that, in addition to the performance in skills, children should have an increased awareness and knowledge of self as related to the acquisition of skill. They feel that children should be better educated regarding movement since movement is a basic factor in the child's day-by-day living. Allenbaugh attempts to show how the experience and knowledge acquired in movement education may be used to meet the demands of any task confronting the individual at any time.[42] She diagrams the information necessary for the foundational aspects of movement education to the specialized acts in Figures 7–30 and 7–31.

There seems to be general agreement that the major emphasis on movement education should be in the elementary school since it is there that the child encounters his first movement experiences. However, there is a place for applying the concepts of movement exploration in secondary physical education. Through the medium of a varied program of activities in the secondary curriculum the student may find the opportunity for creativity and self-expression. As the student learns the

Figure 7–29. A daily program of planned physical education is essential for normal growth and development.

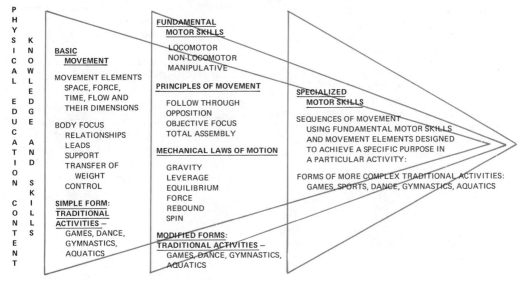

Figure 7–30. Model for movement experiences, foundational to specialized. (Courtesy of Naomi Allenbaugh, Ohio State University.)

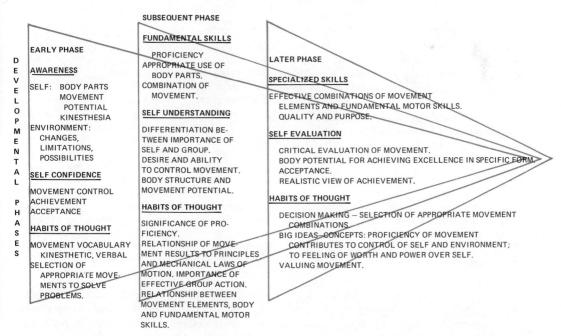

Figure 7–31. Model of developmental phases, related to movement experiences. (Courtesy of Naomi Allenbaugh, Ohio State University.)

skills of dance, basketball and tennis and uses these skills in competition, movement exploration predominates. The neuromuscular mechanisms involved as the individual corrects mistakes, moves from one performance level to another, develops new learnings, has new kinesthetic understanding and new experiences are examples of movement exploration.

Teachers may become confused when they begin to plan content for the movement education program. Logsdon and Barrett simplify the situation by providing a movement analysis form consisting of four categories: *how* the body moves, *what* the body does, *where* the body moves and *with* what relationships. They elaborate on this concept in Figure 7–32. An understanding of the material shown in this figure should clarify some of the confusion which may arise from a study of movement education.

A FUTURE LOOK AT INNOVATIVE TEACHING

Although differences of opinion exist in educational television, programmed instruction, modular scheduling and team teaching, the future will surely show a break from traditional programs to programs that provide quality instruction for all. Probably the most challenging overview of the program of the future is described in the article by J. Lloyd Trump entitled *An Image of a Future Secondary School Health, Physical Education, and Recreation Program.* In this article the author reviews the needs of physical education and recommends new approaches. The approaches grew out of experimental projects sponsored by the National Association of Secondary School Principals which involved 100 junior and senior high schools.

In the school of the future there will be three types of classes based on the purposes and content of instruction. These types are:

1. Classes of 100–150 students for *large group instruction*
2. Classes of 15 or fewer for *small group instruction*
3. Classes of 60, deployable in size at will, for work in laboratories.

The schedule of tomorrow's student will show a minimum of 200 minutes per week with emphasis as follows:

40 minutes—once a week as member of a large group
40 minutes—once a week as a member of a class of 15
120 minutes—twice a week in the laboratory

In the author's school of the future there will be six kinds of staff members: (1) professional teachers, (2) instruction assistants, (3) general aides, (4) clerks, (5) community consultants, and (6) professional consultants. This staffing pattern provides for more individualized instruction, preparation, planning and evaluation.

A number of advantages are achieved from organizing the school of the future using the guidelines shown above. The advantages are:

1. All students every year they are in school will receive motivation and assistance from the most able persons on the staff or in the community.
2. The professional competence, as well as individual differences in teaching strength, of the professional teachers will be utilized.
3. Individual differences among students will be recognized more quickly in classes of fifteen, and in work in the laboratories.
4. Teachers will have more time to plan and evaluate instruction. Clerks and instruction assistants will help them accumulate data and keep better records of individual student needs and accomplishments.
5. The purpose of instruction will be to develop individual responsibility on the part of students for personal programs.
6. What happens in health, physical education, and recreation outside of school will be integrated more closely with what happens inside the classroom.
7. The playing of games in either intramural or interscholastic competition will be an outgrowth of instruction in the classroom rather than the major determinant of how time is spent in the classroom and the nature of the spaces where instruction occurs.
8. Some significant steps will be taken to raise the professional standards of teachers. Teachers will do the teaching, clerks the clerking, instructional assistants and general aides the subprofessional tasks, and machines will automate some parts of teaching.[42]

It is the author's opinion that flexibility within the daily requirement with a wise use of electives is the most satisfactory arrangement for physical education. Those systems that have experimented with this approach find that it meets the needs of

MOVEMENT ANALYSIS

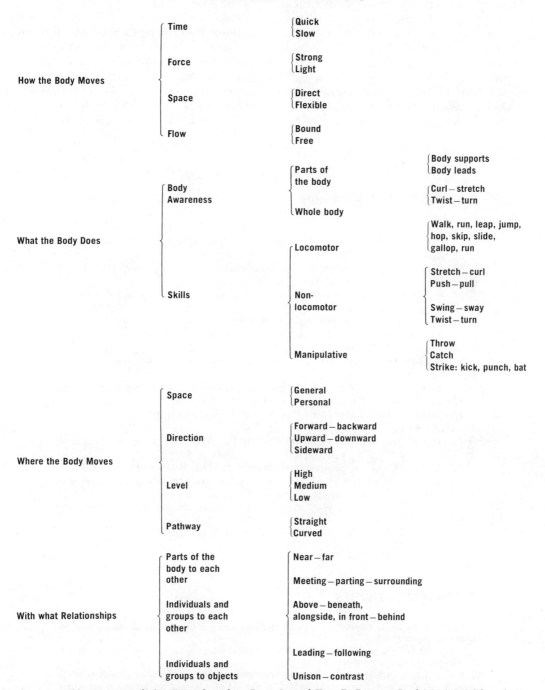

Figure 7–32. Movement analysis. (From Logsdon, Bette J., and Kate R. Barrett: *Ready! Set! Go!*, Bloomington, Indiana: National Instructional Television, 1969, p. 6).

students without creating the problems that arise when physical education deviates from the daily requirement. (See pp. 206–207 in this chapter).

Many pupils will terminate their education at the end of high school. If the program of physical education is to have meaning and attain its objectives, it should offer boys and girls of high school age a program that will encourage their participation in activity beyond the school years.

The discussion of the foundations for effective teaching presented in this chapter has attempted to bring the teacher to the point of organizing the actual class period, which will be covered in more detail in Chapter 10.

The importance of developing the foundations for teaching discussed in this chapter must not be minimized. Hetherington stressed years ago the importance of establishing foundations for effective teaching and emphasized the need for correlating all elements as a working whole in the practical process of teaching, a point of view which is just as valid today.[41]

QUESTIONS FOR DISCUSSION

1. Why is good teaching particularly important in physical education?
2. Why should teachers of physical education have an understanding of child growth and development?
3. What is the basic purpose of physical education in the junior high school? In the senior high school?
4. Compare the characteristics of the junior high school pupil and the senior high school pupil.
5. Discuss the advantages of pupil elective in the senior high school.
6. Why is it important that physical education be required?
7. List the advantages of scheduling pupils by grade.
8. What is a teaching station? How is a teaching station determined in physical education?
9. What are the plans for including content in the physical education curriculum? Discuss the advantages and disadvantages of each.
10. What are the advantages of educational television in physical education? Disadvantages?
11. Would you attempt to use educational television in physical education? Why?
12. What is meant by programmed learning? What is your opinion of it?
13. What is meant by team teaching? What are the advantages and disadvantages of team teaching in physical education?
14. Do you think team teaching may be used to an advantage in physical education? How?
15. What is meant by modular scheduling? What are the advantages and disadvantages?

SUGGESTED ACTIVITIES

1. Construct a yearly calendar for boys for your own school or one with which you are familiar. Construct one for girls.
2. Describe how you would initiate an orientation-pupil choice program in a school which is organized on the 7–5 plan or the 6–6 plan.
3. As a class project, survey one or more of the following groups to determine such items as (1) activities in which they currently participate, (2) whether they learned the activity in secondary school, (3) which activities they would choose to learn if they could go through their high school physical education program again, and (4) whether they had a choice of activity instruction in high school. Groups to be surveyed:

> College graduates — men
> College graduates — women
> High school graduates — men

High school graduates — women
School drop-outs — men
School drop-outs — women

Lists of persons for the various groups might be obtained from local high schools or colleges, or from rosters of professional organizations.

4. Observe one program which utilizes the traditional scheduling arrangement and one which operates on the flexible scheduling plan. List the advantages and disadvantages of each, based on your observations.

REFERENCES

1. *Required Physical Education Must Be Retained in the California Public Schools*, p. 7 (Burlingame: California Association for Health, Physical Education and Recreation, 1961).
2. *A Physical Education Program for Today's Youth* (Washington, D.C.: National Conference for the Mobilization of Health Education, Physical Education and Recreation; American Association for Health, Physical Education and Recreation, March, 1951).
3. *Youth and Fitness: A Program for Secondary Schools*, p. 24 Report of the National Conference on Fitness of Secondary School Youth (Washington, D.C.: American Association for Health, Physical Education and Recreation, 1959).
4. *Youth Physical Fitness*, p. 11 (Washington, D.C.: President's Council on Youth Fitness, Parts I and II, 1961).
5. President's Council on Physical Fitness and Sports: "What Physicians Say About Physical Education," 1972.
6. Lloyd S. Michael, "Time for Teaching Health and Physical Education," *Report of the Seventh National Congress on Physicians and Schools*, p. 18 (Chicago: American Medical Association, 1959).
7. Joseph Gruber, "Exercise and Fitness," pp. 1; 31 (From a paper delivered at the annual convention of the American Association for the Advancement of Science, Dallas, Texas, December, 1968).
8. Greyson Daughtrey and John B. Woods, *Physical Education Program: Organization and Administration*, p. 67 (Philadelphia: W. B. Saunders Company, 1971).
9. *Yearly Calendar* (From materials received through correspondence from the Cedar Rapids, Iowa School System).
10. *Physical Education for Boys, Grades 7–12*, pp. 13–16 (Brooklyn: Board of Education of the City of New York, 1963–1964).
11. *Physical Education, A Guide for Secondary Schools* (Little Rock: Arkansas State Department of Education, 1966).
12. Jay B. Nash, Francis J. Moench, and Jeannette B. Sauborn, *Physical Education: Organization and Administration*, pp. 303; 304 (New York: A. B. Barnes & Company, 1951).
13. Nelson L. Bossing and Roscoe V. Cramer, *The Junior High School*, p. 191 (Boston: The Houghton-Mifflin Company, 1965).
14. *Building Healthier Youth* (a Guidebook), Norfolk Public Schools, Norfolk, Virginia.
15. Don Hermann and Wayne Osness, "A Scientific Curriculum for High School Physical Education," *JOHPER*, pp. 26; 27 (March, 1966).
16. Lois J. McDonald, "An Elective Curriculum," *JOHPER*, pp. 28–29 (September, 1971).
17. "Allowing High School Students to Select Physical Education Activities," *Physical Education Newsletter* (April 1, 1971).
18. *Electing Activities in Physical Education* (From materials received through correspondence from the Grace M. Davis High School, Modesto, California).
19. "Scheduling Activities to Fit Individual Needs," *Physical Education Newsletter* (May 1, 1967).
20. John Scanlon, "Classroom TV Enters a New Era." *In* Paul Woodring and John Scanlon (eds.), *American Education Today*, pp. 220–221 (New York: McGraw-Hill Book Company, 1963).
21. Chris DeYoung and Richard Wynn, *American Education*, 5th ed., pp. 494; 495 (New York: McGraw-Hill Book Company, 1964).
22. Harold Alberty and Elsie Alberty, *Reorganizing the High School Curriculum*, p. 13 (New York: The Macmillan Company, 1962).
23. William C. Trowe, *Teacher and Technology*, p. 87 (New York: Appleton-Century-Crofts, 1963).
24. Roy R. Gray, "Utilization of Educational Television Programs for Physical Education," *JOHPER*, p. 85 (May, 1969).

25. Spencer Klaw, "What Can We Learn from the Teaching Machine?" In Henry Ehlers and Lee Gordon, *Crucial Issues in Education,* p. 355 (New York: Holt, Rinehart and Winston, 1964).

26. John Gardner, "National Goals in Education." In *Goals for Americans.* Report of the President's Commission on National Goals, p. 90 (Columbia University, 1960).

27. Gerald Grant, "Teaching-Aid Market Lures Business," *The Virginian-Pilot* (Norfolk), July 3, 1966.

28. Lawrence F. Locke, "Prepackaged Sports Skills Instruction: A Review of Selected Research," *JOHPER,* p. 57 (September, 1971).

29. "Achieving Excellence in Physical Education Through Team Teaching Techniques," *Physical Education Newsletter* (March 1, 1971).

30. "Team Teaching: An Aid to Planning and Presenting a Vitalized PE Program Geared to Individual Needs," *Physical Education Newsletter* (March 12, 1963).

31. J. Lloyd Trump and Dorsey Baynham, *Guide to Better Schools,* p. 87 (Chicago: Rand McNally and Company, 1961).

32. "An Experiment in Team Teaching," A Committee Report. *The Bulletin of the National Association of Secondary Principals,* pp. 74–76 (December, 1962).

33. James A. Meyers, "Teaming—A First Step for Interdisciplinary Teaching," *The Clearing House,* p. 407 (March, 1967).

34. Gordon F. Vars, "Can Team Teaching Save the Core Curriculum?," p. 260, *Phi Delta Kappan* (January, 1966).

35. J. Galen Saylor and William Alexander, *Curriculum Planning for Modern Schools,* pp. 363–364 (New York: Holt, Rinehart and Winston, Inc., 1966).

36. Harl Douglass, *The High School Curriculum* 3rd ed., pp. 586–587 (New York: The Ronald Press Company, 1964).

37. "Flexible Modular Scheduling in High School PE," *Physical Education Newsletter* (May 1, 1971).

38. Scott D. Thomson, "Beyond Modular Scheduling," *Phi Delta Kappan,* pp. 484; 485 (April, 1971).

39. "California Study Supports Value of Daily Programs," Newsletter, *President's Council on Physical Fitness and Sports* (December, 1971).

40. Robert R. Gard, "A Realistic Look at the Flexible Schedule," *The Clearing House,* p. 429 (Teaneck, New Jersey: Fairleigh-Dickinson University, March, 1970).

41. Clark W. Hetherington, *School Program in Physical Education,* p. 70 (New York: World Book Company, 1922).

42. Naomi Allenbaugh, "Movement Education—An Interpretation," (mimeographed article). Ohio State University, 1968.

43. Bette J. Logsdon and Kate R. Barrett, *Ready! Set! Go!,* p. 6 (Bloomington, Indiana: National Instructional Television, 1969).

44. J. Lloyd Trump, "An Image of a Future Secondary School Health, Physical Education, and Recreation Program," *JOHPER* (January, 1961).

SELECTED READINGS

Biehler, Robert F. *Psychology Applied to Teaching.* Boston: Houghton-Mifflin Company, 1971.

Brown, Camille and Rosaline Cassidy. *Theory in Physical Education.* Philadelphia: Lea and Febiger, 1963.

Cratty, Bryant. *Movement Behavior and Motor Learning,* 2nd ed. Philadelphia: Lea and Febiger, 1967.

Godfrey, Barbara B., and Newell C. Kephart. *Movement Patterns and Motor Education.* New York: Appleton-Century-Crofts, 1969.

Hughes, William L., Esther French, and Nelson Lehsten. *Administration of Physical Education,* 2nd ed. New York: The Ronald Press, 1962.

Irwin, Leslie W. *The Curriculum in Health and Physical Education.* Dubuque: William C. Brown Company, 1969.

Journal of Health, Physical Education and Recreation, September, 1971.

Latchaw, Marjorie and Glenn Egstrom. *Human Movement.* Englewood Cliffs, New Jersey: Prentice-Hall, Inc., 1969.

Nixon, John E. and Anne E. Jewett. *An Introduction to Physical Education,* 7th ed. Philadelphia: W. B. Saunders Company, 1969.

President's Council on Physical Fitness and Sports. *Newsletter.* December, 1971.

Programmed Instruction in Health Education and Physical Education. American Association of Health, Physical Education and Recreation, 1970.

Smith, Hope. *Introduction to Human Movement.* Reading, Massachusetts: Addison-Wesley Publishing Company, 1968.

Trump, J. Lloyd. *Guide to Better Schools, Focus on Change.* Chicago: Rand McNally and Company, 1961.

Willgoose, Carl E. *The Curriculum in Physical Education.* Englewood Cliffs, New Jersey: Prentice Hall, Inc., 1969.

Williams, Jesse F. *Principles of Physical Education,* 8th ed. Philadelphia: W. B. Saunders Company, 1964.

Wessel, Janet. *Movement Fundamentals: Figure, Form, Fun,* 3rd ed. Englewood Cliffs, New Jersey: Prentice-Hall, Inc., 1970.

Chapter 8

LEARNING AND MOTIVATION

Even ordinary man, given a chance, can create.

William Kilpatrick

Courtesy, Washington High School, Germantown, Wisconsin

Motivation is the foundation of education —without it, no learning takes place. Webster defines motivation as "that within the individual, rather than without, which incites him to action; any idea, need, emotion, or organic state that prompts to an action." Moreover, psychologists tell us that learning is a change in the behavior of the learner and that it occurs only when the learner himself is active in the learning process. Therefore, if the purpose of education is to promote learning, then that purpose essentially is to *motivate*; that is, to stimulate within the individual the desire to learn.

Chapter 2 cited the need for motivating the play urge as a crucial issue in physical education. This urge was described in Chapter 5 as one of the basic drives of man and it was shown that this play urge is expressed through the fundamental natural movements. Provision for a desirable manifestation of the play urge was listed as one of the guidelines in the basic philosophy of physical education. It has also been pointed out that although a minimal amount of activity has been established by the medical profession and other authorities as necessary for normal growth and development, the time assigned to physical education within the school day is not

adequate to meet this need. Therefore, as has been shown in previous chapters, physical education must create, through properly selected activities and effective instruction in the classroom, a desire within the pupils to participate in the activities during after-school hours.

It is obviously impossible to cover within the class period the total volume of knowledge in any subject—mathematics, science, or physical education. Pupils must be motivated first to learn, to explore, to rehearse, and to apply after school what he has learned in the classroom. The health and fitness of youth depends on pupil motivation toward these goals and the school cannot delegate its responsibility in promoting this motivation.

Various attempts have been made on a national scale to charge the Boys' Clubs, the Young Men's and Young Women's Christian Associations, the community recreational programs, and other agencies with the responsibility of educating for health and fitness. These organizations, though they have the highest aims and efforts, are totally inadequate for this purpose partly because their programs are permissive programs and reach only a small group and also because their staffs are not trained professional educators. The children who

241

take advantage of these programs do so on a voluntary basis. They participate only if they wish; and, if another activity offers greater appeal, they leave. Frequently these other activities make little or no contribution to health and physical fitness.

The physical education program in our schools is ideally suited to guide all children into a pattern of activity that will contribute to their health and fitness. First, children, with the exception of the severely handicapped, are required by law to attend school; therefore, nearly all children can be reached. Second, schools are organized to bring the appropriate physical facilities and professionally trained personnel together in an environment conducive to learning.

Even with these conditions, motivation remains the greatest task of the teacher, who must find ways of stimulating interest, not only within the class period, but for carry-over to the after-school environment as well.

The modern urban environment, where the majority of our youth live, usually inhibits or prevents the basic play urge from finding its natural expression. Moreover, the situation is usually intensified when the child enters school. If the reader were to consider the changes in his own activity, for example, from the time of early childhood until the present, the chances are that his activity has decreased progressively each year. If so, he fits the usual pattern.

Boys and girls from birth to about six years usually have the opportunity of attaining the minimal three to five hours daily of vigorous activity needed for normal growth and development. They romp, fall down, climb, run, dodge, chase, and rest when nature demands it. Most children satisfy this need in the home or the immediate neighborhood.

At the age of six years most children enter school, and at this point inactivity begins to predominate their day. Approximately five hours are spent in nonmovement tasks during the school day. No longer are they able spontaneously to run, climb, romp, dodge, and engage in the fundamental movements of life as freely as they did before entering school.

As the years pass, the after-school hours as well are filled with inactivity. Riding buses and autos, viewing television and motion pictures, eating, preparing homework, and other nonmovement activity occupy the hours between the close of the school day and retiring. Studies show that about 85 percent of the child's life is spent in nonmovement programs.[1]

We in America have probably the greatest interscholastic and intercollegiate sports program in the world. Each year more emphasis is placed on these programs. Each year more spectators witness them. These programs are important and provide the same opportunity for the physically gifted that honors or advanced study programs provide for the academically gifted. Yet the grass-roots program of sports activities for the masses of boys and girls has not improved very much. The urge for activity continues to be stifled. The schools must counteract this situation by motivating youth through carefully planned, well-equipped, and effectively taught physical education programs.

IMPORTANCE OF QUALITY INSTRUCTION

Another area of concern of physical education (discussed in Chapter 2) is the need to improve instruction. It should be emphasized that motivation of the play urge and the desire to carry it into after-school participation depend upon the excellence of teaching skills in the classroom. Through quality instruction in the skills of sports that may be played after school, boys and girls will be motivated to carry their activity program into the community environment and establish good exercise habits for life.

The essential quality of successful teaching is the ability of the teacher to motivate the student to learn. But, you may ask, can this quality be developed? What is learning, anyway? How do pupils learn? These questions serve as the next point of departure in your own learning process.

Every teacher should have a basic understanding of what is known about the way pupils learn. Considerable research has been conducted through the years in the psychology of learning. Most teacher-preparation programs require a course in this area. It is not our purpose here to duplicate this but instead to give a review of such a course, and to clarify some of the basic concepts about the learning process. Additional sources for further reading are given at the end of this chapter for students who would like a more thorough review.

THEORIES OF LEARNING

At the outset, teachers should understand that most experiments in learning theories have been planned around learning the content of academic subjects. The teaching of physical education activities which consist largely of instruction in motor skills requires different approaches and techniques from those used for teaching academic subjects. However, students of physical education should have an overall knowledge of how students learn and to what extent theories of learning can be adapted to teaching in physical education.

Research in the field of learning has led to the development of a number of theories that will assist the teacher in understanding the learning process. Although we do not yet know how learning actually takes place, two general learning theories now dominate the thinking of educational leaders: the *stimulus-response* theory and the *cognitive* or field theory. Figure 8–1 gives a composite overview of the generally recognized theories of learning.

The Stimulus-Response (Associative) Theory

According to the stimulus-response (S–R) theory, learning is associating and conditioning. The individual is stimulated to perform an act or response, and if the act or response is accompanied by pleasure or satisfaction, it will be remembered and repeated. Thorndike is credited with fostering this theory; through his efforts it has played a dominant role in learning theory for many years.[2] Proponents of this theory believe that the whole is the sum of the parts and that the best way to teach is to teach the parts separately.

Characteristics. The S–R theory has been described in several ways by psychologists, but certain characteristics are common to most of their definitions. The outstand-

ing characteristics of the stimulus-response theory are:

1. Learning is correcting.
2. Learning is remembering.
3. Learning is habit formation.
4. Teaching is the arrangement of situations leading to desirable bonds and making them satisfying.
5. Manipulating is more important than construction.
6. Early learning is more chance than perception.
7. Learning is drill.
8. Learning is passive.

Thorndike was also responsible for the following *laws of learning*, which have through the years had a strong influence on education and the teaching process.

Law of Exercise. The law of exercise states that when the effort (response) made to a situation (stimulus) is satisfying, it becomes linked to the situation; the more it is exercised, the more strongly it becomes linked to the situation.

The law of exercise has had a strong application in the teaching of skills in physical education. Pupils participate in activities that are interesting and that satisfy the basic play urge. It is the responsibility of teachers when teaching the skills of activities to provide the best possible demonstration of skills. They should constantly assist all pupils in improving their performance to keep the learning situation satisfying. Pupils will learn skills quickly and effectively if they are shown the correct form and are taught the procedure correctly. Continual practice in the correct techniques will assure improvement, which in turn will bring about satisfaction. Figure 8–2 illustrates how the law of exercise may be applied to an activity.

Kellog explains the importance of the law of exercise as related to the acquisition of skills in the following statement:

> Improvement in skill is not a matter of finding out what is to be done, but of doing it better and better. Skills may, therefore, be placed under the heading of overlearning. Their single most important principle is the Law of Exercise, upon which their efficiency must ultimately depend.[3]

Law of Effect. The law of effect or operant learning is based on the premise that the associations that connect the situation (stimulus) and the effort (response) are made stronger when the effort is satisfying,

REPRESENTATIVE THEORIES OF LEARN

	I	II	III
	THEORY OF LEARNING	PSYCHOLOGICAL SYSTEM OR OUTLOOK	ASSUMPTION CONCERNING THE BASIC MORAL AND PSYCHOLOGICAL NATURE OF MAN
MIND SUBSTANCE FAMILY	1. Theistic mental discipline	faculty psychology	bad-active mind substance continues active until curbed
	2. Humanistic mental discipline	classicism	neutral-active mind substance to be developed through exercise
	3. Natural unfoldment	romantic naturalism	good-active natural personality to unfold
	4. Apperception or Herbartionism	structuralism	neutral-passive mind composed of active mental states or ideas
CONDITIONING THEORIES OF STIMULUS-RESPONSE (S-R) ASSOCIATIONISTIC FAMILY	5. S-R bond	connectionism	neutral-passive or reactive organism with many potential S-R connections
	6. Conditioning (with no reinforcement)	behaviorism	neutral-passive or reactive organism with innate reflexive drives and emotions
	7. Reinforcement and conditioning	reinforcement	neutral-passive organism with innate reflexes and needs with their drive stimuli
COGNITIVE THEORIES OF GESTALT-FIELD FAMILY	8. Insight	Gestalt psychology	naturally-active being whose activity follows psychological laws of organization
	9. Goal insight	configurationalism	neutral-interactive purposive individual in sequential relationships with environment
	10. Cognitive-field	field psychology or relativism	neutral-interactive purposive person in simultaneous mutual interaction with environment, including other persons

Figure 8–1. Representative theories of learning and their implications for education. (From Bigge, Morris, L.: "Theories of Learning," *Journal of the National Education Association*, March, 1966, p. 18.)

Figure 8–1 continued on opposite page.

D THEIR IMPLICATIONS FOR EDUCATION

IV	V	VI	VII
BASIS FOR TRANSFER OF LEARNING	**MAIN EMPHASIS IN TEACHING**	**KEY PERSONS**	**CONTEMPORARY EXPONENTS**
exercised faculties, automatic transfer	exercise of faculties—the "muscles" of the mind	St. Augustine, John Calvin, J. Edwards	many Hebraic-Christian fundamentalists
cultivated mind or intellect	training of intrinsic mental power	Plato, Aristotle	M. J. Adler, St. John's College
recapitulation of racial history, no transfer needed	negative or permissive education	J. J. Rousseau, F. Froebel	extreme progressivists
growing apperceptive mass	addition of new mental states or ideas to a store of old ones	J. F. Herbart, E. B. Titchener	many teachers and administrators
identical elements	promotion of acquisition of desired S-R connections	E. L. Thorndike	J. M. Stephens, A. I. Gates
conditioned responses or reflexes	promotion of adhesion of desired responses to appropriate stimuli	J. B. Watson	E. R. Guthrie
reinforced or conditioned responses	successive, systematic changes in organisms' environment to increase the probability of desired responses (operants)	C. L. Hull	B. F. Skinner, K. W. Spence
transposition of insights	promotion of insightful learning	M. Wertheimer, K. Koffka	W. Köhler
tested insights	aid students in trial-and-error, goal-directed learning	B. H. Bode, R. H. Wheeler	E. E. Bayles
continuity of life spaces, experience, or insights	help students restructure their life spaces—gain new insights into their contemporaneous situations	Kurt Lewin, E. C. Tolman, J. S. Bruner	R. G. Barker, A. W. Combs, H. F. Wright, M. L. Bigge

Figure 8–1. *Continued.*

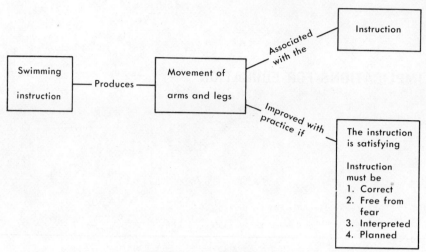

Figure 8-2. Law of Exercise.

successful and pleasant. On the other hand, if the effort is unsuccessful, unpleasant, or unsatisfying, the association is weakened. Figures 8-3 and 8-4 illustrate how the law of effect may be applied to teaching the handspring.

Physical education teachers often express concern about the lack of interest in their classes and about the many problems of discipline and inattention. They might take some lessons from coaches, professional dance teachers and dramatic club directors, successful teachers who seem to have no difficulty with participants reporting on time, dressing quickly, and giving their all for the same activity that was repulsive to them in the instructional class. The diagrams point out the importance of good teaching in the application of the law of effect in a physical education situation.

Law of Readiness. The law of readiness postulates that pupils learn when they are ready to learn. This law points to the need for adjusting the instruction to the level of maturity of the learner, setting the stage for learning by establishing a wholesome teaching climate and applying the principles of growth and development.

The theories of Thorndike have been strongly supported over the years by many leaders in education and psychology, such as Guthrie,[4] Hull,[5] and Skinner. In recent years Skinner probably has been the strongest supporter of the view that learning consists of associations between stimuli and response. He is known for his extensive experiments with rats and pigeons. From these experiments he developed programmed instruction which is prevalent in many schools today.

Skinner is one of the most vocal critics of present day education. He maintains that education is failing and makes the following observations:

1. The most widely publicized efforts to improve education show an extraordinary neglect of method. Learning and teaching are not analyzed, and almost no effort is made to improve teaching as such.

2. It is argued that a good teacher is simply one who knows his subject matter and is interested in it. Any special knowledge of pedagogy as a basic science of teaching is felt to be unnecessary.

3. Education is in more than one sense "compulsory." If a teacher is in any doubt

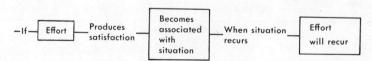

Figure 8-3. Law of Effect.

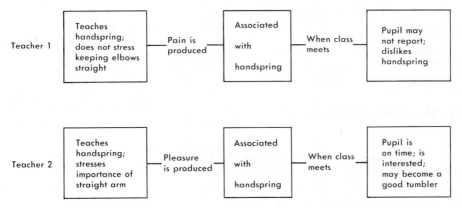

Figure 8–4. Application of the Law of Effect to teaching the handspring.

about his own methods, he should ask himself a few questions. Do my students stop work immediately when I dismiss the class? (If so, dismissal is obviously a release from a threat.) Do they welcome rather than regret vacations and unscheduled days of no school? Do I reward them for good behavior by excusing them from other assignments? Do I punish them by giving them additional assignments? Do I frequently say, "Pay attention," "Now remember," or otherwise gently "admonish" them? Do I find it necessary from time to time to "get tough" and threaten some form of punishment?

4. Perhaps the most serious criticism of the current classroom is the relative infrequency of reinforcement. Since the pupil is usually dependent upon the teacher for being told that he is right, and since many pupils are usually dependent upon the same teacher, the total number of contingencies which may be arranged during, say, the first four years, is of the order of only a few thousand. But a very rough estimate suggests that efficient mathematical behavior at this level requires something of the order of 25,000 contingencies.[6]

Skinner feels that teachers fail because of aversive control, a form of discipline that is less severe but more ingenious than corporal punishment. He elaborates on this method of educational control:

1. The child at his desk, filling in his workbook, is behaving primarily to escape from the threat of a series of minor aversive agents—the teacher's displeasure, the criticism or ridicule of his classmates, an ignominious showing in a competition, low marks, a trip to the office "to be talked to" by the principal, or a word to the parent who may still resort to the birch rod.

2. A much less obvious but equally serious effect of aversive control is plain inaction. The student is sullen, stubborn, and unresponsive.

He "blocks," he refuses to obey. Inaction is sometimes a form of escape (rather than carry out an assignment, the student simply takes punishment as the lesser evil) and sometimes a form of attack, the object of which is to enrage the teacher, but it is also in its own right a predictable effect of aversive control.[6]

Chapter 9 discusses another viewpoint in aversive control and suggests situations in which it can be effectively used.

The reader may draw the obvious conclusion from studying the S–R theory of learning that the teacher is in absolute control of the learning situation. The ultimate in the S–R theory of learning is the teaching machine.

Although the S–R theory is the most widely used in America, it has been vigorously attacked. Some of the criticisms of the associationistic view are discussed by Seagoe:

1. The associationists presuppose specific stimulus-response bonds, whereas the stimulus to any reaction above the reflex level affects a group of cells rather than single units, the response being to a ratio. Actually, there are mutually inhibiting and reinforcing effects present in each situation, determined not only by the nature and complexity of the stimulus but also by the disposition of the learner.

2. The emphasis on the element or part as the primary unit is questionable. Our perceptions are not built up additively, but fall into patterns. Our perceptions are of wholes.

3. The emphasis on chance success and habituation rules out the possibility of intelligent behavior. Understanding and reconstruction have no place in such systems. Learning is really concerned with thinking rather than habituation. It is active, not passive. Many of

the situations were "blind," making intelligent solution impossible.[7]

These criticisms of the S–R theory may serve as a point of departure to the study of the cognitive theory discussed below.

The Cognitive (Field) Theory of Learning

This theory proposes that the response is not to the stimulus but to the learner's inner perception of the reconstruction of the stimulus in terms of the whole situation. The entire process is a sequence of intelligent behavior. Since it involves a broad field of influence, it is also called the "field" theory.

Various psychologists claim that learning is best accomplished when the whole situation is understood. This approach to learning sometimes creates a chaotic situation because it has its basis in the simultaneous perception of the many parts of the whole. The teaching situation may seem hopeless until the pupil suddenly develops the insight to grasp the proper procedure and attain the desired objective.

Characteristics of the Cognitive Theory. Some tenets of the cognitive theory are that learning is:

1. a form of intelligent behavior
2. stimulation of inner forces
3. based on insight
4. not a response to a stimulus but to the learner's inner perception and reconstruction of the stimulus
5. not repetitive
6. based on the whole relationship
7. based on intuitive thinking

An outstanding advocate of the cognitive theory is Jerome Bruner. He advocates the discovery approach and emphasizes the importance of intuitive thinking in classroom situations. Some of his ideas on intuitive thinking are discussed below:

1. The complementary nature of intuitive and analytic thinking should, we think, be recognized. Through intuitive thinking the individual may often arrive at solutions to problems which he would not achieve at all, or at best more slowly, through analytic thinking.
2. In contrast to analytic thinking, intuitive thinking characteristically does not advance in careful, well-defined steps. Indeed, it tends to

involve maneuvers based seemingly on an implicit perception of the total problem. The thinker arrives at an answer, which may be right or wrong, with little if any awareness of the process by which he reached it.
3. It seems unlikely that a student would develop or have confidence in his intuitive methods of thinking if he never saw them used effectively by his elders. The teacher who is willing to guess at answers to questions asked by the class and then subject his guesses to critical analysis may be more apt to build those habits into his students than would a teacher who analyzes everything for the class in advance.[8]

In the cognitive theory of learning, although the teacher still plays an important role in the learning process, the *major emphasis is on the discovery approach.* The teacher using this approach places students in situations in which insight determines the solution to the problem.

The advocates of the cognitive theory oppose the S–R theory on the grounds that too much time is wasted in the classroom on dull routine, boring drill and formality. According to them, children are not allowed to think through a problem or situation but instead are coerced into following authoritarian procedures.

There are many people, however, who look with disfavor upon the cognitive theory. Some of their criticisms are:

1. The criteria of insightful learning do not differentiate insight from trial-and-error as a mode of behavior. Insight refers to the end-product of learning and is not descriptive of the learning process. Apparently insightful learning is that which takes place without overt activity; trial and error is that in which the activity is overt. Essentially they are of the same exploratory and chance-success nature.
2. The stress on whole-relationships is included in stimulus-response versions of learning, which were never as atomistic as the Gestalt psychologists claim. A stimulus has always meant a complex interacting situation and a response a complex form of behavior.
3. The experimentation is somewhat subjective and perhaps over-interpreted. The very fact that it assumes inner reorganization makes it difficult to test experimentally.[7]

Teachers and students as they study the theories of learning are usually confused since it is difficult to apply the theories to the actual physical education classroom situation. Each of the two groups, briefly discussed in the foregoing paragraphs, has distinct value in planning teaching procedures.

Although wide differences seem to exist when the two theories are studied, in reality there are converging similarities. Hilgard shows just how the two theories complement each other with neither complete in itself. He suggests that learning can be graded on a scale with the associative theory placed at one end of the continuum and with the cognitive at the other. Figure 8–5 illustrates such a scale. On the left, habits are learned automatically without awareness and with a minimum of understanding. Tasks that require reasoning and understanding fall to the right of the continuum. The majority of learnings fall somewhere in a "mixture" between the associative and the cognitive.[9]

A practical application of the premise discussed above may be illustrated in learning to serve a tennis ball effectively. Not only does the act involve hitting the ball (associative) but it also entails insight and awareness of the opponent's position on the court, height of the net, position on the court after the serve, placement of the ball in the opponent's court and anticipation of the opponent's type of return (cognitive learnings).

A further study by Garry and Kingsley reveals several points of agreement which are generally accepted. These are:

1. Association and cognitive theorists alike agree on the complexity of stimulus-response relationships. Learning requires identification of the relevant stimuli in a complex field. Where these lack the prominence provided by field-ground relationships or natural groupings, steps to heighten the relevant stimuli are needed.

2. Individual organisms differ in their capacity to recognize or discriminate relevant stimuli. These differences stem from innate organic differences and from previous experiences. Regardless of the course of the differences, the task has to be appropriate to and within the range of competence of the individual.

3. Individual organisms differ in their capacity for making the required responses. Whatever the individual response repertoire, stimulus conditions must be arranged to increase the probability of the occurrence of the desired response relative to other possible responses.

4. Motivation initiates and directs behavior and leads to particular responses organized for the attainment of a particular end, which, if resulting in satisfaction of motives, are more likely to recur. Motives may be organic or acquired, general or specific. Motives may serve to heighten sensitivity to specific stimuli (food or fear), or to provide general arousal (anxiety). Excessive motivation disrupts the complex of

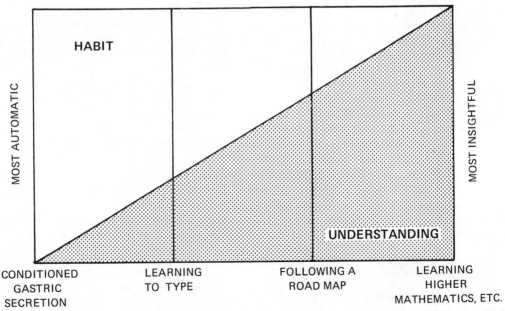

Figure 8–5. Automatic vs. insightful learning. (From Hilgard, Ernest R.: *Introduction to Psychology.* New York: Harcourt, Brace and World, 1962.)

stimulus-response relationships by producing a narrowing of stimulus sensitivity and concomitant emotional response. Acquired motives are subject to principles of learning.

5. The crux of learning lies in the learner's recognizing the appropriateness of his response and modifying future tries in the light of previous experience. This action is dependent upon the ability of the organism to discriminate between differences and generalize between similarities. Direct knowledge of results may suffice. The less the capacity of the organism and the more complex the stimulus-response relationship, the more dependent success will be on the manipulation of rewards and punishment.[10]

Readiness in Learning

While it is generally agreed that a state of readiness for learning must exist, opinions differ as to just how educational programs should be structured to create an atmosphere of readiness for learning. As the growth and development of children and their characteristics at various grade levels become involved at this point, students should review the information in Chapter 6.

In the course of teaching there occur moments in which the student is optimally ready to learn skills. The teacher should attempt to recognize these moments of readiness and take advantage of them in his efforts to make instruction more effective. This is a difficult task, since all students mature at different rates; but if such times are not recognized and attempts are made to force learning at the wrong time, negative attitudes may result.

The teachable moment depends on maturation, relative to which psychologists offer various views. Havighurst believes that children have developmental tasks at various stages of development. He relates these tasks to the teachable moment in the following statement:

When the body is ripe, and society requires, and the self is ready to achieve a certain task, the teachable moment has come. Efforts at teaching which would have been largely wasted if they had come earlier, give gratifying results when they come at the <u>teachable moment</u> when the task should be learned.[11]

A review of the thinking of leaders in psychology regarding the approaches to readiness reveals two concepts that are as distinctly different as they are controversial.

They are described by Biehler as (1) the natural approach and (2) the guided-experience approach.[12]

The Natural Approach. Some educators and psychologists support the premise that the development of the child depends on natural inner growth and maturation. They feel that he should not be subjected to curriculum content until he has reached the level of maturity at which he is ready to benefit by the instruction. Crow and Crow strongly assert that:

Patterns and rate of learning are determined by maturation or internal growth rather than by experience or training. . . . No matter how great the inner urge or the outer pressure may be, the learning process involved in a skill mastery cannot begin effectively until a state of readiness for such learning has been reached.[13]

J. R. Hilgard in her studies showed that older, more mature children learn more rapidly and more easily than younger children. She made her observations from experiments with groups of two and three-year olds who were given training for 12 weeks in buttoning, ladder climbing, and the use of scissors. She concluded that general physiological maturation plus experiences other than specific training had contributed to faster development.[14]

Ernest Hilgard reviews several experiments in maturation in human behavior and arrives at generalizations concerning the relationships of maturation to proficiency through training. These generalizations are given in order to relate maturation to learning:

1. *Skills that build upon developing behavior patterns are most easily learned.* In almost all languages there are words for mother and father with sound patterns similar to pa-pa and ma-ma. The infant may be taught words like these that fit in his natural babling because these words are like the sounds that he makes spontaneously.

2. *The rate of development remains uniform within wide ranges of stimulation.* The maturation of performance often requires environmental support, since growth alone is not enough to account for the resulting behavior. But maturation may still be fundamental in accounting for the rate of development.

3. *The more mature the organism the less training is needed to reach a given level of proficiency.* Many experiments point to faster gains of older children over younger, with the same amount of directed practice. Maturation thus produces a certain *readiness* for specific kinds of learning.

4. *Training given before maturational readiness may bring either no improvement or only temporary improvement.*

5. *Premature training, if frustrating, may do more harm than good.* Although lack of training delays development, the lack appears to do no harm, for the retardation is overcome when practice begins. What is the effect of overstimulation; that is, premature training before maturational readiness? May it also retard development? The child who has been exposed too early to an activity for which he is not ready may lose his natural enthusiasm for the activity when he reaches the stage of development appropriate for it.[9]

On the other hand, some theorists disagree with the natural or maturation view in structuring educational programs. They feel that the guided experience approach is better.

Guided Experience Approach. The proponents of the guided experience approach oppose the natural approach on the grounds that it is permissive. Instead they substitute the view that growth consists of steps and stages of learning and that children should be guided through them. They feel that waiting for children to learn is wasteful and inefficient. It is their belief that children learn more when they are guided through the various stages of instruction with the teacher serving as the leader for accelerating the learning process.

Bruner in his view on readiness for learning speaks of the "spiral curriculum." He feels that:

1. If one respects the way of thought of the growing child, if one is courteous enough to translate material into his logical forms and challenging enough to tempt him to advance, then it is possible to introduce him at an early age to the ideas and styles that in later life make an educated man.

2. If the hypothesis with which this section was introduced is true—that any subject can be taught to any child in some honest form—then it should follow that a curriculum ought to be built around great issues, principles and values that a society deems worthy of continued concern of its members.[8]

Transfer of Learning

A brief discussion of *transfer of learning* would be useful at this point. This term is used to identify and describe the process by which a mental or motor function shows improvement not by direct practice but as a result of practice at some other related activity.[10]

Teachers of physical education are concerned with the transfer of one sport or activity to another. Although there are many instances where transfer exists, there are just as many situations where there is very little transfer. Persons who have learned tennis skills may adapt them to badminton. However, there is little transfer from tennis to basketball.

Although the effectiveness of the educational system is dependent on the degree to which the material learned in class transfers to actual life, the premise has definite limitations. Many of the early beliefs involving transfer have been found to be groundless and fallacious. Some of the earlier beliefs that are no longer acceptable are:

1. Memorizing facts strengthens the mind.
2. Studying "logical" subjects, such as Latin and geometry improves one's powers of reasoning.
3. Educating students for "real life" by teaching them specialized, practical skills is unworkable mainly because it is impossible to anticipate the great variety of skills that will be required of different individuals in a rapidly changing civilization.[12]

Irrespective of the dilemma which seems to exist in transfer of knowledge and skills, there are several principles that may assist in transferring learning to life situations or from one activity to another. Seagoe summarizes the results of laboratory experiments and research in the following paragraphs:

1. *Positive transfer occurs whenever a specific response already learned is to be made in a similar new situation.* A spelling word learned in writing a story is likely to be spelled correctly in a letter. A word learned in reading one page is usually recognized in a different context. A word element which is constant for a group of words may be pointed out and new words worked out more easily as a result. Training in memorizing poetry will help the child to memorize new poems. This is the theory of identical elements. There may be partial identity of content, or the use of a common method in the two.

2. *Positive transfer occurs whenever a generalization already learned applies in a new situation.* An attitude toward arithmetic formed in the third grade may affect a woman's ability to balance her checkbook. Experience in logical reasoning gained in geometry may under

favorable conditions carry over to estimating heights.

3. *Positive transfer is more likely to occur when there is conscious teaching for transfer.* Transfer is not automatic. For transfer, the material must be taught, not as a specific, but for broader use. Wide experience and factual knowledge do not assure transfer. Transfer is the result of conscious effort, of conscious generalization and application while learning.

4. *The more effective the original teaching, the greater the degree of transfer.* Transfer is more likely to occur when the original learning is complete and accurate, when the materials are meaningful and structured, when the transfer situation is highly similar to the learning situation, when the material provides for continuous reconstruction of experience, when the attitudes toward learning both the original and the transferred materials are favorable, and when the time between original learning and transfer is relatively short.

5. *Individual differences are apparent in the ability to transfer.* Bright children and older children generalize easily; hence they are able to transfer their learnings more widely. The extrovert transfers more than the introvert because of the greater range of his experience. In general, how much transfer occurs for a given child depends on the material to be learned, his experience, his desire to learn, and his training in generalization and transfer procedures.[7]

RECENT VIEWS ON LEARNING

More recent views on how children learn question the theories advanced by Thorndike and others. Gagne summarizes the research of several psychologists which shows that in teaching subjects in school repetition is not necessary. It seems that an item once learned is fully learned. The older concept of learning which emphasized strengthening connections is too simple and does not take into account events that transpire in learning both outside and inside the learner.

Gagne suggests that the most important factor to insure learning is the prior learning of prerequisite capabilities. In other words, the student can learn if he is prepared for it.

Conclusions drawn from research in newer ways of learning have definite implications for instruction. Some ways to assist in the learning process are described in the following paragraphs:

1. It is generally recognized that each learner has different prerequisite skills as he attempts to learn a new activity. A complete diagnostic survey should be made of what the child can and cannot do already.

2. The teacher should have available the prerequisites the child has not already mastered.

3. Students do not need additional practice to ensure retention but should be subjected to periodic and spaced reviews.[15]

PRINCIPLES OF LEARNING

From research and study of the ways in which individuals learn, several guiding principles have been developed on which there seems to be general agreement among educators. According to these principles, learning should be:

1. an active process
2. meaningful
3. useful
4. interesting
5. individualized
6. satisfying
7. unified[18]

THEORIES APPLIED TO PHYSICAL EDUCATION

Growing out of the quest for means of learning faster and better, a necessity created by the space age, are new ideas that may throw added light on the way pupils learn and provide new approaches to effective teaching.

Education in our present culture is an everchanging, dynamic function. The constant change is reflected not only in *what* we teach but also in the *way* we teach. Teachers of physical education, therefore, must be not only familiar with the traditional theories of learning, their applications and shortcomings, but must also be alert to improved concepts and new applications in learning mechanisms.

Acquiring Skills

The basic skill movements, such as crawling, walking, running, and climbing, are learned in the course of normal growth. These are kinetic movements which are part of the general kinesthetic pattern established early and instinctively, since movement is usually an essential part of life.

More refined movements, such as serving in tennis, swinging a golf club, pole vaulting, the western roll in high jumping, wrestling techniques, tumbling movements, and hundreds of other skills included in the physical education curriculum, although closely associated with kinesthetic sense, require instruction and guidance. It is to the acquisition of these skills that learning theories must be applied. At the same time, the learning of most skills includes the coordination of muscles which involve both basic and refined movements. As the teacher plans his program, definite principles of learning skills should be followed.

Principles of Skill Learning

Certain recognized principles of skill learning are necessary to assist the teacher in his overall instructional program. Crow and Crow list some which are frequently used. They show that during the process of learning, the learner must be motivated. This being true, the following principles are basic:

1. *Practice.* Accurate and effective practice is important. The practice must be well-planned, have meaning to the learner, and be adjusted to his growth pattern.
2. *Overlearning.* If the skill is to be learned, its movement must be repeated many times, correctly. Correct and accurate practice will result in an automatic, smooth response or movement, which is the aim of teaching skills.
3. *Practice Periods.* Practice periods should be short, particularly for young children and beginners. As learning progresses, the periods may be a little longer but *never so long as to prevent motivation.*
4. *Distribution of Practice Periods.* The practice periods should be distributed over long periods of time rather than being concentrated in a short span of time. The distribution of practice periods depends upon the skill to be taught and the age and ability of the student.[13]

Steps in Teaching Skills

Guided by the four principles shown above, teachers may begin to plan their teaching program. However, it is essential that prescribed steps be followed in the demonstration and practice procedures.

Pupils need to be guided through the learning experience; without expert assistance motivation may not develop. Biehler suggests several steps that teachers should follow in order for learning experiences to proceed smoothly and effectively. They are:

1. If possible and appropriate, analyze the skill to ascertain the specific psychomotor abilities necessary to perform it, arrange these component abilities in order, and help students to master them in this sequence.
2. Provide demonstrations, and as students practice, give verbal guidance to aid mastery of the skill.
   a. Demonstrate the entire procedure straight through, then describe the links of the chain in sequence, and finally demonstrate the skill again step by step.
   b. Allow ample time for students to practice immediately after the demonstrations. (Remember the importance of activity, repetition, and reinforcement.)
   c. As students practice, give guidance verbally or in a way which permits them to perform the skill themselves.
3. Be alert to generalization and interference.[12]

The foregoing discussion of learning theories and teaching of skills has been presented to assist teachers in improving instruction *Underlying all efforts to improve the quality of teaching is the element of motivation. Motivation is the key to all learning, and teachers who are able to motivate children will find teaching more interesting and satisfying.*

Fortunately, physical education teachers do not have the problem of motivation that besets those in academic subjects. Earlier in this chapter it was pointed out that boys and girls are endowed by nature, i.e., self-motivated, to move and play. This play urge continues throughout life in varying degree unless it is inhibited and dampened by poor programs or other factors which interfere with its normal manifestation.

The remainder of the chapter will be concerned with techniques for developing motivation and how these may be applied to physical education.

TECHNIQUES FOR DEVELOPING MOTIVATION

There are many ways of guiding the play urge to motivate the individual into after-school participation. Teachers should be constantly aware that motivation is the basis for all teaching and should be taken advantage of in a way that will yield the best results. Individuals are motivated in different ways; no particular medium is applicable to everyone. Moreover, motivation is a continuous process and the teacher must use a variety of techniques to keep the students motivated. Several techniques that may be used are: (1) maintaining interest, (2) culminating activities, (3) avoidance of overmotivation, and (4) avoidance of failure.

Maintaining Interest

The old adage, "You may lead the horse to the trough but you cannot make him drink," is applicable in teaching skills. Teachers may superimpose what they think the pupils need, but this does not mean that the activity is suitable to all individuals. Interest may be maintained through several media:

1. Satisfactory performance
2. Activity suited to the anatomical, physiological, and psychological needs of pupils
3. Effective teaching procedures
4. Challenging situations
5. Competition
6. Teaching meaningful activities
7. Recognition for accomplishment

Satisfactory Performance. Teachers should teach in such a way that each pupil will have a feeling of satisfaction at the end of each class. This feeling of satisfaction should be great enough that the pupil will want to continue the effort beyond the class period. The author has observed classes in which a great number of pupils dress in their uniforms, come to class, behave themselves, and although they have met all the requirements for the class period, may never have the opportunity of hitting a ball in softball, making a goal in basketball, or serving a ball in volleyball because of faulty organizational procedures. Students gain little, if any, satisfaction from this type of class.

An illustration of this regrettable situation is the manner in which softball is frequently introduced. Teachers will divide a class into two or four groups and tell the pupils to play softball. One group goes into the field and another remains at bat. Day after day the procedure continues, and many of the pupils never field a ball or bat even once. It is impossible to justify such a program. Not only is interest in a generally popular activity killed through such procedures, but the development of fitness is nonexistent. An alternative to this procedure would be to divide the entire class into five groups with five balls and five bats. Each group would have a catcher, a pitcher, three batters, and three fielders. Emphasis would be on teaching skills in which all pupils field and bat many times during the class period.

Suitable Activity. Largely because of certain anatomical limitations, as well as psychological and physiological deviations, boys and girls form desires for certain activities and keen prejudices against others. After a pupil has been subjected to a required program through the elementary school and an orientation program in the junior high school, he is usually qualified to decide what activity he wishes to pursue (see Chapter 7). It is good teaching procedure to allow pupils to participate in the activities appropriate to their capabilities, after proper orientation in a large variety of activities.

Effective Teaching Procedures. The importance of good teaching to motivation has been discussed earlier in this chapter. Effective procedures are an essential part of good teaching and teachers should continually strive to find which procedures are most effective. The use of poor teaching procedures is probably the single most important reason why many pupils dislike physical education class. The teacher who gives a skill test to a class of 40 pupils and allows the entire class to sit while each pupil takes the test is sure to have boredom and disgust as outcomes instead of the interest necessary if the pupils are to be motivated. Moreover, improper teaching procedures often create disciplinary problems; effective teaching procedures, on the other hand, often elicit wholesome behavior from the students.

Challenging Situations. Pupils must be challenged. They enjoy measuring their ability to perform a skill or proficiency test and the instructional period should provide this challenge. An illustration of the way in which this may be done is the procedure employed in giving group proficiency tests. Teachers periodically give fitness tests, such as pull-up and standing broad jump. In order for these tests to be challenging and effective, they must be given in a dignified atmosphere, the procedure must be well organized, and the pupil must understand the purpose of the tests. One way of accomplishing all this is to have posted on the wall close to the testing location the averages for each test by grade (Fig. 8–6). As the pupil takes the test, he sees the average for his grade and is challenged to equal it or to exceed it. These averages are not used for classifying the pupil into a fitness category nor are they used for evaluation. They are used to motivate the pupil to extend himself—which in turn contributes to fitness—within his own potentiality.

Competition. Each skill taught in the instructional period should be placed on a competitive basis. The teacher should be creative in finding ways of doing this. One illustration might be the teaching of dribbling and passing to a class. After the pupils

NORFOLK CITY PUBLIC SCHOOLS
PHYSICAL PROFICIENCY TESTS
BOYS

ACTIVITIES	AVERAGES				
CHIN	6	7	8	10	11
DASH 50 YDS. (Sec. Tenths)	7.5	7.4	7.1	7.0	6.9
SIT-UP (MIN.)	30	34	36	37	39
STD. BRD. JUMP (INCHES)	69	72	78	80	86
AGILITY RUN 40 YDS. (Sec. Tenths)	11.3	10.7	10.1	10.0	9.6

GIRLS

ACTIVITIES					
WALL PUSH (30 SEC.)	20	21	22	23	24
AGILITY RUN 30 YDS. (Sec. Tenths)	8.8	8.6	8.5	8.4	8.3
DASH 40 YDS. (Sec. Tenths)	7.2	7.1	7.0	6.9	6.7
SIT-UP (30 SEC.)	13	14	15	16	17
PULL-UP (MODIFIED)	26	27	28	29	30
GRADES	7	8	9	10	11

BOYS										RECORDS	GIRLS									
7		8		9		10		11		TESTS	7		8		9		10		11	
RECORD	PUPIL	RECORD	PUPIL	RECORD	PUPIL	RECORD	PUPIL	RECORD	PUPIL		RECORD	PUPIL	RECORD	PUPIL	RECORD	PUPIL	RECORD	PUPIL	RECORD	PUPIL
										CHIN										
										DASH										
										SIT-UP										
										STD. BRD. JUMP										
										AGILITY RUN										
										WALL PUSH										

Figure 8–6. Knowledge of class averages in physical proficiency tests motivates the student toward better performance.

have learned the dribble and the pass, the two skills may be combined into a dribble-and-pass relay race. Note, however, that placing the *skill* on a competitive basis does not mean placing the entire *sport* on a competitive basis during the class period.

Meaningful Activity. In order for learning to be effective, it must be transferable to broader fields of activity. Studies have been made in academic subjects showing the lack of retention after the student completes the course. Early studies reveal a serious lack of retention of factual learning in English, mathematics, and science.[16] Today the results are still unsatisfactory.[19] Learning should not stop at the end of the period or term or at graduation. Pupils should be inspired to further their efforts through investigation and activity beyond the school day and school years if the learning is to be effective.

Recognition for Accomplishment. It is basic in our culture to receive some type of award or recognition for practically everything one does. In school, grades are given for different levels of achievement, and monograms or certificates are presented to athletes in recognition of accomplishments.

Community service is recognized by presenting the individual with a citation, certificate or prize. Various organizations, educational and otherwise, have awards ranging from the Phi Beta Kappa key to automobiles and expense-paid trips to Hawaii. Finally, of course, people receive salaries for services rendered.

In education, considerable attention has been focused on the types of rewards for accomplishment that follow the learning process. These rewards may be classified as intrinsic or extrinsic.

INTRINSIC REWARDS. Practical observation supports the claim that people receive many lasting rewards from educational effort that are more valuable than material awards, which are soon forgotten. These lasting rewards are the intangible, or intrinsic, rewards. The intercollegiate football player was the hero of the campus during college years. He received monograms, made speeches at banquets, and was the most sought-after individual on the campus. The third-string tennis player was unknown and never received a monogram. Many years later the monograms and certificates given to the football player were forgotten

Figure 8–7. Basketball relay races are an excellent means of incorporating skills in a competitive event.

and had no value. The intrinsic values acquired by the third-string tennis player carried over into later life and contributed to his health and happiness.

EXTRINSIC REWARDS. Extrinsic rewards are those of a tangible nature and may have monetary value. It has been the practice for many years to give rewards in all aspects of education. Grades, monograms, cups, and certificates are examples. Pupils are aware of awards and, traditionally, expect something for their efforts.

Psychologists show that overemphasizing extrinsic awards may be inadvisable. Seagoe has pointed this out very clearly and lists the reasons:

1. The use of extrinsic forms of motivation is less effective than is commonly supposed. In general, the farther removed an incentive is from the goal, the less effective it will be. Conversely, the nearer an activity is to a continuing goal, the more rapid the learning will be. Motives differ in strength in proportion to their distance from those normally functioning in that situation.

2. Learning under extrinsic motivation tends to be temporary rather than permanent. Extrinsic incentives temporarily increase output by increasing the effort expended per unit of time, but the only permanent incentives are the internal ones which permit the maintaining of efficiency during long work periods and a longer working life.

3. The extent to which extrinsic motivation (as well as motivation in general) is effective is limited by the margin between potential and actual accomplishment. For example, attempts to improve performance on intelligence tests or to improve the range of memorization in accomplished musicians by using extrinsic forms of motivation are relatively fruitless.

4. The effectiveness of extrinsic incentives varies with the degree of emotional stability of the child. The child with a high degree of stability improves little under added extrinsic incentives. The egocentric child does especially well under strong extrinsic pressure.[7]

The failure of extrinsic recognition is illustrated by the use of marks and grades in our schools and colleges. The competition for credit has become so intense that the real values of education frequently are lost. Leaders in education should attempt to place values on dedication to a given field rather than on the credit involved. Intrinsic motivation should precede extrinsic motivation. The desire to excel should precede the award that may be given for excelling.

Culminating Activities

Teachers should arrange for some type of culminating activity at the end of the instructional cycle that will provide the opportunity for pupils to test their ability to participate either by themselves or against other individuals. When pupils continually practice skills without testing their progress, the instructional program becomes stale and lacking in interest. A football team that practices during the week and never participates against an opponent will eventually disintegrate because of lack of interest. There are two means by which individuals may test their progress: competition against themselves or a score and competition against other individuals.

Competition Against Themselves. Psychologists show the advisability of limiting competition for young children to that in which they compete against themselves or a score. Bowling is an illustration of this type of competition. Proficiency tests, such as pull-ups, broad jump, and sit-ups, are illustrations of activities in which the individual participates against himself or against a previous score. Many psychologists feel that there is already enough competition in the present educational system and in our society and that young children benefit more when they compete against their own scores rather than against other individuals. Baker supports this idea:

I believe that in our educational systems throughout the country, there has been built a system of competition. Although I do not object to competition, it is my belief that the child should compete with himself, his record today or compared with his record yesterday in his individual achievement and not with someone else.[17]

Many individuals have an abhorrence for competing physically with another individual; in some, emotional illness may result. Baker shows in a study conducted in Massachusetts that in the last 100 years there has been no significant change in the incidence of schizophrenia, but that the incidence of neuroses has become much higher in the last 50 years. He feels that the atmosphere of competition built up in our schools has contributed to this.[17]

Participating Against Other Individuals. The American system at present is based upon competition. People compete against each other for jobs, recreation, and social

> The democratic invitation to each individual to achieve the best that is in him requires that we provide each youngster with the particular kind of education which will benefit him. That is the only sense in which equality of opportunity can mean anything. The good society is not one that ignores individual differences, but one that deals with them wisely and humanely.
>
> John W. Gardner, Excellence, p. 75.

status. To stop this kind of competition would amount to tampering with the very roots of our culture. The idea is not to eliminate or inhibit competition but to use it wisely.

The majority of individuals benefit by competition with each other in activities that are suited to their normal growth and development and their age level. The qualities acquired from competition on teams or with other individuals—such as perseverance, fortitude, and give and take—parallel the qualities needed for living in a democratic culture. Competition is a great motivator for after-school participation. The successful teacher will study its effects and devise plans to make competition work most effectively in his instruction. Seagoe lists five conclusions from studies of the effects of competition on children:

1. Competition increases the amount of work done, but the quality remains the same or deteriorates.
2. The more personal the competition the greater its effect.
3. The child must think he has a good chance for success in competition to be greatly motivated by it.
4. Older children respond more to competition than younger children.
5. Average or slow children respond more favorably to competition than bright children.[7]

Avoidance of Overmotivation

There are many natural media for motivation in physical education. Unless the teacher is careful, it is comparatively easy to overemphasize an activity. Overemphasis leads to overmotivation, which may retard learning and decrease the child's desire for further participation.

Seagoe lists six guidelines for the avoidance of overmotivation, which the teacher should become familiar with:

1. Learning increases with increased motivation up to a certain point.

2. Maximum gain in learning occurs at a moderate degree of motivation.
3. The point at which maximum gain in learning will be reached depends upon:
    a. complexity of the problem
    b. ability of the learner
    c. degree of concentration of the motivation
    d. the susceptibility of the learner to motivation
4. When tension increases beyond the optimal point, learning is disrupted.
5. An increase in the degree of motivation increases the variability in a group.
6. Altogether, the intermediate degrees of motivation result in the greatest efficiency of learning.[7]

Teachers, coaches, administrators, and parents make a grave error when they superimpose certain types of adult activities upon young children. Studies show the adverse effects of little league baseball, midget football, and other types of activities that are not suitable for young children. These activities vividly illustrate overmotivation and violate all laws of growth and development. If parents would leave children to themselves after organizing programs, the results would be more satisfying.

It was pointed out early in this chapter that the natural play urge of boys and girls will progress under its own drive, but that it needs proper direction as well. However, the play urge may be suppressed if there are too many awards, too much pressure, and too much criticism—all of which have adverse effects on the emotional stability of children.

Avoidance of Failure

Children respond to failure in various ways. Some pupils respond by exhibiting aggressive and antisocial tendencies, whereas others respond by withdrawal from the situation. Withdrawing from reality can lead to psychotic behavior.

Teachers of physical education should try to motivate pupils in such a way that they may have the opportunity of succeeding and expressing themselves. Emphasis should be placed on individual differences, interests of boys and girls, and planning the curriculum to allow for individual improvement and expression. Activities in which a pupil may compete with himself or a score should receive considerable attention in planning the program.

CREATIVITY IN TEACHING

In the instructional period there are many opportunities for the teacher to apply vision and imagination. Creative procedures enhance the prestige of the program and in turn assist in motivation. There are a number of phases in the program through which creative efforts may be developed.

Rhythmical Activities

The basis of all physical education is movement. Constructive movement is manifested through those activities that incorporate the fundamental movements of man discussed in Chapter 5.

Paralleling the natural movements of man are the rhythmic movements, which have been used through the years to express people's conditions and emotions. These rhythmic patterns have been a part of every culture since man was created and are still prevalent today. They have been performed with or without musical accompaniment. Rhythmics provide not only a natural activity but also an opportunity for creativity by both pupils and teacher.

The physical education teacher should guide the rhythmic activities along channels that are educational and in keeping with the best in rhythmic interpretation. Folk, modern, and interpretive rhythms are examples of rhythmic activity that both contributes to health and fitness and allows for creativity.

Teaching Procedure

Vision and creativity are essential factors in good teaching. The traditional procedures involved in teaching skills may be improved when teachers begin to envision new ways of teaching skills more effectively. The old method of using one ball for basketball and volleyball or one shot-put and one

Figure 8–8. Modern dance movements present teaching situations that challenge the creativity of teachers and students. (Courtesy Richmond Senior High School, Richmond, Indiana.)

hurdle for track will be replaced by more functional procedures; for example, many balls will be used for basketball and volleyball skills, and several hurdles for track. In addition, the teacher whose vision provides insight into problems also will quickly see the advantages of such simple techniques as dividing the class into as many small groups as possible for instruction. Teaching will be more effective, and disciplinary problems will diminish for the teacher who employs proper procedures in his work.

Interpretation

Interpreting the program gives unlimited scope to physical education. Assembly pro-grams, playdays, culminating activities, and programs for civic clubs are a few of the many media for developing creativity. Other media for interpreting the program are described in Chapter 3. Teachers should study the various principles of learning, teaching methods, and procedures. When they put these principles into practice, they may find that teaching will not only become easier but will also be more satisfying because the objectives of physical education will be more readily realized. Motivation will automatically follow a good teaching program, because interest will be maintained and boys and girls will become aware of the values of extending the activity program beyond the school hours.

QUESTIONS FOR DISCUSSION

1. What is meant by motivation?
2. Why is motivation important in the teaching of physical education?
3. Discuss the play urge.
4. Distinguish between the two theories of learning.
5. Discuss Thorndike's laws of learning and illustrate how each is applied to physical education.
6. What are the kinds of learning?
7. List several principles of learning.
8. In presenting material for a physical education class, what approach would you use?
9. Discuss several techniques for developing motivation.

SUGGESTED ACTIVITIES

1. Form a committee of three or four members of your class and observe a physical education class in action. Afterward, have the committee list as many learning principles as possible that were observed.
2. Observe a class and list the principles of learning skills that were involved.
3. Study the physical education program of a school and list the techniques for motivation that were observed. Make a report to the class and make recommendations that could be used by you in teaching.

REFERENCES

1. Joseph G. Molner, "Children Get Too Little Exercise," *The Virginian-Pilot* (Norfolk, Virginia), April 22, 1960.
2. Edward L. Thorndike, *Human Learning* (New York: The Century Company, 1931).
3. W. N. Kellog, *An Eclectic View of Some Theories of Learning. In* Lester D. Crow and Alice Crow, *Readings in Human Learning*, p. 188 (New York: David McKay Company, 1963).
4. E. R. Guthrie, "Conditioning: A Theory of Learning in Terms of Stimulus, Response and Association," pp. 17–60. *Yearbook of the National Society for the Study of Education* (1942).
5. C. L. Hull, "Behavior Postulates and Corollaries," pp. 173–180. *Psychological Review,* 1950.
6. B. F. Skinner, *The Technology of Teaching*, pp. 17, 93–96; 15 (New York: Appleton-Century-Crofts, 1968).

7. May V. Seagoe, *A Teacher's Guide to the Learning Process,* 2nd ed., pp. 245; 247–248 (Dubuque, Iowa: William C. Brown Company, 1961).
8. Jerome S. Bruner, *The Process of Education,* pp. 55–62; 52 (Cambridge: The Harvard University Press, 1960).
9. Ernest R. Hilgard, *Introduction to Psychology,* pp. 280; 71–72 (New York: Harcourt, Brace and World, 1962).
10. Ralph Garry and Howard L. Kingsley, *The Nature and Conditions of Learning,* 3d ed., pp. 109–110; 118 (Englewood Cliffs, New Jersey: Prentice-Hall, Inc., 1970).
11. Robert J. Havighurst, *Developmental Tasks and Education,* p. 7 (New York: David McKay Company, 1972).
12. Robert F. Biehler, *Psychology Applied to Teaching,* pp. 30; 269; 281 (Boston: Houghton Mifflin Company, 1971).
13. Lester D. Crow and Alice Crow, *Readings in Human Learning,* pp. 372; 9–11; (New York: David McKay Company, 1963).
14. Josephine R. Hilgard, "Learning and Maturation in Preschool Children," *Journal of Genetic Psychology,* 1932, pp. 40–53.
15. Robert M. Gagne, "Some New Views of Learning and Instruction," *Phi Delta Kappan, Journal of Phi Delta Kappa,* May, 1970, pp. 468–471.
16. James Mursell, *Successful Teaching,* pp. 12–18 (New York: McGraw-Hill Book Company, 1946).
17. Cecil Baker, "The Ill Effects of Competition" (From a lecture delivered at Yankton State Hospital, South Dakota, 1956).
18. Stanley L. Clement, "Seven Principles of Learning. *In* Lester D. Crow and Alice Crow, *Readings in Human Learning,* p. 54 (New York: David McKay Company, 1963).
19. "Little Improvement Seen in Schools in Decade," *Education U.S.A.,* August 7, 1972.

SELECTED READINGS

Biehler, Robert F. *Psychology Applied to Teaching.* Boston: Houghton Mifflin Company, 1971.

Craig, Robert C. *The Psychology of Learning in the Classroom.* London: The Macmillan Company, 1966.

Garrison, Karl C., and Franklin R. Jones. *The Psychology of Human Development.* Scranton, Pennsylvania: International Textbook Company, 1969.

Garry, Ralph, and Howard L. Kingsley. *The Nature and Conditions of Learning,* 3d ed. Englewood Cliffs, New Jersey: Prentice Hall, Inc., 1970.

Guthrie, James W., and Edward Wynne (eds.). *New Models for American Education.* Englewood Cliffs, New Jersey: Prentice Hall, Inc., 1971.

Harlow, H. F. "The Neurophysiological Correlates of Learning and Intelligence." *Psychological Bulletin,* Vol. 33 (1936).

Havighurst, Robert J. *Developmental Tasks and Education.* New York: David McKay Company, 1972.

Hilgard, Ernest R. *Introduction to Psychology.* New York: Harcourt, Brace and World, Inc., 1962.

Kilpatrick, William H. *Philosophy of Education.* New York: The Macmillan Company, 1963.

McClosky, Mildred G. (ed.). *Teaching Strategies and Classroom Realities.* Englewood Cliffs, New Jersey: Prentice Hall, Inc., 1971.

Millon, Theodore. *Theories of Psychopathology.* Philadelphia: W. B. Saunders Company, 1967.

Rippa, S. Alexander (ed.). *Educational Ideas in America.* New York: David McKay Company, 1969.

Saylor, Galen, and William Alexander. *Curriculum Planning for Modern Schools.* New York: Holt, Rinehart and Winston, 1966.

Thayer, V. T.: *The Role of the School in American Society.* New York: Dodd, Mead and Company, 1961.

Thorndike, E. L. *Educational Psychology, Briefer Course.* New York: Teachers College, Columbia University, 1915.

Travers, Robert M. W. *Essentials of Learning.* New York: The Macmillan Company, 1963.

PART THREE

HOW TO TEACH PHYSICAL EDUCATION

Chapter 9

ORGANIZATION OF THE PHYSICAL EDUCATION CLASS

The purpose of planning is to minimize accidental change and to maximize intentional change.

William H. Boyer

Courtesy Washington High School, Germantown, Wisconsin.

Learning is the primary goal of all education, and only when teaching results in learning can it be said to be effective. One has only to observe a few of the programs of physical education today to see the need for improvement of instruction. Where teaching is effective in physical education, the programs maintain a strong position in the school curriculum and the community. On the other hand, in many places physical education has either been abandoned altogether or it is placed in an inferior position in the educational hierarchy, largely because of poor teaching.

It is during the instructional period that physical education serves the needs of the pupils and thereby makes its stand for survival in the curriculum. Nevertheless, in too many instances the period is poorly organized, ineffective, and either serves as a training ground for the interscholastic program or is a free-play program in which the teacher throws out the ball and watches the pupils play. This is not teaching.

The following characteristics of good and poor instructional periods emphasize the importance of good organization. Little things, minor when considered singly, can be compounded into major problems unless they are anticipated and solutions provided beforehand. Teachers should always attempt to eliminate factors that interfere with effective instruction.

CHARACTERISTICS OF A GOOD CLASS PERIOD

1. The pupils are inspired—assemble quickly.
2. All pupils are dressed—no disciplinary problems—morale is high.
3. The instruction is of high quality—has direction—is planned.
4. The activities and instruction show a scientific approach.
5. The teacher is the leader—sets the pace.
6. The program is a participation program—emphasis is on teaching according to individual ability.
7. Emphasis is on teaching skills. All pupils are active—interest is high.
8. The program is planned to motivate and maintain interest.

CHARACTERISTICS OF A POOR CLASS PERIOD

1. Pupils assemble late. Sometimes half the period is lost.

265

2. Many pupils are not dressed. This presents disciplinary problems. Valuable time is wasted checking the reasons for not dressing.

3. The instruction is poor – lacks direction.

4. The activities have been selected without regard for scientific criteria, and instruction has no scientific basis.

5. The teacher disassociates himself from teaching by allowing untrained pupils to assume leadership.

6. The program is regimented – heavy with unscientific calisthenics.

7. The teaching of skills has been abandoned. Emphasis is on playing – many pupils are idle.

8. The program does not motivate.

THE FIRST WEEK OF TEACHING

There are many problems that arise during the first few days of teaching that, if not met and diplomatically solved, may seriously alter the effectiveness of teaching later. Several of the most important are discussed here.

Establish Status

The first time a teacher faces his class he establishes, consciously or not, a relationship that will affect his teaching, for better or for worse. New teachers should never minimize the importance of the first day and the first week of instruction. Invariably the teacher who seeks popularity and who attempts to place himself on the same plane as the pupils loses control of the class and jeopardizes his success as a teacher. The teacher must always maintain his position and status as a teacher with dignity and skill and yet understand and guide pupils in the daily problems that arise. He must be at the same time friendly and firm, informal and forceful. The ability to establish rapport with the pupils early in the term is essential to effective teaching.

Class Control

The success of a teacher is in many instances measured by the discipline maintained. Without proper discipline there can be no instruction. An orderly class can be taught; a disorderly one must be endured. Discipline does not mean that the program

Figure 9–1. A class that is well organized for tumbling instruction.

must be a rigid strait-jacket. Good discipline is measured by the way a class responds to the instruction of the teachers.

Much has been written about disciplinary measures, but little of it can be applied to physical education. An entirely different approach from that used in other subjects must be used in the teaching of physical education. Deep-seated character traits are frequently brought to the surface through competitive activity. Pupils have to learn inhibition, and sportsmanship has to be observed in all phases of the program. Because of these sensitive problems, the physical education instructor has to be a keen practical psychologist. He should be able to analyze the causes of antagonism and guide the boys and girls into selecting the proper course of action.

A teacher's best procedure in meeting discipline problems is to be a human being instead of a tyrant. False dignity is the last resort of the poor teacher. There are pupils in every class who have qualifications of leadership. The qualifications may take the form of boisterousness, exhibitionism, or bullying; however, an instructor's first step should be to win the confidence of these pupils. Having done so, he can then begin to create an atmosphere of orderly conduct and provide a more acceptable outlet for their leadership abilities.

If, at the first meeting of the class, a firm, stable understanding has been reached with the pupils, problems arising later may be easily met. It is much easier for the teacher to relax from a strict beginning than it is to tighten the reins of control once a pattern of informality has been established. The teacher should make every effort to gain the respect of his pupils and maintain discipline through this respect. Usually the little difficulties that arise can be solved by having a frank talk with the pupils. In the endeavor to develop control, the teacher has to be very careful not to set rules and restrictions that are unnecessary. A few rules well enforced will prove to be much more useful than a vast number of slipshod regulations that are not enforced.

The regulations should be thoroughly explained during the first few days of school. Students must be told, for example, whether they will be expected to wear uniforms and, if so, where these may be obtained.

Pupils who do not comply with the regulations—those who are tardy or inattentive or who do not have suits—must, of course, be penalized. There are some pupils in every school who insist on disobeying rules. The teacher must find a way to work with these pupils within the framework of school policy and effective human relations. Having them report after school or during recess brings remarkable results for some teachers but may not work at all for others. Each case must be handled on its own merit.

The problem of discipline should be given a great deal of consideration. It is a problem that the teacher should consider in relation to the environment, the type of pupil, and the seriousness of the misdemeanor. Three essential traits of a good disciplinarian are understanding, firmness, and fairness. If the teacher remembers these traits when working with pupils, the average disciplinary problems can be easily handled.

Finally, two of the greatest deterrents to disorder in the program are good organization and good teaching. Teachers create a disorderly atmosphere by poor organization and poor teaching. If classes are organized properly and the program is one in which instruction is continuous and pupils feel they are making progress, disorder will be reduced to a minimum.

It is our job to guide the basic urge for activity along constructive instructional channels. Failure to do this will not only bring about disciplinary problems, but the health and safety of pupils may also be jeopardized.

Teachers searching for guidance in their discipline problems may find assistance from the evaluation of commonly used procedures outlined by Vineyard and Massey:

1. *Admonition.* Simplest form of control. Desirable for first offenses. When brief, dignified and unemotional, admonition is an effective method of handling mild forms of disorder.

2. *Withdrawal of Privileges.* When the pupil abuses the privilege of, say, watering the plants by squirting water on pupils, withdrawing the plant-watering privilege is a sound tactic. In other words, withdrawal of privileges is effective when the privilege has a direct (or indirect) connection with the offense.

3. *Detention.* One of the most common punishments. Also one of the most abused. It is prob-

ably not effective in cases of dishonesty or poor school work. Detention is justified for pupils who are habitually tardy or waste time in school.

4. *Extra Work.* "A pedagogical blunder." You cannot generate enthusiasm for school work on the part of pupils if extra school work is used as punishment. Extra work is justified in one situation: A student who habitually seeks to escape work may profit from our insistence that he must perform his scholastic tasks consistent with his ability.

5. *Make-up and Pay-up.* Students who damage property or do sloppy work should be asked to make reparations. This is the doctrine of "natural punishment." To ask a student to clean up after an accident caused by carelessness or to pay for a broken easel carelessly used is justifiable.

6. *Lowered Grades.* Lowering a grade because of a pupil's misbehavior doesn't make sense, doesn't improve behavior, and undermines the pupil's confidence in the teacher. "To be heartily condemned."

7. *Forced Apology.* Don't force a child to apologize either in public or in private. Authorities consider the forced apology hypocritical. It stirs additional resentment against the teacher, and may lead to further disobedience and misbehavior. Scratch it out of your book of disciplinary tactics.

8. *Sending to the Principal.* Use with caution. The good teacher attempts to handle minor offenses himself. Hence, before a pupil is sent to the principal, the teacher must use all the skill he has in settling the problem within the classroom. However, don't hesitate to refer serious cases to the front office.

9. *Dismissal from Class.* Effective at times, if used with caution and with proper control. ("Report to me immediately after class.") Dismissal from class is desirable in cases of seriously troublesome behavior, because it saves the rest of the pupils loss of teaching time. To be effective, dismissal should be followed by a pupil-teacher conference.

10. And now we come to the cornerstone in a teacher's efforts to avoid disciplinary actions in the future—The Conference. The conference is not a "talking to" . . . or an admonition in private. It is an exploration of the causes of misbehavior. It is an opportunity for the teacher to know why the pupil acts as he does and for the pupil to know what the teacher thinks of such behavior. It is psychologically sound. It should be effective in preventing and controlling misbehavior.[1]

In addition to the suggestions listed above regarding effective procedures in dealing with disciplinary problems, other studies have been made that are promising. Chapter 8 referred to aversive measures such as physical punishment, sarcasm, and ridicule that are sometimes used for disciplinary purposes. Generally, psychologists and educators feel that this approach to handling unusual behavior should be avoided. Instead, they would substitute a positive approach and endeavor to develop better communication and understanding between the student and the teacher.

Neal, on the other hand, shows in a recent study of aversive control that this approach is receiving new support and attention. He presents evidence to challenge those who feel that the use of such procedures will produce undesirable side effects. He shows that in some instances aversive methods may be effective and that undesirable side effects need not occur.[2]

The author discusses three ways in which aversive control may be used:

1. *Escape Training.* In this case the aversive stimulus is present and the organism must make some specified response to end the stimulus. This is illustrated by the child who would never come to the adult when called. As the child stood barefoot on an electric grid, shock was administered. At the same time the experimenter called, the child moved toward him, and the shock was turned off.

2. *Active Avoidance.* This approach is similar to the escape, except that if a specified response is made, the aversive stimulation will never occur. The child is called and if he moves toward the experimenter, no shock is given. The child avoids the shock by moving toward the adult.

3. *Passive Avoidance.* In this case some specified behavior already exists, the objective being to eliminate it. When the behavior occurs, an aversive stimulus is given.[2]

Warning against brutality, he points to the need for the positive approach mentioned earlier. However, he concludes that:

Enough research on punishment procedures has been conducted to raise serious questions about any legend that says that aversive methods of control are ineffective or necessarily lead to seriously undesirable side effects.[2]

Many delinquents possess great leadership ability. Society could benefit enormously by their seemingly innate ability to influence and guide others. The problem is how to provide them with an environment that will develop their abilities along socially acceptable channels. There are studies to indicate that, among adolescents, at least average physical ability is essential for high group status. It seems that if children are markedly deficient in skill development, an improvement of these skills would provide a better chance for the child to adjust to peer expectations and achieve at least a minimal achievement status.[3]

There is evidence to show that the incorrigible student is often a good leader. Physical education teachers may very well take lessons from an experiment in Woodbourne Junior High School in Baltimore, Maryland. Troublemakers were placed on the Students Security Patrol. Their position on the Patrol was comparable to that of a lawman. The result was that vandalism decreased 99 percent, gang wars were prevented, and drugs almost disappeared. The organizer of the plan, John Pugh, the school security officer, states that:

Basically all kids want to be the good guy. Even the bad kids are just trying to look like big heroes to the other bad kids. The patrol gives them a chance to look like heroes in everyone's eyes.[4]

The problem students in the physical education class have the potential to be good squad leaders and to handle constructive responsibility. The feeling of importance and the provision for them to assume leadership roles not only will provide a valuable education for them, but will also develop a more positive climate in the class.

The positive approach to handling discipline problems is advocated by many education leaders. Those who promote this approach feel that self-discipline is the answer. They place emphasis on the need for teachers and administrators to have faith in students' doing the right thing. Ovard explains self-discipline this way:

The kind of discipline to work in a democracy is self-discipline. Such discipline begins at the earliest years with external authority imposed by parents and teachers and is gradually relaxed as the students finish the secondary school. From a sociological and psychological base, discipline is a learning process whereby the individual progressively learns to develop habits of self-control and recognizes his own responsibility to society.[5]

Many of the behavior problems of students arise from the lack of parental control during the early years and the wrong interpretation of freedom which results. When young children are not provided with proper instruction in responsibility, their relationship to society and their obligations to the rights of others, their interpretation of freedom in later years may be to do as they please. Restrictions must accompany freedom, and educators have a responsibility to see that this relationship is developed. As restrictions are made, awards are necessary to support the restrictions. Since all people need to be complimented for a job well done, such positive efforts are needed to show students that to do the right thing does mean approval.

In promoting the positive approach to discipline, efforts must be made to understand the practices that will be helpful in developing positive behavior patterns in the class. Good student-teacher relationships are necessary. The following practices

---

Parents are deeply concerned about the behavior problems that exist in the schools today. This attitude is shown in the Gallup Poll. The Poll for the years 1970 and 1971 are shown.

	1970 Percent	1971 Percent
Discipline is too strict	2	3
Discipline is not strict enough	53	48
Discipline is about right	31	33
Don't know/no opinion	14	16

The Poll shows that the year 1971 had a small decrease in parental opinion that discipline is not strict enough. Some of the concerns of parents were that teachers lack authority to keep order, students have too much freedom, students have no respect for teachers, rules are not enforced, and vandalism. The report substantiates the premise established earlier that "if the schools and teachers interest the children in learning, most disciplinary problems will disappear."

In 1972 the Gallup Poll showed that discipline was still the number one concern.

were found to be common to all schools with outstanding student-teacher relationships:

1. There was an outstanding apparent recognition of the purposes and values of the standards and rules in force by faculty and students.

2. Emphasis was placed on self-discipline by teachers and students.

3. Good citizenship and conduct were characteristic of the faculty as well as of the student body. Courtesy, consideration, respect, professional dress and manner, and good speech were practiced by the faculty members.

4. Standards and rules were subject to review and change, but were enforced until changed by due process.

5. The emphasis in the treatment of all discipline cases was on the individual involved and not on the act. This represents a significant change in law enforcement in our democracy in the past 50 years. Today society is more concerned with the transgressor than with the crime.

6. Students could expect fair but certain reprimand or punishment for violation of rules and standards. Teachers were confident that their colleagues were also trying to cooperate in maintaining standards.

7. The punishments meted out were fitted to the individual rather than the transgression.

8. Faculty and students cooperated in establishing, maintaining, and revising rules and standards.

9. The program was challenging to all groups.[7]

Throughout this text emphasis is placed on quality instruction. It has been the observation of the author that good teachers have few behavior problems in the class. When teachers plan, understand the content of the activity taught, develop an understanding of individual needs, and use effective teaching methods, few problems of discipline occur in the class. Brown and Phelps contrast the ways in which daily responsibilities are met by poor vs. good teachers:

Poor Teacher	*Good Teacher*
Makes vague assignments or no assignments at all. Pupil doesn't know for certain what he is to do, so does nothing on his assignment. Undesirable activity often results.	Makes a clear and definite assignment. The pupil knows what is expected of him and does it. No time for undesirable activity.
Makes an assignment which is impossible for the child to accomplish. Pupil gives up as he sees no chance of succeeding, does something else — possibly undesirable.	Gears assignments to time allowed and to ability of students. Realizes that learning is tied to a successful completion of an act studiously attempted.
Speaks in a rasping, quarrelsome tone of voice indicating irritation. Talks too much, nags, scolds.	Controls and modulates voice. Remembers that nagging (symbolic drive) diminishes a teacher's effectiveness.
Fails to get attention of every person in his class before proceeding with oral work. Is sometimes competing with students for attention. Respect for teacher lost. Control weakened.	Gets attention pleasantly (if possible), but gets attention of every pupil before proceeding with oral work. There must never be any doubt in any pupil's mind as to who is in charge of the classroom.
Pays inadequate attention to classroom logistics (movement of students, handling supplies, student seating, etc.). Because pupils have not been instructed specifically, they fail to respond specifically. Confusion leads to disorder, which in turn leads to reprimands and ill-feeling.	Is definite in setting up classroom routines. Allows no exception to occur until routines are established. Since the routine is definite and clear, the child has little reason for deviation. The child who deviates is definitely wrong and all the children know it.
Pays insufficient attention to the physical conditions of the room. Pupil discomfort causes restlessness, which in turn forces the teacher into some form of disciplinary action.	Notes physical conditions (heat, light, ventilation) frequently, as these tend to vary with outside conditions during the day. The physically comfortable child gives less trouble.
Does not recognize, or if he does recognize, does not compliment an unusually fine effort on a student's part. Student feels effort was unappreciated, makes less effort on later assignments; may show resentment by unsocial activity.	Recognizes and shows appreciation for honest effort. Feels that failure to commend unusually fine work by a student is bad manners on the teacher's part. Student is inspired to further and better efforts; is not likely to make trouble in class.

Poor Teacher	*Good Teacher*
Is sarcastic in his criticisms. Hurts pupil's sensibilities. Pupils show resentment by being (in turn) ungracious.	Criticizes constructively; shows consideration of pupil's feelings. Always gives a child a chance to "save face."
Is inconsistent. Scolds a pupil for what has been condoned in another. Pupils will forgive anything in a teacher except what they consider to be injustice.	Is consistent although he may not always be right. Pupils recognize fairness in attitude of the teacher. Not inclined to feel resentfulness — one of the principal causes of pupil behavior problems.
Sloughs off reasonable questions or gives a facetious answer. A reasonable (to the child) question is treated as triviality. Pupil feels snubbed, shows resentment through undesirable behavior.	Listens seriously to a reasonable question, but if time is limited suggests the question be brought up again. Pupil pleased, feels important; therefore not inclined to resentfulness.
Plays favorites. Lets it be known when he dislikes a child. Child reacts much as would an adult.	Plays no favorites. Goes out of his way to alleviate a hurt which he may have unintentionally given.
Stops a student curtly when student is seriously discussing or reporting on an assignment. Gives impression that discussion is trivial.	Encourages discussion but controls a situation which is wandering or getting out of hand. Treats children as he would colleagues in same situation.
Disparagingly criticizes community social groups, forgetting pupils' parents may be members of groups. Pupils tell parents. Child may be advised by parents to "tell that teacher off." Result: discipline problem.	Avoids comments or discussions which tend to reflect in a derogatory way on any group or individuals. Teacher remembers that he is serving all of the community.[8]

A general overview of behavior and discipline control has been discussed and some approaches outlined in the foregoing paragraphs. From the discussions, the reader should have developed a philosophy concerning discipline and the factors involved. In addition to this philosophy, a list of specific guidelines is necessary to assist teachers with their daily tasks of maintaining satisfactory class control. Such a list is suggested below:

1. *Be sincere.* Be convinced that you can help all students. Demonstrate the fact that you like all your students. Attempts to disguise negative feelings toward some will be detected, with the result that student faith in you will be lost.

2. *Be cheerful and have a sense of humor.* At the same time do not try to win a teacher popularity contest. Winning cheap popularity at the expense of genuine student respect may lead to a teacher's undoing.

3. *Avoid the use of vindictive punishment;* especially mass punishment for misdeeds done by a few individuals. Punishment for the sake of proving that the teacher is the "boss" is of little consequence in correcting the cause of behavior problems.

4. *Don't use sarcasm or ridicule.* Students cannot be expected to respect a teacher who uses such ruthless tactics. In the opinion of students, sarcasm is one of the most resented actions a teacher could possibly take.

5. *Do not challenge every minor disturbance.* While such disturbances often irritate only the teacher, they may be easily magnified out of proportion so that they affect the entire class.

6. *Don't exhibit angry emotions.* Your mature behavior should be an example for students to emulate.

7. *Learn the names of your students as soon as possible.* When someone begins to misbehave, bring him back into the activity of the moment quickly. For example, get his attention by asking, "Do you agree with Helen's comment, Joe?"

8. *Begin the class activities immediately at the start of the period.* Don't delay by checking attendance or doing other tasks. Do these at a more appropriate time or let students perform them while you begin the important job of teaching.

9. *Work to improve your teaching techniques.* By planning challenging experiences with your students and by using a wealth of instructional materials, there will be fewer opportunities for behavior problems.[9]

Attendance

A major organization pitfall to be avoided during the first week has to do with the

Figure 9–2. Checking the attendance. Attendance may be checked more efficiently when pupils stand in front of numbers painted on the wall. Pupils whose numbers are showing are absent.

recording of attendance. Checking the attendance is one of the most difficult and time-consuming elements in the organization of a physical education class. Many methods are used, but probably the most practical is to have numbers painted on the walls about waist high or on the floor around the gymnasium. The numbers, which should be placed numerically, should be of sufficient range to accommodate the largest class. Each pupil is assigned a number and should report promptly and stand on or in front of his number. At an arranged time, pupils assigned to all exposed numbers are marked absent. Those numbers should be recorded on a slip of paper and placed on the pupil's individual record card or roll book between periods. Arrangements must be made to change the status of pupils who come in late from absent to tardy. A plan such as this is shown in Figure 9–2. Notice that the exposed numbers are 22, 23, and 29. The boys who should be covering these numbers are absent.

Student Accounting

To a large extent the success of the instruction depends on how the daily routine

of recording absences, tardinesses, excuses, and evaluation is handled. Practical tools for assisting teachers with this type of bookkeeping should be available. Usually this information is recorded on individual cards, squad cards, and permanent record cards.

Individual Record Cards. Individual record cards should be filled out the first day the class meets. These cards are the class rolls and are also used for recording other items necessary for proper functioning of the program (Figs. 9–3, 9–4 and 9–5).

Squad Cards. Many teachers prefer to use squad cards. These cards may be used in conjunction with the Individual Record Card. They serve a purpose when the squad plan is predominantly used for the class organization. Usually the cards are designed to include the squad member, attendance, homeroom or grade, test results and other important information that will assist the teacher in organizing the class. Sample squad cards are shown in Figure 9–6.

Daily Check Sheet. A daily check sheet is sometimes practical for keeping daily records of items such as attendance, dress, showers, etc. A form that may serve this purpose is shown in Figure 9–7.

NORFOLK CITY SCHOOLS
HEALTH, PHYSICAL AND SAFETY EDUCATION DEPARTMENT

PUPIL RECORD CARD
-BOYS-

LOCKER NO. _____

SQUAD NO. _____

HOME ROOM _____

PERIOD _____

GRADE _____

NAME _____

ADDRESS _____

HEALTH TEACHER _____

TELEPHONE _____ AGE _____

ATTENDANCE (MARK ONLY WHEN ABSENT)

DATES																					
A–ABSENT T–TARDY X–NO. EQUIP.																					

EVALUATION

	SIX WEEKS	SIX WEEKS	SIX WEEKS	SIX WEEKS	SIX WEEKS	SIX WEEKS	TERM
ACTIVITY INSTRUCTION							
HEALTH INSTRUCTION							
AVERAGE							

NOTE: THE FINAL MARK OR GRADE FOR EACH SIX WEEKS SHOULD BE AN AVERAGE OF THE HEALTH INSTRUCTION AND THE ACTIVITY INSTRUCTION. EACH OF THE TWO AREAS RECEIVES THE SAME WEIGHT.

P.E.-1B

Figure 9–3. Individual record cards for class use. *A* (front of record card) is the same for boys and girls. *B* and *C* show differences in the reverse sides of the cards.

Figure 9–3 continued on pages 274 and 275.

SKILLS TEACHING PROGRESSION

SPORTS	GIVE AS MANY TESTS IN EACH GRADE AS TIME PERMITS					
BASKETBALL	PASSES	DRIBBLE	FOUL	LAY-UP	SET SHOT	PIVOT
BOWLING	GRIP	STANCE	APPROACH	DELIVERY	FOLLOW THRU	AIMING
RHYTHMICS	LOCOMOTION	STEPS	INTERPRETIVE	⟶	⟶	⟶
GOLF	GRIP	STANCE	SWING	FOLLOW THRU	PUTTING	DRIVE
HOCKEY	DRIBBLE	BULLY	PASSING	INTERCEPTION	GOAL SHOOTING	TACKLE
BODY MECHANICS	EXERCISE	BALANCE	ROLLS	WALKS	STUNTS	STUNTS
SOFTBALL	THROWING	HITTING	RUNNING	PITCHING	CATCHING	FIELDING
TABLE TENNIS	GRIP	SERVE	STROKE	DRIVE	CHOP	DOUBLES
TENNIS	GRIP	FORE HAND	BACK HAND	SERVE	VOLLEY	LOB
TRACK	STARTS	DASH	RELAYS	⟶	⟶	⟶
VOLLEYBALL	VOLLEY	SERVE	SET-UPS	SPIKE	BLOCK	RECOVER

GIRLS — PROFICIENCY TESTS — GIRLS

EVENTS	GIVE TESTS FIRST WEEK IN MAY	EVENTS	GIVE TESTS FIRST WEEK IN MAY
MODIFIED PULL-UP (PALMS AWAY)		DASH (40 YDS.)	
WALL PUSH (30 SEC.)		AGILITY RUN (30 YDS.)	
SIT-UP (30 SEC.) (FLEX KNEES)		SEE GUIDEBOOK FOR DESCRIPTION OF TESTS.	

Figure 9–3. *Continued.*

Figure 9–3 continued on opposite page.

SKILLS TEACHING PROGRESSION

SPORTS	GIVE AS MANY TESTS IN EACH GRADE AS TIME PERMITS					
BASKETBALL	PASSES	DRIBBLE	FOUL	LAY-UP	SET SHOT	PIVOT
BOWLING	GRIP	STANCE	APPROACH	DELIVERY	FOLLOW THRU	AIMING
GOLF	GRIP	STANCE	SWING	FOLLOW THRU	PUTTING	DRIVE
SOFTBALL	THROWING	HITTING	RUNNING	PITCHING	CATCHING	FIELDING
TABLE TENNIS	GRIP	SERVE	STROKE	DRIVE	CHOP	DOUBLES
TENNIS	GRIP	FORE HAND	BACK HAND	SERVE	VOLLEY	LOB
T. FOOTBALL	PUNT	PASS	BLOCK	PLACE KICK	B.F.FORMATIONS	LINE
TRACK	STARTS	DASH	HURDLES	R. B. JUMP	SHOT	RELAY
TUMBLING	FWD ROLL	BACK-ROLL	KIP	BALANCE	HAND STAND	HAND SPRING
VOLLEYBALL	VOLLEY	SERVE	SET-UPS	SPIKE	BLOCK	RECOVER
WRESTLING	TAKE DOWNS	COUNTERS	ESCAPES	COUNTERS	REVERSALS	PINS

BOYS—PROFICIENCY TESTS—BOYS

EVENTS	GIVE TESTS FIRST WEEK IN MAY	EVENTS	GIVE TESTS FIRST WEEK IN MAY
PULL-UP (PALMS AWAY)		S. BROAD JUMP (IN.)	
DASH (50 YDS.)		AGILITY RUN (40 YDS.)	
SIT-UP (MIN.) (FLEX KNEES)		SEE GUIDEBOOK FOR DESCRIPTION OF TESTS.	

Figure 9–3. *Continued.*

CINCINNATI PUBLIC SCHOOLS
DEPARTMENT OF PHYSICAL EDUCATION

PERIODS
M. T. W. TH. F.

NAME ____________ HOME ROOM ____________

SQUAD ________ NO. ________ LOCKER ________ LOCK ________ GRADE LEVEL ________

	SEPTEMBER					OCTOBER					NOVEMBER					DECEMBER					JANUARY					SEMESTER
TOWEL FEE:	M.	T.	W.	Th.	F.	M.	T.	W.	Th.	F.	M.	T.	W.	Th.	F.	M.	T.	W.	Th.	F.	M.	T.	W.	Th.	F.	I
ATTENDANCE KEY:																										
	FEBRUARY					MARCH					APRIL					MAY					JUNE					II

											AVERAGE
ATTITUDE											
APPEARANCE											
SHOWERS											
PREPARATORY EXERCISES											
GAMES PROGRAM											
APPARATUS AND TUMBLING											
TRACK AND FIELD											
SWIMMING AND DIVING											

P.E. - 13 BOYS' CLASS CARD—SECONDARY SCHOOLS

Figure 9–4. An individual record card which includes the Pentathlon. (Courtesy Cincinnati Public Schools.)

Figure 9–4 continued on opposite page.

PENTATHLON

NAME _____

SQUAD _____ NO. _____ HOME ROOM _____

CLASSIFICATION _____ EXP. _____

AGE _____ YRS. _____ MOS. _____

HEIGHT _____ INCHES _____

WEIGHT _____ POUNDS _____

TOTAL _____

CLASS _____

EVENTS AND PERFORMANCE

	PULL-UP		TRIPLE JUMP		PUSH-UP		SIT-UP		SQUAT THRUST	
	FALL	SPRING	FALL	SPRING	FALL	SPRING	FALL	SPRING	FALL	SPRING

TRACK AND FIELD

CLASSIFICATION	F	F				E				D				C				B				A			
GRADE	F	D	C	B	A	D	C	B	A	D	C	B	A	D	C	B	A	D	C	B	A	D	C	B	A
60 YARDS		9.7 to 10.5	8.4 to 9.6	7.8 to 8.5	Below 7.8	9.6 to 10.4	8.4 to 9.5	7.7 to 8.3	Below 7.7	9.3 to 10.3	8.0 to 9.2	7.2 to 7.9	Below 7.2	9.2 to 10.2	7.9 to 9.1	7.3 to 7.8	Below 7.3	9.0 to 10.1	7.6 to 8.9	7.1 to 7.5	Below 7.1	9.1 to 10.2	7.6 to 9.0	6.9 to 7.5	Below 6.9
75 YARDS		11.9 to 13.3	10.6 to 11.8	9.8 to 10.5	Below 9.8	11.7 to 13.1	10.2 to 11.6	9.7 to 10.1	Below 9.7	11.2 to 12.9	9.9 to 11.1	9.4 to 9.8	Below 9.4	11.0 to 12.6	9.6 to 10.9	9.0 to 9.5	Below 9.0	10.7 to 12.1	9.4 to 10.6	8.6 to 9.3	Below 8.6	10.8 to 11.8	9.4 to 10.7	8.4 to 9.3	Below 8.4
100 YARDS		15.3 to 16.5	14.1 to 15.2	13.5 to 14.0	Below 13.5	14.7 to 15.9	13.3 to 14.6	12.8 to 13.2	Below 12.8	14.4 to 15.4	13.0 to 14.3	12.3 to 12.9	Below 12.3	14.0 to 15.1	12.7 to 13.9	12.1 to 12.6	Below 12.1	13.7 to 15.0	12.5 to 13.6	11.9 to 12.4	Below 11.9	13.5 to 14.7	12.2 to 13.4	11.6 to 12.1	Below 11.6
220 YARDS		35.8 to 38.0	31.5 to 35.7	30.0 to 31.4	Below 30.0	35.9 to 38.1	32.0 to 35.8	29.9 to 31.9	Below 29.9	34.8 to 37.0	30.9 to 34.7	29.1 to 30.8	Below 29.1	33.8 to 36.1	29.7 to 33.7	28.0 to 29.6	Below 28.0	32.7 to 35.1	28.9 to 32.6	27.1 to 28.8	Below 27.1	32.1 to 34.0	28.5 to 32.0	26.7 to 28.4	Below 26.7
440	ENDURANCE RUN ONLY																								
880	ENDURANCE RUN ONLY																								
MILE	ENDURANCE RUN ONLY																								
S. PUT		12' to 15'	16' to 20'	21' to 24'	Above 24'	15' to 18'	19' to 25'	26' to 28'	Above 28'	17' to 20'	21' to 27'	28' to 30'	Above 30'	19' to 23'	24' to 30'	31' to 35'	Above 35'	21' to 26'	27' to 34'	35' to 37'	Above 37'	24' to 28'	29' to 36'	37' to 42'	Above 42'
H. JUMP		2'8" to 3'0"	3'1" to 3'7"	3'8" to 4'3"	Above 4'3"	2'9" to 3'1"	3'2" to 3'8"	3'9" to 4'4"	Above 4'4"	2'9" to 3'4"	3'5" to 3'9"	4'0" to 4'6"	Above 4'6"	3'0" to 3'5"	3'6" to 4'1"	4'2" to 4'6"	Above 4'6"	3'0" to 3'5"	3'6" to 4'4"	4'5" to 4'9"	Above 4'9"	3'2" to 3'7"	3'8" to 4'6"	4'7" to 4'11"	Above 4'11"
R.B. JUMP		7'2" to 9'1"	9'2" to 11'7"	11'8" to 13'2"	Above 13'2"	7'6" to 9'9"	9'10" to 12'5"	12'6" to 14'0"	Above 14'0"	7'11" to 10'2"	10'3" to 13'7"	13'8" to 15'0"	Above 15'0"	8'2" to 10'10"	10'11" to 14'0"	14'1" to 16'3"	Above 16'3"	8'11" to 11'11"	12'0" to 14'9"	14'10" to 16'7"	Above 16'7"	9'5" to 12'3"	12'4" to 14'11"	15'0" to 16'9"	Above 16'9"

Figure 9–4. *Continued.*

PHYSICAL EDUCATION LOCKER CARD
OMAHA PUBLIC JUNIOR HIGH SCHOOL

1ST SEMESTER   1 2 3 4 5 6 7   M W F   T   TH

2ND SEMESTER   1 2 3 4 5 6 7   M W F   T   TH

NAME   AGE

ADDRESS   PHONE

GROUP   HOMEROOM

LOCKER NUMBER

LOCK SERIAL NUMBER

LOCK COMBINATION   LOCKERMATE

PHYSICIAN

PHYSICAL LIMITATIONS

FEES:

SHIRT NUMBER _____ TOWEL _____ (1ST SEM.) _____ (2ND SEM.)

TRUNKS NUMBER _____ SUIT _____ (1ST SEM.) _____ (2ND SEM.)

SQUAD NUMBER _____ 1ST SEMESTER

SQUAD NUMBER _____ 2ND SEMESTER

TEST RESULTS	1ST	2ND	3RD	4TH
FITNESS				
FLAGBALL				
SOCCER				
SPEEDBALL				
VOLLEYBALL				
BASKETBALL				
TUMBLING				
TRACK				
SOFTBALL				
SWIMMING				
CITIZENSHIP				
ATTENDANCE				
FINAL GRADE				

A

DAVENPORT PUBLIC SCHOOLS—High School Girl's Physical Education

NAME _____ ADDRESS _____ GR. 10 11 12

P.E. PER _____ COUNSELOR _____ H. R. _____ PHONE _____

NO. _____

WEEK 1 WEEK 2 WEEK 3 WEEK 4 WEEK 5 WEEK 6
M T W TH F M T W TH F M T W TH F M T W TH F M T W TH F M T W TH F

WEEK 7 WEEK 8 WEEK 9 WEEK 10 WEEK 11 WEEK 12

WEEK 13 WEEK 14 WEEK 15 WEEK 16 WEEK 17 WEEK 18

ACT.   PRACT.   WRIT.   SHOW.   UNIF.   ABS.   TOTAL   SEM. GRADE

B

Figure 9–5. *A,* A more comprehensive Individual Record Card which, in addition to the usual information, includes space to record test results; *B,* A girl's individual record card. (*A* courtesy Omaha Public Schools, Omaha, Nebraska; *B* courtesy Davenport Public Schools, Davenport, Iowa.)

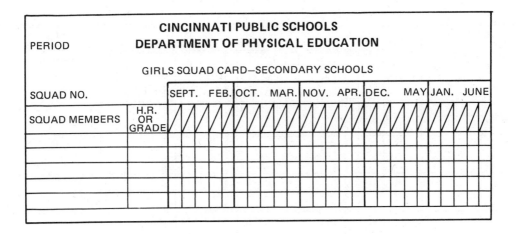

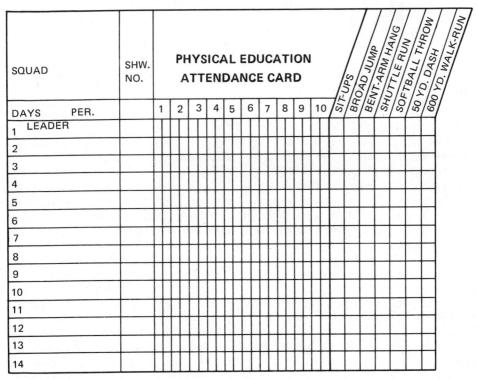

FORM D-64

Figure 9-6. Squad cards. (*Upper*, courtesy Cincinnati Public Schools, Cincinnati, Ohio; *lower*, courtesy Davenport Public Schools, Davenport, Iowa.)

PERIOD ____________ CHEYENNE PUBLIC SCHOOLS WEEK OF __________

DAILY CHECK LIST

1. EXCELLENT
2. GOOD
3. SATISFACTORY
4. UNSATISFACTORY

V–OKAY
T–TARDY
A–ABSENT
E–EXCUSED

NAME	MONDAY					TUESDAY					WEDNESDAY					THURSDAY					FRIDAY					COMMENTS
	ATTENDANCE	DRESS/SHOWER	EXERCISE	CONDUCT	SKILLS	ATTENDANCE	DRESS/SHOWER	EXERCISE	CONDUCT	SKILLS	ATTENDANCE	DRESS/SHOWER	EXERCISE	CONDUCT	SKILLS	ATTENDANCE	DRESS/SHOWER	EXERCISE	CONDUCT	SKILLS	ATTENDANCE	DRESS/SHOWER	EXERCISE	CONDUCT	SKILLS	

Figure 9–7. Daily check sheet. (Courtesy Cheyenne Public Schools, Cheyenne, Wyoming.)

Permanent Record Cards. In the well-planned program of physical education a system is provided for recording the various phases of the program in a permanent form that can be made available years later. Grades, teachers' comments, intramural points earned, and results of special activities are some of the many phases of the program that should be recorded for permanent use. The card in Figure 9–8 shows how these phases of the program can be recorded in a permanent form for yearly examination.

It should be of interest to the reader to notice how the permanent record card shown in Figure 9–9 includes the marks of the student (1–5) which correspond to the letter grades A–F. Teachers also indicate whether the girl has an average (AV), above average (AA), or below average (BA) in skills. In Chapter 7 (Fig. 7–17) the choice of activities of a student is shown.

Excuses

A problem that appears at first glance to be minor can cause many headaches for the teacher whose administrators have not established a firm policy on the matter. This is the problem of excusing students from physical education.

Pupils should be required to have a physician's letter specifying disability in order to be excused permanently from physical education. Temporary excuses from home should first be carried to the nurse for examination and then brought to the teacher. Two or three of these excuses should necessitate a physician's examination and recommendation concerning the student's condition as it pertains to his participation in the physical education program.

Under no circumstances should pupils be excused from physical education to participate in extracurricular activities such as cheerleading, band practice, drill teams, or athletics. If physical education is important for growth and development—as it has been shown to be—then students should not be excused from it to participate in other activities. Physical education teachers too often are prone to permit pupils to take part in extracurricular activities during the class period. This practice eventually undermines physical education instruction; moreover, it is difficult to curtail, once a precedent has been established.

Conant is highly critical of the practice of excusing pupils from physical education to participate in other activities: "I have already mentioned my skepticism of grouping and scheduling based on band membership, and I deplore the substitution of band for physical education."[10]

The Representative Assembly of the

NORFOLK PUBLIC SCHOOLS
HEALTH, PHYSICAL EDUCATION AND SAFETY DEPARTMENT
PERMANENT RECORD CARD

DRIVER EDUCATION
Class Room _____ Mark _____ Teacher _____
Behind-the-Wheel _____ Mark _____ Teacher _____

NAME _____ (Last) _____ (First) _____ (Middle) _____ SCHOOL _____

Address _____ Telephone _____

Parents Name _____

Date of Birth _____ (Month) _____ (Day) _____ (Year) _____ Date of Enrollment _____

SCHEDULE

CLASS	YEAR	HOMEROOM	PERIOD	TEACHER	TERM MARK	REMARKS
7						
8						
9						
10						
11						
12						

A

PHYSICAL PROFICIENCY TESTS
GRADE

BOYS EVENTS	7	8	9	10	11	12	GIRLS EVENTS
PULL-UPS							MODIFIED PULL-UPS
DASH (50 Yds.)							WALL PUSH (30 Sec.)
SIT-UPS (Min.) (KNEES FLEXED)							SIT-UPS (30 Sec.) (KNEES FLEXED)
STANDING BROAD JUMP (In.)							DASH (40 Yds.)
AGILITY RUN (40 Yds.)							AGILITY RUN (30 Yds.)

RECORD TERMINAL TEST FROM PUPIL RECORD CARD EACH YEAR

B

Figure 9–8. Many of the details involved in teaching physical education classes can be recorded on a permanent record card.

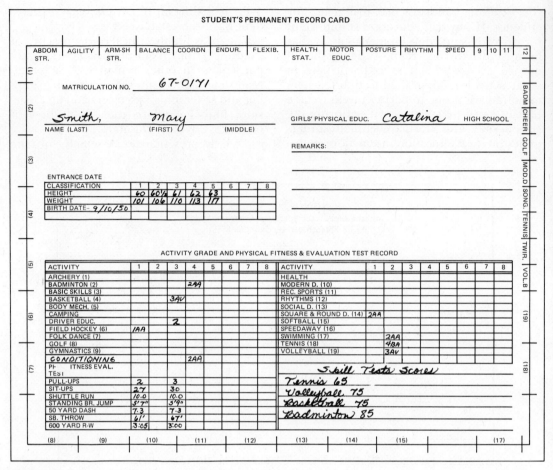

Figure 9–9. Permanent Record Card. (Courtesy of *Physical Education Newsletter*, Croft Educational Services, Inc., May 1, 1967.)

American Association of Health, Physical Education, and Recreation opposed in their resolution the substitution of marching band, baton twirling, and drill team for physical education.[11] This is a logical stand. If pupils are excused for these activities, why should they not be excused for dramatics, choral club, photography, art club, debating team, and many other activities included in the curriculum? The type of activity is not a logical criterion; students building a set for a dramatic club play may get even more exercise than the baton twirler.

Moreover, pupils should not be excused from physical education for athletic competition. Although there are some arguments in favor of this practice, the following reasons show why they are not sound:

1. One of the basic factors in developing athletes is conditioning. After the season is over, there is a tremendous letdown in exercising. Usually the individual "takes it easy" until the following season. If the athlete participates in football, the practice season is entirely too short. In fact, he may have no training at all from the Thanksgiving game until the next September. If he were enrolled in the physical education program, he could continue the conditioning procedure for the remainder of the year.

2. Athletes participating in team sports often miss the important instruction in individual sports offered in the physical education class. In addition to the conditioning they would get in

the class, they would also be learning skills that could be used in later life long after school participation is over.

3. In schools in which physical education is required for credit, teachers cannot justify giving a grade if the pupil does not attend class. A pupil would never be excused from mathematics or other academic subjects and then expect a grade. If this policy does not apply to all subjects alike, it should not apply to physical education.

Frequently, pupils are excused because of some disability that prevents them from participating in the regular program. Decisions regarding these cases should be made only through the recommendation of a physician. In some cases, students should be placed on a modified program which the physician recommends. Special cards or letters should be provided for this. Figures 9–10, 9–11, 9–12, 9–13 and 9–14 describe different types of forms that may be used for this purpose. The form used in

---

DADE COUNTY PUBLIC SCHOOLS
SECONDARY SCHOOL
PHYSICIAN'S RECOMMENDATIONS FOR
MODIFIED PHYSICAL EDUCATION

PUPIL'S
NAME_____ Age_____ Grade_____ School_____
         (Last)   (First)   (Middle)

This is to certify that I have examined the above-named pupil. Diagnosis: (Please be specific) _____

_____

This pupil (is) (is not) at present under continued medical treatment. If pupil is to take specific

medicines while at school, please specify the nature of drugs and regime. _____

_____

(If, in the opinion of the physician, the prescribed medication is considered restricted information, this part of the card need NOT be filled in.)
*Therefore, I recommend that participation in Physical Education be modified as indicated below:

☐ Moderate activity; e.g., volleyball, kickball, dancing, conditioning exercises (moderate), swimming, tennis, jogging (slow trot), officiating.

☐ Restricted activity; e.g., table tennis, ball skills (without running), walking, deck tennis, archery, individual exercises modified as needed, officiating recreational activities, no running or jumping.

Duration: for_____week(s); for_____month(s); for_____

SIGNED: _____M.D.   Phone_____Date_____
                                                                    (Examination)

*Please use the reverse side for additional information on and recommendations in regard to limits of capability and tolerance.

TO THE PARENTS OR GUARDIAN AND TO THE FAMILY PHYSICIAN:
   All pupils are required by the Dade County School Board to take physical education unless the family physician considers such activity detrimental to the pupil's health.
   Your cooperation and support will be invaluable in helping us meet the physical education needs of our pupils.

                                                        JOE HALL, Superintendent

Figure 9–10. Physician's Recommendations for Modified Physical Education. (Courtesy Dade County Public Schools, Dade County, Florida.)

CEDAR RAPIDS COMMUNITY SCHOOL DISTRICT

DEPARTMENT OF PHYSICAL EDUCATION

Family Physician's Request for Special Program in Physical Education

BOYS

Pupil_____ School_____ Grade_____

Home Address_____ Home Telephone_____

Date_____

Dear Doctor:
The above named pupil has requested an excuse from physical education. Since physical education is a required subject, we try to have a program with enough flexibility to meet the needs of most pupils.

Below are listed the various basic activities in our program. Would you please indicate, by check, those activities in which you recommend this boy not participate. Recommendations regarding activities would be appreciated.

Strenuous	Moderate	Light
Touch Football	Softball	Ping Pong
Soccer	Tennis	Social Dancing
Basketball	Volleyball	Gym Games and Relays
Wrestling	Badminton	Archery
Gymnastics	Tumbling	Shuffleboard
Track	Marching	Golf
Swimming	Square Dancing	Officiating

The General Diagnosis:_____

_____

_____

This condition will continue for_____weeks.

Special Recommendations:_____

_____

_____

Signed_____ M.D.

Figure 9–11. Physician's recommendation for modified physical education (boys). (Courtesy Cedar Rapids Community School District, Cedar Rapids, Iowa.)

```
┌─────────────────────────────────────────────────────────────────────┐
│                                                                       │
│          CEDAR RAPIDS COMMUNITY SCHOOL DISTRICT                       │
│                                                                       │
│                 DEPARTMENT OF PHYSICAL EDUCATION                      │
│                                                                       │
│       Family Physician's Request for Special Program in Physical      │
│                              Education                                │
│                                                                       │
│                               GIRLS                                   │
│                                                                       │
│  Pupil_____ School_____ Grade_____        │
│                                                                       │
│  Home Address_____ Home Telephone_____              │
│                                                                       │
│                                        Date_____               │
│                                                                       │
│  Dear Doctor:                                                         │
│  The above named pupil has requested an excuse from physical          │
│  education. Since physical education is a required subject, we try     │
│  to have a program with enough flexibility to meet the needs of       │
│  most pupils.                                                         │
└─────────────────────────────────────────────────────────────────────┘
```

CEDAR RAPIDS COMMUNITY SCHOOL DISTRICT

DEPARTMENT OF PHYSICAL EDUCATION

Family Physician's Request for Special Program in Physical Education

GIRLS

Pupil_____ School_____ Grade_____

Home Address_____ Home Telephone_____

Date_____

Dear Doctor:

The above named pupil has requested an excuse from physical education. Since physical education is a required subject, we try to have a program with enough flexibility to meet the needs of most pupils.

Below are listed the various basic activities in our program. Would you please indicate, by check, those activities in which you recommend this girl not participate. Recommendations regarding activities would be appreciated.

Strenuous	Moderate	Light
Soccer	Volleyball	Ping Pong
Speedball	Softball	Shuffleboard
Track	Badminton	Archery
Field Hockey	Square Dancing	Golf
Basketball	Folk Dancing	Deck Tennis
Swimming	Modern Dance	Stunts
	Gym Games and Relays	Bowling
	Trampoline	
	Tumbling	

The General Diagnosis:_____

_____

_____

This condition will continue for_____weeks.

Special Recommendations:_____

_____

_____

Signed_____M.D.

Figure 9–12. Physician's request for special programs in physical education (girls). (Courtesy Cedar Rapids Community School District, Cedar Rapids, Iowa.)

MOBILE PUBLIC SCHOOLS
Mobile, Alabama

Date_____

Name of student_____ Grade_____ Age_____

Address_____ Phone_____

Parent's or Guardian's Name _____ Business Phone _____

School_____

It is my professional opinion that the above named pupil should participate in the types of activities as checked below for _____ weeks. Thereafter he/she may return to the school's regular program which includes all types of activities.

VIGOROUS ACTIVITY_____	MODERATE ACTIVITY_____	MILD ACTIVITIES_____
_____Apparatus Work	_____Badminton	_____Archery
_____Basketball	_____Deck Tennis	_____Croquet
_____Box Hockey	_____Golf	_____Darts
_____Calisthenics	_____Marching	_____Game Official
_____Field Hockey	_____Softball	_____Horse Shoes
_____Gymnastics	_____Swimming	_____Quoits
_____Relays	_____Tetherball	_____Shuffle Board
_____Soccer	_____Tumbling	_____Table Tennis
_____Speedball	_____	_____
_____Sprinting	_____	_____
_____Square Dance	_____	_____
_____Stunts	_____	_____
_____Tennis	_____	_____
_____Track and Field Events	_____	_____
_____Volleyball	_____	_____
_____Wrestling	_____	_____

QUIET ACTIVITY_____	PRESCRIBED ACTIVITY AS INDICATED BELOW_____	COMPLETE REST_____
_____Equipment Manager	_____	
_____Locker Room Attendant	_____	
_____Score Keeper	_____	
_____Squad Leader	_____	
_____	_____	
_____	_____	
_____	_____	

REMARKS: _____

_____

_____

Approved by: _____ M.D.   Phone_____ Date_____
       (Name of Physician)

Figure 9–13. *See legend on opposite page.*

School .... Address .... Phone ....

Physical Education Director .... Principal ....

To the Family Physician:

    The physical education program for both boys and girls is one which embraces a great variety of activities. It is hoped that this broad program fulfills the needs of the pupils in the areas of physical, emotional, and social growth and development. Physical education is a required subject and each pupil is encouraged to participate to the fullest extent of his or her capacity.

    Below are the various phases of activity offered. Please check the activities in which the pupil under your care may not participate.

☐ Archery	☐ Gymnastics	☐ Softball
☐ Badminton	☐ Jog and Walk	☐ Swimming
☐ Baseball	☐ Lacrosse	☐ Tennis
☐ Basketball	☐ Fitness Testing	☐ Touch Football
☐ Body Building	☐ Push Ball	☐ Track and Field
☐ Calisthenics	☐ Recreational Games	☐ Tumbling
☐ Dancing Activities	☐ Soccer	☐ Volleyball
☐ Field Hockey	☐ Speed Ball	☐ Walking
☐ Folk Dancing	☐ Square Dancing	☐ Weight Training
☐ Golf	☐ Social Dancing	☐ Wrestling

Name of Pupil .... Age .... Grade ....

Nature of Illness/Injury .... Limitation of Activity ....

Date of Return to Normal Activities...

Signature of Physician ....

Address .... Telephone............................

Signature of Parent/Guardian ....

Address .... Telephone............................

Date ....

Figure 9–14. A suggested medical excuse form. (Courtesy of *Physical Education Newsletter,* Croft Educational Services, Inc., December 1, 1967.)

Figure 9–13. Physician's recommendation for modified physical education. (Courtesy Mobile Public Schools, Mobile, Alabama.)

Mobile, Alabama, illustrates how activities may be grouped according to degree of intensity ranging from vigorous activity to complete rest. The other forms are similar but not as comprehensive.

Towel Program

Another part of the overall organization is the provision for cleanliness after participation in activity. One of the essentials is the provision of a towel for each student. There are several ways of providing towels for the daily showering program. Some schools launder the towels in the school. This presents a number of problems. An operator of the washing machines must be employed; when the costs of equipment, water, detergents, and the other items are added in, this can be quite expensive.

Probably the most practical way to handle the problem is to have all pupils pay a small towel fee each year in those systems which allow fees. This money can be kept in a central fund and used to cover the cost of laundering the towels. Indigent students must, of course, be provided for from school funds, welfare, or other sources. Local laundries may bid for the towel laundering contract; they usually make daily deliveries.

Emil Klumpar, Physical Welfare Consultant in the Cedar Rapids (Iowa) Community School District, reports an excellent towel program in which pupils are responsible for towel fees on a prorated basis.

Some school districts prohibit the charging of fees. In such cases, the district usually provides all instructional materials. These, of course, should include towels.

An important aspect of the physical education organization in connection with the towel program is keeping an inventory of the towels. In those schools where local laundries service towels, a strict inventory procedure must be developed. Such a procedure exists in the Cedar Rapids (Iowa) Community School District.

Uniforms

An administrative policy should be established concerning the requirement for appropriate physical education attire for the students. As a rule, student morale, performance, and discipline are improved when students dress uniformly.

Pupils should have a standard uniform: one-piece suits for girls, and trunks and shirts for boys are desirable. These may be provided through local retail stores; some schools order from the manufacturer and distribute them through the school bookstore or through the physical education classes.

Locker Assignments

All locker assignments should be made during the first week. Locker numbers and combinations should be recorded on individual record cards (such as the ones shown on pp. 273 and 278) or on a master sheet filed in the office. In addition, if separate locks are to be obtained by the pupils, regulations concerning these must be explained. Another form that may be used for recording locker information is shown in Figure 9–15. This form may be used when more than one person shares the same locker.

Communication with Parents

Teachers should use every method available to communicate with parents and to interpret the physical education program in such a manner that parents have at least an overview of what goes on in the class. Several media of communication have been proven effective; they are described on the following pages.

Handbook. The handbook is a practical and effective medium for interpreting the program to parents. If used properly it may be the means of securing parental assistance and insuring the teacher of a successful program. Two handbooks are mentioned in this text. One is described in Chapter 3 and should be studied at this point. The other is shown in Figure 9–16. This book has been used for several years and includes all of the necessary details that are involved in organizing a program.

Letters. Sometimes letters may be written to parents describing the program. The

			School		
	Period			Teacher	
Number	Student's Name	Serial Number	Combination	Paid	Returned

Figure 9–15. A master form for keeping locker assignments.

limitations of letters, however, make them less satisfactory than handbooks. A letter usually consists of one page, whereas the handbook consists of several pages. However, if the teacher wishes to acquaint the parent with a limited number of topics, the letter may be an effective medium. Figure 9–17 is one example of how letters may be used.

Reporting to Parents. In addition to sending letters and handbooks to parents, many teachers devise some type of report to give parents an indication of their child's status in the physical education class. Although the usual report card carries a mark in physical education, as for other subjects, something more comprehensive is important if parents are to have a clear understanding of their child's progress. A report of this kind is illustrated in Figure 9–18. Notice that not only are the tests and scores tabulated, but space is provided to show what each test measures and also how to interpret the results.

The Student Leader Corps

In addition to mastering the organizational details of the first week, the teacher must plan for assistance by his students in certain phases of the program. A student leader organization to assist with many of the instructional procedures and many of

Figure 9–16. Physical Education Handbook: an effective medium for interpreting the physical education program to parents. (Courtesy South Bend Community School Corporation, South Bend, Indiana.)

TABLE OF CONTENTS

Figure 9–16. *Continued.*

the routine details that occur in the daily program can be a tremendous help to the teacher. Each class should have a group of students who will be responsible for assisting with routine elements of instruction, such as checking attendance, issuing towels and equipment, recording results, and attending to many other details important to the smooth and effective functioning of the class.

The student leaders from each class should meet periodically. This group of students under the leadership of the teacher should be trained to assist the teacher in the various mechanics of the program. The leaders of each class may be organized as shown in Figure 9–19.

Student Instructors. The teacher should have in each class a group of older, experienced pupils who may assist with the instruction, pupils who have become proficient in certain activities by participating on

the varsity team, in intramurals, or in a community program. For example, it is important in tumbling that one group of pupils check the movements of the pupils performing the skills, in order to prevent accidents. Student instructors should be trained to assist in this procedure.

Assistant Student Instructors. Each class should have several *assistant* student instructors whose chief duty is to work with the class manager and assist the teacher with the overall management of the class.

Student Class Managers. Some students should be selected to serve as class managers. These managers would have as their chief responsibility the issuing of equipment to the squad leaders; the managers would work directly with the squad leaders in the duties outlined for them.

Squad Leaders. Many teachers feel that it is good organizational procedure to divide all classes into squads, each squad

Dear Parents:

The Cooper High School Boys' Physical Education Department plans to offer your son the best physical education program possible. To do this we need your cooperation, help and understanding.

Our program will stress physical fitness with emphasis on physical fitness tests given at the beginning and close of each semester. Every student and parent will be given the opportunity to check the progress made with national standards established by the President's Council of Physical Fitness.

We also plan to stress individual activities such as badminton, tennis, weight training, tumbling and gymnastics plus regular team sports, including touch football, volleyball, basketball, track and field and speedball.

To further meet the physical and leisure needs of your son we will offer an after school intramural program including the activities offered in our physical education classes. We invite you to view these activities as our guest.

Some things we will expect of each student and points on which he will be graded are:

(1) Regular and punctual attendance
(2) In regulation gray uniform each class period
(3) Full participation to the best of his ability
(4) Shower after each class
(5) Written, skill and physical fitness tests
(6) Attitude, (behavior, carrying out assigned jobs, relations with fellow students, etc.)

Please call on me at any time on any question that may arise. My conference period is from 8:30 to 9:30 A.M. in the boys' gym. My phone number is OW 2-5961.

Sincerely,

John Fred Phillips
Boys Physical Education Department

Figure 9–17. Informing parents of school regulations is important in the operation of a successful program. (Courtesy Abilene Public Schools, Abilene, Texas.)

CEDAR RAPIDS COMMUNITY SCHOOLS
Physical Welfare Department
PUPIL PHYSICAL FITNESS REPORT

NAME_____ SCHOOL_____ DATE_____ TEACHER(Fall)_____

PRINCIPAL_____TEACHER(Spring)_____

TO THE PARENTS: A series of physical fitness tests has recently been given to all pupils in grades 4–12. They are being given twice each school year. This is a report on the performance of your child. In each test you may compare your child's score with the performance score of other children throughout the state. The state scores are given in terms of percentile rank. For example, a percentile rank of 75 means that a child's performance surpasses that of 75 per cent of the children of the same grade tested through the state. The state norms were constructed on data obtained by testing boys and girls in 104 schools in Iowa during the 1960–61 school year. Thus, the percentile scores cannot necessarily be interpreted as the ultimate in achievement. They can be assumed to represent the achievements for the 1960–61 school year of those schools where attention was given to motor fitness.

If your child has a low performance score, it might be because of a particular height, weight or other physical characteristic. The important thing is for each child to show continued improvement in his own performance.

This department is making strenuous efforts to assist our young people to attain and maintain health and physical fitness. The physically underdeveloped youngsters are being identified and programs geared to individual needs. We are giving increased emphasis to the more vigorous type activities. It is recommended that parents encourage their children to participate regularly in physical activity.

TEST	WHAT IT TESTS	YOUR CHILD'S SCORE		PERCENTILE RANK		HOW TO INTERPRET THE RESULTS
		Fall	Spring	Fall	Spring	
SIT-UPS	Strength/endurance of abdominal muscles					The object was to do as many as possible in 1 min. (2 min. boys, Gr. 10–12)
STANDING BROAD JUMP	Power in the legs and coordination	in.	in.			The greater distance jumped, the better the performance.
SHUTTLE RUN	Agility					The greater number of trips in a 15 second interval, the better the score.
FORWARD BEND	Flexibility	in.	in.			The higher score (plus) measured in the nearest 1/2", the better the performance.
GRASSHOPPER	Endurance					The object was to do as many as possible in 30 sec. (1 min. boys, Gr. 7 & up.)
DASH	Speed	sec.	sec.			The faster time the better the performance; 40 yd., Gr. 4–6; 50 yds., Gr. 7–12.
PULL-UPS (Boys) BENT ARM HANG (Girls)	Arm, shoulder and upper back strength					Boys—one point each time chin goes above the bar. Girls—the longer the time (in sec.) with arms fully bent, chin above bar, the better the performance.

ARNOLD SALISBURY
Superintendent of Schools

EMIL A. KLUMPAR
Physical Welfare Consultant

Figure 9–18. Reporting to parents. (Courtesy Cedar Rapids Community School District, Cedar Rapids, Iowa.)

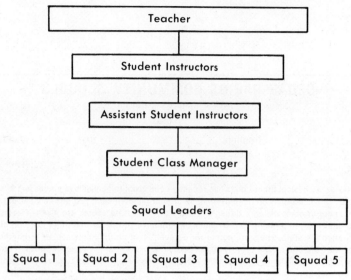

Figure 9–19. Organization of the Student Leader Corps.

having a leader. These squads may be formed by having the entire class nominate a number of students for the leadership position. Those nominated would then select the students who would constitute their squads. The chief function of the squad leaders would be to expedite such procedures as checking attendance, urging members to report on time, and checking uniforms and to provide overall management of their squads.

Wayne Nelson, a teacher at the Fremont Junior High School in Seaside, California, emphasized in a recent article the importance of developing student leaders. He trains leaders to perform such duties as setting up equipment, supervising the locker room, taking the roll, and assisting in demonstrating skills.[12]

A large number of schools and systems throughout the country utilize student leaders to a great advantage. These leaders may assume many of the burdensome details that are present in every class, and thus enable the teacher to devote most of his time to teaching. Several ways in which teachers plan to develop student leaders are described on the following pages. These plans may be used in conjunction with the outline of the student leader corps shown in Figure 9–19.

GRANITE CITY, ILLINOIS. In Granite City Senior High School, Granite City, Illinois, the girls' department of physical education developed a leadership program to provide opportunities for girls to learn how to work with individuals and groups and also to assist teachers with class management. To give an idea of the standards of performance and behavior expected of student leaders, the leadership evaluation form used at Granite City is reproduced below.[13]

GRANITE CITY SENIOR HIGH SCHOOL
Granite City, Illinois

LEADERSHIP EVALUATION

Name of Student

Date _____ Activity_____

Teacher_____

Key: +   Leader is outstanding in this area (Must comment)

/   Satisfactory; rates about the same as other leaders

–   Needs improvement to meet leadership standards (Must comment)

0   Very poor (Must comment)

I. GENERAL APPEARANCE

Well groomed at all times	
Uses good taste in dress, make-up	

P.E. outfit always looks well	
Looks alive, energetic, enthusiastic	
Appears to be confident and poised	
Uses good body mechanics; walks in a graceful manner; stands properly	
Voice is pleasing	
CONSTRUCTIVE SUGGESTIONS	

C. THESE STUDENTS TOWARD THIS LEADER	
Students respond well to leader's direction	
Students are friendly to the leader, seek her help and friendship	
Class worked well when leader was in charge	
CONSTRUCTIVE SUGGESTIONS	

II. PERSONALITY REACTIONS

A. THIS LEADER TOWARD THE TEACHER	
Always friendly and helpful	
Volunteers for extra assignments	
Accepts suggestion and criticism graciously	
CONSTRUCTIVE SUGGESTIONS	

B. THIS LEADER TOWARD THE STUDENTS IN THIS CLASS	
Fair to all students	
Impartial but friendly toward all	
Knows and plays her leadership role properly in relation to students; has status with the students	
CONSTRUCTIVE SUGGESTIONS	

III. LEADERSHIP QUALITIES

Able to follow directions	
Able to control the group	
Punctual (always on time)	
Dependable (did promptly and efficiently what she agreed to do)	
Initiative (capable of going ahead on her own using good judgment)	
Resourceful (suggests new ways of doing things; has ideas for helping the class)	
Tact (does not antagonize)	
CONSTRUCTIVE SUGGESTIONS	

IV. LEADERSHIP LABORATORY SKILLS

Able to organize and direct groups speedily and efficiently	
Can demonstrate the skills well	

Knows rules thoroughly	
Accurate in administering tests, keeping records	
Can play well herself	
Officiates well	
Able to coach when others are playing	
Able to help others analyze their skill difficulties	
Can explain new techniques and new formations easily to group	
Demonstrated pride in and enthusiasm for being a leader in this class	

CONSTRUCTIVE SUGGESTIONS

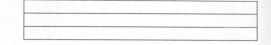

V. WHAT DO YOU CONSIDER THIS LEADER'S ONE MOST OUTSTANDING ATTRIBUTE?

VI. WHAT ONE THING WOULD YOU SUGGEST THIS STUDENT IMPROVE TO BECOME A MORE HELPFUL LEADER?

EAST LYME, CONNECTICUT. Another outstanding program with a student leader plan is used at East Lyme Junior High School, East Lyme, Connecticut. Outstanding students are members of the Leaders Corps, which was organized not only to assist with class management but also to provide an enrichment program for those students who show superior ability. According to Director Bob McLohon, a major objective of the program is to encourage gifted students to choose teaching as a career. Some of the responsibilities of the leaders are to demonstrate skills, assist in clarifying skill teaching points, assist in

---

East Lyme Junior High School Leaders Code

I. STATEMENT OF PURPOSE:
Leaders will, with guidance, assume responsibilities that are commensurate with their level of maturity. Members of the Corps, with supervision, will act as student assistants for their class.

II. RECRUITMENT:
Selection will be based upon outstanding personal qualities, excellent skills ability, a keen interest in sports and a compelling desire for more knowledge in the field of physical education. Candidates will be chosen by the instructor on a volunteer basis. Recruitment will take place in the 7th and 8th year (in the 8th year only when the need arises). Final selection and awarding of emblem will take place after the first marking period of the 8th year. The Leader serves in a candidate status prior to his final election.

III. EAST LYME LEADERS CORPS:
The Leaders Corps will have a President (9th year), Vice President (8th year) and a Secretary (8th or 9th year). All officers will be nominated and elected by members of the corps.

IV. OBJECTIVES OF THE LEADERS CORPS:
1. To assist the instructors
2. To be a master of what you teach and not whom you teach
3. To set an example for your classmates
4. To consider student safety at all times
5. To act as a leader in every possible way to the best of your ability
6. To be fair, to be firm
7. To show a sincere interest in helping all those who need it
   a. Do not discuss a student's progress with another student
   b. Do not converse with fellow students except for the purpose of instruction
8. To respect your elected officers

(Continued on opposite page.)

equipment management, help the teacher with class procedures, such as spotting, and to help teach safety and leadership techniques.

The leaders are taught all the rudiments of class management and instruction, using the school guidebook as a text. Fifty percent of the instruction is on a coed basis.

The leaders are selected by the teachers from a group of volunteers. They meet twice each week on a coed basis during the activity period. The leaders must have a B average and excel in class standards.

The Leaders Corps is highly organized and functions according to the Leaders' Code, reproduced on pages 296 and 297.

ONTARIO, CALIFORNIA. The girls' department of physical education at Chaffey High School, Ontario, California, offers a seminar to assist girls who have expressed desires to become physical education teachers. Girls may take the course for credit but not as a substitute for the regular physical education requirement. The course is offered to girls for two semesters as shown.

First Semester: During this semester the students are required to demonstrate introductory skills to groups and assume leadership roles in the classes. At the end of the semester they must prepare a research paper on the history, philosophy, objectives and age characteristics of the class to which they will be assigned. They are also required to make lesson plans.

Second Semester: The girls are assigned by the chairman to periods and teachers during the second semester. They work in the senior high school with freshmen and sophomores, with junior high school girls, and also in some elementary schools. The assignments for the second semester are:

1. Directing warm-up and conditioning exercises
2. Speaking to classes and other groups
3. Using an audiovisual aid in presenting a new skill or other information to a class or group
4. Assisting in the preparation, administration, and evaluation of a written and practical test
5. Becoming aware of incidental learning problems, and learning to work toward possible solutions
6. Officiating in several sports

V. VIOLATIONS:
1. Lack of respect toward instructor
2. Poor maintenance of high skills standards required of all Corps members
3. Getting below B for Physical Education (Board must invoke penalties 1 to 2)
4. Neglect of student safety
5. Poor leadership techniques
6. Setting poor example
7. Excessive absence from scheduled meetings of the Corps

VI. JUDICIAL PROCEDURE:
There will be five people on the disciplinary board. A disciplinary board will be appointed by the president and be composed of:

9th year GLC Violation	8th year GLC Violation	7th year GLC Violation
3–9th year leaders	3–8th year leaders	2–7th year leaders
1–8th year leader	1–9th year leader	(candidate)
1–7th year leader	1–7th year leader	2–8th year leaders
(candidate)	(candidate)	1–9th year leader

VII. PENALTIES:
1. Elimination from the Corps
2. Suspension—8 weeks
3. Suspension—4 weeks
4. Oral reprimand from President of Corps after reading of violation

VIII.
In order for disciplinary action to be taken an unanimous vote is required by the Board.

IX.
A Leader accused of a violation and penalized may, if he feels the penalty too severe, make a written appeal to the instructor. There may be occasions where personal feelings of students are involved, etc. The teacher will consider the appeal and make a final decision in such cases. If the instructor feels the appeal to be justified, the entire matter will be turned over to a new Board convened by the President.[14]

Objectives of Chaffey's Leadership Program

The leadership training program at Chaffey High School is designed to provide girls with an opportunity:

1. To study the history of physical education and recreation as it has influenced the physical education curriculum of schools today.
2. To develop a better understanding of the values of physical education in the curriculum of the public school.
3. To develop a personal philosophy of physical education which she can apply in her approach to her assignment as a student leader.
4. To study career opportunities in education, physical education, and recreation and the avenues of training.
5. To evaluate the Chaffey High School girls' physical education department procedures, rules and regulations.
6. To study basic techniques of officiating team sports.
7. To study the rules governing three selected team sports.
8. To develop skills in officiating these three team sports and to develop an understanding of the importance of consistent and competent officiating.
9. To develop a confident, effective manner in presenting material to groups.
10. To study audiovisual materials and methods of use in enhancing the learning skills.
11. To develop an understanding of the execution of the basic skills in swimming, tumbling, trampoline, track and field, volleyball, softball, and folk and square dance, and an opportunity to develop the ability to teach these skills to others.[15]

7. Organizing and directing an educational or recreational activity such as a tournament, field trip, service project or campout.

Miss Noreen Kistner, who supervises the program, summarizes the course with the following comments:

In the three years that this program has been in operation, our girls have been assigned as teaching assistants at our own high school, a junior high school, three elementary schools, a school for the mentally retarded, a school for the orthopedically handicapped, and the local American Red Cross Office. We have found them able to teach skills to classes, prepare lesson plans, and adjust to the variety of teaching situations they have been confronted with as the result of the training semester. We feel that this program helps give students a greater understanding of the values of physical education as well as an apprecia-tion of education and related fields. Certainly, they learn something about group dynamics through the program and gain self-confidence through achievement.[15]

After the teacher has completed all of the elements which constitute the first week of organization, he should be ready to begin instruction. At this point, decisions must be made relative to philosophy, procedures and the type of program he will initiate. The teacher needs considerable assistance, since the plans made at this stage of teaching may very well chart the course for the future. One of the most important decisions to be made is determining where the emphasis will be placed. Will teaching be the main objective or will the emphasis be on play? Aids discussed in the following chapter will assist him in making the correct decisions.

QUESTIONS FOR DISCUSSION

1. List some characteristics of a good class period. List the features that characterize a poor class period.
2. Why is the first day of teaching important?
3. What is the best method of establishing good class control? Discuss your answer.
4. Discuss why the teaching of skills is so important.
5. How would you enlist student assistance in a program?

6. Should students be excused from physical education to participate in extracurricular activities? Why or why not?

SUGGESTED ACTIVITIES

1. Visit a local school and observe a program with specific regard for organization techniques. Analyze the program and report to the class.
2. If you have had teaching experience, you can evaluate your effectiveness as a physical education teacher by using the self-appraisal chart on p. 304. What implications do you see for your future professional preparation?
3. Observe a physical education class in the local high school. Evaluate and report your appraisal of class control procedures to the class.

REFERENCES

1. Edward Vineyard and Harold Massey, *Teachers Letter* (March, 1964).
2. Daniel C. Neal, "Aversive Control of Behavior," *Phi Delta Kappan*, pp. 335–337 (February, 1969).
3. Bryant J. Cratty, *Social Dimensions of Physical Activity*, p. 72 (Englewood Cliffs, New Jersey: Prentice-Hall, Inc., 1967).
4. George Karner, "All Kids Want to be the Good Guy," *Parade*, p. 18 (April 18, 1971).
5. Glen F. Ovard, *Administration of the Changing Secondary School*, p. 334 (New York: The Macmillan Company, 1966).
6. George Gallup, "The Third Annual Survey of the Public's Attitudes Toward the Public Schools," *Phi Delta Kappan*, pp. 34; 39 (September, 1971).
7. Lawrence E. Vredevoe, "School Discipline – Third Report on a Study of Students and School Discipline in the United States and Other Countries," *Bulletin of the National Association of Secondary School Principals*, pp. 215–226 (March, 1965). From Glen F. Ovard, *Administration of the Changing Secondary School*, p. 334 (New York: The Macmillan Company, 1966).
8. Edwin John Brown and Arthur Thomas Phelps, *Managing the Classroom – The Teacher's Part in School Administration*, 2nd ed., pp. 121–123 (New York: The Ronald Press Company, 1961).
9. H. Orville Norberg *et al.*, *Secondary School Teaching*, pp. 216–217 (New York: The Macmillan Company, 1962).
10. James Conant, "Excerpts from Dr. Conant." *The Physical Educator*, p. 14 (March, 1961).
11. Report of the Resolutions Committee, *JOHPER*, p. 42 (May–June, 1962).
12. Wayne E. Nelson, "Take Time to Teach Student Leaders," *JOHPER*, p. 22 (April, 1966).
13. Barbara Kerch, "Girls' Leadership Program, Granite City, Illinois." (From mimeographed materials sent by request, undated).
14. "The Squad Leader Corps System in Old Lyme Junior High School," *Physical Education Newsletter* (March 27, 1962).
15. "A Leadership Training Program for High School Girls," *Physical Education Newsletter* (May 15, 1970).

SELECTED READINGS

Cowell, Charles C., and Hilda M. Schwehn. *Modern Principles and Methods in Secondary School Physical Education*, 2d ed. Boston: Allyn and Bacon, 1964.
Davis, Elwood C., and Earl L. Wallis. *Toward Better Teaching in Physical Education*. Englewood Cliffs, New Jersey: Prentice-Hall, Inc., 1961.
Nixon, John E., and Anne E. Jewett. *An Introduction to Physical Education*, 7th ed. Philadelphia: W. B. Saunders Company, 1969.
Vannier, Maryhelen, and Hollis Fait. *Teaching Physical Education in Secondary Schools*, 2d ed. Philadelphia: W. B. Saunders Company, 1964.
Voltmer, Edward, and Arthur Esslinger. *The Organization and Administration of Physical Education*, 4th ed. New York: Appleton-Century-Crofts, 1967.
Williams, Jesse F. *Principles of Physical Education*, 8th ed. Philadelphia: W. B. Saunders Company, 1964.
Williams, Jesse F., Clifford L. Brownell and Elmon L. Vernier. *Administration of Health Education and Physical Education*, 6th ed. Philadelphia: W. B. Saunders Company, 1964.

Chapter 10

AIDS TO EFFECTIVE TEACHING

He who has health, has hope; and he who has hope, has everything.

Arabian Proverb

EMPHASIS ON TEACHING

The future of physical education as a profession and the continuance of the program in the curriculum rest on the *teaching of skills*. In those places where teaching has been the practice, physical education has not suffered. In those places where informal, play-type program has predominated, the program sometimes has been either excluded completely or relegated to an obscure place in the curriculum.

There is no place in the instructional program for play in its true sense. As Hetherington has conclusively pointed out:

The time allotted within the school hours should be regarded as instructional or teaching periods and the time available out of school hours as play, athletic, or training periods. . . . The instructional period within school hours should be devoted primarily to teaching those activities which tend to go on spontaneously during the play or athletic periods.[1]

The National Association of Secondary School Principals emphasizes the importance of teaching in the physical education program:

Partly because of the lack of intramural opportunities and a broad program of interschool athletics and possibly because of inertia, the "play way" of teaching frequently has been overdone. Games were played but not taught. Maybe also for fear of student disinterest in mere instruction without "participation in the whole activity" this process of "throwing out the ball" has been too prevalent. . . . A required physical education class for all students should be, essentially, a learning process.[2]

Oberteuffer explains the relationship of play to instruction:

Perhaps at the risk of oversimplification it may be said that the intramural and interscholastic programs are places where students play: In the physical education class they are expected to learn.[3]

HOMEWORK IN PHYSICAL EDUCATION

The author has shown the value of homework in physical education not only for interpreting the program but for improvement of skills and performance.[4]

Within the school program pupils are screened in objective tests and skill performance; those who do not achieve suggested levels of performance for their age are encouraged to practice at home and report the results to class. This procedure carries the program into the home and assists students in attaining the results demanded of them in the class.

Figure 10-1. Teaching skills is the essence of the physical education program.

CULMINATING ACTIVITIES

Each skill taught in the curriculum should be used in some type of culminating activity. These culminating activities may be in the form of demonstrations, auditorium programs, intramurals, or other activities that bring together many pupils for competition or demonstration of their skills (Fig. 10-2).

TEACHING LARGE CLASSES

Teachers are frequently faced with the problem of teaching fundamental skills to large classes of pupils in small activity areas. Sometimes the problem becomes so acute that teachers abandon desirable activities and resort to informal play, with undesirable results. Teachers must constantly seek effective and interesting ways of teaching skills to motivate the pupils. They must also keep in mind certain principles of organization whenever they are working with large classes. These principles apply to all activities:

1. Teach skills—this should be the objective. Play should take place after school.
2. Divide the class into as many small groups as possible.
3. Use all equipment or tools available. Get more if possible.
4. Classify groups according to ability. Place the more gifted pupils together.
5. Use small groups to simulate actual game situations.
6. Always emphasize the values of the activities to the pupils. Discuss the importance of teaching skills for carry-over and better performance.
7. Use the overflow plan, as shown in the example in Figures 10-3 and 10-4.

Overflow Plan

Many individual sports are difficult to teach because of the need for individualized instruction. While the teacher is working with a few students in the basic activity, the majority of the class may remain idle. This presents a disciplinary problem. In order to teach these large groups, the principle of *overflow* is used. Using this principle, instruction in the skills of a basic activity to one group may be carried on while the remainder of the class participates in a

Figure 10–2. Providing the opportunity for students to demonstrate modern dance movements learned in class is an example of a culminating activity which shows how skills may be placed in competition.

team activity that accommodates large numbers safely and without the need for intensive supervision. Volleyball is the best activity to use for the overflow. Figure 10–3 illustrates the way in which this principle is employed in the teaching of golf to a large class (40 pupils); Figure 10–4 shows a tumbling class using the overflow principle.

See Chapter 12 for the teaching procedures involved.

SELF-EVALUATION

From time to time teachers should evaluate their program to determine whether their teaching practices are leading toward

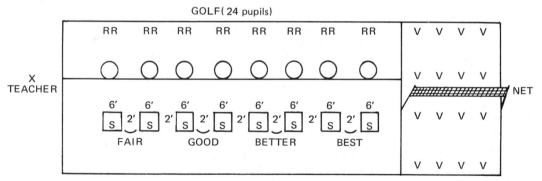

Figure 10–3. The principle of overflow in teaching golf. Pupils are arranged as shown. The golf group has 24 pupils—eight swingers (S) and 16 retrievers (R). The volleyball overflow group has eight on each side. Pupils in the golf swing group practice the stance and swinging at the plastic balls placed in the center of each square. It is imperative that they stay in the square. A swinging golf club is a lethal weapon, and the organization must be such that safety is insured at all times. The retrievers (R) approach the restraining line and throw the plastic balls back to the swingers (S). The swingers periodically change places with the retrievers. Pupils progress from the fair to the best groups according to ability. Periodically either or both overflow groups change with the golf group. The whole method is used throughout this activity with part analysis and explanation.

Figure 10–4. Using the principle of overflow in teaching the skills of tumbling.

desirable goals. In the day-by-day routine of teaching, it is easy for the teacher to deviate from the accepted standards that distinguish a good program from a mediocre one. In any evaluation in education it is wise for the teacher to begin with himself, for good teaching, like charity, begins "at home." Self-appraisal has been found effective in guiding teachers and, when necessary, redirecting their daily teaching efforts.

One school system uses a self-appraisal chart in an effort to improve the quality of teaching. It may be helpful to both the beginning and the experienced teacher to take an inventory of their qualifications, attitudes, and teaching procedures.[5]

TEACHER'S SELF-APPRAISAL CHART

Name_____Date_____

School_____

Note of Explanation: It is not expected that every teacher has done all the things suggested here; rather, this list is intended to serve as (a) an aid in self-evaluation, (b) a guide to improving instruction, and (c) a means of determining the progress made toward the objectives set up by teachers and supervisors.

I. Organization

	Yes	No
a. Are my classes organized to allow maximum time for activity?	___	___
b. Are student leaders a part of my organization?	___	___
c. Are all pupils always participating?	___	___

II. Content

a. Is my program based on the needs and interests of my pupils?	___	___
b. Am I using available facilities in meeting the needs and interests of my pupils?	___	___
c. Do I require each pupil to be exposed to the fundamentals of activities included in the program through orientation?	___	___

(Chart continued on opposite page.)

Yes   No

   d. Do the activities of my program offer carry-over value for later life?.. ___ ___
   e. Do I give my pupil an opportunity to master the activity of his choice?.. ___ ___
   f. Do I allow pupils opportunity to select activities for participation?.. ___ ___

III. Good Will

   a. Good will between student and teacher
      1. Do the majority of my pupils seem to like me?............ ___ ___
      2. Do I enjoy working with my pupils?........................ ___ ___
      3. Do the students cooperate with me?........................ ___ ___
      4. Do I assist pupils with their individual problems?...... ___ ___
   b. Good will between the public and the program
      1. Do I interest the parents in my program?................. ___ ___
      2. Do I publicize the program?.................................. ___ ___
      3. Are there repercussions from my program?............ ___ ___
   c. Good will between teachers and principals
      1. Have I tried to familiarize the principal with my program?.. ___ ___
      2. Is there cooperation between the faculty and the Physical Education Department?........................... ___ ___
      3. Is there cooperation between the teachers in the Physical Education Department?.......................... ___ ___

IV. Safety of Pupils

   a. Do I carry out all the safety precautions within my authority?... ___ ___
   b. Do I teach my pupils all the safety factors involved in physical education?.. ___ ___

V. Supervision

   a. Am I always with my class in the dressing room, gymnasium, and play field?... ___ ___
   b. Do I have student leaders assisting me in supervising my class?... ___ ___

VI. Discipline

   a. Do I handle my own discipline problems?..................... ___ ___
   b. Am I able to maintain the necessary decorum in my class?... ___ ___

VII. Care of Equipment

   a. Do I take care of equipment?.................................... ___ ___
   b. Do I teach students responsibility in care of equipment? ___ ___
   c. Do I keep a record of all equipment received and turned in?.. ___ ___

VIII. Professional Standing

   a. Do I hold membership in professional organizations?... ___ ___
   b. Do I seek self-improvement in my field through workshops, summer school, or committee work?................. ___ ___

IX. Evaluation

In light of the above I feel I am a
Superior Teacher.. ___ ___
Good Teacher.. ___ ___
Fair Teacher.. ___ ___

ACTUAL GAME SITUATION

The ultimate aim of teaching activity skills is to help pupils to participate with enjoyment in the actual game. To make students continually practice without actual participation is a sure way of destroying interest and hindering motivation.

The bulk of participation will, of course, be after school. After-school participation may be intramurals, in a recreation program, in a backyard, or in a roped-off street. No matter where the participation is, skill proficiency is basic for motivation. Lack of knowledge of the skill destroys interest, especially when pupils reach a plateau of performance and are not led further into learning on a higher level.

DAILY HOURS OF EXERCISE NECESSARY FOR NORMAL GROWTH AND DEVELOPMENT

Several authors have studied the number of hours needed daily for normal growth and development. Smiley and Gould have outlined a comprehensive plan for the hours necessary and the desirable activities by ages. They recommend two hours of activity for the junior high school pupils and one and one-half hours daily for senior high pupils.[6] Hetherington recommends that during early adolescence children should have two to three hours of activity daily.[1]

HOW INTENSE SHOULD THE EXERCISE PROGRAM BE?

Within the daily requirement of two to five hours arises the question of how strenuous the exercise should be during the physical education period. The intensity of exercise necessary for health varies with the individual and is based on the play urge of the child. The exercise needed for the development of the interscholastic athlete is not necessary for most of the pupils. No one, not even a physician, is able to say how much running is necessary or how many times a pupil should chin the bar to promote normal growth and development.

Who, then, should determine how intense the exercise should be? The answer is the pupil himself. Each growing child knows his physiological limits because nature has implanted in each person a built-in urge for activity that, if allowed to follow its natural pattern, will provide enough exercise for normal growth and development. The physical education program should provide the motivation—the outlet—for this natural urge.

Teachers are apt to prescribe a certain amount of calisthenics or activity for an entire class. This cannot be justified scientifically because some pupils may not be able to attain the level demanded, while others could easily surpass it. Instead of telling an entire class to do 10 push-ups or 20 sit-ups, it would be better to ask all the pupils to do as many, correctly, as they are able to do. This would allow for individual differences and would provide each individual with activity sufficient to his needs. Such a procedure should be followed in all physical education activities. It should be a challenge to the teacher to explore each activity and to find out how pupils can be motivated to perform within their physiological levels.

Some of the advantages of allowing pupils to follow their own pattern of activity are described in the following paragraphs:

1. The plan in which pupils exercise at their own rate is scientifically sound. The exercise is defined at the pupils' levels and is not a teacher-prescribed movement. Pupils will proceed at their own paces, and the self-interest that grows out of this procedure will motivate them to practice and improve. Because the urge comes from within and not from teacher domination, the interest will be more lasting and the values accrued more beneficial.

2. When pupils practice and perform these movements on their own, the teacher has the opportunity of walking around the class and assisting pupils in their efforts.

3. Teachers are able to conserve their energy and strength, and at the end of the day they are not nearly so exhausted as they were when they dominated each class period.

A Physiological Guide to the Amount of Exercise Required

The American Association of Health, Physical Education, and Recreation made a thorough study of the amount of exercise the individual should have and showed that the ability to recuperate after exercise is a general guide to the amount of exercise necessary for normal growth and development. If the following conditions exist, the individual has been subjected to an overdose of exercise:

1. Breathing and heart rate are still greatly accelerated ten minutes after exercise.
2. Marked weakness or fatigue persists after a two-hour rest period.
3. Restlessness with broken sleep occurs after retiring for the night.
4. A definite sense of fatigue the day following. In this case the exercise has been too severe or too prolonged for the person at his present stage of physical training and strength.[7]

The Recovery Index Test

This is another test designed to check the physiological response of the body to exercise. The test has been described as follows:

The Recovery Index Test consists of stepping up and down on a platform that is 16 inches high; this is done 30 times a minute for four minutes. The height of the platform can vary from 14 inches for short students to 20 inches for tall students. The subject faces the platform and, starting with either foot at the signal "Up," places his foot on the platform. He then steps up so that both feet are on the platform, and immediately steps down again in the same rhythm. The subject then continues stepping up and down in a marching count, "Up—two, three, four;" the signal "Up" comes every two seconds.

After four minutes of this exercise, the subject sits down and remains quiet. One minute later, his pulse rate is taken. Older students, under the supervision of the school nurse or other teachers, can be paired to take each other's pulse rates according to the following schedule:

1. One minute after the exercise for thirty seconds.
2. Two minutes after the exercise for thirty seconds.
3. Three minutes after the exercise for thirty seconds.

To determine the Recovery Index, add the three pulse counts and refer to the table below.

This test is intended to determine the individual's response to moderately strenuous exercise. It helps to select those who do not respond efficiently to exertion, and when repeated on the same boy or girl furnishes a method of measuring individual improvement. When a youth fails to complete the test or scores 60 or less, medical referral may be desirable. The index does not furnish an overall estimate of fitness but merely indicates the quality of the response to this particular test.[8]

Although the test is intended to show how the student responds to moderately strenuous exercise, teachers should take certain precautions before and during the tests. Some precautions that should be taken are the following:

1. Students susceptible to heart disease should not take the test.
2. Students with serious health problems and those who are convalescing should refrain from taking the test.
3. Teachers should watch for signs of distress and should ask the student to stop if he appears in difficulty.
4. Students stopping before the test is completed or who score below 60 should be referred for medical review.

Exercise and Mental Effort

There is concern on the part of educators about the effects of strenuous activity on mental effort in the classroom. Morehouse and Miller state:

The activities during the school period should be short and moderate in order to have a stimulating effect on the capacity for mental work. Severe muscular work should be performed after school in order to avoid the depressing effect on the capacity for classroom work.[9]

When the three thirty second pulse counts total:	The Recovery Index is:	Then the response to this test is:
199 or more	60 or less	Poor
171 to 198	61 to 70	Fair
150 to 170	71 to 80	Good
133 to 149	81 to 90	Very Good
132 or less	91 or more	Excellent

Many teachers have as their objective strenuous exercise plans, subjecting pupils to an exhausting system of activities that do not follow a scientific intensity curve for training and that tax pupils beyond their physiological limits. This is educationally unsound, since our aim is to provide just enough exercise for the health needs of individual pupils. Of all the activities that can be included in the curriculum, the formal, teacher-dominated types are the most exhausting. For exercise to assist normal growth and development, it should be carried on for many hours. To exhaust pupils in a short period of time is not conducive to physiological development and may have adverse effects on the health and fitness of growing children.

The teaching of skills provides an adequate amount of activity for the school day. If motivated properly, the pupil will find the opportunity to participate more vigorously after school within his own particular physiological limits.

CLASS DISCUSSION

Teachers should always explain the purpose of each activity that is being taught. It is not good teaching to walk into the classroom and begin instruction of an activity without explaining why it should be learned. Usually skills and exercises that are uninteresting may become interesting when the teacher explains their importance. Sometimes girls question the need for certain conditioning exercises, particularly those involving the abdominal area. After the purpose of these exercises has been discussed, not only does interest increase but motivation is so great that the pupils will practice the exercises at home.

THE DRESSING ROOM

The physical education class begins in the dressing room. Organization of dressing room procedures is essential to the overall success of teaching in physical education. Charting the flow of traffic, assigning lockers to prevent congestion, efficiently using showers and towels, and planning to save time and prevent disorder are some of the factors that should be considered when one is organizing each period of physical education.

HOW MANY ACTIVITIES SHOULD TEACHERS SUPERVISE SIMULTANEOUSLY?

The factors of safety and effective instruction should always be uppermost in the mind of the teacher. These two factors suggest that the teacher should be concerned with only one activity at a time. Each activity should receive an allotted amount of time, with the teacher concentrating all his efforts on improving the performance in that activity. To teach the skills of basketball in one area and simultaneously allow a group to practice tumbling in another will present safety problems; moreover, such situations are not conducive to good instruction and effective supervision. One exception to this principle is the overflow plan described on page 302.

CLASSIFICATION OF PUPILS

The need for classification of pupils in physical education is emphasized by the Committee on Exercise and Physical Fitness of the American Medical Association. The Committee maintains that unnecessary restriction of physical activity can interfere with the students' development and when good programs exist, excuses from physical education are unnecessary.[10]

The objectives of classification designed to provide for individual needs as established by the Committee are:

1. To safeguard the health of participants. Adequate protective measures are necessary for safe and enjoyable participation.

2. To group pupils for effective learning. Some degree of homogeneity within a group is essential to optimum learning.

3. To equalize competitive conditions. Reasonable matching of players is a requisite for safe and equitable competition.

4. To facilitate progress and achievement. Similar levels of skill among students are helpful to satisfying performance.[10]

The Committee recommended four general categories for classifying all students in physical education. These groups are based on the findings of medical examinations:

1. Unrestricted activity—full participation in physical education and athletic activities.

2. Moderate restriction—participation in designated physical education and athletic activities.

3. Severe restriction—participation in only a limited number of events at a low level of activity.

4. Reconstructive or rehabilitative—participation in a prescribed program of corrective exercises or adapted sports.[10]

In conjunction with the classification of pupils, the Committee strongly recommends cooperation between the school and local physicians. Figure 10–5 shows a form which was developed jointly by physicians and schools and is highly recommended for general use.

Categories two, three, and four are applicable for handicapped students, students who are convalescing and other students who need special attention. Types of classification for the unrestricted category (number one) are discussed in the following paragraphs.

There are several ways in which pupils may be classified for instruction. Teachers should familiarize themselves with them and select the most practical for each situation. A distinction should be made between *classification for instruction* and *classification for intensive competition*. The physical education period should be used for teaching skills; this distinguishes it from the after-school program designed for intensive competition. No program in physical education is complete or adequate if it does not include some sound form of classification. When pupils are classified by using one or several of the criteria shown below, the competition will be fairer, instruction will be more scientific, the program will have more continuity, and the health and safety needs of students will be met.[11]

Height. Pupils may be classified by height in order to insure the best possible instruction. Classification by height is applicable to such activities as basketball and volleyball.

Weight. Activities such as wrestling involve the weight of pupils; it is important that for such activities pupils be classified by weight if the participation is to be fair.

Age. Age is the most common classification because pupils of the same age are usually grouped together in the same grade.

Grade. Grouping pupils by grade is the most practical classification for administrative purposes and scheduling. The disadvantages of this plan can be offset by regrouping after the pupils have assembled.

Ability Grouping. Grouping pupils by ability is a goal sought by all good teachers. Irrespective of how pupils are scheduled for the physical education class, they should be grouped by ability for the best results. Grouping by ability may be done through the use of scores in motor ability tests, fitness tests, and skill tests.

Much publicity has been given to ability grouping in education in recent years. Ability grouping is a lost art in physical education, yet physical education teachers are in a better position to group and teach with this procedure than teachers of any other subject in the curriculum. Because the physical education program is a movement program, an alert teacher can observe and classify pupils into various categories—those with good or poor form, beginners, intermediates, advanced, and so on. There are students with varying degrees of skill performance in each class, and a teacher can place the pupils into as many groups as he wishes, depending on facilities, equipment, ability of the class, and safety factors.

Although in the ideal situation all classes are scheduled by grades, many schools and systems have not as yet reached this stage in scheduling. In those school systems where pupils in two or more grades are scheduled together, the techniques for grouping by ability are the same as those employed when pupils are scheduled by grades.

It is advisable to classify pupils into several ability groups in order to produce the best results in the instructional program. Otherwise, pupils who have attained a high level of proficiency become bored if they have to practice with pupils who are just beginning to learn the skills of an activity. One way in which pupils may be grouped is illustrated with a hypothetical class that is being taught the basketball lay-up shot.

This example illustrates a simple ability-grouping procedure that might be applied throughout the program for teaching skills. Regardless of whether the classes are mixed or scheduled separately, the ability grouping should be used. In junior high school, the ability or performance of a 7th grade boy may be comparable to the performance of a 9th grade pupil. For administrative purposes in physical education, scheduling

*REPORT TO SCHOOL ON SIGNIFICANT FINDINGS OF HEALTH EXAMINATION

This half to be sent to the school

Name of Pupil_____School_____Grade_____

Name of Parent_____Address_____
Physical findings which are of significance to the school

Recommendations to the School:

Is pupil capable of carrying a full program of school work?   Yes_____No_____

Should there be restrictions on up and down stairs travel?   Yes_____No_____

Is special seating recommended?   Yes_____No_____

Would special exercises help to improve posture?   Yes_____No_____

Do you advise supplementary in-between meal feeding?   Yes_____No_____

Does pupil have any irremediable defects?   Yes_____No_____

Is there evidence of emotional upset?   Yes_____No_____
REMARKS:

Classification for Physical Education Activity.   Record Roman Numeral_____
    Code I.   Unlimited activity
    Code II. Slightly modified—under observation
    Code III. Definitely restricted—i.e., cardiac disease, post acute infectious diseases, potential
           chests, etc.
    Code IV. Individual physical education
    Code V.   Rest

Recommendations for the Home (to be used as basis for school-home contact):

Is the present food intake adequate?   Yes_____No_____

If not, what changes are advised?   _____

Is more rest needed?   Yes_____No_____

Do you recommend curtailment of extra-curricular activities?   Yes_____No_____

Should work at home be restricted?   Yes_____No_____

Should a work permit be issued for pupil, if requested?   Yes_____No_____
REMARKS: (please indicate also any specific need for dental, psychiatric, medical or surgical care).

Date_____Signature of Examining Physician_____

Report of Follow-up: (To be filled out by school personnel—please be specific).

_____

*School Health Examinations—A guide for physicians and school authorities.
 School Health Committee of the State Medical Society of Wisconsin. August, 1954.

Sample form for reporting health examination data to schools.

Figure 10–5. "Classification of Students for Physical Education," *JOHPER*, January, 1967, p. 266.

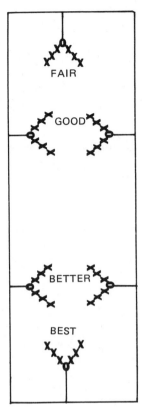

Figure 10–6. Grouping pupils by ability for teaching the lay-up shot: A class of 36 pupils has been scheduled. The class is a mixture of 7th, 8th, and 9th grade pupils. Pupils are arranged by height with the tallest pupil on the left and the shortest at the extreme right. There are six basketball goals in the teaching station; the teacher divides the line into six groups and assigns each group to a goal. The students are shown the correct form in the lay-up shot and then are allowed to practice. After a period of time, the teacher regroups the pupils according to their ability to demonstrate the correct form. Groups at each goal now represent somewhat homogeneous ability. In other words, the teacher may have four stations of pupils each representing a different level of ability to execute the lay-up shot correctly.

pupils by grades is highly desirable and effective; however, when classes are mixed by grades, good teaching can still be accomplished through ability grouping.

Although grouping by ability is rare in physical education, some teachers are successfully developing programs which involve ability grouping. Teachers of girls' physical education at Chief Sealth Junior High School in Seattle, Washington, found grouping by ability to be successful. They grouped all girls by ability based on performances in the Scott Motor Ability Tests. The program functions around three ability groups: high group, middle group, and low group. Special activities were arranged for each group during the first year. The low group was taught body mechanics and fundamental activities; team and individual sports were taught to the middle group and the high group concentrated on individual sports, team sports and recreational leadership.

An evaluation of the program at the end of the first year showed that 96 percent of the students liked ability grouping and 85 percent felt they had accomplished more than the usual class.

Miss Mary R. Carson, the girls' counselor, had this to say about the program:

We felt that we had hit upon one answer to mediocrity in physical education. We felt most of all that the students had been successfully challenged; and better, that the challenge to the faculty had been continuous and rewarding.[12]

Because of the unquestioned success of the girls' program, teachers in the boys' department planned their teaching around ability grouping. One advantage that grew out of this was the development of coed choice units between the two departments.

An excellent example of how students may be successfully grouped for physical education instruction is the plan used in the Dade County, Florida Schools. In this program students are grouped according to performances in the AAHPER tests. Each class usually consists of three groups: Basic, General and Accelerated. Twenty-five percent of the students are in the basic group, 35 percent in the general group, and 40 percent in the accelerated group. The advantages of the program are:

1. Provide for individual differences
2. Focus attention on the different degree of skill in each class
3. Stimulate achievement by setting realistic goals for each group
4. Equalize class competition
5. Give more opportunity for each member of the class to participate
6. Increase interest
7. Improve discipline
8. Show the need for curriculum planning to meet the interest and ability of all students.[13]

Another approach to ability grouping is used in the Harbor Beach Community School, Harbor Beach, Michigan. This highly recommended plan uses the students' knowledge and skill for grouping in badminton, golf, bowling, volleyball, tennis, swimming, riflery, and dancing.

The entire class begins with a lecture by the master teacher, who covers the rules, fundamentals, history, courtesies, strategy and first aid information. The lecture is followed by a written test on material covered in the lecture and an ability test. On the basis of the test scores students are divided into three groups—A, B, and C—with the A group being the top group. The top group spends its time on in-depth study of the unit and in actually playing games. The middle group spends its time in review and fundamentals. The lower group reviews the content of the lecture, games of low organization and skill development.[13]

A strong argument for ability grouping is that when pupils are placed in groups by ability, the incidence of accidents and injuries decreases. Court records list many cases in which pupils have been injured and decisions rendered showing teachers negligent because of improper classification. For example, in wrestling, if a more skillful student is matched with one who has had no instruction and the unskilled student is injured, the courts have found the teacher negligent (see p. 321). This argument alone should stimulate teachers to exert every effort to group students according to their ability, which should be determined by a sound inventory of performance.

THE PHYSICALLY EDUCATED STUDENT

The teacher should have guides to determine how effective the instruction has been. If, after months of teaching and guiding pupils in the acquisition of skills and the knowledge of physical education, there are no standards to show the value of the program, then the value of the instruction may be questioned.

The question may be raised, what is a physically educated person? How does a physically educated student differ from one who has received no formal instruction in physical education? In an effort to answer these questions, the directors and supervisors who attended the fitness conference in 1958 developed certain recognized characteristics of the physically educated student. These characteristics should be of immense value to the teacher in the analysis of his teaching as reflected in the student's personality, his attitude toward physical education, and his performance level in a variety of skills:

Attitudes

1. A strong desire to be healthy
2. Acceptance of the need to exercise daily to maintain physical fitness
3. An awareness of the value of safety procedures in and on the water
4. Appreciation of "change of pace" from work to recreational activities (This is an essential part of healthy living.)
5. A desire to achieve a high degree of excellence in skills to enjoy participation
6. Appreciation of one's strengths and limitations
7. Acceptance of the concept of one's role as a member of a team
8. Positive attitudes and desire for personal cleanliness and safe practices in physical activities
9. Appreciation of wholesome intergroup relationships and respect for the rights of others
10. Appreciation of the values in good sportsmanship and of its fullest application to total living
11. Appreciation of the value of the creative aspects of correct body movements

Knowledge

1. Knowledge of what constitutes body mechanics (acceptable posture) and how this relates to good health
2. Knowledge of the proper functioning of the body and a responsibility to maintain personal fitness
3. Knowledge of the rules of water safety (swimming, rescue, artificial respiration, boating, etc.)
4. Understanding of the nature and importance of physical fitness and knowledge of how to develop and maintain it throughout life

5. Understanding of the rules, strategies, backgrounds, and values of sports and other physical activities
6. Knowledge of proper selection and care of school and personal athletic equipment
7. Understanding and appreciation of the role of physical education in the total education program
8. Knowledge of the proper mechanics of sports and activities
9. Understanding of the importance and the role of physical fitness in successful academic achievement (sound mind, fit body)
10. Knowledge of the scientific and health reasons for proper hygiene and safety practices as applied in physical activities
11. Understanding of one's physical capacities and limitations
12. Knowledge enabling one to be an intelligent spectator of the popular American sports
13. The ability to distinguish between sound and unsound commercial health and exercise practices and programs

Skills
1. Ability to assume good posture and maintain it while sitting, standing, walking
2. Development of skills in at least four seasonal team sports, the level of skill attained being such that there is enjoyment in participation
3. Ability to swim well enough to feel at home in the water (This involves mastery of the different strokes and survival skills.)
4. Development of skills in at least four indoor and outdoor single or dual sports, the level of skill being such that there is enjoyment in participation
5. Development of proper rhythmic response to music, including basic skills in folk, square, modern, and/or social dance
6. Development of skill in one combative activity (boxing excluded) for boys, the level of skill being such that there is enjoyment in participation
7. Ability to apply skills in fundamental body movements — in running, throwing, jumping, lifting, carrying, etc. — to other physical activities
8. Achievement of an adequate level of skill in self-testing activities such as track and field, calisthenics, tumbling, and apparatus.
9. Good habits of cleanliness, personal appearance, and safety practices in all physical activities

Administrative Provisions for Physical Education
1. Physical education activities should be progressively administered from simple to complex levels throughout the secondary school.
2. Appropriate records on all students should be maintained. Marks and credits for graduation should be given on the same basis as in other subjects.
3. Appropriate provisions should be made for the handicapped, the unfit student, and the gifted boy and girl.
4. Comprehensive and effective intramural and interschool programs should supplement the instructional program.[11]

THE WARM-UP

Over the years there has been considerable argument both for and against the warm-up as a part of the instructional program. Some physical educators feel that the warm-up is unnecessary and is a waste of time. They say that nature takes care of this physiological process; and the sooner the basic activity is introduced the better, since time is of the essence in the physical education class. On the other hand, proponents say the warm-up prior to vigorous participation in the activity program is essential. They feel that the sudden demand for vigorous effort by a particular muscle group is physiologically unsound and may produce injury to the muscles involved. A report to the American Heart Association indicated that sudden vigorous activity without prior warm-up may be hazardous to the heart. A group of firemen who participated in sudden running exercises developed abnormal electrocardiograms. When given prior warm-up exercises the symptoms did not occur.[25]

A comprehensive study of 22 research papers on the values of the warm-up reveals that 95 percent of the papers showed that there was improvement in performance when the warm-up was used.[14] Six conclusions were drawn from the study that should be of inestimable value to teachers in their overall planning:

1. Fourteen of 22 studies showed significant improvement in performance following warm-up.

2. Seven of the 22 studies showed improvement in performance following warm-up, but the improvement was not statistically significant.

3. One of the studies showed a decrease in muscular strength following passive warm-up, but muscular endurance was not affected.

4. A vigorous, long warm-up appears to contribute more to better performance than does a moderate, shorter warm-up.

5. A related type warm-up seems to improve performance more than an unrelated warm-up.

6. Attitude appears to have an influence upon the degree of improvement of performance following warm-up.[14]

PRINCIPLES OF MOVEMENT

When the fundamental movements of man are studied scientifically, certain principles of the movement involved are clearly defined. These movements are part of the inherited patterns, which are closely associated with good form and outstanding performances. Williams outlines these as principles of:

1. Opposition
2. Energy-activity ratio
3. Qualitative adjustment
4. Follow-through
5. Objective focus
6. Total assembly

Principle of Opposition. The principle of opposition is the manner in which the arms and legs function in movements in which they are involved. When the right foot moves, the left arm is used, and when the left foot moves, the right arm moves in opposition. In walking, running, and climbing the arms and legs work naturally in opposition to each other.

Activities that contradict the principles of opposition should not be included in the curriculum. The abundance of natural activities that do not violate this principle makes it unwise to take chances on teaching questionable activities.

Principle of Energy-Activity Ratio. This principle involves the economical use of the various parts of the body in order to conserve energy, emphasizing grace and coordination and outlawing clumsy, awkward movements. Teachers should teach the importance of graceful, easy, flowing movements that conserve energy and, because of excellent coordination, are more conducive to better and more economical performance.

Principle of Qualitative Adjustment. This principle is concerned with the quality of the movement. It is generally understood that skill is basic to all movement. After skill has been obtained, it may be followed by applying strength, speed, and endurance in order to produce the desirable quality.

Principle of Follow-Through. The principle of follow-through is essential for achieving performance and is widely accepted in the instruction of sport skills. This principle specifies that in any given skill the movement should continue beyond the point of impact or release. The follow-through assures that the antagonistic muscles are relaxed and that the movement maintains the proper direction without inhibitory action.

Principle of Objective Focus. This principle implies that the performer continually focuses his attention on the object involved without concern for distraction or ultimate goal. The term "keep the eyes on the ball" illustrates the application of this principle.

Principle of Total Assembly. The principle of total assembly requires that the body react as a whole and not as separate parts. All factors involved in a muscular effort are brought together and every emphasis should be applied to this end.[15]

CREATIVITY

The opportunities for developing the creative potential of students in physical education are unlimited. The creative teacher will not only look for creative manifestations by students, but will assist in the development of a creative environment. Torrence, who has devoted considerable time to studying the possibilities of creativity in teaching physical education, lists seven guidelines for developing creativity in the class:

1. Do not leave creative development to chance.

2. Encourage curiosity and other creative characteristics.

3. Be respectful of questions and unusual ideas.

4. Recognize original, creative behavior.

5. Ask questions that require thinking.

6. Build onto the learning skills that your pupils already have.

7. Give opportunities for learning in creative ways.[16]

In the instructional period there are many opportunities for the teacher to apply vision and imagination. Creative procedures enhance the prestige of the program and in turn assist in motivation. There are a number of phases in the program through which creative efforts may be developed.

Rhythmical Activities

The basis of all physical education is movement. Constructive movement is manifested through those activities that incorporate the fundamental movements of man discussed in Chapter 5.

Paralleling the natural movements of man are rhythmic movements that have been used through the years to express people's conditions and emotions. These rhythmic patterns have been a part of every culture since man was created and are still prevalent today. They have been performed with or without musical accompaniment. Rhythmics provides not only a natural activity but also an opportunity for creativity on the part of both pupils and teacher.

The physical education teacher should guide rhythmic activities along channels that are educational and in keeping with the best in rhythmic interpretation. Folk, modern, and interpretive rhythms are examples of types that both contribute to health and fitness and allow for creativity.

The imaginative teacher may find unlimited opportunity for creating new movements to music in the various dance forms. Many innovations in modern dance have grown out of the efforts of individuals who wish to lift their sights beyond the traditional horizon of content and procedure.

Teaching Procedure

There is a great need in teaching procedure for vision and creativity. The traditional procedures involved in teaching skills may be improved when teachers begin to envision new ways of teaching skills more effectively. The old method of using one ball for basketball and volleyball or one shot-put and one hurdle for track will be replaced by more functional procedures; for example, many balls will be used for basketball and volleyball skills, and several hurdles for track. In addition, the teacher whose vision provides insight into problems also will quickly see the advantages of such simple techniques as dividing the class into as many small groups as possible for instruction. Teaching will be more effective and disciplinary problems will diminish for the teacher who employs proper procedures.

Interpretation

Interpreting the program gives unlimited scope to physical education. Assembly programs, playdays, culminating activities, and programs for civic clubs are a few of the many media for developing creativity.

Figure 10–7. Modern dance provides the opportunity for creative effort on the part of students and teachers.

Other media for interpreting the program are described in Chapter 3. Teachers should study the various principles of learning, teaching methods, and procedures. When they put these principles into practice, they may find that teaching will not only become easier but will also be more satisfying because the objectives of physical education will be more readily realized. Motivation will automatically follow a good teaching program because interest will be maintained and boys and girls will become aware of the values of extending the activity program beyond school hours.

TEACHER LIABILITY

Teachers of physical education, even more so than teachers of other subjects, should be aware of their responsibility for the safety and welfare of their students. This is true since the possibility of accidents occurring is greater in physical education than in other areas. For many years accidents occurred in the physical education class with little attention paid to them. They were accepted as a part of the program with very little legal action taken. Parents accepted the situation because they were not aware of tort liability. The result of this long-standing situation was that the physical education class and the athletic field were sites for the majority of accidents in the school.[17] A study of accidents that occurred in 1969 revealed the following statistics:

1. Over 6,000 lawsuits involving schools will be brought before the courts.
2. Seventy percent of all accidents to students from K–12 will occur when they are under school jurisdiction.
3. Nearly half of all reported school accidents will be attributed to activities related to physical education and athletics.[18]

The situation is changing, and teachers can no longer remain ignorant of the legal aspects of accidents which may occur under their supervision. They must become concerned with the importance of careful appraisal of the class environment and the accident potential of each activity they teach.

The enormous increase in accidents in physical education is to a great extent the result of an expanded curriculum, inadequate supervision, and substandard instruction. The curriculum in physical education now includes track, wrestling, football, gymnastics, golf, hockey, tumbling, and many other activities that may be dangerous if not supervised and taught correctly. Inadequate supervision is a major cause of the high incidence of accidents in physical education. When teachers leave their classes unattended, attempt to supervise groups that are too large, or allow students to participate in too many activities at the same time, accidents are most liable to occur. The importance of quality instruction as a deterrent to accidents cannot be overemphasized. Unless correct teaching procedures are followed, accidents and injuries will occur.

Every individual living in the United States has the legal right to be free from physical injury caused by others, whether intentional or because of carelessness. In the physical education class many situations arise in which legal action is initiated by the injured party to determine whether the injury was the result of negligence on the part of the teacher.

Teachers have been sued in many accident cases, and court decisions have been handed down against them. These suits come under the phase of law known as tort. Good described tort as "any negligent or willful and wrongful act of school officers or employees by which pupils or other innocent persons are injured."[19] It must be proved that the teacher was negligent in discharging his duties when the accident occurred.

Although teachers should be ever mindful of the seriousness of accidents, they should at the same time be aware of their own rights in so-called "negligence" cases. A statement from Bolmeier seems appropriate at this point:

Before a school employee can be held liable for an injury sustained by a pupil, there must be sufficient evidence that the alleged negligence is the proximate cause of the injury. Perhaps in the majority of all liability court cases charging negligence of some school officer or employee as the cause of the injury, the defendant has been found to be not liable. In fact, no court has held a defendant liable where there was substantial evidence that the defendant acted with prudence and caution in the performance of his duties.[20]

Teacher liability encompasses a rather complicated aspect of legal procedure. In some states the governmental agencies are immune from suit; this places the entire legal responsibility on the teacher. In other states the responsibility is shared by all parties concerned. Irrespective of what agency is legally responsible, the teacher has the final obligation of conducting the program so that accidents will be reduced to a minimum (Fig. 10–8).

In organizing the program there are several administrative and organizational principles that if followed will contribute to the safety of pupils and reduce the possibility of teacher negligence. These principles are adequate supervision of activities, teaching of safe activities, use of proper teaching methods, effective organization of the class and establishment of a safe teaching environment.

Adequate Supervision of the Activity

Teachers, not realizing the hazards involved, are prone to leave their classes to attend to some personal matter or to some school-related problem. If an accident occurs while they are away, it may be a simple matter to prove negligence since they did not see the accident and could not supervise the activities if they were away at the time it occurred. Teachers should never leave their classes for any reason if they wish to protect themselves against a charge of negligence.

A case of inadequate supervision was reported in the *Wall Street Journal.* A jury returned a verdict of $300,000 against a New Jersey physical education teacher who was shown to be negligent. While the teacher was out of the room during a regular class period, an accident occurred on a springboard.[21]

Recently, courts have handed down decisions involving injuries resulting from assaults and other violent behavior when the teacher leaves the class unsupervised. The courts say that the teachers are aware of the aggressive nature of certain individuals and should provide more supervision and remain with the class. This ruling also applies to injuries by individuals who are not members of a class.[17]

Another kind of poor supervision involves the use of unqualified personnel to serve as substitutes or to teach until a qualified person is available. The importance of using qualified personnel was shown in the case of the unqualified individual who volunteered to take over the duties in wrestling because of the resignation of the regular teacher. The plaintiff, who had no previous experience, was matched with an opponent who was experienced and had injured a boy the year before. The plaintiff was not given instruction in how to escape from a dangerous hold and suffered a severe injury in which the spine was severed. The jury ruled in favor of the plaintiff and awarded him $385,000.[17]

Cases similar to these in which the court has ruled against teachers, administrators and the district should be of concern to all school personnel. Definite action should be taken to insure that there is competent supervision by qualified persons. When this is not possible, then the activity should be discontinued until the qualified teacher is available. Activities such as tumbling, wrestling, golf, and certain track and field events should definitely not be supervised by unqualified and incompetent individuals.

Teaching Safe Activities

Research has shown that certain activities are considerably more dangerous than others and are not any more effective in achieving objectives. An example is the trampoline. The objective of any activity is the development of the highest degree of efficiency possible in the performance of the activity. Yet, as Helen Zimmerman stated in a study of the trampoline, "Based on the number of hours of participation, injuries occurred twice as frequently in colleges as they did in the high schools. Therefore, the teaching of this sport is not only dangerous, but it loses all carryover value for the student."[22] There are other activities, such as tumbling, that meet the objectives of physical education with far fewer accident possibilities.

Boxing is another dangerous sport that is unnecessary in a school physical education program. The basic aim in boxing is to score a knockout. A knockout is the result of a severe blow around the head which causes a concussion of the brain rendering a person unconscious. When a concussion occurs, there is permanent damage to the

LIABILITY OF LOCAL SCHOOL DISTRICTS FOR TORTS

CHART 31

ALABAMA
The state constitution provides that the state is immune from liability for torts. This provision has been interpreted to include school districts.

ALASKA
Insofar as their duties are of a governmental nature, school districts are regarded as immune from liability.

ARIZONA
A decision by the Arizona Supreme Court abrogated the state's immunity from liability for torts. The state legislature subsequently passed a law establishing procedures for filing claims against the state.

ARKANSAS
State law permits school districts to buy general liability insurance & waives immunity up to the amount of the policy. A constitutional provision against liability is avoided by making the insurer, rather than the school district, liable.

CALIFORNIA
State law states that the governing board of a school district is liable for a judgment against the district arising from injury to person or property resulting from negligence of district, its officers or employes. The statute provides procedures for filing claims & limits amount recoverable.

COLORADO
Insofar as their duties are of a governmental nature, school districts are regarded as immune from liability.

CONNECTICUT
Governmental immunity from liability has been abrogated by the state courts. School districts may buy liability insurance, but no statute defines claims procedure or limits the amount of damages that may be recovered.

DELAWARE
Insofar as their duties are of a governmental nature, school districts are regarded as immune from liability.

D.C.
Insofar as their duties are of a governmental nature, school districts are regarded as immune from liability.

FLORIDA
The state constitution provides that the state is not liable for torts. This provision has been interpreted to include school districts.

GEORGIA
Insofar as their duties are of a governmental nature, school districts are regarded as immune from liability.

HAWAII
The state has waived its governmental immunity for the torts of its employes but is not liable for any interest prior to the judgment or for punitive damages.

IDAHO
A decision by the Idaho Supreme Court abrogated the state's immunity for liability for torts.

ILLINOIS
State law waives immunity of local school districts, establishes procedures for filing claims & limits the amount of damages that may be recovered. The state courts have ruled that limits on damages are unconstitutional.

INDIANA
State law permits school districts to buy general liability insurance & waives immunity up to the amount of the policy.*

IOWA
State law waives immunity of school districts & establishes procedures for filing claims but does not limit the amount of damages that may be recovered.

*But school districts that do not buy general liability insurance cannot be held liable.

Figure 10–8. Liability of local school districts for torts. (From You and the Law. *Readers Digest Association*, 1971, p. 448.)

(Figure 10–8 continued on opposite page.)

KANSAS
State law permits school districts to waive immunity up to the amount covered by liability insurance for liability incurred by the negligent operation of motor vehicles by an officer or employe of the school district.*

KENTUCKY
Insofar as their duties are of a governmental nature, school districts are regarded as immune from liability.

LOUISIANA
Insofar as their duties are of a governmental nature, school districts are regarded as immune from liability.

MAINE
State law waives immunity of school districts up to the amount covered by liability insurance for liability incurred by the negligent operation of motor vehicles.*

MARYLAND
Insofar as their duties are of a governmental nature, school districts are regarded as immune from liability.

MASSACHUSETTS
State law provides that all teachers & school personnel are liable for torts committed within the scope of their employment. There are no procedures or limitations on amount of damages that may be recovered.

MICHIGAN
Insofar as their duties are of a governmental nature, school districts are regarded as immune from liability.

MINNESOTA
State law waives immunity of school districts, limits the amount of damages that may be recovered & sets a time limit for bringing suit.

MISSISSIPPI
State law requires a school district to pay $10 annually per school bus into a state fund from which claims may be paid, not to exceed $5,000 per person or $50,000 per accident.

MISSOURI
Insofar as their duties are of a governmental nature, school districts are regarded as immune from liability.

MONTANA
State law permits school districts to buy general liability insurance & waives immunity up to the amount of the policy.*

NEBRASKA
Insofar as their duties are of a governmental nature, school districts are regarded as immune from liability.

NEVADA
State law waives immunity of school districts, limits claims to $25,000 per claimant (award may not include exemplary or interest prior to judgment) & sets a 6-month statute of limitations. Certain actions are barred.

NEW HAMPSHIRE
Insofar as their duties are of a governmental nature, school districts are regarded as immune from liability.

NEW JERSEY
State law waives immunity of school districts but sets no limit on the amount of damages that may be recovered or the time within which a suit must be brought.

NEW MEXICO
State law permits school districts to buy general liability insurance & waives immunity up to the amount of the policy.*

Figure 10–8. *Continued.*

(Figure 10–8 continued on following page.)

NEW YORK
State law waives immunity of school districts & permits school districts to insure pupils against accidents with accident insurance rather than liability insurance.

NORTH CAROLINA
State law permits school districts to buy general liability insurance & waives immunity up to the amount of the policy. School bus claims are exempted from the insurance & are paid from a state school bus fund.*

NORTH DAKOTA
Insofar as their duties are of a governmental nature, school districts are regarded as immune from liability.

OHIO
Insofar as their duties are of a governmental nature, school districts are regarded as immune from liability.

OKLAHOMA
Insofar as their duties are of a governmental nature, school districts are regarded as immune from liability.

OREGON
State law abolishes immunity of school districts & establishes claims procedures. Damages that may be recovered are limited to $25,000 for property, $50,000 per person for injury & $300,000 maximum per accident.

PENNSYLVANIA
Insofar as their duties are of a governmental nature, school districts are regarded as immune from liability.

RHODE ISLAND
Insofar as their duties are of governmental nature, school districts are regarded as immune from liability.

SOUTH CAROLINA
Insofar as their duties are of a governmental nature, school districts are regarded as immune from liability.

SOUTH DAKOTA
Insofar as their duties are of a governmental nature, school districts are regarded as immune from liability.

TENNESSEE
State law requires the purchase of school bus insurance & waives immunity up to the amount of coverage in the policy.

TEXAS
State law makes governmental units liable for damages when personal injury or death is caused by negligence of government employe.

UTAH
State law waives immunity of government employes for injury caused by negligence or omission. The amount of damages that may be recovered is not limited. Some situations are exempted.

VERMONT
State law permits school districts to buy general liability insurance & school bus liability insurance & waives immunity up to the amount of the policies.*

VIRGINIA
Insofar as their duties are of a governmental nature, school districts are regarded as immune from liability.

WASHINGTON
State law abrogates immunity of school districts & other governmental bodies.

WEST VIRGINIA
Insofar as their duties are of a governmental nature, school districts are regarded as immune from liability.

WISCONSIN
State law sets up procedures for filing claims against governmental bodies (including school districts) but sets no limit on the amount of recovery.

WYOMING
State law permits school districts to buy general liability insurance & waives immunity up to the amount of the policy.*

*But school districts that do not buy general liability insurance cannot be held liable.

Figure 10–8. *Continued.*

brain in the form of scar tissue. Any activity in which the objective is to damage the brain is not an educational activity and should be ruled out of the curriculum just as boxing has been deleted from school programs throughout the country. Wrestling meets all the objectives of physical education and is a much safer activity than boxing. There are other activities such as judo, karate, certain gymnastic activities, and calisthenics that fall into the unsafe category. It would not be difficult to prove negligence in any accidents resulting from teaching these activities.

It is foolish to include in the curriculum activities that are inherently dangerous. There can be no valid reason for subjecting children to hazardous activities, since there are hundreds of activities that meet all the objectives which are relatively safe. Teachers should be constantly aware that they are charged with the health and safety of their pupils. They cannot afford to become lackadaisical in their planning, organization, and teaching. Not only are they legally liable, but they are morally obligated to plan and teach so well that pupils will continually progress toward the health objective without injury.

Proper Teaching Methods

There are very definite procedures involved in teaching skills recognized as being sound and safe. If teachers violate these methods they can be held negligent. *Physical Education Newsletter* pointed this out in a case in which the New York City Board of Education was held liable for injuries sustained by a boy who was "over-matched" in a kickball game. The pupils were matched by numbers instead of by height or weight. The teacher and board were held guilty of negligence.[23]

There are many cases involving accidents in tumbling in which teachers have been sued and the courts have ruled in favor of the plaintiff. In most of these cases the grounds for complaint have been improper teaching methods. A case in point involved a girl who was assigned to a tumbling class under protest. She claimed that the teacher did not provide her with adequate instruction in the stunts required and the teacher used students to demonstrate the stunts. Although the defendant school district denied negligence and claimed the girl was guilty of contributory negligence, the court ruled in favor of the plaintiff and awarded her $5000. The court ruled in favor of the plaintiff in a similar case in which a girl was injured while doing a headstand.[17]

In New York City a teacher was charged with negligence when a boy was injured doing a somersault. He claimed that he had received no instruction in tumbling and that he was told to perform the stunt although he was incapable of doing it. Both the trial court and the appellate court ruled in favor of the plantiff.[17]

In New York State a teacher was held negligent for allowing two boys who had never received boxing instruction to box. In the course of the boxing match, one was severely injured.[18]

On the other hand, courts will rule in favor of the teacher in cases where proper teaching procedures have been used. The recognized method of teaching from the simple to the complex is usually sufficient to disprove negligence. This is shown in the case of a 16 year old boy who was practicing take-downs in wrestling. The 30 students in the class were introduced gradually to the various holds, and the boy had practiced these activities. The court ruled against the plaintiff and found that the instruction was competent, having conformed to recognized standards in teaching wrestling.[17]

Another example of the courts ruling in favor of the teacher when adequate teaching procedures had been followed occurred in a New Jersey High School. A student was injured while doing leap frog jumps over a gymnasium horse. The court held that the teacher was not negligent since he had demonstrated the jump, warned the students of the possible danger, and asked that they not participate if they were concerned about being able to perform the activity.[18]

In addition to proper teaching procedures, following a syllabus or teaching guide is of extreme importance. Teachers who do not follow the syllabus and teach activities not included in it may be found negligent. In New York a boy broke his leg when attempting a somersault which was not in the Regents' syllabus. The court ruled for the child, since he had not received instruction in how to perform the stunt.[17]

Teachers should be careful to follow the rules, regulations and standards listed in the syllabus or guidebook. The teacher who deviates from the guidebook must be held responsible for his actions if injuries result.

A final caution concerns teachers' recognition of excuses. Too often teachers ignore notes sent by parents apprising teachers of the physical condition of their children. It is better to have a written policy concerning excuses that will provide some flexibility in dealing with such cases. Teachers will find it difficult to argue against a charge of negligence when notes from parents which have specified physical limitations of their children have been ignored.

Class Organization

The manner in which the class is organized for instruction plays an important role in minimizing accidents and in reducing teacher negligence. An article in *Physical Education Newsletter* noted that a board of education was held liable for negligence when a pupil broke his leg in a softball game. The teacher did not move the spectators from the third base, and one of the players broke his leg by tripping over one of the spectators. The court held that the board sponsored this activity and should have seen to it that the program was organized safely.[23] The teacher who allows benches to be placed behind basketball goals, loose equipment to lie around the gymnasium, and apparatus to be unsupervised is negligent in his organization of the program.

In New York a girl was injured playing indoor line soccer in which a large number of pupils were involved. The court awarded damages to the girl on the grounds that the teacher was more interested in securing active participation by as many students as possible than she was in the safety of her pupils. The court contended that the accident was foreseeable with so many girls involved.[24]

An excellent illustration of the need for careful organization in physical education is a case in which a boy was injured while playing three-man basketball. In the physi-

cal education class 48 boys were participating in various activities of their own choosing in an area 80 feet by 43 feet. The members of the class were participating in eight overlapping areas. The plaintiff was injured when he attempted to shoot and his opponent blocked him. The evidence showed that the injury occurred because the gymnasium was too crowded. The court ruled in favor of the plaintiff and severely criticized the school board.

The overcrowded condition of this gymnasium, with a large number of boys participating simultaneously in a number of games of strenuous activity which required a great deal of movement over a wide area, created a condition of danger which the defendant should have anticipated.[17]

Safe Environment

The environment in physical education includes the gymnasium, the swimming pool and the playground. To attempt to list all of the conditions and situations in these areas in which accidents might occur would be too extensive for this text. However, a few cases which have resulted in court decisions will be discussed. Placement of equipment, types of equipment used, classroom planning, and location are a few factors involved in creating a safe environment for physical education.

A girl was injured in New York when lockers in the gymnasium fell on her. The court awarded damages to her and charged that the school was negligent since it had failed to provide safe facilities.[17]

Similar cases have been recorded. A defective piano fell on a girl and injured her leg; a girl was injured on a defective slide; and the failure to provide protective mats in the gymnasium resulted in the injury of a boy playing dodgeball. In all of these cases the courts ruled in favor of the plaintiffs.[17]

The author, in reviewing cases in which teachers have been found guilty of negligence, found that in many of them there was evidence of little or no instruction in the class. This situation further emphasizes the importance of using the physical education class for an *instructional* program rather than as a period of play. *It is the opinion of the author that the instruction should consist of teaching the skills of the various activities which are included in the physical education program.* Injuries rarely occur when skills are taught properly. Not only does a teaching program (as opposed to a play period) lessen the chances of injury, but it insures that the physical education class is a place where pupils *learn* through the medium of teaching.

In addition to the suggestions mentioned in the preceding paragraphs, there are several other precautionary measures that teachers should take to prevent accidents in their classes. These are:

1. Inspect all equipment and facilities periodically. Report any deficiencies in writing to your building principal, supervisor, and the central office. Things to look for include defective playground equipment, holes and defects in the playground surface, worn-out athletic equipment and materials of all kinds; apparatus and mats that are in unsafe condition; lockers that are loose and not attached to the floor.

2. Be sure that all athletes and physical education students have had recent medical examinations.

3. Require all your athletes to have their parents sign permission to play forms before issuing them equipment and accepting them as candidates for school teams.

4. Keep injured players and students out of practice sessions, games, and class activities until you get clearance to return them to action from your school or team physician. It is better to err on the side of caution than to return a student to action too soon.

5. Remove overly fatigued students from practice, games, or class activities. Research shows that injuries are more apt to occur when students are overly tired. Concentrate on developing endurance and provide extra work in this aspect of fitness for students who need it.

6. Do not permit students to attempt stunts or any other physical education activity until they have been properly taught to execute the maneuver.

7. Follow a definite progression in each activity. Don't permit students to move ahead until they have mastered the previously taught stunt or technique. Make sure your students have mastered particular skills before you require them to use these skills or techniques in class or in a game.

8. Don't overcrowd your individual play areas. Too many students running, jumping, and exercising in any one area can be dangerous and lead to accidents and injuries.

9. Avoid mismatches in class activities and intramurals. Try to group students equally considering such factors as skill, height, weight, fitness, and experience in specific sports, games, and activities.

10. Never leave a class alone, no matter what the reason. This is doubly important when potentially dangerous equipment is being used.[18]

QUESTIONS FOR DISCUSSION

1. Explain what is meant by the overflow principle. Why is it important?
2. What is meant by overflow activities? How would you use them?
3. Why should pupils be grouped by ability in physical education?
4. Discuss the pros and cons of scheduling by mixed groups and graded groups.
5. Why should an entire class not be asked to do 20 push-ups?
6. Are strenuous exercises advisable for the physical education class?
7. What is the maximum number of activities a teacher should supervise at one time? Why?
8. When is a teacher negligent?
9. What is tort?

SUGGESTED ACTIVITIES

1. Visit a local school and observe a program with specific regard for teaching aids listed in this chapter. Analyze the program and report to the class.
2. Have each member of the class participate in some exercise; by applying the criteria listed in the chapter, determine whether the program has been too strenuous. Do the same in a class of high school students and classify them.

3. Visit a class and persuade the teacher to allow you to classify the students by ability. Report results to the class.

4. Observe a class and make a list of situations in which a teacher could be negligent.

REFERENCES

1. Clark Hetherington, *School Program in Physical Education*, pp. 74; 56 (New York: World Book Company, 1932).
2. Karl and Carolyn Bookwalter, "Fitness for Secondary School Youth," *Bulletin, National Association of Secondary School Principals*, pp. 58–59 (March, 1956).
3. Delbert Oberteuffer and Celeste Ulrich, *Physical Education*, 3rd ed., p. 291 (New York: Harper and Row, 1962).
4. Greyson Daughtrey, "Homework in Physical Education," *JOHPER*, p. 23 (October, 1959).
5. "Building Healthier Youth," *Norfolk Public Schools* (Norfolk, Virginia, 1972).
6. Dean F. Smiley and Adrian G. Gould, *A College Textbook of Hygiene*, p. 346 (New York: The Macmillan Company, 1940).
7. Arthur Steinhaus, "The Role of Exercise in Physical Fitness," Committee Report, *JOHPER*, p. 300 (June, 1943).
8. "Report of the Committee on Exercise and Physical Fitness," *American Medical Association*, pp. 6–7 (May, 1965).
9. Laurence E. Morehouse and Augustus T. Miller, *Physiology of Exercise*, 6th ed., p. 255 (St. Louis: The C. V. Mosby Company, 1971).
10. "Classification of Students for Physical Education," *Journal, American Medical Association*, pp. 265; 266 (January 23, 1967).
11. "Youth and Fitness, A Program for Secondary Schools," Report of the National Conference on Fitness of Secondary School Youth, pp. 28–29 (Washington, D.C.: American Association of Health, Physical Education and Recreation, December, 1958).
12. "Chief Sealth Junior High School Groups Physical Education Classes by Ability," *Physical Education Newsletter*, Croft Educational Services, Inc. (February 27, 1961).
13. "Ability Grouping in Physical Education—How and Why," *Physical Education Newsletter*, Croft Educational Services, Inc. (November 1, 1964).
14. Tom Neuberger, "What the Research Quarterly Says About Warm-Up," *Journal, American Association of Health, Physical Education and Recreation*, pp. 75; 77 (October, 1969).
15. Jesse F. Williams, *Principles of Physical Education*, 8th ed., pp. 343–350 (Philadelphia: W. B. Saunders Company, 1964).
16. E. Paul Torrence, "Seven Guides to Creativity," *Journal, American Association for Health, Physical Education and Recreation*, p. 27 (April, 1965).
17. Herb Appenzeller, *From Gym to Jury*, pp. 4; 38; (Charlottesville, Virginia: The Michie Company, 1968).
18. Joseph B. Tremonti, "Legal Liability for Accidents in Physical Education," *Physical Education Newsletter*, Croft Educational Services, Inc. (November 15, 1969).
19. Carter Good, *Dictionary of Education*, p. 573 (New York: McGraw-Hill Book Company, 1959).
20. Edward C. Bolmeier, "Tort Liability and the Schools," American School Board Journal (March, 1958). From Herb Appenzeller, *From Gym to Jury*, p. 31 (Charlottesville, Virginia: The Michie Company, 1968).
21. *Wall Street Journal* (Monday, November 2, 1964).
22. Helen M. Zimmerman, "Accident Experience with Trampolines," *Research Quarterly, of AAHPER*, pp. 452–455 (December, 1956).
23. "In the Courts—Negligence on Playgrounds and in the Gym," *Physical Education Newsletter*, Croft Educational Services, Inc. (October 15, 1963).
24. "Too Many in Mass Games Can Lead to Physical Injuries," *Physical Education Newsletter*, Croft Educational Services, Inc. (August, 1963).
25. "Sudden, vigorous exercise may harm even healthy hearts, scientists warn," American Heart Association News Release, November 18, 1972. (From A.M.A. Health Education Service, American Medical Association, December, 1972.)

SELECTED READINGS

Appenzeller, Herb. *From Gym to Jury*. Charlottesville, Virginia: The Michie Company, 1970.

Bucher, Charles, *et al. Methods and Materials for Secondary School Physical Education*, 3d ed. St. Louis: The C. V. Mosby Company, 1970.

Daughtrey, Greyson, and John Woods. *Physical Education Programs: Organization and Administration.* Philadelphia: W. B. Saunders Company, 1971.

Irwin, Leslie W. *The Curriculum in Health and Physical Education.* Dubuque, Iowa: William C. Brown Company, 1960.

Knapp, Clyde, and Patricia Hagman Leonard. *Teaching Physical Education in Secondary Schools.* New York: McGraw-Hill Book Company, 1968.

Van Der Smissen, Betty. *Legal Liability of Cities and Schools for Injuries in Recreation and Parks.* Cincinnati: The W. H. Anderson Company, 1968.

Willgoose, Carl E. *The Curriculum in Physical Education.* Englewood Cliffs, New Jersey: Prentice-Hall, Inc., 1969.

"You and the Law," *Readers Digest.* Pleasantville, New York: Readers Digest Association, 1971.

Chapter 11

METHODS IN TEACHING PHYSICAL EDUCATION

Coordination is significantly and positively related to intelligence and academic achievement.

Joseph Gruber

METHODS IN TEACHING PHYSICAL EDUCATION

It was explained in Chapter 5 that the various teaching theories designed for the cognitive and affective domains in academic learning are not always applicable to physical education. Attempts have been made to apply these theories to physical education activities, but the results have been confusing. The same problem occurs in methods of teaching. The usual methods employed by general educators are not usually applicable to physical education activities. However, many of the methods may be effectively used in the *knowledge* phase of physical education. Teaching rules of the game, history of sports and physical education, safety in activities, and kinesiology as applied to movement are a few areas in which generally recognized teaching methods may be applied to physical education. In order to prevent confusion, methods will be discussed in two parts: (1) methods in teaching physical education knowledge and (2) methods in teaching physical education skills.

Methods in Teaching Physical Education Knowledge

Many methods successful in the teaching of academic subjects may be used to teach physical education knowledge. Several of these methods may be used for the activity program also. Some of the more commonly used methods are discussed below.

Textbooks. Textbooks are widely used in physical education. Although texts are very important, in some instances they become merely sources from which information is digested and fed back to the teacher without the necessary implementation for retaining the knowledge acquired. Teachers may use the text as a crutch without exploring other methods of teaching. A text is a necessary source of facts and information but should always be used in conjunction with supplementary materials and a guidebook.

The teacher of physical education whose experience has been confined to the activity program, in which the use of texts has been limited to pamphlets and brochures of game rules, may encounter some difficulty in selecting a text for the physical education class. He must have some method of evaluating the text in terms of the philosophy and objectives of the program as well as the appeal it will have for the students. A great deal of improvement has been made in textbooks in recent years; publishers and authors alike are to be commended for their efforts in updating textual materials to reflect as closely as possible both authoritative research findings and prevailing educational philosophies. The job for the teacher is to determine which text will be most effective for developing the proper physical education knowledge and attitudes for the student in his particular situation.

Selection of the text may be made by a state, city-wide, or school committee; in a small school one teacher may have to make the decision. In any case, some guidelines

Figure 11–1. Textbooks are useful in developing effective teaching procedures.

are needed to aid in the selection. In the past, textbook evaluation frequently involved the use of a chart that assigned numerical values to factors that had to be taken into account; this method is rarely used today because of the many variables that arise in each locality. Nevertheless, the factors these charts included still must be considered in selecting a text. The following questions reflect the most important of these factors:

1. Is the content current, factual and objective?
2. Is the content developed logically or in independent units? Is the spiral-of-learning principle evident in unit development?
3. Does the content conform to the pattern of physical education instruction adopted by the school? For example, a text based on the grade placement pattern should be selected in a school that follows this plan of instruction.
4. Is the textbook appropriate in vocabulary, examples, and level of difficulty?
5. Are there appropriate end-of-chapter activities? Are these of the nature and scope to provide for various levels of ability among the students?
6. Is the book sufficiently illustrated, both verbally and graphically, to clarify the material presented?
7. Is the book authoritative? Is there evidence that the authors are qualified both in the specific field and in sound educational principles?
8. Is the book attractive in format and design? Is the type easy to read? Is the size appropriate? Are the cover and binding durable?
9. Is the cost reasonable?
10. Are there supplementary materials available, such as a teacher's manual, workbook, transparencies, or standardized texts?

Although many good texts are available for use in teaching physical education, the book *Physical Education for High School Students* is particularly useful. This text is published by the American Association for Health, Physical Education and Recreation.

Question and Answer. The question and answer method is an effective way to hold attention and keep pertinent topics foremost in the student's mind. Although the question and answer method should not be used too frequently, it has several distinct advantages, such as arousing the interest of certain pupils, getting to the heart of certain problems, serving as a quiz to ascertain extent of knowledge, and promoting discussion. The question and answer method is teacher-orientated and offers very little opportunity for pupil exploration but it may be used effectively in conjunction with other methods.

Its effective use, however, requires considerable skill on the part of the teacher. Not every person has the ability to develop a point or lead to a generalization through questioning. The classic question and answer technique is the Socratic method, in which the teacher asks questions to elicit desired responses from the student. In the hands of the unskilled examiner, however, this practice frequently degenerates into a form of textbook recitation, which is obviously limited as a teaching device.

Lecture. For secondary school teaching, the lecture, except in rare instances, is the poorest method of teaching, as pupils quickly become bored and lose interest. Sometimes, however, when a special topic needs to be presented with authority, the lecture method should be used.

Pupils should have experience in exploring and finding out for themselves the answers to physical education problems. *They* are the ones who should be doing research and ferreting out information. It has been said that the person who learns the most from a lecture is the lecturer himself, but the teacher should already have a good background of knowledge pertaining to the problem. He should make a special effort to guide his pupils toward finding answers themselves. In this way the pupils will retain what they have learned much longer.

Both the question and answer session and the lecture are carry-over methods from the formalized, traditional educational scene of the past. Although both have value for specific instructional situations, their use has for the most part been curtailed in secondary schools in favor of more effective, pupil-oriented methods of instruction.

Group Discussion. Teachers using the discussion method may stimulate the interest of their students so that there is a high level of retention. Because of the challenge to students' intelligence and the development of reasoning in the topics studied, the discussion method is one of the most satisfactory means of teaching on the secondary level. Discussion may be an activity for an entire class, or students may be placed in small groups and topics assigned for discussion. In the latter case, reports are made by leaders from each group. Teachers should be alert to see that unrelated topics are not brought into the discussion, that discussions are summarized, and that conclusions are reached.

The teacher should encourage the timid student to participate and should not allow the talkative, extroverted student to dominate the discussion. Moreover, the teacher should limit his own participation to what is needed to stimulate the students, clarify a point in question, correct the misinformed and summarize what has been discussed. He should be careful not to inhibit students *during* the discussion by criticizing an expression or correcting grammar; constructive criticism is necessary, but it should be given at a more appropriate time.

A variation of the group discussion technique is to have a panel of students discuss a topic before the class and to have a follow-up discussion in which the whole class participates. The panel's presentations may be either prepared or extemporaneous. A summary by a student leader or the teacher may reveal the need for further study and research by the class on the topic discussed, particularly when the technique has been used as an introduction to a unit.

Demonstrations. Physical education instruction can often be made more effective if student effort is portrayed through a demonstration. This technique may be used by the student or the teacher. It must be well planned, and the equipment and materials to be used must be organized at the place where the demonstration is to be given. The demonstration must be timed to coincide with the relevant class instruction, as poor timing may result in an anticlimax, thus preventing the attainment of maximal benefits. Demonstrations also provide a type of visual incentive that may enhance retention.

Projects. Assigning projects to be prepared by students and placed on display is an effective technique when used by an enthusiastic teacher. The physical education curriculum is a fertile field for the development of projects. Safety surveys can be assigned and reported, booklets can be constructed on a competitive basis, and models can be made to illustrate a topic. These are only several of the many projects that are suitable for teaching physical education.

However, a word of caution should be

Figure 11–2. Having small group discussions is one of the better methods of teaching.

Figure 11–3. Demonstrations can be useful in aiding retention.

given to the inexperienced teacher about the use of the project as a teaching device: the project *must* be a meaningful learning experience for the student. All too frequently, projects are mere busy-work assignments which consume more time and energy than they are worth. If a project is assigned, it should be within the ability level of the student and at the same time offer a sufficient challenge to him; it should allow for individual interest relating to the topic; and it should provide the student an opportunity to explore the topic beyond the regular classroom instruction.

Moreover, the project should be reviewed and evaluated by the teacher. A display of the projects in the classroom, elsewhere in the school, or at various places in the community, provides a rewarding experience for the students and should be arranged whenever possible.

Problem Solving. All pupils have health problems which arise daily. Many of the problems of personal hygiene, emotional control, and safety which continually confront pupils have a direct relationship to physical education. Students should be encouraged to discuss their problems in class, or privately with the teacher, whose guidance may be helpful in finding solutions. Developing problem-solving ability is an objective of all education. The teacher should develop his own ability to help students identify their problems, explore alternative solutions with a consideration of the advantages and disadvantages of each, and choose a solution based on the best knowledge available and in keeping with personal values. There are many opportunities for enriching the problem solving experiences of students in physical education.

For example, a student may be overweight and may be developing psychological problems as a result, problems that may last a lifetime if not corrected. From a study of proper diet and exercise, the student may be inspired to consult a physician to direct him in solving his problem. The teacher should be careful not to make any clinical diagnosis or prescribe remedies in such cases, but should encourage the student to talk with his parents and physician about the problem.

Homework. Homework is important in motivating students and assisting in the retention of knowledge. It is a good device for reinforcing what has been learned in

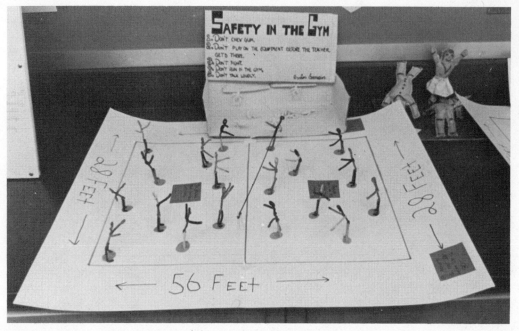

Figure 11–4. Projects constructed by the student motivate interest in acquiring knowledge of physical education.

class, but has been badly abused as a teaching technique. When planned wisely and assigned judiciously, homework can be effective.

Assignments should be timely and purposeful. The practice of saying to the class, "Study Chapter 2 and complete the first three exercises at the end," should be avoided. More meaningful homework assignments are those that review material that has been presented in class and that stimulate the student's curiosity about a topic by requiring him to observe situations, question appropriate individuals, do some research on a point being discussed, or simply think about the point and discuss his reactions in class.

Some schools have policies for homework that establish the length of the assignment and the day on which each subject teacher may assign outside work for his class. The physical education teacher, of course, should be aware of school policies and follow them.

Experiments. Many topics in physical education can lead to a direct classroom or home experiment. This is an excellent way to supplement classroom instruction and aid in the retention of knowledge. For example, an experiment could be conducted by giving psychophysical tests to the pupils and showing the relationship of depth perception, peripheral vision, and reaction time to good performance in physical education.

Care should be taken to see that experiments are limited to those that do not endanger human health. No student should be allowed to participate in a crash diet program, for example, to see how much weight he might lose in a week. On the contrary, the physical education class should point out the dangers of such a practice.

Outside Speakers and Consultants. Social agencies and groups usually are glad to furnish speakers and lecturers to assist teachers in providing instruction in specialized areas. Although the use of guest speakers can provide a valuable instructional medium, certain precautions should be taken to see that the technique meets its potential. The guest should, of course, represent a reputable agency; he should be a recognized authority in his field. Moreover, he should be able to present his ideas to the class effectively and interestingly. A person can be quite an authority in medical research, for example, and yet present his ideas in a vocabulary that is so technical as to be understandable only to other professional workers in his field. Such a presentation would be a waste of time to an average high school physical education class. Many associations and firms have a "speakers' bureau," composed of representatives who have demonstrated their ability to present their topics effectively, matching the presentation to the level of their audience. Before inviting a particular speaker, the teacher should explain to the agency the ages and general backgrounds of the class, the topic being studied, and the type of information that will be helpful in developing the unit. Usually the speaker will be willing to answer questions from the students after his presentation. His willingness to do so should be determined in advance, however; if questions are to be asked, some might be prepared before the guest arrives.

The speaker should be met at the school and escorted to the place where he will meet the class. A letter of thanks from the class following the presentation is also a nice gesture.

Again, school policy should be followed regarding outside speakers at the school, and the principal should be kept informed of the progress of the event.

Methods in Teaching Physical Education Skills

Experiments have been conducted on the teaching of motor skills. Two methods derived from these experimental studies are generally used, both of which teachers should understand before beginning the teaching process.

Whole Method and Part Method in the Activity Program. The premise of the "whole" method of teaching is that teaching the entire movement from the beginning is superior to teaching part of the movement at a time. Proponents of this method feel that the student must visualize the activity in its entirety and that the components should be thought of as a means to an end and not as ends in themselves. This method is the actual utilization of the cognitive theory of learning described earlier.

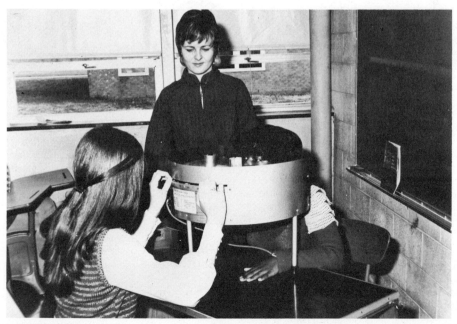

Figure 11–5. Experiments in the use of psychophysical tests stimulate interest in safety instruction. The peripheral vision test shown here is one of the most effective tests for determining the student's ability to adjust to approaching players in basketball and football.

"Part" method teaching is based on the premise that the part is more important than the whole and should therefore receive the most emphasis. The stimulus response theory of learning is employed in the part method procedure.

Shay studied the performances of two classes of college freshmen in an effort to find which of the two methods was more effective for teaching motor skills. He used the kip-up on the horizontal bar. One group was taught by the whole method and the other by learning parts of the kip-up separately. The results showed that the whole method was definitely superior to the part method in the speed with which the skill was acquired.[1]

Kretchmar cites studies of teaching sports skills in which the following observations were made:

Rodgers suggests the effectiveness of teaching certain games by the "whole" method. She points out that no attempt should be made to teach "part game" skills until students have been exposed to the whole game, and recognize the need for these skills.

In experimenting with methods of teaching basketball to 9th grade boys, Cross found the "whole" method more effective in teaching simple unitary functions, such as passing and catching, but the "whole-part" method most effective on some of the more complex functions.[2]

Seagoe lists five generalizations in regard to whole or part methods of presenting material to the learner:

1. Some form of part method is usually preferred by the learner.
2. Units should be clearly and simply structured or patterned.
3. Where the unit is structured, but over-complex for the learner, it is best to present the major outline, isolate one part for attention, then fit it back into the unit within the same learning situation.
4. Conversely, where there is no inherent connection between learnings, they should be taught as independent units.
5. Individual differences and differences in procedure affect these results.[3]

Seagoe also points out that in learning motor skills:

. . . supervised play (the whole method) is superior to formal gymnastics (part method) in promoting general development. In learning to juggle, practice should be on the total process, gradually increasing in complexity, rather than on specific skills.[3]

Neither method can be the best method for all activities. In teaching swimming, it would be absurd to use the whole method at first. A beginning swimmer cannot be thrown in the water without having had some orientation. Not only would fear prevent effective learning, but the individual might drown. On the other hand, in teaching the Western-roll high jump, the whole method must predominate.

The teacher should study each skill in regard to safety, class size, facilities, equipment, and past experiences of the pupils, and use the method that gives the best results. He may find that both methods may be used successfully. Some activities are best taught by the part method followed by the whole method. Other activities should be introduced by the whole method followed by the part method; finally, by putting the parts together and teaching the whole method again, the skill can be refined.

Multisensory Appeal

Research has shown that learning takes place through the senses, especially the visual, auditory, and kinesthetic senses. It has also been shown that the more these three senses are brought into the learning situation, the more effective the retention of knowledge will be. The teacher who effectively combines visual and auditory aids with demonstrations involving movement, will have far greater results than the teacher who appeals to only one sense.

Cratty, after considerable research, found that visual cues are very important in teaching skills. He states:

Thus, it would seem that whenever possible, visual cues in the form of films, demonstrations, or the like are superior to movement cues when learning skills. Attempts to teach a skill by first blindfolding the learner have not seemed as effective as permitting the individual simultaneously to attend to visual cues which may be present.[4]

Approaches to Teaching Physical Education

There have been several approaches to teaching physical education activities. We will describe three approaches that have been used widely.

Formal Approach. This approach is just what the name signifies. Everything in the class is done by command from the teacher. Exercises are given and activities are taught by command, resulting in a formal, regimented program that rules out individualism and limits activity to the pattern set by the teacher. This type of teaching dominated physical education in this country until the early 1920's.

Informal Approach. The informal approach provides opportunity for the individual to progress at his own rate as he acquires various skill techniques. The teacher presents the subject in an informal manner, taking into consideration individual differences within each class.

Sharman has shown that the informal approach has an advantage over the formal approach in the teaching of skills.[5] However, one criticism of the informal approach is the faulty manner in which many teachers interpret and apply it. The informal approach does not mean free play or the "throwing out the ball" type of physical education.

The Compromise Approach. This is a combination of the two mentioned above: the formal approach is used for some activities while the informal is used for others. For example, when conditioning exercises are given to a group, they should be formally and precisely presented in order to save time and attain the desired results. However, in teaching basketball, the informal approach is more effective, although certain *aspects* of teaching basketball skills may be formal. The compromise approach employs whichever part of the formal or informal approaches that is appropriate to the specific learning situation.

The compromise approach also provides the inquiry and discovery so important in effective teaching. The teacher, after demonstrating the skill, allows the students to practice in the various ability groups. As they learn by trial and error, with occasional assistance from the teacher, they are able to experience the satisfaction of accomplishment in each particular skill.

Kinds of Learning

Educational leaders generally agree that three kinds of learning are involved in any learning situation — *primary, associated,* and *concomitant.*

Primary Learning. Primary learning in physical education constitutes the body of fundamental technical skills of each activity in the program. The basic movements in a skill or activity, such as punting a football, serving a tennis ball, or learning the crouch start or the forward roll, are all examples.

Associated Learnings. Associated learnings are those acquired after the student has mastered the primary movements. Having learned the *skills* of golf, for example, the pupil needs to learn the rules of the game, selection of clubs, and playing procedures and courtesies essential for participation in golf. He should also have an in-depth knowledge of the history and values of golf.

Concomitant Learnings. Concomitant learnings are those that are acquired *concurrently* with the primary learning process. These learnings may reflect the desirable outcome of the program beyond proficiency in skills. In physical education, the effective teacher will take the whole individual into consideration and will take advantage of the fact that concomitant learnings during the learning process are outgrowths of qualities innate in all individuals. Attitudes of character and sportsmanship, the evaluation of the teacher, and the appraisal of the fellow student or competitors are outgrowths of the primary learnings.

TOOLS FOR EFFECTIVE TEACHING IN PHYSICAL EDUCATION

The teacher must employ many aids to assist with the challenge of effective teaching. Page 334 points out the need for multisensory appeals in the learning process. Audiovisual instructional materials extend the teacher's ability to meet this need.

Audiovisual Aids

The sources for audiovisual aids related to the various areas of physical education are almost unlimited. Teachers should plan instructional units that will incorporate these aids, as many pupils learn more readily through these media than through

Figure 11-6. Instant replay units provide powerful tools for effective teaching. (Courtesy SONY Corporation of America.)

the verbal approach. In combination, verbal and audiovisual aids greatly enhance the learning situation.

Films. Films are available in almost every area of physical education. Some are full length; many are loaned for extended periods, free of charge. Films are very effective in introducing a new area of instruction. They should not be considered as a substitute for the teacher or as a time for the teacher to take a "break." Their main value is to stimulate interest.

Filmstrips and Slides. Filmstrips and slides, which are readily available, are a powerful teaching device. They are more effective than films for specific instruction. They may be flashed on the screen for as long as needed, allowing ample time for discussion, and they can easily be returned for review. They serve well for introducing, developing, and reviewing a unit.

Videotapes and Cassettes. Videotapes and cassettes are innovations that are gaining popularity in assisting teachers with teaching skills. These aids are available commercially in most activities that are taught

in the physical education program, and are very useful as a teaching supplement.

Guidelines for Use of Audiovisual Aids. Although audiovisual aids are very effective teaching devices, certain guidelines must be observed if they are to be effective. Some of these guiding principles are discussed in the following paragraphs:

1. The audiovisual aids should be carefully selected and timed in relation to the subject matter and interests of the pupils. (See Appendix A for suggested sources of audiovisual aids.)

2. Films and filmstrips should motivate and supplement instruction. They should never replace the planned sequential procedures but should extend the instruction.

3. Planning well in advance for the showing of films or filmstrips is very important. Such routine procedures as examining the screen and projector, locating outlets, providing extension cords, and insuring proper lighting, should be checked prior to the meeting of the class. The film or strip should be threaded and ready for projection before the class assembles.

4. The audiovisual aids should be previewed to acquaint the teachers with the content and to allow them to formulate plans to raise questions,

comment, and anticipate questions from students. This is essential to relate the content to the unit of instruction.

5. Class discussion should follow immediately after showing the film. Discussion may also take place during the filmstrip.

6. The film or strip may be shown again, if necessary, to clarify details and to reemphasize various points.

7. The film or strip should be evaluated by the teacher and the students to determine the extent of its contribution to the unit of instruction.

8. After the projection and discussion of the film or strip, the planned class procedures should be continued, relating the contents of the film or strip to the remainder of the instructional unit.

Visual Aids

Bulletin Boards.   Bulletin boards can be a strong teaching device. The teacher may appoint committees to keep the board filled with information pertaining to the area being taught; the items should be changed frequently to keep the information up-to-date. Portable boards may be used to illustrate talks before civic clubs, parent-teacher associations, and other groups.

Wall Charts.   Wall charts are almost indispensable in presenting facts about physical education. They are invaluable when used to illustrate various aspects of physiology, for example. There is usually an abundant supply from many sources, such as school safety charts from the American Automobile Association.

Magnetic Boards.   There are several areas of physical education in which magnetic boards may be used to assist in the instruction. These boards may be purchased or they may be constructed locally.

Chalk Boards.   Although the chalk board has lost its popularity as a teaching tool because of better teaching aids, it remains unsurpassed as a tool for instant emphasis. The teacher can always rely on the effectiveness of the chalk board to reinforce or clarify a statement. Many occasions arise in the class when instant visual illustrations are necessary. For this purpose the chalk board is a most effective tool.

Flannel Board.   The flannel board, with careful preparation and planning, is an excellent tool for presenting physical education material. Diagrams may be used to illustrate a topic, or varicolored charts may be arranged to provide vivid emphasis on a particular problem.

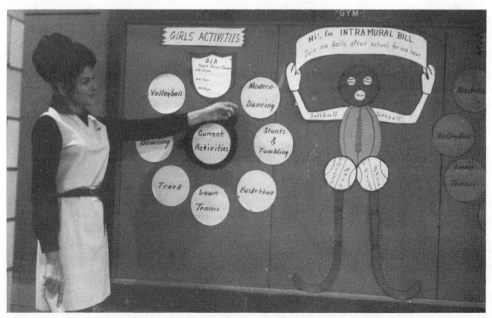

Figure 11–7.   The bulletin board may be used effectively as a teaching device.

Enriching Instruction Through Free Materials

There are many schools that would develop physical education instruction if the cost of materials to assist with the instruction were not prohibitive. Although standard textbooks are desirable, they are not mandatory; and when they are used, it is considered a good teaching practice to use supplementary materials as well. Some systems use texts in some areas and free materials in others. Areas and topics are outlined in the guidebook of instruction, but teaching units are developed around free materials and textbooks.

Many agencies will furnish free materials in quantities great enough to provide a copy for each student. Not only does the introduction of these materials enrich the instructional offering, but it provides both pupil and teacher with the results of the latest research in many areas.

In addition to the educational and public relations values derived from the use of free materials, economic aspects are important as well. The use of these free materials, if planned wisely, may save the schools thousands of dollars annually. Some materials and items of equipment are quite costly and would put a considerable burden on the school budget.

The alert teacher can enhance the effectiveness of his instructional program by investigating the possibilities of using free materials. Some of the agencies that furnish these materials are listed in Appendix A.

Criteria for Selecting Supplementary Materials

Although there is an abundance of supplementary material available for physical education, the teacher should have some standards by which he can judge those that are most effective for his purposes. In the professional literature in general education the teacher will find various criteria for determining the value of supplementary materials for classroom use. The criteria most appropriate for selecting physical education materials include the following:

1. *The material must be factual.* It is particularly important that physical education materials be reliable. Because the physical education area is vulnerable to quackery in medical and pharmaceutical claims, special care must be taken to select only the very best materials. The teacher may need to set up a medical-dental advisory board to help him with this task.

2. *The material must be current.* Medical research results in frequent and important changes in physical education knowledge. Supplementary materials should reflect the most current thinking.

3. *The material must be relevant.* Common sense dictates that the materials be related to the unit being studied.

4. *The materials must aid in developing understanding, abilities, and attitudes.* One should select only those materials that serve as an extension of the text or the teacher's instruction to help the student understand the unit, broaden his knowledge, and improve his attitudes in physical education.

5. *The material must be appropriate for classroom use.* Materials that go beyond the scope of the unit objectives should be excluded. This is obviously true in such areas of instruction as isometrics.

6. *The material must be appropriate to the level of difficulty.* The teacher should review the materials with the abilities of the students in mind. Generally speaking, lower-ability students need more graphically illustrated material than students with high verbal ability; this is also generally true for students in lower grades. Vocabulary as well as illustrations should be evaluated to determine the level of difficulty of the materials. It is through this evaluation that the teacher plans for individual differences, for he can select materials over a range of difficulty comparable to the ability range of his class.

7. *The material must be within the financial means of the school.* There is an abundance of free materials in physical education from which the teacher can make selections. Commercially prepared materials, however, may be desirable but may be too expensive for the school's budget. It is usually not difficult to find free or inexpensive substitutes to be used with the unit until more desirable materials are within the means of the school.

8. Other factors of less critical importance should also be considered in selecting supplementary materials. For example, the materials should be attractively prepared with good format and readability. They should also be of a size and type that make handling and storing relatively easy.

CLASSIFICATION AND TIME ALLOTMENTS FOR PHYSICAL EDUCATION ACTIVITIES

The physical education program draws from thousands of activities that may be included in the curriculum. Teachers should be familiar with the classification of activities in order to discuss the merits of the program, to assure a balance of activities in the program, and to facilitate research.

Activities have been classified by many authors and professional groups in the professional literature through the years. Several of the outstanding classification lists are the following:

COWELL AND SCHWEHN

These authors classify all activities into seven large divisions which are listed below:

1. *Games, sports, and athletics:* individual activities such as archery, golf, track and field events, and bowling; dual activities such as tennis, badminton, wrestling, and fencing; team games such as football, hockey, and baseball.

2. *Rhythmic activities:* athletic, clog, square, tap, folk, social, and modern creative dance.

3. *Aquatics:* swimming, lifesaving, diving, sailing, boating, canoeing, and similar activities.

4. *Self-testing activities:* tumbling, stunts on the apparatus, pyramid building, achievement tests in track and field events.

5. *Camping and outdoor activities:* boating, cycling, canoeing, hiking, cook-outs, camping, skating, skiing, skin and skuba diving, tobogganing, and equestrian activities.

6. *Social-recreational activities:* picnicking, playdays, mixers, skating parties, social activities of the girls' athletic association, corecreational sports activities.

7. *Body-building, corrective and preventive activities* (adapted physical education): body mechanics instruction, special conditioning or developmental exercises, therapeutic exercises.[6]

VOLTMER AND ESSLINGER

A more modern classification by these authors, which includes time allotments, consists of five groups in grades 7–12:[7]

BOOKWALTER

This author recommends seven classifications: administrative, hygienic, sports, rhythmic, formal, remedial, and self-testing. The classifications and time allotments for these groups for junior and senior high school boys and girls are shown in Figure 11–8.

Chapter 7 includes other classification and time allotment plans. These plans should be reviewed before proceeding with the lessons described in this chapter.

For practical purposes and simplicity, activities may be classified and placed under two groups—individual activities and group activities. Although some activities may fall in both classes, most are clearly in one or the other.

Individual Activities

Individual activities are those activities in which performance is based entirely on the individual's prowess. He may be a part of a team of individual performers who represent a school, but his individual accomplishment is not dependent upon another person. Bowling is an illustration. Although the participant may be a member of a team, his score is not dependent upon the activity of others.

The need for individual sports is quite apparent. Too often the curriculum consists of a program in team sports, and very little attention is given to those activities that will carry over beyond school years. As was pointed out in Chapter 5, one of the basic objectives of physical education is to prepare students for worthy use of their

	Grade 7		Grade 8		Grade 9	
	Girls	*Boys*	*Girls*	*Boys*	*Girls*	*Boys*
1. Rhythms	25%	15%	25%	15%	25%	15%
2. Team Sports	25	30	25	30	25	30
3. Individual Sports	20	20	20	20	20	25
4. Gymnastics	20	25	20	25	20	20
5. Aquatics	10	10	10	10	10	10
	Grade 10		Grade 11		Grade 12	
	Girls	*Boys*	*Girls*	*Boys*	*Girls*	*Boys*
1. Rhythms	25%	10%	25%	10%	25%	10%
2. Team Sports	25	30	25	30	25	25
3. Individual Sports	25	25	25	25	25	35
4. Gymnastics	15	25	15	25	15	20
5. Aquatics	10	10	10	10	10	10

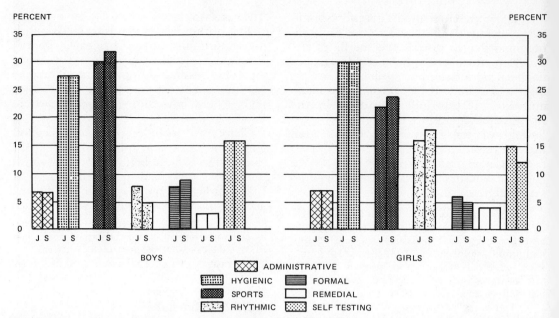

PERCENT

PERCENT

BOYS

GIRLS

▨ ADMINISTRATIVE

▦ HYGIENIC   ▬ FORMAL

▦ SPORTS   ☐ REMEDIAL

▧ RHYTHMIC   ▨ SELF TESTING

Figure 11–8. Suggested time allotments for physical education activities for secondary school boys and girls. (From Bookwalter: *Physical Education in Secondary Schools.* New York: The Center for Applied Research in Education, Inc., 1964, p. 54.)

future leisure time. Team sports have excellent immediate value, but they have very little value for carry-over participation after the school years. This point of view has been advanced by leaders for many years; nevertheless, probably because of the impact of interscholastic competition in the team sports, it has been suppressed. As a result, individual sports such as golf, bowling, tennis, swimming, table tennis, tumbling, and handball—which have great participation value for later years—have been by-passed.

A recent issue of the *Physical Education Newsletter* reported a study by David Clark of the University of Maryland, which showed that 80 percent of the nation's public schools do not include instruction in golf, tennis, bowling, or badminton in the physical education curriculum. This report also stated that four out of five high school graduates receive no training in carry-over sports. This means that many boys and girls will be handicapped in their recreation pursuits in the years ahead.[8]

There is overwhelming evidence—from doctors, school administrators, teachers, psychologists and actual participants—to support the inclusion of individual sports instruction in the physical education cur-

riculum. Williams,[9] Karl and Carolyn Bookwalter,[10] and Brownell and Hagman[11] are a few of the many physical education leaders who have emphasized the importance of instruction in individual sports. Bucher summarizes the general thinking about individual sports this way:

Team sports such as football, basketball and baseball perform a great service in providing an opportunity for students to develop physical power and enjoy exhilarating competition. However, in many school programs of physical education, they dominate the curriculum at the expense of various individual and dual sports, such as tennis, swimming, badminton, handball and golf. In so doing, the student is being deprived of the opportunity of developing skills in activities which he can play until the time he dies. It has been estimated that only one out of every one thousand students that play football, for example, ever play the game again after they leave school.[12]

Medical opinion advocating instruction in individual sports is plentiful. R. A. McQuigan, a medical advisor, comments: ". . . it is of vastly more importance to produce an individual who is able to play games he can continue to play in adult life than to produce a star athlete in a sport he cannot use later."[13] A survey of parental opinion showed an overwhelming preference for individual sports.[14]

The Lifetime Sports Foundation was organized in February, 1965, for the purpose of promoting and interpreting the need for individual sports. This organization will have an important role in increasing the number of individual sports to be included in the physical education curriculum.

One of the reasons that individual sports have received little attention is the difficulties that arise in teaching them. New building programs invariably include adequate facilities for basketball and football; there are probably not many high schools in the United States today that do not have gymnasia planned for the basketball team. However, rarely does one find provision made for tennis, bowling, golf, wrestling, and other individual activities.

The teacher who wishes to teach tennis skills will find it difficult to provide a program when only a basketball court and a football field (frequently restricted to football use) are available. It is not difficult to teach volleyball or basketball skills to a class of 40 pupils in an average gymnasium. However, to teach tennis skills effectively in this situation requires a great deal of organizational ability. To show the teacher how to teach the skills of individual sports effectively is the purpose of this chapter.

Group Activities

Group activities are those in which the successful performance of the individual depends upon close teamwork with another person or persons. An end in football cannot receive a pass unless the passer forwards the pass properly. Individuals cannot play football without other individuals. Although individual sports are of the greatest importance for their carry-over value, they do not, as a rule, provide the rugged physiological development that comes from team sports. For growing boys and girls, team sports are essential. The strength, speed, skill, and endurance developed through hockey, touch football, soccer, or basketball are not acquired in many of the individual activities.

Team activities have for years dominated the physical education curriculum. Their importance, when kept in perspective, cannot be questioned. For immediate carry-over and for physiological development, they are unexcelled. They are of inestimable importance for normal growth and development. Moreover, team competition develops qualities of cooperation, leadership, and teamwork, and provides emotional release and social acceptance—qualities essential for health and personality development.

It is impossible to measure the extent of the deterrent effect that a well-planned intramural program of team activities may have on delinquency. Association with other pupils and intelligent adult supervision and guidance while participating as a member of a team cannot be replaced by any other effort in developing personality. As Clark Hetherington stated, "Play gone wrong is the source of most of the bad habits known to children and youth."[15] It is natural and normal for children of all ages to form groups and play together. The gregarious drive and the play urge are two of the basic drives. A combination of these two urges brings children together on the playground, in the gymnasium, and in areas near the home. It is the responsibility of physical education teachers to organize and guide the activities of these groups along socially accepted channels.

With an overview of the two types of activities that may be included in the physical education curriculum, the teacher is now ready to learn how selected activities from these two classifications may be taught. The remainder of this chapter is devoted to showing how this is done.

BASIC LESSON PLAN

Probably one of the most important aspects of good teaching is careful planning for each day's work. A review of Chapters 9 and 10 may help to emphasize this for the reader. Teachers should have a daily outline of how each moment of the day's lesson will be utilized. Plans should not only outline daily procedures but they should also include weekly and monthly goals. It cannot be emphasized too strongly that teachers must always have at their finger tips a knowledge of how each moment will be used. Careful planning is essential if the goal of excellence of teaching is to be reached, motivation generated, and pupil interest maintained.

Each period should have a step-by-step plan or procedure in which each step is given a definite time allotment. Many of the characteristics of a poor instructional period can be eliminated by following a basic time pattern for each period. It is the purpose of this section to show how to put a daily lesson plan for a 60-minute period into effect. A well-organized period should consist of four distinct phases: *introductory, developmental, teaching skills,* and *closing.*

Introductory Phase (Five to 10 Minutes)

This is the phase in which the teacher must be aggressive and thorough in his planning or inferior teaching may result. The following items are ones that usually cause trouble and are time consuming; they should be carefully planned out before the teacher comes to class:

1. *Dressing.* Pupils should be given a definite time limit for dressing and reporting to the gymnasium. All pupils should be dressed within that time and penalized if they are not.

2. *Roll call.* This should take no more than one or two minutes. There are several plans that are designed to expedite the effectiveness of checking attendance. Probably the best is one in which numbers are placed on either the floor or the wall. Each pupil is assigned a number; when he reports, he stands on the number or in front of it, depending upon where it is placed. The numbers showing at the end of a specified time represent pupils who are absent (Fig. 11–9).

3. *Announcements.* These should be brief, concise explanations of what will take place during the period.

4. *Class formation.* Teachers should select a practical plan for bringing the class into formation in order that the second phase of the lesson may function effectively. A highly recommended plan is to have pupils count off by fours, beginning from the left end of the line, and at a given command take the number of steps forward as shown in Figure 11–10. From this position, exercises can be given effectively.

Another commonly used method is that in which the class is divided into squads and each squad is assigned a definite place to assemble on the floor (Fig. 11–11).

Developmental Phase (10 Minutes)

Exercises that should be included in this phase have been discussed in Chapter 6. It was pointed out that many popular exercises taught in this part of the lesson are contraindicated. Present knowledge about the suggested exercises that follow indicates that they are safe; they may be used

Figure 11–9. Class arrangement for checking the roll.

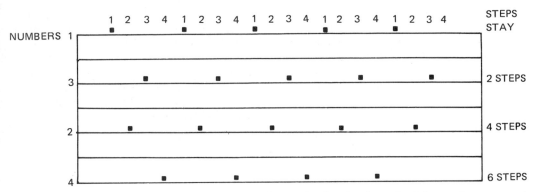

Figure 11–10. Class formation from a single line. An efficient plan for class formation is for pupils to open order by counting off by fours and taking steps forward.

Figure 11–11. For conditioning exercises, pupils may assemble by squads at prearranged spots in the gymnasium.

for this developmental phase. There are also many others that may be used, but any exercise chosen should be selected scientifically.

Suggested Exercises. Exercises should be scientifically selected for each period so that they "warm up" the muscles used in the particular activity being taught that day (Fig. 11–12).

Exercise Commands. Exercises should be given by the teacher and the commands should be clear and forceful. Commands always consist of three parts: (1) explanation; (2) pause; and (3) execution.

Example: Hands on hips....................place!
          (1)   (2)   (3)

Teaching Skills Phase (30 Minutes)

The teaching of skills is the nucleus of the entire program. It has already been emphasized that teaching skills calls for all the training and knowledge the teacher has. Good programs depend on the manner in which the teacher organizes and imparts to his pupils the scientific procedures in the teaching of basic skills.

Activities for this phase should be selected according to practical and scientific criteria. The inclusion of unscientific activities may impair the health of many pupils and destroy the overall effectiveness of instruction. Chapter 6 described the scientific approach to the selection of activities. The procedures

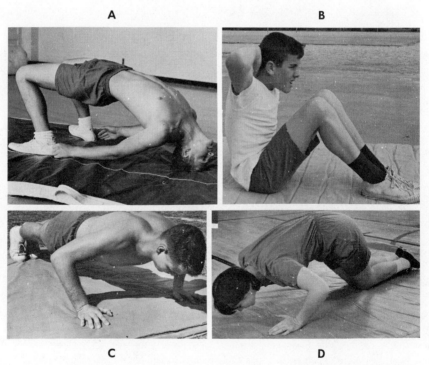

Figure 11–12. Warm-up exercises. *A*, Neck. *B*, Abdominal muscles. *C*, Arms and chest (boys). *D*, Arms (modified push-up for girls).

Figure 11–12 continued on opposite page.

outlined in that chapter should be reviewed. The following outline should be used in the order shown for teaching the skills of each activity in the curriculum.

Orientation

1. Acquaint the class with the history and importance of the activity and emphasize the need for learning the skills thoroughly before participation is attempted.

2. Use visual aids and have pupils read about the activity in newspapers and magazines. A textbook would be helpful.

3. Allow pupils to participate briefly with a superior player.

4. Initiate discussion about the activity.

5. Determine the extent of previous experience of the class in the sport or activity.

6. Have the pupils bring news clippings to class.

7. Outline the rules and discuss them with the class.

8. Help the pupils to learn how to keep score.

Demonstration

1. Have the skill demonstrated by the teacher or by pupils who are able to perform the skill well.

2. Analyze the skill and discuss it with the class.

3. Determine whether the whole or part method should be used (p. 333).

4. Use members of the varsity team, professionals, or other outstanding performers to demonstrate the skills.

E   F

G   H

Figure 11–12. *Continued. E,* Legs (Jumping Jack). *F,* Thighs (half-knee bend). *G,* Trunk. *H,* Back and shoulders.

5. Use films, filmstrips, and slides to demonstrate the skills.

6. Use bulletin boards, wall charts, and pictures shown through an opaque projector or transparencies on an overhead projector.

Organization for Instruction

1. Organize the class, continually keeping in mind how to make the best use of the available time (Figs. 11–14, 11–15, and 11–16).

2. Divide the class into as many groups as space, facilities, and equipment permit.

3. Emphasize the need for allowing pupils to perform the skill as many times as possible.

4. Motivate the pupils to practice beyond the school hours.

Inventory

1. Allow each member of the class to try the skills.

2. Encourage pupils to try the skills in groups when possible, so that no pupil remains idle.

3. Walk around the groups and point out faulty techniques but also comment on good and improved techniques.

4. Inventory the group periodically. Move pupils as needed from groups of lesser ability to those of more advanced ability.

5. Provide individualized instruction.

Ability Grouping

1. Group pupils, according to ability, into as many sections as space, facilities, and safety permit (Fig. 11–17).

2. Allow pupils to practice the skill and advance from the less proficient group to the most proficient group, or from one component of an activity to another, as in a tumbling sequence.

3. Allow pupils who perform skills well to assist others or to serve as checkers in activities such as tumbling.

4. Evaluate the pupils subjectively through continuous observation.

5. Use individualized instruction throughout this phase of the period. Particular attention should be given to the exceptional child.

Skills Laboratory. All skills taught should be used in a competitive activity at the end of the period. Relays, games requiring little organization, or any activity that places the skill in a competitive situation is indicated for this part of the plan. Teachers should be creative and devise many activities involving the skill best suited for large group participation. One illustration is the basketball dribble-and-shoot relay race, which places the dribbling and shooting skills in a competitive activity (Fig. 11–18).

Evaluation of the Skills Taught. Periodically, pupils should be evaluated on the skills taught in a series of lessons. It is important for pupils to know what progress they have made and where their weaknesses lie. Teachers should refer to Chapter 14 for suggested evaluative procedures.

Closing Phase (10 Minutes)

In this phase pupils should assemble (fall in) for announcements and a brief discussion of the next day's lesson. During this phase, activity comes to a close and movement is inhibited, allowing pupils to proceed to other classes refreshed and relaxed.

Intensity Curve

Classes should follow a definite exercise pattern: beginning with an absolutely quiet formation at the beginning of the period, there should be a gradual increase in the vigor and intensity of movement until a maximal peak of intensity of effort is

(*Text continued on page 353*)

Figure 11–13. Demonstrating a hockey skill.

Figure 11–14. Organizing the class for teaching. *A*, Line organization. *B*, Circle organization. *C*, Shuttle formation. *D*, Columns for organization. *E*, Organizing by small groups. *F*, Buddy system. *G*, Tandem organization. *H*, Organization as a large group. (*E*, *F*, and *G* courtesy Los Angeles Public Schools.)

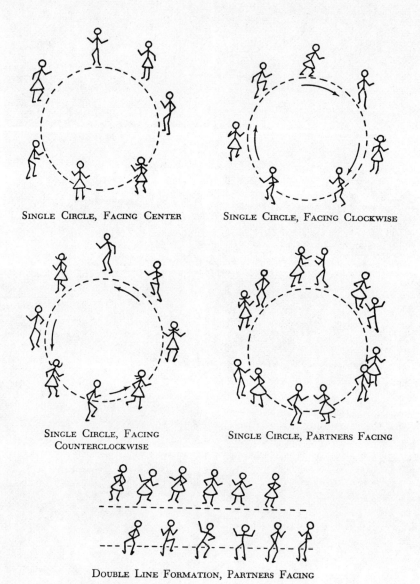

SINGLE CIRCLE, FACING CENTER

SINGLE CIRCLE, FACING CLOCKWISE

SINGLE CIRCLE, FACING
COUNTERCLOCKWISE

SINGLE CIRCLE, PARTNERS FACING

DOUBLE LINE FORMATION, PARTNERS FACING

Figure 11–15. Formations for folk dances and square dances. (Adapted from Salt, Fox, and Stevens: *Teaching Physical Education in the Elementary School.* New York: The Ronald Press, 1960.)

Figure 11–15 continued on opposite page.

LARGE CIRCLE, SQUARE DANCE

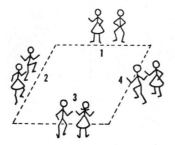

QUADRILLE, SQUARE DANCE

Figure 11–15.   (Continued.)

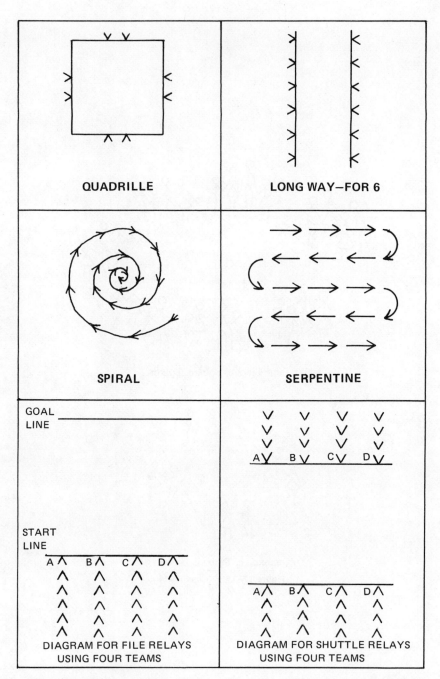

Figure 11–16.   Formations used in organizing class for teaching. (From Sharman: *Introduction to Physical Education.* New York: A. S. Barnes and Company, 1934.)

Figure 11–16 continued on opposite page.

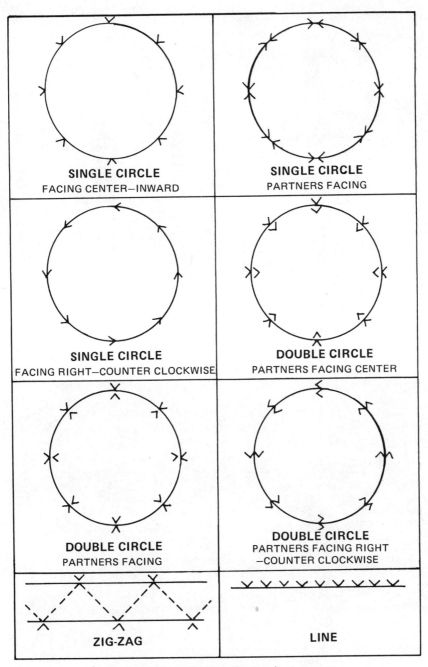

SINGLE CIRCLE
FACING CENTER—INWARD

SINGLE CIRCLE
PARTNERS FACING

SINGLE CIRCLE
FACING RIGHT—COUNTER CLOCKWISE

DOUBLE CIRCLE
PARTNERS FACING CENTER

DOUBLE CIRCLE
PARTNERS FACING

DOUBLE CIRCLE
PARTNERS FACING RIGHT
—COUNTER CLOCKWISE

ZIG-ZAG

LINE

Figure 11–16. (*Continued.*)

Figure 11-17. A class learning to volley in volleyball is placed into four groups based on ability. The teacher on court 2 is working with the inexperienced group while the remaining groups practice. A student teacher is on court 3.

Figure 11-18. The dribble-and-shoot relay race is one of many group activities that may be used in the skills laboratory phase of the class.

reached. After a period of sustained movement at this level, the exercise program should diminish in intensity until the effort is inhibited as it was at the beginning of the period. From this intensity curve, the daily lesson guide described in the preceding paragraphs is formed. (Fig. 11–19).

TEACHING THE ATYPICAL CHILD*

The material contained in the first part of this chapter and in Chapter 10 is designed for the majority of students. However, every school has some children who, because of various types of handicaps, should receive special attention regarding their physical education program. Many names and terms have been used to describe the program of physical education for these children. Such terms as physical education for the handicapped, corrective physical education, remedial physical education, preventive physical education, modified physical education, special physical education, adapted physical education, and developmental physical education have evolved. In an effort to minimize the confusion arising from such divergence in terminology, this text will use the term *atypical child.*

Definition and Purpose

Noll and Scannell define the exceptional child as "either unusually gifted or perhaps

*Much of the material in this section is taken from Daughtrey, Greyson, and Woods, John B., *Physical Education Programs: Organization and Administration.* Philadelphia: W. B. Saunders Company, 1971, Chapter 14.

handicapped in some way that interferes with normal participation and success in activities of various sorts."[16] Since many children are different to a marked degree, special attention is necessary if they are to receive benefits from the physical educational offering.

In a democratic culture every individual has the right to be educated regardless of anatomical, psychological, or physiological deviations. Thus, *all* individuals must be included in the physical education program. The fact that some children deviate from an established pattern defined as "normal" should not deprive them of the opportunity to improve their health and fitness, even if including them in the class necessitates changes in program content or development of special types of activities.

Recent court actions have focused attention on the importance of physical education teachers becoming knowledgeable in methods of teaching the exceptional child. The district court recently ruled that all already identifiable handicapped children in Washington, D.C. schools had to be enrolled in the public schools within 30 days. The ruling also stipulated that a comprehensive plan for providing special education facilities and identifying these children had to be completed within 45 days. A court decision in Pennsylvania led to the recent placing of between 8000 and 10,000 retarded children in public schools.

These court rulings will probably be followed by others throughout the country, and their far-reaching implications for physical education cannot be underestimated. Physical education programs for these children must be provided, and teachers must become familiar with the

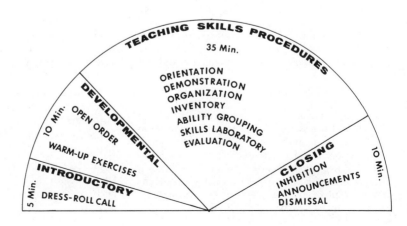

Figure 11–19. The intensity curve determines the sequence of the daily lesson plan.

necessary procedures and content involved in teaching them.[16a]

Since no two individuals are alike, it can be stated in broad terms that *all* physical education programs are special programs. Following this line of reasoning, it may be said that all programs in physical education are *guidance* programs. Normal pupils have to be guided, through instruction, from a lower level of skill performance to a higher level. This principle is applicable to both the normal and the atypical child.

A survey of students in a given secondary school will reveal that, with a few exceptions, the regular program in physical education suffices to meet the needs of the students in the school. If the program consists of a variety of activities, and the ability grouping procedure (Chapter 12) is followed, it becomes relatively easy to provide activity for all but a few children in each class. Keeping in mind that the regular physical education program provides adequate opportunity for *all* students, with a few exceptions, we will now proceed with a discussion of physical education for the atypical child.

Scheduling Atypical Children for Physical Education

One of the problems in planning physical education programs for atypical children is that of scheduling, which may be solved in several ways. Generally, the procedures for assigning such children in physical education fall into one of the following categories:

1. The students may be excused from physical education and assigned to study halls or other areas of instruction.

2. They may be assigned to special work, such as checking attendance, issuing and collecting towels, officiating, keeping score, keeping records, maintaining bulletin boards, and other menial tasks which require no vigorous activity that would contribute to their health and fitness.

3. Some schools provide programs for atypical children which consist of remedial and therapeutic classes involving prescribed individualized exercises designed to restore function of a muscle or increase the range of a joint. These programs are usually referred to as *"corrective"* programs. Many physical education leaders and physicians feel that these programs have no place in the physical education curriculum unless teachers have had special training in the field and unless the program has constant medical supervision.

The entire field of correctives should be studied carefully before the teacher embarks on such a program. If corrective physical education is to be interpreted literally, it involves correcting physical defects, rehabilitation, and other functions that should be under the supervision of a physician. If the term "correctives" is used loosely to include body-building exercise and instruction in games and sports to assist in physical development, then the physical education teacher is the one for the job. However, the physician is the only person *legally qualified* to diagnose and treat individuals for the correction of many types of physical defects.

4. In many places, *adaptive* programs are provided in which atypical children are assigned to regular physical education classes with modified activities or to special classes with individualized instruction, followed by admittance to the regular physical education class when improvement justifies the transfer. It is with this group that physical education is primarily concerned and for whom future programs for atypical children hold great promise.

"Adaptives" is that phase of physical education dealing with individuals who need special programs. Just who should participate in such a program is debatable. If the program in physical education is limited and includes only a few activities, many pupils will be unable to participate. However, if the program is varied—if pupils are grouped by ability in many activities such as table tennis, golf, bowling, and swimming—and if the emphasis is on teaching skills progressively, then the need for a special program is unnecessary and adaptives become a part of the regular physical education class with emphasis on individual differences. In the final analysis, all teaching of skills is concerned with adaptives in varying degrees.

Program Modifications

It was pointed out earlier that by modifying the existing physical education program the needs of most atypical children could be met. An effective and educationally sound plan for modifying the program, which meets not only the needs of atypical children but also those of the normal child, is *ability grouping*. An effective instructional program in physical education would incorporate ability grouping for all pupils in the overall planning. This teaching procedure is discussed earlier in this chapter and also in Chapter 10.

We will use the skill of passing in basketball to illustrate the ability grouping method. After an inventory of the pupils in a class, the performance level was found to vary so greatly that six groups could be formed, as follows:

Fair	Fair	Good	Good	Very Good	Excellent
Pupils 6	6	6	6	6	6

The inventory of the pupils' basketball passing skill revealed a broad range of abilities with a majority in the average group, following the normal curve of distribution. Among the pupils of highest and lowest abilities, there were several children classified as atypical by virtue of their physical endowments. Those who were placed in the "fair" group were pupils who, though not physically retarded, had not developed skill for basketball passing. Those who showed a gift for performing the skill were placed in the "excellent" group. Also in this group were students who, though not physically gifted, may have been playing basketball and may have developed skills in this activity beyond normal expectancy. The point is this: except in extreme cases, *atypical children should be accommodated in the regular physical education class with normal children* where, through ability grouping, all children have equal opportunity for participation. (Fig. 11–20).

Activity Modifications

In conjunction with grouping pupils by ability, several *specific* modifications may be made to provide greater opportunity for the atypical child without affecting the structure of the regular program. Although careful planning is necessary, it is not particularly difficult. Some possible modifications are outlined by Wheeler and Hooley:

1. Shorten time periods.
2. Shorten distances.
3. Change the type of signals.
4. Use guidewires, handrails, etc.
5. Soften landing spots with mats.
6. Allow two hands instead of one where accuracy or power is involved.
7. Change rules, deleting limiting conditions which lessen success (shot circle).
8. Lower nets, baskets (volleyball).
9. Increase the size of the striking implement and the targets (large bat or racquet).
10. Increase or decrease the size of the projectile, such as the ball, discus, etc.
11. Permit body positions, such as sitting, which increase stability in games usually played in a standing position.[17]

Figure 11–20. Grouping a class of pupils into four ability groups for the basketball pass. Atypical children may be placed in the appropriate group depending upon the level of performance of the atypical child and of the group.

Such modifications can be incorporated with minimal effort, time, and cost. Moreover, the element of safety will be enhanced. Modification of activities to meet the needs of all students really makes only two demands on the teacher: (1) an understanding of the activity needs and potentials of the various ability groups, and (2) a little imagination.

CLASSIFICATION AND ACTIVITIES FOR THE ATYPICAL CHILD

In planning physical education programs for atypical children, the teacher must study the particular activities suitable for the various classifications. All atypical children fall into three general categories: (1) the physically handicapped; (2) the emotionally disturbed; and (3) the mentally exceptional. It has been stated that the majority of handicapped children can participate in the activities which comprise the regular physical education program provided that (1) the program consists of a large variety of skills and activities; (2) the activity skills are modified through ability grouping or, in some cases, through modification of the activity itself and (3) there is emphasis on individualized instruction. The following discussion shows which activities may be used for the three categories of atypical children named above.

The Physically Handicapped

Children in the physically handicapped group are usually children who have problems of orthopedics, anemia, asthma, diabetes, tuberculosis, overweight and underweight, epilepsy, heart, cerebral palsy, vision, hearing, or hernia. The physical educator needs to have an understanding of these problems and of the desirable activities for each.

Structural or Orthopedic. These pupils have structural defects that prohibit them from attaining the level of performance of normal children. Some children in this group may be so crippled by disease at birth that they gain very little from attending regular physical education classes. On the other hand, the majority of children in

this group may participate in a modified program, either at the outset or after a period of attending a special class. Wheeler and Hooley list four conditions to which the greater majority of these cases may be attributed:

1. Congenital, as in scoliosis, clubfoot, spina bifida, and dislocation of shoulder or hip.
2. Osteochondrosis (as in Morquio's disease), which tends to render insufficient the functioning of the ossification centers of the body. It is seen most frequently as Perthes' hip, in which the head of the femur undergoes dystrophy, then recalcification.
3. Injury resulting in the loss of function of all or part of the limb and pressure on a portion of the nervous system. Amputation is a frequent result of such injury cases.
4. Diseases such as tuberculosis of the bone, osteomyelitis, and despite the availability of vaccine, poliomyelitis.[17]

Activities for the Structurally Handicapped. It has been pointed out that many activities in the regular physical education program may be used, either in their natural or a modified state. These activities will be discussed in two categories: (1) those for the lower extremity and (2) those for the upper extremity.

The lower extremity. When the upper extremity is affected, activities in this group may include dancing, running, soccer, and skating. In addition to these, others such as golf, tennis, basketball, horseshoes, badminton, casting, bowling, and table tennis may be used when only one arm is affected.

The upper extremity. When the lower extremities are affected and the arms are normal, the activities such as table tennis, bowling, weights, shot-put, archery, casting, billiards, bag-punching, stunts, croquet, horseshoes, swimming, and basketball shooting and dribbling are appropriate. These activities are suggested when the individuals are ambulatory and movement is accomplished either from a chair or with crutches. If only one leg is afflicted, the same activities may be performed more proficiently and in some instances without modification.

Activities for the Anemic. Anemic children do not have the strength and endurance of normal children. To place them in situations with children who have sufficient strength and endurance may produce psychological reactions that will be detrimental to their development. Children suffering from anemia should participate in activities requiring skill performance. To excel in skills will develop the confidence and self-assurance necessary for motivating them to continue with the program. Some activities that are suitable for the anemic child are dancing, archery, billiards, bowling, golf, horseshoes, table tennis, skating, softball, field events such as putting the shot and discus-throw, tumbling, volleyball, and basketball (half court). All of these activities should be planned in moderation, allowing for frequent rest periods.

Activities for the Asthmatic. Asthmatic children not only suffer from physiological disturbances, but also have emotional problems relating to exercise. Activities demanding increased respiration and competition with other children may bring on an attack. Activities involving skill, in which they may participate by competing against a score rather than against another individual, may be appropriate. Bowling is a typical activity in which the asthmatic may become involved without adverse effects. Other activities from which children may gain pleasure and confidence are golf, horseshoes, billiards, archery, shuffleboard, and croquet.

Activities for the Diabetic. The diabetic may participate in activities that do not involve intense competition and prolonged effort. With proper supervision, plenty of rest, and the elimination of body contact, the diabetic may eventually participate in most of the activities included in the usual physical education curriculum. Tennis (with frequent rest periods), golf, bowling, softball, and horseshoes are particularly suitable for the diabetic.

Activities for the Tubercular Pupil. Children with tuberculosis should never be allowed to participate in activities that require prolonged effort, endurance, and strength. If activities are properly supervised and if the pupil realizes that sufficient rest is necessary, the post-tubercular pupil may dance, play golf and tennis, swim, and participate in other individual sports such as bowling, horseshoes, and badminton. The highly contagious nature of this disease, rather than the pupil's ability to participate, requires that medical approval be secured before the pupil is placed with a class. Referral of suspected cases by the teacher is vital.

Activities for the Overweight Pupil. The obese child presents one of the most difficult problems for the physical educator. Not only is he unable to achieve success in sports and physical activity as normal children do, but his handicap sometimes produces emotional reactions that may seriously handicap him in all walks of life. In conjunction with prescribed physical activity, the overweight child must be placed on a diet by a physician. Unless a glandular condition exists, overeating and lack of exercise are the usual causes of overweight.

In planning the program for overweight children, the teacher should avoid selecting, at first, activities that place emphasis on the endurance involved in prolonged running and on activities involving contact, such as football. Emphasis should be placed on activities that progressively develop strength, endurance, speed, and skill. Eventually, with the establishment of proper eating habits and properly supervised programs of progressive exercise, the child may participate in the usual physical education program. Such activities as tennis, golf, bowling, horseshoes, basketball, dancing, volleyball, softball, and swimming are recommended for the overweight child.

Activities for the Underweight Child. Children who are underweight should be thoroughly examined to determine the cause of the condition. They may suffer from such problems as malnutrition, ulcers, tuberculosis, or glandular disturbances. Heredity may be a cause; if so, this should be determined as soon as possible.

Because underweight children usually tire easily, a medical examination is indicated before participation in the program. Underweight children, like those in other categories, should be placed in a classification group that involves children of similar ability and size.

Children who are underweight usually like and excel in individual sports, such as tennis, golf, bowling, swimming, and some track events. Various rhythmic activities are also recommended for these children.

Activities for the Epileptic Child. In selecting activities for the epileptic child, safety should always be the major criterion. Although warnings usually occur before a seizure, sometimes they may be too late to prevent a tragedy. Activities which are intensely vigorous, such as basketball, football, distance running, and contact sports may possibly be followed by a seizure and therefore should be avoided. All aquatic sports are contraindicated unless there is supervision at all times. Activities in which gravity and height are involved, such as tumbling, trampoline, parallel bars, and horizontal bars, are contraindicated. A seizure occurring during the performance of any of these activities might result in death.

With the exceptions listed in the foregoing paragraph, the usual physical education activities may be included in the program for the epileptic. Individual sports, such as golf, tennis and bowling, are recommended. All forms of dancing and rhythms are permitted. However, close and constant supervision must always prevail throughout the life of an epileptic, and the teacher cannot be too careful in planning the program, with safety as a major criterion.

Activities for the Cardiac Child. Planning programs for children with cardiac handicaps is extremely difficult. Irrespective of the degree of handicap, the child must be under constant supervision. To exclude the pupil from class completely is not recommended except in extreme cases; nevertheless, without expert planning, supervision, and constant awareness of the individual's problem, it would be better to excuse the child. One simple mistake in the type of exercise or supervision provided might be fatal.

Notwithstanding these problems of the cardiac child, when the safeguards described above prevail in the conduct of the program, these children may be scheduled for physical education. Careful study of each case reveals that children with heart abnormalities fall into one of the following four classes:

1. No restriction of usual activity.
2. Slight restriction of physical activity.
3. Marked restriction of physical activity.
4. Severe restriction of physical activity.

The teacher should be familiar with these divisions and the types of activity suitable for each group.

Pupils in the first class usually are able to play with normal children in the usual physical education activities with the exception of highly competitive activities and activities involving extreme endurance.

Modification in activities, play areas,

distances, and equipment are the criteria for the selection of activities in class two. Highly emotional situations and strenuous tournaments and contests should be avoided. Moderate and carefree games and sports which provide movement based on individual capacity are suitable. Provision for frequent rest and relaxation should be part of the planning. Golf putting, tennis doubles rather than singles, croquet, limited table tennis, bowling, paddle tennis, horseshoes, skating, swimming in warm water, and boating are activities that may be permitted, though with frequent rest periods.

For class three, requiring marked restriction of activities, golf, croquet, horseshoes, moderate dancing, archery, bowling, hiking, moderate skating, and table tennis are examples of activities that may be used to advantage. Children placed in this group should be under constant supervision. The program should provide time for frequent rest periods, freedom from strenuous competition, moderate movement, and a climate free of tension and pressure.

The teacher should follow several distinct steps in planning programs for the cardiac pupil. Wheeler and Hooley suggest the following:

1. Read the health history and whatever other records are available concerning the past activity and academic experience of the child.
2. Discover the interests and attitudes of the child by a conference with him.
3. Discover, by a personal interview with the physician, the classification of the child, as well as the exact activities in which he may participate and to what degree. The teacher should inquire about unusual symptoms or other aspects of the case which might help him in working with the child.
4. Get to know the child further through apparently casual interviews, by watching him in action, and from reports which parents, physicians, or teachers may submit.
5. Encourage the child to adopt and follow health practices which are particularly beneficial to him; e.g., rest, exercise, and recreation.[17]

Activities for the Cerebral Palsied. Pupils who suffer from cerebral palsy need continual guidance to develop confidence and assurance in their ability to participate in the moderate exercise in modified physical education activities. These children may find pleasure and success in dancing, bowling, croquet, golf, horseshoes, table tennis,

tennis, moderate tumbling, swimming, and archery. Modification to include rest periods and moderate competition to meet varying needs of the cerebral palsied are the criteria that should have high priority in the selection of activities.

Activities for Children with Sight Handicaps. Too often pupils who have sight difficulties are excused from physical education. This is regrettable because they are deprived of the many opportunities that play and movement offer in programs planned to meet their needs.

Children with sight problems fall into two groups, the totally blind and the partially blind.

Partially blind children, when placed in situations free from hazardous equipment and unsafe activities, may participate in the usual program of physical education. They must be under strict supervision, and the teacher must be constantly aware of their limitations. Activities that are suitable for their limited participation are basketball, bowling, horseshoes, skating, track and field events, tumbling, volleyball, and wrestling.

Totally blind children present a much greater problem for physical education teachers than the partially blind. However, in several places progress has been made in providing physical education instruction for the totally blind. Charles Buell reports many instances in which blind athletes have participated safely in interschool wrestling, football, track, gymnastics, ice skating, and bowling. The annual international blind golf tournament is a notable success. Blind children have also been very successful in horseback riding.[19]

Dorothy Hyman has been successful in teaching archery to blind students at the college level. The same procedures are adaptable to the secondary school physical program. Here is an outline of the teaching procedures used:

1. Proper selection of bows and arrows.
2. The correct way of nocking the bow to the arrow.
3. Placement of arrows in the front of pupil.
4. Explanation of foot position.
5. Nocking the bow to the arrow; drawing bow until the string was touching the lips.
6. Actual shooting and direction are explained by devising a tow line. A rope was suspended from the middle of the top of the target to a nail attached to the student's footboard. This enabled the student to walk to the target by herself and to keep the bow straight up and down by placing it against the rope.
7. A system was devised to enable the student to identify her own arrows. This was done by covering each color of the target with an unusual texture of material. The materials were sand paper for gold, satin for red, terry cloth for blue, cotton for black and the white portion left as it was.[20]

By following these procedures, the student gained confidence through the success attained by approaching the target, by ascertaining the number of arrows that hit the target, and by noting how many points were scored. She returned to the footboard, recorded her score in braille, and began the second round of her competition.

Activities for Children with Hearing Difficulties. Hearing difficulties range from slight hard-of-hearing to total deafness. Teachers should be aware of those students with hearing problems, since such disabilities are sometimes difficult to detect. These students may have lost interest in the program or developed hostility toward it, since they may not have been able to follow instructions or perceive the various cues necessary in all physical education classes. These students may have poor balance, may not enjoy team activity, and may seem uncooperative, all because they cannot hear. Teachers should use many kinds of visual aids and demonstrations in teaching these children. Instructions should be given in a normal manner.

Children in this group will, if given individualized instruction, learn about as fast as normal children. They can participate in the regular skill activities included in the curriculum, such as basketball, volleyball, swimming, bowling, and tennis. Rhythms are recommended, since through kinesthetic sense they may develop an understanding of this type of movement. Some contraindicated activities are boxing, trampoline, and tumbling. Boxing is not recommended even for normal children, and participation in this activity may compound the already existing hearing condition. The other contraindicated activities may present problems because of involvement of the semi-circular canals.

Activities for Children with Hernia. Students who have hernia problems may participate in the regular program of physical education, although common sense should, of course, prevail in deciding the extent of participation. Exhausting activities, activities which involve blows around the hernia, and movements involving heavy lifting should be avoided. Skills of individual sports, such as horseshoes, tennis, bowling, golf (if a cart is used), badminton, swimming and dancing, and team sports, such as volleyball, softball, touch football, and basketball, are acceptable. Contraindicated activities are trampoline, boxing, parallel bars, tumbling, wrestling, and lifting weights.

The Emotionally Disturbed

The intense pressures of living in the nuclear age, competition for grades and academic excellence, permissiveness resulting from affluence, and apprehension of the future are producing enormous numbers of emotionally disturbed children. Since the environment in which they live was created by adults, it is the responsibility of adult leaders to develop programs for helping these children to understand the world in which they live and to adjust to acceptable social standards both in school and in the various phases of community life. Children have a natural drive for play and activity. This drive may be channeled into activities that are purposeful and socially acceptable, or it may lead to anti-social behavior. It is the responsibility of parents, teachers, and educational leaders to channel this play urge into socially acceptable activities through supervision and guidance.

Although many factors such as parental pressure and the environmental conditions discussed above are cited as the reasons for emotional disturbance, some authors feel that organic factors are the major cause. Arnheim believes that "mental disturbances are due to faulty physiology of the nervous system."[21] He further asserts:

Disorders of the mind should be restored through procedures acting on the basic physiological mechanism that determines behavior. If this is the case, one might speculate that physical activity would be important therapy for the emotionally disturbed. It is known that volitional motor activity induces proprioceptive impulses that, in turn, effectively activate the hypothalamic cortical system, a powerful determinant of behavior.[21]

Principles of Teaching the Emotionally Disturbed. Teachers need specific guidelines to assist them in teaching emotionally disturbed children. Many children in physical education classes have emotional problems and still participate as part of a group, but there are some that must have special attention. In addition to grouping such children by ability with other students, certain guiding principles are necessary. Arnheim lists eleven:

1. Provide overstimulation for emotionally disturbed children, with the exception of the hyperactive disturbed child.
2. Use a variety of methods of teaching and a variety of games that will accommodate children who function at different physical, social, and emotional developmental levels.
3. Remove distracting objects.
4. Manual guidance has proved to be an excellent method of teaching basic skills to younger emotionally disturbed children.
5. Limits should be required in regard to use of equipment, facilities, and conduct.
6. Motor skills and games should be within the child's ability to achieve some degree of success.
7. Know when to encourage a child to approach, explore, and try a new activity or experience.
8. Discourage sterotyped play activities that develop rigid behavioral patterns.
9. It is not essential to strive for control in all situations.
10. Inappropriate interaction among specific children in the class may result in conflicts that disrupt the whole class.
11. Provide activities capable of coping with individual abilities and levels of development.[21]

The physical education teacher is in a strategic position to observe the emotionally disturbed child. Participation in physical education activities reveals deep, primitive characteristics, and the physical education teacher through careful guidance is able to assist the disturbed child not only to understand himself better, but also to adjust to life situations.

Through play and movement, a normal outlet is found for frustrations, pent-up energy, and aggressiveness. Hostile children may find normal expression in swimming, batting a tennis ball, driving a golf ball, slamming a handball, hitting a baseball, and kicking a football. These children may be allowed to participate until their aggressiveness is dissipated.

Some disturbed children find expression through *team* sports, such as volleyball, basketball, touch football, rhythms, and soccer. Again, the importance of ability grouping cannot be overemphasized. The emotionally disturbed child must develop feelings of success and accomplishment. This is possible only when pupils of similar ability are grouped together.

Teaching Procedures for Extreme Aggression. Some students in certain situations react to instruction in aggressive and disturbing ways. The usual classroom procedures are not effective in teaching children, and different techniques are necessary. The following methods have been found to be effective:

1. *Planned ignoring:* Much of children's behavior is designed to antagonize the teacher. If this behavior is not contagious, it may be wise to ignore the behavior and not gratify the child.

2. *Signal interference:* The teacher may use nonverbal controls such as hand clapping, eye contact, facial frowns and body postures to indicate to the child the feeling of disapproval and control.

3. *Proximity control:* The teacher may stand next to a child who is having difficulty. This is to let the child know of the teacher's concern regarding the behavior.

4. *Interest boosting:* If a child's interest is waning, involve him actively in class activities of the moment and let him demonstrate the skill that is being performed or discussed.

5. *Reduction of tension through humor:* Humor is often able to penetrate a tense situation, with the end result of everyone becoming more comfortable.

6. *Hurdle lesson:* Sometimes a child is frustrated by the immediate task he is requested to perform. Instead of asking for help, he may involve his peers in disruptive activity. In this event, structure a task in which the child can be successful.

7. *Restructure the classroom program:* If the teacher feels the class is irritable, bored, or excited, a change in program may be needed.

8. *Support from routine:* Some children need more structure than others. Without these guideposts they feel insecure. Structure programs for those that need it.

9. *Direct appeal to value areas:* Appeal to certain values that children have internalized. Some of these values may be relationship between the teacher and child, reality consequences, an awareness of peer reaction, or appeal to the teacher's power of authority.

10. *Remove seductive objects:* It is difficult for the teacher to compete against balls, bats, objects that can be manipulated, or equipment that may be in the vicinity of instruction. Either the objects have to be removed, or the teacher has to accept the disorganized state of the group.

11. *Verbal removal:* When a child's behavior has reached the point where he will not respond to verbal controls, he may have to be asked to leave the room (to get a drink, wash up, or deliver a message—not as punishment).

12. *Physical restraint:* It may be necessary to restrain a child physically if he loses control and becomes violent.[31]

The Mentally Exceptional

It was shown earlier that children in this category fall into two classes: (1) the mentally retarded and (2) the "gifted" child. Selected activities for these two groups, described in the following paragraphs, provide opportunities for these children to participate in a movement program.

The Mentally Retarded. The *degree* of retardation determines whether these children should be placed in the regular physical education class or in a separate class. Of the three types of mentally retarded—educable, trainable, and totally dependent—the first two present a challenge for the physical educator. When classes are planned properly, many of the educable and trainable children may be assigned as other children are; and the educable group may even excel in various activities. The trainable group needs encouragement and a feeling of accomplishment, and fun should be an objective. The totally dependent child should be assigned to special classes either in school or out of school.

Mentally retarded children who are assigned to physical education may participate in the regular program, provided all pupils are grouped by ability. Dancing, progressive movements involving balls, all types of relays, elementary track events, progressive swimming movement, and movement exploration are a few of the activities these children may safely enjoy.

Recent studies show that the physical education program makes unique contributions to the education of mentally retarded children. Again attention should be focused on the play urge and the importance of organized play activities in the development of boys and girls. Chapter 1 describes the relationships of play and exercise in the mental, physical, and emotional development of all children.

Most leaders in health and physical education agree that the program should be designed to meet the needs of all pupils and not the gifted few alone. This premise focuses the attention of physical education teachers on the need for planned programs for the mentally retarded. Research has established a few guideposts that show the importance of health and physical education to the mentally retarded. Stein lists some of these guideposts:

1. For a given age and sex, normal children are superior to the mentally retarded on most measures of motor proficiency.

2. In spite of underachievement with respect to motor function, the mentally retarded are much nearer the norm physically than mentally.

3. Physical proficiency can be improved in the retarded as a result of planned and systematic programs of physical education.

4. There are real differences to be expected in working with institutionalized retardates vs. those enrolled in public school special classes.

5. The mentally retarded achieve better in activities characterized by simple rather than complex neuromuscular skills.

6. Achievement in the area of physical fitness development apparently does not result in corresponding differential gains with regard to sociometric status.

7. Significant IQ gains have been achieved by EMR boys participating in programs of planned and progressive physical education activities.

8. Motor proficiency and intelligence are more highly correlated in the retarded than in normal children.[22]

In an effort to bring the need for activity programs to the attention of the American people, The Project on Recreation and Fitness for the Mentally Retarded was launched on July 1, 1965, by the American Association for Health, Physical Education, and Recreation with a grant from the Joseph P. Kennedy, Jr. Foundation.

The project lists three objectives that serve as guidelines for planning:

1. *Leadership preparation* (help organize and conduct clinics, institutes, and workshop programs).

2. *Research* (organize and conduct a status study of existing programs for the mentally retarded).

3. *Interpretation and program development* (develop publications, produce materials and conduct a matching grant program.[23]

Several areas in the country have initiated programs for the mentally retarded. In 1957, the University of Maryland developed a Children's Physical Development Clinic to meet the needs of the Washington, D.C., area.[23] Graduates of the University of Maryland program were instrumental in starting similar programs at the University of Southwest Louisiana and the Louisiana State University at New Orleans.

Probably the greatest obstacle in the development of programs for the mentally retarded is the lack of understanding of these children. The average teacher has had very little training in the techniques of teaching children who are apparently unable to adjust to existing programs in physical education.

Briefly there are two procedures currently used in working with mentally retarded children. Usually, special classes have been arranged for these children, and they have been kept apart from the normal pupils. In some places, attempts have been made to integrate them, as much as possible, into the regular programs in physical education. The latter plan has a great deal of promise. Stein reports:

. . . **Studies have shown that the mentally retarded respond and progress as much as normal boys and girls when given specialized training or instruction in a systematic and progressive physical education program.**[24]

The United States Office of Education reports that 83 percent of the retarded are educable. Current research shows that, in order to be educated, mentally retarded children must be taught how to play; once they are taught, the resulting movements are smooth and quick.[25]

Some teaching guidelines for teachers are suggested by Joan Nelson, Assistant Professor at Ferris State College, and Gail A. Harris, Consultant for the Michigan Department of Public Instruction. They show that mentally handicapped children participate in most of the activities in which normal children participate. Their suggested guidelines are:

1. Progress slowly, offering familiar activities first. Use repetition, because these students need reinforcement of learning.

2. Introduce new activities during the early part of class before the class gets tired.

3. Be kind, firm and patient, using a positive approach.

4. Be clear in directions without talking down to the class. Use concrete examples.

5. Attempt to keep each child active.

6. Demonstrate and take part in the activities.

7. Offer activities which could be useful at recess time, after school, and later on in life.

8. Remember the characteristics of the children and consider individual abilities and attention spans.

9. Let children compete with themselves. Some simple tests and measurement devices provide an incentive.

10. Give the children goals in which they can have some measure of success, and use praise as often as possible.

11. Allow them to have some choice of activities, and allow them to suggest activities.

12. Include rhythmical activities, such as simple folk and square dancing.

13. Aid the children in developing skills such as running, jumping, and ball handling.

14. Correlate good health habits with physical education.

15. Keep records of physical fitness.

16. Aim for progression in social and physical skills.[18]

Emphasis on providing opportunity for the mentally retarded is still in the experimental stage. However, the future is bright, and all indications show that as teachers learn more about the mentally retarded, they will show greater interest in programs for them. As interest increases and programs develop, attention should be given to a *teaching* program. Recent research shows that, although normal children play voluntarily, mentally retarded pupils need to be taught how to play.[24]

The Mentally Gifted. The mentally gifted find their greatest problems in social acceptance. Too often, since they excel in mental pursuits, they are encouraged to spend all available time in academic activities. When placed with average students, they may not be immediately accepted. Although their potential in physical activity is normal, at the outset they need guidance, encouragement, and a feeling of accomplishment comparable to that derived from academic achievement.

These children perform their best in individual sports, such as golf, tennis, bowling, swimming, and rhythmics. They should be encouraged to participate in team activities in order that they may learn about teamwork, about adjusting to other situations and people, and about the habits and personalities of the average child. Play brings out the best and the worst in all individuals; and the gifted child, through the medium of play, may not only add to his reservoir of mental attainment but also develop skills that will contribute to his total health throughout life.

SPECIAL CLASSES FOR ATYPICAL CHILDREN

Some children need to be temporarily assigned to a special class in physical education. The traditional plan of scheduling presents difficulties in arranging such classes. Chapter 7 describes an innovation in scheduling, usually referred to as *modular scheduling*, that provides a relatively easy plan for including the atypical child within the physical education program but not in the regular class.

GUIDELINES FOR PLANNING PROGRAMS FOR THE ATYPICAL CHILD

It is extremely important that all programs in physical education be planned carefully. However, it is *imperative* that programs for the handicapped be so planned. The following guidelines are essential in this planning:

1. All students should receive periodic medical examinations. The results of these examinations should be made available to school authorities with recommendations of the types of activities needed, and the degree of allowable participation in these activities (no restriction, moderate restriction, or severe restriction).

2. There should be constant communication between the teacher and the physician.

3. Classes should be organized by ability grouping in order to allow all pupils, including the handicapped, to find opportunity for participation on their ability level.

4. Handicapped children should be under constant supervision and guidance throughout their years in the scheduled physical education program. This is necessary not only to watch for

improvement, but also to insure that safety measures are always enforced.

5. Handicapped children should be assigned to the regular physical education classes whenever possible. If the handicap is severe and special classes are indicated, children in these classes should be assigned to the regular program, either on a part-time basis or permanently, as soon as possible. The social contact with other children makes a great contribution to the emotional development of these children and their outlook on life.

6. Although ability grouping will meet the needs of the majority of these children, sometimes it may be necessary to modify the activity itself. Modifying procedures are outlined on page 355.

7. In the initiation of programs for the handicapped, it is extremely important to begin the program as early in the pupil's life as possible.

8. Handicapped children should be encouraged frequently and progress, even though slight, should be brought to the attention of the child.[26]

HOMEWORK FOR THE ATYPICAL CHILD

Monroe Junior High School, Omaha, Nebraska, has developed a program designed to further the instruction for atypical children. In addition to the regular class work, each student is given homework assignments which are placed on a homework sheet. He takes this sheet home and enlists the assistance of his parents in performing the assignment. Figure 11–21 shows the exercises and daily results of the test performances.

Certain procedures were followed during the early stages of the program:

NAME *ERIC NELSON*   DATE *11-6-61*   WEIGHT *137*

EXERCISES	MON.	TUES.	WED.	THURS.	FRI.	SAT.	SUN.
1. Jumping Jacks	14	16	17	18	19	20	22
2. Leg Extention	6	7	8	9	10	11	12
3. Mod. Pull-Ups	2	2	3	3	4	5	6
4. Propellers			45	seconds			
5. Curl Ups	15	17	19	21	24	27	30
6. Seal	3	3	4	5	6	8	10
7. Squat Thrusts	14	16	18	20	22	24	25

SKILLS

A. Pass							
B. Punt	Football						
C. Catch							

EXPLANATION:

    Exercises 1 and 7 are designed to build stamina and speed.

    Exercises 2 and 6 are designed to develop flexibility, agility and balance.

    Exercises 3, 4, and 5 are designed to develop muscular strength and endurance.

    Skill practice will be assigned according to units of work.

    Remember the exercise routine must be followed regularly and exactly if improvement is to be made.

PARENTS SIGNATURE *Mrs. Nelson*

COMMENTS:

HOMEWORK SHEET FOR MONROE JUNIOR HIGH STUDENTS

Figure 11–21. Homework sheet. (Courtesy Monroe Junior High School, Omaha, Nebraska.)

1. Students were chosen for the class through the regular fitness testing program skill tests and through personal observations of the physical education teachers.

2. A meeting for eligible students was held to explain the program in detail.

3. Letters were sent to parents stating briefly the reasons why the class was being offered, and inviting them to a meeting to learn what it could do for their child.

4. At the meeting with the parents, a detailed chart of the entire year's work was explained, with parents being encouraged to ask questions. This led to parental endorsement, with the course being established soon after.[27]

THE TEACHER AND THE PHYSICIAN

Teaching handicapped pupils is a challenge that demands all of the professional training, courage, and dedication the teacher can muster. Not only should the teacher have a sound background in the field of physical education and adaptives, but he should also have the vision to plan and the ability to adjust the program to the individual's handicap and need.

To insure that the two types of programs, described as the adaptive program and the corrective program, are conducted on a medically sound basis, there must be complete cooperation between the teacher and the physician. The first principle in conducting programs for the handicapped is to seek and follow the guidelines established by the physician. Adaptive programs designed for providing general modified activity for the minor handicapped are recommended as part of the regular physical education challenge. However, it is inadvisable to initiate programs which involve corrective activities unless both qualified teachers and medical supervision can be supplied. Children placed in such a group need specific corrective exercises and for proper care should be under regular medical supervision.[26]

THE PHYSICIAN'S REPORT

Usually all pupils are examined by a physician several times during their school years. These examinations should reveal the exceptional child and his academic education needs.

When the examination discloses that the pupil needs special attention in the physical education program, a report showing the physician's recommendation is sent to the physical education teacher. The report should designate in which of the two programs, modified or normal, the child should be enrolled, the type of activities involved, and the intensity of the exercise program. Figure 11-22 is an example of a card that may be used for physician's recommendations. (See Chapter 9 for other examples.)

The need for greater communication between physical education teachers and physicians is apparent in the many discussions that have arisen regarding the classification of students for physical education. Some of the conclusions reached by physicians, educators, and public health leaders attending the National Conferences on Physicians and Schools are these:

1. There is a great need for better communication among all interested parties. Physicians need to be fully informed about all aspects of the local physical education program.

2. It is important that the physician provide all pertinent information on why an excuse has been issued. This can be done without divulging privileged information by providing an interpretation of the condition rather than medical findings.

3. Inadequate physical education programs must be strengthened, since pupil resistance to physical education often stems from lack of proper equipment, facilities, and teaching personnel.

4. There is need in many localities to widen the physical education offerings by increasing the variety of available activities, so that more young people will be able to experience satisfying physical recreation which contributes to their well-being.

5. Every pupil should have the kind of exposure to physical education which promotes understanding of the significance of physical activity in maintaining health and in motivating the individual to regular physical activity.

6. Modification of a youth's physical education program in terms of his special needs should be substituted for blanket excuses.[32]

It is logical to assume that the more efficiently the physical education class is organized and administered, the greater will be the opportunity for the atypical child. Physical education classes that provide for the classification of pupils, ability

CINCINNATI PUBLIC SCHOOLS
ADAPTED PHYSICAL EDUCATION PROGRAM
JUNIOR AND SENIOR HIGH SCHOOLS

Home Room_____

Name of Pupil_____ School_____

Signature of
Parent or Guardian_____ Telephone_____

Signature of Principal_____ Date_____

To the Examining Physician:

The procedure described on the reverse side has been approved by the Commissioner of Health, Cincinnati, Ohio, and the Director of Health and Safety Services for adapting the physical education instructional program in special cases.

Supervisor of Health and Physical Education

This form is to be kept on file in the physical education office.

Cat. No. 7807

ADAPTED PHYSICAL EDUCATION PROGRAM

Home Room_____

For a period of _____ months, an adapted program for _____
(pupil's name)
is to be arranged for these medical reasons:

_____

_____

☐ **Group I**   This pupil may participate in the type of activities checked (✔) below:

Vigorous	Moderate	Mild
☐ Calisthenics	☐ Archery	☐ Ball Kicking
☐ Chinning	☐ Basketball Fundamentals	☐ Calisthenics
☐ Hockey-Soccer	☐ Badminton-Tennis Skills	☐ Corrective Exercises
☐ Rope or Pole Climb	☐ Calisthenics	(prescribed by physician)
☐ Side Horse Vaulting	☐ Corrective Exercises	☐ Foul Shooting
☐ Support Movements	(prescribed by physician)	☐ Horseshoes
☐ Swimming	☐ Dance Activities	☐ Jogging
☐ Tag Football	☐ Swimming	☐ Swimming
☐ Tumbling Skills	☐ Volleyball	☐ Throwing and Catching

☐ **Group II**   Omit physical activity but pupil should remain with class and take notes, score, or perform duties in the physical education office.

☐ **Group III**   Pupil must be excused and may be assigned elsewhere by principal.

Signature of Physician_____ Date_____

Address_____ Telephone_____

Back

Figure 11–22. Physician's recommendations for special programs for the atypical child. (Courtesy Cincinnati Public Schools.)

grouping, and a variety of activities are readily adaptable for the inclusion of the atypical child.

PROGRAMS OF PROMISE FOR THE ATYPICAL CHILD

Throughout the country efforts are being made to provide programs for handicapped children. Many schools, cities, and states have shed the shackles of tradition and have joined the movement to provide equal opportunity for all children irrespective of emotional, physical, and mental handicaps.

New Jersey has advanced the opportunity for the handicapped and exceptional child on a state-wide basis. Thomas M. Vodolo, head of a joint committee of the New Jersey Youth Commission and of the state's Health, Physical Education, and Recreation Association, reports the results of a survey and program of action involving 592 public school districts. The joint committee asked for information concerning the number of schools offering developmental and adaptive physical education and also the types of workshops and clinics that physical education teachers and administrators felt were needed to initiate programs. The respondents expressed their need for help in the following areas:

1. How would one schedule classes?
2. Is special certification necessary to teach developmental and adapted physical education in New Jersey?
3. What liability risks are involved?
4. How can this kind of program be conducted with limited facilities?
5. What special facilities are needed?
6. What kind of tests are used to identify and classify students?
7. What equipment is needed for the program?
8. What is the school nurse's role?
9. What is the physician/instructor relationship in establishing and conducting this type of program?
10. What criteria are used to determine the need for such a program?
11. How does one sell such a program to the community?
12. Are federal funds available to establish such programs?[28]

Based upon the results of the survey, workshops were planned, showing teachers how to arrange testing programs, how to screen pupils, and how to classify them. The ultimate aim of the program is the development of an awareness throughout the state of the need for sound physical education programs for exceptional children.

Wilmington, Delaware, initiated a program for the handicapped, involving both corrective and adaptive programs. John Jenny describes the steps necessary for the implementation of the program:

1. A survey of medical records to determine the needs.
2. Examination of the offerings in the regular physical education programs.
3. Arrangement of their own screening programs by physical education teachers.
4. Establishment of workshops for physical education teachers.[29]

The program in Wilmington, which has been in existence for many years, is an example of what combined efforts of school officials and community groups can do for the education of the handicapped.

In a revised program of physical education in Salt Lake City, Utah, provision is made for the atypical student. The program developed as a result of cooperative efforts on the part of the home, the school, and the family physician. The health examinations in the 7th and 10th grades determine which students are assigned to the classes. Students who are overweight, have postural defects, postoperative and congenital problems, cardiac irregularities, and emotional problems constitute the classes. Figure 11–23 provides an overview of the program.

1. To eliminate the deconditioning phenomenon that accompanies extended periods of inactivity.
2. To overcome physical handicaps that are either temporary or permanent in nature.
3. To teach the use of mechanical devices (aids) necessary for everyday living.
4. To adjust to everyday living psychologically, socially and vocationally within the limits of physical capability.
5. To adjust program needs to student disabilities.[30]

Participation in some form of physical education can be an important experience. Properly guided, it can contribute greatly toward developing feelings of adequacy, security, and belonging.

PROGRAM OF SECONDARY SCHOOL PHYSICAL EDUCATION

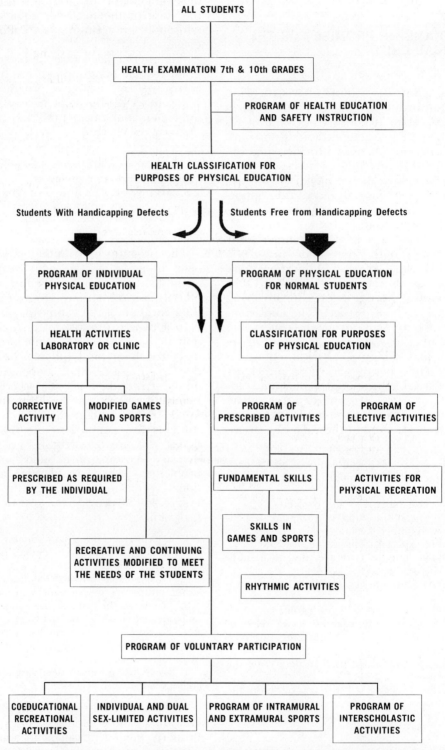

Figure 11–23. Salt Lake City's New Physical Education Program for Normal and Handicapped Children. (Courtesy of *Physical Education Newsletter*, "Highland High Pilots a New Adapted Program." Croft Educational Services, Inc., May 27, 1959.)

QUESTIONS FOR DISCUSSION

1. What, in your opinion, are the best methods in teaching physical education knowledge? Why?

2. What are the advantages of using textbooks for teaching? Disadvantages?

3. What are the advantages of using methods involving student participation in teaching? List several methods involving student participation.

4. Do you feel that the lecture method is appropriate for teaching in the secondary school? When?

5. What are the methods used in teaching skills? Which would you use? Why?

6. In presenting material for teaching skills, which approach would you use?

7. Describe the kinds of learning.

8. List some tools in teaching physical education. Which do you feel is the most important?

9. Why is it important to classify and allot time to physical education activities?

10. In your opinion, which is the most important—group activities or individual activities?

11. Why is it important to follow a basic lesson plan in teaching physical education?

12. What are the phases of the basic lesson plan?

13. What is the intensity curve? How does it relate to the basic lesson plan?

14. What is an "atypical" child?

15. What are the major classifications of atypical children?

16. What is the teacher's responsibility in programs for the physically handicapped? Why?

SUGGESTED ACTIVITIES

1. Visit a physical education class and list the methods used in teaching physical education knowledge. Discuss their effectiveness.

2. Observe a class which is teaching the skills of a physical education activity and develop a chart showing (a) methods used; (b) approaches used; and (c) tools used.

3. Construct a chart listing the kinds of learning. Visit a class and list some items which you feel are learned in each of the kinds of learning.

4. Construct a basic lesson plan for (1) group activity and (2) individual activity.

5. Plan a physical education lesson plan and show how atypical children may be taught in the regular program.

6. Secure permission to visit a school and assist with the periodic medical examination of a class. Use these findings and classify all pupils according to the categorical groupings shown in this chapter.

REFERENCES

1. Clayton Shay, "The Progressive Part vs. the Whole Method of Learning Motor Skills," *Research Quarterly*, p. 62 (December, 1934).

2. R. T. Kretchmar, H. L. Sherman, and Ross Mooney, "Survey of Research in the Teaching of Sports," *Research Quarterly*, p. 244 (October, 1949).

3. May V. Seagoe, *A Teacher's Guide to the Learning Process*, 2nd ed, pp. 141–147 (Dubuque, Iowa: William C. Brown Company, 1961).

4. Bryant J. Cratty, *Movement Behavior and Motor Learning*, 2nd ed., p. 56 (Philadelphia: Lea and Febiger, 1967).

5. Jackson Sharman, *The Teaching of Physical Education*, pp. 114–115 (New York: A. S. Barnes and Company, 1939).

6. Charles Cowell and Hilda Schwehn, *Modern Principles and Methods in Secondary School Physical Education*, 2nd ed., p. 96 (Boston: Allyn and Bacon, 1964).

7. Edward F. Voltmer and Arthur A. Esslinger, *The Organization and Administration of Physical Education*, 4th ed, pp. 130–135 (New York: Appleton-Century-Crofts, 1967).

8. Editorial, *Physical Education Newsletter*, (Croft Educational Services, Inc., January 1, 1967).

9. Jesse F. Williams, *Principles of Physical Education*, 8th ed., p. 479 (Philadelphia: W. B. Saunders Company, 1964).
10. Karl and Carolyn Bookwalter, "Fitness for Secondary School Youth," *Bulletin of the National Association of Secondary School Principals*, p. 52, 1956.
11. Clifford Brownell and Patricia Hagman Leonard, *Physical Education Foundations and Principles*, p. 24 (New York: McGraw-Hill Book Company, 1951).
12. Charles Bucher, *Foundations of Physical Education*, 5th ed., p. 264 (St. Louis: The C. V. Mosby Company, 1968).
13. R. A. McQuigan, "Athletics for Children," Transactions of the Sixth Annual Meeting, American College of Sports and Medicine, Atlantic City, 1959, p. 61.
14. Greyson Daughtrey, "Sports Preferences of 16,000 Parents" (unpublished paper).
15. Clark Hetherington, *School Program in Physical Education*, p. 87 (New York: World Book Company, 1922).
16. Victor H. Noll and Dale P. Scannell, *Introduction to Educational Measurement*, 3rd ed., p. 546 (Boston: Houghton Mifflin Company, 1972).
16a. "Education, U.S.A.," *Bulletin of the National School Public Relations Association*, p. 230, August 7, 1972.
17. Ruth Hook Wheeler and Agnes M. Hooley, *Physical Education for the Handicapped*, pp. 241; 297; 259 (Philadelphia: Lea and Febiger, 1969).
18. Joan Nelson and Gail A. Harris, "Teaching Suggestions," *JOHPER*, p. 27 (April, 1966).
19. Charles Buell, "Is Vigorous Physical Activity Feasible for Blind Children in Public Schools?" *JOHPER*, pp. 97–98 (February, 1969).
20. Dorothy Hyman, "Teaching the Blind Student Archery Skills," *JOHPER*, pp. 85–86 (April, 1969).
21. Daniel D. Arnheim *et al.*, *Principles and Methods of Adapted Physical Education*, pp. 289; 291; 297 (St. Louis: The C. V. Mosby Company, 1969).
22. Julien Stein, "What Research Says About Psychomotor Function of the Retarded," *JOHPER*, pp. 37–38 (April, 1966).
23. "Recreation and Fitness for the Mentally Retarded," *Bulletin of the American Association for Health, Physical Education and Recreation* (December, 1965).
24. Julian Stein, "The Potential of Physical Activity for the Mentally Retarded Child," *JOHPER*, p. 25 (April, 1966).
25. John Throne, "Everybody's Problem," *JOHPER*, p. 24 (April, 1966).
26. Greyson Daughtrey and John B. Woods, *Physical Education Programs: Organization and Administration*, pp. 378; 384; 385 (Philadelphia: W. B. Saunders Company, 1971).
27. "Monroe Junior High Uses Homework in its Remedial Program," *Physical Education Newsletter* (Croft Educational Services, Inc., December 12, 1961).
28. "New Jersey's Youth Commission and Health, Physical Education and Recreation Association Cooperate to Provide Programs for the Handicapped," *Physical Education Newsletter* (Croft Educational Services, Inc., April 1, 1969).
29. John H. Jenny, "Remedial Adaptive and Corrective Physical Education," *Physical Education Newsletter* (Croft Educational Services, Inc., 1967).
30. "Highland High Pilots a New Adapted Program," *Physical Education Newsletter* (Croft Educational Services, Inc., May 27, 1959).
31. Nicholas V. Long and Ruth G. Newman, "A Differential Approach to Management of Surface Behavior of Children in School," *Teachers' Handling Of Children In Conflict*, Bulletin of the School of Education, Indiana University, Vol. 37 (July, 1961), pp. 47–61.
32. "Classification of Students for Physical Education." A.M.A., January 23, 1967, p. 267.

SELECTED READINGS

Arnheim, Daniel D., *et al. Principles and Methods of Adapted Physical Education*. St. Louis: C. V. Mosby Company, 1961.
Biehler, Robert F. *Psychology Applied to Teaching*. Boston: Houghton Mifflin Company, 1971.
Bookwalter, Karl W., and Harold J. Vanderzwaag. *Foundations and Principles of Physical Education*. Philadelphia: W. B. Saunders Company, 1969.
Bucher, Charles A. *Foundations of Physical Education*, 5th ed. St. Louis: The C. V. Mosby Company, 1968.
Davis, Elwood C., and Earl L. Wallis. *Toward Better Teaching in Physical Education*. Englewood Cliffs, New Jersey: Prentice-Hall, Inc., 1961.
Franklin, C. C., and William H. Freeburg. *Diversified Games and Activities of Low Organization for Mentally Retarded Children*. Carbondale, Illinois: Southern Illinois Press.
Garrison, Karl C., and Franklin R. Jones. *The Psychology of Human Development*. Scranton, Pennsylvania: International Textbook Company, 1969.
"Guide for Programs in Recreation and Physical Education for the Mentally Retarded." Washington, D.C.: AAHPER, 1968.
Hilgard, Ernest R. *Introduction to Psychology*, 3d ed. New York: Harcourt, Brace and World, 1962.

Jones, John Walker. *The Visually Handicapped Child.* Washington, D.C.: United States Department of Health, Education and Welfare, 1969.

Knapp, Clyde, and Patricia Hagman Leonard. *Teaching Physical Education in Secondary Schools.* New York: McGraw-Hill Book Company, 1968.

"Mental Retardation Activities." Washington, D.C.: United States Department of Health, Education, and Welfare; Superintendent of Documents, United States Government Printing Office.

"Physical Activities for the Mentally Retarded." Washington, D.C.: AAHPER, 1968.

"Recreation and Physical Activity for the Mentally Retarded." Washington, D.C.: Council for Exceptional Children and the AAHPER, 1966.

Seagoe, May V. *A Teacher's Guide to the Learning Process,* 2nd ed. Dubuque, Iowa: William C. Brown Company, 1961.

Wheeler, Ruth H., and Agnes M. Hooley. *Physical Education for the Handicapped.* Philadelphia: Lea and Febiger, 1969.

Chapter 12

TEACHING INDIVIDUAL AND GROUP ACTIVITIES

The secret of success is constancy to purpose.
Disraeli

DAILY LESSON PLANS FOR SELECTED ACTIVITIES

The lesson plans included in this section provide guidelines of the necessary sequential procedures for teaching skills of selected individual and group activities. Although the plans are designed for classes of 40 students, they may be adapted to varying class loads. To ensure that the instruction is evaluated adequately the objectives are written in terms of performance. The examples shown illustrate how performance objectives may be written. The teacher should use these examples for assistance in writing others which relate to the particular situation. Reference should be made to Chapter 5 for a review of performance objectives.

Five daily plans are developed for each activity, covering progression for one week. However, these plans may be used for varying time periods. In some instances the five plans might cover two weeks or even a month depending on the physical education background of the students. The purpose of the plans is to provide teachers with practical procedures and approaches for teaching large groups of students effectively and safely.

Students and teachers should review the overflow principle described in Chapter 10.

This approach to teaching skills to large groups is used throughout this section. Volleyball is selected for the overflow activity since large numbers may be used safely with a minimum of supervision. When planning the overflow activity, the teacher should be flexible and not concerned with a fixed official number of participants on a side, in order to accommodate the group not immediately participating in the basic instructional activity. The overflow activity may be informal or highly organized, according to the discretion of the teacher.

In all plans, emphasis is placed on grouping by ability or performance. The importance of this procedure is discussed in Chapter 10. The number of groups depends on the size of the class, the previous experience of each member of the class, the size of the teaching station, and the equipment available. The teacher should group by ability and arrange his teaching plans accordingly.

An important part of successful teaching is choosing the method to be used. The discussion of the whole and part methods in Chapter 11 should be reviewed at this time. Teachers, as they analyze the skill to be taught, should determine which method can be used most effectively.

Individualized Instruction

The goal of effective teaching is to develop plans and procedures in such a way that the teacher may spend considerable time helping each student develop his potential. Mass instruction may be used in some instances but providing individualized instruction is the only way interaction between student and teacher can be developed to prepare the student for the challenge of tomorrow. In earlier chapters, innovative plans such as modular scheduling, team teaching, and elective programs were discussed. These plans may set the organizational stage for individualized instruction. This chapter is concerned with ability grouping which is a measurable approach for providing the opportunity for students to make decisions and realize their potential. Students, by achieving the goals in one group, may, with the help of the teacher, advance to a new level of performance compatible with their potential.

Each lesson on the following pages is planned for 40 pupils and will follow a general outline, as shown:

I. History
II. Values of the Activity
III. Rules, Scoring, Strategy and Courtesies
IV. Safety Precautions
V. Equipment Needed
VI. Basic Skills
VII. Teaching Skills Procedures
    A. Introductory
    B. Developmental
    C. Teaching Skills
       1. Orientation
       2. Demonstration
       3. Organization
       4. Inventory
       5. Ability Grouping
       6. Skills Laboratory
       7. Evaluation
    D. Closing

Material for parts of the outline is shown in each plan; any material not included in the plan may be found in the references at the end of the chapter.

The teacher should at this point review the basic lesson plan which is discussed in Chapter 11. Having followed this suggestion, he is now ready to apply his knowledge of how to teach to the first activity which is tennis.

Teaching Tennis Skills

GENERAL OBJECTIVES:
  A. Psychomotor. The students will demonstrate the correct form in executing the intricate skills of tennis.
  B. Cognitive. The students will demonstrate their knowledge of tennis by checking the correct answers among a list of choices on a knowledge test.
  C. Affective. The students will demonstrate their ability to:
      Control emotions under stress.
      Show good sportsmanship.
      Exhibit team loyalty.
      Accept responsibility.
      Assume leadership.
      Respect decisions of officials.

I. HISTORY OF TENNIS
(See references at end of chapter.)

II. VALUES OF TENNIS
Leisure time values
Social potential
Development of physiological fitness

III. RULES, SCORING AND STRATEGY

IV. SAFETY PRECAUTIONS

Warm up to prevent muscle injury.
Hold ball until instruction begins.
Be careful in using racquets.
Stay in assigned area.

V. EQUIPMENT NEEDED

Racquets   Areas or courts
Balls   Nets or ropes

VI. BASIC SKILLS

Grips — Eastern   *Strokes* — Hitting the ball
      Western   Forehand
      Continental   Backhand
                            Serve
                            Volley
                            Lob

VII. TEACHING SKILLS PROCEDURES

    A. Introductory — see page 342
    B. Developmental — see page 342
    C. Teaching skills
        1. Orientation — see page 345
        2. Demonstration — see page 345
        3. Organization — see page 346
        4. Inventory — see page 346
        5. Ability Grouping — see page 346
        6. Skills Laboratory — see page 346
        7. Evaluation — see Chapter 14 (p. 346)
           (made in terms of behavior)
    D. Closing — see page 346

HOW TO LAY OUT A TENNIS COURT

First spot place for net posts, 42 feet apart. Measure in on each side 7-1/2 feet and plant stakes 27 feet apart at points A and B in diagram.

Then take two tape measures and attach to each peg—one tape 47 feet 5 inches, the other 39 feet. Pull both taut in such directions that at these distances they meet at point C. This gives one corner of the court. Interchange the tapes and again measure to get point D. Points C and D should then be 27 feet apart. Put in pegs at C and D and measure 18 feet toward net and put in pegs to denote service lines.

Proceed in same way for the other half of court and add center line from service line to service line—distance 42 feet. Then add 4-1/2 feet on each side for alleys. Alleys should then be 3 feet inside posts on each side. Put in permanent pegs to mark all corners.

Measure to outside edge of boundary lines.

CENTER OF COURT

SERVICE LINE

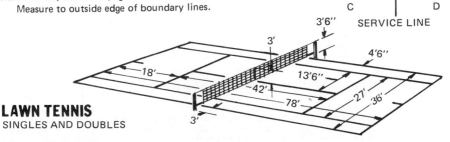

LAWN TENNIS
SINGLES AND DOUBLES

Figure 12–1. Tennis court. (Courtesy Wilson Sporting Goods Company.)

LESSON ONE

PERFORMANCE OBJECTIVES:

Psychomotor. The student will demonstrate the correct form in bouncing the ball with the racquet a distance of 30 feet and back without losing possession of the ball.

Cognitive. The student will list advantages of each of the three grips as discussed in class.

Affective. The student will exhibit inhibition and control when he loses the ball in the relay race.

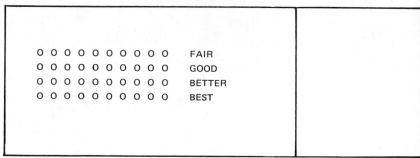

Figure 12-2. Grip and hitting ball formation.

The class is arranged as shown. The first student in each line is given a ball and racquet, using the correct grip. Each pupil walks to the line, bouncing the ball. He touches line, walks back, and gives ball and racquet to next person. This procedure continues until all students have tried. Students are asked to run and bounce the ball. For variation, repeat procedure with pupils bouncing ball in the air. For motivation the same plan may be used in competitive relay races.

LESSON TWO

PERFORMANCE OBJECTIVES:

Psychomotor. The student will demonstrate the correct position of the feet and arms in executing the forehand and backhand return, three out of five times.

Cognitive. The student will describe the footwork in the forehand and backhand return in one paragraph on a written test.

Affective. The student displays patience while learning to execute the forehand and backhand return.

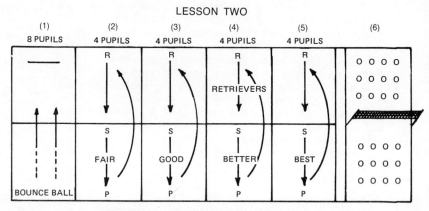

Figure 12-3. Forehand and backhand return.

The class is divided into six groups: (1) those who did not show improvement in bouncing the ball; (2) fair; (3) good; (4) better; (5) best in the backhand and forehand; and (6) volleyball overflow. Each of the four players (P) is given a racquet. The set-up (S) students have six balls each, which they throw with one bounce to the players, who practice making a forehand or backhand return in their lane. The retrievers (R) throw the balls to the set-up pupils. After the players (P) have practiced sufficiently, they rotate as shown in the figure. This continues with students advancing from group 2 toward group 5 as they improve. Students in group 1 continue practicing and are advanced to group 2 as they improve. As group 5 becomes crowded, group 1 will have advanced leaving section 1 open for another advanced group (5). The tennis groups periodically change with the volleyball groups.

LESSON THREE

PERFORMANCE OBJECTIVES:

Psychomotor. The student will serve the ball into the left and then the right service area, seven out of 10 times.

Cognitive. The student will discuss why the power serve in tennis is essential for championship tennis.

Affective. The student displays self-control after failing to serve the ball in the service court.

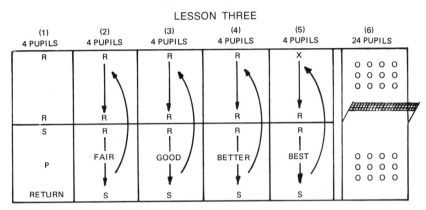

Figure 12–4. Teaching the serve.

The class is divided into six groups: (1) those who need more practice in returning the ball; (2) fair; (3) good; (4) better; (5) best who are ready for practice in serving; and (6) the volleyball overflow group. Each of the four servers (S) is given a racquet and two balls. They practice placing the serve over the net in their lane. The retrievers (R) throw the balls to the server. After practicing the serve sufficiently, the servers rotate, as shown in diagram. This continues with students advancing from group 2 toward group 5 as they improve. As group 5 becomes crowded, group 1 will have advanced to group 2, leaving section 1 open for another advanced group (5). All students in groups 1 through 5 change with the volleyball overflow group after practicing tennis skills sufficiently and follow the same serving procedure.

LESSON FOUR

PERFORMANCE OBJECTIVES:

Psychomotor. The student will successfully volley the ball from a position close to the net, three out of five times.

Cognitive. The student will list three advantages of the volley in tennis.

Affective. The student displays control of his temper if hit by the ball while attempting to volley it.

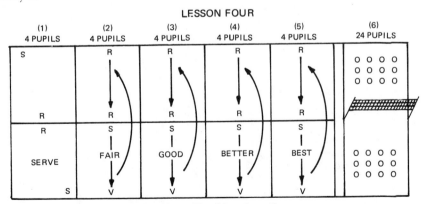

Figure 12–5. Teaching the volley.

The class is divided into six groups: (1) those who did not progress too well with the serve; (2) fair; (3) good; (4) better; (5) best; and (6) volleyball overflow. Each of the four volleyers (V) is given a racquet. The four set-up (S) students are given about six balls each. They toss the balls so that the students who are volleying are able to return the ball in their lanes. Retrievers (R) gather the balls for their lane and throw them to the set-up students. The volleying groups rotate within their lanes. This continues with students advancing from group 2 toward group 5 as they improve. Students in group 1 advance to group 2 as they improve. As group 5 becomes crowded, group 1 will have advanced to group 2, leaving this space open for another advanced group. All students in groups 1 through 5 change places with volleyball overflow group 6 after they have practiced tennis skills sufficiently.

LESSON FIVE

PERFORMANCE OBJECTIVES:

Psychomotor. The student will successfully lob the ball from mid-court over the opponent's head, three out of five times.

Cognitive. The student lists champions in tennis who used the lob to advantage.

Affective. The student exhibits kindness to the opponent who fails to return the lob.

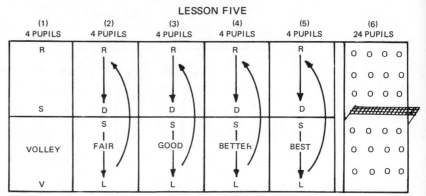

Figure 12-6. Teaching the lob.

The class is divided into six groups: (1) students from the last lesson who continue to practice the volley; (2) fair; (3) good; (4) better; (5) best—students who progressed enough to practice the lob; and (6) the volleyball overflow. Each of the four students (L) who will practice the lob is given a racquet. Each of the four defense (D) students nearest the net is given a racquet. The set-up (S) students are given several balls and make a one bounce toss to the lobbers. The lobbers (L) attempt to return the ball over the heads of the defense students (D). After the lobbers have practiced sufficiently, they rotate as shown in the figure. This continues with students advancing from group 2 toward group 5 as they improve. Students in group 1 advance to group 2 as they improve. As group 5 becomes crowded, group 1 will have advanced to group 2, leaving that space open for another advanced group (5). After sufficient practice all students in groups 1 through 5 change with volleyball group (6).

Figure 12-7. One example of how students may be grouped for the demonstration phase in teaching tennis.

Teaching Bowling Skills

GENERAL OBJECTIVES:

  A. Psychomotor. The students will perform correctly the basic movements in bowling as described in class.

  B. Cognitive. The students will demonstrate knowledge of bowling by matching the correct statements in a written test.

  C. Affective. The students will demonstrate their ability to:

Control emotions under stress.

Show good sportsmanship.

Exhibit team loyalty.

Accept responsibility.

Assume leadership.

Respect decisions of officials.

I. HISTORY OF BOWLING

(See references at end of chapter.)

II. VALUES OF BOWLING

Social and recreational values

Family participation

Develops coordination

Leisure time values

III. RULES, SCORING AND COURTESIES

IV. SAFETY PRECAUTIONS

Stay away from flying pins.

Always watch balls when returned.

Stop ball with foot (improvised alleys).

Roll balls slowly.

Remove balls from rack properly, keeping fingers away from oncoming balls.

Release ball only when pin setter is away (improvised alley).

Control ball at all times.

V. EQUIPMENT NEEDED

Six alleys (improvised—see Figure 12–14)

60 pins—18 balls

Six pieces of indoor-outdoor carpeting, 40 to 60 feet long

Score sheets

VI. BASIC SKILLS

Grip	Release
Stance	Delivery
Approach	Follow-through

VII. TEACHING SKILLS PROCEDURES

A. Introductory—see page 342

B. Developmental—see page 342

C. Teaching Skills

  1. Orientation—see page 345

  2. Demonstration—see page 345

  3. Organization—see page 346

  4. Inventory—see page 346

  5. Ability Grouping—see page 346

  6. Skills Laboratory—see page 346

  7. Evaluation—see Chapter 14 (p. 346) (made in terms of behavior)

D. Closing—see page 346

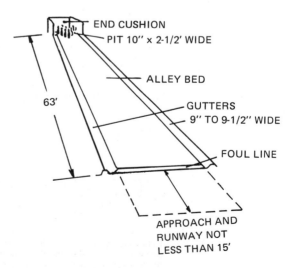

Figure 12–8. Dimensions of a bowling alley. (Armbruster, David A., *et al.: Basic Skills in Sports for Men and Women.* St. Louis: The C. V. Mosby Company, 1971, p. 72.)

LESSON ONE

PERFORMANCE OBJECTIVES:

Psychomotor.   The student will demonstrate the correct form in the delivery from the starting position by hitting the headpin, three out of five times.

Cognitive.   The student lists five values of bowling in a written test with a time limit of five minutes.

Affective.   The student displays control over his emotions when he fouls as the ball is released.

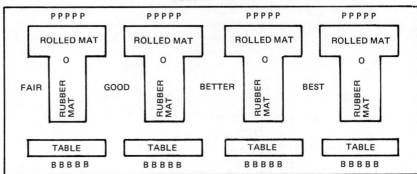

Figure 12-9.   Grip—stance—release—follow-through.

Students are arranged in ability groups of five as shown. The B's are bowlers; they are seated on benches behind the tables. The P's are pin-setters who roll the balls slowly on the rubber runners back to the bowlers. One pin is used. Each bowler walks to the foul line, places his left foot on it, and releases the ball, aiming it at the pin and following through. Each bowler repeats this many times. Bowlers then change places with pin-setters. Students are grouped by ability into one of the four groups. Bowlers advance from one group to another as they improve.

LESSON TWO

PERFORMANCE OBJECTIVES:

Psychomotor.   Using the four step approach, the student hits the headpin, three out of seven times.

Cognitive.   The student gives an oral report of the four step approach to the class.

Affective.   The student displays emotional control as he fouls when releasing the ball.

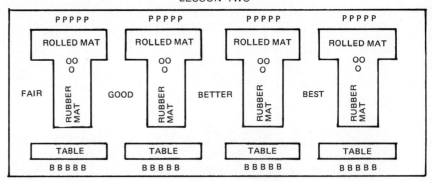

Figure 12-10.   The approach.

Follow the same organizational procedure outlined in lesson one, using three pins instead of one. Students practice the four step approach instead of releasing the ball from the stationary position. Bowlers advance from the fair group to the best group as they improve.

LESSON THREE

PERFORMANCE OBJECTIVES:

Psychomotor. The student demonstrates the correct form in the hook delivery by hitting the 1–3 pocket, four out of 10 times.

Cognitive. The student writes a description of the straight delivery showing the advantages.

Affective. The student displays courtesy to an opponent whose ball has rolled into his alley.

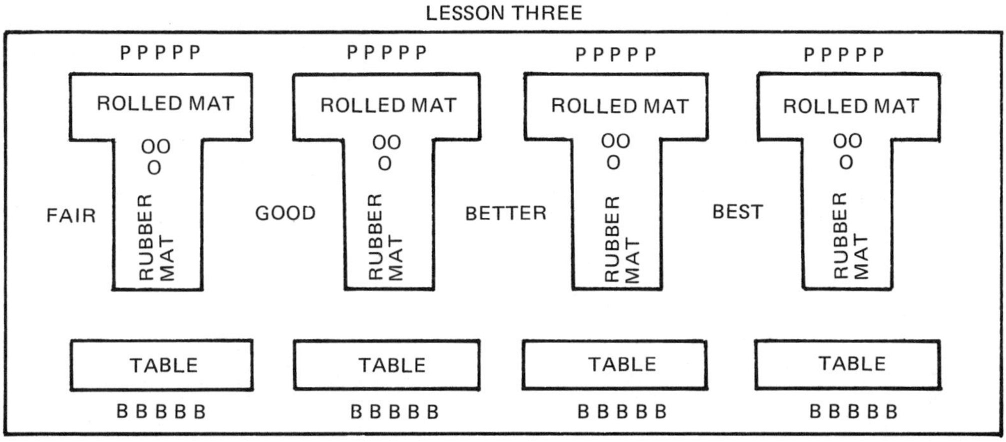

LESSON THREE

Figure 12–11. The delivery.

Students are organized as shown in lesson one. Three pins are used. Emphasis is on the hook and straight deliveries. They advance from one group to another as they improve.

LESSON FOUR

PERFORMANCE OBJECTIVES:

Psychomotor. The student after selecting a spot 15–20 feet from the foul line hits the 1–3 pocket, three out of seven times.

Cognitive. The student prepares a one page paper on the advantages and disadvantages of the two types of aims.

Affective. The student controls his temper when he fails to hit the proper pin in spot aiming.

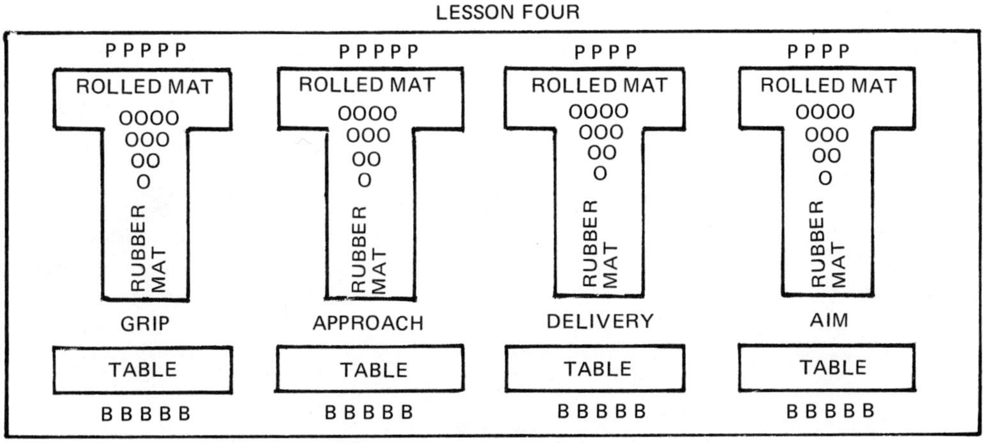

LESSON FOUR

Figure 12–12. The aim.

The organizational plan for the preceding lessons is used. All ten pins are used. Students practice the two types of aim—head pin and spot aiming. They advance as they improve.

LESSON FIVE

PERFORMANCE OBJECTIVES:

Psychomotor. The student, using the four steps in bowling—the grip, approach, delivery and aim—hits the 1–3 pocket, six out of 10 times.

Cognitive. The student identifies the correct form in the four stages from a list of pictures which show both correct and incorrect form.

Affective. The student shows good sportsmanship when consistently missing strikes.

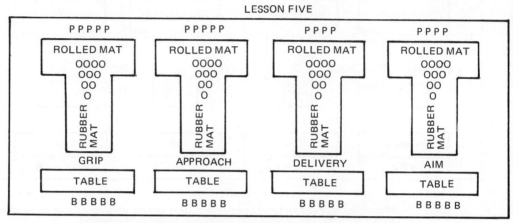

Figure 12–13. Teaching all skills: grip—approach—delivery—aim.

Students are placed in groups as shown above based on the inventory. They should practice those skills in which they are weakest. All pins are used.

Figure 12–14. Demountable bowling backstops provide a practical and efficient method for teaching bowling skills.

Teaching Golf Skills

GENERAL OBJECTIVES:
  A. *Psychomotor.* The students will exhibit correct form in the complex movements in golf as described by the teacher and demonstrated by a professional who will visit the class.
  B. *Cognitive.* The students will demonstrate their knowledge of golf in checking correct answers on a true or false test.
  C. *Affective.* The students will demonstrate their ability to:
        Control emotions under stress.
        Show good sportsmanship.
        Exhibit team loyalty.
        Accept responsibility.
        Assume leadership.
        Respect decisions of officials.

    I. HISTORY OF GOLF

      (See references at end of chapter.)

   II. VALUES OF GOLF

      Leisure time values
      Social values
      Develops coordination

  III. RULES, SCORING AND COURTESIES

   IV. SAFETY PRECAUTIONS

      Always be aware of danger of swinging clubs.
      Stay in individual squares while swinging.
      Stay away from other pupils who are practicing.
      Golf requires intensive supervision at all times.

    V. EQUIPMENT NEEDED

      Eight rubber mats or pieces of indoor-outdoor carpeting
      Plastic balls
      Clubs

   VI. BASIC SKILLS

      Grip   Pivot
      Stance   Follow-through
      Swing   Putt

  VII. TEACHING SKILLS PROCEDURES

      A. Introductory—see page 342
      B. Developmental—see page 342
      C. Teaching Skills
          1. Orientation—see page 345
          2. Demonstration—see page 345
          3. Organization—see page 346
          4. Inventory—see page 346
          5. Ability Grouping—see page 346
          6. Skills Laboratory—see page 346
          7. Evaluation—see Chapter 14
             (p. 346) (made in terms of
             behavior)
      D. Closing—see page 346

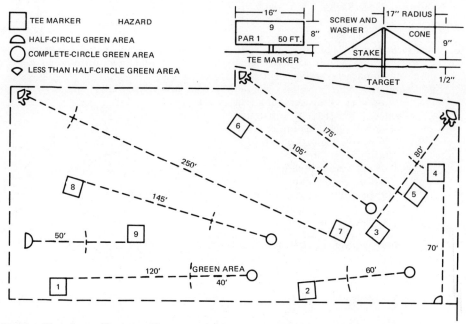

Figure 12–15. The plug golf course. (Courtesy of The Athletic Institute: *Planning Areas and Facilities for Health, Physical Education, and Recreation.* Chicago: Merchandise Mart, 1966.)

LESSON ONE

PERFORMANCE OBJECTIVES:

Psychomotor. Following instruction in class, the student will execute a golf swing emphasizing the stages in the lesson, three out of seven times.

Cognitive. The student will draw a diagram showing the position of player in order to insure safe practice.

Affective. The student shows tolerance for his classmates when they violate rules of safety.

LESSON ONE

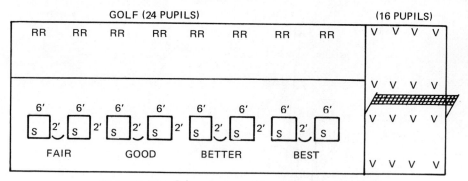

Figure 12–16. Grip — stance — swing — follow-through (indoors).

Students are arranged as shown. The golf group has 24 students — eight swingers (S) and 16 retrievers (R). The volleyball overflow group has eight on each side. Students in the golf swing group practice the stance and swinging at the plastic balls placed in the center of each square. It is imperative that they stay in the square. A swinging golf club is a lethal weapon, and the organization must be such as to insure safety at all times. The retrievers (R) approach the restraining line and throw the plastic balls back to the swingers (S). The swingers periodically change places with the retrievers. Students progress from the fair to the best groups based on ability. Periodically overflow groups change with the golf group.

LESSON TWO

PERFORMANCE OBJECTIVES:

Psychomotor.   Using the circle as a target, the student, with an iron, will hit a plastic ball in it, three out of five times.

Cognitive.   The student will identify the functions of the irons by matching the correct iron with the yardage shown on a chart.

Affective.   The student will respect the safety of his classmates by remaining in his circle while practicing.

LESSON TWO

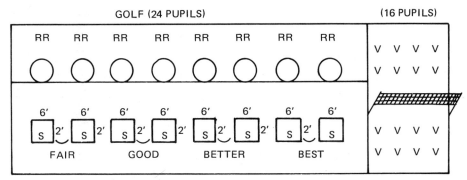

GOLF (24 PUPILS)   (16 PUPILS)

Figure 12–17.   Accuracy (outdoors).

The same plans are used as shown in lesson one. Students attempt to place the ball in the circle corresponding with their squares. Plastic balls are used. Students advance from the fair group to the best group as they improve.

LESSON THREE

PERFORMANCE OBJECTIVES:

Psychomotor.   The student, using a regular golf ball and a selected iron, hits the ball in the circle, three out of five times.

Cognitive.   The student describes the reason for using the iron rather than a wood during early instruction.

Affective.   Using the terms discussed in class, the student demonstrates proper courtesy before hitting the ball.

LESSON THREE

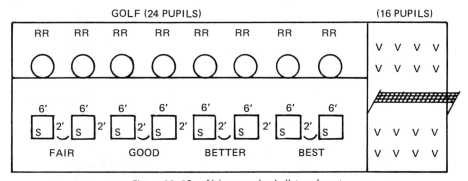

GOLF (24 PUPILS)   (16 PUPILS)

Figure 12–18.   Using regular ball (outdoors).

The students are organized as in lesson two. Students use regular balls and attempt to place them in the circles. The previous teaching procedures were arranged for either indoors or outdoors using plastic balls. Lesson three is designed for outdoors using the regular ball. The circles are drawn farther from the practice squares than for indoors. Students advance as they improve.

LESSON FOUR
PERFORMANCE OBJECTIVES:

Psychomotor.   Using a putter, the student puts the ball in the metal cup (or hole), three out of seven times.

Cognitive.   The student will describe the stance used in putting and explain how it differs from the other stances.

Affective.   The student will show courtesy for his classmate by waiting his turn for putting.

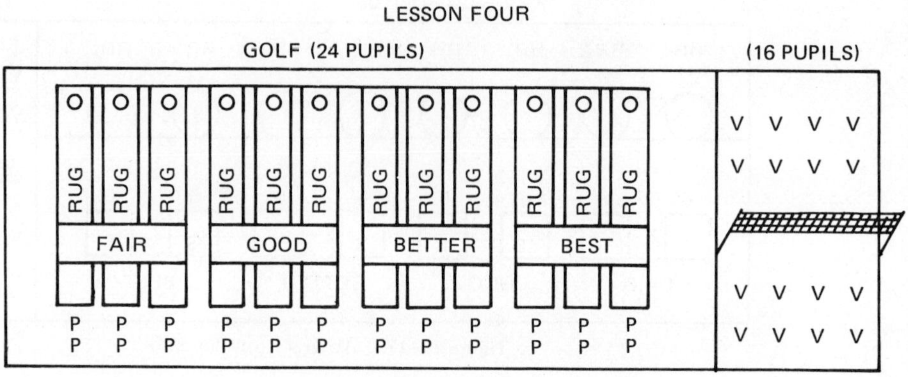

Figure 12-19.   Putting, indoors or outdoors.

The students are organized into two groups as shown. The golf group consists of 24 putters (P), and the volleyball overflow group (V) consists of 16 students with eight on each side. Students practice putting on the rugs that have metal cups at the end of each rug. The students advance from the fair group to the best group based on their ability. Periodically the volleyball overflow groups change with the golf group. Regular balls are used.

LESSON FIVE
PERFORMANCE OBJECTIVES:

Psychomotor.   The student will score par for the pitch and putt course, three out of five times.

Cognitive.   In the selection of his club, the student will orally state the reason for his selection.

Affective.   The student will show tolerance and empathy for the classmate who has poor coordination.

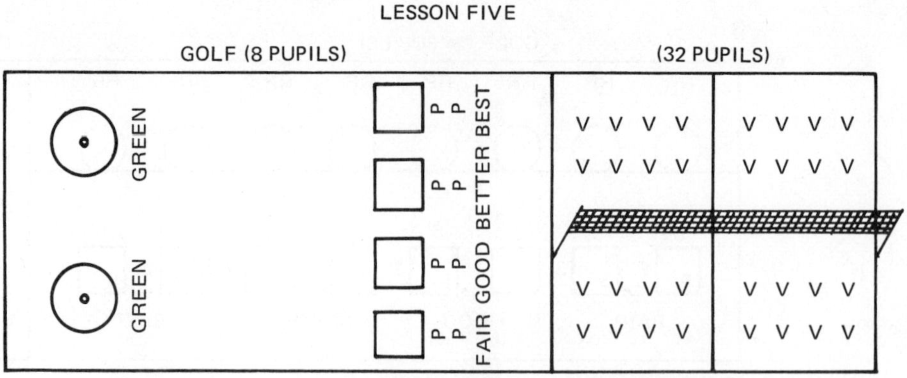

Figure 12-20.   Pitch and putt (outdoors).

Students are arranged in two groups as shown. The golf group (P) has eight students, and the volleyball overflow group (V) has 32 players with two courts or areas. The golfers pitch and putt and are grouped from fair to best based on ability. The volleyball groups and the golfers change places periodically. Regular balls are used. Golfers advance from fair to best group as they improve.

Figure 12–21 Teaching golf skills safely and effectively. Retrievers are not shown in the picture.

Teaching Tumbling Skills

GENERAL OBJECTIVES:
  A. Psychomotor. The students will correctly demonstrate the various skills of tumbling as described by the teacher and practiced in class.
  B. Cognitive. The students will demonstrate their knowledge of tumbling in a true or false test by checking the correct answers.
  C. Affective. The students will demonstrate their ability to:
>   Control emotions under stress.
>   Show good sportsmanship.
>   Exhibit team loyalty.
>   Accept responsibility.
>   Assume leadership.
>   Respect decisions of officials.

I. HISTORY OF TUMBLING

   (See references at end of chapter.)

II. VALUES OF TUMBLING

   Safety values for other sports
   Contributes to emotional stability
   Contributes to physiological fitness
   Leisure time values.

III. RULES, SCORING AND COURTESIES

IV. SAFETY PRECAUTIONS

Never leave group unsupervised.
Follow recommended sequence in teaching.
Always use spotters in all skills.
Do not allow students to overextend their efforts.
Do not urge students to progress too fast.
Check mats for unseen objects.
Always have students warm up.
Always have students complete a movement; do not allow them to hesitate.
Have student stay off mat until tumbler in front is off.

V. EQUIPMENT NEEDED

Two 20-foot mats   Teaching aids
Two safety belts   Test

VI. BASIC SKILLS

Forward roll   Front handspring
Backward roll   Back handspring
Kip-up   Front somersault
Head stand

VII. TEACHING SKILLS PROCEDURES

A. Introductory—see page 342
B. Developmental—see page 342
C. Teaching Skills
   1. Orientation—see page 345
   2. Demonstration—see page 345
   3. Organization—see page 346
   4. Inventory—see page 346
   5. Ability Grouping—see page 346
   6. Skills Laboratory—see page 346
   7. Evaluation—see Chapter 14
     (p. 346) (made in terms of
     behavior)
D. Closing—see page 346

Figure 12–22. If the class is organized properly, two 5 ft. by 20 ft. mats may be sufficient for teaching tumbling effectively.

LESSON ONE

PERFORMANCE OBJECTIVES:

Psychomotor. The student demonstrates the correct form in the forward roll, which was taught and demonstrated in the class, three out of five times.

Cognitive. The student will show in proper sequence the steps in performing the forward roll.

Affective. The student will follow instructions given by the teacher to insure safety of his classmate.

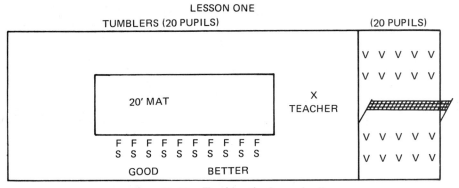

Figure 12–23. Teaching the forward roll.

The class is divided into two groups as shown. The tumbling group consists of ten tumblers, who will practice the forward roll (F), and ten spotters (S). The volleyball overflow group (V) consists of two teams with ten on each team. The forward roll has been demonstrated in the second part of the teaching procedure and the pupils are ready to begin, with the spotters beside them and assisting them. As they improve, the "better" group becomes larger and the "good" group is absorbed. As students improve in the simple forward roll, they may add a dive. The tumbling group changes with the volleyball overflow group either several at a time or as a group at the discretion of the teacher.

LESSON TWO

PERFORMANCE OBJECTIVES:

Psychomotor. The student exhibits the correct form in the backward roll, demonstrated in the film strip shown in the class, seven out of 10 times.

Cognitive. The student will exhibit his knowledge of the backward roll which he learned by reading the recommended text.

Affective. The student demonstrates tolerance for the poor performance of his classmate and assists him in the correct form.

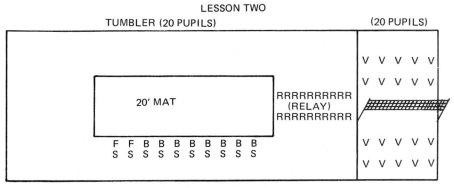

Figure 12–24. Teaching the backward roll.

Students are grouped as shown. Students (F) who failed to execute the forward roll continue to practice, and those who learned the forward roll practice the backward roll (B) with spotters (S). The tumbling group changes with the volleyball group, either several at a time or as a group at the discretion of the teacher. Spotters change with learners at the discretion of the teacher. A forward roll relay race may be used as shown.

LESSON THREE

PERFORMANCE OBJECTIVES:

Psychomotor. The student demonstrates the correct form in the headstand by maintaining it for 25 seconds.

Cognitive. The student exhibits his knowledge of the headstand by assisting a classmate to perform it correctly.

Affective. The student shows his appreciation of the teacher's instruction by following instructions.

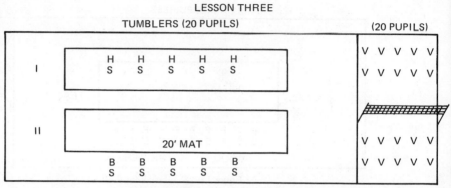

Figure 12–25. Teaching the headstand.

Students are arranged in two sections as shown. The mat is placed against the wall and the students learning the headstand (H), assisted by their spotters (S), place their head and hands on the mat and their feet against the wall. A mat is not necessary for this activity but is desirable if available. At the teacher's discretion the spotters change with those learning the headstand. Students who failed to execute the backroll in the previous lesson practice on mat II with their spotters. Tumbling sections change with volleyball sections either in pairs or as a group.

LESSON FOUR

PERFORMANCE OBJECTIVES:

Psychomotor. The student performs the kip-up correctly, three out of five times.

Cognitive. The student exhibits his understanding of the kip-up by observing a classmate and pointing out what he does wrong.

Affective. The student demonstrates good sportsmanship by overlooking remarks made by a classmate.

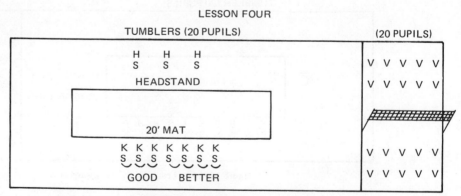

Figure 12–26. Teaching the kip-up.

Students are grouped as shown with those who failed to execute the headstand (H) practicing and those who are ready to practice the kip-up (K) starting with the spotters (S) helping them. Students progress as they improve from headstand to "good" and from "good" to "better." A constant interchange, either in pairs or by entire groups, goes on between the tumbling group and the volleyball overflow. Spotters change with learners at the discretion of the teacher.

LESSON FIVE
PERFORMANCE OBJECTIVES:

Psychomotor. The student correctly executes the handspring in proper sequence without hesitating, three out of five times.

Cognitive. Using a series of pictures made by students, the student identifies those who are using correct form.

Affective. The student shows kindness toward a poorly coordinated classmate and assists him in performing the handspring.

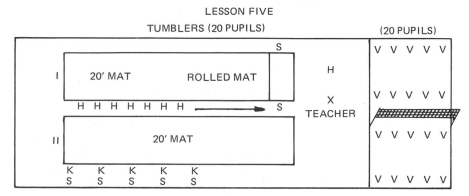

Figure 12–27. Teaching the front handspring.

Students are grouped into two sections: the tumblers with 20 students and the volleyball overflow with 20 students. The eight students learning the handspring (H) assisted by the two spotters (S) begin to execute the handspring over a rolled mat. These students have executed the kip and are ready to learn the handspring. Students who did not execute the kip correctly continue to practice on mat II as shown. As students learn the kip, they advance to the handspring. As the handspring group learn the skill satisfactorily, they change with one of the volleyball overflow groups. Spotters change with learners at the discretion of the teacher.

Figure 12–28. Tumbling may be taught without the volleyball overflow provided there is good organization.

Teaching Handball Skills

GENERAL OBJECTIVES:

A. Psychomotor. The students will correctly demonstrate the various skills of handball as described in the audiovisual aids shown in the class.

B. Cognitive. The students will exhibit their knowledge of handball in a matching test prepared and administered by the teacher.

C. Affective. The students will demonstrate their ability to:

Control emotions under stress.
Show good sportsmanship.
Exhibit team loyalty.
Accept responsibility.
Assume leadership.
Respect decisions of officials.

I. HISTORY OF HANDBALL

(See references at end of chapter.)

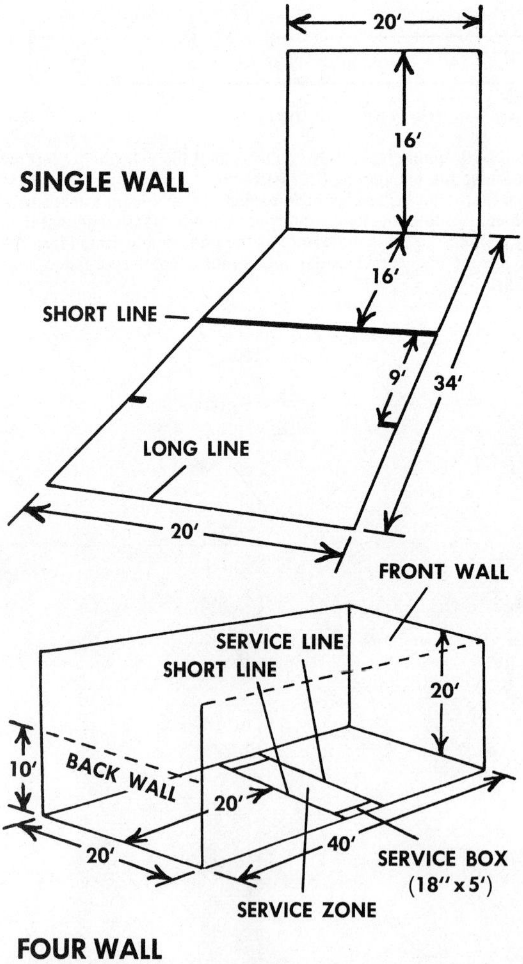

II. VALUES OF HANDBALL

Physiological development
Carry-over value
Contributes to emotional stability

III. RULES, SCORING AND COURTESIES

IV. SAFETY

Wear proper shoes.
Always keep eye on the ball.
Warm up before playing.

V. EQUIPMENT NEEDED

Handballs
Films and strips
Texts

VI. BASIC SKILLS

Hand positions
Serve
Return strokes

VII. TEACHING SKILLS PROCEDURES

A. Introductory—see page 342
B. Developmental—see page 342
C. Teaching Skills
1. Orientation—see page 345
2. Demonstration—see page 345
3. Organization—see page 346
4. Inventory—see page 346
5. Ability Grouping—see page 346
6. Skills Laboratory—see page 346
7. Evaluation—see Chapter 14 (p. 346) (made in terms of behavior)
D. Closing—see page 346

Figure 12–29. Handball court. (Hase, Gerald J., and Irwin Rosenstein: *Modern Physical Education.* New York: Holt, Rinehart & Winston, Inc., 1966, p. 109.)

LESSON ONE

PERFORMANCE OBJECTIVES:

Psychomotor.   The student demonstrates the correct stance as taught and described in class, three out of five times.

Cognitive.   The student will give a written description of the correct stance in handball.

Affective.   The student will assist his classmate in learning the stance instead of ignoring his faulty movements.

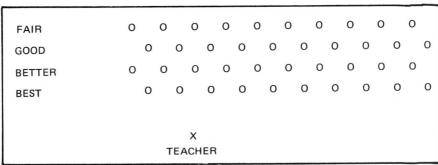

Figure 12–30.   The stance and hand positions.

Students are arranged in open order as shown. The teacher leads the entire class in executing the stance and the hand positions. Students advance from the fair group to the best group as they improve.

LESSON TWO

PERFORMANCE OBJECTIVES:

Psychomotor.   The student bounces the ball on the floor and correctly hits it against the wall, two out of three times.

Cognitive.   The student will draw a diagram of the correct form in hitting the ball.

Affective.   The student will respect the safety of his classmate by carefully following the safety instructions described by the teacher.

Figure 12–31.   Hitting the ball.

Students are placed in ability groups as shown. The first player (P) in each line hits the ball against the wall and runs behind his classmate. The second player returns the ball and runs behind his classmate. This procedure is continued. Lines are made on the floor and wall with masking tape. Students advance from the fair to best group as they improve.

LESSON THREE

PERFORMANCE OBJECTIVES:

Psychomotor. The student will serve the ball correctly in an area marked on the wall, two out of five times.

Cognitive. The student will discuss the correct form in serving the ball.

Affective. The student controls his temper when hit by the ball which was served by his opponent.

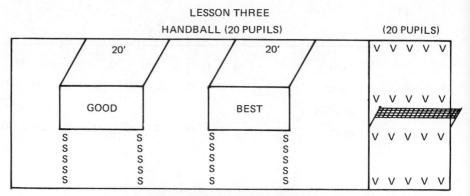

LESSON THREE

HANDBALL (20 PUPILS)   (20 PUPILS)

Figure 12–32.   Teaching the serve.

The class is divided into two sections as shown. Students in section I (S) are placed in four groups as shown; they practice the serve with the first students in each line serving the ball and running to the end of the line. The volleyball players change with the handball groups periodically at the discretion of the teacher. Students advance from the fair group to the best group as they improve.

LESSON FOUR

PERFORMANCE OBJECTIVES:

Psychomotor. The student will return the ball with proper form, three out of five times.

Cognitive. The student will list the advantages of using the correct form in returning the ball.

Affective. The student shows kindness to an opponent who fails to return the ball.

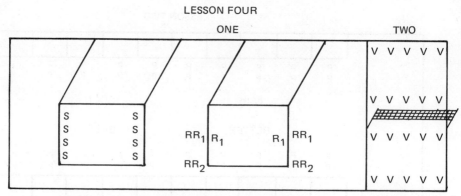

LESSON FOUR

ONE   TWO

Figure 12–33.   Return strokes.

The class is divided into two sections as shown. The students in section I form two groups—those who need more serving practice (S) and those who are ready to learn the return (R). The first player in the R_1 group enters the court, serves the ball, and runs to the end of the R_2 line. The first player in the R_2 groups enters the court, returns the ball, and runs to the end of the R_1 line. The volleyball players change with the handball group at the discretion of the teacher. If enough courts are available, the return group may be divided into ability groups.

LESSON FIVE

PERFORMANCE OBJECTIVES:

Psychomotor. The student demonstrates correct court strategy as described by the teacher, three out of seven times.

Cognitive. The student describes in writing several strategies which have been used in class.

Affective. The student shows respect for the teacher who gives a poor demonstration of a court strategy.

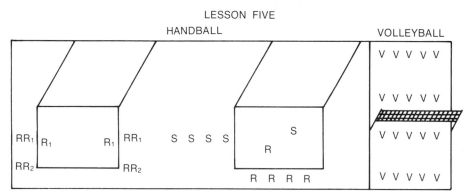

LESSON FIVE

Figure 12–34. Teaching court strategy.

The class is organized in two sections as shown. The handball section is composed of two groups: (1) those who need practice in returning the ball, and (2) those learning court strategy. In the second group the servers (S) serve the ball and those returning the ball (R) practice using the various strategies. The volleyball section and the handball section change at the discretion of the teacher. If space is available, the strategy group may be divided into ability groups.

Figure 12–35. Good class organization is essential for effective instruction in handball skills.

Teaching Swimming Skills

GENERAL OBJECTIVES:
  A. Psychomotor. The students will exhibit the correct form in the complex movements of swimming as described and demonstrated by the visiting professional.
  B. Cognitive. The students will demonstrate their knowledge by giving the correct answers on a true or false test.
  C. Affective. The students will demonstrate their ability to:
      Control emotions under stress.
      Show good sportsmanship.
      Exhibit team loyalty.
      Accept responsibility.
      Assume leadership.
      Respect decisions of officials.

I. HISTORY OF SWIMMING

  (See references at end of chapter.)

II. VALUES OF SWIMMING

  Safety values
  Physiological development
  Recreational values

III. RULES

IV. SAFETY PRECAUTIONS

  Never go in pool alone.
  Wear swim suit at all times to be ready to aid students.
  Do not permit dangerous behavior such as pushing, ducking, and climbing in water.
  Use the "buddy system."
  Do not allow students to dive in water unless the depth is known.
  Do not allow students to run around the pool.
  Always have life preservers available.

V. EQUIPMENT NEEDED

  Pool or tank   Films and strips
  Swim suits   Texts

VI. BASIC SKILLS

  Learning to swim: Breath control
                    Submerging
                    Face floating
                    Flutter kick
                    Arm stroke

Strokes: Crawl
Back crawl
Breast
Side

VII. TEACHING SKILLS PROCEDURES

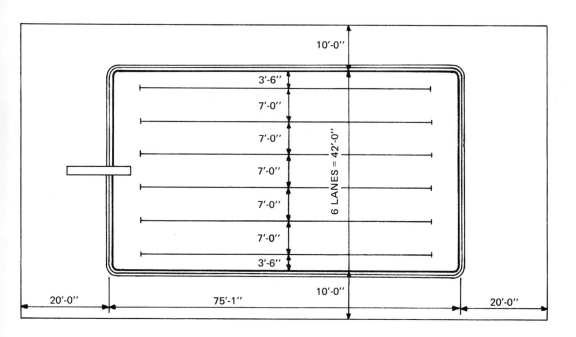

Figure 12–36. Specifications for a six-lane pool. (Courtesy Oliver & Smith, AIA, Norfolk, Virginia.)

LESSON ONE

PERFORMANCE OBJECTIVES:

Psychomotor. The student exhibits the proper way of bobbing by holding his breath and remaining under water for three seconds.

Cognitive. Using the films and instructions of the teacher, the student describes in writing the importance of bobbing.

Affective. The student exhibits understanding of his "buddy's" fear of water and helps him to "bob" properly.

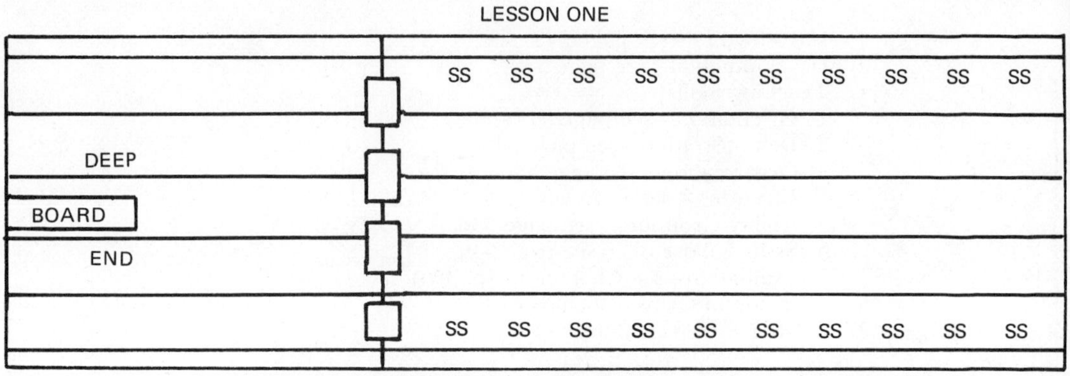

LESSON ONE

	SS	SS	SS	SS	SS	SS	SS	SS	SS	SS
DEEP										
BOARD										
END										
	SS	SS	SS	SS	SS	SS	SS	SS	SS	SS

Figure 12–37. Dispelling fear of water.

The entire class of 40 students is grouped in pairs ("buddy system"). The students enter the shallow water and practice "bobbing" or submerging to dispel the fear of water. This is done in a leisurely manner without pressure, since the fear of water is one of the biggest impediments in teaching swimming. Once students have become accustomed to the water and no longer fear it, they should begin to practice rhythmical breathing.

LESSON TWO

PERFORMANCE OBJECTIVES:

Psychomotor. The student demonstrates the correct form in floating by pushing from the side of the pool and floating at least 30 seconds.

Cognitive. The student shows his knowledge of floating by scoring eight correct answers out of 10 in a true or false test.

Affective. The student shows respect for the teacher by following his instructions in floating the requested distance without complaining.

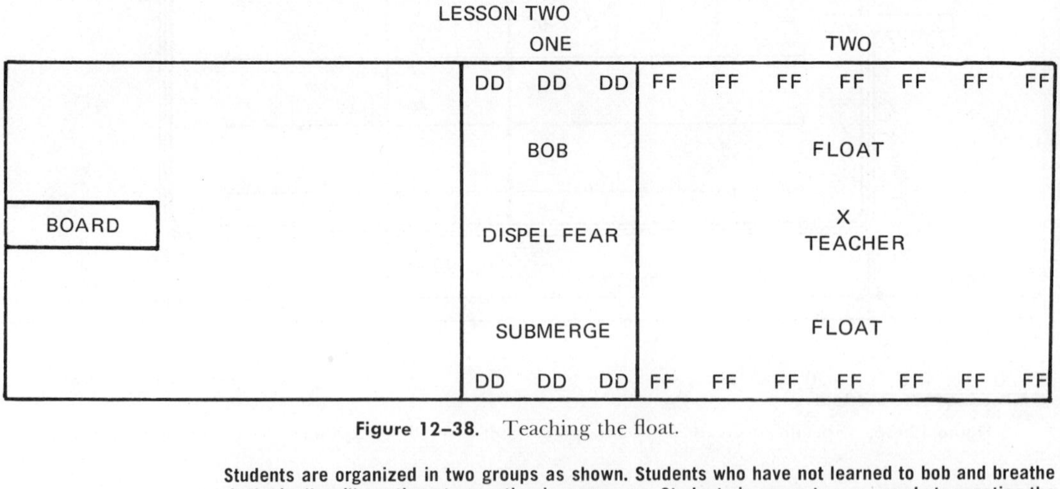

LESSON TWO

	ONE			TWO						
	DD DD DD	FF	FF	FF	FF	FF	FF	FF
BOARD	BOB		FLOAT
	DISPEL FEAR		X TEACHER
	SUBMERGE		FLOAT
	DD DD DD	FF	FF	FF	FF	FF	FF	FF

Figure 12–38. Teaching the float.

Students are organized in two groups as shown. Students who have not learned to bob and breathe rhythmically will continue to practice in group one. Students in group two are ready to practice the dead man's float by holding their breath and pushing off from the side of the pool with arms outstretched. Breathing may be practiced in conjunction with the floating procedure. Students in group one practice floating as they improve in the bobbing and submerging. Because of lack of proper buoyancy, all students may not be able to float without slight arm and leg movements. However, practicing floating is important in preparing for swimming.

LESSON THREE

PERFORMANCE OBJECTIVES:

Psychomotor. The student demonstrates the flutter kick by holding his breath, grasping the edge of the pool and with knees straight executing the flutter kick for 15 seconds.

Cognitive. By answering correctly the statements on a true-false test, the student demonstrates his knowledge of the flutter kick.

Affective. Overcoming the fear of water, the student performs the flutter kick without hesitation.

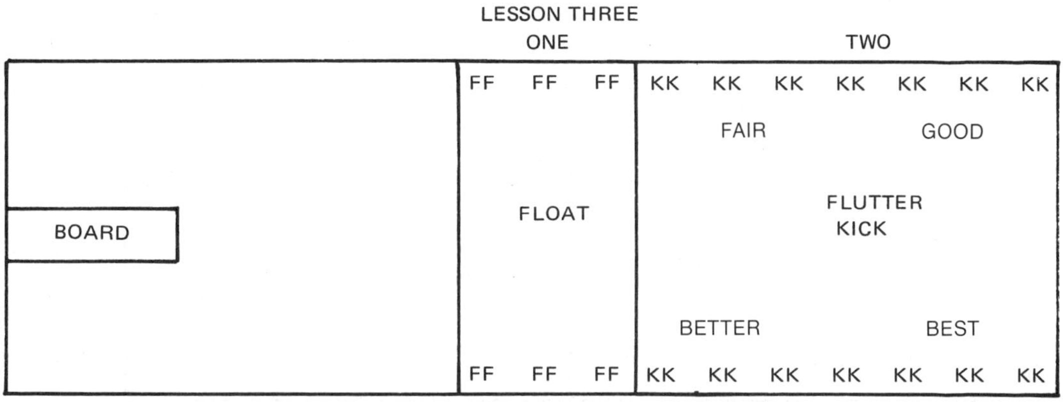

LESSON THREE

	ONE			TWO							
	FF	FF	FF	KK	KK	KK	KK	KK	KK	KK	
					FAIR			GOOD			
		FLOAT				FLUTTER					
BOARD						KICK					
					BETTER			BEST			
	FF	FF	FF	KK	KK	KK	KK	KK	KK	KK	

Figure 12–39. Teaching the flutter kick.

Students are grouped in two groups as shown. Students in group one continue practicing the float (FF) and as they improve they advance to group two. Students in group two are ready to learn the flutter kick (KK), and are divided into two ability groups. Students grasp the edge of the pool and practice the flutter kick first with the head out of water and then with it under water. They advance as they improve.

LESSON FOUR

PERFORMANCE OBJECTIVES:

Psychomotor. The student demonstrates how to push off from the pool and by using the flutter kick propels himself the width of the pool.

Cognitive. By observing his classmates, the student displays his knowledge of the push-off by pointing to incorrect procedures.

Affective. The student shows respect for a teacher who may lack confidence in demonstrating the push-off.

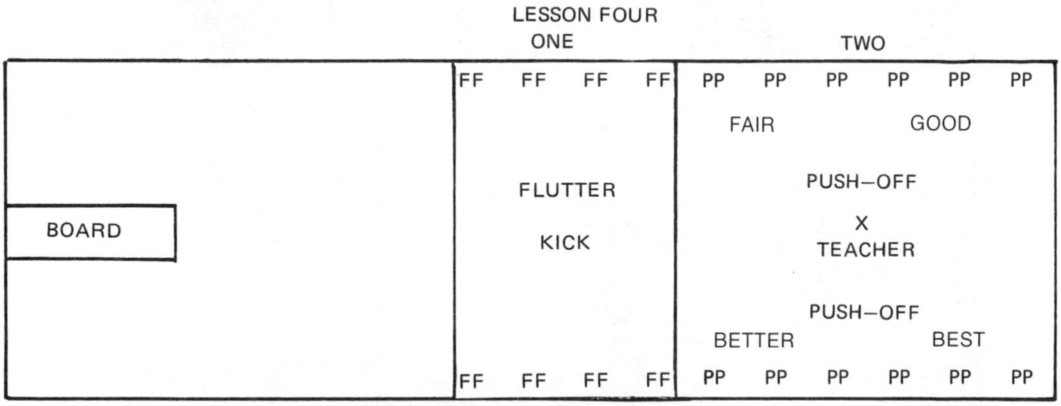

LESSON FOUR

	ONE				TWO					
	FF	FF	FF	FF	PP	PP	PP	PP	PP	PP
						FAIR			GOOD	
		FLUTTER					PUSH–OFF			
BOARD							X			
		KICK					TEACHER			
							PUSH–OFF			
						BETTER			BEST	
	FF	FF	FF	FF	PP	PP	PP	PP	PP	PP

Figure 12–40. Teaching the push-off.

Students are placed in two groups as shown. Students in group one (FF) continue to practice the flutter kick, and as they improve they advance to group two. Students in group two are ready to learn the push-off (PP) and are divided into four ability groups. One student from each of the pairs (PP) takes a deep breath and pushes off with outstretched arms and with his head under water. The flutter kick is executed vigorously as the pupils try to travel the width of the pool. Finally, they push off, flutter, and use two or three strokes with their arms. They advance as they improve.

LESSON FIVE

PERFORMANCE OBJECTIVES:

Psychomotor. The student demonstrates the correct form in the crawl stroke by coordinating the arms and legs.

Cognitive. The student demonstrates his knowledge of the crawl stroke by comparing the form of classmates with films shown in the class.

Affective. The student shows sympathy for a classmate who has trouble mastering the crawl stroke.

LESSON FIVE

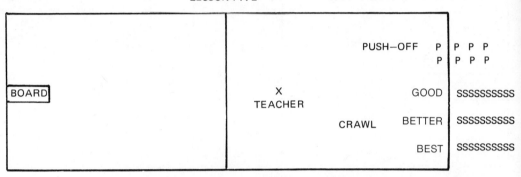

Figure 12–41. Teaching the crawl stroke.

The class is organized in two groups as shown. The students who failed to execute the push-off in the preceding lesson continue to practice. Those who learned the push-off are ready to practice the crawl with the first student in each group swimming to the teacher, to the side of the pool, and out. This goes on with the push-off group advancing to the crawl group as they improve. Students advance from the fair group to the best group as they improve.

Figure 12–42. The use of the buddy system in teaching swimming is essential for safe and effective instruction. (Courtesy Los Angeles Public Schools.)

Teaching Track Skills

GENERAL OBJECTIVES:

A. Psychomotor. The students will demonstrate the correct form in the various track events as shown in the audiovisual aids used in class.

B. Cognitive. The student will describe in writing the form recommended for the various track events.

C. Affective. The students will demonstrate their ability to:

Control emotions under stress.

Show good sportsmanship.

Exhibit team loyalty.

Accept responsibility.

Assume leadership.

Respect decisions of officials.

I. HISTORY OF TRACK

(See references at end of chapter.)

II. VALUES OF TRACK

Development of speed, strength, skill and endurance

Development of individual initiative

Carry-over value (immediate)

III. RULES

IV. SAFETY PRECAUTIONS

Always warm up before participating in any track event.

Do not jump when someone is in the pit.

Do not run hurdles back to starting line.

Do not stand in front of shot-put—stay behind while waiting.

V. EQUIPMENT NEEDED

Ten starting blocks

Ten hurdles

Two jumping pits (filled with sawdust)

Ten old bowling balls (used for shots)

Films and strips

Texts

VI. BASIC SKILLS

Sprints	*Broad Jump*	*Shot-put*
Start	Approach	Holding the shot
Body angle	Take-off	Stance in circle
Leg action	Arm action	Travel
Arm action	Leg action	Release
Stride		Follow-through
Finish		

Hurdles	*High Jump*	*Relays*
Form	Approach	Shuttle
Low hurdles	Check marks	Standard (220 to 440)
High hurdles	Form	
Sprint form	Arm action	
(above)	Leg action	
	Roll	
	Landing	

VII. TEACHING SKILLS PROCEDURES

A. Introductory—see page 342

B. Developmental—see page 342

C. Teaching Skills
1. Orientation—see page 345
2. Demonstration—see page 345
3. Organization—see page 346
4. Inventory—see page 346
5. Ability Grouping—see page 346
6. Skills Laboratory—see page 346
7. Evaluation—see Chapter 14 (p. 346)
   (made in terms of behavior)

D. Closing—see page 346

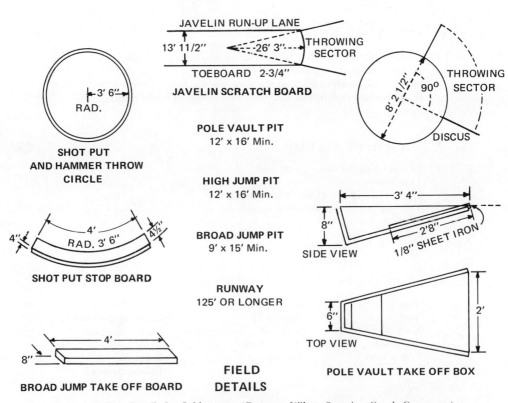

Figure 12-43. Details for field events. (Courtesy Wilson Sporting Goods Company.)

LESSON ONE

PERFORMANCE OBJECTIVES:

Psychomotor. The student demonstrates the correct form of the crouch start by employing the proper action of arms and legs for 25 yards as described by the teacher in class.

Cognitive. The student exhibits his knowledge of the proper technique in sprinting by drawing pictures of the sprint sequence using observations of varsity sprinters as a source.

Affective. In a 50-yard sprint, the student, after losing the dash, congratulates the winner.

LESSON ONE

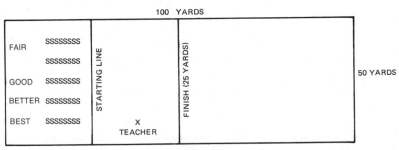

Figure 12–44. Teaching the skills of starting.

Students are placed in five lines as shown (S). On commands from the teacher, the first student in each line takes the mark! Get set! Go! They run to the 25-yard finish line, go outside the running area, and stride back to the end of their lines. This goes on as long as the teacher feels it necessary. At the end of the period pupils run 50 yards instead of 25 yards. Students advance from the fair group to the best group as they improve.

LESSON TWO

PERFORMANCE OBJECTIVES:

Psychomotor. The student exhibits the correct form in running a hurdle by using the standard number of steps and by employing the hurdling form described in class, two out of three times.

Cognitive. By placing a check mark on one of several pictures, the student demonstrates his knowledge of correct form in hurdling.

Affective. The student after winning a hurdle race displays kindness to the loser by encouraging him to practice more.

LESSON TWO

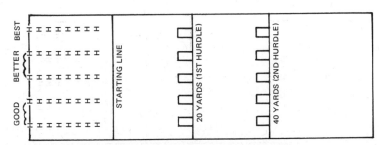

Figure 12–45. Teaching hurdling.

Students are placed in five groups of eight pupils (H) as shown. The first student in each group using the crouch start jumps the first hurdle, leaves the hurdling area, and strides back to the end of his line. After this has been done several times the students start and jump both hurdles, returning to the end of their lines. Finally, they jump both hurdles and run 100 yards. Pupils are grouped by ability as shown, and advance as they improve.

LESSON THREE

PERFORMANCE OBJECTIVES:

Psychomotor. Using instruction acquired in the class, the student executes the hitch kick in the long jump correctly, three out of six times.

Cognitive. The student exhibits his knowledge of the long jump by describing its advantages to the class.

Affective. The student demonstrates his respect for the teacher by abiding by the safety rules which were described in class.

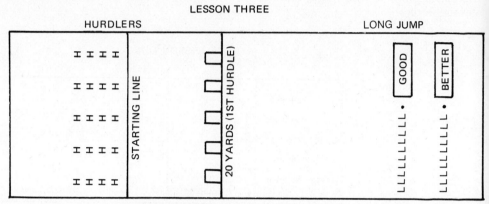

Figure 12–46. Teaching the long jump.

Students are placed in two sections as shown. Those who did not learn how to hurdle continue practicing (H). The long jumpers (B) form lines 25 yards from the take-off board and practice jumping. The hurdlers advance to the long jump as they improve and the long jumpers advance from the good group to the better group.

LESSON FOUR

PERFORMANCE OBJECTIVES:

Psychomotor. Using the demonstration made in the class as a guide, the student will exhibit the correct form in the Western roll high jump by clearing a 4-foot bar, two out of three times.

Cognitive. The student, by describing the correct sequence in the Western roll high jump, demonstrates his knowledge of the event.

Affective. After missing a 4-foot height in the Western roll the student displays emotional control by refraining from showing anger.

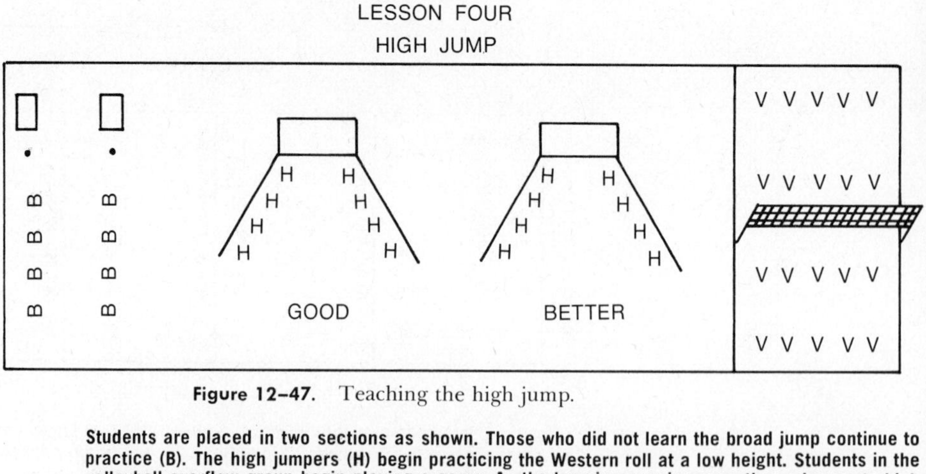

LESSON FOUR

HIGH JUMP

Figure 12–47. Teaching the high jump.

Students are placed in two sections as shown. Those who did not learn the broad jump continue to practice (B). The high jumpers (H) begin practicing the Western roll at a low height. Students in the volleyball overflow group begin playing a game. As the long jumpers improve, they advance to high jumping. The volleyball groups change with the high jumpers at the discretion of the teacher. Emphasis is on form and not height. Students advance from the good group to the better group as they improve.

LESSON FIVE

PERFORMANCE OBJECTIVES:

Psychomotor.   The student will demonstrate the correct form in putting the shot as described in class, two out of three times.

Cognitive.   The student demonstrates his knowledge of putting the shot by describing to the class in slow motion the sequence involved.

Affective.   The student shows respect for the teacher by following the safety precautions discussed in class.

LESSON FIVE

					V V V V V
NO ONE STANDS BEYOND THIS LINE					V V V V V
O	O	O	O		
S	S	S	S		V V V V V
S	S	S	S		
S	S	S	S		
S	S	S	S		
S	S	S	S		
GOOD	BETTER	BEST			V V V V V

Figure 12–48.   Teaching the shot-put.

Students are placed in two sections as shown. The shot-putters (S) form four groups and, using old bowling balls, begin to practice. The first player in each line steps in the circle and puts the shot. All four students put balls at the same time, run, and bring them back at the same time. They are grouped by ability as shown, and advance as they improve. The shot-putters change with the volleyball groups at the discretion of the teacher.

Figure 12–49.   Knowing how to start properly is a basic skill in track.

Teaching Rhythms

GENERAL OBJECTIVES:

A. Psychomotor.   After studying a film on rhythms, students demonstrate correct form in these movements.

B. Cognitive.   The students demonstrate their knowledge of rhythms by writing two-page essays on these activities.

C. Affective.   The students will demonstrate their ability to:

Control emotions under stress.
Show good sportsmanship.
Exhibit team loyalty in demonstrations.
Accept responsibility.
Assume leadership.

I. HISTORY OF RHYTHMS

(See references at end of chapter.)

II. VALUES OF RHYTHMS

Has tremendous social value
Develops poise, grace, and confidence
Develops physiological fitness
Provides emotional release of tension

III. SAFETY PRECAUTIONS

Intricate movements should be taught progressively.
All pupils should warm up before beginning movements.

IV. EQUIPMENT NEEDED

Record player with microphone
Records
Tomtoms
Drums
Piano

V. TYPES OF RHYTHMS

Basic movements: Running   Hopping
                   Walking   Skipping
                   Leaping   Sliding
                   Jumping   Galloping
Folk dancing
Square dancing
Modern dancing
Social dancing

VI. TEACHING SKILLS PROCEDURES

A. Introductory—see page 342
B. Developmental—see page 342
C. Teaching Skills
    1. Orientation—see page 345
    2. Demonstration—see page 345
    3. Organization—see page 346
    4. Inventory—see page 346
    5. Ability Grouping—see page 346
    6. Skills Laboratory—see page 346
    7. Evaluation—see Chapter 14 (p. 346)
        (made in terms of behavior)
D. Closing—see page 346

Figure 12–50. A folding partition provides a practical teaching station for teaching modern dance. An auxiliary station (shown through the small door in the background) is also adequate.

LESSON ONE

PERFORMANCE OBJECTIVES:

Psychomotor. The student, after viewing a film in basic dance steps, demonstrates the proper form in leaping, three out of five times.

Cognitive. The student exhibits his knowledge of the basic dance movements by sketching them on the chalkboard for the class.

Affective. The student exhibits inhibition by controlling his temper when the teacher strongly criticizes him for a poor performance.

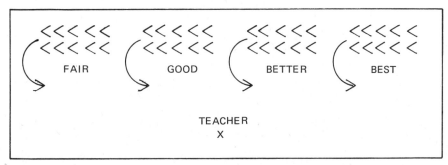

Figure 12–51. Basic dance movements.

Teaching dance movements to large groups does not present a procedural problem, because it is an activity that is easily adapted to large groups. Teaching procedures for large rhythmic groups are generally known. In teaching basic movements the class is organized as shown. Students form two lines and execute the various movements around the gymnasium. They may or may not hold hands. Students should be classified by ability as shown and advance from the fair group to the best group as they improve.

LESSON TWO

PERFORMANCE OBJECTIVES:

Psychomotor.   After listening to a muscial number, the student demonstrates the correct form in the allemande movement, two out of three times.

Cognitive.   The student demonstrates his knowledge of square dancing by writing a paper.

Affective.   The student demonstrates positive character traits developed in the class by assisting his awkward partner in performing an intricate movement.

LESSON TWO

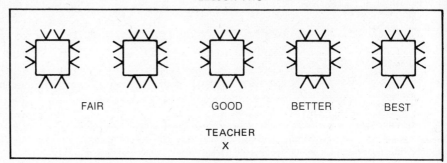

Figure 12–52.   Square dance formations.

Teaching square dancing does not present procedural problems. There are many formations that may be used. When the quadrille formation is used, students may be placed as shown. They should advance from the fair group to the best group as they improve.

LESSON THREE

PERFORMANCE OBJECTIVES:

Psychomotor.   The student demonstrates correct form in the mazurka, which was taught in the class, three out of seven times.

Cognitive.   The student exhibits his knowledge of folk dancing by relating its history to the class.

Affective.   The student shows respect for the teacher when corrected for a poor performance.

LESSON THREE

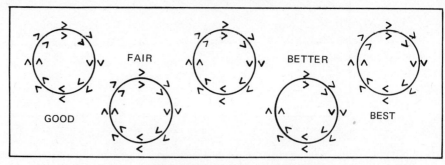

Figure 12–53.   Folk dance formations.

There are many variations in the formations for teaching folk dancing. It was pointed out that teaching the various dance forms presents no procedural problem. The procedures shown here can be used for all dances involving double circles. Students should be placed in ability groups as shown, and advance as they improve.

LESSON FOUR

PERFORMANCE OBJECTIVES:

Psychomotor. The student, after studying a film, demonstrates correct form in the waltz step, four out of eight times.

Cognitive. The student exhibits his knowledge of the waltz by writing a paper describing the evaluation of this step.

Affective. The student assumes leadership in performing the waltz with his partner without showing embarrassment.

LESSON FOUR

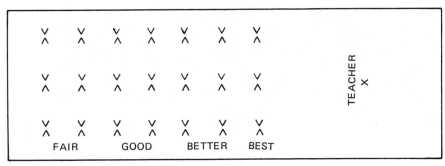

Figure 12–54. Formation for social dancing.

In teaching social dancing students may be grouped in pairs as shown. They may progress from the fair group to the best group as they improve. Teaching social dancing does not present a procedural problem.

LESSON FIVE

PERFORMANCE OBJECTIVES:

Psychomotor. After watching a professional demonstrate in class, the student exhibits correct form in flexion, three out of six times.

Cognitive. The student displays knowledge of modern dance by describing it before the class.

Affective. The student overcomes a feeling of embarrassment in performing the steps of modern dance by seeking assistance from a classmate.

LESSON FIVE

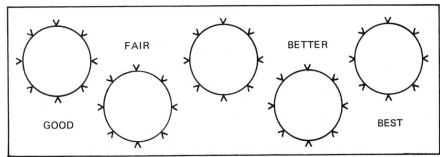

Figure 12–55. Modern dance formations.

Procedures in fundamental forms of modern dance may be approached in two ways: (1) Group the entire class as shown in lesson four and teach the same movement to all or (2) break the class into several groups and allow them to interpret the music as they feel it. The figure above shows a class divided into five groups with eight in each group. They will interpret the same musical composition as they feel it. Students advance from the fair group to the best group as they improve.

Figure 12–56. Using balls makes modern dance more interesting. (Courtesy Richmond Senior High School, Richmond, Indiana.)

Teaching Wrestling Skills

GENERAL OBJECTIVES:

A. Psychomotor. Students execute correctly the intricate techniques of wrestling, which were studied in class, several times.

B. Cognitive. Students exhibit knowledge of wrestling by identifying the various holds when they are flashed on the screen.

C. Affective. The students will demonstrate their ability to:

Control emotions under stress.
Show good sportsmanship.
Exhibit team loyalty.
Accept responsibility.
Assume leadership.
Respect decisions of officials.

I. HISTORY OF WRESTLING

(See references at end of chapter.)

II. VALUES OF WRESTLING

Has great fitness value
Develops strength, speed, skill and endurance
Immediate carry-over values
Develops confidence
Tremendous self-defense value

III. RULES AND SCORING

IV. SAFETY PRECAUTIONS

Students should be matched by weight and ability.
In physical education classes, wrestling should be limited to maneuvers from the referee's position.
Mats should be adequately padded and cleaned frequently.

V. EQUIPMENT NEEDED

Mats   Covers

VI. BASIC SKILLS

Referee's position   Pin holds
Breakdowns   Escapes
  Advantage   Counters
  Disadvantage

VII. TEACHING SKILLS PROCEDURES

   A. Introductory—see page 342
   B. Developmental—see page 342
   C. Teaching Skills
      1. Orientation—see page 345
      2. Demonstration—see page 345
      3. Organization—see page 346
      4. Inventory—see page 346
      5. Ability Grouping—see page 346
      6. Skills Laboratory—see page 346
      7. Evaluation—see Chapter 14 (p. 346)
        (made in terms of behavior)
   D. Closing—see page 346

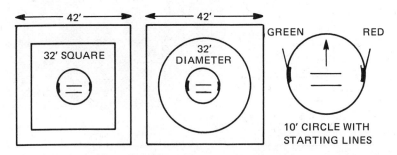

MINIMUM MAT SIZE PROVIDES FOR A CIRCLE WITH A DIAMETER OF 28′ AS A LEGAL WRESTLING AREA OR A 24′ SQUARE WRESTLING AREA WITH A MAT AREA OF AT LEAST 5′ IN WIDTH EXTENDING ROUND WRESTLING AREA PROPER.

Figure 12–57. Wrestling mat. (Armbruster, David, *et al.: Basic Skills in Sports for Men and Women,* 5th ed. St. Louis: C. V. Mosby Company, 1971, p. 372.)

LESSON ONE

PERFORMANCE OBJECTIVES:

  Psychomotor. The student, having watched a demonstration, correctly executes the spinning movement, circling his partner 30 seconds without stopping.

  Cognitive. The student will describe the spinning maneuver using the chalk board to illustrate it.

  Affective. The student will protest to the teacher when violations of the safety rules occur.

Figure 12–58. Spinning.

Teaching wrestling skills does not present a procedural problem. The average class can be accommodated on the standard mat. Students should be matched according to ability and weight, as shown in the figure, and should advance as they improve.

LESSON TWO

PERFORMANCE OBJECTIVES:

Psychomotor. The student, after observing the referee's position, will demonstrate it with a classmate, two out of three times.

Cognitive. The student will draw a diagram of an official wrestling mat listing the correct dimensions.

Affective. The student will display in class a positive attitude toward the teacher.

LESSON TWO

Figure 12–59. Referee's position.

Wrestling maneuvers from the referee's position are recommended for physical education classes because they are safer and require less space. In the plan above, students are arranged around the mat in pairs according to ability. They advance from the fair group to the best group as they improve.

LESSON THREE

PERFORMANCE OBJECTIVES:

Psychomotor. The student, after observing a demonstration, performs the rear-wrist breakdown correctly, three out of five times.

Cognitive. The student will explain in sequential order the steps in executing the rear-wrist breakdown.

Affective. The student will not lose his temper when pinned.

LESSON THREE

Figure 12–60. Maneuver from position of advantage.

From the referee's position there are many breakdowns that may be used. The one shown above is the rear-wrist breakdown. Students should practice this hold and, at the discretion of the teacher, change from the position of advantage to the position of disadvantage. They progress from the fair group to the best group at the discretion of the teacher.

LESSON FOUR
PERFORMANCE OBJECTIVES:

Psychomotor. The student, after observing a film, will demonstrate correctly the set-out maneuver, three out of five times.

Cognitive. The student will write a paper describing the correct form in the set-out and switch maneuver.

Affective. The student will not exhibit rowdiness in class while learning the set-out and switch maneuver.

LESSON FOUR

Figure 12–61. Maneuver from position of disadvantage.

As in the maneuvers from the position of advantage, there are many movements from the position of disadvantage. The set-out and switch maneuver shown above is one illustration. Students are grouped by ability in pairs and advance from the fair group to the best group as they improve.

LESSON FIVE
PERFORMANCE OBJECTIVES:

Psychomotor. The student, using the information acquired in class, correctly executes the half-nelson and rear leg combination, three out of five times.

Cognitive. The student will describe to the class in sequential order the steps involved in the half-nelson.

Affective. The student will display respect for the teacher by reporting to class on time.

LESSON FIVE

Figure 12–62. Pin holds (half-Nelson and near-leg combination).

There comes a moment in a match when the opponent may be pinned. There are many holds that may be used to do this, one of which is shown above. Students are grouped as shown and progress from the fair group to the best group as they improve.

Figure 12–63. An entire class may be taught wrestling skills effectively when students are grouped properly.

Teaching Basketball Skills

GENERAL OBJECTIVES:
  A. Psychomotor. Students will demonstrate the correct form in the various basketball skills studied in class, several times.
  B. Cognitive. Students will demonstrate knowledge of basketball by identifying the various shots when demonstrated by other students.
  C. Affective. The students will demonstrate their ability to:
       Control emotions under stress.
       Show good sportsmanship.
       Exhibit team loyalty.
       Accept responsibility.
       Assume leadership.
       Respect decisions of officials.

  I. HISTORY OF BASKETBALL

    (See references at end of chapter.)

 II. VALUES OF BASKETBALL

    Physiological development
    Develops skill, speed, and endurance
    Immediate carry-over value
    Develops teamwork
    Contributes to emotional stability

III. RULES, SCORING AND STRATEGY

    (See references at end of chapter.)

IV. SAFETY PRECAUTIONS

    Conduct warm-up drills before activity to prevent pulled muscles.
    Hold balls when whistle blows.
    Roll balls on the floor when asked for by instructor or student instructor.
    Report all injuries, blisters, floor burns, and bruises to the instructor.
    Have properly fitted shoes.
    Note any obstructions on the floor.
    Be conscientious about training rules; take care of your body.

V. EQUIPMENT NEEDED

Ten balls   Films and strips
Six baskets   Texts
Court (inside or
     outside)

VI. BASIC SKILLS

Dribbling   Guarding
Passing   Pivoting
Rules and scoring   Strategy
Shooting

VII. TEACHING SKILLS PROCEDURES

A. Introductory—see page 342
B. Developmental—see page 342
C. Teaching Skills
     1. Orientation—see page 345
     2. Demonstration—see page 345
     3. Organization—see page 346
     4. Inventory—see page 346
     5. Ability Grouping—see page 346
     6. Skills Laboratory—see page 346
     7. Evaluation—see Chapter 14 (p. 346)
          (made in terms of behavior)
D. Closing—see page 346

BASKETBALL COURT DIAGRAM

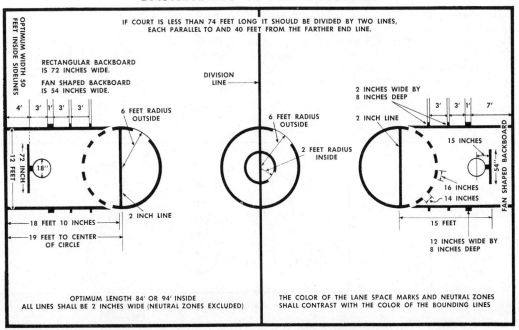

Figure 12–64. Official dimensions of a basketball court. (Courtesy of The Athletic Institute.)

LESSON ONE

PERFORMANCE OBJECTIVES:

Psychomotor. The students will demonstrate the correct form in dribbling by running the length of the court while dribbling the ball, without losing possession.

Cognitive. The student will draw a diagram of a basketball court listing the dimensions and height of the goal.

Affective. The student will wait his turn in the relay race without creating a disturbance.

LESSON ONE

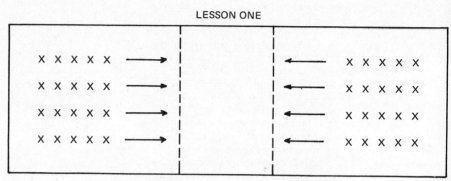

Figure 12–65. Teaching the dribble.

Students are arranged in eight lines of five each as shown. Each line has a ball. The first student in each line dribbles to the line and back, passing the ball to the next dribbler and returning to the end of the line.

LESSON TWO

PERFORMANCE OBJECTIVES:

Psychomotor. The student will demonstrate the correct form in the bounce pass, four out of five times.

Cognitive. The student will write a description of the bounce pass.

Affective. While waiting for his turn to pass the ball, the student will refrain from interfering with class procedure.

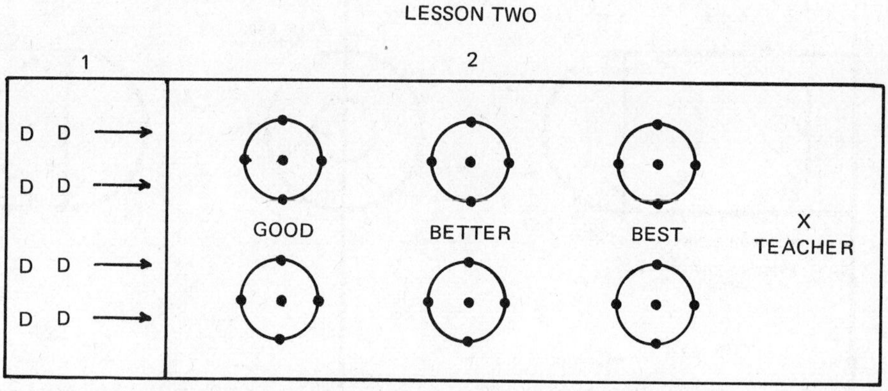

LESSON TWO

Figure 12–66. Teaching the pass.

The class is divided into two sections as shown. In section one the students who failed to learn how to dribble (D) continue to practice dribbling to the line and back. The students who are ready to learn the passes are grouped in circles of five. The various passes are used with the inside student passing to the outside students, who pass back; this should be done in standing formation. Then the outside students should walk around the circle and finally run as the passing routine continues. Students should progress from the dribble to the pass, and they should progress from the good to better and best as they improve.

LESSON THREE

PERFORMANCE OBJECTIVES:

Psychomotor. The student, using the form taught in class, will shoot a basketball through the goal seven out of 10 times, standing on the foul throw line.

Cognitive. The student will describe the form he uses in foul shooting and list the advantages of it.

Affective. After failing to score the required number of foul shots, the student demonstrates tenacity of purpose by practicing after school.

LESSON THREE

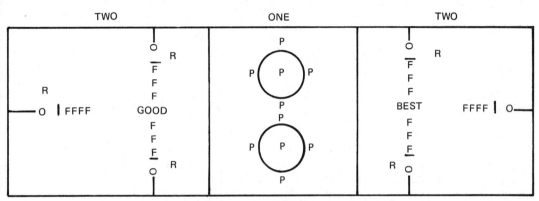

Figure 12–67. The foul shot.

Students are organized in two sections as shown. Section one consists of the students who failed to learn the pass (P). They continue to practice. Students in section two are ready to learn the foul shot (F) with the retrievers (R) passing the ball back. They may be grouped by ability as shown and advance as they improve. The passers advance to the foul shot lines as they improve.

LESSON FOUR

PERFORMANCE OBJECTIVES:

Psychomotor. The student, using the set shot, will shoot the basketball through the goal, seven out of 10 times, standing 20 feet from the goal.

Cognitive. The student will describe the situations in which the set shot would be used.

Affective. The student displays willingness to assist other students in mastering the form in the set shot.

LESSON FOUR

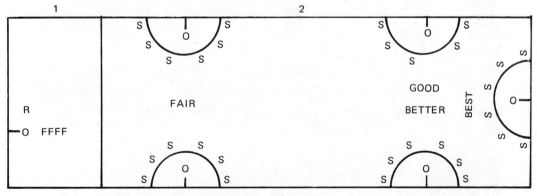

Figure 12–68. The set shot.

Students are placed in two sections as shown. In section one the students who did not learn the foul shot (F) continue to practice. In section two, students who have mastered the foul shot practice the set shot and progress from the fair to the best group as they improve. The students in the foul shot advance to the set shot group as they improve.

LESSON FIVE

PERFORMANCE OBJECTIVES:

Psychomotor. The student will execute the correct placement of the ball on the backboard, four out of five times.

Cognitive. The student will describe in sequence the steps involved in the lay-up shot.

Affective. The student recognizes the need for following safety precautions in executing the lay-up shot.

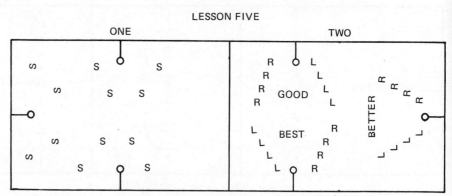

Figure 12–69. Teaching the lay-up shot.

Students are grouped in two sections as shown. Those who failed to perform the set shot are placed in section one (S) and continue to practice. Students ready to learn the lay-up shot are placed in section two with L's executing the lay-up shot and R's retrieving and passing to L's. Both L's and R's run to the end of the opposite lines. In the next step the ball is shot from the left side of the basket using the same procedure. Students advance from the good to the best group as they improve.

Figure 12–70. Dividing a class into small groups by ability provides greater opportunity for individualized instruction.

Teaching Volleyball Skills

GENERAL OBJECTIVES:
A. **Psychomotor.** The student will demonstrate the complex skills involved in the game of volleyball.
B. **Cognitive.** The student will demonstrate his knowledge of volleyball by identifying and describing the various techniques as they are flashed on the screen.
C. **Affective.** The students will demonstrate their ability to:
    Control emotions under stress.
    Show good sportsmanship.
    Exhibit team loyalty.
    Accept responsibility.
    Assume leadership.
    Respect decisions of officials.

I. HISTORY OF VOLLEYBALL
(See references at end of chapter.)

II. VALUES OF VOLLEYBALL
Emotional release
Recreational and carry-over value
Aid to good posture
Developmental value

III. RULES, SCORING AND STRATEGY
(See references at end of chapter.)

IV. SAFETY PRECAUTIONS
Conduct vigorous warm-up exercises before the instruction.
Assign pupils carefully to areas to prevent collisions.
Organize practice around spikers, passers, and retrievers.
Provide nonslippery playing surfaces.
Clear area of benches, chairs, and other obstacles.
Provide correct instruction in footwork to prevent sprained ankles.
Require proper clothing and shoes.

V. EQUIPMENT NEEDED
Three nets or rope
Concrete area, 80 × 120 feet (turf area may be used)
Inside area
30 balls
Films and strips
Texts

VI. BASIC SKILLS
Passing
Serving
Set-up and spike
Blocking and net recovery
Strategy
Rules and scoring

VII. TEACHING SKILLS PROCEDURES
A. Introductory—see page 342
B. Developmental—see page 342
C. Teaching Skills
  1. Orientation—see page 345
  2. Demonstration—see page 345
  3. Organization—see page 346
  4. Inventory—see page 346
  5. Ability Grouping—see page 346
  6. Skills Laboratory—see page 346
  7. Evaluation—see Chapter 14 (p. 346)
    (made in terms of behavior)
D. Closing—see page 346

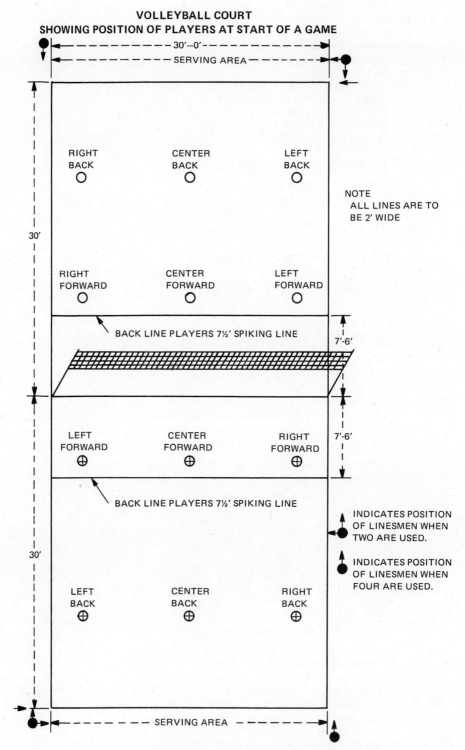

VOLLEYBALL COURT
SHOWING POSITION OF PLAYERS AT START OF A GAME

Figure 12–71. Volleyball court. (Courtesy of The Athletic Institute.)

LESSON ONE

PERFORMANCE OBJECTIVES:

Psychomotor. The student will execute as many passes over a line on the wall as possible in 30 seconds.

Cognitive. The student orally describes the volleyball pass to the class, pointing out the important features involved.

Affective. The student recognizes the variance in performance of his classmates and volunteers to assist where he is needed.

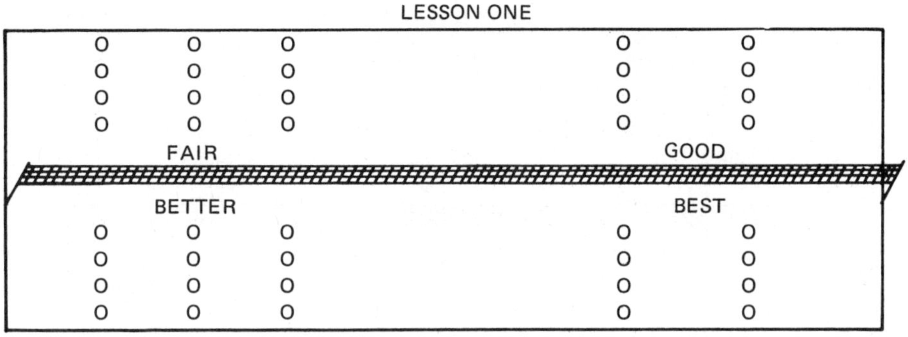

LESSON ONE

O	O	O		O	O
O	O	O		O	O
O	O	O		O	O
O	O	O		O	O
	FAIR			GOOD	

	BETTER			BEST	
O	O	O		O	O
O	O	O		O	O
O	O	O		O	O
O	O	O		O	O

Figure 12–72. Teaching the pass.

Four students are placed in each group – a total of ten groups; five groups are on each long side of the gymnasium, single file, facing the wall. The first student in each line passes the ball high on the wall and runs to the end of the line. The second student replaces the first and passes the ball, followed by the third, and so on until all students have practiced sufficiently. Students are grouped by ability. Alternate Plan: Students face each other across the net in the same formation. The first student in each line passes the ball over the net and runs to the end of the line. The first person in each line across the net returns the ball and runs to the end of the line. This is done many times, the object being to keep the ball from falling to the floor. Another plan is to divide the class into ten circles with four students in each circle. One student of each circle stands in the center and passes the ball to the outside students, who pass it back to him. In both plans students advance as they improve.

LESSON TWO

PERFORMANCE OBJECTIVES:

Psychomotor. The student will serve the volleyball over an 8-foot net, seven out of 10 times, using the overhand serve.

Cognitive. The student describes the merits of the overhand serve to the class.

Affective. The student cooperates with the teacher by reporting to class on time.

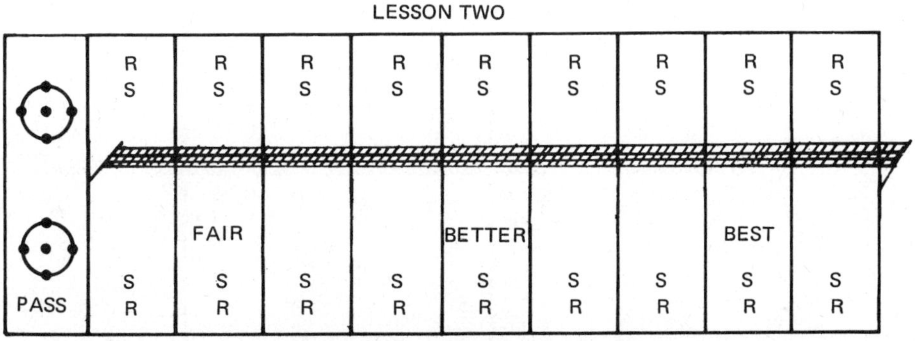

LESSON TWO

	R S	R S	R S	R S	R S	R S	R S	R S	R S
	FAIR			BETTER			BEST		
PASS	S R	S R	S R	S R	S R	S R	S R	S R	S R

Figure 12–73. Teaching the serve.

On each side of the net or rope there are ten groups with two in each group (group one has five on each side). The two students directly across from the other (S) will be serving to each other; the others are retrievers (R). The servers change places with the retrievers periodically. Students who showed little progress in lesson one are placed in the first group and continue practicing the pass. If space is a problem, the number assigned to each group can be increased. Students progress from fair to best groups.

LESSON THREE

PERFORMANCE OBJECTIVES:

Psychomotor. The student correctly spikes the ball into the opponents' territory, seven out of 10 times.

Cognitive. The student describes his knowledge of the spike to the class by showing two classmates how to execute it.

Affective. The student volunteers to assist the teacher in teaching the spike to the class.

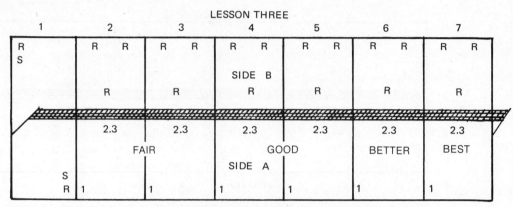

Figure 12–74.   Set-up and spike.

The class is divided into seven groups as shown. Students in group one continue practicing the serve. Students in the remaining groups practice the set-up and spike. The retrievers (R) throw the balls back to the other side. Number 1 passes to number 2, who sets up for number 3, who spikes. The students on side A rotate clockwise after each spike. After sufficient practice, side A pupils become retrievers and side B pupils practice the skill. Students advance as they improve.

LESSON FOUR

PERFORMANCE OBJECTIVES:

Psychomotor. The student successfully blocks the opponents' ball, six out of 10 times.

Cognitive. The student displays emotional control when he fails to block the ball and it hits him on the head.

Affective. The student exhibits cooperation by assisting with the collection of equipment at the end of the period.

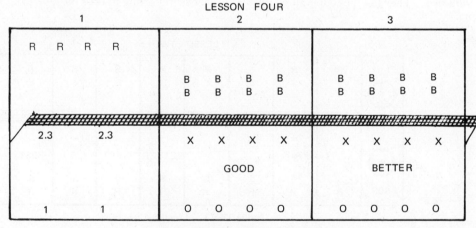

Figure 12–75.   Teaching blocking.

The class is divided into three groups based on the inventory. Students in group 1 continue to practice the set-up and spike, since they showed very little progress in previous lesson. Students in groups 2 and 3 practice the block as follows: O sets up for the spiker X, and B's are the blockers. After practicing these skills sufficiently, the students on both sides of the net change skills. The students practicing the set-up and spike gradually begin practicing the block. Students advance from the good group to the better group as they improve.

LESSON FIVE

PERFORMANCE OBJECTIVES:

Psychomotor. The student successfully removes the ball from the net, three out of six times.

Cognitive. The student, by diagramming on the chalkboard the steps involved in the net recovery, demonstrates his knowledge of the recovery.

Affective. The student assumes leadership in situations such as injury to a boy recovering the ball from the net.

LESSON FIVE

A	B	C	D	E
B B B B	O O X O	O O X O	O O X O	O O X O
X X O O	O X O O FAIR	O X O O GOOD	O X O O BETTER	O X O O BEST

Figure 12–76. Net recovery.

The class is divided into five groups based on the inventory. Students in group A continue to practice blocking, since they showed little progress in previous lesson. Students in B, C, D, and E practice the net recovery as follows: X throws the ball into net and the first O runs forward and recovers to X. X and O rotate clockwise. This practice continues until all pupils show improvement. The students in group A gradually begin practicing the net recovery and advance to group B. Students advance from fair to best as they improve.

Figure 12–77. Ability grouping is essential for effective instruction. Four groups are shown. This arrangement allows the teacher to provide more individualized instruction.

Teaching Touch Football Skills

GENERAL OBJECTIVES:

A. Psychomotor. The student will demonstrate the complex motor skills involved in touch football by performing movements which incorporate these skills.

B. Cognitive. The student will demonstrate his knowledge of touch football by describing the various skills involved in the game.

C. Affective. The students will demonstrate their ability to:

> Control emotions under stress.
> Show good sportsmanship.
> Exhibit team loyalty.
> Accept responsibility.
> Assume leadership.
> Respect decisions of officials.

I. HISTORY OF TOUCH FOOTBALL

(See references at end of chapter.)

II. VALUES OF TOUCH FOOTBALL

Physiological fitness
Carry-over value (immediate)
Develops teamwork
Contributes to emotional stability

III. RULES, SCORING AND STRATEGY

(See references at end of chapter.)

IV. SAFETY PRECAUTIONS

Always supervise the groups.
Do not permit misconduct.
Wear proper uniforms.
Use safe playing areas.
Use simple rules.

V. EQUIPMENT NEEDED

Footballs
Kicking tees

Films and strips
Texts

VI. BASIC SKILLS

Forward passing
Receiving
Kicking
Centering
Ball handling

Running with the ball
Blocking
Offensive stance
Defense

VII. TEACHING SKILLS PROCEDURES

A. Introductory—see page 342
B. Developmental—see page 342
C. Teaching Skills
　1. Orientation—see page 345
　2. Demonstration—see page 345
　3. Organization—see page 346
　4. Inventory—see page 346
　5. Ability Grouping—see page 346
　6. Skills Laboratory—see page 346
　7. Evaluation—see Chapter 14 (p. 346)
　　(made in terms of behavior)
D. Closing—see page 346

FOOTBALL

(11-MAN) MEASURE TO INSIDE EDGE OF BOUNDARY LINES.

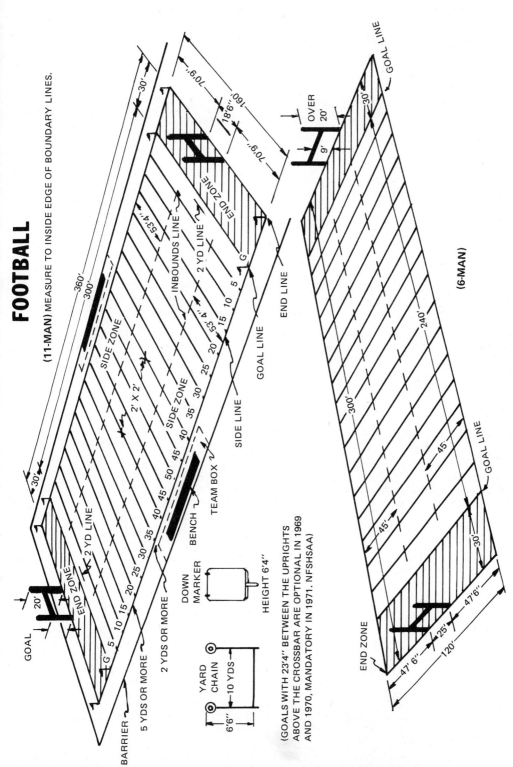

(6-MAN)

Figure 12-78. Football field. (Courtesy Wilson Sporting Goods Company.)

LESSON ONE

PERFORMANCE OBJECTIVES:

Psychomotor. The student demonstrates the correct form in passing, six out of 10 times.

Cognitive. After observing several demonstrations of passing, the student describes the one which is correct.

Affective. The student displays sportsmanship qualities by assisting a classmate who may be poorly coordinated.

LESSON ONE

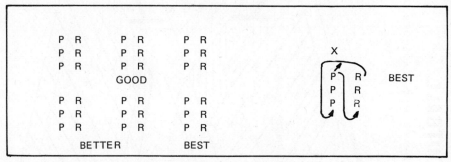

Figure 12–79. Passing and receiving.

The class is divided into seven groups of six students each. The passers (P) pass the ball to the receivers (R) and run to the end of the receivers' line. The receivers receive the ball at X and run to the end of the passers' line. Pupils advance from good to better to best groups as they improve.

LESSON TWO

PERFORMANCE OBJECTIVES:

Psychomotor. The student punts the football into an area marked on the field, six out of 10 times.

Cognitive. The student describes, in proper sequence, the stages of punting the football correctly.

Affective. Having tried unsuccessfully to punt the football in the proper area, the student exhibits self-control by not showing his dissatisfaction.

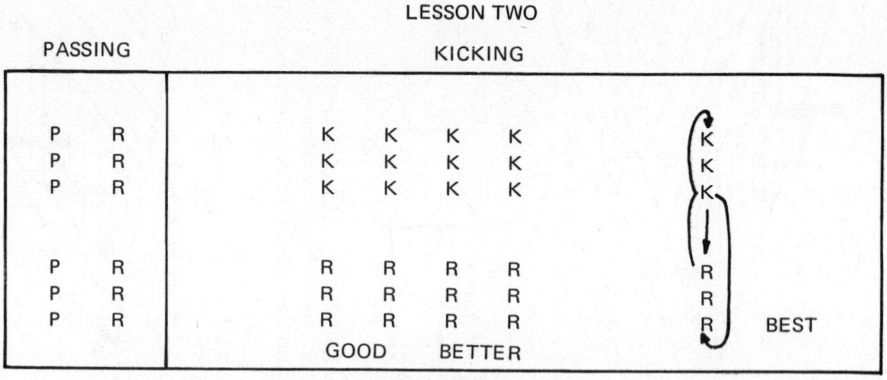

LESSON TWO

Figure 12–80. Teaching the kick.

The class is divided into two sections as shown. Those who did not learn how to pass and receive continue to practice and advance to the kicking group as they improve. The kickers (K) punt the ball to the receivers (R) and run to the end of the receiving line. The receivers catch the ball, run it back to the head of the kicking line, and then run to the end of the line. Students advance from good to better to best as they improve.

LESSON THREE

PERFORMANCE OBJECTIVES:

Psychomotor. The student correctly passes the ball from the center position to the receiver, eight out of 10 times.

Cognitive. The student, after viewing several passes from the center, selects the correct one and describes it to the class.

Affective. The student shows admiration for the classmate who excels in this pass by congratulating him.

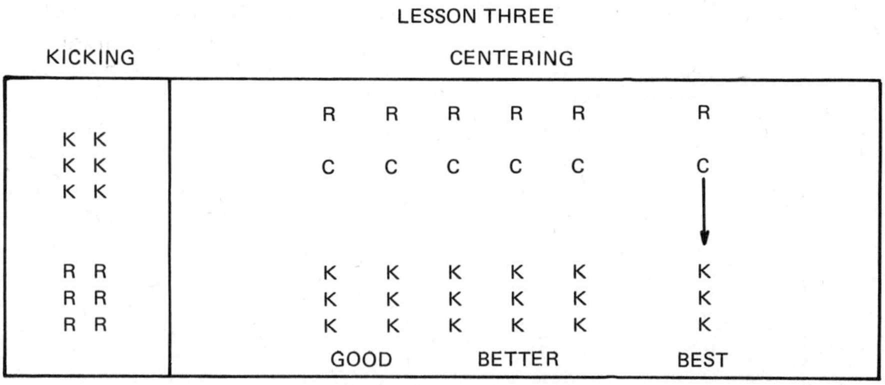

LESSON THREE

KICKING		CENTERING					
K K		R	R	R	R	R	R
K K		C	C	C	C	C	C
K K							↓
R R		K	K	K	K	K	K
R R		K	K	K	K	K	K
R R		K	K	K	K	K	K
		GOOD		BETTER			BEST

Figure 12–81.   Teaching how to center.

Students are placed in two sections as shown. Those who failed to learn kicking continue to practice. The centering group practices with the centers (C) snapping the ball to the kickers (K), who kick to the receivers (R). The centers run to the receiving position, the kickers to the center position, and the receivers to the end of the kicking line. Students advance from the good to better to best group as they improve.

LESSON FOUR

PERFORMANCE OBJECTIVES:

Psychomotor. The student correctly demonstrates the block, three out of five times.

Cognitive. In an oral report to the class, the student describes the proper steps in blocking.

Affective. The student exhibits self-control when he is hurt in blocking.

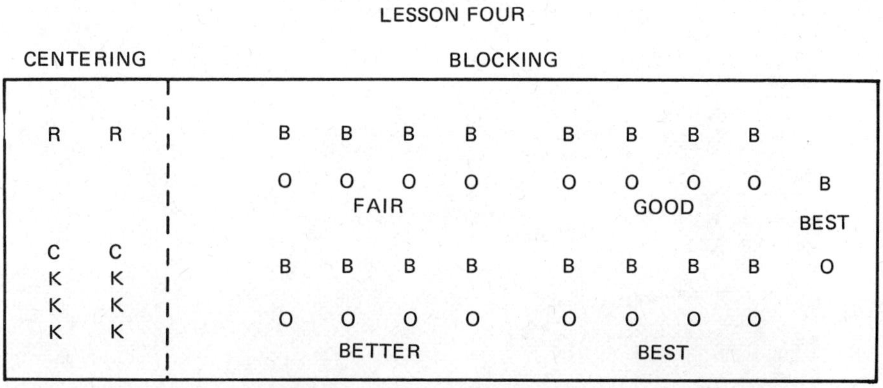

LESSON FOUR

CENTERING		BLOCKING								
R R		B	B	B	B	B	B	B	B	
		O	O	O	O	O	O	O	O	B
			FAIR				GOOD			BEST
C C		B	B	B	B	B	B	B	B	O
K K										
K K		O	O	O	O	O	O	O	O	
K K			BETTER				BEST			

Figure 12–82.   Teaching how to block.

Students are placed in two sections as shown. Those who failed to learn how to center continue to practice. Students who learned to center and punt are arranged in two groups, the blockers (B) and the opponents (O). They advance from fair to good to better to best as they improve.

LESSON FIVE

PERFORMANCE OBJECTIVES:

Psychomotor.   The student in an offensive play demonstrates how to handle the ball correctly, six out of 10 times.

Cognitive.   The student presents a written report on the offensive movements discussed in class.

Affective.   The student shows cooperation with his classmates by passing the ball when he could have run with it.

LESSON FIVE

BLOCKING

OFFENSIVE PLAY

```
B    B                    |
O    O                    |
                         |
                         |
                         |
                         |   L L L    L L L L    L L L L L    L L L L L L L
                         |    B B      B B B      B B B        B B B B
B    B                   |   5 MAN     7 MAN      8 MAN        11 MAN
O    O                   |
                         |
```

Figure 12–83.   Teaching offensive play.

Students are placed in two sections as shown. Those who failed to learn blocking continue to practice and advance to offensive play as they improve. The students in section two are placed in four groups as shown. Those groups reflect the types of teams that boys organize when playing touch football away from school under their own organization plans. It is difficult to form complete 11-man teams and they are usually organized in numbers varying from three to 11. From the formations shown above, the teacher can use all the types of offensive maneuvers that may be used when students play after school.

Figure 12–84.   Division of a class into four ability groups for effective instruction.

Teaching Soccer Skills

GENERAL OBJECTIVES:

A. Psychomotor.   The students will demonstrate the complex skills and techniques of soccer by executing the movements involved.

B. Cognitive.   The students will demonstrate their knowledge of soccer by correctly answering questions on a true or false test.

C. Affective.   The students will demonstrate their ability to:

> Control emotions under stress.
> Show good sportsmanship.
> Exhibit team loyalty.
> Accept responsibility.
> Assume leadership.
> Respect decisions of officials.

I. HISTORY OF SOCCER

(See references at end of chapter.)

II. VALUES OF SOCCER

Contributes to physical fitness
Develops teamwork
Provides immediate carry-over value

III. RULES, SCORING AND STRATEGY

(See references at end of chapter.)

IV. SAFETY PRECAUTIONS

Always warm up before practicing skills.
Be careful to protect head when opponent kicks ball.
Learn to relax.
Avoid collisions with opponents.

V. EQUIPMENT NEEDED

Ten soccer balls
Films and strips
Texts

VI. BASIC SKILLS

Dribbling	Intercepting
Kicking	Heading
Passing	Chesting
Trapping	Tackling
One foot	
Both feet	

VII. TEACHING SKILLS PROCEDURES

A. Introductory—see page 342
B. Developmental—see page 342
C. Teaching Skills
  1. Orientation—see page 345
  2. Demonstration—see page 345
  3. Organization—see page 346
  4. Inventory—see page 346
  5. Ability Grouping—see page 346
  6. Skills Laboratory—see page 346
  7. Evaluation—see Chapter 14 (p. 346)
    (made in terms of behavior)
D. Closing—see page 346

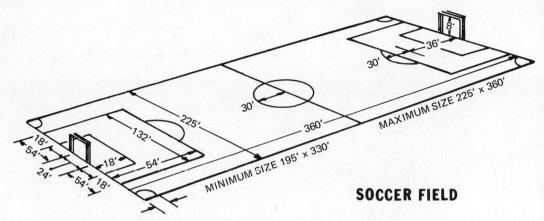

Figure 12–85.   Soccer field (Courtesy Wilson Sporting Goods Company.)

LESSON ONE
PERFORMANCE OBJECTIVES:

Psychomotor.   The student will dribble a soccer ball in a zigzag manner for 50 yards in 30 seconds.

Cognitive.   The student, after observing several demonstrations of the dribble, selects the correct one and describes it.

Affective.   The student exhibits respect for the teacher after being reprimanded for unnecessary roughness.

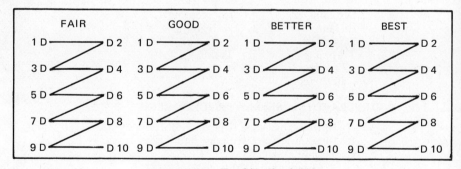

Figure 12–86.   Teaching the dribble.

The class is divided into eight groups of five each. The number 1 student in each group is given a soccer ball and dribbles as shown in diagram (number 1 to number 2 and takes his place; number 2 to number 3 and takes his place; finally number 10 replaces number 1). Students may be grouped according to ability as shown and advance from the fair to the best group as they improve.

LESSON TWO

PERFORMANCE OBJECTIVES:

Psychomotor. The student will kick a soccer ball within five feet of a class-mate 20 yards away, three out of five times.

Cognitive. The student will draw a diagram on the chalkboard showing the correct form in kicking the ball.

Affective. The student protests a violation of the rules laid down by the teacher for this event.

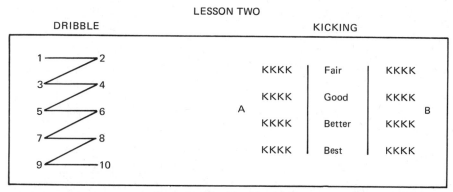

Figure 12-87. Teaching kicking.

The class is divided into two sections as shown. Those who failed to learn the dribble continue practicing and advance to the kicking section as they improve. The first students in the A groups kick to the first students in the B groups and run to the end of the line. The first students in the B groups kick to the second students in the A groups and run to the end of the line. Students may be grouped by ability as shown and advance from the fair to the best group as they improve.

LESSON THREE

PERFORMANCE OBJECTIVES:

Psychomotor. The student, using the inside of the foot, passes to a target point 20 feet away, 3 out of 5 times.

Cognitive. The student demonstrates his knowledge of soccer by identifying the various passes and describing the value of each.

Affective. The student offers no alibis for a poor performance, after having studied the pass in class.

LESSON THREE

SECTION A	SECTION B

```
                                              1
                     P   P    P   P      P   P   P   P
   K   K    K   K     P   P    P   P      P   P   P   P

                            GOOD           BETTER

                     P   P    P   P      P   P   P   P
   K   K    K   K     P   P    P   P      P   P   P   P
                                 2
```

Figure 12-88. Teaching passing.

The class is divided into two sections as shown. Section A includes students who did not learn the kicking skills. Section B consists of students who learned how to kick and are ready to learn passing skills. The first pairs in group 1 of section B are given a ball. They pass to each other, advance the ball to the first pairs in group 2, and run to the end of the line. The first pairs of the opposite group 2 pass to each other, advance the ball back to group 1, and run to the end of the line. As this procedure continues, the teacher points out mistakes and assists with instruction. Students advance from the good group to the best group as they improve.

LESSON FOUR

PERFORMANCE OBJECTIVES:

Psychomotor. The student will trap the ball, which was kicked by his class-mate, three out of five times.

Cognitive. The student will demonstrate his knowledge of trapping by showing two boys how to properly execute it.

Affective. The student cooperates with the teacher by assisting in the distribution of equipment.

LESSON FOUR

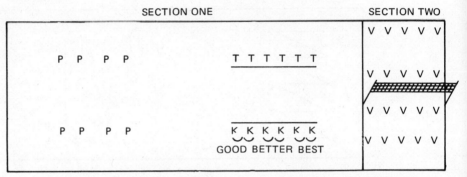

Figure 12–89. Teaching trapping.

The class is divided into two sections as shown. In section one those who failed to learn the pass (P) continue to practice and advance to the trappers as they improve. The kickers (K) kick the ball in an effort to cross the trapper's line. The trappers (T) attempt to trap the ball and kick it back to the kickers. This procedure continues. Students may be grouped by ability as shown and advance from the good to the best group as they improve. The volleyball overflow group changes with the soccer group at the discretion of the teacher.

LESSON FIVE

PERFORMANCE OBJECTIVES:

Psychomotor. The student successfully intercepts a soccer ball, four out of five times.

Cognitive. The student, after viewing a film on soccer, identifies an interception and describes what is wrong with the execution.

Affective. The student controls his temper after being tripped.

LESSON FIVE

SECTION ONE (TRAPPING)	SECTION TWO (INTERCEPTING)
T T T T	GOOD
K K K K	BETTER BEST

Figure 12–90. Intercepting.

The class is divided into two sections as shown. Students who did not learn how to trap continue practicing and advance to the interception group as they improve. Students learning how to intercept are placed in six groups with five in each group. The center player in each group is given a ball and throws it so that the other players in the circle may head or chest the ball. The object of the procedure is to keep the ball in the air as long as possible. Students advance from the good to the best groups as they improve.

Figure 12–91. Soccer dribbling relays motivate interest in learning skills.

Teaching Softball Skills

GENERAL OBJECTIVES:
  A. Psychomotor. The student will demonstrate the complex motor skills involved in softball by executing the movements incorporating them.
  B. Cognitive. The student will demonstrate his knowledge of the game by identifying and describing the various skills involved from a large list of techniques.
  C. Affective. The students will demonstrate their ability to:
    Control emotions under stress.
    Show good sportsmanship.
    Exhibit team loyalty.
    Accept responsibility.
    Assume leadership.
    Respect decisions of officials.

  I. HISTORY OF SOFTBALL

    (See references at end of chapter.)

  II. VALUES OF SOFTBALL

    Carry-over value
    Develops skill

  III. RULES, SCORING, AND STRATEGY

    (See references at end of chapter.)

  IV. SAFETY PRECAUTIONS

    Always stay clear of the batter.
    Swing the bat in the designated area only.

  V. EQUIPMENT NEEDED

    Ten softballs and bats   Films and strips
    Bases   Texts

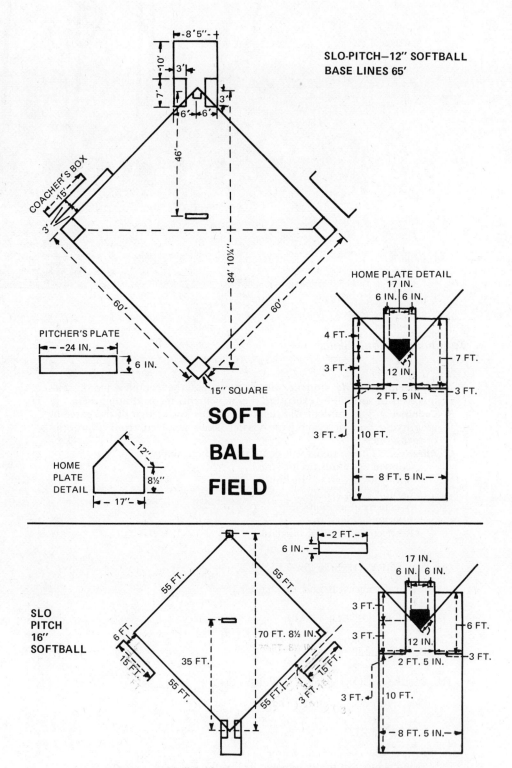

SLO-PITCH—12″ SOFTBALL
BASE LINES 65′

COACHER'S BOX

PITCHER'S PLATE

HOME PLATE DETAIL

HOME
PLATE
DETAIL

SOFT
BALL
FIELD

SLO
PITCH
16″
SOFTBALL

Figure 12-92.   Softball field. (Courtesy Wilson Sporting Goods Company.)

VI. BASIC SKILLS

Throwing and catching
Fielding
Pitching

Batting
Base running

VII. TEACHING SKILLS PROCEDURES

A. Introductory—see page 342
B. Developmental—see page 342
C. Teaching Skills
    1. Orientation—see page 345
    2. Demonstration—see page 345
    3. Organization—see page 346
    4. Inventory—see page 346
    5. Ability Grouping—see page 346
    6. Skills Laboratory—see page 346
    7. Evaluation—see Chapter 14 (p. 346)
       (made in terms of behavior)
D. Closing—see page 346

LESSON ONE
PERFORMANCE OBJECTIVES:
   Psychomotor. The student will catch a ball thrown by his classmate for a distance of 15 yards, seven out of 10 times.
   Cognitive. The student gives an oral presentation to his class on the proper form in catching a fly ball.
   Affective. The student, after missing a fast ground ball, displays self-control by running for it.

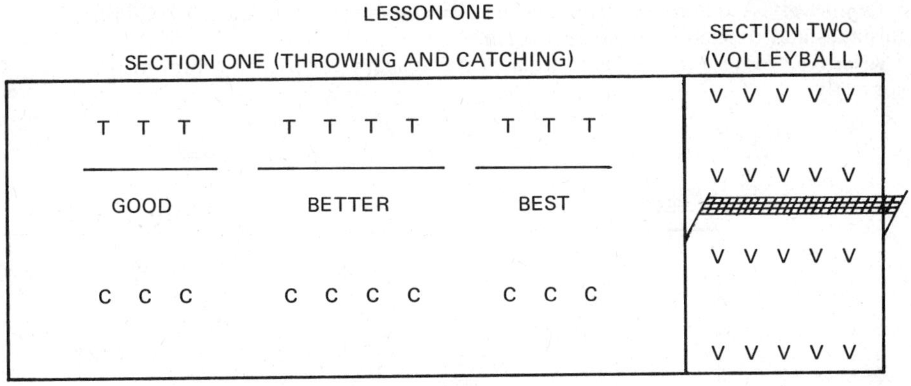

LESSON ONE

SECTION ONE (THROWING AND CATCHING)

SECTION TWO
(VOLLEYBALL)

T T T	T T T T	T T T
GOOD	BETTER	BEST
C C C	C C C C	C C C

V V V V V

V V V V V

V V V V V

V V V V V

Figure 12–93. Throwing and catching.

Students are placed in two sections as shown. The throwers (T) are given balls and practice throwing to the catchers (C). This continues with the good players advancing to the best groups as they improve. The volleyball groups change with the throwing and catching groups at the discretion of the teacher.

LESSON TWO

PERFORMANCE OBJECTIVES:

Psychomotor. The student, at a distance of 20 yards, will use the correct form in fielding the ball, four out of seven times.

Cognitive. The student illustrates the correct form in fielding by drawing stick figures on the chalkboard.

Affective. The student displays interest in his classmate by assisting him in learning how to field the ball.

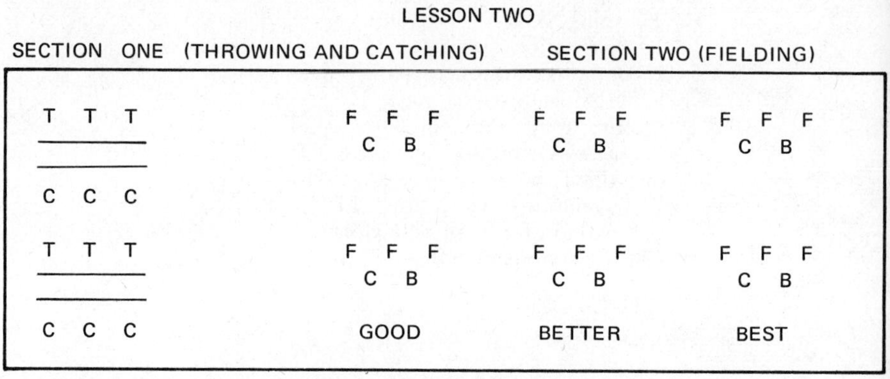

LESSON TWO

SECTION ONE (THROWING AND CATCHING)   SECTION TWO (FIELDING)

Figure 12–94. Teaching fielding.

Students are divided into two sections as shown. Those who failed to learn how to throw and catch continue practicing and advance to the fielding group as they improve. The batter (B) in each of the fielding groups is given a bat and ball. He hits the ball to one of the fielders, who fields the ball and throws it to the catcher (C), who gives it to the batter. This is repeated many times. The catcher and batter rotate around the fielders. Pupils are grouped by ability as shown and advance as they improve.

LESSON THREE

PERFORMANCE OBJECTIVES:

Psychomotor. The student, emphasizing in sequence the stages of pitching, will execute the pitch from the mound correctly, four out of six times.

Cognitive. After viewing pitches by his classmates, the student identifies mistakes and describes the correct form.

Affective. The student congratulates the teacher for assisting him to pitch correctly.

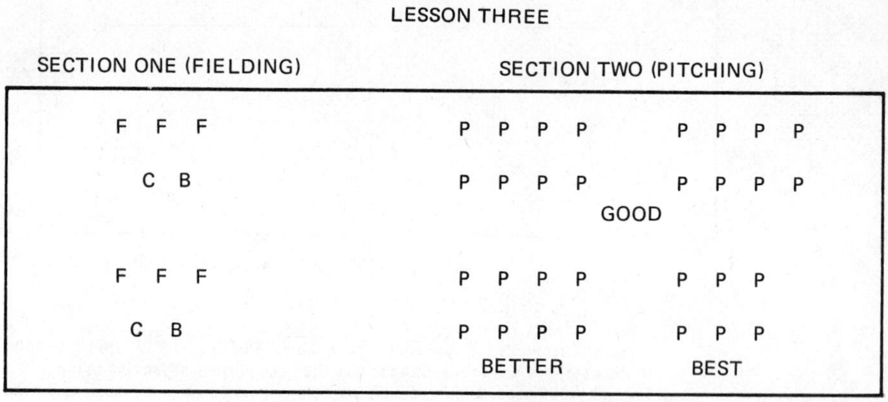

LESSON THREE

SECTION ONE (FIELDING)   SECTION TWO (PITCHING)

Figure 12–95. Teaching pitching.

Students are divided into two groups as shown. Those who did not learn the fielding skills continue practicing and advance to the pitching group as they improve. Each of the four groups of pitchers is given a ball, and they practice pitching the ball back and forth. Students are grouped by ability as shown and advance as they improve.

LESSON FOUR

PERFORMANCE OBJECTIVES:

Psychomotor. The student will hit a fair pitch from a distance of 46 feet into fair territory, three out of seven times.

Cognitive. The student writes a paper on the correct form in batting.

Affective. The student, after striking out several times, congratulates the pitcher.

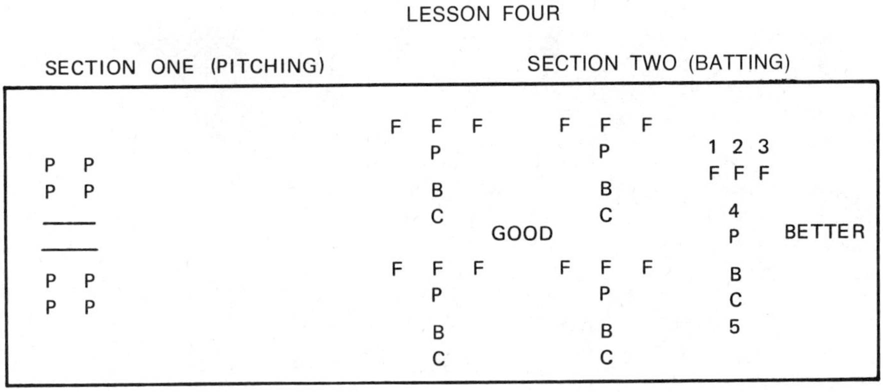

LESSON FOUR

SECTION ONE (PITCHING) SECTION TWO (BATTING)

Figure 12-96. Teaching batting.

The class is divided into two sections as shown. Students in section one continue to practice pitching, and those in section two are placed in five groups of six each. The pitcher (P) and batter (B) in each group are given a ball and a bat. The batter hits the ball, and the fielders (F) attempt to catch the ball and throw it back to another fielder or catcher (C). This continues with the students rotating as shown. Number 1 goes to number 2, who goes to number 3. Number 3 goes to (P), and (P) goes to (C), who becomes the batter. (B) goes to number 1 in the outfield. Students are grouped by ability as shown and advance as they improve. Those who failed the pitching (P) continue to practice and advance to the batting groups as they improve.

LESSON FIVE

PERFORMANCE OBJECTIVES:

Psychomotor. The student will bunt the ball in a designated zone, three out of five times.

Cognitive. The student gives an oral report on the importance of bunting.

Affective. The student, after being hit by the ball, maintains self-control and assumes the stance for the next pitch.

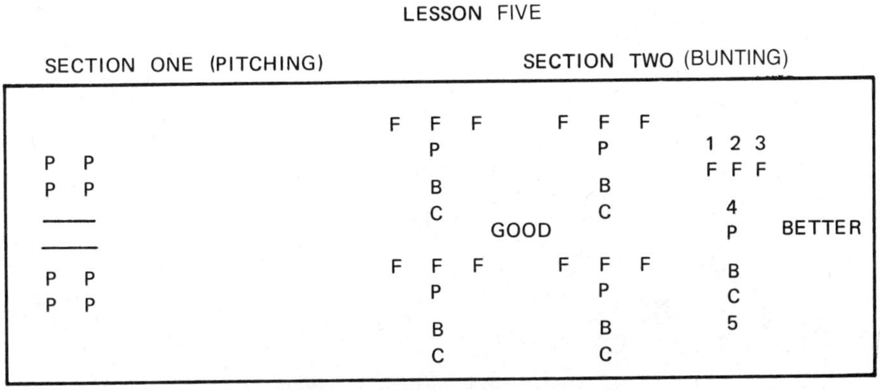

LESSON FIVE

SECTION ONE (PITCHING) SECTION TWO (BUNTING)

Figure 12-97. Teaching bunting.

The class is divided into two sections. The students in section one continue to practice pitching while those in section two are placed in five groups as shown. The teaching procedure is identical to that followed in Figure 12-96 (Lesson Four).

Figure 12–98. Throwing and catching are basic skills in softball, and are taught best in small ability groups.

Teaching Field Hockey Skills

GENERAL OBJECTIVES:

A. Psychomotor. The students will demonstrate the complex motor skills involved in field hockey by executing the movements which incorporate them.

B. Cognitive. The students will demonstrate knowledge of the game by identifying and describing the various skills involved from a large list of techniques.

C. Affective. The students will demonstrate their ability to:

Control emotions under stress.
Show good sportsmanship.
Exhibit team loyalty.
Accept responsibility.
Assume leadership.
Respect decisions of officials.

I. HISTORY OF FIELD HOCKEY

(See references at end of chapter.)

II. VALUES OF FIELD HOCKEY

Contributes to emotional stability
Physiological development
Carry-over value
Develops teamwork and cooperation

III. RULES, SCORING AND STRATEGY

(See references at end of chapter.)

IV. SAFETY PRECAUTIONS

Warm up adequately before participating.
Learn to handle the stick correctly.
Never hit a moving ball.
Never strike in the direction of another player.
Use shin-and-ankle guards and glasses if necessary.

V. EQUIPMENT NEEDED

40 sticks	Films and strips
20 balls	Ankle guards
Pinnies	Shoes
Goal-keeper equipment	Texts
Shin guards	

VI. BASIC SKILLS

Dribble	Dodging
Drive	Right
Straight	Left
Left	Triangular Pass
Right	Scoop
Fielding	Bully
Push Pass	Corner
Flick	Long corner
Tackling	Short corner
Left-hand lunge	Free Hit
Front or straight	Roll-in
Circular	Strategy
	Rules and scoring

VII. TEACHING SKILLS PROCEDURES

   A. Introductory — see page 342
   B. Developmental — see page 342
   C. Teaching Skills
      1. Orientation — see page 345
      2. Demonstration — see page 345
      3. Organization — see page 346
      4. Inventory — see page 346
      5. Ability Grouping — see page 346
      6. Skills Laboratory — see page 346
      7. Evaluation — see Chapter 14 (p. 346)
        (made in terms of behavior)
   D. Closing — see page 346

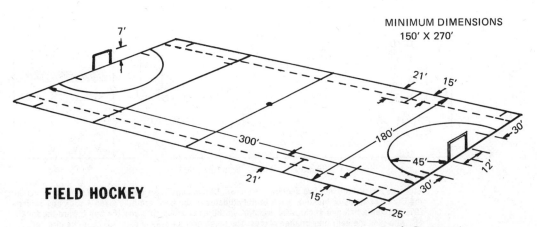

Figure 12–99.   Field hockey field. (Courtesy Wilson Sporting Goods Company.)

LESSON ONE

PERFORMANCE OBJECTIVES:

Psychomotor. The student correctly executes the dribble, by evading an opponent three out of five times.

Cognitive. The student orally describes the dribble to the class, pointing out the importance of mastering this skill.

Affective. The student displays self-control when the opponent strikes him on the shin with the hockey stick.

LESSON ONE

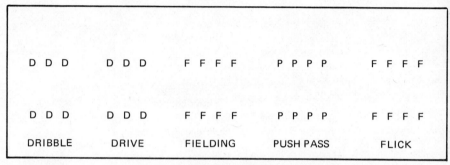

Figure 12–100. Teaching the strokes.

Students are divided into groups as shown. Each student is given a stick; as many balls as possible should be provided for each group. The dribbling group, using as many balls as possible, dribbles back and forth. The driving group practices the drive using as many balls as possible. The fielding group works back and forth with one group passing and the other fielding. The push-pass group practices back and forth as does the flick group. As the skill of each stroke is learned students rotate until all have mastered all strokes adequately. An alternative to this procedure would be to take each stroke separately, teach it, and move to another skill after each stroke is mastered.

LESSON TWO

PERFORMANCE OBJECTIVES:

Psychomotor. The student gains control of the ball from the advancing dribbler, two out of three times.

Cognitive. The student, using the chalkboard, draws the stages involved in the tackle.

Affective. The student shows cooperation with the teacher by assisting in the distribution of equipment.

LESSON TWO

SECTION ONE (TACKLING)

SECTION TWO (VOLLEYBALL)

D D D D

T T T T

FRONT OR STRAIGHT

DT DT DT DT

LEFT HAND LUNGE

D^T D^T D^T D^T

CIRCULAR

V V V V

V V V V

V V V V

V V V V

Figure 12–101. Teaching tackling.

Students are divided into two sections as shown. Section one is divided into three groups, each learning the three types of tackling. Each of the students in the front group is given a stick and each pair (DT) is given a ball and sticks. The dribblers in the front group (D) carry the ball toward the tacklers (T), who stop the ball; they change places. The lunge group works in pairs (DT) and the circular group (DT) works in pairs with the student in possession of ball (D) placed on the right of the tackler (T). The dribbler carries the ball in the direction of arrows, and the tackler (T) attempts to capture the ball. Students change with volleyball overflow at the discretion of the teacher. An alternative would be to teach each skill separately using ability grouping.

LESSON THREE

PERFORMANCE OBJECTIVES:

Psychomotor. The student executes the triangular pass correctly, three out of five times.

Cognitive. After viewing several executions of the triangular pass, the student spots errors and describes the correct performance.

Affective. The student volunteers to assist a poorly coordinated classmate in learning how to dodge.

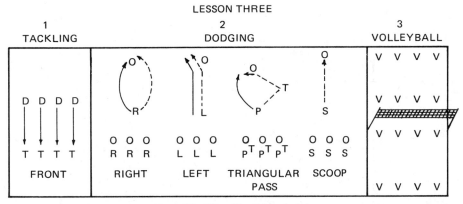

Figure 12–102. Teaching dodging.

Students are divided into three sections as shown. Students in section one continue practicing tackling. Section two is divided into four groups with each group practicing the skills of the types of dodge shown. The students (R and L) in the right dodge and left dodge are given sticks and balls. The diagrams at the top illustrate the path of the ball (----->), the player (→), and the opponent (O). In the triangular pass the player (P) with the ball passes to teammate (T), who returns it to the player behind the opponent (O). In the scoop each scooper (S) is given a ball and stick and carries the ball (----->) toward the opponent. Students change with the volleyball overflow group at the discretion of the teacher. An alternative would be to teach each skill separately using ability grouping.

LESSON FOUR

PERFORMANCE OBJECTIVES:

Psychomotor. The student executes the bully correctly, three out of six times.

Cognitive. The student makes an oral report to the class on the proper execution of the bully.

Affective. The student controls his temper when a classmate violates a safety precaution in the use of the hockey stick.

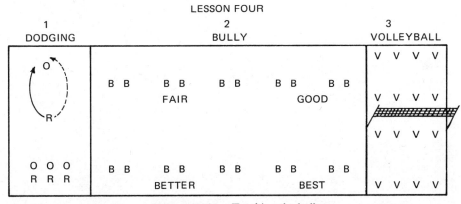

Figure 12–103. Teaching the bully.

The class is divided into three sections as shown. The students in section one continue practicing dodging, and those in section two are divided into ten pairs with each pair practicing the bully. Students advance from the fair group to the best group as they improve. The hockey group changes with the volleyball group at the discretion of the teacher.

LESSON FIVE

PERFORMANCE OBJECTIVES:

Psychomotor.   After observing a demonstration by a varsity player, the student executes the roll-in, four out of seven times.

Cognitive.   The student identifies and describes the roll-in from a list of hockey techniques flashed on the screen.

Affective.   The student assumes leadership in settling a dispute between two classmates who collided during a roll-in.

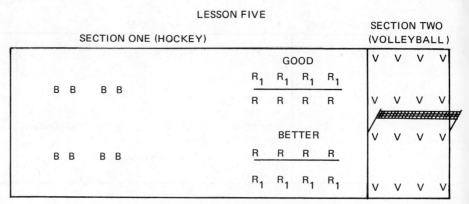

Figure 12–104.   Teaching the roll-in.

Students are divided into two sections as shown. In section one the bully group (BB) students continue practicing until they have improved enough to advance to the roll-in group (R_1). Students in the roll-in group (R_1) practice the roll-in. The retrievers (R) roll the ball back to the roll-in group. Students advance from the good to better group as they improve. The roll-in group changes with the volleyball group at the discretion of the teacher.

Figure 12–105.   When taught correctly, hockey skills become more meaningful and interesting. The class shown above is divided into three ability groups. Students in the background have advanced to the actual playing situation.

QUESTIONS FOR DISCUSSION

1. What is the importance of including individual activities in the curriculum? Group activities?

2. Why should teachers divide their classes into specific teaching phases? List each phase and discuss the purpose of each.

3. What is meant by the intensity curve? Draw one and place the component parts in the proper section.

SUGGESTED ACTIVITIES

1. Select an activity and plan to spend two lessons teaching it. Plan for the two lessons using the procedures outlined in this chapter. Present the plans to the class.

2. Visit a physical education class. List the teaching procedures involved. Describe how they could be improved.

3. Select a skill in five activities and compile games and relays that might be incorporated in the skills laboratories phase involving these skills.

4. Select an activity and use the class for a teaching laboratory. Have each member evaluate your teaching in writing. Present the results to the class.

SELECTED READINGS

Ainsworth, Dorothy S. *Individual Sports for Women*, 4th ed. Philadelphia: W. B. Saunders Company, 1966.

Armbruster, David A., *et al. Basic Skills in Sports*, 5th ed. St. Louis: The C. V. Mosby Company, 1971.

Barnes, Mildred, *et al. Sports Activities for Girls and Women*. New York: Appleton-Century-Crofts, 1967.

Barrett, Marcia, *et al. Foundations for Movement*, 2d ed. Dubuque, Iowa: William C. Brown Company, 1968.

Fait, Hollis, John Shaw, and Katherine Ley. *A Manual of Physical Education Activities*, 3d ed. Philadelphia: W. B. Saunders Company, 1967.

Fox, Grace, and Kathleen Merrill. *Folk Dancing in High School and College*. New York: The Ronald Press Company, 1957.

Gates, Alice A. *A New Look at Movement: A Dancer's View*. Minneapolis: Burgess Publishing Company, 1968.

Hall, J. Tillman. *Dance! A Complete Guide to Social, Folk and Square Dancing*. Belmont, California: Wadsworth Publishing Company, Inc., 1963.

Harris, Jane, Anne Pittman, and Marlys Waller. *Dance a While*, 4th ed. Minneapolis: Burgess Publishing Company, 1968.

Hawkins, Alma. *Creating Through Dance*. Englewood Cliffs, New Jersey: Prentice-Hall, Inc., 1964.

Hayes, Elizabeth R. *An Introduction to the Teaching of Dance*. New York: The Ronald Press Company, 1964.

Hayes, Elizabeth R. *Dance Composition and Production for High Schools and Colleges*. New York: A. S. Barnes & Company, 1955.

Humphrey, Doris. *The Art of Making Dances*. New York: Grove Press, 1962.

Lockhart, Aileene, and Esther Pease. *Modern Dance*. Dubuque, Iowa: William C. Brown Company, 1966.

Meyer, Margaret H., and Marguerite M. Schwarz. *Team Sports for Girls and Women*, 4th ed. Philadelphia: W. B. Saunders Company, 1965.

Norris, Dorothy E. K., and Reva P. Shiner. *Keynotes to Modern Dance*, 3d ed. Minneapolis: Burgess Publishing Company, 1969.

Physical Education Curriculum Guide, 7–12. Clark County School District, Las Vegas, Nevada, 1971.

Physical Education for High School Students, 2d ed. AAHPER, 1970.

Seaton, Don C., *et al. Physical Education Handbook*, 5th ed. Englewood Cliffs, New Jersey: Prentice-Hall, Inc., 1969.

Stanley, D. K., and I. F. Waglow. *Physical Education Activities Handbook*. Boston: Allyn and Bacon, 1966.

Smith, Hope M. *Introduction to Human Movement*. Reading, Massachusetts: Addison-Wesley Publishing Company, 1968.

Vannier, Maryhelen, and Holly Poindexter. *Individual and Team Sports for Girls and Women*, 2d ed. Philadelphia: W. B. Saunders Company, 1968.

Wessel, Janet A. *Movement Fundamentals: Figure, Form, Fun*, 3d ed. Englewood Cliffs, New Jersey: Prentice-Hall, Inc., 1970.

Chapter 13

THE INTRAMURAL LABORATORY

The young child perhaps learns more and develops better through play than through any other form of activity.

Herbert S. Jennings

An important phase of the total physical education program is the division of intramural sports. This program is becoming more popular each year because of the emphasis placed on the importance of activity for all and not for the gifted few alone.

PURPOSES OF INTRAMURAL SPORTS

The purposes of the intramural sports program are: to serve as an extension of the instructional program; to motivate pupils to exercise after school; to provide the opportunity for hours of vigorous activity essential for normal growth and development; to provide supervision for competition; and to provide facilities for the program.

Extension of the Instructional Program

The required class program does not provide sufficient time for the two to five hours of vigorous activity needed daily by children for normal growth and development. No matter how vigorous the physical education instructional program may be there remains the problem of providing several additional hours of exercise based

on individual needs. The intramural program provides this extension of instruction which allows pupils to carry the exercise programs beyond the school.

Motivation for Exercise After School

Pupils often learn the skills of an activity in the instructional period and then find it difficult to put these skills to use in an actual game situation. When intramural sports are planned and organized properly, pupils are encouraged to further their exercise program and to continue practicing the skills taught in class.

Opportunity for Play

If the urge for play is inhibited for several years, it may never be revived. Boys and girls are born with the urge for play and movement, but usually their daily routine does not provide the opportunity for vigorous play activities. They may have the desire and the time but the opportunity to be with children of their own age, to be a part of a group, to learn cooperation and teamwork in physical activity, is not available. The intramural program may provide this opportunity by organizing tournaments and informal activities and by making space, equipment, and leadership available.

445

Supervision for Competition

There should always be adult supervision of intramural sports. Without involving himself too much in the actual playing, an adult should be available to insure a safe environment, settle disputes, and see that the objectives of the program are met.

Provide Facilities for the Program

It is the responsibility of the school administration to provide adequate space, equipment, supplies and personnel for the intramural program. Schools are designed for use by all students, but in too many instances play areas are used exclusively for the varsity athletic program. This misuse of facilities cannot be justified.

NEED FOR INTRAMURALS

Never before in the history of this country has there been a greater need for intramural programs. It has been pointed out that during the formative years boys and girls need large blocks of time for vigorous muscular movement. The interscholastic programs in the schools are not adequate because they put a definite ceiling on the number of pupils allowed to participate. No matter what the size of a school is, whether its enrollment is 100 or 2000, there can be only five boys on the basketball team or 11 on the football team. The first job of the coach is to cut the squad and reduce the numbers involved as soon as possible. The job of the intramural director is to *add* to the numbers involved and increase the numbers participating. The interscholastic program obviously cannot replace intramurals; there is no substitute for a well-planned intramural program.

The instructional period alone is not enough since time is limited. A good teacher may be able to organize the class so well that he is able to find 40 minutes out of a 60-minute period for teaching. Nevertheless, this amount of time is several hours short of the time necessary for activities that promote normal growth and development. This means, then, that the physical education period *must* be used to teach skills that may be carried over *beyond* the class period into after-school participation.

Intramural sports, if organized and planned properly, can be the answer to one of the major needs of American youth today—time for vigorous activity under adult supervision for all boys and girls.

ADMINISTRATIVE STRUCTURE

For the intramural program to be organized properly it should be planned as an extension of the required physical education program and financed by school board appropriation; the administrative arrangement of the Cincinnati Public Schools (Fig. 13–2) provides a good working example of this arrangement.

TYPES OF INTRAMURALS

A great deal of vision is needed in planning the intramural program—merely organizing a basketball league with eight teams playing one game per week is not sufficient. There must be enough basketball teams to provide opportunity for all pupils to participate every day. A well-rounded program should include several types of intramurals.

Organized Intramurals

Organized intramurals have been the basis for most programs in the past. The first effort usually made by the intramural director is to organize groups into leagues, play a round robin or elimination tournament, and present awards to the winning team. Assuming that there are eight teams in the basketball league, this means that only 40 boys may participate in the tournament. This is an excellent plan for the 40 boys who are gifted in basketball, but how about the four or five hundred who are not desirous of participating on one of the teams but who enjoy practicing the skills of basketball? Another type of intramural organization is needed for this group.

Informal Participation

Many pupils in a school would rather participate in an informal skills program

Figure 13–1. Adequate facilities are necessary for conducting a varied intramural laboratory.

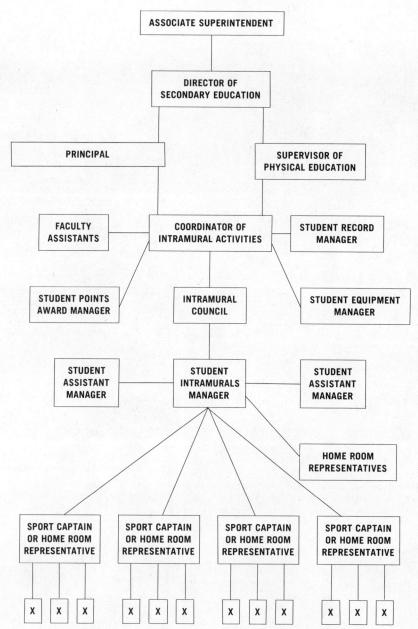

Figure 13–2. Organization of the intramural program. (Courtesy Cincinnati Public Schools, Cincinnati, Ohio.)

than belong to a team. Informal participation in conjunction with the league plan may increase intramural participation in many situations by 1000 percent. Informal participation is particularly applicable to activities which involve little teamwork, such as table tennis, basketball shooting, tennis, and track events.

Too often the pattern used for varsity programs is imposed on the intramural organization, limiting participation to a few gifted individuals. There is nothing wrong with planning activities for the gifted, as long as programs are also planned for all other pupils, irrespective of their degree of excellence in performance (Fig. 13–3).

Figure 13–3. Informal basketball play is one type of activity that may be used for before-school participation.

ELMER MITCHELL
Elmer Mitchell, known as the "Father of Intramural Sports," was a leader in this area of physical education for many years.

UNITS FOR ORGANIZING THE INTRAMURAL LABORATORY

The physical education class is for instruction, not play and so class time should not be used for intramurals. However, the physical education class may be used as a unit of organization of teams for later participation. Several units may be used to group pupils for intramural competition.

Homeroom

Effective group organization and planning is probably best carried out in the homeroom, which is already organized and easy to reach when notices and communication are necessary.

Grade

Another unit frequently used is the grade level. Pupils from various grades may form teams and participate against other pupils in the same grade. This plan is most useful in small schools with few homerooms, or in schools where there is an insufficient number of pupils in a single room to form a team.

Weight Classes

Some intramural activities should be organized on the basis of the weight of the participants. Wrestling is an obvious example of a sport that should be planned according to weight.

One-Day Tournaments

When a sport is in the process of development and the degree of performance is not too great, the one-day tournament plan is very useful. One afternoon is set aside for a particular sport, and all pupils interested in playing will be asked to report. Teams are formed on the spot; a straight elimination tournament is played; and the winner is determined that day. Events may be held periodically, ideally following the conclusion of a unit or skill in the classroom. The one-day tournament can be used for any sport or activity.

The Physical Education Class

Teams for after-school participation may be *formed* in the physical education class, but *class time should be reserved for instruction—not for intramural competition.*

Pupil-Choice Teams

Pupils may arbitrarily form teams and elect a captain. The teams' rosters are turned in to the physical education office and organized for tournament play. Entry blanks such as the one shown in Figure 13–12 may be used.

Department Teams

Pupils in the various departments of the school such as vocational, science, mathematics, and social studies, may organize teams for intramural competition.

TIME SCHEDULE FOR INTRAMURALS

The time chosen for intramural participation is of great importance. Many pupils are not able to participate after school because they live too far away and transportation difficulties prevent their enrollment in the program. Some of the more popular time periods are discussed below.

After School

Most of the intramural participation takes place immediately after school. This is the ideal time, but transportation problems, other athletic programs, and after-school jobs prevent many pupils who might otherwise be interested in the program from participating.

Before School

Early morning programs are becoming popular; the programs are usually informal and many pupils may take advantage of the opportunity they offer (Fig. 13–3). East Orange High School, East Orange, New Jersey, schedules a 50-minute recreation period each morning between 7:30 and 8:30. The program includes competition in football, basketball, volleyball, softball, and bowling. Tournaments are held in tennis, table tennis, basketball, push-up, sit-up, and rope climbing.[1]

During School

Intramural programs may take place during school hours; for example, during periods set aside for club organization. If there is ample time, recesses may provide opportunity for informal intramural participation, although care must be taken for proper timing of eating and activity. The boys' physical education department at Crockett Junior High School, Beaumont, Texas, conducts such a program, providing a period for intramural play under adult supervision in flag football, basketball, volleyball, and softball. Leagues are developed around the homeroom concept, and students officiate each game. One feature of the program that deserves to be mentioned is the mandatory substitution rule by which the action is stopped every 11 minutes to allow substitutes to enter the game. This provides for 400 participants rather than just spectators.[2]

Away From School

One objective of the intramural program is to provide opportunity for students to practice skills learned in class; programs away from school may provide this opportunity. One such plan is the *One Goal Challenge Basketball* program developed in Norfolk, Virginia. The skills of basketball may be practiced at home, in areas near the home and on community playgrounds.

The captain of each winning team each day brings the results of the afternoon's play to the physical education teacher. The results are kept over a two-month period; the team with the highest number of wins is given a trophy and each member receives a certificate (Fig. 13–4).

A program at Riverside High School, Sioux City, Iowa, under the direction of Mr. Raymond Abraham, illustrates how intramurals away from school may be used to counteract the adverse effects of television. The program is described by Mr. Abraham as follows:

Use of Television Commercials as a Motivational Device for Exercise

Television viewing has become a very important part of our young students' lives. The effects of television viewing are showing up in a number of ways, some good, some bad. From a physical education standpoint, the bad effects are poor posture and inactivity. In order to combat this effect and to motivate interest in push-ups and sit-ups and other exercises, I have started the following program.

A survey is made at the beginning of the school year to find out which television program is most popular. After the program is selected, the two main commercials are timed. The first commercial is the push-up commercial and the second is the sit-up commercial.

A large chart is placed on the bulletin board in the locker room where the boys record their number of push-ups or sit-ups. If one student feels that someone has reported a greater number than he can do, he can challenge him to prove his score.

At the end of the school year a little trophy is given to the boy in each class that has the highest score. The trophy is called "Television Exercise Emmy."[3]

ORGANIZATION FOR COMPETITIVE PLAY

There are a number of instruments that have been used to place pupils into competition after teams have been determined. Some of the most effective are reviewed here.

Tournaments

Tournaments are the most popular instrument for determining winners. Four types are generally used: single elimination, consolation elimination, double elimination and round robin.

Single Elimination. When time is limited, the single elimination type may be used. The teams or individuals participating are placed in brackets as shown in Figure 13–5. As long as the number of contestants exists in powers of two (2, 4, 8, 16, and 32), the first round presents no problem. However,

HEALTH, PHYSICAL EDUCATION AND SAFETY DEPARTMENT
NORFOLK CITY PUBLIC SCHOOLS

ONE-GOAL CHALLENGE BASKETBALL

This is to certify that _____ won a ONE-GOAL CHALLENGE BASKETBALL game
                          Team Captain

played at _____
                 Place

_____   _____
   Winning Captain   Losing Captain

ONE-GOAL CHALLENGE BASKETBALL

RULES:
  TIME: One hour

  DATE: March 1 – May 1

  PLACE: Any place after school

  PLAYING AREA: One goal

  TEAM: Three players

  WINNER: Team with most points at end of one hour wins game.

  SCHOOL WINNER: Team with most wins on May 1st wins.

Figure 13–4. Pupil instructions in one-goal basketball.

Figure 13-5. Single elimination tournament with contestants in powers of two.

when the number of players is not in powers of two, the first round should have "byes." The number of byes is determined by subtracting the number of players from the next power of two. For instance, if there are five players or teams, the next power of two is eight. Five subtracted from eight is three; therefore, there must be three byes in the first round, as shown in Figure 13-6.

Consolation Elimination. In the consolation elimination, the losers of the first round begin a loser's tournament the next day (Fig. 13-7). Although this type of tournament provides more playing opportunity, it is not very popular—the idea of losers playing each other does not appeal to many pupils.

Double Elimination. In this type of elimination tournament, the losers in all rounds continue to play a loser's tournament. The losers from the championship brackets drop down and play the winners in the loser's bracket (Fig. 13-8).

Round Robin. The round robin is the most popular of all tournaments because of the number of times each individual or team plays. This type of tournament is the most generally used for team play and for league competition. It requires a great deal of time, so teachers should first determine the number of games that will have to be played. Below is a simple formula:

The round robin schedule should not be planned for more than eight teams because of the time involved. If there are more than

$$\frac{(\text{Number of teams}) \times (\text{Number of teams} - 1)}{2} = \text{Number of games to be played}$$

Example: Number of teams = 8

$$\frac{8 \times 7}{2} = 28 \text{ games played}$$

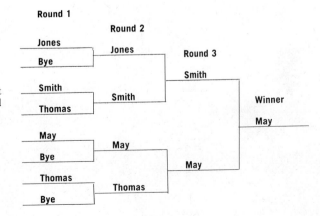

Figure 13-6. Single elimination tournament with byes. This means that Jones, May and Thomas do not play in the first round.

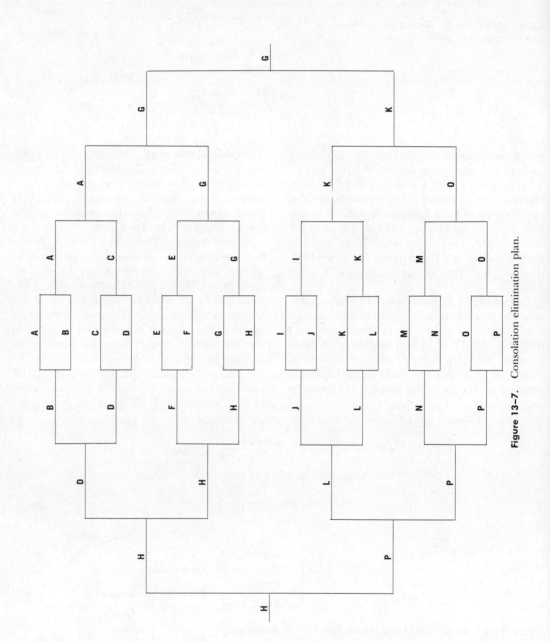

Figure 13–7. Consolation elimination plan.

Figure 13–8. Double elimination tournament. If team 5 defeats team 3, team 5 is the tournament winner. However, if team 3 defeats team 5, these two teams must play another game since this is the first game that team 5 has lost.

eight teams, a different league should be formed.

After the number of teams has been determined, the teacher has to arrange a schedule, the simplest way being to arrange all teams in two columns:

$$1-4$$
$$2-5$$
$$3-6$$

If there is an even number of teams, number 1 remains stationary and the other teams are rotated around number 1 either clockwise or counterclockwise. If we take the six teams shown and rotate them clockwise, the following schedule is formed:

Round 1	Round 2	Round 3
1−4	1−2	1−3
2−5	3−4	6−2
3−6	6−5	5−4

Round 4	Round 5
1−6	1−5
5−3	4−6
4−2	3−2

When teams are uneven, they are arranged in two columns with the bye placed either at the bottom or the top and the other teams rotating clockwise. With five teams, the schedule would be as follows:

Round 1	Round 2	Round 3
1−bye	2−bye	3−bye
2−4	3−1	5−2
3−5	5−4	4−1

Round 4	Round 5
5−bye	4−bye
4−3	1−5
1−2	2−3

ADMINISTRATION OF THE INTRAMURAL LABORATORY

Intramural programs must be organized carefully and therefore require a competent administrative staff. Some of the personnel to be considered are discussed in the following paragraphs (see Figure 13–9).

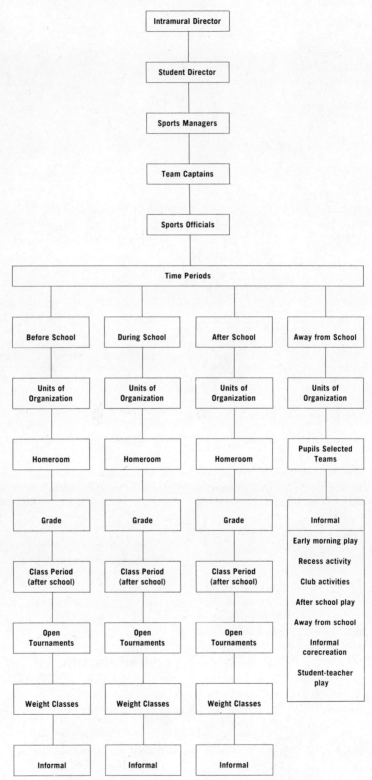

Figure 13-9. Organization of the intramural program.

Intramural Director

The success of the program largely depends on who directs it. The physical education teacher is the logical person to assume this leadership role; he should be freed from other after-school duties, since directing an intramural program is a full-time after-school job. Howard Denike, in a survey of 105 high schools, found that the vast majority assigned the responsibility of directing the program to the physical education teacher who had been trained in this field.[4]

Duties of the Director. The intramural director must:

1. Spend a specified amount of time outside the regular school day in organizing, supervising, and promoting the intramural program.

2. Keep accurate records of each activity on permanent record cards.

3. Accompany the intramural teams when games are scheduled away from school.

4. Keep up to date with the intramural awards system.

5. Know the mechanics of the city-wide tournaments and cooperate closely with the city-wide chairman. He should be present at all city-wide events.

6. Submit the name, division, and sex of each school winner to the city-wide chairman at least one week prior to city-wide meets. (City-wide chairmen should submit a copy of winners immediately to the Physical Education Office and call in the results of the tournaments to the newspapers.)

7. Obtain parental permission slips from all pupils who are to participate in city-wide tournament prior to tournament. All pupils should have insurance in case of accident. Many schools and school systems have special inexpensive arrangements with reputable insurance companies so that pupils pay only a small premium for this protection.

8. Keep a record of the number of participants and submit a report of the results of the school intramural program. Blanks are furnished for this report.

9. Plan the program; arrange all schedules; plan meetings of those individuals responsible for conducting the program; provide officials; and finally, prepare and administer the budget.

Student Director

A student who has worked with the program for at least one year should be selected to assist in the overall direction of the program. He can assist in recording daily results, procuring officials, working with the sports managers, and keeping track of equipment and supplies. It would be a good policy to select someone from the senior class at the beginning of each year; in this way, a number of students can be trained in their freshman, sophomore and junior years, assuring the teacher of capable assistance at all times.

Sports Managers

Each sport should have a manager who is responsible for the proper functioning of the sport. He should work with the captain in procuring equipment for the particular sport and assisting with the assigning of officials.

Team Captains

Each team should have a captain to represent his team in all situations in which his team is involved. The captain should assist the manager in approving and securing officials for each game.

Officials

Good officials are necessary for the proper functioning of the program. Older pupils and sometimes members of the varsity team may be trained to officiate: because of their youth and alertness, they make good officials if they are trained properly.

The program of the Ector County Independent School District in Odessa, Texas, is an outstanding example of how students may be trained to officiate in intramurals. Eighty boys and girls are selected to officiate all games and contests. These students achieve status and receive awards as varsity athletes do. In order to receive awards, the student officials must meet certain requirements, described below:

Intramural Official's Badge

1. Earn 100 points as an official (Fig. 13–10).
2. Officiate in some capacity in at least two different sports.

3. Officiate in some capacity in at least five games.
4. Have an official's pinnie to wear in each game.

Intramural Two Gold Stars
1. Earn 150 points as an official.
2. Attend clinics in each sport officiated.
3. Pass requirements under "Intramural Official's Badge."

Intramural Three Gold Stars
1. Earn 200 points as an official.
2. Pass a written test in all sports officiated.
3. Receive a rating of excellent, good, or average by coaches.
4. Pass requirements under "Intramural Two Gold Stars."

Intramural Four Gold Stars
1. Earn 300 points as an official.
2. Wear a regulation official's shirt or pinnie.
3. Pass requirement under "Intramural Three Gold Stars."[5]

The Ector Physical Education Department developed an Intramural Officials Point System which is used to determine which students are eligible for awards. Figure 13–10 lists the assignments and the activities in which points are awarded.[5]

Officials should be given written notices on the date and time of each game or activity (Fig. 13–11).

The boys' physical education department at Cooper High School, Abilene, Texas, solved its officials problem by training interested boys to officiate in four sports: football, basketball, softball, and track. Before beginning their assignment they must pass an extensive examination.

The advantages of the plan are:
1. It gives a boy who has been active in sports, but who can't make the team in his junior or senior year, an opportunity to remain active.
2. It gives him an opportunity to achieve status and recognition, especially from younger boys whose games he officiates. (All officials wear uniforms which give them a professional appearance and enhance their stature on the field.)
3. It enables the district to use qualified officials at no expense in the intramural and interscholastic program below the high school level.
4. It serves as a training ground for future officials. Many of the boys currently being trained in the program will continue their interest after graduation and become high school and college officials.[6]

ECTOR COUNTY INDEPENDENT SCHOOL DISTRICT

Physical Education Department

Assignments	Football	Basketball	Volleyball	Softball	Soccer	Tennis	Track & Field	Swimming	Badminton	Baseball	Wrestling	Gymnastics
Referee	10	10	10		10						10	10
Umpire	7	7	7	10	7	10			10	10		
Head Linesman	7											
Timer	3	3	3		3		7	7			7	7
Starter							10	10				
Judges	7						7	7				7
Score Keeper	3	3	3		3	7	10	10			10	10
Down Box-Chain	3											
Base Umpire				7						7		
Announcer							5	5			5	
Clerks							10	10				10

*INTRAMURAL OFFICIALS POINT SYSTEM

*Student officials receive double the number of points for working extramural games.

Figure 13–10. Intramural officials point system. (Courtesy Ector County Independent School District, Odessa, Texas.)

INTRAMURAL DEPARTMENT

_____High School

OFFICIAL'S NOTICE

NAME_____ HOME ROOM _____ WEEK OF _____

You are scheduled to REFEREE, SCORE and TIME a BASKETBALL or WATER POLO game at_____
on the following circled days this week: (time)

| Monday | Tuesday | Wednesday | Thursday | Friday |

If you cannot fulfill this assignment, please notify the intramural coordinator immediately.

Thank you,

Intramural Manager

Figure 13–11. Officials' notice. (Courtesy Cincinnati Public Schools, Cincinnati, Ohio.)

Mechanics of Organizing the Program

Several procedures are involved in the overall organization of the intramural program.

Securing Participants. The teacher has to find some medium for acquainting the pupils with the details of the program (dates, time of play, and activities). Probably the best medium is the physical education class. All announcements may be made in class and entry blanks for team organization may be distributed. These blanks, to be returned to the teacher, should include the names of players and captains (Figs. 13–12 and 13–13).

NORFOLK PUBLIC SCHOOLS
HEALTH, PHYSICAL EDUCATION AND SAFETY DEPARTMENT

INTRAMURAL ENTRY BLANK

_____
Sex

| Sport | H. R. Number | Captain | School |

PLAYERS	PLAYERS

Homeroom Director

Homeroom Teacher

Figure 13–12. Intramural entry blank.

NORFOLK CITY PUBLIC SCHOOLS
HEALTH, PHYSICAL EDUCATION AND SAFETY DEPARTMENT

INTRAMURAL ENTRY BLANK

| (Sport) | H. R. Number | Captain | School |

PLAYERS	PLAYERS

Home Room Director

Home Room Teacher

(*Front*)

Figure 13–13. An intramural entry blank including rules and regulations, adapted from the Cincinnati Public Schools. (Courtesy Cincinnati Public Schools, Cincinnati, Ohio.)

Figure 13–13 continued on opposite page.

<u>REGULATIONS</u>

Table Tennis

Who Participates — Any student enrolled in the intramural program.
Entries — One winner (single) from each grade level — 7th, 8th & 9th.
Game — 21 — Winner must have a two point advantage.
Tournament — All games will be single elimination except the final. Finals will be best 2 out of 3 games.

Tennis

Who Participates — Any student enrolled in a physical education class who is enrolled in the intramural program.
Entries — Four representatives from each school — two 9th & 10th, two 11th & 12th.
Tournament — Double elimination.

Field Hockey

Who Participates — Any student enrolled in a physical education class who is enrolled in the intramural program.
Entries — One team from each school — open competition grades 9–12.
Game — 20 min. — two 10 min. halves — 3 min. half time.
Tournament — Single Elimination.

Volleyball

Who Participates — Any student enrolled in the intramural program.
Entries — One team from each grade — 7th, 8th & 9th.
Height of Net — 8 ft. for 8th & 9th grades; 7 ft. for 7th grade.
No. of Players — 6 per team.
Points Per Game — 15 points (Winning Team must have a 2 point advantage.) 7 min. time limit.
Tournament — Single elimination — all rounds except finals — finals best 2 out of 3 games.

(Back)

Figure 13–13. *Continued.*

Posting Schedules. After the teacher has secured the teams, schedules should be made up and posted. The student director should be familiar with the schedules and work with the sports managers and the homeroom captains to give the teams the necessary information.

Cumulative Records. The teacher and the student director working together should keep accurate records of all results. These records, which may be kept on four by six cards, should be kept in a filing cabinet alphabetically arranged by name for easy reference (Fig. 13–14).

Motivation. Although an intramural program may be carefully planned, it will be a failure if a large number of students do not participate. Some techniques for stimulating interest are suggested:[6]

1. Appoint a qualified and enthusiastic person from the physical education department to organize and direct the program.

2. Include coeducational activities as a part of the program. Individual sports such as bowling, tennis, and golf are suitable, as well as team sports such as softball and volleyball.

3. Provide time periods other than the regular after-school program for students who cannot attend at this time; early morning programs should be developed for students who work after school.

4. Informal programs should be planned as an integral part of the total intramural schedule. Organized sports may be too demanding of students' time, particularly in the senior high school.

5. Schedule straight elimination tournaments in as many activities as possible. These are desirable for students who cannot spare the time necessary for round robin play.

6. Provide an elaborate awards system which allows each individual the opportunity of receiving some recognition for participation.

7. Use every means available for publicizing the program. Bulletin Boards, the school paper, special announcements, and local papers should be used to announce winners, coming events, and special achievement or recognition (Figs. 13–15, 13–16 and 13–17).

8. Arrange special contests between winning teams and faculty teams. Bringing teachers into the program often increases interest.

9. Arrange city-wide tournaments for winning teams for each school or neighboring schools, which will provide added incentive for students to participate.

10. Have as many classifications as possible in arranging tournaments. Plan tournaments for winners in the various grade levels; develop special schedules for short boys, tall boys, or fat boys.

11. Arrange programs for the different types of handicapped students.

12. Performance records that can be objectively measured should be kept in individual activities, such as track. This is one of the best motivational media available in intramurals. Mr. John F. Phillips, Director of Physical Education at Cooper High School in Abilene, Texas, keeps yearly records in track and field events (meets are held after school and on Saturday mornings):

440 dash	57.0
440 relay	46.1
880 run	2:05.1
880 relay	1:37.1
100-yard dash	10.5
50-yard dash	5.6
One-mile run	4:58.9
High jump	5'9"
Broad jump	20'5"
Discus	131'10"
Shot-put (12 lb.)	39'3"

Intramural directors should secure parental permission for all students who participate in the intramural program (Fig. 13–18). This will assist the director in coping with the many problems which may arise and will also let the parent know where the child is.

The teacher who plans carefully and uses many tools, such as record cards and official entry blanks, will be more successful in organizing the program. Slipshod organization will result in a slipshod program. Student leaders and assistants enjoy working out many of the details involved in developing a program, and they should be given opportunities to assist.

CONTENT OF THE INTRAMURAL PROGRAM

A well-planned intramural program serves as an extension of the physical education instruction during the school day. Joint planning of the instructional program and intramural programs will result in achievement of the objectives of both. Ac-

NORFOLK PUBLIC SCHOOLS
HEALTH, PHYSICAL EDUCATION AND SAFETY DEPARTMENT
Intramural Sports Record

Name...

Address...

School...

Intramural Awards Record

Date	Awards	Date	Awards

INTRAMURAL RECORD

ACTIVITIES	7	8	9	10	11	12	REMARKS
Archery							
Basketball							
Bowling							
Rhythmics							
Foul Shots							
Golf							
Hockey							
Managers							
Officials							
Rapid Shooting							
Softball							
Swimming							
Table Tennis							
Tennis							
Touch Football							
Track							
Tumbling							
Volleyball							
Wrestling							
Body Mechanics							
Fitness Meet							
TOTAL POINTS							

LEGEND:
Enter 5 points for 1st place—3 points for 2nd place, and 2 points for 3rd place winners.
1 point for participating, but not winning 1st, 2nd, or 3rd place.
17 points—Monogram.

Figure 13–14. Intramural sports records.

Figure 13–15. The bulletin board is an excellent medium for developing motivation.

Figure 13–16. Posting photographs of intramural participants and winners motivates intramural participation. (Courtesy Richmond Senior High School, Richmond, Indiana.)

INTRAMURAL NEWS

_____ HIGH SCHOOL

| 1963–64 | Issue 1 | Monday, October 6 |

BASKETBALL

Intramural Basketball starts this week for all grades. There is a total of 21 teams entered in the competition.

7th GRADE VOLLEYBALL

Results of games through Oct. 1.
134 defeated 120   35–7
 36 defeated 113   16–15
 34 defeated 119   forfeit

PARENTAL APPROVAL FORM

A reminder to home room representatives to turn in the intramural permission slips in room 104. No boy will be permitted to participate in intramural activities

BOWLING

A new high 2 game total record was set last Wednesday when Gary Smith rolled a total of 360 on games of 184 and 176. The previous record, set last year, was 336 held by Vernon Ralls. Other scores were as follows:

Racy Borinstein   155 and 139
Gary Lamb   141 and 129
Mark Smith   140 and 129
Terry Lamb   129
Ed Walker   121

The "Mets" continue to lead the league with a record of 8 wins

Figure 13–17. Publications such as this newsletter can be prepared and distributed to the home rooms each week, to provide motivation and keep the intramurals at a high level. (Courtesy Cincinnati Public Schools, Cincinnati, Ohio.)

tivities included in the intramural laboratory should be the same as those taught in the physical education class and should be scheduled in the same season in which they are taught. The activities included in several intramural programs are shown on the following pages.

The program in Norfolk, Virginia, is an extension of the instructional program and operates on the following monthly basis:

PARENTAL APPROVAL FORM

_____ HIGH INTRAMURALS

Date_____

This is to inform you that my child _____ is to the best of my knowledge physically fit and has my permission to participate in the intramural sports program

at _____ during the year 1964–65.

Signed _____

(After having this signed, fill in the information below and return to the Intramural Coordinator.)

HOME ROOM_____ GRADE_____ NAME_____

Figure 13–18. Parental Approval form. (Courtesy Cincinnati Public Schools, Cincinnati, Ohio.)

	BOYS		GIRLS	
Month	*Activities*	*Place*	*Activities*	*Place*
September	Touch football (begin)	School	Hockey (begin)	School
	Bowling practice	School	Bowling (practice)	School
	Table tennis (begin)	School	Table tennis (begin)	School
October	Touch football (cont.)	School	Hockey (cont.)	School
			Table tennis (cont.)	School
	Bowling (begin)	Local	Bowling (begin)	Local
	(Oct. 1–Feb. 1)	alleys	(Oct. 1–Feb. 1)	alleys
	Wrestling (begin)	School	Volleyball (begin)	School
	Volleyball (begin)	School	Basketball (begin)	School
	Basketball (begin)	School	Rhythmics (begin)	School
	Table tennis (cont.)	School		
November	Bowling (cont.)	Local	Bowling (cont.)	Local
		alleys		alleys
			Rhythmics (cont.)	School
	Wrestling (cont.)	School	Volleyball (cont.)	School
	Volleyball (cont.)	School	Hockey (cont.)	School
	Basketball (cont.)	School	Basketball (cont.)	School
December	Bowling (cont.)	Local	Bowling (cont.)	Local
		alleys		alleys
	Wrestling (cont.)	School	Volleyball (cont.)	School
	Volleyball (cont.)	School	Basketball (cont.)	School
	Basketball (begin)	School	Foul shooting (begin)	School
	Foul shooting (begin)	School	Rhythmics (cont.)	School
January	Bowling (cont.)	Local	Bowling (cont.)	Local
		alleys		alleys
	Wrestling (cont.)	School	Rhythmics (cont.)	School
	Volleyball (cont.)	School	Volleyball (cont.)	School
	Basketball (cont.)	School	Basketball (cont.)	School
	Foul shooting (cont.)	School	Foul shooting (cont.)	School
February	Basketball (cont.)	School	Rhythmics (cont.)	School
	Tumbling (begin)	School	Basketball (cont.)	School
	Rapid shooting (begin)	School		
March	Basketball (cont.)	School	Basketball (cont.)	School
	Tumbling (cont.)	School	Swimming (begin)	Pool
	Track (begin)	School	Tennis (begin)	School
	Tennis (begin)	School	Golf (begin)	School
	Golf (begin)	School	Archery (begin)	School
April	Track (cont.)	School	Swimming (cont.)	
	Tennis (cont.)	School	Tennis (cont.)	School
	Golf (cont.)	School	Golf (cont.)	School
	Horseshoes (begin)	School	Archery (cont.)	School
	Softball (begin)	School	Horseshoes (begin)	School
May	Track (cont.)	School	Swimming (cont.)	
	Tennis (cont.)	School	Tennis (cont.)	School
	Golf (cont.)	School	Golf (cont.)	School
	Horseshoes (cont.)	School	Horseshoes (cont.)	School
	Softball (cont.)	School	Softball (cont.)	School
			Archery (cont.)	School

Note: Informal programs every morning at 8 o'clock in all schools.

Ray Welsh, Director of Physical Education at the East Orange (New Jersey) High School, has devised a comprehensive yearly calendar of intramural activities:

I. Calendar of intramural activities for the school year.

    A. *September*
        1. Touch football league Tuesday and Thursday.
        2. After-school recreation period every day except Friday from 3:00 to 4:45 P.M. Open to any boy in school (boy's gym). Gym shoes and gym suit a requisite.

    B. *October*
        1. Continuation of touch football league Tuesday and Thursday.
        2. After-school recreation period every day except Friday—3:00 to 4:45 P.M.
        3. 7:30 to 8:20 A.M. recreation period and physical education *make-up.*

    C. *November*
        1. Continuation of touch football league Tuesday and Thursday (closes on Tuesday, November 6).
        2. Bowling league at the Bowl-O-Drome every Friday for a 12-week period starting Friday, November 16, at 80c for two games including shoes.
        3. Fall rope climbing championships Thursday, November 15, at 3:10 P.M. (timed).
        4. Two-rope, hands-only climbing championship.
        5. Push-up championship (2 minutes).

    D *December*
        1. Continuation of the bowling league on Fridays.
        2. Ping-pong practice, gym corridor, Tuesday and Thursday (6 tables).
        3. Freshman basketball league.
        4. Upper-class basketball league.
        5. Three and four are open to all boys except varsity, junior varsity, and freshmen varsity players. There are to be no less than eight boys on each squad. (3:00 P.M. sharp)

    E. *January*
        1. Continuation of the bowling league on Fridays.
        2. Ping-pong and Knobby Pool practice gym corridor Tuesday and Thursday.
        3. Continuation of the freshmen and upper-class basketball leagues.
        4. Pull-up championships. Based on the number you can do.
        5. Push-up championships. Based on the number you can do in one minute.
        6. Sit-up championships. Based on the number you can do in one minute.

    F. *February*
        1. Continuation of the bowling league on Fridays.
        2. Ping-pong and Knobby Pool practice, gym corridor, Tuesday and Thursday.
        3. Continuation of the freshmen and upper-class basketball leagues.
        4. Speed-bag punching championship.
        5. "Sweet Georgia Brown" dribbling contest done to music.
        6. Red and Blue Night (February 7).

    G. *March*
        1. Freshmen volleyball league.
        2. Upper-class volleyball league.
        3. Ping-pong singles and doubles tournament.

    H. *April*
        1. Olympic weight lifting competition.
        2. Rope jumping championship.
            a. Based on (5 minute) deductions on each miss.
            b. The number of jumps is your computed score.
        3. Indoor track and field meet.
        4. Badminton tournament singles and doubles.
        5. Softball league Tuesday and Thursday.

    I. *May*
        1. Outdoor track and field meet.
        2. Physical fitness test champion.
        3. Continuation of softball league.
        4. Indoor tennis tournament; you must *furnish* your own racquet.

    J. *June*
        1. Intramural softball league champions vs. junior varsity baseball team at Martin Stadium (baseball game—seven innings).

In the Cedar Rapids, Iowa, Community School District, Mr. Emil Klumper has proposed an extensive program. The program includes three divisions of activities: (1) clubs, (2) corecreational, and (3) informal. These activities are shown below.[7]

The Charlotte-Mecklenburg Schools schedule intramurals before school, during school, after school, at night, and on Saturday mornings. The objective of the program is to provide balanced and diversified intramural competition for all students regardless of ability. One feature of the program is the allocation of one hour after school for intramurals. Varsity athletes spend this hour studying and conferring with academic teachers. A partial list of activities in the program is shown above:[8]

Tag Football	Swimming
Soccer	Shuffleboard
Basketball	Paddle Tennis
Volleyball	Bowling
Softball	Deck Tennis
Track and Field	Handball
Horseshoes	Wrestling
Table Tennis	Baseball
Foul Shooting	Kickball
Tumbling	Folk Dancing
Gymnastics	Social Dancing
Modern Dancing	Field Hockey
Tennis	Speedball
Golf	Archery

The Clark County School District in Las Vegas, Nevada, designed the following program of sports participation, designed to meet the needs of all students (p. 469).[9]

SUGGESTED SECONDARY ACTIVITIES GRADES 7–12 BY SEASON

★ Activities suited to the "club" type of organization.

★★ Activities which lend themselves to development of co-recreation.

★★★ Example of informal activities: free play, practice periods.

FALL	WINTER	SPRING
Football (touch)	★★★Basketball	Track and field
★★★Softball	★★Volleyball	★★★Softball
★Tennis	★★★	★Tennis
★★	★Wrestling	★★
★★★	★Swimming	★★★
Soccer	★★	★Golf
Speedball	★★★	★★
★Golf	★Life saving	★Archery
★★	★Tumbling	★★
★Archery	★Gymnastics	★Fly and spin casting
★★	★Social, square and	★★
Field ball	★★ folk dancing	
	★Trampoline	*Misc. Activities*
Misc. Activities	Water show	★★Horseshoes
Accuracy throw	★Physical fitness	★★★
★Hiking	★Bowling	Paddle tennis
★★	★★	★Hiking
Kickball		★★
★Camp craft	*Misc. Activities*	★Camp craft
★★	Table tennis	
	Aerial darts	
	★Badminton	
	★★	
	★★★	
	Deck tennis	
	★Riflery	
	★★Skating	
	★Shuffleboard	
	★★	
	★Handball	

Figure 13-19. Modern dance demonstrations are popular intramural activities for girls.

CLARK COUNTY SCHOOL DISTRICT
INTRAMURAL PROGRAM

Date	Girls	Coeducational	Boys
Oct.	Basketball Foul Shooting League Bowling		Basketball Foul Shooting League Bowling
Nov.	Chess Club *Lee's Canyon Trip Basketball Volleyball Drill Team		Chess Club *Lee's Canyon Trip Basketball Flag Football Drill Team
Dec.	Volleyball *Roller Skating	Volleyball	Flag Football Volleyball *Roller Skating
Jan.	Table Tennis Badminton Deck Tennis *Rec. Games Shuffleboard Quiet Games *Ice Skating	Table Tennis Badminton Deck Tennis *Rec. Games Shuffleboard Quiet Games *Ice Skating	Table Tennis Badminton Deck Tennis *Rec. Games Shuffleboard Quiet Games *Ice Skating Wrestling
Feb.	Square Dance	Square Dance	Square Dance
March	Square Dance	Square Dance	Square Dance
April	*Bicycling Softball		*Bicycling Softball
May	Tennis		Tennis

*Special Events
Chess and Drill Team activities go on all year round
Some of the activities listed for January also go on in February and March

The Cincinnati Public Schools operate a tournament program which includes several recreational activities such as chess and checkers. The calendar includes the sports, divisions for competition, types of activities, entries, times and dates for competition, and places the events will be held (Fig. 13–20).

INTRAMURAL FORMS

Appropriate printed or mimeographed forms should be used to record data important to intramural competition. Scoring forms for basketball, bowling, diving, table tennis, tumbling, and volleyball are essential. One sample of an effective score card is shown in Figure 13–21.

AWARDS FOR INTRAMURALS

There are two points of view concerning the giving of awards in intramurals: (1) that interest in the competition and the fun derived from participation are sufficient rewards; (2) that inexpensive awards would increase motivation. What is important is that there should be some type of recognition for everyone.

The most popular awards are medals, monograms, trophies, plaques, and certificates. The first four types mentioned are too expensive for a large program with many students. Attractive certificates are inexpensive and may be framed and displayed in the home to provide a constant reminder of the pupil's participation.

Point System

A sound, fair and practical point system is essential for an effective awards program. The following is an example of how an awards program may be planned.

In team and individual activities, there must be individual school competition in order that points be awarded to members of the winning team or individual winners. Points may be awarded as follows, to school winners only:

First place winners: Five points awarded to each winner.

Second place winners: Three points awarded to each winner.
Third place winners: Two points awarded to each winner.
Participation: One point awarded to each participant not winning first, second, or third place. The one point for participation will not be used for monogram points if the pupil wins first, second, or third place in an activity.

Rules for Awarding Points:
  a. There is to be no transferral of monogram points from junior high school to senior high school.
  b. Monogram points are not awarded to city-wide winners.
  c. *Certificates.* Pupils earning 17 intramural points shall receive a certificate. Points accumulated but not sufficient for a monogram may be carried over to the next term, but points may not be transferred from junior high school to senior high school.
  d. *Monograms.* Pupils receiving eight points over the 17 will be awarded a monogram. Points may not be transferred to the senior high school.
  e. *Stars.* Pupils will be awarded a star for every 10 points earned above the 25.
  f. Scoring for track and swimming—school meets:
    (1) The individual scoring the highest number of points in these events will receive five monogram points.
    (2) Individual scoring second highest number of points will receive three monogram points.
    (3) Individual scoring third highest number of points will receive two monogram points.

Certificates for Awards

Many cities have found certificates to be extremely satisfactory. A few illustrations of the types of certificates used are shown in Figure 13–22.

Monogram and Felt Awards

Monograms and felt awards are awarded universally to show accomplishment in intramural competition. They range in size from four to 12 inches and are made of felt

High School Intramurals Sports Calendar 19___–19___

Sports	Division	Type	Entries	Time	Competition	Place
Tennis Clinic	Jr & Sr	Indiv.	None	A S	Sept. 13	GG
Tennis Tournament	Jr & Sr	Indiv.	None	A S	Sept. 16 to comp	Tennis Courts
Flag Football	7th & 8th	Team	Sept. 23–24	A S	Sept. 30–Nov. 1 (MF)	Playfield
Water Polo	9th only	Team	Sept. 23–24	A S	Oct. 1–Oct. 18 (TWTh)	Pool
Basketball	Sr	Team	Sept. 17–18	A S	Oct. 1–Nov. 8	GG & BG
Faculty Table Tennis Tournament		Indiv.	Oct. 29–30	A S	Nov. 5 & 6	Auditorium
Table Tennis Tournament	Jr & Sr	Indiv	None	A S	Nov. 13 to comp	North Lunch
Basketball	Jr	Indiv	None	Sat	Nov. 16–Feb. 15	GG & BG
Spot Shot Tournament	Jr & Sr	Indiv	None	B S	Dec. 17–18–19	GG & BG
Golf Clinic	Jr & Sr	Indiv	None	A S	Jan. 7–23 (TTh)	North Lunch
Weight Lifting	Jr & Sr	Indiv	None	A S	Dec. 11–Feb. 28 MWF	Room 401
Wrestling	Jr & Sr	Indiv	None	A S	Dec. 11–Feb. 28 TTh	Room 401
Volleyball	Jr & Sr	Team	Dec. 17–18	B S	Jan. 6–31	GG & BG
Roller Skating	Jr & Sr	Indiv	Jan. 28–29	B S	Feb. 3–28	GG
Gymnastics	Jr & Sr	Indiv	None	B S	Feb. 3–21	BG
Bowling	Jr & Sr	Indiv	Feb. 26–27	A S	Mar. 2–26 (MTh)	St. George
Foul Shooting Contest	Jr & Sr	Indiv	None	A S	Mar. 26–27	GG & BG
Pentathlon Contest	Jr & Sr	Indiv	None	A S	April 1–2	BG
Chess Tournament	Jr & Sr	Indiv	None	A S	April 8 to comp	North Lunch
Checker Tournament	Jr & Sr	Indiv	None	A S	April 8 to comp	North Lunch
Sweet Georgia Brown	Jr & Sr	Indiv	None	A S	May 4	BG
Golf Hole-in-One	Jr & Sr	Indiv	None	A S	May 6–7	Playfield
Badminton Tournament	Jr & Sr	Team	May 4–5	A S	May 11 to comp	GG & BG
Field Day	Jr & Sr	Team	None	A S	May 7	Playfield

Code: Jr = Junior High   A S = After School   BG = Boys Gym   Indiv = Individual
     Sr = Senior High   B S = Before School   GG = Girls Gym

M = Monday   T = Tuesday   W = Wednesday   Th = Thursday   F = Friday

Figure 13–20. High School Intramural Sports Calendar. (Courtesy Cincinnati Public Schools, Cincinnati, Ohio.)

HUGHES VOLLEYBALL INTRAMURAL SCORE CARD

Grade

Date _____ Court _____ Team _____ Vs Team _____

Full Name of Players	H.R.	Full Name of Players	H.R.

1 2 3 4 5 6 7 8 9 10 11 12 13 14 15 16 17 18 19 20 21 22
23 24 25 26 27 28 29 30 31 32 33 34 35 36 37 38 39 40

1 2 3 4 5 6 7 8 9 10 11 12 13 14 15 16 17 18 19 20 21 22
23 24 25 26 27 28 29 30 31 32 33 34 35 36 37 38 39 40

Officials

_____ HR

_____ HR Scorer _____ HR

Figure 13–21. A volleyball intramural score card which includes the rules and regulations. (Courtesy Cincinnati Public Schools, Cincinnati, Ohio.)

Figure 13–21 continued on opposite page.

VOLLEYBALL RULES AND REGULATIONS

TEAM

Six boys shall compose a team. However, a team may play with any lesser number. All players and substitutes must have their names on the score sheet before entering the game.

GAME

The team which has the most points at the end of the regulation playing time will be declared the winner. In case of tie games at the end of period the team that scores one point first is the winner.

PLAYING SCHEDULE

FIRST GAME		SECOND GAME
7.30 a.m.	Start of game	7.50 a.m.
7.35 a.m.	End first quarter	7.55 a.m.
7.40 a.m.	End first half	8.00 a.m.
7.45 a.m.	End third quarter	8.05 a.m.
7.50 a.m.	End of game	8.10 a.m.

SERVICE

The captains shall toss for court or service. The winner of toss may choose the service or the court. At the start of the game the ball shall be put in play by the player in the "Right Back" position. A service is putting the ball in play by batting it over the net into the opponents court in any direction with one hand (open or closed) and while in a position with both feet wholly behind the right one-third of the back line of the court.

SERVER

Each server shall continue to serve until the referee calls "Side Out." Points shall be called when the team receiving fails to return the ball legally to opponents' court.

SIDE OUT

"Side Out" shall be called when the team serving fails to win its point or plays the ball illegally.

ROTATION

The team receiving the ball for service shall immediately rotate one position in the usual manner — clockwise.

SIDE OUT

When a served ball touches the net, passes under the net, or touches any player, surface or object before entering the opponents' court is side out.

OUT OF BOUNDS

The ball is out of bounds when it touches any surface or object or the ground outside of the playing court. A ball touching the boundary line is good.

CATCHING OR HOLDING

When the ball momentarily comes to rest in the hands or arms of a player, he shall be considered as catching or holding the ball. The ball must be clearly batted.

DRIBBLING

A player touching the ball more than once with any part of the body is dribbling, which is illegal.

CHANGE COURTS

Teams shall change courts mid-way between the playing game, namely at 7:40 for first game and 8:00 for second game.

NUMBER OF HITS

The ball may be touched only three times by one team before being returned over the net. This does not prevent a boy from playing the ball twice providing he does not play it twice in succession. All other regulation rules will apply.

Figure 13–21. *Continued.* (Reverse of card shows rules and regulations.)

Figure 13–22.   Intramural certificates are inexpensive and make satisfactory awards for intramural competition.

Figure 13–22 continued on opposite page.

C

Cooper Senior High School
ABILENE, TEXAS
INTRAMURAL AWARD
PRESENTED TO

In_____

Year_____

| INTRAMURAL DIRECTOR | PHYSICAL EDUCATION DIRECTOR | PRINCIPAL |

YOUTH FITNESS PROGRESS AWARD

Presented To

_____

in recognition of a demonstrated increase in physical fitness efficiency from September 19___ to May 19___ as measured by the Omaha Fitness Test.

Signed this   day of   , 19 .

| Physical Education Teacher | Principal |

Tom Hallstrom
Supervisor of Physical Education

Paul A. Miller
Superintendent of Schools

D

Figure 13–22. *Continued.*

or chenille. In order to lower the cost of the monograms, pupils in the homemaking department may be willing to make them as a class project.

Participation Awards

To motivate students to join in intramural competition, all participants should receive *some* recognition whether they win or not. Figure 13–23 illustrates such an award.

ELIGIBILITY RULES

Rules governing the conduct of intramural sports should be put in writing and posted conspicuously. Sound and specific rules and regulations will prevent misunderstandings and embarrassment later. The following rules illustrate areas that need coverage:

1. All students who are enrolled in school are automatically eligible to enjoy all intramural privileges, unless they fail to comply with the other eligibility rules.

2. No scholastic requirements are enforced unless a student is so far behind the average of his class that all his spare time is needed for study.

3. Any student who is or has been a member of a varsity or junior varsity team and has participated in one or more scheduled games or practice games shall be ineligible to compete in that particular intramural sport. The same regulation applies to pupils who bowl on civic league bowling teams or swim on any organized teams. This rule shall be strictly enforced.

4. A player may be ruled ineligible to compete in future contests because of unsportsmanlike conduct, refusal to abide by the decision of an official, or use of improper language.

5. Upon the decision of the intramural director, students may be ruled ineligible to compete for infractions of any rules of the program or for any conduct that might cause embarrassment to the school.

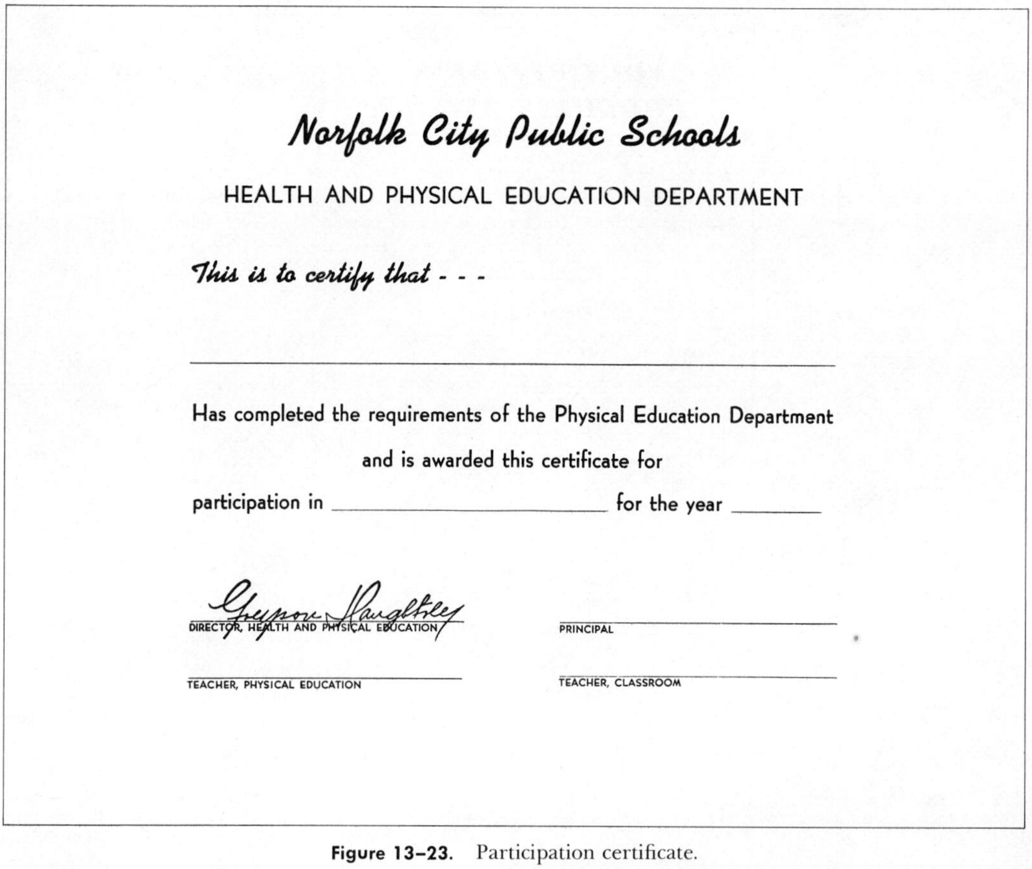

Norfolk City Public Schools

HEALTH AND PHYSICAL EDUCATION DEPARTMENT

This is to certify that - - -

_____

Has completed the requirements of the Physical Education Department

and is awarded this certificate for

participation in _____ for the year _____

DIRECTOR, HEALTH AND PHYSICAL EDUCATION   PRINCIPAL

TEACHER, PHYSICAL EDUCATION   TEACHER, CLASSROOM

Figure 13–23. Participation certificate.

General Regulations for Intramural Participation

The rules just given apply to the pupils in the school. There are several further general regulations concerning policy that should be printed and posted:

1. *No admission charge for intramurals.*
2. *Intramural competition must be limited to groups within the school.* If intramurals were to assume the competitive aspects of interscholastics, their existence would be unnecessary. (One exception to this, the city-wide tournaments, will be discussed later.)
3. *Intramurals must be scheduled outside of class periods.*
4. *Forfeits.* Forfeits are unnecessary if programs are planned properly. However, they should be anticipated and arrangements made to consider them.
5. *Postponements.* Contests postponed because of weather conditions and administrative conflicts should be rescheduled as soon as possible.
6. *Protests.* A committee should be established to develop policies pertaining to protests.

COEDUCATIONAL ACTIVITIES

Many activities in the physical education curriculum are suitable for joint play by boys and girls—when well organized, properly supervised, and played in wholesome environments, they make a tremendous contribution to the overall objectives of education. Psychologists and sociologists have for many years advocated vigorous physical activity for the release of pent-up energy and the development of emotional stability. Moreover, when boys and girls are playing together in an acceptable manner, greater respect for the opposite sex is developed.

Coeducational intramurals should be planned and administered differently from those activities segregated by sex. Placing boys and girls together in competitive situations necessitates new codes of behavior, emphasis on the scientific selection of activities, and intensive supervision. Some guidelines for developing coeducational intramurals are:

1. The regulations that govern the traditional intramural program should be followed.
2. The coeducational program should be voluntary.

3. Activities involving body contact should not be included in the program.
4. Rules should be modified to provide desirable participation by both sexes.
5. Activities should be scientifically sound and selected by the same criteria that are used for the instructional program.
6. Student interest should be the basic criterion, providing that guideline number five is followed.
7. Supervision of the program should be a joint function of men and women teachers or directors.
8. Careful supervision is important to insure desirable behavior by participants of both sexes.[10]

CULMINATING ACTIVITIES

A well-balanced intramural program should include, at the end of a season, a program incorporating several activities that have been featured in the tournaments and other competitive media. These culminating programs may be in the form of school-wide tournaments, demonstrations, field days, or May Days. Miss Barbara Kerch, Supervisor of Physical Education for the Community School District in Granite City, Illinois, reports an annual May Day event that illustrates an effective culminating activity. The cover and contents are shown in Figure 13–25.

Another noteworthy culminating activity is an event designed by Mrs. Mary Elizabeth Miller, head of the girls' physical education department, Richmond Senior High School, Richmond, Indiana. The title of this yearly demonstration is "Fitness and Femininity." The performance, which involves approximately 400 girls, is part of the total effort of the girls' physical education staff. Since its inception in 1967, "Fitness and Femininity" has provided an evaluation of the program at Richmond High School by the citizens of the community. Figure 13–26 shows the cover of the 1971 program.

Women physical education teachers at William Allen High School, Allentown, Pennsylvania, conduct annual demonstrations with a central theme. Recently, 1400 girls participated in a program entitled "Gaslight Follies," which included such activities as dancing, tumbling, and free exercise. The purpose of the event is to promote satisfaction and pleasure for stu-

Figure 13–24. Co-recreational programs are popular in both junior and senior high schools and assist in developing wholesome attitudes between boys and girls. (Courtesy Los Angeles City Schools.)

dents and to acquaint the parents with the physical education program.[11]

Culminating activities must be carefully planned to be successful. Definite guidelines are needed, of which the following should be helpful.

1. The demonstration should reflect the activities taught in the physical education program.

2. The demonstration should be carefully planned. If it is a yearly event, mistakes made should be recorded and corrected the following year.

3. A checklist should be devised showing the equipment, supplies, procedures, and all details involved in conducting the program.

4. Class time should not be used for practicing and rehearsing the events.

5. It is desirable to have a theme for the demonstration.

6. Programs should be printed if possible. Mimeographed programs may be used, but they are not as attractive as the printed programs.

7. The content of the demonstration should reflect the local philosophy of physical education.

8. In order to interpret the program, information relative to the program should be disseminated through public relations media, such as television and the newspapers.[10]

Planning a successful demonstration is a most time-consuming and intricate task. If demonstrations are not organized well in advance of the date in which they are held, confusion may result. Some additional guides to assist directors with their planning are outlined below:

1. The demonstration should represent activities that are taught in the instructional program. This not only serves as a true interpretation of the physical education program; it also does not infringe on instructional time.

2. A checklist of all items of equipment needed for the demonstration should be kept.

3. As many students as possible should be included in the demonstration.

4. Advanced planning is essential. Some of the factors that have to be arranged are (1) a place to hold the demonstration, (2) a date, (3) use of the public address system, (4) the arrangements for persons on the program, such as guest speakers (see Figure 13–27), and (5) transportation.

5. All participants should be neatly dressed. If the school uniform is used, it should be cleaned before use.

6. Activities in the demonstration should have a time limit. If this is not done, the program may drag on indefinitely, which means that

many spectators will leave. The program should move quickly and should include activities that can be explained to the spectators.

7. Adequate publicity should be given the event by television, newspapers, and announcements to teachers and administrators.

8. A printed program is essential for giving the demonstration status. If the financial outlay is prohibitive, a sponsor may be found to assume the cost.

9. The superintendent or a school board member should be given an important responsibility on the program. They may not come if they do not have a responsibility, and they are the very individuals who should know about the program (see Figure 13–27).

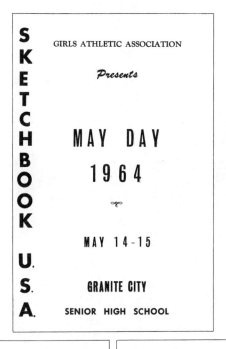

Figure 13–25. May Day program, promoting the annual "Sketchbook U.S.A.," consists of 21 events. (Courtesy of Barbara Kerch, Supervisor of Physical Education, Community Unit School District, Granite City, Illinois.)

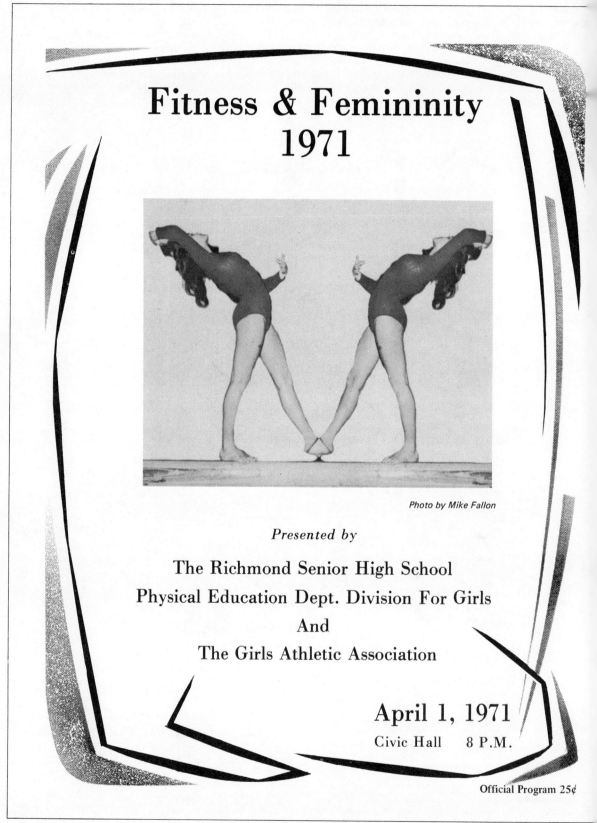

Fitness & Femininity
1971

Photo by Mike Fallon

Presented by

The Richmond Senior High School

Physical Education Dept. Division For Girls

And

The Girls Athletic Association

April 1, 1971

Civic Hall   8 P.M.

Official Program 25¢

Figure 13–26.   Fitness and Femininity, 1971. (Courtesy Richmond Senior High School, Richmond, Indiana.)

Figure 13–26 continued on opposite page.

We proudly present our

1970-71 Intramural Champions

Photos
by
Mike Fallon

SINGLES CHAMPION, TENNIS: Ida Russell, Senior.
(47 girls participated)

DOUBLES CHAMPIONS, TENNIS: Juniors Carlyss Soulier and
Donna Jones. (23 teams participated)

DOUBLES CHAMPIONS, BADMINTON: Gwen
Grimes, junior; Debbie Grimes, sophomore. (64 teams
participated)

RHS GIRLS A.A. BOWLING CHAMPIONS: GUTTER
GIRLS; Sophomores Nila Sandusky, capt., Cathy
Wagner, Nancy Stilwell, Dianne Bennett. (8 teams, 32
girls participated)

DOUBLES CHAMPIONS' TABLE TENNIS:
Seniors, Ida Russell and Missy Garrett. (24
teams participated.

*Winning entry in Fitness
and Femininity 1971
Photo-Art Contest by Gail
Richardson.*

SINGLES CHAMPION, TABLE TENNIS:
Senior, Marsha Ruble. (47 girls participated)

Figure 13-26. *Continued.*

HEALTH AND PHYSICAL EDUCATION DEPARTMENT

Annual City-Wide
Junior High School Intramural

VOLLEYBALL TOURNAMENT

On the broad and firm foundation of health alone can the loftiest and most enduring structures of the intellect be reared.   Horace Mann (1845)

BLAIR JUNIOR HIGH SCHOOL

Wednesday, January 9, 1962   3:30 P.M.

Figure 13–27. Participants in the program for an intramural tournament.

Figure 13–27 continued on opposite page.

PROGRAM
(Boys)

NATIONAL ANTHEM

PLEDGE OF ALLEGIANCE TO THE FLAG

INVOCATION .... Mr. Robert J. Steckroth
Principal, Blair Junior High School

WELCOME .... Mr. E. L. Lamberth
Superintendent of Schools

OPENING REMARKS .... Mr. Stanley Walker
Member, Norfolk City School Board

CHAIRMAN .... Mr. Kenneth Fulghum
Physical Education Teacher

OFFICIALS .... Arnold Davis, R. C. Street, Lionel Meredith
and James Thomas

PARTICIPANTS .... Winners of the 7th, 8th and 9th grade
tournaments in Azalea, Blair, Northside,
Norview Jr. and Willard.

PROGRAM
(Girls)

NATIONAL ANTHEM

PLEDGE OF ALLEGIANCE TO THE FLAG

INVOCATION .... Mr. John Klousia
Director of Instruction

WELCOME .... Mr. W. L. Robison
Assistant Superintendent of Schools

OPENING REMARKS .... Mrs. C. E. Griffin
Member, Norfolk City School Board

CHAIRMAN .... Miss Donna Doyle
Physical Education Teacher

PARTICIPANTS .... Winners of the 7th, 8th and 9th grade
tournaments in Azalea, Blair, Northside,
Norview Jr. and Willard.

OFFICIALS .... Mary Barnes, Jayne Bennett, Jeanette Elmore
and Roxanne Teaford

Figure 13-27. *Continued.*

Intramural Reports

It is important at the conclusion of the intramural program that reports be made by individual schools showing the number of students that participated. These reports should be sent to the director of physical education with copies to the principal and other administrators. The reports are necessary for publicity purposes, evaluation of the program and other items necessary for perpetuating the program. A participation report that has been used successfully is shown in Figure 13–28.

A summary of the total participation in all schools of a city is necessary for making yearly comparisons of the intramural program. A form that may be used for this purpose is shown in Figure 13–29.

CITY-WIDE PROGRAMS

Beyond the individual school performance and just below the level of the varsity program exists a group of pupils who have a degree of excellence in performance that should receive attention. These are the gifted pupils who should be allowed to further their participation beyond the competitive challenge offered in the school. To organize these pupils in one-day competitive contests is in keeping with recognized educational procedures. One criticism of junior high school interscholastics is the formation of leagues, the keeping of percentages, and the capitalizing on the extreme emotionalism of junior high school boys and girls to further the competitive effort. To allow the winners of the

---

CEDAR RAPIDS COMMUNITY SCHOOL DISTRICT

Physical Welfare Department
Cedar Rapids, Iowa

INTRAMURAL PARTICIPATION REPORT

To: All School Intramural Instructors

In order to have a uniform annual report on activities which can be made into a complete report for the Superintendent of Schools, will you please fill out the form below. The report should cover the entire school year. All reports must be completed and forwarded before the last week of the school year. Send all reports to the Physical Welfare Office. A duplicate report should be left with your principal.

School _____ Teacher _____

Date forwarded _____

List Activities (indicate boys, girls or co-recreational)	No. of Teams	No. of Pupils Partici- pating	Season of Year	Average No. of Games per Pupil	Type of Tournament (1)	Time of Day (2)	Grade Level of Participants

(1) Round robin — elimination, ladder, etc.　(2) Hour of day when play was conducted.

Figure 13–28. Intramural Participation Report. (Courtesy Cedar Rapids Community School District, Cedar Rapids, Iowa.)

CEDAR RAPIDS COMMUNITY SCHOOL DISTRICT

Physical Welfare Department
Cedar Rapids, Iowa

JUNIOR AND SENIOR HIGH SCHOOL
INTRAMURAL PUPIL PARTICIPATION SUMMARY REPORT
(Fall, Winter, and Spring)

This is a quantitative report only, indicating number of pupils participating in each activity.

	BOYS										GIRLS								CO-ED			
	Football (touch)	Softball	Wrestling	Tennis	Soccer and Speedball	Basketball	Volleyball	Tumbling and Trampoline	Swimming and Life Saving	*Misc. Games and Activities	Touch Football and/or Soccer, Field Hockey	Softball	Tennis	Basketball	Volleyball	Tumbling and Trampoline	*Misc. Games and Activities	Swimming and Life Saving	Volleyball	Water Show	Swimming and Life Saving	*Misc. Games and Activities
Franklin	78	56	46	22	47	79	32				36	86	41	157	150	30	71				65	
McKinley	186	183	63	22	268	218	224			111	80	55	22	200	60	100	191		276		61	396
Roosevelt	38	30	63	15		240	233				87	95	35	100	96	70	57		515		65	
Wilson	23	34	12	14	14	80		18		33	73	75	25	65		15	75		45		5	
Jefferson	64	180	21	10		350		24	40	95	20		10	50	60		426	130		85	200	350
Washington			43			387			151					252					935	52	118	320
TOTALS	**389**	**483**	**248**	**83**	**329**	**1354**	**489**	**42**	**191**	**239**	**296**	**311**	**133**	**824**	**366**	**215**	**820**	**130**	**1771**	**137**	**514**	**1066**

*Miscellaneous games and activities include: table tennis, aerial darts, badminton, kickball, bowling, physical fitness, deck tennis, ice skating, hiking, track, dancing, cheerleading, pep club, officiating, golf, archery, GRA, and campout.

Figure 13–29. Intramural Participation Summary Report. (Courtesy Cedar Rapids Community School District, Cedar Rapids, Iowa.)

school intramurals and tournaments to compete with one another on a one-day basis seems to be the answer to the problem.

Objectives of City-Wide Programs

City-wide intramural programs should:

1. Serve as a culmination of a seasonal sport.
2. Further stimulate interest, which in turn motivates participation beyond the school day.
3. Provide opportunity for the gifted to participate in competition with other students nearer their ability.

Organizing the City-Wide Program

The overall pattern for the city-wide organization is the responsibility of the city director or supervisor. A suggested plan that has been satisfactory is shown in the following sections. Each city-wide contest is assigned a chairman. All school winners

are sent to him, and he serves as the host for the contest that is held in his school.

It is the teacher's responsibility to see that the actual winners of school tournaments participate in the city-wide contests. In some instances intramural directors select the best players from a grade and allow them to participate in the city-wide contests. This practice defeats the purpose of the program, since the aim of all intramurals is to have as many players as possible.

Yearly Calendar. A yearly calendar should be made showing the sport, chairman and host, date, and other details. This calendar should be sent to all school directors as early in the school year as possible. As teachers may be asked to participate in the construction of this calendar, they should be familiar with the mechanics involved. One example of such a calendar for city-wide tournaments follows.[12]

MONTH	BOYS	GIRLS	PLACE	HOST
November	Volleyball Tues. 27 Wed. 28	Volleyball Tues. 27 Wed. 28	Granby	Sigler
				Zettlemoyer
January	Fitness meet Tues. 15	Fitness meet Tues. 15	Maury	Bryant
				Pulley
February	·Basketball Tues. 12 Thurs. 14	Basketball Tues. 12 Thurs. 14	Norview	Holloway
				Fardette
	Bowling Tues. 5	Bowling Tues. 5		Holloway
				Fardette
March	Tumbling Wed. 20	Body Mechanics Wed. 13	Granby	Slaughter
			Granby	Beach
	Wrestling Wed. 27		Granby	Slaughter
April	Tennis Wed. 24	Tennis Wed. 24	Lake Taylor	Sims
				Meacom
May	Track Wed. 22		Lake Taylor	Sims
	Table tennis Thurs. 23	Table tennis Thurs. 23	Maury	Peters
				Haywood

Records

All results of the city-wide contests should be sent, on special forms, to the physical education director immediately after the event. It is important that the lists of winners be kept from year to year.

General Rules Governing City-Wide Intramurals

It is strongly recommended that definite policies and rules governing the intramural program be formulated and enforced. Some of the rules might be the following:

1. Participants must have participated in and won the school competition before entering any city-wide tournament.
2. The junior high schools should participate separately from the senior high schools.

3. All pupils must have written parental permission to participate in the city-wide program.
4. All city-wide tournament participants must have insurance such as that provided by the school system.
5. All entries for the city-wide contests must be sent by the intramural director to the city-wide chairmen one week prior to the contest.
6. The city-wide contest chairmen are responsible for tournament arrangements and the procuring of officials.
7. All tornament results should be compiled and sent to the physical education office the day after the tournament.
8. Any pupil who has had varsity or junior varsity experience and who is a member of community leagues or any other league or organized group is ineligible for participation in that activity.
9. All participants should be insured.
10. In order to insure greater participation, the city-wide events should be organized on a grade-level basis.

Figure 13–30. City-wide intramural demonstrations not only provide controlled competition for many students, but also inform parents of the purposes of the program.

Awards for City-Wide Programs

The same problems complicating individual school awards apply to the city-wide contests. Extensive programs, involving a greater number of pupils and events, and thus requiring numerous award cups, trophies, medals and the like, are very costly. Again, the use of inexpensive certificates is an excellent solution (Fig. 13–31).

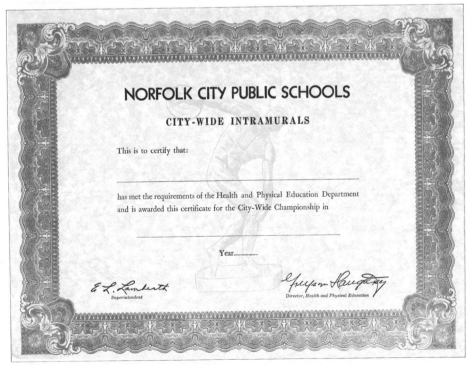

Figure 13–31. Certificate used as a city-wide intramural award.

Types of City-Wide Events

Demonstrations. The demonstration is an important type of city-wide activity. The events may be varied, and there is no limit to the number of pupils that may be involved. The Norfolk Public Schools hold a yearly demonstration involving hundreds of pupils and many events. The program, called "Building Healthier Youth," is described in Figure 13–32.

Mr. Tom Hallstrom, Director of Physical Education for the Omaha Public Schools, reports outstanding public relations accomplishments through an annual Youth Spectacular. His statistics show that about 3000 pupils participate in a three-night demonstration, attended by over 10,000 parents.

The Charlotte-Mecklenburg School District, Charlotte, North Carolina, sponsors an annual system-wide physical education demonstration. The program, entitled "Keeping Fit is Fun," includes exercises and dances to music, volleyball, badminton, field hockey, wrestling, tumbling, rope skipping, and other activities taught in the instructional class.[13]

Rhythmic demonstrations in which each school enters outstanding groups, have tremendous educational value for both students and teachers (Fig. 13–33). Teachers see creative effort by other teachers and are stimulated to improve their own instruction for the next year.

Meets. The Omaha Public Schools Physical Education Department has developed a unique and effective city-wide "postal" track meet. The event is described on page 490.

KHEDIVE SHRINE TEMPLE
OFFICERS

Illustrious Potentate..................Mr. Charles W. Davis
Chief Rabban.............................Mr. Judson H. Rodman
Assistant Rabban.....Mr. Herman F. Drummond, Jr.
High Priest
& Prophet.........................Mr. Robert H. Foxwell, Jr.
Oriental Guide.....................Mr. James H. Boyles, Jr.
Treasurer............................Mr. Bernard C. Murden, P.P.
Recorder...............................Mr. Robert E. Mayes, Jr.

Mr. Charles O. Philpotts
Director of Uniformed Units

Mr. Edward J. Blankenship
Assistant Director
of Uniformed Units

Khedive Drum & Bugle Corps
Mr. Weldon G. Barnes
Director

Mr. Wallace E. Ballard
Assistant Director

Meyer Legum, M.D.
Director, Medical Unit

EVENTS
Gross Motor Activities

These are activities involving the large muscles of the body and are the nucleus of all physical education programs.

FITNESS TESTS—The contestants tonight are the winners in the recent 5th Grade City-Wide Physical Proficiency Telephonic Meet involving elementary schools. The teachers are: Mr. Victor Roberts, Mrs. Geraldine Burney, Mr. Elsmer Stewart, Mr. William Reavis, and Mr. Richard Parker from Carey, Suburban Park, Marshall, Roberts Park, Sherwood Forest and Madison Elementary Schools.

BASKETBALL RELAYS—The seventh grade pupils, from Lee, Ingleside, Marshall, Easton, Lansdale, Liberty Park, Coleman Place, Ocean View and Stuart Elementary Schools, participating tonight are winners in the City-Wide Basketball Relays. The teachers are Mr. Rudolph Olds, Mr. Craig Schoulda, Mr. Elsmer Stewart, Mrs. Dorothy Cooper, Mrs. Pamela Drant, Mr. Raymond Smith, Miss Love Dishman, Mr. Charles Minton and Mr. Michael Smith. These relays provide a medium for placing masses of pupils in competitive basketball situations.

CAGEBALL RELAYS—First grade pupils from Larchmont, Granby, Lakewood, Taylor, Norview Annex and Oakwood Elementary Schools are competing tonight. The teachers are: Mr. Michael Grinder, Mr. William Adams, Mrs. Judith Daniel, Mrs. Pamela Drant and Mr. James Thomas. These relays provide an interesting medium for developing skills and endurance.

DEVELOPMENTAL EXERCISES — Music motivates interest in developmental exercises. Pupils from Rosemont Junior High School demonstrate various

---

PROGRAM

MASTER OF CEREMONIES........................Mr. Curtis Brooks, Director
Norfolk Convention and Visitors' Bureau
Chamber of Commerce

AMERICA THE BEAUTIFUL......Pupils, Camp Allen Elementary School

PLEDGE OF ALLEGIANCE........................Mr. Curtis Brooks, Director

INVOCATION..Mr. Eugene Gordman, President
Norfolk City Federation of
Parent-Teachers Associations

INTRODUCTION OF SHRINE OFFICERS.............Mr. Charles W. Davis
Illustrious Potentate

WELCOME...Dr. Robert Forster
Assistant Superintendent
Norfolk City Public Schools

ADDRESS...................................Honorable G. William Whitehurst
Member of Congress

DRUM AND BUGLE CORPS......................Mr. Weldon G. Barnes
Director

PROGRAM DIRECTOR...................Mr. Greyson Daughtrey, Supervisor
Health and Physical Education
Norfolk City Public Schools

PROGRAM COORDINATOR.........................Mr. Walter B. Clay
Assistant Supervisor
Health and Physical Education
Norfolk City Public Schools

SOUND ENGINEER....................Mr. Jack Gillentine, Teacher-Advisor
Health and Physical Education
Norfolk City Public Schools

AREAS OF EMPHASIS IN PHYSICAL EDUCATION

Physical education emphasizes the teaching of skills in three areas of instruction. They are: Gross Motor Activities, Perceptual-Motor Skills and Artistic Movements. The program tonight includes activities in the three areas.

EVENTS (Continued)

movements. Mrs. Sue Vance and Mrs. Jean Barham are the teachers.

CAGE VOLLEYBALL—Sixth grade pupils from Calcott and Stuart Elementary Schools play an exhibition game. This game is a variation of volleyball. The teachers are Mr. Leo Wood and Mr. Michael Smith.

Volleyball Demonstration—Maury High School, the winners of the Annual City-Wide Intramural Tournament, plays a team from the Tidewater Volleyball Association. Mr. Bruce Peters is the teacher.

WRESTLING—Wrestling develops the four components of fitness, strength, speed, skill and endurance. Pupils from Lake Taylor Junior High School demonstrate wrestling techniques. Mr. William Tugwell is the teacher.

Perceptual-Motor Activities

Activities in this group emphasize the awareness of the sensory processes as well as motor or muscle movements. Many children enter school without having had the opportunity of developing these coordinations. In many instances inability to read and write can be traced to deficiencies in these skills.

TUMBLING (Elementary)—Tumbling has no equal for development of balance, body relationships to space and kinesthetic awareness. Pupils from Bay View Elementary School illustrate the extent in which perceptual-motor skills may be developed. Mr. Wayne Whitson is the teacher.

SKIPPER-ETS—Rope skipping develops skill and coordination and when performed to music becomes more effective and meaningful in sensory perception. Third and fourth grade pupils from Larrymore Elementary School, under the direction of Mr. Albert Boyd, demonstrate these skills.

BASKETBALL SKILLS—Pupils develop precise directionality, laterality and kinesthetic awareness through performance in basketball skills. Pupils from Willard Junior High School demonstrate this. Mr. Gene Byerly directs the event.

BALL RHYTHMS AND BASIC MOVEMENTS—Young children begin perceptual-motor development by learning ball handling and other movements to music. Second grade pupils from Camp Allen Elementary School demonstrate these skills under the direction of Mr. Dale Williamson.

Artistic Movements

A well-balanced program in physical education includes many movements of an artistic nature. These skills are involved in the following activities.

RHYTHMS — Lindenwood pupils attending Camp Young demonstrate elementary movements. Miss Patricia Babine is the teacher.

MODERN DANCE—(Junior High School)—The group appearing tonight depicts the creativity that is involved in modern dance. Pupils from Northside Junior High School portray this theme. The teachers are Mrs. Sybil Stone and Miss Margaret Smart.

MODERN DANCE (Senior High School)—Not only is modern dance a creative activity, but it is an innovated dance form that is typically American. Granby Senior High School pupils, under the direction of Mrs. Janet Zettlemoyer, demonstrate the movements that constitute modern dance.

NOTICE: You Are Invited to Visit the Military Circle Shopping Mall to See the Health Education Fair, May 10-16

A

Figure 13–32. One thousand students perform before 6000 spectators in this annual demonstration. *A*, The program; *B*, Activities and participants.

Figure 13–32 continued on opposite page.

B

Figure 13–32. *Continued.*

Figure 13-33. Modern dance demonstrations provide an interesting medium for city-wide intramural programs.

POSTAL TRACK MEET
OMAHA PUBLIC SCHOOLS
OMAHA, NEBRASKA

The following plans for a "postal" track meet have been made after consultation with several of the senior high men physical education teachers.

Participating Schools. Benson, Beveridge, Central, North, South, Tech.

Participants. All boys enrolled in physical education classes except those on the track or baseball squads. Boys will compete at their own age level.

Events. 100, 220, 440, 880, high jump, broad jump, triple jump, shot-put (12 lb.), pull-ups, football throw.

Limit on Events. A boy may enter *all* of these events. *BUT* his time or distance may be submitted on only *five* events.

Reporting. Results of the top three performances in each event will be submitted *on the attached form* no later than *Friday, May 15.*

Awards. On a "time" comparison basis, the top six performers in the city for each age group will receive a very fine ribbon.

Team Scores. None will be kept.

Event Regulations. Same as regular track and field rules. Pull-ups start from a dead hang with the palms facing away from the body. *Note:* This is different from the fitness test.

A run is permitted on the football throw.

Other Regulations. None. For example, the number of trials of each boy is unlimited.

The motivational value of this program is directly proportional to the ingenuity and interest of each teacher.

The telegraphic track meet has proved to be successful in some places. Cortez High School in Phoenix, Arizona, has sponsored this type of city-wide participation. Developed by Richard King, the contestants are not limited to Phoenix alone, but include entries from other states.

Operation of the program is simple. The results of an intramural meet held in an individual school are sent to Mr. King by May 15; he tabulates the results and announces the winners by the end of the year.[14]

The events included in the meet are:

Track Events	*Field Events*	*Relays*
100-yard dash	High jump	440 yards
200-yard dash	Broad jump	880 yards
300-yard dash	Hop, step, and jump	Mile
600-yard dash	Shot-put	Mile medley
1320-yard dash	Discus	(440–220–220–880)
120 yard low hurdles (five hurdles, 20 yards apart)		
60 yard high hurdles (three hurdles, 15 yards apart)		

Tournaments. City-wide tournaments provide an opportunity for the more gifted boys and girls to participate—the pupils form lasting associations and are motivated to continue their competitions beyond the school years.

An illustration of the enthusiasm created by city-wide tournaments is the bowling program in the Norfolk public schools. Each year, all of the 16,000 boys and girls in the secondary schools are given bowling instruction, made possible by the use of portable bowling alleys set up in each school (Fig. 13–34). In conjunction with the instruction, each school has an intramural bowling program, held in the local bowling alleys. At the conclusion of the season a city-wide tournament is held in which the outstanding bowlers from each school meet and bowl for the city championship. Invitations are sent to parents and important city and school officials.

Planning for City-Wide Programs

Planning for city-wide programs presents a challenge to the teachers who are responsible for the initial groundwork. Participants must be familiarized with the surroundings, officials must be briefed, the areas must be marked properly, and numerous other details must be taken care of.

An illustration of a demonstration involving several schools should be helpful to the teacher. The following plan describes a physical education demonstration involving 2000 participants, 54 schools and 5 events. The total time for completing the program was two hours. The demonstration illustrates how the physical education department, teachers, administrators, principals, the local college, and parents combine efforts to provide boys and girls with the opportunity of participating in a program designed to contribute to their health and fitness.

It is relatively easy to plan a demonstration for a small number of schools, but planning for many schools presents a complex problem. To illustrate a method of planning for many schools, an example is drawn from an elementary school program. The plans include the seventh grade, which is normally the first grade of the junior high school, and various parts of the plan are used interchangeably for secondary schools. Items such as regulations for events, entry lists, checklists, division groups, officials and responsibilities, marking the site, and compilation of records are the same for both elementary and secondary schools. The purpose of the following description is to provide a demonstration plan that may be used effectively for several schools, with adjustments for the local situation.

Preliminary Planning. A committee consisting of supervisors, principals, physical

Figure 13–34. Portable bowling backstops can be used to simulate actual bowling situations. They serve as an inexpensive tool for instruction.

Figure 13–35. Annual city-wide tournaments provide an opportunity for pupils and teachers to see the value of intensive instruction and the need for more constructive intramural programs.

education teachers, and classroom teachers should determine the overall policy for organizing the demonstration. Such items as time, day, date, events, transportation, site, and purpose might comprise the list that the committee should study.

After decisions have been made regarding these items, they should be presented to the superintendent, and a letter from his office should be sent to all principals and other persons who are involved. The following letter illustrates how the decisions of the committee may be announced by the superintendent:

March 10, 1973

MEMORANDUM

To: Principals, Teachers, and Parent-Teacher Presidents

From: Superintendent of Schools
           Assistant Superintendent for Curriculum and Instruction
           Director of Health and Physical Education

Topic: Annual Health and Physical Education Demonstration

Our annual health and physical education demonstration will be held on Tuesday, May 17, at 1:00 P. M., Foreman Field. In the event of rain the demonstration will be held on Wednesday, May 18, at 1:00 P.M.

There is grave concern on the part of our leaders relative to the physical fitness of the boys and girls in this country, and we are exceedingly anxious to provide an adequate physical education program for the boys and girls in Norfolk. We feel that the demonstration which has been planned for this year will serve as a great motivating influence and will increase interest on the part of boys and girls for taking exercise.

Enclosed you will find a copy of the regulations governing the demonstration. Every effort has been made to simplify the technique involved in holding an affair of this nature, and the whole program should be finished by the time school is normally dismissed. Approval has been obtained from the Superintendent to excuse all participants at 12:30 P. M. on the afternoon of the demonstration. Each participant will be required to have a parental approval permit which will be furnished by the Health, Physical Education and Safety Department.

We assume that the parent-teacher organizations will assist with the transportation for the demonstration as they have done in the past, and we will appreciate their assistance with this phase of the program.

We sincerely hope that you will cooperate with us on this project as you have done in the past, and any information not included in the enclosed paragraphs will be sent to you upon request from your physical education teacher or by calling our office.

Details of the Demonstration. At a later date, an announcement should be sent to all persons concerned with organizing the demonstration. It should contain specific information relative to the preliminary planning. The announcement that follows outlines some of these items:

A N N O U N C I N G

ANNUAL

HEALTH AND PHYSICAL EDUCATION DEMONSTRATION

AT FOREMAN FIELD

Tuesday, May 17, 1973

1:00 P. M.

IMPORTANT

1. If weather is unsuitable, the demonstration will be held Wednesday, May 18, at 1:00 P.M.

2. Permission of parents must be secured on forms furnished by the Department.

3. Approved entry blanks must be collected by the physical education teacher on or before Thursday, May 12.

4. Each contestant must wear identification tags pinned to front and back of shirt. The tag on the front will show school and grade and the back will show school and lane number assigned. The tags will be furnished by the Health, Physical Education, and Safety Department.

5. Each contestant may compete in only one event.

6. If the first place participant is unable to compete, the second place participant will be allowed to enter.

7. Scoring — First Place, five (5) points — Second Place, three (3) points — Third Place, one (1) point.

8.   Awards—Ribbons, First, Second, and Third Place Winners.

Certificates will be awarded to all participants in the demonstration.

A Rotating Trophy will be awarded to division winners.

9.   Physical education teachers and physical education majors from the Old Dominion College, Norfolk, will score and officiate the demonstration.

10. All contestants and spectators will please enter from the west side of the stadium. All cars and buses will park on west side of the stadium.

11. Contestants cannot wear any type of shoes with spikes or cleats.

Regulations and Entry Lists. Teachers should select the participants in the demonstration and should be given sufficient time o select them fairly. The regulations for each event should be explained and posted in a conspicuous place. The following form illustrates one way this can be done.

Regulations for Events

1. Pull-ups (boys)

a. Pupil must go all the way up and down.
b. No swinging, kicking or jerking—normal body movement only.
c. Pupil must touch bottom of chin to top of bar.
d. Pupil may use any grip.

2. Hop, Step, Jump (girls)

a. The pupil must start on one foot—other foot may swing.
b. The pupil must end jump on both feet.
c. The part of the body nearest starting line will be where measurement is made. For example: If a girl falls back on her hands, the measurement will be made from hand.

3. Potato Race (boys and girls)

a. Crouch start is compulsory for the start of the race.
b. The block must be in the circle.
c. The pupil should pick up first block—return it to the starting circle—pick up second block—place it in starting circle—return first block to second circle—return second block to first circle and cross finish line. (See Diagram)

```
S
T   X  _____34 feet_____→   1     2
A
R      _____42 feet_____→
T
```

Note: If a contestant is disqualified by crossing over into another lane and picking up block, the race will stop immediately, and the person disqualified shall be eliminated and the race rerun.

HEALTH AND PHYSICAL EDUCATION DEMONSTRATION
NORFOLK CITY PUBLIC SCHOOLS

ENTRY LIST

School _____ Division _____ Sex _____

Teacher Representative _____

This entry list should be properly filled in, collected by the health and physical education teacher and delivered to the Health, Physical Education, and Safety Office one week before the demonstration. Parental permission slips must be obtained for all participants.

HOP, STEP, JUMP (GIRLS) PULL-UPS (BOYS)

GRADE	FIRST PLACE	SECOND PLACE
4		
5		
6		
7		

POTATO RACE

GRADE	FIRST PLACE	SECOND PLACE
4		
5		
6		
7		

SHUTTLE RELAY

4th	5th		6th	7th

DASH

GRADE	FIRST PLACE	SECOND PLACE
4		
5		
6		
7		

Principal _____ Phys. Ed. Teacher _____

Figure 13–36. Official entry blank for annual physical education demonstration.

4. Shuttle Relay (boys and girls)

   a. Crouch start is compulsory for the start of race.
   b. Baton must be passed with right hand to the right hand of teammate.
   c. Pupil must stay in lanes—he is disqualified if not.
   d. Pupil must stay behind line until he or she gets baton.
   e. Pupil may go back to get baton if dropped.
   f. 40 yards.
   g. Each grade team will consist of four pupils from the same classroom.

5. Dash (boys and girls)

   a. Crouch start is compulsory.
   b. Pupil must stay in lanes—he is disqualified if not.
   c. 40 yards

After the participants have been determined, they should be placed on an official entry blank such as the one shown in Figure 13–36.

Parental Approval. Individuals selected to participate in the demonstration should be given parental approval forms (Fig. 13–37), to be taken home, signed by the parents, and returned promptly to the teacher.

Division Groupings. To provide fairer competition and to ease handling of large groups of pupils in the various events, all schools should be grouped in divisions based on their size. Instead of one large group of pupils waiting for their turn to participate in an event, there would be several groups (six in the plan outlined) participating simultaneously. Instead of a program's lasting an entire afternoon, which would be boring to both participant and spectator, the entire program would last only two hours.

The following plan on the opposite page shows how all of the schools in a system may be grouped.

Officials' Orientation. As the plans progress, it is extremely important to meet with the officials who have been selected for the demonstration. In those localities where a teacher training institution exists, the institution may be willing to cooperate and allow one of the professional classes to assist with the officiating. Such an experience is invaluable to students who intend to teach when they graduate.

HEALTH, PHYSICAL EDUCATION AND SAFETY DEPARTMENT

Norfolk Public Schools

Parental Approval Permit

I hereby give my permission for _____ to

participate in the health and physical education demonstration, _____
                                                            (Date)

I understand that all precautions will be taken to prevent accidents and I will not hold school authorities responsible for any injury resulting from his/her participation.

_____   _____
     Date   Signature of Parent or Guardian

Figure 13–37. Parental approval form.

DIVISION ASSIGNMENT
FOR
ANNUAL HEALTH AND PHYSICAL EDUCATION DEMONSTRATION
FOREMAN FIELD
TUESDAY, MAY 17, 1973 — 12:30 P. M.

All participants will run races in the lane assigned below. Divisions were determined by total 4–6 grade memberships shown on December, 1972, monthly report.

Lane No.	Division I	Lane No.	Division IV
1	E. Ocean View	28	Goode
2	Pretty Lake	29	Chesterfield
3	Campostella Hgts.	30	Liberty Park
4	Smallwood	31	Fairlawn
5	Coronado	32	Lansdale
6	Campostella Jr.	33	Larchmont
7	Tidewater Park	34	Madison
8	Pineridge	35	Norview
9	Lafayette	36	Poplar Halls

Lane No.	Division II	Lane No.	Division V
10	Ballentine	37	Tarrallton
11	Rosemont	38	Lindenwood
12	Oakwood	39	Lincoln
13	Taylor	40	Sherwood Forest
14	Carey	41	Titus
15	Ingleside	42	Larrymore
16	Easton	43	Calcott
17	Young Park	44	Lakewood
18	Meadowbrook	45	Ocean View

Lane No.	Division III	Lane No.	Division VI
19	Titustown	46	Stuart
20	Tucker	47	Granby
21	Diggs Park	48	Bowling Park
22	Gatewood	49	Coleman Place
23	Roberts Park	50	Monroe
24	Lee	51	Bay View
25	Suburban Park	52	Crossroads
26	West	53	Marshall
27	Oceanair	54	Little Creek

If there is *not* a teacher training institution available, officials may be selected from students in the high school. There should be several meetings with the officials to explain their duties and distribute their assignments, which should be printed or mimeographed and given to them early during the planning period (Fig. 13–38). Representatives from the school system meet with the college group, outline responsibilities, acquaint them with the regulations of each event, and give each student an assignment sheet.

Check List. There should be a check list to determine the items needed for holding the demonstration. Mistakes that are made during the demonstration should be noted and placed in the check list file and also placed on the list for the following year. The following check list on page 501 includes the items that are usually involved in a demonstration.

ANNUAL HEALTH AND PHYSICAL EDUCATION DEMONSTRATION—
FOREMAN FIELD
OFFICIALS

DIVISION I	DIVISION II
Division Official	**Division Official**
_____—Teacher in charge	_____—Teacher in charge
Awards	**Awards**
_____—Teacher in charge	_____—Teacher in charge
PULL-UPS	**PULL-UPS**
1. _____—Teacher in charge	1. _____—Teacher in charge
2. _____—Student	2. _____—Student
3. _____—Student	3. _____—Student
HOP, STEP, JUMP	**HOP, STEP, JUMP**
_____—Teacher in charge	_____—Teacher in charge

	DIVISION I		DIVISION II
Grade 4	1. _____—Student	Grade 4	1. _____—Student
	2. _____—Student		2. _____—Student
Grade 5	1. _____—Student	Grade 5	1. _____—Student
	2. _____—Student		2. _____—Student
Grades 6 & 7	1. _____—Student	Grades 6 & 7	1. _____—Student
	2. _____—Student		2. _____—Student

RACES	RACES
DIVISION I	**DIVISION II**
Starter: _____—Student	Starter: _____—Student
Timer: _____—Student	Timer: _____—Student
Judges: Place 1. _____—Student	Judges: Place 1. _____—Student
2. _____—Student	2. _____—Student
3. _____—Student	3. _____—Student
4. _____—Student	4. _____—Student
Line-Up	**Line-Up**
1. _____—Teacher	1. _____—Teacher
2. _____—Teacher	2. _____—Teacher
3. _____—Teacher	3. _____—Teacher
4. _____—Teacher	4. _____—Teacher

Figure 13–38. Schedule of assignments of officials for annual physical education demonstration.

Figure 13–38 continued on opposite page.

ANNUAL HEALTH AND PHYSICAL EDUCATION DEMONSTRATION— FOREMAN FIELD
OFFICIALS

DIVISION III

Division Official

_____ —Teacher in charge

Awards

_____ —Teacher in charge

PULL-UPS

1. _____ —Teacher in charge
2. _____ —Student
3. _____ —Student

HOP, STEP, JUMP

_____ —Teacher in charge

Grade 4   1. _____ —Student
           2. _____ —Student

Grade 5   1. _____ —Student
           2. _____ —Student

Grades 6 & 7   1. _____ —Student
              2. _____ —Student

RACES

DIVISION III

Starter: _____ —Student

Timer: _____ —Student

Judges: Place 1. _____ —Student
            2. _____ —Student
            3. _____ —Student
            4. _____ —Student

Line-Up

1. _____ —Teacher
2. _____ —Teacher
3. _____ —Teacher
4. _____ —Teacher

DIVISION IV

Division Official

_____ —Teacher in charge

Awards

_____ —Teacher in charge

PULL-UPS

1. _____ —Teacher in charge
2. _____ —Student
3. _____ —Student

HOP, STEP, JUMP

_____ —Teacher in charge

Grade 4   1. _____ —Student
           2. _____ —Student

Grade 5   1. _____ —Student
           2. _____ —Student

Grades 6 & 7   1. _____ —Student
              2. _____ —Student

RACES

DIVISION IV

Starter: _____ —Student

Timer: _____ —Student

Judges: Place 1. _____ —Student
            2. _____ —Student
            3. _____ —Student
            4. _____ —Student

Line-Up

1. _____ —Teacher
2. _____ —Teacher
3. _____ —Teacher
4. _____ —Teacher

Figure 13–38. *Continued.*

Figure 13–38 continued on following page.

ANNUAL HEALTH AND PHYSICAL EDUCATION DEMONSTRATION—
FOREMAN FIELD
OFFICIALS

DIVISION V

Division Official

_____ —Teacher in charge

Awards

_____ —Teacher in charge

PULL-UPS

1. _____ —Teacher in charge
2. _____ —Student
3. _____ —Student

HOP, STEP, JUMP

_____ —Teacher in charge

Grade 4 1. _____ —Student
        2. _____ —Student

Grade 5 1. _____ —Student
        2. _____ —Student

Grades 6 & 7 1. _____ —Student
        2. _____ —Student

RACES

DIVISION V

Starter: _____ —Student

Timer: _____ —Student

Judges: Place 1. _____ —Student
        2. _____ —Student
        3. _____ —Student
        4. _____ —Student

Line-Up

1. _____ —Teacher
2. _____ —Teacher
3. _____ —Teacher
4. _____ —Teacher

DIVISION VI

Division Official

_____ —Teacher in charge

Awards

_____ —Teacher in charge

PULL-UPS

1. _____ —Teacher in charge
2. _____ —Student
3. _____ —Student

HOP, STEP, JUMP

_____ —Teacher in charge

Grade 4 1. _____ —Student
        2. _____ —Student

Grade 5 1. _____ —Student
        2. _____ —Student

Grades 6 & 7 1. _____ —Student
        2. _____ —Student

RACES

DIVISION VI

Starter: _____ —Student

Timer: _____ —Student

Judges: Place 1. _____ —Student
        2. _____ —Student
        3. _____ —Student
        4. _____ —Student

Line-Up

1. _____ —Teacher
2. _____ —Teacher
3. _____ —Teacher

Figure 13–38. _Continued._

HEALTH AND PHYSICAL EDUCATION DEPARTMENT
NORFOLK CITY SCHOOLS

CHECK LIST OF ITEMS NEEDED FOR THE
ANNUAL HEALTH AND PHYSICAL EDUCATION DEMONSTRATION

GENERAL:

1. Requisition for using public address system with record player-alternate system.

2. Clear date and use of field with Recreation Department, college; request Recreation Department to install pull-up bars.

3. Letter to principals, purpose, date, place, transportation, description of events, entry sheet and parental permission slips for participants, diagram of field and seating arrangements, list of times and records for preceding year to use as standards.

4. School markers and district markers for stands.

5. List of officials and assignments.

6. Pupil tags:

	Front		Back
4″	School / Grade	4″	School / Grade
	8″		8″

SPECIFIC:

1. TO TEACHERS:
   Parents' permission slips; pupil tags; copies of letter and materials and extra copies of entry sheets; certificates.

2. MARKING FIELD:
   Line, line marker, nails, tape, string, hammer, 3–10″ round cut-outs for marking potato race circles.

3. DIVISION BOXES:
   Tape measures (3 each) and staples to hold down; yardsticks (6 each), potato race blocks, rubber relay batons, pencils, clipboard with completed scoring sheets for each activity, ribbons, stop watches, starting gun and blanks, nails to remove empty shells.

4. DAY OF DEMONSTRATION:
   Rotating trophies, school markers installed, tables for demonstration of exercises, speaker's stand with steps, P.A. set up with record player, alternate system.

Marking the Field. Marking the field for the thousands of pupils involved requires careful consideration. The majority of the pupils may never have seen the site where the event is to be held. In most instances, the mechanics or organization are unrehearsed. Stadium or field markings for assembly of the pupils, division markings, lanes for individual event assembly, speaker's stand, and other details are shown in Figure 13–39.

Scoring Sheets. Printed or mimeographed scoring sheets should be available for smooth operation and the keeping of official records. Figures 13–41, 13–42, and 13–43 show scoring forms that should be

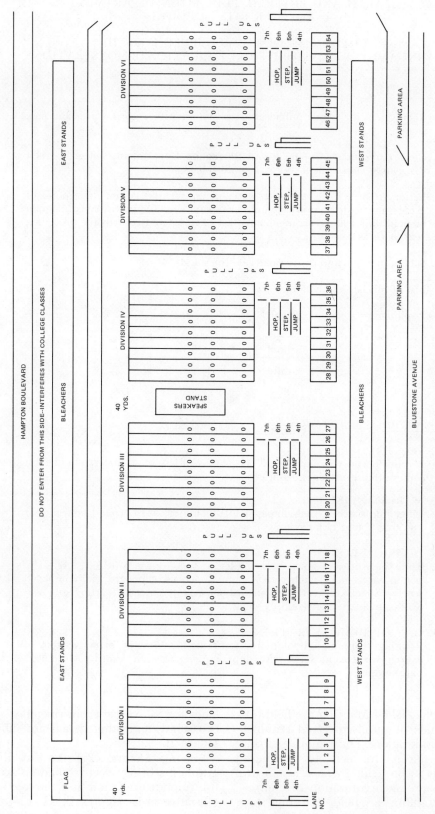

Figure 13–39. Marking the field for demonstrations.

Figure 13–40. A well-marked field facilitates the organization of a physical education demonstration. The illustration shows the placement of two divisions described in the demonstration outlined in this chapter: the lane for dashes; alignment of pupils; location of pull-up bars; markings for hop, step, and jump; announcer's stand; areas for folk dancing; and seating arrangements for participants are shown.

provided prior to the day the demonstration is held.

Auxiliary Personnel

DEMONSTRATION DIRECTOR. One person, preferably an experienced teacher, should be selected to direct the entire demonstration. This person should have adequate knowledge of the various facets involved and should have had previous experience with demonstrations of this kind.

ANNOUNCER. The announcer should have experience in talking over a public address system and should also have had experience with this type of demonstration. The demonstration director may or may not be assigned to this responsibility.

NURSE. Although accidents are rare, a nurse or physician should be available at all times.

TRAFFIC CONTROL. One or two policemen should be used to prevent traffic congestion and assist in maintaining order.

Programs. Printed programs add dignity and give pupils and spectators a more comprehensive understanding of the demonstration. The program should include the official ceremony, events, purpose of the demonstration, and other details that would be of interest to the public (Fig. 13–44).

Public Relations in City-Wide Programs

Representatives from local newspapers and television stations should be invited to the demonstration and the results should be compiled and given to reporters. Usually local newspapers and television stations will provide adequate space and time for acquainting the public with the results.

Representatives from civic clubs and parent-teacher organizations should be invited, along with other school administrators. The program should include the names of the superintendent, members of the board, and other persons of influence.

Groups and individuals interested in school programs should be acquainted with the purposes of city-wide contests. Chapter 3 on public relations should be reviewed and the media discussed in the chapter should be applied to the city-wide programs.

Intramurals are the windows of the physical education program through which the public can view the content, activities, philosophy, and objectives of the physical education offering. Alert directors of physical education may present a broad panorama of the entire program if they desire. In addition to the media outlined in

NORFOLK CITY PUBLIC SCHOOLS
HEALTH AND PHYSICAL EDUCATION DEPARTMENT

ANNUAL PHYSICAL EDUCATION DEMONSTRATION

RESULTS

Year

Division   Sex

Event	Grade	Place	Name	School	Record

Figure 13–41. Form for recording results of annual physical education demonstration.

NORFOLK CITY PUBLIC SCHOOLS
ANNUAL PHYSICAL EDUCATION DEMONSTRATION

RUNNING AND FIELD EVENTS

Event	Division	Sex	Grade

Score

NAMES	CHIN or H.S.J.	SCHOOL	POINTS AND PLACE			RECORD
			1	2	3	

Officials

1. Write number of points earned in point and place column.
2. Enter top score for event in record column.
3. Each girl will do the hop, step, jump twice, consecutively. Enter only the highest score attained in score column for hop, step, jump.
4. Enter score for contestant's pull-ups in appropriate column.

_____

OFFICIAL

Figure 13–42. Form used for running and field events.

NORFOLK CITY PUBLIC SCHOOLS
HEALTH AND PHYSICAL EDUCATION DEPARTMENT

DIVISION_____   SEX_____

Division Results Tabulation Form

	Boys	Girls	Totals	Chin — Grade 4	Chin — Grade 5	Chin — Grade 6–7	Hop, Step, Jump Grade 4	Hop, Step, Jump Grade 5	Hop, Step, Jump Grade 6–7	Potato Race Grade 4	Potato Race Grade 5	Potato Race Grade 6–7	Shuttle Relay Grade 4	Shuttle Relay Grade 5	Shuttle Relay Grade 6–7	Dash — Grade 4	Dash — Grade 5	Dash — Grade 6–7
TOTALS																		

INSTRUCTIONS   1. Points: First — 5   Second — 3   Third — 1
2. In the event of a tie, the points are added and the participants are awarded one-half of the total.
Example: Two-way tie for first place — 5 + 3 = 8 ÷ 2 = 4 points to each participant.

Figure 13–43. Division results form.

Chapter 3, there are other media involved in a good public relations program that merit consideration; these are discussed in the following paragraphs.

Sponsors. It is relatively easy to find clubs and groups interested in sponsoring school programs. Most civic clubs have youth committees that are responsible for activities that contribute to the improvement of the health and welfare of boys and girls. For example, Norfolk has the co-operation of three outstanding organizations that lend their support to the city-wide events. (See p. 507.)

Although school systems in many instances do not need the financial support, they do need the good will of these groups. Such groups, by investing a little money and assisting with the events, become strong supporters of the program. Figure 13–45 illustrates one way a civic group may assist in promoting city-wide intramurals.

Bulletin Boards. Attractive and well-planned bulletin boards are one of the greatest assets in promoting public relations, acquainting pupils with results, and providing an overview of the entire program.

Pupils may be appointed to construct these boards; not only will they welcome the challenge but some of their ideas will enhance the promotion of the program.

Club	Activity Sponsored	What Club Does
Kiwanis	One goal basketball tournament	Furnishes trophies
Rotary	Leisure time fitness program	Furnishes trophies and bulletins; officiates
Shrine	City-wide demonstration	Leases city arena, and pays for filming of event

Announcements. In order to interpret and acquaint the public with the city-wide programs, well-planned announcements should be prepared well in advance of the events. Printed programs are inexpensive and may contain much valuable information that will assist teachers and administrators in their efforts to interpret the school program to the public (see Figure 13–46).

Other Media. Chapter 3 outlines in detail other media that may be used in interpreting the program; these should be reviewed.

INTRAMURAL SPORTS AND RECREATION

Although intramural sports serve as an extension of the instructional program, they also play a significant role in motivating pupils to continue exercising in later life. Intramural sports serve as a medium for immediate carry-over and as a laboratory for the instructional program. However, when school days are over, pupils must find another medium for organized play activity—the recreational programs.

The teacher of physical education sometimes is asked to assist with the planning of recreational programs. The informed teacher can be of great assistance in serving as an ex-officio member of the recreation board or as a consultant in developing programs. It is important also that teachers provide the opportunity for participation in those activities that are popular during the school years but that also may be a part of recreational life in later years. For this, guidelines are needed; Zeigler lists some areas in which the teacher has a responsibility for working with the community in developing recreational programs:

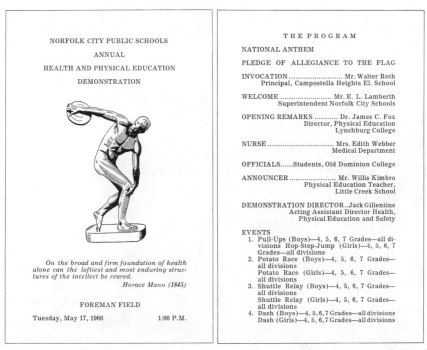

Figure 13–44. A printed program adds dignity to the demonstration and provides a source of information for participants and parents.

1. He can serve on the recreation commission as a responsible individual who is qualified professionally in part of the recreation field.

2. He can develop proper attitudes in his students toward the learning of recreational skills for use in post-school life.

3. He can teach sports skills to his students and thereby allow subsequent recreation programs to meet other needs.

4. He can develop future part-time and volunteer leaders for the physical recreation program by using leaders' corps in his physical education program.

5. He can call to the attention of the recreation director those atypical children who might need special attention during the summer program.

6. He can help the recreation director set up classification tests for physical recreational activities similar to those which operate in the school program.[15]

EVALUATION OF THE INTRAMURAL SPORTS PROGRAM

The basic criterion for evaluating the intramural program is the number of pupils participating. This chapter has been written with this aim in view. Too often teachers are apparently satisfied to organize an eight-team basketball league and plan for one or two games each day. This means that approximately 40 boys will profit from the program. Programs operating with this limited scope do not meet the objectives of intramurals.

There are evaluative criteria that may be used to assist teachers in appraising their efforts. Howard Parsons at Charles Maclay Junior High School, Pacoima, California, has devised an intramural checklist that should be helpful to teachers in evaluating their program:

Before the Season

1. Do I have adequate facilities?
2. Do I have adequate supplies and equipment?
3. Have I a good storage system?
4. Are all items marked and identified?
5. Have I planned for adequate safety supervision?
6. Have I scheduled a variety of seasonal sports?
7. Have I informed my administrator as to what we plan to do?
8. Have I involved as many faculty members as possible?
9. Have I informed and involved the PTA whenever practical?
10. Have I advertised the program by daily bulletins, PE class announcements, signs, posters, and newspaper releases?
11. Have I checked all community agencies to reduce conflicts in scheduling?
12. Have I planned seasonal activities that are neither too long nor too short?
13. Am I really enthusiastic about the program?
14. Do I have a standings bulletin board in a prominent place?
15. Have I posted clear-cut rules governing all activities for all to see and do I insist that everyone understand and follow the rules?

Figure 13–45. Providing trophies for the winners is an excellent way for local groups to support the city-wide intramural program. (Courtesy Richmond Senior High School, Richmond, Indiana.)

Figure 13–46. Well-planned announcements give prestige and status to the program.

16. Have I posted a schedule of all proposed intramural activities?

17. Do I have well-trained student officials?

18. Do I have good captains who know their jobs?

19. Do the captains and team members know the rules of the league and the sport they're playing?

Seasonal Organization and Operation

1. Have I organized teams using a system that will work in our school?

2. Have I planned so that all who want to participate may participate?

3. Have I included activities for all grades and abilities?

4. Have I made being on a team attractive for all?

5. Do I have an effective means of checking attendance?

6. Do all teams know whom, when, and where they play?

7. Have I developed a system to control absenteeism?

8. Do I have a plan to reorganize leagues if teams drop out?

9. Do I have a method of publicizing games (photography and journalism clubs)?

After the Season

1. Do I have a good awards program?

2. Have I based my awards on attendance and participation as well as ability?

3. Do I have team awards and trophies?

4. Do I have an all-star vs. league champion-ship game at the end of each season in each sport?

5. Do I have an awards day (father-son night, letter day)?

6. Have I kept up-to-date records?

7. Do I have sports clinics in all activities?

8. Have I evaluated the program to improve it?

9. Have I written thank you notes to all who have helped during the season?[16]

INTRAMURALS IN THE EMERGING SCHOOL PROGRAM

Recent developments throughout the country have led to greater demands for programs for *all* pupils and not for the gifted few alone. The President's Council for Physical Fitness and Sports, The Lifetime Sports Foundation, and the federal govern-ment's appropriation of large sums of money for the educationally deprived are examples of group efforts to provide pro-grams for many children who would other-wise be ignored.

Intramural programs that include rec-reational activities may be the solution to the problem of inadequate physical activity for leisure time. Educators and leaders in sociology and psychology have for many years subscribed to the objectives of inter-school athletics, which they feel are neces-sary for the gifted few. If it is educationally sound to provide programs for the academi-cally gifted, then it seems logical that pro-grams be developed for the physically gifted — the interschool sports program does this.

However, just as academic programs are necessary for the masses of average pupils, so are programs needed for physically average individuals. Intramural programs with a broader philosophy than interschool athletics have opened up an entirely new field of participation. The emphasis is no longer on spectator sports but on participa-tion sports. Bowling alone provides op-portunity for thousands of people to par-ticipate with very little spectatorship.

As the working public is granted more leisure time, intramural programs play a more important role in developing proper attitudes and providing recreational expe-rience during the school years for carry-over to this leisure time. The school pro-gram that includes instruction in such carry-over sports as bowling, golf, and tennis and then provides for intramural participation in these sports is assisting boys and girls in planning their recreational activity for later years.

Present social trends are reëmphasizing the importance of the individual and his relationship to the democratic way of life. World tension and current social problems existing in the country are making greater demands on the individual as a citizen. More important decisions must be made, and these decisions may affect the entire social order for years to come. In order to make the right decision, the individual must be emotionally stable, physically sound, and mentally alert; above all, he must remain healthy.

The wise use of leisure time is important in maintaining a well-balanced outlook on life and life's many problems. The rapid pace at which we live makes it difficult to find time for the recreation necessary for optimal health. However, when the desire for recreational experiences is coupled with the knowledge and background established in the school intramural program, the individual may more easily find the oppor-tunity for recreation.

QUESTIONS FOR DISCUSSION

1. What is the purpose of intramural sports?

2. Why has the need for intramural sports become so important in the past ten years?

3. What are the types of intramural activities? Discuss each.

4. Discuss the units for organizing intramurals. Point out the most desir-able unit and explain your selection.

5. What is the best time for intramural competition?

6. What is the difference between single elimination and round robin tournaments?

7. What are some areas that need to be covered by intramural regulations?

8. Is the class period a good time for intramurals? Why?
9. Define city-wide intramurals. What is their purpose?
10. What are some types of city-wide intramurals?
11. What is the physical education teacher's role in promoting recreation?

SUGGESTED ACTIVITIES

1. The local school system offers no program in intramural sports. In answer to your inquiry, officials state that an interscholastic program is offered and that there is insufficient money to sponsor intramural competition. What would be your response? List several items consistent with good public relations that you would use in a campaign to change the situation.

2. Construct a point system for a high school intramural program.

3. Outline the procedure for organizing a city-wide volleyball tournament.

4. Survey the facilities of a high school and plan an intramural program for boys and girls.

REFERENCES

1. "Games, Sports, Tumbling, Gymnastics Before, During and After School," *Physical Education Newsletter* (Croft Educational Services, Inc., April 1, 1965).
2. "A Tasty Diet of Intramurals for Lunch," *Physical Education Newsletter* (Croft Educational Services, Inc., September 15, 1967).
3. Raymond Abraham, "Use of Television Commercials as a Motivational Device for Exercise." *Report* made in graduate school, University of South Dakota, 1966.
4. Howard R. De Nike, "How Good Is Your Intramural Sports Program?" *The Physical Educator,* p. 117 (Phi Epsilon Kappa, Indianapolis, October, 1955).
5. "Student Officials Play a Vital Role in Intramurals," *Physical Education Newsletter* (Croft Educational Services, Inc., April 15, 1968).
6. "Student Officials Handle High School Intramurals and Interscholastics for Grades 6–8," *Physical Education Newsletter* (Croft Educational Services, September 15, 1965).
7. "Suggested Intramural Activities," Cedar Rapids, Iowa Community School District. From materials sent to the author through correspondence.
8. "Scheduling Intramurals Before School, During School, After School, at Night and on Saturday Mornings," *Physical Education Newsletter* (Croft Educational Services, Inc., June 1, 1966).
9. "Everybody Gets a Chance to Play in Intramurals," *Physical Education Newsletter* (Croft Educational Services, Inc., March 1, 1965).
10. Greyson Daughtrey and John B. Woods, *Physical Education Programs: Organization and Administration,* p. 341 (Philadelphia: W. B. Saunders Company, 1971).
11. "Show and Explain Your Program to the Public," *Physical Education Newsletter* (Croft Educational Services, Inc., January 1, 1966).
12. *Building Healthier Youth.* A guidebook in health and physical education, 1972 (Norfolk Public Schools, Norfolk, Virginia).
13. "Demonstration Ideas That Score," *Physical Education Newsletter* (Croft Educational Services, Inc., April 1, 1967).
14. "Telegraphic Track Meet Gives Students Incentive," *Physical Education Newsletter* (Croft Educational Services, Inc., November 1, 1963).
15. Earle Ziegler, "Education for Leisure, Whose Job?", p. 39 *JOHPER* (March, 1963).
16. Howard Parsons, "An Intramural Evaluation Check List," *Physical Education Newsletter* (Croft Educational Services, Inc., March 1, 1966).

SELECTED READINGS

"Intramurals for the Junior High School," Athletic Institute, Chicago, 1964.
"Intramurals for the Senior High School," Athletic Institute, Chicago, 1964.
Kleindienst, Viola and Arthur Weston. *Intramural and Recreation Programs for Schools and Colleges.* New York: Appleton-Century-Crofts, 1964.
Leavitt, Norman M. and Hortley D. Price. *Intramural and Recreational Sports for College.* New York: The Ronald Press Company, 1958.
Means, Louise. *Intramurals.* Englewood Cliffs, New Jersey: Prentice-Hall, Inc., 1963.
Mueller, Pat and Elmer Mitchell. *Intramural Sports.* New York: The Ronald Press Company, 1960.
Sapora, Allen V. and Elmer D. Mitchell. *The Theory of Play and Recreation,* 3rd ed. New York: The Ronald Press Company, 1961.
"School Athletics—Problems and Policies," Educational Policies Commission, National Education Association, Washington, D.C., 1954.

Chapter 14

EVALUATION

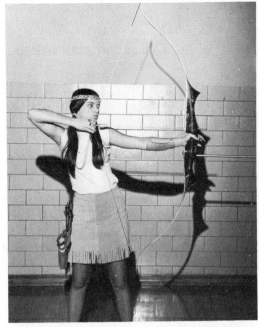

There may be too great devotion to a measure which is final in form but quite incomplete in nature.

Jesse F. Williams

Courtesy Richmond Senior High School, Richmond, Indiana.

OVERVIEW OF THE EVALUATIVE FUNCTION

Literature in all areas of education reveals the need for determining the quality of instruction offered throughout the country. The increasing interest of the taxpayers in the costs of education has focused the attention of educators on the importance of assuring the public of a wise use of the tax dollar in conducting educational programs. Sound techniques of appraisal are necessary for providing parents and others with evidence that educators are providing the best possible education for today's students.

The material in this chapter is centered around three techniques which are used to determine the quality of the educational program. The techniques are *evaluation, measurement,* and *testing.* Barrow defines each:

Evaluation is a process of education which makes use of measurement techniques, which, when applied to either the product or process, result in both qualitative and quantitative data expressed in both a subjective and objective manner and used for comparisons with preconceived criteria.

Measurement is a technique of evaluation which makes use of procedures which are generally precise and objective, which will generally result in quantitative data, and which characteristically can express its results in numerical form. It may be applied to qualitative procedures, however, when its techniques are objectified.

A test is a specific tool of measurement and implies a response from the person being measured.[1]

Various instruments are shown on the following pages which may be used in evaluating (1) the school program; (2) the teacher; and (3) student performance.

EVALUATION OF THE SCHOOL PROGRAM

Certain criteria are necessary for evaluating the school program in which the teacher is engaged. The teacher, if he is to meet the daily challenge successfully, must be familiar with the various phases of the curriculum and the administration of physical education in his particular school. An instrument that provides material for such an appraisal has been devised by the Colorado State Department of Education. This instrument is a self-appraisal type of evaluation, consisting of 19 questions to assist the teacher in determining the quality of the program.[2]

A Question and Answer Evaluation of Your Program

As the year moves toward the homestretch, take a critical look at your PE program. Pinpoint the deficiencies of the past; plan to overcome them in the future. Begin this process by considering each of the following questions and recording your answers in the appropriate boxes. The more Yes answers the better the status of physical education in your school or district. When you finish your self-evaluation, resolve that some of the No answers will be changed to Yes next year and in the years ahead.

	Yes	No
1. Are physical education classes taught or supervised by properly certificated teachers who have the necessary training or competence in physical education?	☐	☐
2. Are medical examinations required before all new students participate in physical education?	☐	☐
3. Are all students required to have a medical examination every third year or more frequently?	☐	☐
4. Do all students from kindergarten through grade 12 have physical education every day?	☐	☐
5. Are class periods long enough to permit you to teach activities in sufficient depth?	☐	☐
6. Are class sizes consistent with the pupil/teacher ratio in other subjects?	☐	☐
7. Does your curriculum include—at appropriate grade levels—the following activities:		
Rhythmics (folk, square, social, and modern dance)?	☐	☐
Mimetics?	☐	☐
Lead-up games?	☐	☐
Relays?	☐	☐
Team sports and games?	☐	☐
Self-testing activities, including tumbling and apparatus?	☐	☐
Conditioning exercises, including calisthenics, weight training, isometrics, and combatives?	☐	☐
Individual and dual carry-over sports?	☐	☐
Aquatics, including swimming, lifesaving, rescue and survival activities using school, community, or private pools?	☐	☐
8. Are fitness, skills, and written knowledge tests a regular part of your program?	☐	☐
9. Do you have a curriculum guide containing a flexible and workable scope and sequence up through the grades?	☐	☐
10. Do you offer co-educational activities in the class and extracurricular program?	☐	☐
11. Does your intramural program involve a high percentage of the total enrollment of boys and girls?	☐	☐
12. Do you provide a broad program of interscholastic athletics at the secondary level involving a substantial percentage of the male enrollment?	☐	☐
13. Do you offer an athletic program for girls based on the new AAHPER guidelines?	☐	☐
14. Do you have an intramural program for boys and girls in grades four through six which includes individual and team activity that is designed to encourage mass participation?	☐	☐
15. Do you group your physical education classes on the basis of skill and maturity?	☐	☐
16. Do you have books, film strips, other audio-visual and text materials on physical education and athletics for use by both teachers and students?	☐	☐
17. Do you have a policy which prohibits the substitution of athletics, marching band, ROTC, driver education, baton twirling, cheer leading, and other activities for participation in the physical education program?	☐	☐
18. Do you have adequate space, facilities, equipment, and supplies to carry out your program? (For guidance, see Planning Areas and Facilities for Health, Physical Education, and Recreation—Athletic Institute and AAHPER, 1965.)	☐	☐
19. Is group accident insurance provided or recommended as a parental responsibility?	☐	☐

These questions were adapted from evaluation materials prepared by the Colorado Department of Education under the direction of Dr. John C. Thompson, consultant for health, physical education, safety, and driver education.

Another comprehensive instrument for evaluating the school program is contained in the *Evaluation for Physical Education,* a project of the Ohio Association for Health, Physical Education and Recreation. The entire plan is constructed on the self-appraisal concept. The document includes an evaluation scale of five steps: 0, 1, 2, 3, 4 in 7 areas (1) Philosophy and Principles, (2) Organization and Administration, (3) Class Management, (4) The Staff, (5) The Curriculum, (6) Facilities and Equipment, and (7) The Elective Program. The Instrument is reproduced in its entirety beginning on page 516.

Recent attacks on physical education in the *Los Angeles Times,* the *New York Times* and *Family Health* have focused attention on the part administrators should have played in order to produce quality programs. Chapter 2 discusses many areas in physical education in which poor practices have contributed to the inferior programs that presently exist. In addition to these areas of concern, *Physical Education Newsletter* has compiled several administrative failures which need to be corrected if physical education programs are to improve:

1. Scheduling large classes so that teaching and learning are often impossible.
2. Providing too little equipment to get the job done. Making one or two balls suffice for a class of 30 or more so that most of the children stand around and wait for a chance to shoot a basket or throw the ball.
3. Failing to schedule at least 30 minutes of physical education a day—or a weekly average of at least 30 minutes a day.
4. Depending upon elementary classroom teachers to teach physical education without sufficient guidance from physical education specialists. This had led to an overemphasis on games or recess, and a lack of movement education, rhythm, fitness, ball skill, and coordination activities geared to individual growth patterns of elementary school youngsters.
5. Allowing the physical education curricula to be structured down from the high school level rather than up from the elementary level. This failure to build on a sequential body of knowledge or skills has impeded teaching, learning, and enthusiasm for physical education and led to undue emphasis on team sports and competition at too young an age.
6. Building elementary schools without gymnasiums or outdoor play areas.
7. Choosing unqualified and physically inept teachers to handle physical education when no certified or qualified physical education instructors were available.
8. Failing to provide adequate budgets.
9. Overlooking the fact that a youngster's earliest learnings are motor-oriented as a result of running, jumping, climbing, skipping, reaching, and similar activities—and that these are vital to later intellectual accomplishments.
10. Using physical education as a dumping ground so that the pupil load for physical education teachers is from 50 to 100 percent greater than for teachers of other subjects, including required music.
11. Emphasizing interscholastic sports so that gymnasiums, athletic fields, and pools are monopolized by the school teams after school, which cuts down on the use of the facilities by other students who can benefit substantially by participating in intramural activities.[3]

EVALUATION OF THE TEACHER

The physical education teacher in many places either is not evaluated by an adequately constructed instrument or, if an instrument is used, it is usually a general device designed for evaluating teachers of academic subjects. Not only should teachers be aware of how administrators evaluate them but they should demand an evaluative device which is specially designed for physical education. Such a device is shown in the form used by the Thornton Fractional High School, South Lansing, Illinois (Fig. 14–1).

The Parma Public Schools, Parma, Ohio, developed an evaluation instrument for appraising physical education teachers that includes such desirable qualities as (1) teaching personality; (2) professional qualities; (3) class management; and (4) teaching performance (Fig. 14–2).[4]

Just as administrators have been attacked for failure to provide basic essentials in physical education programs, teachers have in turn been criticized for not using their technical knowledge and experience to produce quality programs. Some of the failures of teachers are discussed in the *Physical Education Newsletter.* These failures were compiled from the criticisms of physical education already mentioned, recently published in such news media as the *Los Angeles Times,* the *New York Times,* and *Family Health.* Teachers should study these

(Text continued on page 526)

EVALUATIVE CRITERIA FOR PHYSICAL EDUCATION

A SELF-APPRAISAL CHECKLIST
FOR
OHIO SECONDARY SCHOOLS

The following evaluative criteria have been prepared in the form of a self-appraisal checklist appropriate for physical education programs for both boys and girls in secondary schools. Each statement is presented in the form of a standard. The evaluator(s) will read each statement and determine the extent to which there is compliance with the accepted standard.

EXPLANATION OF COLUMN HEADINGS

0. Non-compliance; provisions missing or not functioning.
1. Very limited compliance in provisions or function.
2. Limited or partial compliance; adequacy of provisions or function questionable.
3. Adequate compliance regarding provisions or function.
4. Full compliance; provisions extensive, function excellent.

The above five point progressive scale can be used in arriving at an evaluative judgment. For purposes of guidance, a rating of zero or one would be *unsatisfactory;* a two represents the *borderline between unsatisfactory and satisfactory;* a three or four would be *satisfactory.* The scale should be applied to the standard under question and the estimate of degree of compliance indicated by placing an "X" in the appropriate column.

When the checklist has been completed, the needed improvements should be listed under the proper heading. This list may then serve as a blueprint for improving the quality of services to students through physical education.

EVALUATIVE CRITERIA FOR PHYSICAL EDUCATION IN OHIO SECONDARY SCHOOLS

I PHILOSOPHY AND PRINCIPLES

Possible Score = 56 points
Actual Score = ___ points

Evaluation Scale

	0	1	2	3	4
1. There exists in writing a clear statement of the philosophy and principles upon which the physical education program is based.					
2. The belief is held that physical education is education through the medium of the physical, rather than education of the physical.					
3. The point is clearly understood that physical education in our society is primarily a developmental experience and a mode of expression through movement and not a series of unplanned play periods.					
4. Physical education is regarded as an integral part of education and consecrated to the same aim—the fullest possible development of each student in accordance with his capacities.					

	0	1	2	3	4

5. The belief is held that physical education is concerned with social, mental, and emotional outcomes, as well as the physical aspects of pupil development.

6. The present and future total needs of the students are considered in planning the desired outcomes of the program as well as the program content itself.

7. The biological, psychological and social foundations of physical education are recognized and consciously utilized in planning and teaching.

8. The characteristics and values of the high school age student are considered when determining the scope and sequence of the program.

9. To meet the student's needs the program provides learning experiences which will help each pupil to:
    a. develop basic skills in a variety of games, sports, rhythms, aquatic and gymnastic activities
    b. understand rules, techniques and strategies as related to the above types of activities
    c. develop social standards, ethical behavior, appreciations and wholesome attitudes through direct teachings, example and participation
    d. incorporate into his daily living the activities learned in physical education classes
    e. understand the basic principles of physiology of exercise and body mechanics.

10. In planning the program, major consideration is given to providing opportunities for pupils to acquire knowledges and understandings regarding the development and maintenance of the human organism as the result of physical education activities.

TOTAL _____

II ORGANIZATION AND ADMINISTRATION

Possible Score = 76 points
Actual Score = ___ points

Evaluation Scale

	0	1	2	3	4

1. All students in the junior and senior high school, grades 7–12, are enrolled in physical education classes and participate in an organized and progressive program of activities.

2. Pupils are *not* permitted to substitute other curricular or extracurricular phases of the school program (i.e., band, intramural athletics, clerical work) for participation in physical education instructional classes.

	0	1	2	3	4

3. Students participating in any sport of the school's inter-scholastic athletic program are enrolled and take part in a regular physical education class.

4. Class rank and the findings of the medical examination are major factors in assigning pupils to physical education classes.

5. Atypical students unable to participate in the activities of the general program because of low physical vitality or disability are assigned to adapted physical education sections or rest, depending upon the physician's recommendations.

6. Excuses from the physical education program are allowed only upon a physician's request. This request includes a statement of the pupil's problem and covers a specific period of time.

7. Students are classified for physical education classes according to:
    a. grade
    b. developmental levels
    c. health status determined by findings of medical examination.

8. Instruction for boys and girls is offered in separate classes, but there are frequent co-educational and co-recreational periods involving activities appropriate for such occasions.

9. Although ideal facilities may be lacking, maximum use is made of all available outdoor and indoor space.

10. Instructional activities are planned on a progression from grade to grade.
    a. There is a written up-to-date course of study for each grade.
    b. Within each course of study there are units of instruction.
    c. Daily lesson plans are made up from the units of instruction.

11. Units of instruction are planned as a block or unit of work with the length of time for each unit being determined by the level of learning of the pupils, amount of time available and the nature of the activity.

12. The minimum time allotment for class instruction is two regular class periods per week.

13. One quarter unit credit is granted upon the successful completion of one year's work in the required physical education course; one full unit of credit is granted upon successful completion of the four-year course.

14. An attempt is made to remove or reduce all hazards related to facilities, equipment, curriculum content and teaching methods.

15. With the aid of medical consultation, an accident policy has been developed which includes prevention, first aid treatment, other necessary procedures, and a plan for reporting.

TOTAL _____

III CLASS MANAGEMENT

Evaluation Scale

Possible Score = 96 points
Actual Score = ___ points

0	1	2	3	4

1. Class sizes are kept to a minimum with no more than 30–35 assigned to one teacher for any class.

2. Teacher load, including class instruction and after-school responsibilities, does not exceed:
   a. six clock hours per day
   b. 250 students per day.

3. The daily class period arrangement approximates the following: (45 minute periods)
   a. dressing and roll, 4–6 minutes
   b. instructional program, 29–33 minutes*
   c. shower and dressing, 8–10 minutes

4. Class experience is primarily conceived as systematic and progressive instruction.

5. Students have a voice in planning class activity.

6. Classes are conducted in an orderly but informal atmosphere.

7. Appropriate teaching aids such as films, slides, charts, and demonstrations are used with moderate frequency.

8. Both pupils and instructors are required to wear appropriate costumes for all class work.

9. All students take a cleansing shower following vigorous class activity.

---

*For 60 minute periods, at least 44 minutes are allowed for instruction.

0	1	2	3	4

10. Student leadership is utilized and developed whenever possible by providing opportunities for teaching, coaching, managing, officiating, planning and demonstrating.

11. Evaluation of student progress is based on:
    a. observation
    b. tests—skill, fitness, written
    c. total performance ability (e.g., playing the whole game of volleyball)
    d. conferences with students
    e. desirable changes in social, emotional, and health behavior
    f. knowledge of the effects of activity on the human organism.

12. The criteria for evaluation are directly related to the objectives being sought.

13. A separate grade for each unit of instruction is combined into a single semester grade.

14. The grading or marking system is based upon established criteria for measuring pupil progress.

15. The grading plan indicates the extent to which each student has achieved the objectives of the course.

16. The entire physical education class program is organized and conducted as an orderly and progressive teaching-learning process.

TOTAL _____

IV THE STAFF

Possible Score = 40 points
Actual Score = ___ points

0	1	2	3	4

1. Coaches of interscholastic athletics should possess a philosophy in harmony with the stated philosophy of the school's department of physical education and should meet minimum state requirements.

2. All physical education teachers meet state certification standards for teaching physical education in secondary schools.

3. Staff members are effective with respect to:
    a. planning and organizing class work
    b. establishing and maintaining fine student-teacher relationships
    c. a knowledge of the curriculum areas of physical education
    d. methods of teaching
    e. relationship with other teachers
    f. participating in community life.

0	1	2	3	4

4. Staff members are following a plan for personal and professional growth through participation in graduate work, workshops and conferences, meetings and conventions, and independent study.

5. The school has a definite well-organized in-service education program for improving the quality of instruction in the physical education classes.

TOTAL _____

V THE CURRICULUM

Evaluation Scale

Possible Score = 76 points
Actual Score = ___ points

0	1	2	3	4

1. The content of the curriculum ranges over the five areas of gymnastics and tumbling, rhythms, aquatics, individual and dual sports, and team sports including knowledge and understandings of the effects of these activities on the human organism.

2. The program for each grade is specifically constructed around the needs and interests of the students.

3. The program is as broad as facilities and personnel will permit.

4. The boys' program is arranged so that the course of study for a given year is *approximately* as follows:
   a. Rhythmic activities 10–15%
   b. Team sports 30–35%
   c. Individual and dual sports 30–35%
   d. Gymnastics 15–20%
   e. Aquatics (when available) 10%
   f. Games and relays 5%

5. The girls' program is arranged so that the course of study for a given year is *approximately* as follows:
   a. Rhythmic activities 25%
   b. Team sports 25–30%
   c. Individual and dual sports 25–30%
   d. Gymnastics 10%
   e. Aquatics (when available) 10%
   f. Games and relays 5%

6. Up-to-date sources of curriculum materials are available for the staff.

7. Recognition is made of the fact that many students terminate their formal education upon graduation from high school and they need basic instruction in adult type of dual and individual sports, such as bowling, golf, tennis, and badminton.

0	1	2	3	4

8. A course of study committee (men and women) gives consideration annually to needed revisions in the program.

9. The school is making continuous effort to upgrade its program by striving for daily instruction in physical education for each pupil and for facilities, staff and equipment commensurate for such a program.

TOTAL _____

VI FACILITIES AND EQUIPMENT

Evaluation Scale

0	1	2	3	4

Possible Score = 48 points
Actual Score = ____ points

1. The Board of Education allocates sufficient money for supplies and equipment needed in the physical education program.

2. Indoor and outdoor facilities are designed to include use for community recreational programs.

3. The outdoor area is adjacent to the school building and is large enough to provide for a full-scale outdoor program.

4. The outdoor area is properly surfaced, graded, drained, enclosed, and free from safety hazards.

5. The gymnasium and auxiliary indoor teaching stations meet the following criteria: hardwood floors, properly painted lines, free of safety and health hazards, large enough to accommodate all pupils in the school, ceilings at least 20 to 22 feet in height, and proper storage space.

6. Sufficient teaching stations are provided to enable the school to schedule physical education for all the pupils in the school for a minimum of two periods each week.

7. Dressing, shower and toilet facilities are clean, sanitary, in good working order, and in sufficient quantity to handle the peak class load.
    a. There is a storage locker or basket for each student.
    b. There is one shower head for each 4 students during the peak load.
    c. There are adequate benches, mirrors in the dressing rooms.
    d. Enough full length lockers are provided to permit each pupil to be assigned a locker for storing street clothes during peak load.

8. A satisfactory towel system has been worked out which meets good hygienic and sanitary standards.

9. There is an adequate supply of games and activity equipment such as balls, bats, nets, paddles, clubs, archery tackle, mats, gymnastic pieces, and officiating materials.

TOTAL _____

VII THE ELECTIVE PROGRAM

Possible Score = 44 points
Actual Score = ___ points

	Evaluation Scale				
	0	1	2	3	4

1. A comprehensive program of intramural activities is provided for students and faculty.

2. Opportunities are provided for clubs (hiking, bait casting, archery, cycling, etc.) and recreational activities.

3. The above programs are evaluated on:
   a. time allocated, such as before school, after school, noon hours and in cooperation with community agencies
   b. opportunity provided for all students to participate
   c. competitive playing experience offered in most of the activities taught in class
   d. emphasis placed on participation and recreation
   e. preliminary training periods provided for the strenuous sports
   f. opportunity offered for student leadership
   g. units of competition such as homerooms used, thereby making possible the greatest amount of participation
   h. strong faculty leadership provided
   i. an award system provided in keeping with the purposes of intramural sports.

TOTAL _____

****
```
SCORE

Part    I          (56)          _____

Part    II         (76)          _____

Part   III         (96)          _____

Part   IV          (40)          _____

Part    V          (76)          _____

Part   VI          (48)          _____

Part  VII          (44)          _____


TOTAL             (436)          _____
```
****

RATING OF TEACHER

Name of the Teacher _____ Date _____

Teaching Responsibility _____

RATING SCALE:
No. 1 = Teaching is poor
No. 2 = Teaching is below average
No. 3 = Teaching is average
No. 4 = Teaching is above average
No. 5 = Teaching is excellent

PERSONAL QUALITIES:	SCALE				
	1	2	3	4	5
1. General appearance					
2. Voice					
3. Enthusiasm					
4. Poise and self-control					
5. Initiative and self-reliance					
Total					

PROFESSIONAL TRAITS:					
1. Scholastic ability					
2. Cooperation					
3. Interest in the unit					
4. Use of good English					
5. Attitude toward pupils					
Total					

TEACHING TECHNIQUE:					
1. Daily preparation					
2. Skill in motivating work					
3. Provisions for individual differences					
4. Variations in methods of procedure					
5. Ability to use illustrative and supplementary materials					
Total					

CLASS ADMINISTRATION:					
1. Classroom control					
2. Ability to keep students busy					
3. Ability to challenge students					
4. Teacher-pupil relationship					
Total					

COMMENTS: _____

Evaluator _____

Title _____

Figure 14–1. Rating of health and physical education teachers. (Courtesy Thornton Fractional High School, South Lansing, Illinois.)

PARMA PUBLIC SCHOOLS
DEPARTMENT OF ATHLETICS, PHYSICAL EDUCATION AND RECREATION

OBSERVATION FORM

Teacher _____ Date _____

School _____ Subject _____

The prime object of this Observation Form is to serve as a constructive means of helping staff members to improve their teaching competencies.

Where deemed necessary, appropriate assistance or follow-up will be provided by the Director of Athletics, Physical Education and Recreation.

Desirable Qualities for Health and Physical Education Teachers

✔ = this item needs strengthening

I. **Teaching Personality**

Self control and poise.
Appropriate sense of humor.
Emotional stability.
Vitality and good health.
Enthusiasm in working with students
Appearance (neat and appropriate dress)
Punctuality in attendance.
Voice quality.
English usage (grammar)

II. **Professional Qualities**

Has harmonious relationship with other
  staff members.
Participates in staff meetings and
  discussions.
Upholds departmental and school policies,
  rules and regulations.
Follows planned prescribed program.
Cooperates with co-teachers and department
  chairman.
Willingness to assume extra duties.
Relationship with parents.
Written reports (on time and organized)

III. **Class Management**

Prompt in meeting class.
Supervises locker room before and after
  activity.
Makes maximum time available for
  instruction.
Utilizes every opportunity for instruction.
Demonstrates care of equipment and
  facilities.
Class discipline and control (based on
  respect not fear of reprisal.)
Utilization of student leaders as assistants
  (not in place of the teacher).
Commands respect by example in appear-
  ance, manners, behavior and language.

IV. **Teaching Performance**

Well versed in subject matter content.
Provides for individual as well as group
  instruction and activity.
Demonstrations to class kept to a minimum
  — keeps entire class active.
Recognizes individual differences and
  abilities.
Is sympathetic; fair, tolerant and patient
  with students.
Is well versed in and practices safety
  procedures.

V. Willing to serve on Physical Education Curriculum Committee. _____ _____

                                                          Yes   No

VI. Constructive suggestions: _____

_____

_____

_____

_____

Completed by _____

Figure 14–2. Observation form for physical education teachers. (*Physical Education Newsletter,* "Improving Teaching Through Observation and Evaluation." Croft Educational Services, Inc., Dec. 1, 1969.)

criticisms and use them as guides to evaluate their professional efforts:

1. Being concerned only with the athletes—the top 10 percent of the student body from a physical education point of view.

2. Failing to provide imaginative programs; repeating the same activities each year.

3. Not using existing natural facilities such as nearby lakes or ski areas to teach carry-over sports and activities.

4. Overlooking the principles of child development in planning physical education programs, particularly in the primary grades.

5. Pushing children into competition too quickly, before they're ready for it.

6. Being coaches and not teachers. The publications charged physical educators with failing to plan classes—and being preoccupied with their coaching assignments.

7. Teaching the same old thing in the same old way. Calisthenics, more calisthenics—and taking the roll on the same old numbers on the same old blacktop.

8. Adding exercise to normal assignments as discipline, thus cheapening it in the eyes of students by making it a punishment.

9. Failing to stimulate and motivate the average child to achieve.

10. Being unable to relate to inner-city children and imposing middle class values on ghetto students.

11. Overlooking and ignoring the best interests of about 41 million children—including the overweight, underweight, shy, scrawny, awkward, handicapped, poorly coordinated, and just plain normal.[3]

EVALUATION OF STUDENT PERFORMANCE

One of the most important phases of education is the measurement of pupil progress. Because it is often misunderstood, the results are unscientific, invalid, and unfair. Referring to the need for improvements in education, Dr. Benjamin Fine points out that ". . . the whole system of grading and testing must be changed."[5] The traditional plan of measuring pupils in physical education by comparing them with others is not fair. A better measure of pupil progress would be to grade the pupil on his *own* ability and improvement in an assignment. Fine explains that the present unscientific method of grading or marking largely contributes to the dropout problem confronting educational leaders today.[5] The National Education Association's pro-

ject on dropouts substantiates these claims. In a report on the project, Dr. Robert Strom pointed out that the school curriculum is usually geared to the average pupil; those pupils who cannot meet the standards arbitrarily established by teachers become disheartened, finally lose all interest, and usually drop out of school.[5]

The loss of interest and the dropout problems are serious, but an appalling problem which exists for the remaining students should be mentioned at this point: cheating. A study made by *Look Magazine* revealed that in a study made by Columbia University of 5000 college students in 99 United States colleges, 50 percent of them admitted cheating. The author of the study estimated that the evidence of cheating in high schools is even higher. The article shows that the *intense emphasis on testing and marks is the underlying cause of the increase in cheating throughout the country*. The situation is summarized in the following statement:

Actually, the present situation, with its heavy emphasis on tests and its insane pressure for grades, is less an invitation to learn than an invitation to cheat. Just as heavy testing is a symptom of what is wrong with our schools, cheating is a symptom of what is wrong with testing.[6]

The alarming results which have grown out of testing and marking in the United States should draw attention toward the need for more realistic measuring techniques, which might help to alleviate the conditions described above.

Probably the most far-reaching criticism of present evaluative systems appeared in the *American Association of Colleges for Teacher Education*. The article reported the results of the National Advisory Council on Education Professions Development. Some statements from the report follow:

Evaluation of the wrong kind, at the wrong time, and for the wrong reasons has characterized too much of the current effort to appraise educational reforms. Meaningless evaluation is ruining the cutting edge of educational innovation.

It is becoming increasingly clear that a number of policies and practices . . . are having an adverse effect on efforts to provide genuine innovation and improvement. Among such practices and policies, we cite for special note the following . . .

1. Premature evaluation of a project or venture before it is fully operational.

2. Preoccupation with so-called "hard data" developed by mass use of standardized tests.

3. Too much concern with final results alone leads to lack of effort to determine why project objectives were or were not met.

4. Lack of imagination in selecting types of evaluation policies that are applicable to the special nature, purposes, or stage of development of an educational activity.

5. Requirements that all projects in a program make financial provisions for project evaluation.

6. A tendency to construe tentative findings as "proof".[7]

As a result of the conditions stated in the preceding paragraphs, students develop hostility toward the traditional types of evaluation. Biehler lists the four general criticisms that are most frequently heard:

1. Too much emphasis on tests and grades limits creativity and individuality of expression. Consequently, grades may discourage rather than encourage learning that is personally relevant to the student.

2. Tests and grades put too much pressure on the student. Learning should be an enjoyable experience; it is too often a tension-filled, disagreeable one. Students should not be forced to compete with each other to earn high grades.

3. Information learned for a test is only a means to an arbitrary end—a grade. Much of what has been learned will be forgotten as soon as the grade is achieved.

4. Teachers are too authoritative. Students are forced to spit back exactly what the book or professor says. This is not only degrading; it involves punishment if a student doesn't learn what he has been told to learn.[8]

The criticisms discussed by Biehler were aimed at academic subjects, yet many of these criticisms apply to physical education. Too often marks given to students in physical education are based either on an invalid testing program or on subjective evaluation without a formal testing plan.

Irrespective of the criticisms of testing, when the advantages and disadvantages are weighed, the resulting evidence strongly indicates the need for objective testing and marking based on the results of the testing program. As Gardner explains:

It must never be forgotten that ours is one of the few societies in the history of the world in which performance is a primary determinant of status. What the individual can "deliver" in the way of performance is a major factor in how far he can rise in the world.[9]

Biehler strongly feels that in order to provide fairer and more accurate evaluations, formal testing procedures are essential. He lists the following potential advantages of tests and grades:

1. Evaluation provides feedback, which often functions as reinforcement, which in turn is an essential part of learning.

2. Tests and grades help guarantee that a student will master basic facts and skills en route to mastery of concepts and general abilities.

3. In studying for exams, students usually overlearn. Such overlearning helps assure that material will be remembered. Furthermore, distortions and faulty generalizations are cleared up when wrong answers are corrected.

4. Exams require students to try out their ideas under rigorous circumstances that limit "fudging." In the absence of such control, many students might never really test their ideas (or their abilities) in a literal sense.

5. Tests and grades may be the only, if not the best, way to get many pupils to learn many important things. Test scores and grades function as specific goals. Most students need incentives even to approach their full potential. Sometimes a student who studies to pass an exam discovers a new interest.

6. Capable students often thrive on competition. Tests and grades may inspire them to work closer to their capacity. Specific feedback also permits a student to compete against himself.

7. Grades and test performance provide a detailed analysis of the strengths and weaknesses of pupils. This information can be used in a variety of ways by teachers, counselors, and students themselves. Evaluation also assists a teacher to improve her own performance. In the absence of a feedback, it is practically impossible for a teacher to make systematic efforts to change things for the better, whereas the very process of writing and reading exams aids the organization and presentation of subject matter.[8]

It is the opinion of the author that formal testing and marking programs are basically important for a successful program of physical education. However, these programs should be carefully studied, using such criteria as adequate test items, administration of tests, validity of the tests, and other procedures so necessary for an accurate and fair appraisal of student performance. The remainder of this chapter will be devoted to suggesting procedures and aids for the teacher who wishes to initiate such a program.

CLASSIFICATION OF TESTS

In evaluation of physical education, each individual authority develops his own classification of tests. The lack of unanimity of test classifications may be confusing to teachers and students. However, an in-depth knowledge of these classifications and the various tests that may be used in each classification should be acquired by all teachers and students. On the following pages are shown two general classifications of tests and one classification with the various tests that have been made in that classification.

Haskins[10]
Strength
Endurance
Physical Fitness
Motor Ability
Posture
The Concomitants
Sports Skills

Barrow[1]
Motor Ability and Achievement
Fitness and Endurance
Specific Sports Skills
Posture and Nutrition
Knowledges and Understandings
Concomitant Learnings

Mathews[11]
STRENGTH TESTS
Cable-Tension Strength Tests
Kraus-Weber Strength Tests
MOTOR FITNESS TESTS
AAHPER Youth Fitness Test
Indiana Motor Fitness Test for High School and College Men
Indiana Physical Fitness Test for High School Boys and Girls
Elementary School Motor Fitness Test
Youth Physical Fitness Test
JCR Test
Division for Girls' and Women's Sports Tests (DGWS)
Army Air Force Physical Fitness Test (AAF Test)
Navy Standard Physical Fitness Test
Army Physical Efficiency Test

GENERAL MOTOR ABILITY
Classification Indexes
Tests of Motor Ability
Humiston Motor Ability Test
Newton Motor Ability Test
Scott Motor Ability Test
Barrow Motor Ability Test
Cozens' Test of General Athletic Ability
Larson Motor Ability Test
Strength Tests of Motor Ability
Oberlin College Test

Sigma Delta Psi Test
McCloy's General Motor Ability Tests
Tests of Running Endurance
Motor Educability
Iowa-Brace Test
Johnson Test of Motor Educability
Johnson-Metheny Test
Latchaw Motor Skills Test
Perceptual Motor Evaluation
SPORTS SKILL TESTING
Hyde Archery Test
Lockhart and McPherson Badminton Test
Miller Wall Volley Test
Boys' Baseball Classification Plan
Achievement Level in Basketball Skills for Women
Johnson Basketball Ability Test
Knox Basketball Test
Lehsten Basketball Test
Bowling Norms
Borleske Touch Football Test
Cornish Handball Test
McDonald Soccer Test
Broer-Miller Tennis Test
Dyer Tennis Test
Brady Volleyball Test
Russell-Lange Volleyball Test
French-Cooper Volleyball Test
CARDIOVASCULAR TESTS
Blood Pressure Measurement
Balke Treadmill Test
Modified Treadmill Test for Children
Barach Index
Burger Test
Carlson Fatigue Curve Test
Crampton Blood Ptosis Test
Foster's Test
Gallagher and Brouha Test for High School Boys
Gallagher and Brouha Test for Girls
Harvard Step Test
Pack Test
Schneider Test
Sloan Test
Tuttle Pulse-Ratio Test
The Ohio State University Step Test
NUTRITIONAL MEASUREMENTS AND SOMATOTYPE
Measuring Nutritional Status
Subjective Evaluation
Objective Measurement
EVALUATION OF BODY MECHANICS
Early Posture Tests
Recent Posture Tests
Static Anteroposterior Posture Tests
Screening Tests
Functional Body Mechanics Appraisal
Refined Posture Appraisal
Muscle Power and Holding Power Measurements
Evaluation of the Feet
Evaluation of Flexibility

After studying the pros and cons of testing and the various classifications, the teacher should be ready to initiate a program of testing. He should be primarily concerned with two broad testing areas: (1) Physical Education Knowledge Tests and (2) Physical Education Performance Tests. There are other means, as shown on the preceding pages, which may be used in developing the testing program; but the two just mentioned are the most generally used.

TESTING AREAS

Physical Education Knowledge Tests

Pupils may be given written tests to determine to what extent they have retained the facts pertaining to the material covered. These tests should be given periodically to determine progress, to bring out those topics that need clarification, and to provide the teacher with an instrument for future pupil-teacher planning and evaluation. The tests are generally classified into two types, subjective and objective.

Subjective Tests. The most common type of written subjective test is that which asks the pupil to discuss a topic or to give his point of view and justify it. Considerable time is required to evaluate this type of test and it is usually not practical for large classes. However, subjective tests do tap the pupil's reservoir of learning by making him think through a problem, justify his reactions, and express himself concisely and clearly. For some types of learning, therefore, subjective tests are more effective than objective tests.

Objective Tests. Written objective tests are those which call for specific answers. The most common are the true-false, completion, multiple choice, and matching tests. These are practical and can be corrected quickly; teachers with large classes usually find them more convenient. The following test may serve as a guide in preparing objective tests:

C. H. McCLOY
Dr. McCloy was a leader and prolific writer in the field of testing in physical education.

Tennis

Part I. True-False

Directions: Read the following sentences carefully. If a statement is true, place a (+) in the parenthesis before the sentence. If the statement is false, place a (−) in the parenthesis.

( )   1. Tennis began as handball in Greece.
( )   2. The term "love" means no score.
( )   3. In tennis the server's score is always given first.
( )   4. To win a game a player must be four points ahead.
( )   5. In the forehand stroke the body is turned sideways.
( )   6. In the backhand both hands should be used.
( )   7. In the volley, the ball is returned before the first bounce.
( )   8. Tennis is primarily a girl's sport.
( )   9. In the serve the server stands facing the net.
( ) 10. A let ball entitles the server to another serve.

Part II. Multiple Choice

Directions: Read each question and answer carefully. Then place the letter of the correct answer in the parenthesis before the sentence.

( ) 1. Scoring in tennis originated in:
      a. France   c. Germany
      b. Netherlands   d. England

( ) 2. When playing, the player should look:
      a. At the ball   c. In the direction ball is hit
      b. At the opponent   d. At his partner

( ) 3. The deuce in tennis means that:
      a. The opponent is ahead   c. The score is even
      b. You are ahead   d. The game is over

( ) 4. A fault means:
      a. A served ball   c. A served ball out of court
      b. A missed ball   d. A lost ball

Part III. Completion

Directions: From the list of words at the bottom of the section select one that completes the sentence. Write the number of the word in the parenthesis. Do not use a word more than once.
1. In the volley the ball is hit before it touches the ( ).
2. The drop shot usually has a reverse ( ).
3. ( ) is the term used when a player wins three points.
4. Hitting a ball in such a way that the opponent cannot retrieve it is a ( ).
5. A served ball touching the net and falling on the proper court is a ( ).

     1. Ground   6. Backhand
     2. Let   7. Party
     3. Backcourt   8. Chop
     4. Base line   9. Kill
     5. Spin

Part IV. Matching

Directions: In the left-hand column place the number from the right-hand column that matches.

a. A no-spin ball is a
b. Lawn tennis was started by
c. The international matches are called
d. A delicate and dangerous shot is
e. An easy shot is the

1. Flat
2. Round
3. Ball
4. Love
5. Major Wingfield
6. Davis Cup
7. Return
8. The drop
9. The chop
10. Court

Physical Education Performance Tests

Although knowledge in physical education may be measured by some written tests, performance tests in physical education demand an entirely different procedure. There are so many factors involved in testing physical education activities that the teacher needs to study the entire field of testing thoroughly before initiating a program. Certain procedures should be followed in planning performance tests.

What to Test. The teacher must decide what he wants to test. To give a test just for the sake of testing is not justifiable. If the teacher wishes to test for physiological fitness, then the factors of strength, speed, skill, and endurance should be included in the testing program. If he wishes to test knowledge of sports and activities, then a test similar to the objective tennis test on pages 530–531 may be used. If the teacher wishes to measure motor ability, however, he must devise a test that encompasses a much broader field.

Testing for a Purpose. Each test must serve a definite purpose in the instructional program. Too often, tests in physical education are given to masses of pupils, scored, and the results recorded, filed, and never seen again. Time spent in this manner is wasted.

Tests should be given for a reason. If a test is given in the 100-yard dash, for example, the teacher should know why he

Figure 14–3. Objective testing is an integral part of a physical education program.

is giving the test and the pupil should be told the purpose of the test.

Determining physical fitness should *not* be the reason for giving performance tests. Shaffer explains why:

It is doubtful that the so-called fitness tests, which are given these days in schools and elsewhere, really measure fitness at all. They do reveal motor skills, but there is nothing in them to disclose dynamic fitness; i.e., the cardiovascular response to all-out or just intense effort; nor do they tell anything about medical or organic fitness.[12]

Reasons for Giving Performance Tests

The reasons for giving performance tests include motivation, marking, comparison of scores, and teacher information.

Motivation. It is the author's opinion that motivation should be the real reason for all testing. If a pupil takes a test and at the end of the class period loses all interest in the activity, the test contributes very little to his health and fitness. On the other hand, if the test stimulates him to practice some activity beyond the school day, then its value extends to the effective domain.

Marking. Teachers may wish to use tests to provide some indication of the pupils' achievement to assist in marking for the report cards. However, arbitrary marking based on performance tests is not desirable. For example, some pupils may have anatomical handicaps that might prevent satisfactory performance. In such cases, the teacher should be very careful in marking the pupil. The basic objective of health and physical education is to contribute to the health and fitness of boys and girls. A pupil who is handicapped by weight and cannot chin the bar one time is not necessarily unfit; he may be in excellent health and should not be marked low because of this poor performance.

Comparison of Scores. It may be advantageous to have individual scores and even room scores posted so that pupils may make comparisons. However, this should be done purely for the sake of motivation.

Teacher Information. The teacher should have a general knowledge of the pupil's performance and ability. When tests are given and recorded, the teacher may study them in order to assist in developing a more effective instructional and guidance program. If an entire class of pupils or many pupils in a class are unable to perform the 50 yard dash in less than ten seconds, this situation merits a thorough study. These pupils may not be getting sufficient rest or food for some reason, and there may be a need for medical attention or, more probably, better instruction.

Tests Should Measure Objectives

All tests should measure the degree to which the objectives are being fulfilled. Too often teachers list their objectives somewhere at the beginning of the unit and never refer to them again. If an objective of volleyball is to learn the serve, the tests should measure how well the teaching process is improving the performance of pupils in this skill. The use of performance objectives in testing in this area is highly recommended. Performance objectives are discussed in Chapter 7; Chapter 12 shows ways in which they may be written.

Characteristics of a Good Test

All tests must have certain characteristics to be effective. Although factors such as cost and ease of administration should be considered in preparing or selecting a test, the essential criteria of a good test are reliability, validity, objectivity, simplicity, and norms.

Reliability. A reliable test is one that the teacher can depend upon to produce consistent results. If the same test is given to a group of pupils at different times, the reliability of the tests is determined by the degree to which pupils seem to hold their same relative positions in both tests.

Validity. In order to be valid, a test must measure what it is supposed to measure. A test used to measure knowledge of nutrition of 8th grade pupils would be valid for 8th grade pupils, but if used to test 10th or 12th graders it would be invalid. A valid test should give an accurate picture of whatever it is intended to measure.

Objectivity. An objective test is one that rules out the opinion, judgment, or influence of the scorer. An essay test scored by one teacher could very well be scored quite differently by another teacher.

Simplicity. Because of the large classes in physical education and the complexity of many physical education test items, the testing program should be simple. Many dedicated teachers lose interest in testing their students when the testing program becomes too time-consuming.

Norms. A good test should have norms so that students can compare their test results with those of students in other areas.

Examples of Local Performance Tests

Just as locally constructed knowledge tests in academic subjects are desirable, so are locally planned tests in physical education. These tests are usually prepared and given by the local teacher, who can control the testing conditions in test-retest situations. For 24 years the Norfolk schools have given locally prepared proficiency tests to all junior and senior high school pupils. These tests are used solely to increase motivation and are not in any way reflected in the pupil's grade (Fig. 14–4).

To spur motivation, norms are established by grades, and the test results are placed on large posters fastened to the walls near the area in which the test is given (Fig. 14–5).

Howard Price, a teacher of physical education at Haverford Junior High School in Havertown, Pennsylvania, has developed a comprehensive testing program. The test pattern consists of ten items, which constitute a decathlon:

Decathlon

Description of Events

1. **Football Throw for Distance:** Each boy is allowed two throws. 100' = 5 pts.; 90' = 4 pts.; 80' = 3 pts.; 65' = 2 pts.; 50' = 1 pt.
2. **Foul Shooting:** Boys may use the underhand, one-hand or two-hand shot. If a boy misses the first shot, he may call it a practice shot. Each boy must shoot 10 shots at the basket. 6-7-8-9 or 10 out of ten = 5 pts.; 5 out of 10 = 4 pts.; 4 out of 10 = 3 pts.; 3 out of 10 = 2 pts.; 2 out of 10 = 1 pt.
3. **Thirty Second Shooting:** The first shot is taken from the foul line. The next nine shots are taken anywhere outside a semi-circle having a 7½ foot radius, with its center the same as used for measuring for the foul line. Each boy must shoot 10 shots at the basket within 30 seconds. If he does not complete 10 shots at the basket, his score does not count. Example: A boy making 9 shots out of 9 would receive zero points. 7-8-9 or 10 out of ten = 5 pts.; 6 out of 10 = 4 pts.; 5 out of 10 = 3 pts.; 4 out of 10 = 2 pts.; 3 out of 10 = 1 pt.
4. **Rope Climbing:** Each boy must start from a standing position with his hands on or off the rope. The scissor climb is recommended. 10 seconds or less = 5 pts.; 11 to 15 seconds = 4 pts.; 16 to 20 seconds = 3 pts.; 21 to 25 seconds = 2 pts.; more than 25 seconds = 1 pt.
5. **Chinning:** Each boy may use either the forward or reverse grip. He must start his chin from a straight arm hang, bringing his chin above the bar and then lowering himself to a straight arm hang. He may not kick as an aid to chinning. He should raise both legs slightly on the way up to stop him from swinging. 10 or more = 5 pts.; 9 or 8 = 4 pts.; 7 or 6 = 3 pts.; 5 or 4 = 2 pts.; 3 or 2 = 1 pt.
6. **Standing Broad Jump:** This activity may be held either indoors or outdoors. We conduct it in the gymnasium on a 5' × 20' mat that is marked for easy scoring. 7'6" = 5 pts.; 7' = 4 pts.; 6'6" = 3 pts.; 6' = 2 pts.; 5'6" = 1 pt.
7. **Running Broad Jump:** Each boy has a minimum of two jumps. 14' = 5 pts.; 12'6" = 4 pts.; 11' = 3 pts.; 9'6" = 2 pts.; 8' = 1 pt.
8. **High Jump:** Each boy is allowed one miss for each height. If he misses twice on any height, he receives the points for the height he has cleared. He may use either the roll, scissors or hurdle style of jump. He may not dive over the bar. 4'2" = 5 pts.; 3'9" = 4 pts.; 3'3" = 3 pts.; 2'10" = 2 pts.; 2'6" = 1 pt.
9. **50 Yard Dash:** Boys use the sprinter's start. 7 seconds or less = 5 pts.; 7.1-7.2-7.3 = 4 pts.; 7.4-7.5-7.6 = 3 pts.; 7.7-7.8-7.9 = 2 pts.; 8-8.1-8.2 = 1 pt.
10. **100 Yard Dash:** Boys use the sprinter's start. 13 seconds or less = 5 pts.; 13.1 to 13.5 = 4 pts.; 13.6 to 14 = 3 pts.; 14.1 to 15 = 2 pts.; 15.1 to 16 = 1 pt.

Figure 14–4. Physical proficiency tests given yearly to all secondary pupils of the Norfolk Public Schools since 1951. The tests are *A*, boys' pull-up; *B*, girls' wall push; *C*, dash; *D*, boys' push-up; *E*, sit-up; *F*, girls' pull-up; *G*, agility run; and *H*, boys' standing broad jump. Unless otherwise indicated, boys and girls take the same tests.

Determining Decathlon Winner

About the middle of May the decathlon is completed and the points for each of the ten events are added to determine the total each boy has accumulated. Qualification for the "Decathlon Certificate" is determined in the following manner:

1 — any 7th grader accumulating 35 or more points
2 — any 8th grader accumulating 42 or more points
3 — any 9th grader accumulating 45 or more points

Honorable mention is given for:

1 — Any 7th grader receiving 30 to 34 points
2 — Any 8th grader receiving 35 to 41 points
3 — Any 9th grader receiving 40 to 44 points

The following are the averages for each grade:

1 — 7th grade averages approximately 20 points
2 — 8th grade averages approximately 28 points
3 — 9th grade averages approximately 35 points

Tom Hallstrom, Director of Physical Education in the Omaha Public Schools, uses a physical fitness battery consisting of the push-up, sit-up, pull-up, jump and reach, and squat thrust. Norms are determined for boys and girls. The test battery and norms are shown in Figure 14–6.

A motor efficiency pentathlon test for boys in the secondary schools of Cincinnati, under the direction of Rudolph Memmel, is an excellent illustration of testing for a purpose (Fig. 14–7).

In Lexington High School, Lexington, Massachusetts, a battery of six tests is used.

(*Text continued on page 542*)

Figure 14–5. Posting physical proficiency norms near the testing area stimulates interest in the test.

OMAHA PHYSICAL FITNESS SCORE CARD (Boys)

Omaha Public Schools

Name.. School ....

PHYSICAL FITNESS TEST ITEMS	Sept. 19......		May 19......		Sept. 19......		May 19......		Sept. 19......		May 19......		Sept. 19......		May 19......	
	Test Score	Points	Test Score	Points	Test Score	Points	Test Score	Points	Test Score	Points	Test Score	Points	Test Score	Points	Test Score	Points
1. Push-Ups																
2. Sit-Ups 3 Minutes																
3. Pull-Ups																
4. Jump Reach																
5. Squat Thrusts 2 Minutes																
Totals																
Point Average		5–7 = 1			8–12 = 2			13–17 = 3			18–22 = 4			23 up = 5		
Final Classification																

Achievement Awards given in May to all boys in (1) classification.
Progress Award in May to all boys who improve 100 or more in the test score column from September to May.

Figure 14–6. A battery of test items. (Courtesy Omaha Public Schools, Omaha, Nebraska.)

BOYS AGE NORMS FOR OMAHA FITNESS TEST					
CLASSIFICATION	1	2	3	4	5
BOYS AGE 11					
1. Push-Ups	26 up	20–25	14–19	8–13	0–7
2. Sit-Ups 3 minutes	80 up	65–79	50–64	35–49	0–34
3. Pull-Ups	11 up	8–10	5–7	2–4	0–1
4. Jump Reach	18 up	16–17	14–15	12–13	0–11
5. Squat Thrusts 2 minutes	60 up	50–59	40–49	30–39	0–29
BOYS AGE 12					
1. Push-Ups	30 up	24–29	18–23	12–17	0–11
2. Sit-Ups 3 minutes	85 up	70–84	55–69	40–54	0–39
3. Pull-Ups	12 up	9–11	6–8	3–5	0–2
4. Jump Reach	19 up	17–18	15–16	13–14	0–12
5. Squat Thrusts 2 minutes	62 up	52–61	42–51	32–41	0–31
BOYS AGE 13					
1. Push-Ups	34 up	28–33	22–27	16–21	0–15
2. Sit-Ups 3 minutes	90 up	75–89	60–74	45–59	0–44
3. Pull-Ups	13 up	10–12	7–9	4–6	0–3
4. Jump Reach	20 up	18–19	16–17	14–15	0–13
5. Squat Thrusts 2 minutes	64 up	54–63	44–53	34–43	0–33
BOYS AGE 14					
1. Push-Ups	38 up	32–37	26–31	20–25	0–19
2. Sit-Ups 3 minutes	95 up	80–94	65–79	50–64	0–49
3. Pull-Ups	14 up	11–13	8–10	5–7	0–4
4. Jump Reach	21 up	19–20	17–18	15–16	0–14
5. Squat Thrusts 2 minutes	66 up	56–65	46–55	36–45	0–35

Figure 14–6. *Continued.*

Figure 14–6 continued on following page.

BOYS AGE 15					
1. Push-Ups	42 up	36–41	30–35	24–29	0–23
2. Sit-Ups 3 minutes	100 up	85–99	70–84	55–69	0–54
3. Pull-Ups	15 up	12–14	9–11	6–8	0–5
4. Jump Reach	22 up	20–21	18–19	16–17	0–15
5. Squat Thrusts 2 minutes	68 up	58–67	48–57	38–47	0–37

BOYS AGE 16					
1. Push-Ups	46 up	40–45	34–39	28–33	0–27
2. Sit-Ups 3 minutes	105 up	90–104	75–89	60–74	0–59
3. Pull-Ups	16 up	13–15	10–12	7–9	0–6
4. Jump Reach	23 up	21–22	19–20	17–18	0–16
5. Squat Thrusts 2 minutes	70 up	60–69	50–59	40–49	0–39

BOYS AGE 17					
1. Push-Ups	50 up	44–49	38–43	32–37	0–31
2. Sit-Ups 3 minutes	110 up	95–109	80–94	65–79	0–64
3. Pull-Ups	17 up	14–16	11–13	8–10	0–7
4. Jump Reach	24 up	22–23	20–21	18–19	0–17
5. Squat Thrusts 2 minutes	72 up	62–71	52–61	42–51	0–41

BOYS AGE 18					
1. Push-Ups	54 up	48–53	42–47	36–41	0–35
2. Sit-Ups 3 minutes	115 up	100–114	85–99	70–84	0–69
3. Pull-Ups	18 up	15–17	12–14	9–11	0–8
4. Jump Reach	25 up	23–24	21–22	19–20	0–18
5. Squat Thrusts 2 minutes	74 up	64–73	54–63	44–53	0–43

Points	5–7 = 1	8–12 = 2	13–17 = 3	18–22 = 4	23 up = 5

Figure 14–6. *Continued.*

Figure 14–6 continued on opposite page.

GIRLS AGE NORMS FOR OMAHA FITNESS TEST					
CLASSIFICATION	1	2	3	4	5
GIRLS AGE 11					
1. Push-Ups	40 up	30–39	20–29	10–19	0–9
2. Sit-Ups 3 minutes	70 up	55–69	40–54	25–39	0–24
3. Pull-Ups	25 up	19–24	13–18	7–12	0–6
4. Jump Reach	15 up	13–14	11–12	9–10	0–8
5. Squat Thrusts 2 minutes	40 up	30–39	20–29	10–19	0–9
GIRLS AGE 12					
1. Push-Ups	42 up	32–41	22–31	12–21	0–11
2. Sit-Ups 3 minutes	75 up	60–74	45–59	30–44	0–29
3. Pull-Ups	27 up	21–26	15–20	9–14	0–8
4. Jump Reach	16 up	14–15	12–13	10–11	0–9
5. Squat Thrusts 2 minutes	42 up	32–41	22–31	12–21	0–11
GIRLS AGE 13					
1. Push-Ups	44 up	34–43	24–33	14–23	0–13
2. Sit-Ups 3 minutes	80 up	65–79	50–64	35–49	0–34
3. Pull-Ups	29 up	23–28	17–22	11–16	0–10
4. Jump Reach	17 up	15–16	13–14	11–12	0–10
5. Squat Thrusts 2 minutes	44 up	34–43	24–33	14–23	0–13
GIRLS AGE 14					
1. Push-Ups	48 up	36–45	26–35	16–25	0–15
2. Sit-Ups 3 minutes	85 up	70–84	55–69	40–54	0–39
3. Pull-Ups	31 up	25–30	19–24	13–18	0–12
4. Jump Reach	18 up	16–17	14–15	12–13	0–11
5. Squat Thrusts 2 minutes	46 up	36–45	26–35	16–25	0–15

Figure 14–6. *Continued.*

Figure 14–6 continued on following page.

GIRLS AGE 15

1. Push-Ups	48 up	38–47	28–37	18–27	0–17
2. Sit-Ups 3 minutes	90 up	75–89	60–74	45–59	0–44
3. Pull-Ups	33 up	27–32	21–26	15–20	0–14
4. Jump Reach	19 up	17–18	15–16	13–14	0–12
5. Squat Thrusts 2 minutes	48 up	38–47	28–37	18–27	0–17

GIRLS AGE 16

1. Push-Ups	50 up	40–45	30–39	20–29	0–19
2. Sit-Ups 3 minutes	95 up	80–94	65–79	50–64	0–49
3. Pull-Ups	35 up	29–34	23–28	17–22	0–16
4. Jump Reach	20 up	18–19	16–17	14–15	0–13
5. Squat Thrusts 2 minutes	50 up	40–49	30–39	20–29	0–19

GIRLS AGE 17

1. Push-Ups	52 up	42–47	32–41	22–31	0–21
2. Sit-Ups 3 minutes	100 up	85–99	70–84	55–69	0–54
3. Pull-Ups	37 up	31–36	25–30	19–24	0–18
4. Jump Reach	21 up	19–20	17–18	15–16	0–14
5. Squat Thrusts 2 minutes	52 up	42–51	32–41	22–31	0–21

GIRLS AGE 18

1. Push-Ups	54 up	44–53	34–43	24–33	0–23
2. Sit-Ups 3 minutes	105 up	90–104	75–89	60–74	0–59
3. Pull-Ups	39 up	33–38	27–32	21–26	0–20
4. Jump Reach	22 up	20–21	18–19	16–17	0–15
5. Squat Thrusts 2 minutes	54 up	44–53	34–43	24–33	0–23

Points	5–7 = 1	8–12 = 2	13–17 = 3	18–22 = 2	23 up = 5

Figure 14–6. *Continued.*

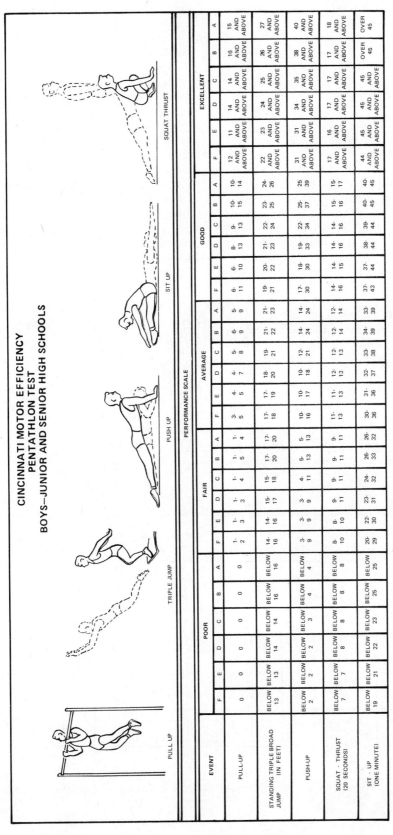

Figure 14–7. Using test items to develop a pentathlon is a unique way of administering motor efficiency tests. (Courtesy Cincinnati Public Schools, Cincinnati, Ohio.)

The battery consists of the agility run, rope climb, standing broad jump, sit-ups, pull-ups, and dips; statistical norms have been developed. The battery and the point conversion table are shown in Figures 14–8 and 14–9.

Standardized Tests

Sometimes teachers wish to compare the physical performances of their pupils with those in other sections of the country. Although in some areas of the curriculum this procedure may be satisfactory, it is questionable whether standardized testing procedures in physical education performance produce the desired results.

One reason is that there are too many variables in physical education activities for them to be subjected to standardized testing programs. These tests are given by many different people in different sections of the country under different conditions with different types of motivation. This makes effective control of the testing conditions almost impossible and obviously affects the validity and reliability of the tests. Environmental conditions also affect performance factors in physical education activities.

Standardized tests are excellent if they are used for the purpose of motivating students. However, if the tests are used merely for passing or failing pupils, or for attempting to classify a pupil into "fit" or "unfit" groups, the results may be extremely undesirable. It is therefore suggested that standardized tests be given strictly for *motivation*, in conjunction with locally prepared tests in both health instruction and physical education instruction. The American Association for Health, Physical Education, and Recreation publishes a test battery that may serve this purpose.

CONDUCTING THE TESTING PROGRAM

Careful consideration should be given to the procedures involved in conducting a

LEXINGTON HIGH SCHOOL PHYSICAL EDUCATION FITNESS CARD

LAST NAME	FIRST NAME	INITIAL	UNIT-H.R.	CLASS

	CLASSIFICATION TESTS							AAHPER TESTS						
GRADE	TOTAL SCORE	AGILITY RUN	STANDING BROAD JUMP	20 FOOT ROPE CLIMB	PULL-UPS	DIPS	60 SEC. SIT-UPS	50 YARD DASH	600 YARD RUN	PULL-UPS	SIT-UPS 100 MAX.	STANDING BROAD JUMP	AGE	REMARKS
9														
10														
11														
12														

Figure 14–8. Score card for test items. (Courtesy Lexington High School, Lexington, Massachusetts.)

	SOPHOMORES	
Agility Run	**Standing Broad Jump**	**Rope Climb (20 ft.)**
32.0 – Under 10	7'9 – Above 10	8.0 – Better 10
32.1 – 34.0 9	7'6 – 7'8 9	8.1 – 9.0 9
34.1 – 36.0 8	7'3 – 7'5 8	9.1 – 10.0 8
36.1 – 38.0 7	7'0 – 7'2 7	10.1 – 11.0 7
38.1 – 40.0 6	6'9 – 6'11 6	11.1 – 12.0 6
40.1 – 42.0 5	6'6 – 6'8 5	12.1 – 13.0 5
42.1 – 44.0 4	6'3 – 6'5 4	13.1 – 14.0 4
44.1 – 46.0 3	6'0 – 6'2 3	14.1 – 15.0 3
46.1 – 48.0 2	5'9 – 5'11 2	15.1 – 16.0 2
48.1 – 50.0 1	5'6 – 5'8 1	16.1 – 17.0 1
50.1 – Over 0	5'5 – Below 0	17.1 – Above 0
Pull-Ups	**Sit-Ups (60 Sec.)**	**Dips**
10 10	49 – Above 10	11 – Above 10
9 9	46 – 48 9	10 9
8 8	43 – 45 8	9 8
7 7	40 – 42 7	8 7
6 6	37 – 39 6	7 6
5 5	34 – 36 5	6 5
4 4	31 – 33 4	5 4
3 3	28 – 30 3	4 3
2 2	25 – 27 2	3 2
1 1	22 – 24 1	2 1
0 0	21 – Below 0	1 – Below 0
	FRESHMEN	
Agility Run	**Standing Broad Jump**	**Rope Climb (20 ft.)**
34.0 – Under 10	7'6 – Above 10	9.0 – Better 10
34.1 – 36.0 9	7'3 – 7'5 9	9.1 – 10.0 9
36.1 – 38.0 8	7'0 – 7'2 8	10.1 – 11.0 8
38.1 – 40.0 7	6'9 – 6'11 7	11.1 – 12.0 7
40.1 – 42.0 6	6'6 – 6'8 6	12.1 – 13.0 6
42.1 – 44.0 5	6'3 – 6'5 5	13.1 – 14.0 5
44.1 – 46.0 4	6'0 – 6'2 4	14.1 – 15.0 4
46.1 – 48.0 3	5'9 – 5'11 3	15.1 – 16.0 3
48.1 – 50.0 2	5'6 – 5'8 2	16.1 – 17.0 2
50.1 – 52.0 1	5'3 – 5'5 1	17.1 – 18.0 1
52.1 – Over 0	5'2 – Below 0	18.1 – 19.0 0
Pull-Ups	**Sit-Ups (60 Sec.)**	**Dips**
10 10	46 – Above 10	10 – Above 10
9 9	43 – 45 9	9 9
8 8	40 – 42 8	8 8
7 7	37 – 39 7	7 7
6 6	34 – 36 6	6 6
5 5	31 – 33 5	5 5
4 4	28 – 30 4	4 4
3 3	25 – 27 3	3 3
2 2	22 – 24 2	2 2
1 1	19 – 21 1	1 1
0 0	18 – Below 0	0 0

Figure 14–9. Test Battery Conversion Table. (Courtesy Lexington High School, Lexington, Massachusetts.)

successful testing program. A program that has not been carefully planned cannot provide a valid measurement of the items selected to be tested. General testing procedures are discussed in the following paragraphs.

Preliminary Planning

The teacher should study all aspects of the school program before initiating a testing program. Many of the problems that occur during administration of the test items may be prevented if sufficient time is allowed for pre-planning. Some of the factors that should be considered before the testing program begins are:

1. The purpose of the testing program should be stated. If the test is designed to test motor ability, then a statement should be made stating the *reason* and *purpose* for testing motor ability.
2. A careful selection of the test items should be made based on the purpose and objectives of the program.
3. Announcements should be made concerning the testing program and the dates in which they will be given.
4. A clear and concise explanation of the test items should be made to the students.
5. Students should be made aware of the purpose and importance of the test program.
6. A survey should be made of the existing equipment, and all necessary items should be procured.
7. Assignment of teachers and student aides should be made in writing.
8. A survey of the necessary space for conducting the test items should be made and the space marked accordingly.
9. Safety factors should be considered in planning for the administration of all tests.

Organizing the Class

Organization of the class is an important procedure in administering tests. Large classes and the time involved in conducting the program necessitate the careful arrangement of students to prevent unnecessary waste of time. Several plans for organizing the class for conducting the program are discussed below.

Mass Testing. Some test items may be conducted in large groups. Items such as the sit-up and the push-up may be administered to an entire class. The class may be divided into two groups, with one taking the test while the other scores (Fig. 14–10). Figure 14–11 illustrates mass testing of the pull-up, using many items of equipment.

Squad Organization. Organizing the class into squads is a popular plan for administering tests. Students move from one test station to another in squads. Figure 14–12 shows a floor plan for testing basketball skills. The results of the tests are recorded on a squad card. (See Chapter 9.)

Individual Testing. Some teachers prefer to test each individual and record the results on an individual record card. Figure 14–14 illustrates one type of individual card that may be used. Students move from one testing station to another singly instead of by squads. After completing all test items, they report to an overflow activity for active participation. This procedure allows the teacher to concentrate on testing and provides purposeful activity for students after they have completed the test items. With this plan, problems of discipline are lessened and the incidence of accidents is reduced.

Conducting the Test. Teachers should exert every effort to administer the tests smoothly and accurately. Students should be motivated to perform their best by procedures such as the posting of averages of the test items near the test area. Having the norms near the test area motivates each student to equal or surpass the norm which is displayed (Fig. 14–5).

Teachers should explain the importance of the test, demonstrate proper form in taking the test, and discuss safety procedures.

Final Procedures. There are several procedures that must follow completion of the tests. Score cards must be collected and properly filed; results of the tests should be studied and used to plan future testing programs; the tests should be analyzed to determine whether the objectives developed in the pre-planning stage have been used properly; and finally, the degree to which test results will influence students' grades must be carefully determined. Because the importance of this step cannot be overemphasized, the remainder of the chapter will be devoted to marking in physical education.

Figure 14-10. Mass testing of an entire class in the sit-up.

Figure 14-11. The pull-up may be administered to large groups by providing additional equipment.

FLOOR PLAN - GOLF and TENNIS

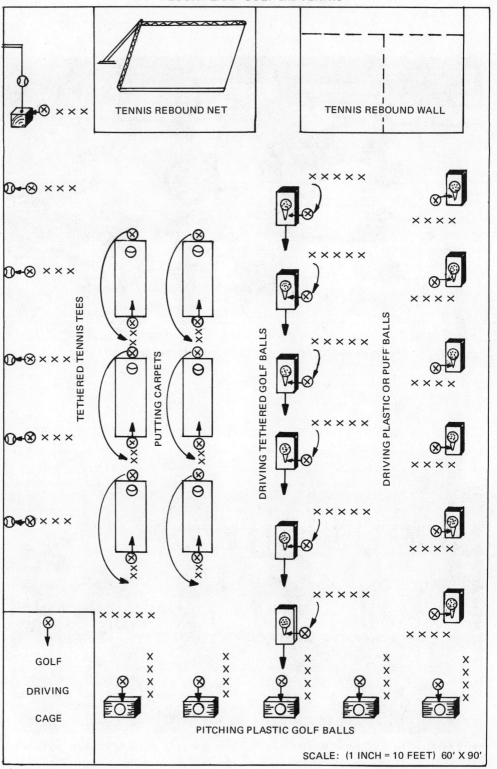

Figure 14-12.   A floor plan for testing and teaching golf and tennis skills. (Courtesy New York City Public Schools.)

CEDAR RAPIDS COMMUNITY SCHOOLS

Physical Welfare Department

IOWA TEST OF MOTOR FITNESS

Cumulative Individual Record Form

Name____________________ Sex_____ School__________________ Teacher__________________

Date	Grade	Age	Height	Weight	Sit-Up	Stand Broad Jump	Shuttle	Forward Bend	Grass-hopper	Dash	Pull-Up	Bent Arm Hang	Percentile Total and Remarks
Fall / /6													
Spring / /6													
Fall / /6													
Spring / /6													
Fall / /6													
Spring / /6													

NOTE: The bottom half of each recording space under each test item is for the percentile rank at each grade level.

Figure 14–13. A practical form for recording test results.

INDIVIDUAL PHYSICAL FITNESS TEST RECORD

Division of Curriculum and Instruction
Mobile Public Schools

Name _____ School _____
　　　　Last　　　　First　　　　Middle

Address _____ Phone _____ Date _____

EVENT	H. R. Grade_____ Sec._____ Wt_____ Ht_____ Age_____			H. R. Grade_____ Sec._____ Wt_____ Ht_____ Age_____			H. R. Grade_____ Sec._____ Wt_____ Ht_____ Age_____		
Age/Classification Index	Sept	Jan	May	Sept	Jan	May	Sept	Jan	May
Push-Ups (Boys) (Knee Push-Ups Girls)									
Sit-Ups									
Squat Jumps									
Pull-Ups (Modified for Girls)									
Run-Walk 220 yds 600 yds 440 yds 880 yds									
Squat Thrusts (30 sec)									
50 yd Dash									

Figure 14–14. Individual record card for recording results of test items. (Courtesy Mobile Public Schools, Mobile, Alabama.)

MARKING IN PHYSICAL EDUCATION

One of the most difficult problems in physical education is the assigning of marks to pupils. Unlike many other areas in the curriculum, physical education involves a great many variables. The physical education teacher has to be concerned with such problems as students' dressing and taking showers in addition to evaluating knowledge and performance.

Marking in physical education is extremely difficult, but it is here to stay. Parents will always want to know just what their children are achieving and how they compare with other children. Many teachers need some form of marking to control students, to motivate students to work, to classify students, and to justify their decisions to parents when their methods and instructional competencies are questioned. Students will always want a mark as long as our society continues to place emphasis on competitive achievement for entering college. One must conclude that as long as the school system requires marking, physical education should conform.

Probably the two greatest obstacles to marking in physical education are oversized classes and the frequency of marking periods. Adding to these difficulties is the complicated nature of the test items in physical education. The overwhelming complexity of marking in physical education leads to disagreement as to what should be tested, how tests should be given, and what techniques should be used. Because of these conditions, valid and reliable techniques frequently are not used because they are too time-consuming. As a result, teachers often compensate by using unjustifiable test items and techniques. Instead of marking students on instruction and achievement, teachers may evaluate them on items such as attendance, showers, dress, attitudes, sportsmanship, discipline and other factors that have no bearing on achievement. A recent survey of marking practices reported by 50 practice teachers revealed that in 80 percent of the school systems the pupils' grades were based solely on attendance and dress.[11] It is difficult to justify marking pupils on such items, even though they do play a significant role in the teaching assignment; they are a reflection of overall school policy and should not be used to determine marks. Pupils should be evaluated on the basis of those elements that make up the learning situation. Skill tests, knowledge tests, and proficiency tests *are* measurable, and are the best yardsticks of the learning situation. If a pupil is absent or does not dress, he should not be allowed to participate; but the mark should be lowered not because of failure to dress but because he could not participate, and therefore could not score on the test or the day's lesson.

In an effort to bring some direction to the search for valid marking in physical education, some physical educators have attempted to study the causes of confusion and offer suggestions for teachers to help them to mark students more fairly. The establishment of certain guidelines or principles to assist teachers would greatly improve the situation and should be the first step in initiating a new marking system for physical education. McGraw offers several principles that may adequately serve as guidelines for marking in physical education:

1. Grades given to students should be based on all of the objectives of the course, such as skills, physical fitness, attitudes, appreciation, and knowledge. These factors should be weighed according to the emphasis given in the instruction; however, a major portion of the grade should be based on skill and/or physical fitness with a minimum standard of achievement for each of the other objectives.

2. The grade for a student should be determined by the extent to which he attains the objectives with ample consideration given to attainment in terms of capacity and to improvement during the instructional period.

3. The grading procedure used for physical education should be consistent with that for other subjects in the school or school system. This includes the use of symbols (A, B, C, D, F; S or U; or Pass or Fail), distribution of grades, and the inclusion of grades in the computation for the honor roll.

4. The grade assigned to a student should be based on his performance in relation to the objectives of the course and not in comparison with other students. There can be no justification in applying the so-called curve system to assigning grades in physical education.

5. The same basic principles and plan should govern the grading procedure in all physical education classes in the school system. These principles and plan should be developed cooperatively by all teachers.

6. A variety of instruments, both subjective and objective, should be used in the evaluating process. The selection of these instruments should be in terms of extent to which they are valid, reliable, and objective; ease with which they are understood, administered, and scored; economy in time and equipment; availability of norms and/or standards; and extent to which they serve a useful purpose; i.e., meet the purposes of tests.

7. Evaluative instruments should not be used solely or even primarily for assigning grades. Other purposes are to: provide a basis for classifying students for instruction; determine needs of students in terms of specific objectives or competencies; motivate students to attain objectives; provide a method of instruction, i.e., in taking the test the student is drilling on the skill; provide the teacher with material for self-evaluation of teaching effectiveness; provide the teacher with additional data for reporting to parents, school administrators, and the public the achievement of students in physical education.

8. Students should be informed of the procedure to be used for assigning grades in physical education. Notification should be made in writing at the beginning of the unit, semester, or school year as appropriate.[13]

After the teacher has studied the *general* principles of marking, his next step is to study the *local* situation and determine just how he may apply these principles to develop a marking plan that will be valid and not too time-consuming. Solley offers some suggestions that should be helpful, discussed in the following paragraphs:

1. It is unnecessary to grade students in physical education each six or nine-week period of the school year. A single, comprehensive

report of pupil achievement once or twice each year is adequate in meeting the purposes of grading students. To report grades at frequent intervals simply to conform to patterns set for other subjects is not logical, particularly in the light of the limitations to good evaluation at the local level.

2. Grading frequently directs all evaluation processes toward a grade. Reducing grading periods makes it possible to improve the quality of the grading process and at the same time it enables the teacher to direct evaluation toward other goals, such as pupil guidance and motivation.

3. Each major goal of the program should be evaluated only when warranted. One or two assessments of physical fitness per school year is adequate. Achievement in specific sports skills and abilities can be determined during each unit. Tests of knowledge can be minimized in each unit; a single consolidated test once each semester suffices for grading purposes. Attitudes and habits related to the personal-social objective develop slowly, and to turn continuous observations in this area into grades frequently is a waste of time.

4. The techniques employed in using evaluation devices in physical education can be changed. While the teacher will always be responsible for the accuracy and truthfulness of any evaluation result used in teaching, this does not mean that all measurement and evaluation must be done by the teacher. Use of student leaders, partner methods of administration and scoring, and other time-saving techniques are encouraged, particularly for testing in physical fitness and sports skill. The teacher should assume complete responsibility for the training of all involved in the testing procedure.

5. Under the unit system of teaching, the only major objective requiring frequent, time-consuming evaluation procedures is sports skill and ability. Such measurement is not difficult with trained assistance, even when done on an individual basis.[14]

The teacher is now in a position to proceed with the third step in developing a marking program—determining what areas should be tested for marking students. The marking program should be based on the student performance with relation to course objectives. The teacher at this point should review the objectives of physical education discussed in Chapter 5.

The remainder of this chapter will be concerned with marking in the areas of proficiency, sports skills, emotional development, and social adjustment. The final grades should also take the student's *improvement* and *effort* into consideration.

Marking on Improvement

There is a great deal of merit in marking pupils on their degree of improvement. Initial tests in a selected number of activities might be given at the beginning of each marking period. After a six-week period of teaching the same tests should be given again and the pupils evaluated on progress made during this interval. There are, however, some disadvantages to this procedure. Here are suggestions for overcoming two of the most important ones:

1. If pupils are aware that the test-retest technique is being used, they may deliberately score low on the initial test in order to make a high score on the terminal test. This tendency may be overcome by giving the tests without any announcements about marking based on improvement. Pupils should be told that these tests are only part of the total testing program and that they should do their best.

2. Pupils with natural ability who score high may be penalized because the more accomplished a pupil is, the more difficult it is to improve. As illustration, consider Pupils A and B. Pupil A has had considerable experience in football and Pupil B has had none. In the initial test, A punts the football 50 yards and B punts it only 20. After instruction, the terminal test is given to each pupil. Pupil A punts 55 yards while Pupil B punts 40 yards. Pupil B shows more improvement and would receive a better mark based on improvement. This criticism of the plan may be offset by grouping the pupils on the basis of ability before the initial test. Each ability group would have a different range of testing performances; this would place Pupil A in a performance division in which as much weight would be awarded to a 5 yard improvement as to the 20 yard improvement of Pupil B. Figure 14–15 illustrates the use of ability grouping in a performance test.[15]

Marking on Effort

The effort made by pupils should receive consideration in marking. Many pupils have ability and good physiological health but are unable to score well on the tests. Body type plays a tremendous role in performance; merely because a pupil with a certain

GROUP	INTERVAL	INITIAL TEST TALLY		TERMINAL TEST TALLY	
1	1 — 19	ʇʜʜ ʇʜʜ	10	ʇʜʜ /	6
2	20 — 39	ʇʜʜ ʇʜʜ ʇʜʜ	15	ʇʜʜ ʇʜʜ ʇʜʜ /	16
3	40 — 59	ʇʜʜ ʇʜʜ	10	ʇʜʜ ʇʜʜ //	12
4	60 — 79	ʇʜʜ	5	ʇʜʜ /	6

IMPORTANT

Pupils grouped into four ability sections, based on the initial test.

Each group is evaluated on improvement as determined by the terminal test, based on scale shown below.

SCALE FOR EVALUATION

Group 1
20 yds. improvement — excellent
15 yds. improvement — very good
10 yds. improvement — good
5 yds. improvement — fair

Group 3
10 yds. improvement — excellent
5 yds. improvement — very good
3 yds. improvement — good
Below 3 yds. improvement — fair

Group 2
15 yds. improvement — excellent
10 yds. improvement — very good
5 yds. improvement — good
Below 5 yds. improvement — fair

Group 4
5 yds. improvement — excellent
3 yds. improvement — very good
2 yds. improvement — good
1 yd. improvement — fair

Figure 14–15. Football punt administered to a class of 40 pupils grouped by ability.

SCORE SHEET

PUPIL'S NAME	ABILITY GROUP	INITIAL TEST	TERMINAL TEST	YARDS IMPROVED	MARK
Frank Jones	1	10 yds.	30 yds.	20 yds.	Excellent
Joe Thomas	2	25 yds.	30 yds.	5 yds.	Good
Tom Luck	3	40 yds.	48 yds.	8 yds.	Very good
Jack Tabb	4	60 yds.	65 yds.	5 yds.	Excellent

body type cannot attain certain standards in the kip-up or the mile run does not mean that he should fail. If he makes the effort and is seriously trying, the final mark should reflect this. Although unable to perform the skills of the test battery, he probably can work all day, ride a bicycle well, or skate proficiently.

A test for the 100 yard dash will illustrate this point. Six pupils are to run the dash. Twelve seconds has been established as the average for the grade or class. One of the pupils is short and fat; one is tall and skinny; one is of medium build; one has a slight limp; one is an all-round athlete; and one has exceptionally long legs and fast repetition time. This group is typical of the variety found in all heterogeneously grouped classes in physical education. The six run the dash and finish in the following times:

Pupil with long legs and fast repetition time	11.5 seconds
All-round athlete	11.7 seconds
Slight limp	11.9 seconds
Medium build	12 seconds
Tall and skinny	12.3 seconds
Short and fat	12.5 seconds

According to the scale used by the teacher, the short fat boy might receive a failing grade. From a physiological point of view, all the runners benefited equally. Because the short fat boy was handicapped as a sprinter, he probably exerted more effort than the boy who won. How can a teacher justify failing this boy when he derived physiologically as much health benefit as the others? This point emphasizes the value of considering effort as an integral part of the marking system.

Suggested Marking Plans

One reason why difficulty is experienced when efforts are made to evaluate pupils in physical education is that physical education leaders disagree as to what should be evaluated. Earlier in this chapter we explained why including attendance, showering, and dressing in the grades that are sent home to parents is indefensible; we also pointed out that the *basic* element for evaluation should be skill performance. Other factors that should be considered in marking are knowledge, physical profi-

ciency, emotional development, social adjustment, improvement in performance, and effort.

Other Marking Plans

Some schools have made constructive efforts to devise marking plans which are acceptable for use in determining pupil achievement. The program in physical education at Levelland Junior High School, Levelland, Texas, includes testing as an integral part of the overall planning. The teachers and principal developed a marking scale in which 90 percent of the student's grade is based on ability and knowledge of games and rules, and 10 percent is based on his attitude, participation, and other similar factors. Skills and written tests are given at the end of each six-week marking period. Students are given tests on three items in each skill test and are graded by quartiles in each element of the test as follows:

Fourth quartile	— 4 points
Third quartile	— 3 points
Second quartile	— 2 points
First quartile	— 1 point

A student in the fourth quartile in all three skills receives a maximum of 12 points and the student who scores in the first quartile in the three skills gets a minimum of three points. The following scale is used for point conversion:

12 equals 98%		7 equals 81%	
11 equals 95%		6 equals 78%	
10 equals 91%		5 equals 75%	
9 equals 89%		4 equals 71%	
8 equals 85%		3 equals 68%	

Other schools, such as Harbor Beach Community School, Harbor Beach, Michigan, and Fife Junior and Senior High School, Tacoma, Washington, have developed testing programs to upgrade physical education. In the Harbor Beach School, students in grades 7 through 12 are grouped by ability for each activity. Boys and girls are placed in three groups: top, middle, and low. Each group spends proportionate time on seminar study and participation in the actual activity. Fifty percent of the student's grade in each unit is based on improvement in skills and written tests. In addition to skills tests, students are given the AAHPER tests.[17]

At Fife Junior and Senior High School, students are given fitness tests, and skills and knowledge tests in football, basketball, volleyball, wrestling, badminton, and track and field. The Fife fitness test, given four times each year, includes push-ups, pull-ups, burpees, sit-ups, bar dips, vertical hang, rope climb, 600-yard run and walk, man lift and carry, extension press-ups, and overhead ladder crawl.

The skills and fitness tests are based on a 10-point scale which is translated into letter grades as follows:

10 = A		5 = C+
9 = A−		4 = C
8 = B+		3 = C−
7 = B		2 = D
6 = B−		1 = D−

The final mark for each unit and fitness battery is determined by dividing the number of points scored by the number of tests given. If a boy scored 32 points in the four-item basketball test, his mark would be 8, or B.[17]

Moriarity developed a plan for testing in physical education which deserves attention. She maintains that marking should be awarded on the basis of successful attainment of purposeful objectives.[18] Moriarity feels that the objectives of the program should determine how much the measurable items should count. Factors such as achievement and knowledge should be studied in light of their *relative* value. If achievement is more important than knowledge, then equal weight should not be given to both factors. It is suggested that letter grades, and their numerical values might be A−5, B−4, C−3, D−2, and E−1. The weight given the factors might be achievement−3, ability−2, knowledge−1 and attitude−1. In the following example the sum of the marks earned by a pupil in each area is 28, which, when divided by the total of the weights, seven, gives a score of four or a grade of B:[18]

The marking plan used in the Dade County Public Schools reflects overall performance by the student in the physical education class. The plan includes student grouping, screening tests, cardiovascular tests, fitness tests, standard tests, and sports skill tests. The results of the tests are recorded on a permanent record card (Fig. 14–16) which includes attendance, conduct, effort, test results, and other factors that make up the daily routine of teaching physical education.

Roxborough High School in Philadelphia has for many years followed a plan for measuring student status in physical education based on a point system in three suggested areas. These areas with the points involved and their descriptions are shown below:

1. *Physical Fitness* (64 out of 100 points).

Eight standardized tests per year—two in each report period—measure the components of strength, endurance, power, speed, agility and coordination. Pupils are put into five homogeneous groups according to age-height-weight exponents calculated in each teaching period. Because of this grouping it does not matter in the rostering how the pupils come to gym—grades 7–8–9, or 10–11–12 may all be in the same class. Marking aims A–B–C–D–E–F, with an appropriate number of points for each, have been standardized in each of the tests for all of the five homogeneous groups. Pupils' records are kept on a three by five gym record card which is also used for attendance. It takes about one period to test an average sized class in one test.

2. *Skills* (24 out of 100 points).

The areas of games, sports skills, apparatus and dancing are measured in this group. Four skills are tested in the school year, one in each report period. The skills used at Roxborough are found on the gym record card. These skills could be different in each school and could be selected according to the facilities available and neighborhood needs. The 24 points allotted for a year give six points for each skill and are rated A–6; B–5; C–4; D–3; E–2; F–1. Some of these skills are rated objectively and some subjectively.

Factors	Weight	Marks	Points
Achievement (Skills)	3	B (4)	3 × 4 = 12
Ability (Motor Ability)	2	A (5)	2 × 5 = 10
Knowledge	1	C (2)	1 × 3 = 3
Attitude	1	C (1)	1 × 3 = 3

STUDENT FITNESS TEST RECORDS

				Three Screening Tests					AGE	CARDIOVAS-CULAR TEST	RATING	STANDARD TESTS		
			AGE	Flex. A or Pull-up	Stand. B. J.	Shutt. Run	Total					Rope Skipping		
Date								1.						
Height												600 yard Run-Walk		
Weight		1st						2.						
Vision W/O Glasses	R L											Rope Climb		
Vision with Glasses	R L	2nd						3.						

	GROUPING – LEVEL	FITNESS TESTS		AGE	Flex. A or Pull-up	60 sec. Sit-up	Shutt. Run	Stand. B. J.	50 yds. Dash	Softball Throw	600 Run-W.	Total %ile	Comp. Score	Pull-ups — Arm Flexed H.		
Dates	1 2 3 4 5	1st	%ile											Push-ups		
____	___ ___		Score													
____	___ ___	2nd	%ile										Bar Dips		
____	___ ___		Score										60 Sec. Sit-up		

COMMENTS:

_____

_____

_____

_____

_____

_____

_____

_____

SPORTS SKILL TESTS (Three Basic)	1.	2.	3.

NAME: _____ LAST _____ FIRST _____ PHONE _____ SECTION _____

PHYSICAL EDUCATION STUDENT GRADE CARD

Instructor's Name _____

		Skills	Obs. Skills	Written T.	Soc. & Per.	Daily Av.	Subject	Effort	Conduct	Absences	Tardies
Sept.	Oct.										
Date 4 5 6 7 8 11 12 13 14 15 18 19 20 21 22 25 26 27 28 29	2 3 4 5 6 9 10 11 12 13 16										
1ST Six Weeks											
Oct. Nov. Dec.		Skills	Obs. Skills	Written T.	Soc. & Per.	Daily Av.	Subject	Effort	Conduct	Absences	Tardies
Date 17 18 19 20 23 24 25 26 27 30 31 1 2 3 6 7 8 9 10 13 14 15 16 17 20 21 22 27 28 29 30 1 4											
2ND Six Weeks											
Dec. Jan.		Skills	Obs. Skills	Written T.	Soc. & Per.	SEM. EXAM	Subject	Effort	Conduct	Absences	Tardies
Date 5 6 7 8 11 12 13 14 15 18 19 20 21 22 1 2 3 4 5 8 9 10 11 12 15 16 17 18 19 22 23 24 25 26											
3RD Six Weeks											
Feb. Mar.		Skills	Obs. Skills	Written T.	Soc. & Per.	Daily Av.	Subject	Effort	Conduct	Absences	Tardies
Date 29 30 31 1 2 5 6 7 8 9 12 13 14 15 16 19 20 21 22 23 26 27 28 29 1 4 5 6 7 8											
4TH Six Weeks											
Mar. Apr.		Skills	Obs. Skills	Written T.	Soc. & Per.	Daily Av.	Subject	Effort	Conduct	Absences	Tardies
Date 11 12 13 14 15 18 19 20 21 22 25 26 27 28 29 1 2 3 4 5 8 9 10 11 12 15 16 17 18 19 22 23 24 25 26											
5TH Six Weeks											
May June		Skills	Obs. Skills	Written T.	Soc. & Per.	Final EXAM	Subject	Effort	Conduct	Absences	Tardies
Date 29 30 1 2 3 6 7 8 9 10 13 14 15 16 17 20 21 22 23 24 27 28 29 30 31 3 4 5 6 7 10											
6TH Six Weeks											

Roll No.	Comp. Score	NAME						Subject	Effort	Conduct
	Level		Period	Locker No.	Combination					
		Last	First	Grade & Sec.	IBM No.	Student Classification	Fees	Final Average		

Form 252 1967-68   M & M PRESS

Figure 14–16. *Legend on opposite page.*

3. *Floorwork* (12 out of 100 points).

The pupil's attendance, preparation and cooperation are measured in this group. Twelve points for each year, or three points for each report period is allotted each pupil. The teacher deducts one point for suit cuts, lateness, or lack of cooperation to commands (discipline). The teacher keeps this record in the attendance section of the gym record card.[19]

Results of the tests are kept in a central file and used for improvement of parent-pupil-principal-teacher relationships.

Cedar Rapids Community School District, Cedar Rapids, Iowa, uses a marking system which includes the weighted factors of participation, skill, progress, citizenship, and knowledge. These factors with their weights are shown below:[20]

Participation	40%
Skill	25%
Progress	20%
Citizenship	10%
Knowledge	5%

Hanson advocates that marks be determined by the student's achievement in accomplishing the basic objectives. He rules out such factors as improvement, level of fitness, good citizenship, uniforms, showers, attendance, effort, and discipline. His plan would include motor skills and physical fitness as basic objectives, and he believes that knowledge and achievement in these areas should be the basis for marking. He suggests the following as the basis for a marking plan for students in physical education:[21]

Objectives	*Weight*
Motor Skills	50%
Physical Fitness	25%
Knowledge	25%
Understanding sports	
techniques	
Rules	
Strategy	
Whys of Physical Education	

A marking theory that is advocated by some physical education teachers is the pass-fail plan. In this plan the traditional letter system is abolished, and the student either passes or fails. The teachers at Thornton Fractional High School, South Lansing, Illinois, point out the following advantages of the pass-fail concept:

1. It eliminates many of the inequities inherent in any grading system in that one decision is better than placing students in five arbitrary categories.

2. Pass-fail is practical. It does not require intricate measurements or evaluation. Good judgment still has to be made of a student's competence.

3. Students will be encouraged to participate more willingly without the external stimulus of low grades.

4. Students should learn course content through motivation, not through the mere desire for high grades.

5. Many students become problems because they feel they cannot compete with the more skilled students.

6. Pass-fail systems of grading at college level are being accepted on a wider scale than ever before; hence our pass-fail grading would not be affected in any way by the admissions offices of colleges.

7. A pass in this plan is construed to be equivalent to at least a D grade in the regular grading system.

8. Successful completion of a course on pass or fail basis should result in a pass grade being recorded in the student's record, the credit earned being added to his credit total to fulfill his graduation requirement.

9. Unsuccessful completion in a pass-fail course should yield a fail grade, which is recorded in the student's record. At the junior-senior level he will be held accountable for satisfactory passing of the course in physical education.[22]

The physical education marking system at Thornton Fractional High School is shown for the junior and senior years:

Figure 14–16. Comprehensive permanent record card showing overall performance of the student in physical education. (Courtesy Dade County Public Schools, Florida.)

THE PHYSICAL EDUCATION PROGRAM FOR THE JUNIOR YEAR

Activity	Point Value	Required	Pass	Fail
1. Touch Football	½			
2. Soccer	½			
3. Rugby	½			
4. Swimming-safety	1	x		
5. Volleyball (intermediate)	½			
6. Health, communicable diseases	2	x		
7. Hockey	½			
8. Handball	½			
9. Progressive body building	1	x		
10. Basketball, team play	½			
11. Softball	½	x		
12. Wrestling (intermediate)	1	x		
13. Track, running, endurance, physical testing and fitness	1	x		
Total Activity Points	10	6		

Junior year credit. One credit for graduation is composed of six activity units. The basic required courses plus any of the electives can be used to earn one credit for graduation. SEMESTER GRADES HAVE NO FURTHER MEANING. All courses are graded on a pass-fail basis. Failure of a required course necessitates retaking the course and passing it successfully.

THE PHYSICAL EDUCATION PROGRAM FOR THE SENIOR YEAR

Activity	Point Value	Required	Pass	Fail
1. Running, endurance, physical fitness	1	x		
2. Swimming (recreational)	½			
3. Volleyball (recreational)	½			
4. Health, mental hygiene, emotions, personality, etc.	2	x		
5. Handball (advanced)	½			
6. Badminton	1	x		
7. Basketball (recreational)	½			
8. Golf	1	x		
9. Softball (recreational)	½			
10. Soccer	1	x		
11. Touch football	½			
12. Wrestling (advanced)	1	x		
Total Activity Points	10	6		

Senior year credit. One credit for graduation is composed of six activity units. The basic required courses plus any of the electives can be used to earn one credit for graduation. SEMESTER GRADES HAVE NO FURTHER MEANING. All courses are graded on a pass-fail basis. Failure of a required course necessitates retaking the course and passing it successfully.

PHYSICAL EDUCATION CREDITS

Credits. Each student will receive one credit for each year duing the 11th and 12th years of school. One credit is composed of six activity units. At the end of the two required years, if a student has successfully completed 12 activity units, he shall receive the necessary two credits for graduation. If a required course is not fulfilled (passed), the student receives a fail grade and remains in the program until all requirements are met. The student who has not passed a required activity may make up the deficiency in the following manner:
1. Passing a written test; later attempt, apart from the unit just taken.
2. Retaking the course until meeting the test.
3. Taking a proficiency battery of tests designed by the instructor and passing satisfactorily.[22]

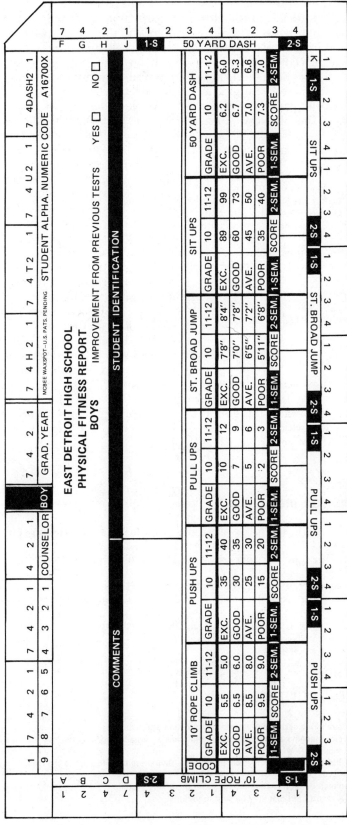

Figure 14-17. Reporting plan to parents, showing improvement from one test period to the next. (*Physical Education Newsletter*; "How Detroit Uses Report Cards to Spark Interest in Fitness." Croft Educational Services, March 15, 1965.)

In those schools where physical education is not granted academic credit for graduation, the pass-fail concept has a great deal of merit. Many schools throughout the country have placed physical education on a par with academic subjects and require physical education credit for graduation. In these schools the pass-fail concept would adversely affect the physical education program.

Biehler has this to say about the pass-fail concept:

1. The standard in pass-fail systems gravitates toward the level of those who just pass. In rare institutions with highly selected students, this level may be respectable. In most schools and colleges it is mediocre.

2. The pass-fail system is unreliable. . . . The likelihood that a given teacher will come up with a different grade on a second evaluation of borderline students, or that different teachers will assign different grades, increases as the number of categories decreases.[8]

Reporting to Parents

After the student has been tested and marks given, teachers are faced with the problem of reporting to parents. It is doubtful that the letter grade which usually appears on the periodical report card is sufficient to provide parents with adequate information regarding their child's achievement in the class. Many plans are used throughout the country to provide parents with an evaluation of student progress in physical education, several of which are discussed below.

A plan devised at East Detroit High School, East Detroit, Michigan, shows improvement from one test period to the next, which should give parents an indication of the physical fitness status of their children. The report is sent to parents each semester, with emphasis on stimulating interest which would motivate the student to improve his performances in the test battery. The items used for the test are the 10-foot rope climb, push-ups, pull-ups, standing broad jump, sit-ups and 50-yard dash. The report card (Fig. 14-17) simulates a small IBM card.

The report card sent to parents by the Cedar Rapids Community School District, Cedar Rapids, Iowa, consists of a test battery which includes the sit-up, standing broad jump, shuttle run, forward bend, grasshopper, dash, pull-up and bent-arm hang. The card shows the student's fall and spring scores, with a section for interpreting the results (see Chapter 9, Fig. 9-18).

QUESTIONS FOR DISCUSSION

1. Why should the teacher be familiar with evaluation instruments in physical education?

2. What is the difference between evaluation and testing? between evaluation and marking?

3. What are the advantages of locally constructed tests?

4. Why are standardized tests used? Discuss the advantages and disadvantages of these tests.

5. What is your reaction to marking in physical education? Do you think marks should be given? Justify your answer.

SUGGESTED ACTIVITIES

1. Develop a marking system for a physical education program.

2. Test several students in the chin, dash, and standing broad jump. Can you say that one pupil is more fit than another? Why?

3. Devise a battery of tests for physical proficiency. Give these tests to a group of pupils. Formulate averages.

4. Using the material in this chapter, construct a marking system.

5. Develop a report card that may be sent to parents.

REFERENCES

1. Harold M. Barrow and Rosemary McGee, *A Practical Approach to Measurement in Physical Education*, pp. 19; 9–11 (Philadelphia: Lea and Febiger, 1964).
2. "A Question and Answer Evaluation of Your Program," *Physical Education Newsletter* (Croft Educational Services, Inc., April 1, 1967).
3. "Physical Education Teachers and Programs Attacked," *Physical Education Newsletter* (Croft Educational Services, Inc., January 1, 1971).
4. "Improving Teaching Through Observation and Evaluation," *Physical Education Newsletter* (Croft Educational Services, Inc., December 1, 1969).
5. Benjamin Fine, "School Revisions Needed," *Virginian-Pilot*, Norfolk, Virginia (November 26, 1964).
6. George B. Leonard, "Testing vs. Your Child," *Look Magazine*, p. 64 (March, 1966).
7. "In-depth Study Faults Evaluation Policies," *American Association of Colleges for Teacher Education*, p. 5 (Washington, D.C., July–August, 1969).
8. Robert Biehler, *Psychology Applied to Teaching*, pp. 374; 381; 408 (Boston: Houghton Mifflin Company, 1971).
9. John W. Gardner, *Excellence*, p. 68 (New York: Harper and Row, 1961).
10. Mary Jane Haskins, *Evaluation in Physical Education*, pp. V–VI (Dubuque, Iowa: William C. Brown Company, 1971).
11. Donald Mathews, *Measurement in Physical Education*, 4th ed. pp. 8–10; 374 (Philadelphia: W. B. Saunders Company, 1973).
12. Thomas Schaffer, "Misconceptions in Athletics and Physical Education," *Journal of School Health*, p. 348 (October, 1963).
13. Lynn W. McGraw, "Principles and Practices for Assigning Grades in Physical Education," *JOHPER*, p. 24 (February, 1964).
14. William H. Solley, "Grading in Physical Education," *JOHPER*, pp. 35–36 (May, 1967).
15. Greyson Daughtrey and John B. Woods. *Physical Education Programs: Organization and Administration*, p. 186 (Philadelphia: W. B. Saunders Company, 1971).
16. "The Grade in Physical Education: How to Make It More Meaningful," *Physical Education Newsletter* (Croft Educational Services, Inc., February 15, 1964).
17. "And Here's How Schools Are Using Physical Education Tests to Upgrade Physical Education," *Physical Education Newsletter* (Croft Educational Services, Inc., October 15, 1965).
18. Mary J. Moriarity, "How Shall We Grade Them?" *JOHPER*, pp. 27; 55 (January, 1954).
19. W. H. Grigson, *Editorial* in *The Physical Educator* (Phi Epsilon Kappa, December, 1965).
20. Cedar Rapids Community School District, Cedar Rapids, Iowa (materials sent to author).
21. Dale L. Hanson, "Grading in Physical Education," *JOPHER*, p. 37 (May, 1967).
22. Adolph Gentile, Chairman, Department of Physical Education, Thornton Fractional High School, South Lansing, Michigan (materials sent to author).

SELECTED READINGS

Barrow, Harold M., and Rosemary McGee. *A Practical Approach to Measurement in Physical Education*. Philadelphia: Lea and Febiger, 1964.

Bookwalter, Karl W., and Harold J. Vanderzwaag. *Foundations and Principles of Physical Education*. Philadelphia: W. B. Saunders Company, 1971.

Clark, H. Harrison. *The Application of Measurement to Health and Physical Education*, 4th ed. Englewood Cliffs, N.J.: Prentice-Hall, Inc., 1967.

Clark, H. Harrison. *Physical Education and Motor Tests in the Medford Boys Growth Study*. Englewood Cliffs, New Jersey: Prentice-Hall, Inc., 1971.

Haskins, Mary Jane. *Evaluation in Physical Education*. Dubuque, Iowa: William C. Brown Company, 1971.

Latchaw, Marjorie, and Camille Brown. *The Evaluation Process in Health Education, Physical Education and Recreation*. Englewood Cliffs, New Jersey: Prentice-Hall, Inc., 1962.

Mathews, Donald K. *Measurement in Physical Education*, 4th ed. W. B. Saunders Company, 1973.

Scott, M. Gladys, and Esther French. *Measurement and Evaluation in Physical Education*. Dubuque, Iowa: William C. Brown Company, 1959.

Smithells, Philip and Peter E. Cameron. *Principles of Evaluation in Physical Education*. New York: Harper and Row, 1962.

Chapter 15

FACILITIES, EQUIPMENT AND SUPPLIES

*Build better school rooms
for "the boy" than cells
and gibbets for "the man"!*
Eliza Cook

FACILITIES

In order for any area of instruction in the curriculum to fulfill its objectives, adequate facilities are necessary. Just as adequate facilities are needed for effective instruction in other subjects, so are they needed for successful teaching in physical education.

It was pointed out in Chapter 2 that the lack of adequate teaching stations and play areas is one of the reasons that poor programs in physical education still exist throughout the country. This does not imply that good programs cannot be carried on in older and apparently inadequate facilities. It does imply that at least enough space should be available in which to teach a class effectively. Some of the finest programs exist in old facilities, and some of the worst programs exist in modern beautiful stations.

Many books and articles have been written about physical education facilities and equipment; it would be impossible in this chapter even to outline adequately all the specific information available. Nevertheless, teachers are expected to be well informed about all phases of their special field and are often asked to make recommendations on facilities and equipment.

It is the purpose of this chapter to give an overview of the facilities needed for physical education and to list several references for more extensive study in these two areas.

The main principle the teacher should press for is that he be allowed to participate in the *planning* of the facility. This is of extreme importance. After final plans are drawn and approved, the school program must adjust to the facility irrespective of whether the final construction is functional.

PRINCIPLES OF PLANNING

Principles of planning are important if the aim of construction is to provide functional areas for teaching. Some principles that may be used by administrators and architects in developing plans for construction of the physical education plant are these:

1. All persons concerned with the use of the facility—administrators, ·directors, supervisors, and teachers—should be involved in the initial planning.
2. A variety of teaching stations is necessary for a program in physical education. Auxiliary gymnasiums, health classrooms, rhythm rooms,

and swimming pools are examples of areas that may be used for teaching stations.

3. One standard gymnasium is basic, since it may be used jointly for physical education and interschool athletics. The space occupied by bleachers may be converted into a teaching station when the bleachers are rolled back.

4. Folding partitions, particularly in the large gymnasium, may be used to provide additional stations.

5. Factors such as cost, location of the stations, storage, shower and dressing facilities, locker areas, toilets, and accessibility by both inside and outside groups should be carefully studied and designed to conform to state and local codes.

6. Immediate and future use may be more fully realized when the physical education facility is constructed as a separate plant or located in a wing of the building.

7. The physical education facility should be designed as a separate entity and not in conjunction with the auditorium, cafeteria, or other school facilities. The multi-purpose facility is not recommended. Experience and study have shown that conjunctive arrangements are unsatisfactory because of scheduling difficulties.

8. The physical education facility should be designed to meet present and future needs of both school and community programs. This premise places emphasis on adequate bleacher space for spectators, functional location of toilets and entrances, functional entrance and egress routes, and sufficient stations to meet adequately the needs of future programs.[1]

The use of these guidelines in planning should provide a framework within which administrators and teachers can plan functional physical education facilities.

PROCEDURES IN PLANNING

There is a trend to bring teachers into the planning and to use their suggestions to assist in effecting a more functional design for physical education. Several important factors are involved in planning facilities for the physical education program, and the teacher should be familiar enough with them to plan them sequentially.

Size of School

For a new building, one should estimate what the enrollment of the school will be in order to determine the number of teaching stations needed. This is a crucial factor. One gymnasium may be adequate for 200 pupils (40 pupils per period, five periods daily), but for more than this number the architect and the administration must begin to think in terms of more stations or spaces. Page 570 discusses the procedures involved in determining the number of stations needed.

General Recommendations

The teacher should make general recommendations as to the needs of the program. The number of teaching stations needed and a general plan for location of stations, showers, and other items should be given to the architect. It is helpful if a rough sketch can be made of these needs to be presented with the recommendations.

Review of the General Plan

The architect should study the recommendations of the teacher and use them in planning the building. After he has drawn a rough sketch of the entire facility, he should ask the teacher to review the plans.

Specific Recommendations

At this point the teacher should be ready to make specific recommendations regarding the size of the teaching stations, showers, storage, towel room, lockers, and other items that are necessary in a functional facility. It costs no more to design a building for functional use than to design it so that teachers and pupils are handicapped in the day-by-day operations.

An authoritative check list should be tremendously helpful to the teacher in discussing the specific details involved in constructing physical education facilities. A check list developed by the Athletic Institute is shown.[2]

CHECKLIST FOR PLANNING FACILITIES

As an aid to those responsible for planning facilities for physical education, health education, and recreation, a check list has been prepared. The application of this check list may prevent unfortunate and costly errors.

Place the appropriate letter in the space indicated in the right-hand margin after each statement:

A — The plans meet the requirements **completely.**
B — The plans meet the requirements **only partially.**
C — The plans **fail** to meet the requirements.

Soundly-conceived plans for areas and facilities are not achieved by chance or accident, but by initiative and action of knowledgeable people acting individually, in groups, and as agencies.

GENERAL

1. A clear-cut statement has been prepared on the nature and scope of the program, and the special requirements for space, equipment, fixtures, and facilities dictated by the activities to be conducted. _____

2. The facility has been planned to meet the total requirements of the program as well as the special needs of those who are to be served. _____

3. The plans and specifications have been checked by all governmental agencies (city, county, and state) whose approval is required by law. _____

4. Plans for areas and facilities conform to state and local regulations and to accepted standards and practices. _____

5. The areas and facilities planned make possible the programs which serve the interests and needs of all the people. _____

6. Every available source of property or funds has been explored, evaluated, and utilized whenever appropriate. _____

7. All interested persons and organizations concerned with the facility have had an opportunity to share in its planning (professional educators, users, consultants, administrators, engineers, architects, program specialists, building managers, and builder—a team approach). _____

8. The facility and its appurtenances will fulfill the maximum demands of the program. The program has not been curtailed to fit the facility. _____

9. The facility has been functionally planned to meet the present and anticipated needs of specific programs, situations, and publics. _____

10. Future additions are included in present plans to permit economy of construction. _____

11. Lecture classrooms are isolated from distracting noises.

12. Storage areas for indoor and outdoor equipment are adequately sized. They are located adjacent to the gymnasiums. _____

13. Shelves in storage rooms are slanted toward the wall. _____

14. All passageways are free of obstructions; fixtures are recessed. _____

15. Facilities for health services, health testing, health instruction, and the first-aid and emergency-isolation rooms are suitably interrelated. _____

16. Buildings, specific areas, and facilities are clearly identified. _____

17. Locker rooms are arranged for ease of supervision. _____

18. Offices, teaching stations, and service facilities are properly interrelated. _____

19. Special needs of the physically handicapped are met, including a ramp into the building at a major entrance. _____

20. All "dead space" is used. _____

21. The building is compatible in design and comparable in quality and accommodation to other campus structures. _____

22. Storage rooms are accessible to the play area. _____

23. Workrooms, conference rooms, and staff and administrative offices are interrelated. _____

24. Shower and dressing facilities are provided for professional staff members and are conveniently located. _____

25. Thought and attention have been given to making facilities and equipment as durable and vandalproof as possible. _____

26. Low-cost maintenance features have been adequately considered. _____

27. This facility is a part of a well-integrated master plan. _____

28. All areas, courts, facilities, equipment, climate control, security, etc., conform rigidly to detailed standards and specifications. _____

29. Shelves are recessed and mirrors are supplied in appropriate places in rest rooms and dressing rooms. Mirrors are not placed above lavatories. _____

30. Dressing space between locker rows is adjusted to the size and age level of students. _____

31. Drinking fountains are conveniently placed in locker-room areas or immediately adjacent thereto. _____

32. Special attention is given to provision for the locking of service windows and counters, supply bins, carts, shelves, and racks. _____

33. Provision is made for the repair, maintenance, replacement, and off-season storage of equipment and uniforms. _____

34. A well-defined program for laundering and cleaning of towels, uniforms, and equipment is included in the plan. _____

35. Noncorrosive metal is used in dressing, drying, and shower areas except for enameled lockers. _____

36. Antipanic hardware is used where required by fire regulations. _____

37. Properly-placed hose bibbs and drains are sufficient in size and quantity to permit flushing the entire area with a water hose. _____

38. A water-resistant, coved base is used under the locker base and floor mat, and where floor and wall join. _____

39. Chalkboards and/or tackboards with map tracks are located in appropriate places in dressing rooms, hallways, and classrooms. _____

40. Book shelves are provided in toilet areas. _____

41. Space and equipment are planned in accordance with the types and number of enrollees. _____

42. Basement rooms, being undesirable for dressing, drying, and showering, are not planned for those purposes. _____

43. Spectator seating (permanent) in areas which are basically instructional is kept at a minimum. Roll-away bleachers are used primarily. Balcony seating is considered as a possibility. _____

44. Well-lighted and effectively-displayed trophy cases enhance the interest and beauty of the lobby. _____

List continued on following page.

45. The space under the stairs is used for storage. _____

46. Department heads' offices are located near the central administrative office, which includes a well-planned conference room. _____

47. Workrooms are located near the central office and serve as a repository for departmental materials and records. _____

48. The conference area includes a cloak room, lavatory, and toilet. _____

49. In addition to regular secretarial offices established in the central and department-chairmen's offices, a special room to house a secretarial pool for staff members is provided. _____

50. Staff dressing facilities are provided. These facilities may also serve game officials. _____

51. The community and/or neighborhood has a "round table"—planning round table. _____

52. All those (persons and agencies) who should be a party to planning and development are invited and actively engaged in the planning process. _____

53. Space and area relationships are important. They have been carefully considered. _____

54. Both long-range plans and immediate plans have been made. _____

55. The body comfort of the child, a major factor in securing maximum learning, has been considered in the plans. _____

56. Plans for quiet areas have been made. _____

57. In the planning, consideration has been given to the need for adequate recreation areas and facilities, both near and distant from the homes of people. _____

58. Plans recognize the primary function of recreation as being enrichment of learning through creative self-expression, self-enhancement, and the achievement of self-potential. _____

59. Every effort has been exercised to eliminate hazards. _____

60. The installation of low-hanging door closers, light fixtures, signs, and other objects in traffic areas has been avoided. _____

61. Warning signals—both visible and audible—are included in the plans. _____

62. Ramps have a slope equal to or greater than a one-foot rise in 12'. _____

63. Minimum landings for ramps are 5' x 5', they extend at least one foot beyond the swinging arc of a door, have at least a 6-foot clearance at the bottom, and have level platforms at 30-foot intervals on every turn. _____

64. Adequate locker and dressing spaces are provided. _____

65. The design of dressing, drying, and shower areas reduces foot traffic to a minimum and establishes clean, dry aisles for bare feet. _____

66. Teaching stations are properly related to service facilities. _____

67. Toilet facilities are adequate in number. They are located to serve all groups for which provisions are made. _____

68. Mail services, outgoing and incoming, are included in the plans. _____

69. Hallways, ramps, doorways, and elevators are designed to permit equipment to be moved easily and quickly. _____

70. A keying design suited to administrative and instructional needs is planned. _____

71. Toilets used by large groups have circulating (in and out) entrances and exits. _____

CLIMATE CONTROL

1. Provision is made throughout the building for climate control—heating, ventilating, and refrigerated cooling. _____

2. Special ventilation is provided for locker, dressing, shower, drying, and toilet rooms. _____

3. Heating plans permit both area and individual-room control. _____

4. Research areas where small animals are kept and where chemicals are used have been provided with special ventilating equipment. _____

5. The heating and ventilating of the wrestling gymnasium have been given special attention. _____

ELECTRICAL

1. Shielded, vaporproof lights are used in moisture-prevalent areas. _____

2. Lights in strategic areas are key-controlled. _____

3. Lighting intensity conforms to approved standards. _____

4. An adequate number of electrical outlets are strategically placed. _____

5. Gymnasium and auditorium lights are controlled by dimmer units. _____

6. Locker-room lights are mounted above the space between lockers. _____

7. Natural light is controlled properly for purposes of visual aids and other avoidance of glare. _____

8. Electrical outlet plates are installed 3' above the floor unless special use dictates other locations. _____

9. Controls for light switches and projection equipment are suitably located and interrelated. _____

10. All lights are shielded. Special protection is provided in gymnasiums, court areas, and shower rooms. _____

11. Lights are placed to shine between rows of lockers. _____

WALLS

1. Movable and folding partitions are power-operated and controlled by keyed switches. _____

2. Wall plates are located where needed and are firmly attached. _____

3. Hooks and rings for nets are placed (and recessed in walls) according to court locations and net heights. _____

4. Materials that clean easily and are impervious to moisture are used where moisture is prevalent. _____

5. Shower heads are placed at different heights—4' (elementary) to 7' (university)—for each school level. _____

6. Protective matting is placed permanently on the walls in the wrestling room, at the ends of basketball courts, and in other areas where such protection is needed. _____

7. An adequate number of drinking fountains are provided. They are properly placed (recessed in wall). _____

8. One wall (at least) of the dance studio has full-length mirrors. _____

9. All corners in locker rooms are rounded. _____

CEILINGS

1. Overhead-supported apparatus is secured to beams engineered to withstand stress. _____

2. The ceiling height is adequate for the activities to be housed. _____

3. Acoustical materials impervious to moisture are used in moisture-prevalent areas. _____

4. Skylights, being impractical, are seldom used because of problems in waterproofing roofs and the controlling of sun rays (gyms). _____

List continued on opposite page.

5. All ceilings except those in storage areas are acoustically treated with sound-absorbent materials. _____

FLOORS

1. Floor plates are placed where needed and are flush-mounted. _____

2. Floor design and materials conform to recommended standards and specifications. _____

3. Lines and markings are painted on floors before sealing is completed (when synthetic tape is not used). _____

4. A coved base (around lockers and where wall and floor meet) of the same water-resistant material used on floors is found in all dressing and shower rooms. _____

5. Abrasive, nonskid, slip-resistant flooring that is impervious to moisture is provided on all areas where water is used —laundry, swimming pool, shower, dressing, and drying rooms. _____

6. Floor drains are properly located and the slope of the floor is adequate for rapid drainage. _____

GYMNASIUMS AND SPECIAL ROOMS

1. Gymnasiums are planned so as to provide for safety zones (between courts, end lines, and walls) and for best utilization of space. _____

2. One gymnasium wall is free of obstructions and is finished with a smooth, hard surface for ball-rebounding activities. _____

3. The elementary-school gymnasium has: one wall free of obstructions; a minimum ceiling height of 18'; a minimum of 4,000 square feet of teaching area; and a recessed area for housing a piano. _____

4. Secondary-school gymnasiums have: a minimum ceiling height of 22'; a scoreboard; electrical outlets placed to fit with bleacher installation; wall attachments for apparatus and nets; and a power-operated, sound-insulated, and movable partition with a small pass-through door at one end. _____

5. A small spectator alcove adjoins the wrestling room and contains a drinking fountain (recessed in the wall). _____

6. Cabinets, storage closets, supply windows, and service areas have locks. _____

7. Provisions have been made for the cleaning, storing, and issuing of physical education and athletic uniforms. _____

8. Shower heads are placed at varying heights in the shower rooms on each school level. _____

9. Equipment is provided for the use of the physically handicapped. _____

10. Special provision has been made for audio and visual aids, including intercommunication systems, radio, and television. _____

11. Team dressing rooms have provisions for:

   a. hosing down room _____

   b. floors pitched to drain easily _____

   c. hot- and cold-water hose bibbs _____

   d. windows located above locker heights _____

   e. chalk, tack, and bulletin boards, and movie projection _____

   f. lockers for each team member _____

   g. drying facility for uniforms _____

12. The indoor rifle range includes:

   a. targets located 54" apart and 50' from the firing line _____

   b. 3' to 8' of space behind targets _____

   c. 12' of space behind firing line _____

   d. ceilings 8' high _____

   e. width adjusted to number of firing lines needed (1 line for each 3 students) _____

   f. a pulley device for target placement and return _____

   g. storage and repair space _____

13. Dance facilities include:

   a. 100 square feet per student _____

   b. a minimum length of 60 linear feet for modern dance _____

   c. full-height viewing mirrors on one wall (at least) of 30'; also a 20' mirror on an additional wall if possible _____

   d. acoustical drapery to cover mirrors when not used and for protection if other activities are permitted _____

   e. dispersed microphone jacks and speaker installation for music and instruction _____

   f. built-in cabinets for record players, microphones, and amplifiers, with space for equipment carts _____

   g. electrical outlets and microphone connections around perimeter of room _____

   h. an exercise bar (34" to 42" above floor) on one wall _____

   i. drapes, surface colors, floors (maple preferred), and other room appointments to enhance the room's attractiveness _____

   j. location near dressing rooms and outside entrances _____

14. Training rooms include:

   a. rooms large enough to administer adequately proper health services _____

   b. sanitary storage cabinets for medical supplies _____

   c. installation of drains for whirlpool, tubs, etc. _____

   d. installation of electrical outlets with proper capacities and voltage _____

   e. high stools for use of equipment such as whirlpool, ice tubs, etc. _____

   f. water closet, hand lavatory, and shower _____

   g. extra hand lavatory in the trainers' room proper _____

   h. adjoining dressing rooms _____

   i. installation and use of hydrotherapy and diathermy equipment in separate areas _____

   j. space for the trainer, the physician, and for the various services of this function _____

   k. corrective-exercise laboratories located conveniently and adapted to the needs of the handicapped _____

15. Coaches' rooms should provide:

   a. a sufficient number of dressing lockers for coaching staff and officials _____

   b. a security closet or cabinet for athletic equipment such as timing devices _____

   c. a sufficient number of showers and toilet facilities _____

   d. drains and faucets for hosing down the rooms where this method of cleaning is desirable and possible _____

   e. a small chalkboard and tackboard _____

   f. a small movie screen and projection table for use of coaches to review films _____

INDOOR FACILITIES

Planning indoor facilities to provide for functional operation is extremely important. Often the entire responsibility for this planning is left to the architect, who may not have had experience in planning for physical education programs. As a result, he usually resorts to traditional plans for a gymnasium designed for the varsity basketball team. This type of planning is nonfunctional and usually results in inadequate space for effective teaching in physical education.

Probably the most crucial area of planning is for indoor facilities. A group of 40 or 50 pupils may have had adequate outdoor space, but when the group comes inside for instruction, problems arise. The allotted indoor space usually determines the activity.

At this point the term "adequate" should be discussed. A teacher will often say facilities are inadequate, when in reality they are adequate—it is a matter of changing the activity. As an illustration, let us consider a class of 40 pupils that has been outside for touch football instruction. The outside space is usually adequate—almost every school in the country has a football field. If the class is divided into several groups, the football area will be large enough for all pupils to learn the skills of touch football. Now this same group, which

had ample room for sufficient movement outside, comes inside to a one-gymnasium situation. At this point many teachers will say that the space is inadequate because all 40 pupils cannot "play" basketball at the same time; it would take four gymnasia to permit 40 pupils to "play" basketball. In such a situation the alert and creative teacher would *teach the skills* of basketball. Instantly, the situation changes. The class is divided into many groups: four with ten pupils, five with eight pupils, eight with five, or any division of pupils consistent with the number of balls available. Not only is the situation now entirely adequate, but the objectives of physical education are more nearly attained. Remember that the teaching of skills is the reason physical education teachers are needed.

There is still another situation that may arise. Let us assume that another group of pupils is assigned to physical education (either boys or girls). Teachers might say that it is impossible to teach 80 or 100 pupils in the one gymnasium. Again this is not a fair statement. A folding door can be used to divide the gymnasium into two teaching stations with a group on each side, as shown in Figure 15–2. Again the answer to the problem is the teaching of skills, not "play" during the instructional period.

The divided-gymnasium plan discloses the possibility of including many activities

Figure 15–1. Large numbers of people can be accommodated on one station when skills are taught and sufficient equipment is provided. (Courtesy Chicago Public Schools, Chicago, Illinois.)

Figure 15–2. Teaching 80 to 100 pupils in a standard gymnasium is possible with a folding door forming two stations. The class in the foreground is beginning the sit-up before learning volleyball skills. The class on the far side of the folding door is learning the skills of basketball.

in the program. In this plan, effective instruction may be accomplished in volleyball, rhythms, basketball, tumbling, wrestling, table tennis, or bowling—in either or both stations.

A third illustration of the use of facilities is a situation in which the administration of the school attempts to schedule an additional group (40 to 50 pupils) in the same standard-size gymnasium. At this point the facilities become inadequate, and the teaching program is jeopardized. The teacher and administrators must find a third station and a third teacher. This type of arrangement, if not corrected, will contribute to the eventual breakdown of the program. A recommended solution to the problem of the third teaching station is the auxiliary gymnasium. Figure 15–3 shows how an auxiliary gymnasium may be used. A three and four station facility is shown (Fig. 15–5).

Outstanding leaders in building design are leading the way in recommending adequate stations for physical education. Trump predicts that in the school of tomorrow:

> Health–physical education–recreation laboratories will contrast with the gymnasium in today's schools, which is planned basically for basketball. The HPER laboratories will be places where students develop and practice health, physical fitness and recreational activities that will be further followed in out-of-school hours.[3]

In Figure 15–4, Trump shows how a physical education facility of tomorrow should look.

Teaching Stations

In the preceding paragraphs the term "teaching stations" has been used. These teaching stations, or classrooms, are essential, in numbers that are comparable to those in all classroom subjects, if physical

Figure 15–3. The auxiliary gymnasium can be used for many purposes. The performing group here is presenting its interpretation of a rhythms number before the class. Each class is divided into several groups and each group has an opportunity to present its interpretation.

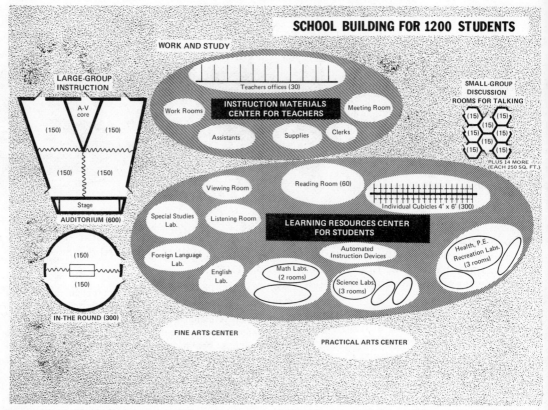

Figure 15–4. Physical education facilities of tomorrow. (From Trump, J. Lloyd, and Dorsey Bayham: *Focus on Change.* Chicago: Rand McNally and Company, 1961, p. 336.)

education instruction is to be effective and successful. Teaching stations have been described as any space or area used for physical education and health instruction. The stations do not have to be of the traditional gymnasium type. Teachers frequently think of the standard gymnasium with the high ceiling as the only area for physical education instruction. As a matter of fact, the only sport requiring a high ceiling is basketball. All other activities can be taught successfully in stations with 12- to 14-foot ceilings.

The Auxiliary Gymnasium. In schools with large enrollments, auxiliary teaching stations are recommended. These stations should be about 25 to 40 feet wide and 50 to 70 feet long with ceilings 12 to 14 feet high. These auxiliary stations may be used for wrestling, tumbling, rhythms, bowling, archery, table tennis, and other activities that do not require a high ceiling.

Improvised Teaching Stations. The teach-er in quest of teaching stations should study the building and attempt to find some old room, corridor, or oversized dressing room that can be converted into a teaching station. Obviously the result will not be ideal, but such improvised stations are better than blaming inadequate facilities for poor teaching. An illustration of one method of converting a dressing room into a teaching station is shown in Figure 15–6. This area is used three periods daily for teaching physical education. Other stations are located in different places in the building. The use of this area for a third teaching station makes the difference between an adequate instructional program and no program at all.

Erle Johnson, Program Specialist in Physical Education, Sacramento City Unified School District, Sacramento, California, reports a revolutionary idea for the dual use of the girls' locker room for dressing and auxiliary physical education purposes.

Figure 15–5. With the use of folding partitions, a three-station facility is possible. In the photograph above, in addition to the three stations, a fourth station is shown through the opening in the background.

Figure 15–6. A locker room may be converted into a teaching station-locker room combination.

Overhead clothes racks are used for hanging street clothes. These racks are raised and lowered in a manner similar to that used for lowering and raising basketball standards. As a result of this arrangement an auxiliary gymnasium is provided, which may be used for tumbling and rhythmics and other activities not requiring a high ceiling.

PLANNING FOR NEW CONSTRUCTION

Because teachers are often asked to assist in planning for a new building, they should have a general background that will enable them to assist the architect in designing physical education facilities. We have already noted that the first and most important step in planning facilities is to determine the number of teaching stations needed. When one is planning teaching stations, the school enrollment, the size of classes, and the number of periods per day must be taken into consideration. Below is one formula that can be used to determine the number of teaching stations needed.

When new buildings are planned, teachers should be careful to provide the best available information in their efforts to assist the architect. Sometimes, for the sake of economy, teachers and administrators are prone to compromise and approve construction that is nonfunctional and impractical. An illustration is the trend in some parts of the country to combine the gymnasium with the lunchroom or the auditorium. None of these combinations has ever been satisfactory; indeed, the conflicts resulting from the joint use of these facilities frequently demoralize students, teachers, administrators, lunchroom employees, and outside groups who use the auditorium. Only chaos can result from such a situation; effective use of the combined facilities by any group becomes impossible.

Research shows that another mistake in planning in some places has been the multiple-purpose room.[4] This arrangement may cause a complete breakdown in the programs involved. Those classes that meet intermittently may use these rooms to advantage, but classes in subjects that are offered daily, such as physical education, usually suffer.

If the physical education program is to approach the desired objectives, there must be a sufficient number of stations to meet the needs of the program without interference from or conflict with other subjects in the curriculum.

Teaching Station Plans

Figure 15–7 illustrates the use of a teaching-station plan in the overall planning in a school system having 11 junior high schools and five senior high schools. In this case the planning for 1200 pupils in grades 7 to 9 indicated the need for six stations with six teachers in a program requiring daily classes in health and physical education with credit throughout the three years.

When health rooms are not included as part of the total teaching-station arrangement, they may be designed as shown in Figure 15–8 (assuming a 400- to 500-pupil school with equal numbers of boys and girls).

If health instruction is a part of the program, the teaching-station plan would look like that in Figure 15–9.

For a school of 800 to 1000 pupils (400 to 500 boys and 400 to 500 girls), the teaching-station plan might be like that shown in Figure 15–10.

If health instruction is part of the program the teaching-station plan would be as shown in Figure 15–11.

If there are 1200 to 1400 pupils (600 to

$$\frac{\text{Total school enrollment} \times \text{No. periods per week}}{\text{Class size} \qquad \times \text{No. periods per week}} \times \text{Extra class load} = \text{No. stations needed}$$
$$\text{Each station can be used}$$

Example: A school with 800 pupils, class size of 40 pupils, and six periods per day, five days per week (30 periods)

$$\frac{800 \times 5 \text{ periods per week}}{40 \times 30 \text{ periods per week}} \times 1.25 \text{ extra class load} = \frac{4000}{1200} \times 1.25 = 4.16 \text{ or four stations}$$

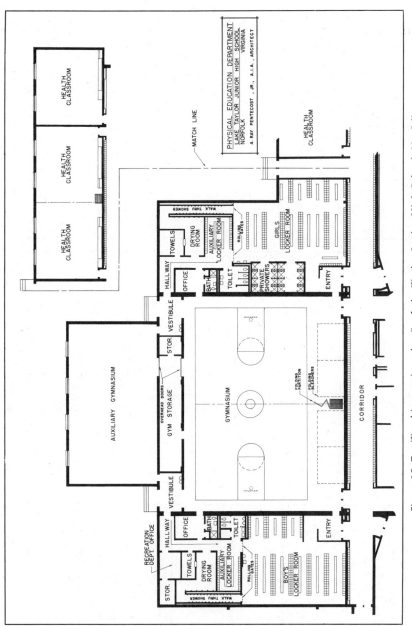

Figure 15–7. Teaching station plan for Lake Taylor Junior High School, Norfolk.

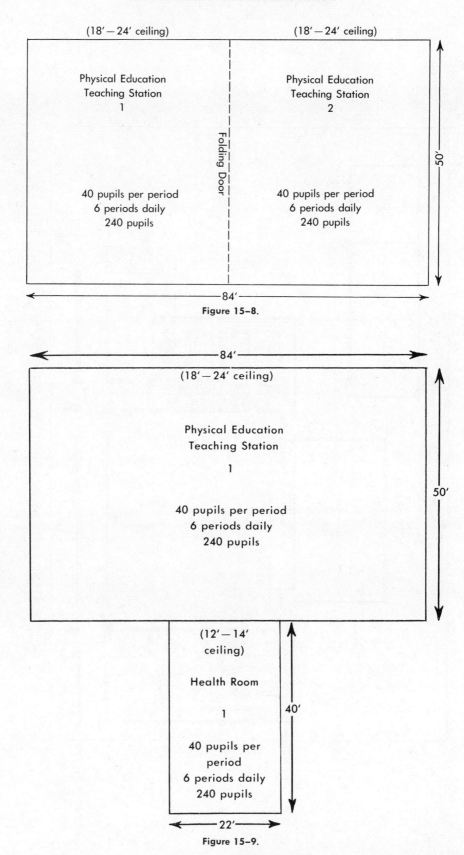

Figure 15–8.

Figure 15–9.

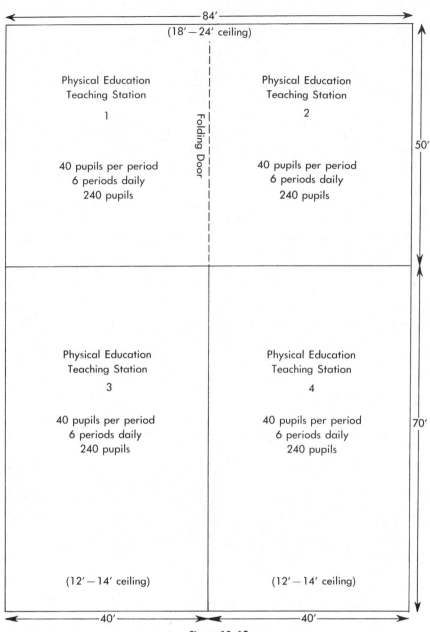

Figure 15–10.

700 boys and 600 to 700 girls), the plan might look like that in Figure 15–12.

If health instruction is a part of the program the teaching stations would look like those in Figure 15–13.

The plans shown in these illustrations outline the ideal situation.

It is important to note that the inclusion of health instruction as a part of the total program will greatly decrease costs, since a health classroom is less expensive than a physical education station.

Teachers should always seek a sufficient number of teaching stations. Next to the physical education requirement, provision for adequate teaching areas is the most important part of the health and physical education structure.

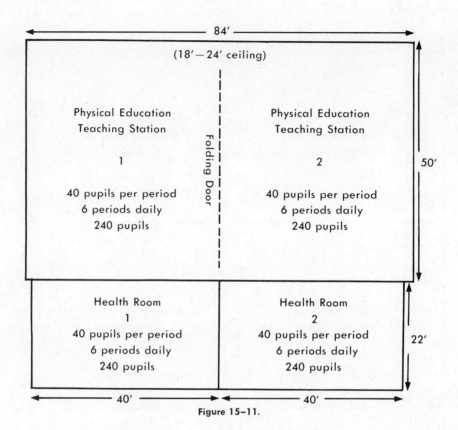

Figure 15–11.

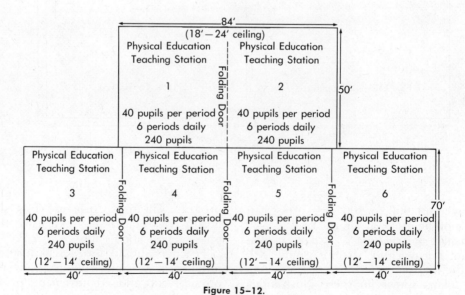

Figure 15–12.

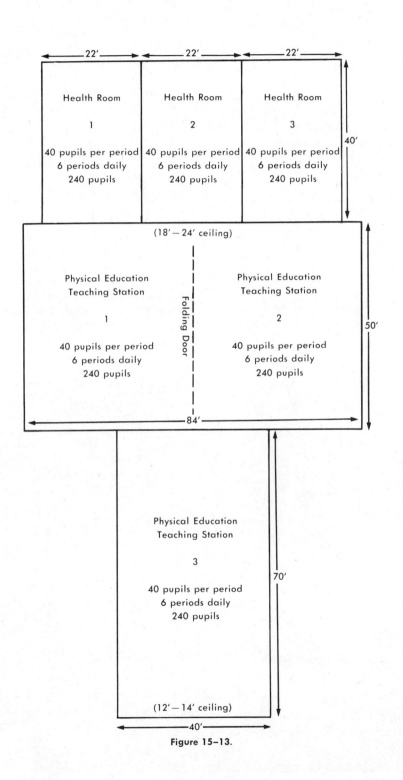

Figure 15–13.

Small Schools

Teachers may question how a small school in a suburban community with a low economic base can ever hope to obtain facilities similar to those we have shown. The answer is that a small school is usually in a better position than a large school. There is probably not a small high school in America that does not have a fairly adequate area designed for varsity basketball. This being true, any school with an enrollment up to 400 pupils will automatically have two stations by using a folding partition. A school with an enrollment of 800 pupils, by securing two rooms for health instruction, may have an excellent teaching arrangement that will be adequate for effective teaching in health and physical education.

Lockers

Many types of lockers may be used both for storage of clothes while the student is in his physical education uniform and for storage of uniforms. Teachers may have to decide just which is the best locker arrangement for the program. Experience has shown that the basket system is not as satisfactory as the box-locker arrangement. The baskets are easily damaged and the contents stolen. Probably the most satisfactory arrangement is the box locker–storage locker unit (a $5' \times 12'' \times 12''$ dressing locker with $12'' \times 12'' \times 12''$ storage lockers attached). Figure 15–14 illustrates one such unit.

The lockers should have padlock attachments and combination locks should be used. After the enrollment has been determined, it is relatively easy to ascertain the number of units needed. There should always be enough dressing lockers to accommodate the highest number of pupils who will dress at the same time. For instance, if two scheduled classes of 80 are the day's peak load, there should be a minimum of 80 dressing locker units (40 pupils per class). This would provide 480 storage lockers for

Figure 15–14. The box locker–storage locker unit offers a practical arrangement for the physical education program.

Figure 15–15. Box locker storage room is shown in the background with the dressing lockers in the foreground.

480 pupils to store their shoes and uniforms in during a six-period day.

Another locker arrangement is to have all the storage units in a separate room. Pupils enter the box-locker storage room, take their uniforms and locks from their box lockers, and enter the dressing room. There must be enough dressing lockers to accommodate the largest class. This plan is recommended in situations in which outside groups use the dressing facilities. The room in which the box lockers are located should be locked to prevent outside groups from entering (Fig. 15–15).

Showers

Showers are important in planning for new buildings. The walk-around shower is both practical and economical. These showers are placed five feet high on two sides of a corridor; the water is controlled by a master valve in the physical education office. Pupils walk through the corridors as water sprays on them from both sides. An entire group of 100 pupils can pass through the showers in three minutes. This type of shower plan has several advantages:

1. *Costs Less.* The initial cost is considerably less because of the small amount of space necessary compared with the space required for individual showers.

2. *Saves Time.* An entire class can pass through in three or four minutes. There is no loitering.

3. *Prevents Discipline Problems.* Since pupils are given limited time, there is no opportunity for loitering and misbehavior in the showers.

4. *Lowers Water Cost.* The entire system is controlled by a master valve in the physical education office. When the valve is closed by the teacher, there is no chance of pupils leaving showers on and wasting water.

Figure 15–16 shows the walk-around type of shower arrangement.

Showers for girls present a different situation. Modesty and other considerations make it advisable to have individual showers and booths for girls who wish privacy, in addition to the walk-around shower. The type of showers shown in Figure 15–17 is both practical and satisfactory for girls.

Storage

It is essential to provide adequate storage space for physical education equipment and supplies. Many new buildings do not allow sufficient room for storage and this can present a serious problem for the teachers. A large area should be planned to store mats, table tennis tables, and other heavy equipment. In addition, a smaller area is needed for balls, bats, golf clubs, etc.

Figure 15–16.   Towel room and walk-around showers.

Figure 15–17.   The arrangement of a girls' shower room. The foreground shows the dressing room with a section of individual showers in the background.

Figure 15-18. A well-planned storage room. The mobile counter is an innovation; the teacher rolls it to the door on the right and uses it to issue equipment. The box in the foreground is used to take equipment to the field and it can be locked between periods.

Three factors that should be considered in planning storage facilities for small equipment are security, accessibility, and portability. See Figure 15–18.

Towels

A towel room should be included with a check-out window at the exit end of the showers. The room should be large enough to store towels and allow freedom of movement for one person to issue towels. Used towels can be placed in carts or bins to be picked up for laundering (see Fig. 15–16).

The Gymnasium

Usually when buildings are planned, the gymnasium is designed for varsity competition and is to be used in conjunction with the physical education department. The gymnasium should be of regulation size for varsity competition, but it should have a folding partition to provide two separate stations for the physical education program. Some of the items that architects should include in their plans are shown below.

One aspect of planning indoor teaching stations that requires particular attention is the material to be used for constructing floors. For many years the standard material used for floors was wood and in some instances tile. Recent experimentation with synthetic surfacing gives teachers, administrators, and architects new ideas for the construction of gymnasium floors.

One such material is Tartan, which was developed by the Minnesota Mining and Manufacturing Company. Figures 15–19 and 15–20 show schools that are using this type of surfacing.

The Health Classroom

Classrooms for health and safety instruction should be slightly larger than the average classroom, which is 22 × 34 feet. A good size is 22 × 40 feet. The room should have storage space, counter space, chalkboards, and tackboards (Fig. 15–21).

Dimensions for Indoor Areas

Indoor dimensions are adequately shown in Table 15–1.

Backboards for basketball goals	Recessed lights
Heating and ventilation	Floor or wall electric outlets
Mountings for bars, ropes, etc.	Bulletin boards
Drinking fountains	Floor markings
Safety mats behind goals	Wall numbers for roll checks
Bleachers	Public address outlets and horns

Figure 15-19. School using "Tartan," a synthetic surfacing. (Courtesy Minnesota Mining and Manufacturing Company.)

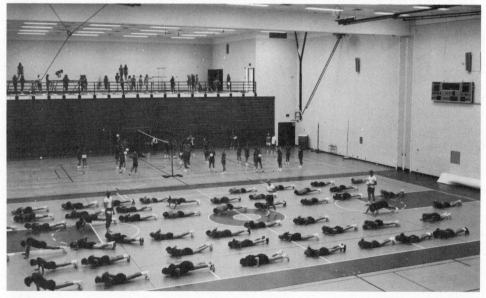

Figure 15-20. School using "Tartan," a synthetic surfacing. (Courtesy Minnesota Mining and Manufacturing Company.)

TABLE 15-1.   SPACE FOR SELECTED INDOOR ACTIVITIES IN SECONDARY SCHOOLS

Activity	Play Area in Feet	Safety Space in Feet*	Total Area in Feet
Badminton	20 x 44	6s, 8e	32 x 60
Basketball			
Jr. High instructional	42 x 74	6s, 8e	
Jr. High interscholastic	50 x 84	6s, 8e	
Sr. High interscholastic	50 x 84	6s, 8e	62 x 100
Sr. High instructional	45 x 74	6s, 8e	57 x 90
Neighborhood El. Sch.	42 x 74	6s, 8e	54 x 90
Community Junior H. S.	50 x 84	6s, 8e	62 x 100
Community Senior H. S.	50 x 84	6s, 8e	62 x 100
Competitive—DGWS	50 x 94	6s, 8e	62 x 110
Boccie	18 x 62	3s, 9e	24 x 80
Fencing, competitive	6 x 40	3s, 6e	12 x 52
instructional	3 x 30	2s, 6e	9 x 42
Rifle (one pt.)	5 x 50	6 to 20e	5 x 70 min.
Shuffleboard	6 x 52	6s, 2e	18 x 56
Tennis			
Deck (doubles)	18 x 40	4s, 5e	26 x 50
Hand	16 x 40	4½s, 10e	25 x 60
Lawn (singles)	27 x 78	12s, 21e	51 x 120
(doubles)	36 x 78	12s, 21e	60 x 120
Paddle (singles)	16 x 44	6s, 8e	28 x 60
(doubles)	20 x 44	6s, 8e	32 x 60
Table (playing area)			9 x 31
Volleyball			
Competitive and adult	30 x 60	6s, 6e	42 x 72
Junior High	30 x 50	6s, 6e	42 x 62
Wrestling (competitive)	24 x 24	5s, 5e	36 x 36

*Safety space at the side of an area is indicated by a number followed by "e" for end and "s" for side.

Table 15–1 is from "Planning Areas and Facilities for Health, Physical Education and Recreation," p. 85. The Athletic Institute and AAHPER, 1966.

The Swimming Pool

Many of the details in planning a swimming pool require the help of specialists. Factors involved in the construction of the pool can make the structure both nonfunctional and extremely costly. Some of the factors requiring expert attention are discussed in the following paragraphs.

Type of Pool.   Teachers and administrators must decide what type of pool is needed and the purpose for which it will be used. Usually the pool for the secondary schools is used jointly for physical education instruction and athletic competition. If this combination is needed, the pool should be planned for swimming and diving meets as well as for

the teaching of swimming. Several types of pools may be used: (1) the all-purpose pool with the instructional and diving areas in the same unit; (2) the instructional area located in a separate unit; (3) the diving area in a separate unit; and (4) the diving, swimming, and instructional areas all planned separately.

The most practical plan for the secondary school is one combining the instructional, swimming, and diving areas in one unit. The pool shown in Figure 15–22 meets this requirement.

Location of Pool.   The pool should be planned in conjunction with the physical education dressing rooms and showers to

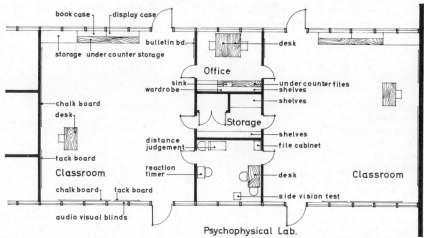

Figure 15–21.   A well-planned health and safety classroom. (Courtesy Riverside Unified School District, Riverside, California.)

facilitate use and to lower the cost. Location is one of the most important factors in planning the pool if the overall cost is to be kept at a minimum. If the pool is planned as a separate unit, separate showers, dressing rooms, and lockers must be incorporated in the unit; this may increase the cost by one third.

Size of the Pool.   Pools designed for instruction and interscholastic competition may vary in size. The width should always

be planned with several lanes 7 feet apart and with buffer space on each side. The length may vary from 60 to 75 feet or more. A pool 30 feet wide should provide four 7-foot lanes with a buffer of 1 foot on each side. A practical and adequate pool should be 75′1″ by 42′, providing six lanes as shown in Figure 15–22.

Check List for Planning the Pool.   Authoritative information should be secured in the following items:[2]

Figure 15–22.   A practical pool for secondary school programs. (Courtesy Lockport Senior High School, Lockport, New York.)

SWIMMING POOLS

1. Has a clear-cut statement been prepared on the nature and scope of the design program and the special requirements for space, equipment, and facilities dictated by the activities to be conducted?

2. Has the swimming pool been planned to meet the total requirements of the program to be conducted as well as any special needs of the clientele to be served?

3. Have all plans and specifications been checked and approved by the local Board of Health?

4. Is the pool the proper depth to accommodate the various age groups and types of activities it is intended to serve?

5. Does the design of the pool incorporate the most current knowledge and best experience available regarding swimming pools?

6. If a local architect or engineer who is inexperienced in pool construction is employed, has an experienced pool consultant, architect, or engineer been called in to advise on design and equipment?

7. Is there adequate deep water for diving (minimum of 9' for one-meter boards, 12' for 3-meter boards, and 15' for 10-meter towers)?

8. Have the requirements for competitive swimming been met (7-foot lanes; 12-inch black or brown lines on the bottom; pool 1 inch longer than official measurement; depth and distance markings)?

9. Is there adequate deck space around the pool? Has more space been provided than that indicated by the minimum recommended deck/pool ratio?

10. Does the swimming instructor's office face the pool? And is there a window through which the instructor may view all the pool area? Is there a toilet-shower-dressing area next to the office for instructors?

11. Are recessed steps or removable ladders located on the walls so as not to interfere with competitive swimming turns?

12. Does a properly-constructed overflow gutter extend around the pool perimeter?

13. Where skimmers are used, have they been properly located so that they are not on walls where competitive swimming is to be conducted?

14. Have separate storage spaces been allocated for maintenance and instructional equipment?

15. Has the area for spectators been properly separated from the pool area?

16. Have all diving standards and lifeguard chairs been properly anchored?

17. Does the pool layout provide the most efficient control of swimmers from showers and locker rooms to the pool? Are toilet facilities provided for wet swimmers separate from the dry area?

18. Is the recirculation pump located below the water level?

19. Is there easy vertical access to the filter room for both people and material (stairway if required)?

20. Has the proper pitch to drains been allowed in the pool, on the pool deck, in the overflow gutter, and on the floor of shower and dressing rooms?

21. Has adequate space been allowed between diving boards and between the diving boards and sidewalls?

22. Is there adequate provision for lifesaving equipment? Pool-cleaning equipment?

23. Are inlets and outlets adequate in number and located so as to insure effective circulation of water in the pool?

24. Has consideration been given to underwater lights, underwater observation windows, and underwater speakers?

25. Is there a coping around the edge of the pool?

26. Has a pool heater been considered in northern climates in order to raise the temperature of the water?

27. Have underwater lights in end racing walls been located deep enough and directly below surface lane anchors, and are they on a separate circuit?

28. Has the plan been considered from the standpoint of handicapped persons (e.g., is there a gate adjacent to the turnstiles)?

29. Is seating for swimmers provided on the deck?

30. Has the recirculation-filtration system been designed to meet the anticipated future bathing load?

31. Has the gas chlorinator (if used) been placed in a separate room accessible from and vented to the outside?

32. Has the gutter waste water been valved to return to the filters, and also for direct waste?

INDOOR POOLS

1. Is there proper mechanical ventilation?

2. Is there adequate acoustical treatment of walls and ceilings?

3. Is there adequate overhead clearance for diving (15' above low springboards, 15' for 3-meter boards, and 10' for 10-meter platforms)?

4. Is there adequate lighting (50 footcandles minimum)?

5. Has reflection of light from the outside been kept to the minimum by proper location of windows or skylights (windows on sidewalls are not desirable)?

6. Are all wall bases coved to facilitate cleaning?

7. Is there provision for proper temperature control in the pool room for both water and air?

8. Can the humidity of the pool room be controlled?

9. Is the wall and ceiling insulation adequate to prevent "sweating"?

10. Are all metal fittings of noncorrosive material?

11. Is there a tunnel around the outside of the pool, or a trench on the deck which permits ready access to pipes?

OUTDOOR POOLS

1. Is the site for the pool in the best possible location (away from railroad tracks, heavy industry, trees, and open fields which are dusty)?

2. Have sand and grass been kept the proper distance away from the pool to prevent them from being transmitted to the pool?

3. Has a fence been placed around the pool to assure safety when not in use?

4. Has proper subsurface drainage been provided?

5. Is there adequate deck space for sunbathing?

6. Are the outdoor lights placed far enough from the pool to prevent insects from dropping into the pool?

7. Is the deck of nonslip material?

8. Is there an area set aside for eating, separated from the pool deck?

9. Is the bathhouse properly located, with the entrance to the pool leading to the shallow end?

10. If the pool shell contains a concrete finish, has the length of the pool been increased by 3 inches over the "official" size in order to permit eventual tiling of the basin without making the pool "too short"?

11. Are there other recreational facilities nearby for the convenience and enjoyment of swimmers?

12. Do diving boards or platforms face north or east?

13. Are lifeguard stands provided and properly located?

14. Has adequate parking space been provided and properly located?

15. Is the pool oriented correctly in relation to the sun?

16. Have windshields been provided in situations where heavy winds prevail?

Portable Pools. Lawrence Houston, Administrator of the Health, Physical Education, Safety and Youth Services for the Los Angeles Public Schools, has experimented with a portable swimming pool for teaching swimming (Fig. 15–23). The pool is assembled, disassembled, and transported from school to school during the summer. The pilot program using a prototype facility and experimental techniques was well received. Houston's evaluation follows:

1. Reception was enthusiastic to overwhelming by both children and parents. It was not possible to accommodate the numbers seeking instruction or the schools desiring the pool.
2. Enrollment ranged from 165 to 214 pupils per school with an attendance rate of 93.3 per cent. Parent spectators averaged 57 per day.
3. 7184 pupil lessons were given in 42 teaching days.
4. Children lost their fear of water and learned the basics of water safety; many learned to swim.
5. Because elementary schools are within walking distance of every child, these schools provided convenient sites.[5]

OUTDOOR FACILITIES

Teachers frequently feel that if there is not a large amount of space available for outdoor activity, they will be unable to have an effective program in physical education.

Such reasoning does not survive the application of logic to the situation. If a survey is made of available outdoor space, it will be found that there usually is sufficient area to conduct a program that meets all objectives of physical education. Effective use depends on the activities to be taught. Many activities can be taught successfully in limited areas. For instance, volleyball skills may be taught in an area of 90 × 60 feet. But when teachers think of outside activities, they usually think of football, track, or softball. These activities are desirable, but it is not imperative that they be taught in order to attain the objectives of physical education. If volleyball and softball are compared, it will be found that the values derived from volleyball far exceed those of softball. Surely a teacher who finds the school without a golf course would not say that there could be no program in physical education.

A thorough survey of the existing space should be made to determine what activities can be taught in the area. Earlier in the chapter, it was pointed out that when teachers begin to place emphasis on the teaching of skills, the entire situation changes; they often find that a good program can be conducted in small areas.

In planning for the outdoor program where a sufficient amount of space is available, the following guidelines may assist teachers.

Figure 15–23. The portable pool is an innovation for providing swimming instruction.

Surfaces

The surface used for outdoor areas is important. Teachers should have a general knowledge of the surfaces that are needed for the program. There are many types, but the most generally used are turf, asphalt, and concrete.

Turf. Turf is the most common surface for all field games, such as softball, touch football, hockey, soccer, speedball, and lacrosse. Considerable attention must be given to upkeep and maintenance. In many climates a great amount of water must be applied to prevent grass from dying and to promote its growth.

Asphalt. Asphalt surfaces are popular for multiple-use areas and small play spaces, and asphalt is relatively inexpensive. However, these areas should be treated to prevent grass from growing in them.

Concrete. Concrete surfaces are widely used for multiple-play areas and small play spaces. Many physical education leaders and administrators prefer this surface because of the little maintenance required, the all-weather usage, and the comparatively low cost.

Synthetic Surfaces. The use of synthetic surfaces for all outdoor areas is becoming more popular each year. The trade names of Astroturf, Poly-turf, Uniturf, Synthoturf, Robbinsturf, Dynaturf, Proturf, and Axonturf are examples of synthetic surfacing that may eventually replace the surfaces discussed above. The *Physical Education Perspective* reports many advantages of using these artificial turfs:

1. Continuous use—eliminating the need for many practice and intramural fields since the synthetic material makes it possible to use the fields without harming them.
2. All-year use—outdoor sports can be played all year long on artificial turf simply by placing an inexpensive bubble over the field or facility. Without a bubble, it is still useable, except, of course, when covered by snow.
3. Reduction of injuries—synthetic surfaces cut down on injuries in contact sports such as football. Players can wear shoes with soccer-type cleats (shorter) which provide traction without digging into the surface. When a player wearing regular football shoes on natural grass is hit, his body twists, feet cannot turn, and he often tears ligaments and breaks bones.

4. Lower maintenance costs—there is no mud, surfaces can be cleaned easily, and maintenance crews can be reduced. There's no problem with mowing, fertilizing, or spraying.
5. Better use of audiovisuals—coaches have found that game movies stand out better on artificial turf and television viewers made the same observation.[6]

Multiple-Use Areas

Probably the most practical outside space is the multiple-use area providing for several activities on one hard surface. These areas are usually surfaced with concrete or asphalt and are usable the year round. The properly planned multiple-use area may be used for teaching the skills of basketball, tennis, and volleyball (Fig. 15–24).

Areas for Fixed Equipment

The surfacing around fixed equipment, such as chinning-bars, ropes, and apparatus, should be of soft materials. Considerable experimentation is in progress with rubber, cork, sponge, and air cell materials to determine which provides the greatest safety features. (See Figure 15–25.)

Golf Area

Instruction in golf is extremely difficult if teachers are not skilled in handling large groups effectively. Again attention must be given to the teaching of skills employing the overflow principle described in Chapter 10. Figure 15–26 illustrates how golf can be taught to a large class effectively when the instructional area is planned properly. Figure 15–27 shows how a par three course may be constructed.

Other Areas

Adequate space for touch football, track, softball, and tennis is desirable in a well-rounded physical education program. The amount of space needed for these playing areas is given in Table 15–2; the lay-out diagrams are shown in Chapter 12.

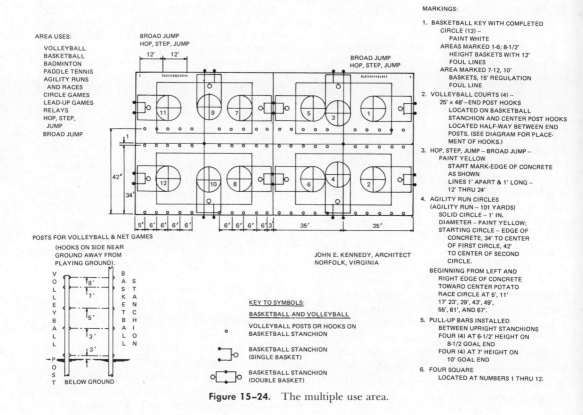

Figure 15–24. The multiple use area.

Figure 15–25. Hard-surfaced areas for multiple use placed adjacent to soft-surfaced areas for fixed equipment are a practical arrangement for the instructional program. (Courtesy Los Angeles City Schools.)

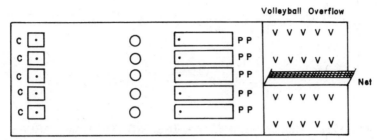

Figure 15–26. If the areas to be used are planned properly, golf instruction can be effective and safe. C, Chippers; □, squares for chippers to hit plastic balls; ○, circles for balls to fall into; □, skinned grass putting areas with cans placed in ground; PP, putters; V, volleyball overflow pupils.

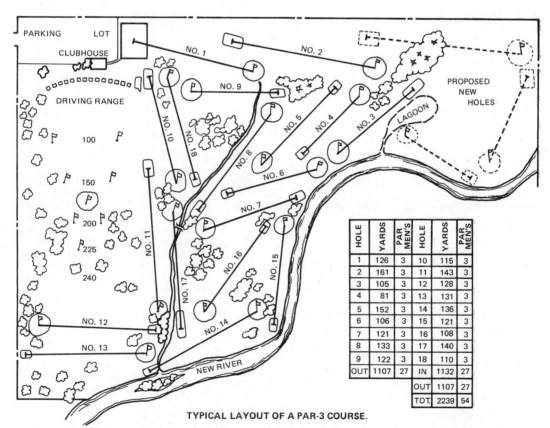

TYPICAL LAYOUT OF A PAR-3 COURSE.

HOLE	YARDS	PAR MEN'S	HOLE	YARDS	PAR MEN'S
1	126	3	10	115	3
2	161	3	11	143	3
3	105	3	12	128	3
4	81	3	13	131	3
5	152	3	14	136	3
6	106	3	15	121	3
7	121	3	16	108	3
8	133	3	17	140	3
9	122	3	18	110	3
OUT	1107	27	IN	1132	27
			OUT	1107	27
			TOT.	2239	54

Figure 15–27. Layout of a par three course. (From Gabrielsen and Miles: *Sports and Recreation Facilities for School and Community.* Englewood Cliffs: Prentice-Hall, Inc., 1958, p. 284.)

TABLE 15–2. RECOMMENDED DIMENSIONS FOR GAME AREAS*

Games	Elementary School	Junior High School	High School (Adults)	Area Size (Including Buffer Space)
Basketball	40' × 60'	50' × 84'	50' × 84'	7,200 sq. ft.
Basketball (College)			50' × 94'	8,000 sq. ft.
Volleyball	25' × 50'	25' × 50'	30' × 60'	2,800 sq. ft.
Badminton			20' × 44'	1,800 sq. ft.
Paddle Tennis			20' × 44'	1,800 sq. ft.
Deck Tennis			18' × 40'	1,250 sq. ft.
Tennis		36' × 78'	26' × 78'	6,500 sq. ft.
Ice Hockey			85' × 200'	17,000 sq. ft.
Field Hockey			180' × 300'	64,000 sq. ft.
Horseshoes		10' × 40'	10' × 50'	1,000 sq. ft.
Shuffleboard			6' × 52'	640 sq. ft.
Lawn Bowling			14' × 110'	1,800 sq. ft.
Boccie			15' × 75'	1,950 sq. ft.
Tetherball	10' circle	12' circle	12' circle	400 sq. ft.
Croquet	38' × 60'	38' × 60'	38' × 60'	2,200 sq. ft.
Roque			30' × 60'	2,400 sq. ft.
Handball (Single-wall)	18' × 26'	18' × 26'	20' × 40'	1,200 sq. ft.
Handball (Four-wall)			23' × 46'	1,058 sq. ft.
Baseball	210' × 210'	300' × 300'	400' × 400'	160,000 sq. ft.
Archery		50' × 150'	50' × 300'	20,000 sq. ft.
Softball (12" Ball)**	150' × 150'	200' × 200'	275' × 275'	75,000 sq. ft.
Football			160' × 360'	80,000 sq. ft.
Touch Football		120' × 300'	160' × 360'	80,000 sq. ft.
6-Man Football			120' × 300'	54,000 sq. ft.
Soccer (Men) Minimum			165' × 300'	65,000 sq. ft.
Maximum			240' × 360'	105,000 sq. ft.
Soccer (Women)			120' × 240'	40,000 sq. ft.

*Table covers a single unit; many of above can be combined. Table 15–2 is from "Planning Areas and Facilities for Health, Physical Education and Recreation," p. 18. The Athletic Institute and the AAHPER, 1966.
**Dimensions vary with size of ball used.

Recommended Outdoor Facilities

Teachers need some guidelines when they are assisting with the planning of outdoor facilities. California has been a pioneer in planning outdoor facilities. The Bureau of Health, Physical Education and Recreation of the State of California recently issued a bulletin stressing the need for establishing standards for planning adequate outdoor facilities for a school with a potential enrollment of 1440 pupils. The suggested standard for facilities is described as follows:

Outdoor Instructional Facilities

1. *Field space.* A minimum of four field spaces—two field spaces for each class using the fields during any period—should be provided for activities such as softball, hockey, speedball, soccer, and touch football. The area of each field should be 190 feet × 420 feet or 7.3 acres.

2. *Hard-surfaced area.* There should be eight basketball courts 46 feet × 84 feet. With space between courts, the total dimensions would be 416 feet × 92 feet or 38,272 square feet. There should also be six volleyball courts 30 feet × 60 feet. With space between courts the total dimensions would be 218 feet × 72 feet or 15,696 square feet. The total hard-surfaced area should be 53,968 square feet or 1.24 acres.

3. *Tennis courts.* Space should be provided for eight courts with backboards for eight practice stations or for six courts with backboards for 16 practice stations. A hard surface should be provided for both the play and practice areas. The total tennis area for eight courts should be 55,600 square feet or 1.28 acres.

4. *Areas for modified physical education classes, school and community recreation.* Hard-surfaced and turfed areas, a golf green, and a landscaped area should be provided for these purposes and space should be set aside for back-yard type games.

The hard-surfaced area should contain about 14,400 square feet for modified activities. In addition, another 4,000 square feet should be provided for four shuffleboard and outdoor bowling alleys. The total hard-surfaced area should be 18,400 square feet.

In the turfed area, there should be two croquet courts each 4,750 square feet and four horseshoe courts, each 624 square feet. The total turfed area should be 11,996 square feet.

In the modified PE and recreational area, the California Department of Education also recommends that 6,417 square feet (69 feet × 93 feet) be set aside for a golf putting course or green.

The department also suggests that a landscaped area of eight acres be set aside as an outdoor classroom equipped with tables and a barbecue pit for parties and picnics. Part of this area should be planned for use as an outdoor theater.

The aquatics center used in the instructional program during the day and for community recreation during out-of-school hours should be located here. The State Department of Education recommends a two-pool complex. One pool of near constant depth should be 75 feet, 1 inch long, 45 feet wide, and 3½ to 5 feet deep. This pool should be used for instruction and competition. The second pool, 60 feet long, 35 feet wide, and 12 feet deep, should be used for water polo, diving, and similar activities.

The total space suggested for modified physical education classes and school and community recreation is 9.64 acres.

5. *Archery and golf driving areas.* If possible, separate areas should be provided for these activities. However, the bulletin suggests that you can use space provided for other activities. An area of 20,000 square feet—50 feet × 400 feet—should be allowed for an archery range.

When teaching golf, an area of between 150 and 230 yards should be used for a driving range.

The total space recommended for all outdoor instructional facilities is 11.46 acres.

Additional Facilities

In addition to the space provided for regular instruction and recreation, the bulletin recommends that an additional 11.4 acres be set aside for interscholastic and intramural activities. Recommended are:

1. A football field with a quarter mile track circling it and provision for a 220-yard straightaway; also bleacher space. Total space—five acres.

2. A baseball field with a hooded backstop and bleacher space. Total space—three acres.

3. Space for two practice fields each 190 feet × 420 feet for use by freshmen and junior varsity teams and for instructional and intramural purposes. Total space—3.4 acres.

In addition, the bulletin notes that the tennis courts provided for class instruction should be used for the interscholastic and intramural programs and that instructional facilities should be used by both boys and girls in intramurals, playdays, sports days, aquatics days, and other special events.[8]

In Odessa High School, Odessa, Texas, the students and teachers constructed a removable nine-hole golf course that enables all high school students to practice skills learned in class. The course is laid down on one of the football fields and consists of plywood, old rugs or carpeting, glue and sta-

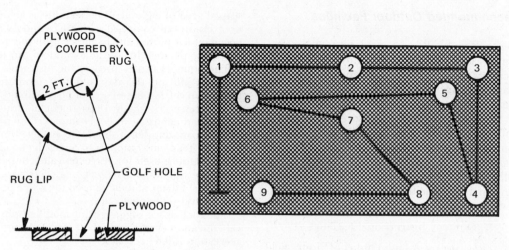

Figure 15-28. Outdoor golf course. (Courtesy Odessa High School, Odessa, Texas.)

ples, and may be easily constructed by following these steps (see Figure 15-28).

1. Take a quarter-inch plywood and cut a circle with a two-foot radius from the center of the board.

2. Cut a hole in the center of the plywood the size of a regulation golf hole. The piece of plywood will be round like an archery target.

3. Cut the rug six inches larger than the edges of the plywood circle to create a lip to hang over the plywood.

4. Cut a hole in the center of the rug to match the hole in the plywood.

5. Glue rug to plywood. Part of the rug should hang over the plywood. This is extremely important when placing the green on the ground, since this part fits over the green or ground, making it possible for a golf ball to roll onto your green fairly smoothly.

6. Take a stapling machine and tack the rug around the edges and also around the hole. This holds the rug more securely to the plywood.[7]

EQUIPMENT AND SUPPLIES

Teachers of physical education are usually responsible for initiating requisitions for the purchase of equipment and supplies. They should be familiar with the types of equipment that are scientifically adequate for the program. In addition teachers should know how to prepare the inventory, budget wisely, requisition equipment and supplies, and care for equipment and supplies.

The Inventory

At the end of each year a detailed inventory should be made. This inventory is of inestimable value in assisting the teacher with the many problems of selecting equipment and determining the budget. Teachers are expected to know how much equipment is on hand and are responsible for maintaining accurate accounts of where the equipment is. Damaged and unusable materials should be stored and should show up in the inventory. Figure 15-29 shows an inventory check list that may be used.

Budgeting

A yearly budget should be prepared showing the allocation of money for each activity. By referring to the inventory one can determine the quantity of materials needed. There is usually a stipulated amount of money set aside for the health and physical education budget. The teacher must work within this budget in determining the allocation for each activity in the program.

One particularly widespread practice should be mentioned at this point. In many school systems the budget for physical education is dependent upon the income from gate receipts of the athletic program. This practice is not a recommended procedure. The instructional program in physical education is of vital importance for the health and fitness of all boys and girls. Therefore, the effectiveness of the program should not be dependent upon fluctuating income from athletic contests. Physical education is the only phase of the school program that is faced with this problem, and steps should be made to correct it. However meager the allocation may be, it should be made from the same instructional source from which other subjects derive their support.

Requisitioning Equipment and Supplies

Determining what items should be requisitioned may present a problem for teachers. Materials should not be requested without considering some determining factors that may be used to justify the need. The type and amount of equipment and supplies needed for the program are determined by (1) the instructional content of the program and (2) the teaching procedures used.

The Instructional Content as a Determinant. For each activity taught there should be ample equipment and supplies to enable the teacher to do an acceptable teaching job. One of the criteria in the selection of activities for the instructional program on the local level is the availability of equipment and supplies. In the curriculum shown in Chapter 5, there should be available equipment and supplies for each activity shown. For example, bowling cannot be taught unless there are pins, balls, and alleys available. If they are not available, the teacher should make every effort to procure them so that the activity can be included in the curriculum. Local bowling establishments are usually willing to furnish used balls and pins at little or no cost. Locally constructed bowling traps or backstops can be made, and rubber runners can be used to provide direction for the release of balls and to keep the balls off the floor (see Figure 12–14).

The approach described in the foregoing paragraph should be used in making supplies and equipment available for any activity that is a desirable addition to the curriculum.

Teaching Procedures as a Determinant. The teaching approach will always determine the quantity of supplies and amount of equipment needed for the program. If the teacher is content with a play program in basketball, for instance, two or three balls will suffice. However, if the teacher is eager to teach effectively, then the class should be divided into eight or ten groups with a ball for each group. This will require more supplies, but only by working with small instructional groups can teachers effectively teach skills.

After determining the materials necessary the teacher should be careful in the selection of items. He should try to find the most reliable sources of materials and place all orders on bid. Specifications should be written concerning quality, design, and safety factors. Locally devised forms are helpful in requisitioning the equipment and supplies needed for the program. Figure 15–30 illustrates two forms that may be used.

Improvising

A considerable quantity of equipment is necessary for teaching effectively, and the cost of providing it may be great. However, many items used in the instructional program can be constructed or secured locally for a portion of the usual cost. Some examples of the types of equipment that may be constructed locally are starting blocks, hurdles, jumping standards, table tennis tables, bowling alley backstops, table tennis nets (made from canvas), basketball backstops, table tennis paddles, archery racks, batons, volleyball standards, and rope equipment.

Rope-Tug-o-War. John Jenny, Director of Health and Physical Education in the Wilmington (Delaware) Public Schools, reports the use of a four-way tug-o-war rope, which may be used for large classes (Fig. 15–31). The rope tug-o-war is relatively inexpensive and provides a practical solution for rainy day activity, intramural programs, and corecreation.

Indoor Bowling Equipment. With a small expenditure of money, bowling backstops can be constructed to provide for adequate instruction in the physical education classes. Figure 12–14 shows a group of folding bowling backstops used in the Norfolk schools. These backstops, constructed locally, are used in all junior and senior high schools.

Rubber runners are used to prevent damage to the gymnasium floor and score sheets

Figure 15–29. An inventory form helps the teacher to keep records for all equipment and assists in preparing the requisition.

Figure 15–29 continued on opposite page.

C

FILM STRIPS

REQ	INV	JUNIOR HIGH ONLY	REQ	INV	JUNIOR HIGH ONLY
		The Skin, Hair and Nails			Your Teeth
		How Vitamins Help Man			Man's Battle Against Disease
		Human Respiration			Safety in the Home
		Salk Vaccine			Preventing Accidents in the Home
		Work of Louis Pasteur			Fire Prevention at Home and in School
		How Hormones Control the Body			Safety Coming to School and in School
		Antibiotics - Disease Fighting Champions			Safety in School Shop & Gymnasium
		Battle Report: War Against Cancer			Safety on the Streets and on Vehicles
		How Your Body Fights Diseases			Safety in Outdoor Sports
		Man's Senses in Action			Outboard Motor Boat Handling
		Our Heart and Circulation			Confidence - You Understand Menstruation
		Nutrition: Energy, Growth and Repair			SENIOR HIGH ONLY
		Mechanics of Breathing			Alcohol and You - Part 1
		Digestion of Foods			Alcohol and You - Part 2
		Food and Nutrition			Narcotics and You - Part 1
		Care of the Feet			The Digestive System
		Control of Body Temperature			Respiratory System
		Communicable Diseases			Circulatory System
		Bacteria, Good & Bad			Endocrine System
		Insect Pests and Disease			The Nervous System
		Safety Behind the Wheel			Bones and Muscles
		Your Eyes			Dangers of Narcotics
		Your Ears and Hearing			Work of the Blood
		First Aid Series			What Is Behavior?
		Fighting Cancer			Narcotics and You - Part 2
		Communicable Disease			

D

FILM STRIPS

Junior and Senior High Schools

REQ	INV	SPORTS	REQ	INV	DRIVER EDUCATION
		Basketball, Beginning			General Motors Kit (8)
		Basketball, Girls			Ford Kits (3)
		Bowling, Beginning			
		Golf, Beginning			
		Tennis, Beginning			
		Track and Field, Beginning			
		Tumbling, Beginning			
		Tumbling, Advanced			
		Volleyball, Beginning			
		Wrestling, Beginning			
		Field Hockey, Beginning			INSTRUCTIONAL RECORDS
		Table Tennis			Rhythmic Activity, Basset-Chestnut
					Rhythms DP1 Album 1 Dietrick
					Rhythms DP2 Album 2 Dietrick
					Barefoot Ballerina
					Strauss Waltzes
					Nutcracker Suite
					Quiet Village
					West Side Story
-	-				Physical Fitness Activities 16-A
					Exodus
					Sound of Music
					Basic Rhythms - Ruth Evans
					Book, Basic Rhythms for BRI Evans
					Magical World of Melody (4 albums, Readers Digest)

*Do not destroy equipment. All unusable equipment should be turned in to the Physical Education Office.

*The June report, under the requisition column, should show all supplies and equipment and items ordered for the following year.

Figure 15–29. *Continued.*

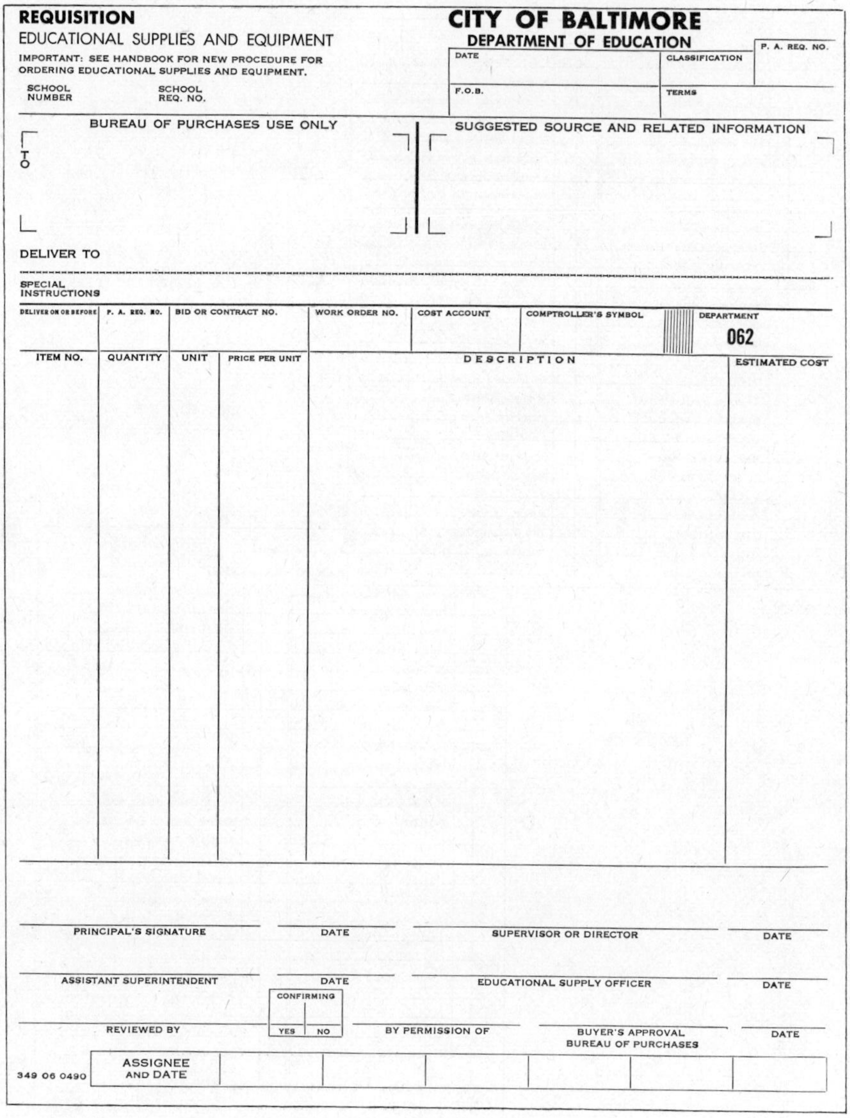

REQUISITION
EDUCATIONAL SUPPLIES AND EQUIPMENT
IMPORTANT: SEE HANDBOOK FOR NEW PROCEDURE FOR ORDERING EDUCATIONAL SUPPLIES AND EQUIPMENT.

SCHOOL NUMBER | SCHOOL REQ. NO.

CITY OF BALTIMORE
DEPARTMENT OF EDUCATION

DATE | CLASSIFICATION | P. A. REQ. NO.
F.O.B. | TERMS

BUREAU OF PURCHASES USE ONLY

TO

SUGGESTED SOURCE AND RELATED INFORMATION

DELIVER TO

SPECIAL INSTRUCTIONS

DELIVER ON OR BEFORE	P. A. REQ. NO.	BID OR CONTRACT NO.	WORK ORDER NO.	COST ACCOUNT	COMPTROLLER'S SYMBOL	DEPARTMENT 062

ITEM NO.	QUANTITY	UNIT	PRICE PER UNIT	DESCRIPTION	ESTIMATED COST

PRINCIPAL'S SIGNATURE | DATE | SUPERVISOR OR DIRECTOR | DATE

ASSISTANT SUPERINTENDENT | DATE | EDUCATIONAL SUPPLY OFFICER | DATE

REVIEWED BY | CONFIRMING YES NO | BY PERMISSION OF | BUYER'S APPROVAL BUREAU OF PURCHASES | DATE

349 06 0490 | ASSIGNEE AND DATE

A

Figure 15–30. *A*, Requisition form for supplies and equipment. *B*, Requisition for repairs (buildings and grounds). (Courtesy Baltimore Public Schools.)

Figure 15–30 continued on opposite page.

700542 B-54-2

	REQ. CLERK CHARGED TO
CLASS **B** FOR	**BALTIMORE PUBLIC SCHOOLS** BALTIMORE, MARYLAND **REQUISITION** REPAIRS (Buildings and Grounds)	1_____ 2_____ 3_____ 4_____ 5_____ 6_____

Necessary repairs to buildings, heating plants, plumbing, lighting or any building or grounds improvement which requires labor. Emergency calls must be followed by written requisition marked "confirmatory," giving date of call. Make in duplicate. Mail original to Business Office. Retain duplicate.

ALWAYS MENTION YOUR REQUISITION NUMBER WHEN REFERRING TO SAME

YOUR REQ. NO. **B**	DATE	SCHOOL NO.	PRINCIPAL OR SUPERVISOR SIGN HERE

LOCATION IN BUILDING

Nature of work to be done (state fully)

DO NOT WRITE BELOW THIS LINE

_____
Chief, Maint. Bureau

APPROVED	DATE	CHARGE	OFFICE DATA
For Supt.		7.	Job No.
Asst. Supt. (Educational)			P. A.
Director			S. O.
Asst. Supt. (Business)			CODE

B

Figure 15–30. *Continued.*

Figure 15–31. With a little imagination teachers may improvise to meet local needs. The picture illustrates a four-way tug-of-war rope. (Courtesy Health and Physical Education Department, Wilmington Public Schools, Wilmington, Delaware.)

may be placed on tables or on the wall adjacent to each alley. Local bowling establishments furnish old pins and balls at no cost.

Balance Beam.   Paula Drake, Director of the Girls' Physical Education Program at Cape Elizabeth High School, Cape Elizabeth, Maine, has devised a balance beam that was constructed in the industrial arts shop of the high school. The beam is used in the intramural program (Fig. 15–32).

Nets.   Nets used jointly by the school and community usually undergo severe treatment, leading to costly repair jobs. The nets usually used for this purpose, including the rugged wire nets, have proved to be unsatisfactory. Pupils sit on them and it is difficult to prevent their deterioration. One innovation which has proved to be successful is shown in Figure 15–33. The net is made of the heavy wire used for building fences, with 3/4-inch pipe stretched across the top and posts installed at intervals to provide rugged support.

Miscellaneous Items

Many small items of equipment may be constructed to supplement the equipment purchased through the regular school budget. Teachers in the physical education department, School District 65, Evanston, Illinois, spend holidays and Saturdays designing and making equipment for the department. Table 15–3 itemizes and gives the approximate cost of equipment they made.[10]

CARE OF EQUIPMENT AND SUPPLIES

The equipment and supplies used in the health and physical education program are expensive. With proper care these materials will withstand hard wear. However, when these items are abused the teacher may find that before the season is over the supply of materials is exhausted and the budget depleted. There are several guidelines that may assist the teacher in caring for equipment and supplies:

1. The teacher should establish a plan for issuing equipment and supplies each period.

2. Someone should be responsible for the return of materials at the end of each period.

3. Equipment should be kept clean.

4. All equipment and supplies should be carefully repaired and properly stored at the end of the season.

5. The equipment room should be kept clean, orderly, and free from moisture. (See Figure 15–18).

Figure 15–32. The balance beam is an excellent example of equipment that can be constructed locally. (Courtesy Cape Elizabeth High School, Cape Elizabeth, Maine.)

Figure 15–33. A net that will withstand severe treatment. (Courtesy Norfolk City Schools, Norfolk, Virginia.)

TABLE 15-3.   A GUIDE TO LOCAL SUPPLEMENTATION OF EQUIPMENT*

Item	Grade Level	Can be made with basic hand tools	Requires shop and/or power tools	Outside help needed in part	Considerable outside help needed	Material cost per unit (approx.)	Construction time (approx.)	Single purpose	2-3 Activities	Multi-purpose	Commercially manufactured
Redwood Balance Beam	3-8	X			X	$28.00 pr.	1 hr.		X		Yes
Bases—Outdoor	1-8	X				.50-1.00	15 min.	X	X		No
Basketball Rebound Developer	6-8		X			$ 5.10	3 hrs.	X			Yes
Bench—Playground	K-8		X	X		$12.37	4 hrs.		X	X	Yes
Bongo Board	6-8	X				$ 1.00	1 hr.	X			Yes
Bowling Pin	K-8	X	X	X		.22	35 min.			X	Yes
Canvas Pillow Fight Bag	4-8	X			X	$13.60 pr.	10 min.	X			No
Canvas Sled	2-8				X	$ 3.60		X			Yes
Captain Ball Stands	4-6	X				$ 4.00	2 hrs.		X		No
Climbing Rope Disc	2-8	X				$ 1.00	1 hr.	X			No
Drive Ball Target Disc	4-8	X				$ 2.30	2 hrs.	X			No
Field Markers	2-8	X	X	X				X			Yes
Goal Post Target	4-8	X		X		$ 9.40	2½ hrs.		X		No
Hand Stand Practice Blocks	5-8		X			$ 1.00 pr.	2 hrs.		X		Yes
High Jump and Hurdle Standard	3-8		X			$ 5.10 pr.	8 hrs.		X		Yes
Hockey Stick	4-8	X				.78	½ hr.	X			Yes
Isometric Test Scale	5-8	X			X	$ 8.00	10 min.	X			No
Jump Rope	1-8	X				.56	3 min.	X			Yes
Lemi Stick	2-8		X			.12	15 min.		X		Yes
Paddle	4-8		X			.20	20 min.		X		Yes
Parallel Bar Platform	6-8		X			$11.75	4 hrs.		X		No
Philippine Poles	4-8	X		X		$ 1.40 pr.	20 min.	X			No
Portable Ping Pong Table	6-8		X	X		$40.00	8-10 hrs.	X			Yes
Pull-up Bar	2-8		X	X		$10.50	4 hrs.			X	No
Ring Ride	7-8		X	X		$100.00		X			No
Safety Hurdle	4-8		X	X		$ 7.20 pr.	3 hrs.		X		No
Scooter Carts	K-8	X				$ 4.30	45 min.		X		Yes
Strength Test Device	4-8	X				$16.50	1 hr.	X			No
Tire Stand	K-8		X			$ 2.00	2 hrs.			X	No
Training Parallel Bars	6-8		X	X		$19.00	6-8 hrs.		X		Yes
Wall Peg Board	4-8		X			$ 6.30	4 hrs.	X			Yes
Welded Steel Bucks	3-8				X	$27.20				X	No
Weight Lifting Bar	6-8		X	X		$ 2.00	½ hr.	X			Yes
Weighted Hurdle Rope	2-8	X				.65	10 min.	X			No

*Courtesy of *Physical Education Newsletter,* Croft Educational Services, Inc., December 15, 1958.

SCHEDULING THE USE OF PHYSICAL EDUCATION FACILITIES

The large increase in enrollment in the physical education instruction program, the expansion of community activities, the broadening of the athletic program, and the tremendous growth of intramurals have placed heavy demands on the use of physical education facilities. Gymnasia and playfields in many places are used from early morning through the late evening hours. Probably the trend that places the heaviest demands on the use of facilities is the broadening of community programs. The concept of the school plant is changing. It was once considered an exclusive facility of the educational system; now it is viewed as community property, which should be used around the clock by many groups. This change plays an important role in the use of school facilities.

As the demands for use of physical education facilities increase, the necessity for planning, supervision, and scheduling well in advance also increases. The larger the program, the greater the need for careful planning to avoid conflict and misuse of the facilities.[2] The following chart shows the interrelationships involved when planning the use of facilities. In those places where there are no supervisors, the teacher assumes the supervisor's role as described in the chart. (See Figure 15-34.)

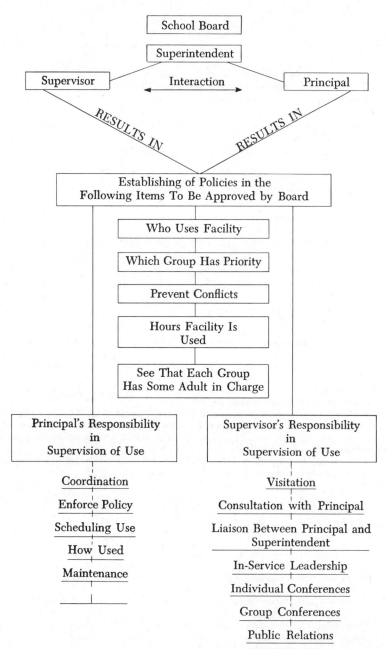

Figure 15–34. The proper use of physical education facilities requires planning and scheduling well in advance. (From Daughtrey, Greyson: Use of physical education facilities. In *Current Administrative Problems* [Elmon L. Vernier, Chairman]. Bulletin of the National Association of Secondary School Principals, 1960, p. 73.)

QUESTIONS FOR DISCUSSION

1. Which is better: to employ an experienced architect to plan a facility by himself or to have teachers work cooperatively with him? Explain your answer.

2. What are the procedures in planning for a new facility?

3. What is the relationship between the program and the facilities?

4. What is a teaching station?

5. How many teaching stations are needed for a school with an enrollment of 1300 pupils?

6. Discuss two types of lockers.

7. What is a walk-around shower? What are its advantages?

8. Why should girls have individual showers?

9. What are the points to be considered in swimming pool plans?

10. What types of surfaces are suitable for outdoor areas? What are the advantages of each?

11. What is a multiple-use area? How does it differ from a multiple-purpose room?

12. Discuss the two determinants of teaching supplies.

13. What is the teacher's responsibility for the equipment and supplies needed in the physical education program?

14. In what way do teaching procedures affect the quantity of equipment and supplies needed for the program?

15. Should the physical education budget be included in the athletic budget? Why?

SUGGESTED ACTIVITIES

1. Make a survey of the physical education facilities in the community. Report your findings to the class.

2. Prepare a layout of outside facilities for a 400-pupil school. Include all areas needed and draw to scale.

3. Prepare indoor plans for a new school with an enrollment of 1200 pupils. Show the teaching stations needed, showers, lockers, storage, and other items.

4. Interview a local school principal to determine the use of the school facilities. Make a list of the users during the current semester. In a report to the class, discuss some of the problems you see in the community-school concept. How can these problems be solved? What implications do you envision for health and physical education?

5. Prepare a budget for a high school with four teachers and 800 students. Submit it to the class.

6. Prepare a schedule for the use of facilities by outside groups.

REFERENCES

1. Greyson Daughtrey and John B. Woods, *Physical Education Programs: Organization and Administration*, pp. 207–208 (Philadelphia: W. B. Saunders Company, 1971).

2. "Planning Areas and Facilities for Health, Physical Education and Recreation," The Athletic Institute. p. 256; 259 (1966).

3. Lloyd Trump and Dorsey Baynham, *Focus on Change, Guide to Better Schools*, p. 39 (Chicago: Rand McNally and Company, 1961).

4. "Administering City and County School Programs," p. 65, American Association for Health, Physical Education and Recreation (Washington, D.C., 1956).

5. Lawrence Houston, Los Angeles City Schools, from printed materials.

6. "Advantages of Synthetic Surfaces," *Physical Education Perspective* (Croft Educational Services, Inc., January, 1971).

7. "Recipe for a 'Gridiron' Golf Course: Plywood, Carpet, Staples, and Glue," *Physical Education Newsletter* (Croft Educational Services, Inc., September 1, 1966).

8. "Recommended Outdoor Facilities for High School Physical Education Athletics and Recreation," *Physical Education Newsletter* (Croft Educational Services, Inc., February 1, 1966).

9. Greyson Daughtrey, "Use of Physical Education Facilities," p. 73, *The Bulletin of the National Association of Secondary School Principals* (May, 1960).

10. "Stretching the Physical Education Budget by Making Some of Your Own Equipment," *Physical Education Newsletter* (Croft Educational Services, Inc., December 15, 1968).

SELECTED READINGS

Carter, Joel: *How to Make Athletic Equipment.* New York: The Ronald Press Company, 1960.

Castaldi, Basil: *Creative Planning of Educational Facilities.* Chicago: Rand McNally & Company, 1969.

Daughtrey, Greyson, and John B. Woods: *Physical Education Programs: Organization and Administration.* Philadelphia: W. B. Saunders Company, 1971.

Gabrielsen, M. Alexander, and Caswell N. Miles: *Sports and Recreation Facilities.* Englewood Cliffs, New Jersey: Prentice-Hall, Inc., 1958.

Kelsey, Lamar, *et al.*: "New Generation Gyms," *Nation's Schools.* New York: McGraw-Hill Book Company, December, 1969.

"Planning Areas and Facilities for Health, Physical Education, and Recreation," *The Athletic Institute,* 1966.

APPENDICES

Appendix A

SOURCES FOR AUDIOVISUAL AIDS IN PHYSICAL EDUCATION

Space limitations prevent the listing of the hundreds of specific items that are available. The companies shown in the following list are more than glad to mail descriptive catalogues, and some will submit materials for trial on request.

Activities and Teaching for Early Childhood
2754 San Gabriel
San Bernardino, California 92404

Aetna Life Affiliated Companies
Public Education Department
151 Farmington Avenue
Hartford, Connecticut 06115

AIMS Instructional Media Services
P.O. Box 1010
Hollywood, California 90028

All American Production
P.O. Box 801
Riverside, California 92502

American and National Leagues
  of Professional Baseball Clubs
64 East Jackson Boulevard
Chicago, Illinois 60604

American Film Registry
831 South Wabash Avenue
Chicago, Illinois 60605

American Medical Association
535 North Dearborn Street
Chicago, Illinois 60610

Associated Film Services
3419 W. Magnolia Boulevard
Burbank, California 91505

Association Films, Inc.
600 Madison Avenue
New York, N.Y. 10022

Athena Films, Inc.
165 West 46th Street
New York, N.Y. 10019

The Athletic Institute
805 Merchandise Mart
Chicago, Illinois 60654

Audio Film Center
2138 E. 75th Street
Mount Vernon, N.Y. 10550

Bailey Film Association
11559 Santa Monica Boulevard
Los Angeles, California 90025

Bell and Howell Company
1801 Larchmont Avenue
Chicago, Illinois 60613

Ben Bearson Film Library
421 North Altadena Drive
Pasadena, California 91107

BFA Educational Media
2211 Michigan Avenue
Santa Monica, California 90404

Bonnie Pick Foundation
1101 Harrison Street
Park Ridge, Illinois 60068

Brandon Films, Inc.
200 West 57th Street
New York, N.Y. 10019

British Information Service
45 Rockefeller Plaza
New York, N.Y. 10020

Bureau of Audio-Visual Instruction
Extension Division
State University of Iowa
Iowa City, Iowa 52240

Carl F. Mahnke Productions
215 E. Third Street
New York, N.Y. 10018

Chicago Tribune
Motion Picture Bureau
33 West Madison Street
Chicago, Illinois 60602

Coca-Cola Company
P.O. Drawer 1734
Atlanta, Georgia 30301

Colburn Film Distributors, Inc.
P.O. Box 470
668 N. Western Avenue
Lake Forest, Illinois 60045

Columbia University Press
Communication Materials Center
562 W. 113th Street
New York, N.Y. 10025

Connecticut College for Women
Department of Physical Education
New London, Connecticut 06320

Coronet Instructional Films, Inc.
65 E. South Water Street
Chicago, Illinois 60601

Dartmouth College Films
Mr. J. B. Watson, Director
Hanover, N.H. 03755

Duckpin Bowling Council
1420 New York Avenue, N.W.
Washington, D.C. 20005

Eastman Films: Eastman Kodak Co.
Informational Films Division
343 State Street
Rochester, N.Y. 14650

Educational Activities, Inc.
P.O. Box 392
Freeport, N.Y. 11520

Film Associates
11559 Santa Monica Boulevard
Los Angeles, California 90025

FilmFair Communications
10946 Ventura Boulevard
Studio City, California 91604

Film Marketing Division of Syracuse University
1455 East Colvin Street
Syracuse, N.Y. 12310

Film Trends
8060 Melrose Avenue
Los Angeles, California 90046

Ford Motor Company
3000 Schaefer Road
Dearborn, Michigan 48122

G. N. Productions
1019 N. Cole Avenue
Hollywood, California 90038

General Motors Corporation
Department of Public Relations
Film Distribution Center
3044 W. Grand Boulevard
Detroit, Michigan 48202

General Sportcraft Company, Limited
215 Fourth Avenue
New York, N.Y. 10003

Holt, Rinehart, and Winston, Inc.
383 Madison Avenue
New York, N.Y. 10017

Instructional Media Center (VIB)
University of Texas
Drawer W
University Station
Austin, Texas 78712

International Film Bureau, Inc.
332 S. Michigan Avenue
Chicago, Illinois 60604

Jan-Or Pictures, Inc.
890 Napoli Drive
Pacific Palisades, California 90272

Journal Films, Inc.
909 West Diversey Parkway
Chicago, Illinois 60614

McGraw-Hill Book Company
Test Film Department
230 West 42nd Street
New York, N.Y. 10018

Minneapolis-Honeywell Regulator
Merchandising Division
2747 4th Avenue South
Minneapolis, Minnesota 55403

Modern Talking Picture Service, Inc.
1212 Avenue of the Americas
New York, N.Y. 10036

Mohawk Productions
Players Theater
New Hartford, N.Y. 13413

Museum of Modern Art Film Library
11 West 53rd Street
New York, N.Y. 10019

National Alcoholic Beverage Control
   Association, Inc.
Suite 1610
5454 Wisconsin Avenue, N.W.
Washington, D.C. 20015

National Basketball Coaches Association
Visual Committee
University of Wisconsin
Madison, Wisconsin 53706

National Bowling Council
1420 New York Avenue, N.W.
Washington, D.C. 20005

National Federation of State
   High School Athletic Associations
7 S. Dearborn Street
Chicago, Illinois 60603

National Film Board of Canada
680 Fifth Avenue
Suite 819
New York, N.Y. 10019

National Foundation, Inc.
120 Broadway
New York, N.Y. 10005

National Instructional Television Center
Box A
Bloomington, Indiana 47401

National Society for the Prevention
   of Blindness
79 Madison Avenue
New York, N.Y. 10016

NET Film Service
Indiana University
Audio-Visual Center
Bloomington, Indiana 47401

Northeast Regional Supplementary
   Educational Center
8 South Platt Street
Plattsburgh, N.Y. 12901

Nu-Art Films, Inc.
247 W. 46th Street
New York, N.Y. 10036

Official Films, Inc.
Grand and Linden Avenues
Ridgefield, N.J. 07657

Official Sport Film Service
7 South Dearborn Street
Chicago, Illinois 60603

Paul Burnford Film Production
9417 W. Pico Boulevard
Los Angeles, California 90035

Paul Parker Productions
11 West 42nd Street
New York, N.Y. 10018

Perry-Mansfield
15 West 67th Street
New York, N.Y. 10023

Phillips Petroleum Company
Advertising Department
Adams Building
Bartlesville, Oklahoma 74003

Public Relations Department
Sears, Roebuck and Co.
7401 Skokie Boulevard
Skokie, Illinois 60076

Pyramid Films
Box 1048
Santa Monica, California 90406

RKO Pictures, Inc.
Rockefeller Center
New York, N.Y. 10020

Simensen and Johnson
Educational Consultant Service
P.O. Box 34
College Park, Maryland 27040

Sterling Movies USA, Inc.
375 Park Avenue
New York, N.Y. 10022

Stuart Finley, Inc.
3428 Mansfield Road
Falls Church, Virginia 20041

Sunkist Growers, Inc.
P.O. Box 2706, Terminal Annex
Los Angeles, California 90054

Teaching Film Custodians, Inc.
25 West 43rd Street
New York, N.Y. 10036

T. N. Rogers Productions
2808 East Slauson Avenue
Huntington Park, California 90255

United States Golf Association
40 East 38th Street
New York, N.Y. 10016

United States Rubber Company
Advertising Department
1230 Avenue of the Americas
New York, N.Y. 10020

United World Films, Inc.
Educational Film Department
221 Park Avenue, South
New York, N.Y. 10003

Universal Education and Visual Art
221 Park Avenue, South
New York, N.Y. 10003

University of Illinois
Division of University Extension
Visual Aids Service
Champaign, Illinois 61820

Wholesome Film Service, Inc.
48 Melrose Street
Boston, Massachusetts 02116

Young American Films, Inc.
18 East 41st Street
New York, N.Y. 10017

Zurich-American Insurance Companies
135 South LaSalle Street
Chicago, Illinois 60603

Appendix B

MANUFACTURERS OF EQUIPMENT AND SUPPLIES

Sports Equipment

Adirondack Bats, Inc.
McKinley Avenue
Dolgeville, N.Y. 13329

Air-Tech Industries, Inc.
9 Brighton Road
Clifton, N.J. 07012

American Athletic Equipment Co.
Pinet and McKinley Streets
Jefferson, Iowa 50129

American Lock Co.
Exchange Road and Kedzie Avenue
Crete, Illinois 60417

American Playground Device Company
P.O. Drawer 2599
Anderson, Indiana 46011

Atlas Athletic Equipment Co.
2115 Locust Street
St. Louis, Missouri 63103

Ball-Boy Co.
27 Milburn Street
Bronxville, N.Y. 10708

Ballet Barres
P.O. Box 717
Sarasota, Florida 33578

Bike Athletic Products Division
The Kendall Co.
309 W. Jackson Boulevard
Chicago, Illinois 60606

Birdair Structures
1800–10 Broadway
Buffalo, N.Y. 14212

Cran Barry, Inc.
P.O. Box 488
2 Lincoln Avenue
Marblehead, Massachusetts 01945

Dayton Racquet Co.
936 Albright Street
Arcanum, Ohio 45304

DeBourgh All American
9300 James Avenue South
Minneapolis, Minnesota 55431

Dudley Sports Co., Inc.
12–12 37th Avenue
Long Island City, N.Y. 11101

Educational Media, Inc.
3191 Westover Drive, S.E.
Washington, D.C. 20020

Form Incorporated
12900 West Ten Mile Road
South Lyon, Michigan 48178

Gametime, Inc.
903 Anderson Road
Litchfield, Michigan 49252

Garrett Tubular Products, Inc.
802 E. King Street
Garrett, Indiana 46738

Gym Master Co.
3200 South Zuni Street
Englewood, Colorado 80110

Gymnastic Supply Co., Inc.
P.O. Box 1470
San Pedro, California 90733

Hillyard Chemical Co.
302 N. Fourth Street
St. Joseph, Missouri 64502

Jamison, Inc.
Playground and Athletic Field Equipment
Box 275
Grinnell, Iowa 50112

Jayfro Athletic Supply Co., Inc.
30 Hynes Avenue
Groton, Connecticut 06340

J. A. Preston Corporation
71 5th Avenue
New York, N.Y. 10003

J. C. Hall Dance Supplies
210 Pearl Street
Hartford, Connecticut 06103

J. L. Hammett Company
Physical Education Division
Box 4125
Lynchburg, Virginia 24502

Kenneth C. Hart Company
1323 Magnolia Avenue
Norfolk, Virginia 23508

Adolph Kiefer McNeil Corp.
1775 Winnetka Avenue
Northfield, Illinois 60093

Leflar
6840 S.W. Macadam Avenue
Portland, Oregon 97219

MacGregor/Brunswick
Division of Brunswick Corp.
Interstate 75 at Jimson Road
Cincinnati, Ohio 45215

Marcy Gym Equipment Company
1736 Standard Avenue
Glendale, California 91201

Master Lock Company
2600 N. 32nd Street
Milwaukee, Wisconsin 53245

Miracle Equipment Co.
P.O. Box 275
Grinnell, Iowa 50112

Mitchell Rubber Products
Division of Amerco, Inc.
2130 San Fernando Road
Los Angeles, California 90065

National Sports Co.
362 N. Marquette Street
Fond du Lac, Wisconsin 54935

Nevco Score Board Co.
Greenville, Illinois 62246

New York Athletic Supply Co.
321 E. 149th Street
Bronx, N.Y. 10451

Nissen Corp.
930 27th Avenue S.W.
Cedar Rapids, Iowa 52406

Ocean Pool Supply Co., Inc.
17 Stepar Place
Huntington Station, N.Y. 11746

Ben Pearson
Dept. J
Pine Bluff, Arkansas 71601

Pennsylvania Athletic Products
The General Tire & Rubber Co.
P.O. Box 951
Akron, Ohio 44309

Physical Education Aids
P.O. Box 5117
San Mateo, California 94402

Pipo Table Tennis Balls
882 Massachusetts Avenue
Indianapolis, Indiana 46204

Porter Athletic Equipment Co.
9555 W. Irving Park Road
Schiller Park, Illinois 60176

Premier Products Corp.
Rivervale, N.J. 07675

The Program Aids Co., Inc.
161 MacQuesten Parkway
Mount Vernon, N.Y. 10550

Protection Equipment
Division of Vogt Manufacturing Corporation
100 Fernwood Avenue
Rochester, N.Y. 14621

Rawlings Sporting Goods Co.
2300 Delmar Boulevard
St. Louis, Missouri 63166

Recreation and Athletic Products
3M Company
3M Center
St. Paul, Minnesota 55101

Resilite Sports Products, Inc.
P.O. Box 442
Sunbury, Pennsylvania 17801

Saunders Archery Co.
P.O. Box 476
Columbus, Nebraska 68601

The Seamless Rubber Co.
253 Hallock Avenue
New Haven, Connecticut 06503

Seron Mfg. Co.
15 W. Jefferson Avenue
Joliet, Illinois 60431

Skill Development Equipment
1340 N. Jefferson
Anaheim, California 92806

Snitz Manufacturing Company
104 South Church Street
East Troy, Wisconsin 53120

Sorensen-Christian Industries, Inc.
P.O. Box 1
Highway 210W
Angier, N.C. 27501

A. G. Spalding & Bros., Inc.
Meadow Street
Chicopee, Massachusetts 01014

Sportsman Shop
130 West Plume Street
Norfolk, Virginia 23510

Sterling Recreation Products
164 Belmont Avenue
Belleville, N.J. 07109

W. J. Voit Rubber Corp.
3801 S. Harbor Boulevard
Santa Ana, California 92704

Wilson Sporting Goods Co.
2233 West Street
River Grove, Illinois 60171

Wittek Golf Range Supply Co., Inc.
3650 Avondale Street
Chicago, Illinois 60618

Wolverine Sports Supply
745 State Circle
Ann Arbor, Michigan 48104

Wyandotte Chemicals Corp.
J. B. Ford Division
Wyandotte, Michigan 48192

Costumes, Suits, Shoes, and Leotards

Aldrich and Aldrich, Inc.
1859 Milwaukee Avenue
Chicago, Illinois 60647

Ballet Barres
P.O. Box 717
Sarasota, Florida 33578

Baum's Inc.
106–112 S. 11th Street
Philadelphia, Pennsylvania 19107

Stanley Bowmar Co., Inc.
12 Cleveland Street
Valhalla, N.Y. 10595

Tom Broderick Co., Inc.
P.O. Box 6096
Glendale, California 91205

Capezio
1855 Broadway
New York, N.Y. 10023

Castello Fencing Equipment Co., Inc.
30 E. 10th Street
New York, N.Y. 10003

Champion Knitwear Co., Inc.
115 College Avenue
Rochester, N.Y. 14607

Converse Rubber Co.
392 Pearl Street
Malden, Massachusetts 02148

Felco Athletic Wear Co., Inc.
113–119 Fourth Avenue
New York, N.Y. 10003

The Fred Gretsch Mfg. Co.
60 Broadway
Brooklyn, N.Y. 11211

Herbert Dancewear
1657 Broadway
New York, N.Y. 10019

Jean Lee Originals, Inc.
P.O. Box 207
Goshen, Indiana 46526

J. C. Hall
210 Pearl St.
Hartford, Connecticut 06103

S. D. Kirch, Inc.
47 W. 56th Street
New York, N.Y. 10019

Kling's Theatrical Shoe Co.
218 S. Wabash Avenue
Chicago, Illinois 60604

Loshin's Costume Center, Inc.
215 E. Eighth Street
Cincinnati, Ohio 45202

E. R. Moore Co.
7230 N. Caldwell Avenue
Niles (Chicago), Illinois 60648

National Sportogs Co.
821–823 Arch Street
Philadelphia, Pennsylvania 19107

New Balance Athletic Shoe Company
2402 Massachusetts Avenue
Cambridge, Massachusetts 02140

Ocean Pool Supply Co., Inc.
17 Stepar Place
Huntington Station, N.Y. 11746

Selva and Sons, Inc.
1607 Broadway
New York, N.Y. 10019

Art Stone Theatrical Corp.
73 Fifth Avenue
New York, N.Y. 10003

United States Rubber Company
1230 Avenue of the Americas
New York, N.Y. 10020

Wilton Manufacturing Company, Inc.
East Main Street
Ware, Massachusetts 01082

Records

Ballet Barres
P.O. Box 717
Sarasota, Florida 33578

Dance Records
1438 Springvale Avenue
McLean, Virginia 22101

Educational Activities, Inc.
P.O. Box 392
Freeport, N.Y. 11520

Educational Recordings of America
P.O. Box 6062
Bridgeport, Connecticut 06606

Folkraft
1159 Broad Street
Newark, N.J. 07114

Hoctor Dance Records, Inc.
P.O. Box 38
Waldwick, N.J. 07463

Leo's Advance Theatrical Co.
32 W. Randolph Street
Chicago, Illinois 60601

Kathleen Merrill Dance Records
6484 S.W. 25th Street
Miami, Florida 33155

Kimbo Education Records
P.O. Box 246
Deal, N.J. 07723

Freda Miller Records for Dance
131 Bayview Avenue
Northport, N.Y. 11768

J. Lowell Pratt & Company
15 E. 48th Street
New York, N.Y. 10017

Record Center
2581 Piedmont Road, N.E.
Atlanta, Georgia 30324

Rhythms Productions Records
P.O. Box 34485
Los Angeles, California 90034

Russell Records, Inc.
P.O. Box 3318
Ventura, California 93003

Stepping Tones Records
2506 Overland St.
Los Angeles, California 90064

Art Stone Theatrical Corp.
73 Fifth Avenue
New York, N.Y. 10003

Windsor Records Company
5530 N. Rosemead Boulevard
Temple City, California 91780

Appendix C

SOURCES OF OFFICIAL RULES*

ACTIVITY	SOURCE OF RULES
Aerial Tennis	Sells Aerial Tennis Co. Box 42, Kansas City, Kan., 66103
Archery (Field)	National Field Archery Assn. Rte. 2, Box 514, Redlands, Calif., 92373
Archery (Target)	National Archery Assn. 23 E. Jackson Blvd., Chicago, Ill., 60604
Archery (Indoor)	American Archery Council 23 E. Jackson Blvd., Chicago, Ill., 60604
Archery (See DGWS listing)	
Badminton	American Badminton Assn. Donald Richardson, 20 Wamesit Rd., Waban, Mass., 02168
Badminton	Dayton Racquet Co., 302 S. Albright St., Arcanum, Ohio, 43504
Badminton (See DGWS listing)	
Banball (Rules included)	General Sportcraft Co., Ltd. 33 New Bridge Rd., Bergenfield, N.J.
Baseball (Non-professional) Guide Annual w/rules	National Baseball Congress Wichita, Kansas
Baseball (Copyrighted Rules)	National Baseball Congress Wichita, Kansas
Baseball (American Legion)	American Legion, Box 1055 Indianapolis, Ind., 46206
Baseball, Babe Ruth League	Babe Ruth League, Inc. 524½ Hamilton Ave., Trenton, N.J., 08609
Baseball, Little League	Little League Baseball, Inc. P.O. Box 925, Williamsport, Pa., 17704
Baseball, Little League (Umpire's Handbook)	Little League Baseball, Inc. P.O. Box 925, Williamsport, Pa., 17704
Baseball, Bronco-Pony-Colt	Boys Baseball, Inc. P.O. Box 225, Washington, Pa., 15301

*Courtesy of The Athletic Institute, Chicago, Illinois.

ACTIVITY	SOURCE OF RULES
Baseball, "Knotty Problems of Baseball" (Professional Rules)	The Sporting News 2018 Washington Ave., St. Louis, Mo., 63166
Baseball (Professional Rules Only)	The Sporting News 2018 Washington Ave., St. Louis, Mo., 63166
Baseball (See NCAA listing)	
Baseball Umpire's Handbook (Does not include actual rules)	American Amateur Baseball Congress P.O. Box 44, Battle Creek, Mich., 49016
Baseball Scorer's Handbook (Does not include actual rules)	American Amateur Baseball Congress P.O. Box 44, Battle Creek, Mich., 49016
Baseball, Rules in Pictures	American Amateur Baseball Congress P.O. Box 44, Battle Creek, Mich., 49016
Baseball, Tournament Manual	American Amateur Baseball Congress P.O. Box 44, Battle Creek, Mich., 49016
Baseball, League Organization	American Amateur Baseball Congress P.O. Box 44, Battle Creek, Mich., 49016
Baseball (See High School listing)	
Basketball (See AAU listing)	
Basketball (See High School listing)	
Basketball (See NCAA listing)	
Basketball (See DGWS listing)	
Basketball (Biddy)	Jay Archer, 701 Brooks Building, Scranton, Pa., 18501
Basketball, Balanced (Height Equalization)	John L. McHale, 66 Dale Road Eastchester, N.Y.
Bicycling	Bicycle Institute of America 122 E. 42nd St., New York, N.Y., 10017
Billiards (Rules & Records)	Billiard Congress of America 20 N. Wacker Dr., Chicago, Ill., 60606
Bocce	General Sportcraft Co., Ltd. 33 New Bridge Rd., Bergenfield, N.J.
Bocce	Lignum-Vitae Products Corp. 96 Boyd Ave., Jersey City, N.J.
Bowling (Duck Pin)	National Duck Pin Bowling Congress 1420 New York Ave., N.W. Washington, D.C., 20005
Bowling (Ten Pin)	American Bowling Congress 1572 E. Capitol Dr., Milwaukee, Wisc., 53211
Bowling (See DGWS listing)	
Bowling, Women (Ten Pin)	Women's International Bowling Congress, Inc. 1225 Dublin Rd., Columbus 12, Ohio

ACTIVITY	SOURCE OF RULES
Boxing (See AAU listing)	
Casting (Official Rules for Fly and Bait Casting)	American Casting Education Foundation P.O. Box 51, Nashville, Tenn., 37202
Corkball	Rawlings Sporting Goods Co. 2300 Delmar Blvd., St. Louis, Mo., 63166
Croquet	General Sportcraft Co., Ltd. 33 New Bridge Rd., Bergenfield, N.J.
Dartball	Wisconsin State Dartball Comm. c/o E. Dorow, Pres. 9333 W. Lincoln Ave., West Allis, Wisc.
Darts	General Sportcraft Co., Ltd. 33 New Bridge Rd., Bergenfield, N.J.
Deck Tennis	General Sportcraft Co., Ltd. 33 New Bridge Rd., Bergenfield, N.J.
Fencing	Amateur Fencer's League of America William Latzko, 33–62nd Street, West New York, N.J.
Fencing (See DGWS listing)	
Field Hockey (See DGWS listing)	
Field Hockey	General Sportcraft Co., Ltd. 33 New Bridge Rd., Bergenfield, N.J.
Floor Tennis	U.S. Floor Tennis Assn. 1580 Sherman Ave., Evanston, Ill.
Football (See NCAA listing)	
Football (Junior League)	Pop Warner Football 3664 Richmond St., Philadelphia, Pa., 19134
Football (Six-Man) (See High School listing)	
Football (See High School listing)	
Golf	U.S. Golf Assn., 40 E. 38th St., New York, N.Y., 10016
Gymnastics (See AAU listing)	
Gymnastics (See NCAA listing)	
Gymnastics (See DGWS listing)	
Handball (See AAU listing)	
Handball	U.S. Handball Assn. 4101 Dempster St., Skokie, Ill.
Horseshoes	General Sportcraft Co., Ltd. 33 New Bridge Rd., Bergenfield, N.J.
Horseshoes (Professional)	National Horseshoe Pitchers Assn. of America, c/o Elmer Beller 9725 Palm St., Bellflower, Calif.

ACTIVITY	SOURCE OF RULES
Ice Hockey (See NCAA listing)	
Ice Skating	Amateur Skating Union of the U.S. c/o Edward J. Schmitzer 4135 N. Troy St., Chicago, Ill., 60618
Indoor Hockey	Cosom Corp., 6030 Wayzata Blvd. Minneapolis, Minn., 55416
Lacrosse (See DGWS listing)	
Lawn Bowling	American Lawn Bowling Association c/o John W. Deist, Secretary 1525 Ridge Court, Wauwatosa, Wisc., 53213
Marbles Shooting	National Marbles Tournament Cleveland Press Bldg., Cleveland, Ohio
Outings (See DGWS listing)	
Paddle Tennis	General Sportcraft Co., Ltd. 33 New Bridge Rd., Bergenfield, N.J.
Paddleball	Rodney J. Grambeau, Sports Bldg. University of Michigan, Ann Arbor, Mich.
Quoits	General Sportcraft Co., Ltd. 33 New Bridge Rd., Bergenfield, N.J.
Riding (See DGWS listing)	
Roller Hockey	National Roller Hockey Assn. of the U.S. 97 Erie St., Dumont, N.J.
Roque	American Roque League, Inc. 4205 Briar Creek Lane, Dallas, Tex., 75214
Scoopball (Rules for 26 different games)	Cosom Industries, 6030 Wayzata Blvd., Minneapolis, Minn., 55416
Shooting (See National Rifle Assn. listing)	
Shuffleboard (Deck)	General Sportcraft Co., Ltd. 33 New Bridge Rd., Bergenfield, N.J.
Shuffleboard (Table)	American Shuffleboard Leagues, Inc. 533 Third St., Union City, N.J., 07087
Skating (Figure)	U.S. Figure Skating Assn. 575 Boylston St., Boston, Mass., 02116
Skating (Roller)	U.S. Amateur Roller Skating Assn. 120 W. 42nd St., New York, N.Y., 10036
Skating (Speed)	Amateur Skating Union of the U.S. c/o Edward J. Schmitzer 4135 N. Troy St., Chicago, Ill., 60618
Skeet Shooting	National Skeet Shooting Assn. 3409 Oak Lawn Ave., Suite 219, Dallas, Tex., 75219
Skiing (See NCAA listing)	
Skiing (Downhill, Slalom, Giant Slalom, Jumping & Cross-Country, FIS and USSA Rules)	U.S. Ski Assn., c/o Gloria C. Chadwick Executive Secy., Broadmoor Colorado Springs, Colo.

ACTIVITY	SOURCE OF RULES
Skin Diving, Competitive (See AAU listing)	
Smash	Smash, 1024 North Blvd., Oak Park, Ill.
Soccer (See NCAA listing)	
Soccer (See DGWS listing)	
Softball (12″ — fast and slow pitch)	Amateur Softball Assn., Suite 1300, Skirvin Tower, Oklahoma City, Okla.
Softball (16″)	Umpires Protective Assn. of Chicago c/o Edw. Weinstein, Chairman Rules Committee, Apt. 710 3550 Lake Shore Dr., Chicago, Ill.
Softball (See DGWS listing)	
Speed-A-Way	Marjorie S. Larsen, 1754 Middlefield Stockton, Calif., 95204
Speedball (See DGWS listing)	
Spiral Tennis	General Sportcraft Co., Ltd. 33 New Bridge Rd., Bergenfield, N.J.
Squash	U.S. Squash Racquets Assn. 200 E. 66th St., New York, N.Y., 10021
Swimming (See AAU listing)	
Swimming (See NCAA listing)	
Swimming (Synchronized — See AAU listing)	
Table Tennis	General Sportcraft Co., Ltd. 33 New Bridge Rd., Bergenfield, N.J.
Table Tennis (Instructions)	U.S. Table Tennis Assn., 210 Saturn Dr. North Star, Newark, Del.
Table Tennis (Rules)	U.S. Table Tennis Assn., 210 Saturn Dr. North Star, Newark, Del.
Table Tennis (Instructions & Rules)	Nissen-Sico, 930–27th Ave., S.W. Cedar Rapids, Iowa
Takraw Game	General Sportcraft Co., Ltd. 33 New Bridge Rd., Bergenfield, N.J.
Tennis (Includes Guide)	U.S. Lawn Tennis Assn., 51 E. 42nd St., New York, N.Y., 10017
Tennis (Rules Only)	U.S. Lawn Tennis Assn., 51 E. 42nd St., New York, N.Y., 10017
Tennis (See DGWS listing)	
Tennis	Dayton Racquet Co., 302 S. Albright St. Arcanum, Ohio 45304
Tennis Umpire's Manual (Includes Rules)	U.S. Lawn Tennis Assn., 51 E. 42nd St. New York, N.Y., 10017
Tetherball (Inflated Ball)	W. J. Voit Rubber Corp. 3801 S. Harbor Blvd. Santa Ana, Calif., 92704

ACTIVITY	SOURCE OF RULES
Tetherball (Inflated Ball)	General Sportcraft Co., Ltd. 33 New Bridge Rd., Bergenfield, N.J.
Tether Tennis	General Sportcraft Co., Ltd. 33 New Bridge Rd., Bergenfield, N.J.
Touch Football	The Athletic Institute 805 Merchandise Mart Chicago, Ill., 60654
Track & Field (See AAU listing)	
Track & Field (See High School listing)	
Track & Field (See NCAA listing)	
Turf Bowling (Bocce)	Lignum-Vitae Products Corp., 96 Boyd Ave., Jersey City, N.J.
Volleyball (Includes Rules)	U.S. Volleyball Assn., USVBA Printer P.O. Box 109, Berne, Ind., 46711
Volleyball (See DGWS listing)	
Water Polo (See AAU listing below)	
Weight Lifting (See AAU listing below)	
Winter Sports (See DGWS listing below)	
Wrestling (See NCAA listing below)	

NCAA RULEBOOKS AND GUIDES — National Collegiate Athletic Bureau
Box 757, Grand Central Station
New York, N.Y., 10017

Baseball	Ice Hockey
Basketball	Skiing
Football	Soccer
Football Rules Interpretations	Swimming
Gymnastics	Track & Field
	Wrestling

DGWS OFFICIAL GUIDES FOR
WOMEN'S SPORTS, INCLUDING RULES — Division for Girls' and Women's Sports
1201 Sixteenth St., N.W.,
Washington, D.C., 20036

Aquatics	Soccer-Speedball
Archery-Riding	Softball
Basketball	Tennis-Badminton
Bowling-Fencing-Golf	Track & Field
Field Hockey-Lacrosse	Volleyball
Gymnastics	Winter Sports & Outing Activities

HIGH SCHOOL ACTIVITIES — National Federation of State High School
Athletic Assns., 7 S. Dearborn,
Chicago, Ill., 60603

Basketball:	Football:
Rules	Rules
Casebook	Casebook
Player Handbook	Player Handbook
Officials' Manual	Officials' Manual
Baseball:	
Rules	
Casebook	Football, Touch Football
Umpires' Manual	Six-Man Football
	Track & Field, Rules & Records

ACTIVITY	SOURCE OF RULES
OFFICIAL AAU RULE BOOKS AND GUIDES	Amateur Athletic Union of the U.S., 231 W. 58th St., New York, N.Y., 10019

AAU Handbook	Swimming (Synchronized)
Basketball	Swimming, Water Polo, & Diving
Boxing	Track & Field
Gymnastics	Weight Lifting
Handball	Wrestling
Judo	

NRA AND INTERNATIONAL SHOOTING UNION RULE BOOKS	National Rifle Assn., 1600 Rhode Island Ave., N.W., Washington, D.C., 20036

NRA High-Power Rifle	ISU Center-Fire Pistol
NRA Pistol	ISU Rapid-Fire Pistol
NRA Smallbore Rifle	ISU Running Deer
NRA Shotgun	ISU Running Roebuck & Boar
ISU Constitution	ISU Clay Pigeon
ISU General Regulations	ISU Skeet
ISU SB Rifle & Free Pistol	ISU Bound Vol. (all rules)
ISU Free Rifle & Army Rifle	

Appendix D

HEIGHT AND WEIGHT INTERPRETATION GROWTH AND DEVELOPMENT FORMS

Registering height and weight progress. Assume May is now one year older. At age 5 years 4 months she weighed 50 pounds and had a height of 46 inches, at age 5 years 8 months she weighed 52 pounds and was 46.5 inches tall, and now at age 6 years she weighs 55 pounds and is 47.5 inches in height. Further, assume that points representing these records have been plotted correctly on May's chart. Having status records at more than one age, it becomes possible to draw *individual growth curves,* or lines of progress. May's progress between ages 5 years and 6 years can be depicted by drawing lines connecting (a) her points in the height part of the chart and (b) her points in the weight part of the chart.

Following the same procedure, height and weight progress of any individual girl may be portrayed over part or all of the period from age 4 years to age 18 years.

Interpreting status. (1) The figures written above or below the plotted points readily describe each girl's overall body size at the age or ages measures have been obtained.

(2) The channels in which a girl's height and weight points for a given age are located indicate her standings with reference to schoolmates of like age. The illustrative values given at age 6 years show May to be moderately tall and moderately heavy.

(3) When a girl's height and weight points do not lie in corresponding channels, the discrepancy may denote normal slenderness or stockiness of build, or it may reflect an undesirable state of health. Assume the chart shows a new pupil to be "average" in height and "light" in weight. She should be screened for medical study to determine whether she is a "satisfactorily healthy" girl of slender build, or a "medically unsatisfactory" girl with an incipient infection, a nutritional deficiency, or an unsuitable activity program.

Interpreting progress. (1) The difference between a girl's recorded heights (or weights) at two different ages gives the amount of change in the intervening period. For example, May Atkin between 5 and 6 years of age gained 2.5 inches in height and 7 pounds in weight.

(2) During the childhood span from age 4 years to age 9 years, normality of growth progress is indicated by approximately-parallel relationship of the individual's height and weight lines with the channel lines of the chart. Suppose that Ruth Tweed has been measured successively from age 5 years to age 8 years. Her height line runs along the middle of the "average" height channel, while her weight line runs fairly close to the middle of the average weight channel until age 7 years then takes a steep turn upward. Ruth should be screened for medical investigation—her disproportionate gain in weight may reflect the need for a prescribed diet, a change in daily regimen, or drug therapy.

(3) Interpretations of growth progress after age 9 years are made on the same basis as earlier except that allowance must be made for individual differences in age of the circumpuberal "spurt" in height and weight. Suppose (a) Harriet and Elise are nearly alike in height and weight at each age from 5 to 9 years, and (b) the time of rapid adolescent growth in these measures begins before 10 years for Harriet and after 12 years for Elise. In the early teens when Elise is continuing to grow in height and weight at childhood rates, this growth should not be appraised as "unsatisfactory."

About the chart. The height and weight measurements for constructing the chart were collected in 1961 on white girls attending public and private schools in Iowa City, Iowa. To obtain the channels, age distributions for height and weight were subdivided as follows: Upper 10 per cent (Tall, Heavy), next 20 per cent, middle 40 per cent (Average), next 20 per cent, and lower 10 per cent (Short, Light).

HEIGHT WEIGHT INTERPRETATION FOLDER FOR GIRLS*

Uses of folder. This folder (1) provides each girl a personal chart designed to accompany her from grade to grade and give a graphic record of her growth in height and weight, (2) furnishes the teacher a guide for interpreting each pupil's height and weight records as indicators of growth status and growth progress, and (3) brings the attention of school health workers to certain height and weight findings suggestive of deviations from satisfactory health.

Determining weight. Obtain the weight of each pupil in September, January, and May. Wherever possible use beam-type, platform scales. Before each weighing period check the scales; if they do not balance correctly, adjust them. Have the girl remove her shoes and as much other clothing as practicable (the weight measures used in developing the chart were taken on girls wearing undergarments only). With the girl standing near the center of the platform of the scales, her hands hanging free, determine weight to the nearest one-half pound.

Determining height. Use a metric measure fixed in the upright position, and a wood headpiece. The measure may be a yardstick, metal tape, or paper scale; it should be fastened firmly to an upright board or to a smooth wall with no wainscoting. (An accurate paper scale may be purchased from the Institute of Child Behavior and Development, State University of Iowa.) Although a chalk box can serve as the headpiece, this is not recommended for regular use. A more satisfactory headpiece is easily made in the school workshop by joining at right angles the shorter edges of two pieces of seasoned wood 7 inches x 5 inches, and mounting within the 90° angle a triangular wood brace having an opening for insertion of the fingers.

Measure height with shoes removed. Have the girl stand with heels, buttocks, and upper part of back in contact with the wall or board; feet almost together but not touching each other; arms hanging at the sides; heels in firm contact with the floor; head facing straight forward; and chin lifted but not tilted up. When she is positioned, place one face of the headpiece against the upright scale and bring the other face down, keeping it horizontal, until it crushes the girl's hair and makes contact with the top of her head. Take two separate measurements and record height to the nearest one-fourth inch.

Registering height and weight status. Assume you have determined the height and weight of May Atkin. May weighs 48 pounds, is 45 inches in height, and will have her fifth birthday tomorrow. Find age 5 below the *height* portion of the chart and 45 inches along its left-hand margin. Plot a point above 5 years and opposite 45 inches. Below this dot on the height portion of the chart write "45.0."

Next, find age 5 years below the *weight* portion of the chart and 48 pounds along its left-hand margin. Plot a point above 5 years and opposite 48 pounds. Above this mark in the weight portion of the chart write "48.0."

With the completion of these directions, the height and weight status of May Atkin at age 5 years is fully registered. At any age from 4 years to 18 years, the status of other girls can be registered similarly.

---

*Prepared for the Joint Committee on Health Problems in Education of the NEA and AMA by Howard V. Meredith and Virginia B. Knott, State University of Iowa. Additional copies may be secured through the order departments of the American Medical Association, 535 N. Dearborn St., Chicago, Illinois 60610, or of the National Education Association, 1201 Sixteenth St., N. W., Washington, D. C. 20036.

_____   _____   Grade: K   1   2   3   4   5   6   7   8   9   10   11   12

(girl's name)   (date of birth)   (encircle present grade)

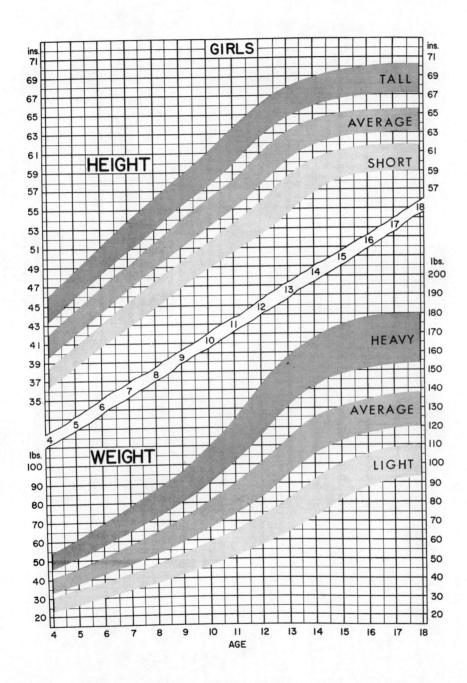

Registering height and weight progress. Assume Ned is now one year older. At age 5 years 4 months he weighed 52 pounds and had a height of 46 inches, at age 5 years 8 months he weighed 55 pounds and was 46.5 inches tall, and now at age 6 years he weighs 58 pounds and is 47.5 inches in height. Further, assume that points representing these records have been plotted correctly on Ned's chart. Having status records at more than one age, it becomes possible to draw *individual growth curves,* or lines of progress. Ned's progress between ages 5 years and 6 years can be depicted by drawing lines connecting (a) his points in the height part of the chart and (b) his points in the weight part of the chart.

Following the same procedure, height and weight progress of any individual boy may be portrayed over part or all of the period from age 4 years to age 18 years.

Interpreting status. (1) The figures written above or below the plotted points readily describe each boy's overall body size at the age or ages measures have been obtained.

(2) The channels in which a boy's height and weight points for a given age are located indicate his standings with reference to schoolmates of like age. The illustrative values given at age 6 years show Ned to be moderately tall and moderately heavy.

(3) When a boy's height and weight points do not lie in corresponding channels, the discrepancy may denote normal slenderness or stockiness of build, or it may reflect an undesirable state of health. Assume the chart shows a new pupil to be "average" in height and "light" in weight. He should be screened for medical study to determine whether he is a "satisfactorily healthy" boy of slender build, or a "medically unsatisfactory" boy with an incipient infection, a nutritional deficiency, or an unsuitable activity program.

Interpreting progress. (1) The difference between a boy's recorded heights (or weights) at two different ages gives the amount of change in the intervening period. For example, Ned Barth between 5 and 6 years of age gained 2.5 inches in height and 8 pounds in weight.

* (2) During the childhood span from age 4 years to age 9 years, normality of growth progress is indicated by approximately parallel relationship of the individual's height and weight lines with the channel lines of the chart. Suppose that Paul Stone has been measured successively from age 6 years to age 10 years. His height line runs along the middle of the "average" height channel, while his weight line runs fairly close to the middle of the average weight channel until age 9 years then takes a steep turn upward. Paul should be screened for medical investigation—his disproportionate gain in weight may reflect the need for a prescribed diet, a change in daily regimen, or drug therapy.

(3) Interpretations of growth progress after age 11 years are made on the same basis as earlier except that allowance must be made for individual differences in age of the circumpuberal "spurt" in height and weight. Suppose (a) Eric and Gerald are nearly alike in height and weight at each age from 5 to 11 years, and (b) the time of rapid adolescent growth in these measures begins before 13 years for Eric and after 15 years for Gerald. In the early teens when Gerald is continuing to grow in height and weight at childhood rates, this growth should not be appraised as "unsatisfactory."

About the chart. The height and weight measurements for constructing the chart were collected in 1961-1963 on white boys attending public and private schools in Iowa City, Iowa. To obtain the channels, age distributions for height and weight were subdivided as follows: Upper 10 per cent (Tall, Heavy), next 20 per cent, middle 40 per cent (Average), next 20 per cent, and lower 10 per cent (Short, Light).

*Line should read: During the childhood span from age 4 years to age 11 years, ...

B

HEIGHT WEIGHT INTERPRETATION FOLDER FOR BOYS*

Uses of folder. This folder (1) provides each boy a personal chart designed to accompany him from grade to grade and give a graphic record of his growth in height and weight, (2) furnishes the teacher a guide for interpreting each pupil's height and weight records as indicators of growth status and growth progress, and (3) brings the attention of school health workers to certain health findings suggestive of deviations from satisfactory health.

Determining weight. Obtain the weight of each pupil in September, January, and May. Wherever possible use beam-type, platform scales. Before each weighing period check the scales; if they do not balance correctly, adjust them. Have the boy remove his shoes and as much other clothing as practicable (the weight measures used in developing the chart were taken on boys wearing underclothing only). With the boy standing near the center of the platform of the scales, his hands hanging free, determine weight to the nearest one-half pound.

Determining height. Use a metric measure fixed in the upright position, and a wood headpiece. The measure may be a yardstick, metal tape, or paper scale; it should be fastened firmly to an upright board or to a smooth wall with no wainscoting. (An accurate paper scale may be purchased from the Institute of Child Behavior and Development, State University of Iowa.) Although a chalk box can serve as the headpiece, this is not recommended for regular use. A more satisfactory headpiece is easily made in the school workshop by joining at right angles the shorter edges of two pieces of seasoned wood 7 inches x 5 inches, and mounting within the 90° angle a triangular wood brace having an opening for insertion of the fingers.

Measure height with shoes removed. Have the boy stand with heels, buttocks, and upper part of back in contact with the wall or board; feet almost together but not touching each other; arms hanging at the sides; heels in firm contact with the floor; head facing straight forward; and chin lifted but not tilted up. When he is positioned, place one face of the headpiece against the upright scale and bring the other face down, keeping it horizontal, until it crushes the boy's hair and makes contact with the top of his head. Take two separate measurements and record height to the nearest one-fourth inch.

Registering height and weight status. Assume you have determined the height and weight of Ned Barth. Ned weighs 50 pounds, is 45 inches in height, and will have his fifth birthday tomorrow. Find age 5 below the *height* portion of the chart and 45 inches along its left-hand margin. Plot a point above 5 years and opposite 45 inches. Below this dot on the height portion of the chart write "45.0."

Next, find age 5 years below the *weight* portion of the chart and 50 pounds along its left-hand margin. Plot a point above 5 years and opposite 50 pounds. Above this mark in the weight portion of the chart write "50.0."

With the completion of these directions, the height and weight status of Ned Barth at age 5 years is fully registered. At any age from 4 years to 18 years, the status of other boys can be registered similarly.

(boy's name)   (date of birth)   Grade: K 1 2 3 4 5 6 7 8 9 10 11 12

(encircle present grade)

Prepared for the Joint Committee on Health Problems in Education of the NEA and AMA by Howard V. Meredith and Virginia B. Knott, State University of Iowa. Additional copies may be secured through the Model School Department of the American Medical Association, 535 N. Dearborn St., Chicago, Illinois 60610, or of the National Education Association, 1201 Sixteenth St., N.W., Washington, D.C. 20036.

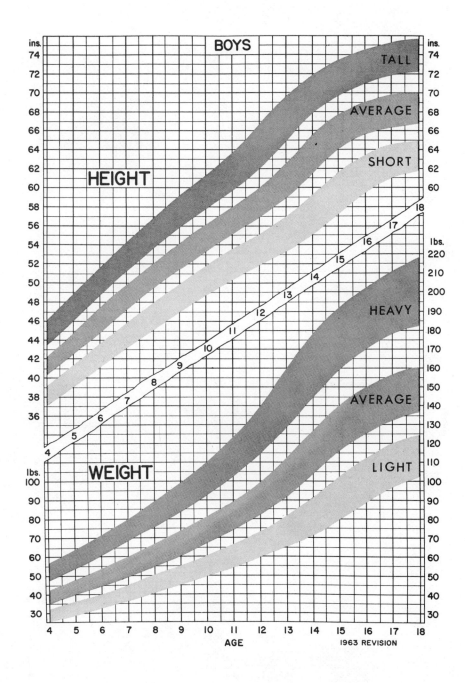

INDEX